BOONE AND CROCKETT CLUB'S

25th Big Game Awards
2001-2003

▼ ▼ ▼ ▼ ▼ ▼ ▼

Boone and Crockett Club's 25th Big Game Awards, 2001-2003
Edited by George A. Bettas, Eldon L. "Buck" Buckner, and Jack Reneau

Copyright © 2004, by the Boone and Crockett Club

Library of Congress Catalog Card Number: 2004104576
ISBN: 0-940864-46-0
Published September 2004

Published in the United States of America
by the
Boone and Crockett Club
250 Station Drive
Missoula, Montana 59801
Phone (406) 542-1888
Fax (406) 542-0784
Toll-Free (888) 840-4868 (book or merchandise orders only)
www.booneandcrockettclub.com

BOONE AND CROCKETT CLUB'S

25th Big Game Awards
2001-2003

▼   ▼   ▼   ▼   ▼   ▼   ▼

A Book of the Boone and Crockett Club
Containing Tabulations of Outstanding North American
Big Game Trophies Accepted During the
25th Awards Entry Period of 2001-2003

Edited by
George A. Bettas
Eldon L. "Buck" Buckner
Jack Reneau

2004

Boone and Crockett Club

Missoula, Montana

Photograph courtesy of Jack Reneau

Boone and Crockett Club President, Bob Model, presented long-time Boone and Crockett Club member, Arthur C. Popham, with an Honorary Life plaque at the Welcoming Dinner in Kansas City. Art had the opportunity to hunt with Jack O'Connor and George Parker years ago and has contributed immensely to hunting and conservation throughout his life.

FOREWORD

▼ ▼ ▼ ▼ ▼ ▼ ▼ ▼ ▼

ROBERT MODEL

President of the Boone and Crockett Club

Congratulations to all on the 25th Triennial Awards! We had an impressive showing in Kansas City in June. My special thanks to Eldon "Buck" Buckner for setting the example and appropriate tone for the Club in this new century. To quote Buck, "we are putting dignity, formality and respect back into the Awards program." Through Buck's leadership, we accomplished this. This is very important because it goes along with the respect that the Club shows not only for the animal, but also for the ethics of the pursuit and collection of prey. Buck was correct to note that as we find ourselves in the middle of the first decade of the 21st century, it is appropriate to discuss the different roles of the Club, as we seem them. It is clear that Boone and Crockett has a role to play in defining the future, and maybe the survival, of our hunting, naturalist, and conservation legacy.

It is clear as we transition to the 21st century the needs are different from when our forefathers transitioned to the 20th century. At that time, the population was much smaller. We were consuming our natural resources at an unsustainable level and by doing so, almost destroyed our big game populations in the process. Through the farsightedness of our early members, led by George Bird Grinnell, Theodore Roosevelt, and others, the Club almost single-handedly put into motion the mechanism that would put the brakes on the wholesale slaughter of our wildlife populations. The Club, led by our members and their debates, had the clear vision to ensure our National Parks would be protected. Our early members were responsible for the creation of these treasured lands. Simultaneously, they had the additional vision to make sure wildlife refuges were set aside, not only for the protection of those creatures and the land on which they lived, but also that those lands were to remain open to the public for hunting, fishing, and recreation on a sustainable basis. We are fortunate to reap the benefit of those early struggles. In 2003 we saw the Centennial Celebration of our National Refuge System. One hundred years ago, Boone and Crockett started this program; 100 years later Boone and Crockett was still here, represented by past B&C President, Dan Pedrotti, at the special centennial celebration.

In 2005, we celebrate our National Forest Centennial. These national forest lands were part and parcel of the vision of Roosevelt, Grinnell, Pinchot, and other early Boone and Crockett members. Boone and Crockett will be the key participant in the celebration of the agency founded by the Club to care for what is now known as the National Forest Systems. Currently this system comprises an impressive 192 million acres of multiple use lands for the enjoyment of all the American people. These lands all were protected under the principle of "the greatest good for the greatest number of American people."

My appreciation also goes to Keith Balfourd for giving us ethical goals to attain through the Hunt Fair Chase program. This great program came as a direct result of leadership from members Dan Pedrotti and Val Geist.

My good friend and mentor, Bill Spencer, was responsible for engaging the Club and challenging members to be relevant again on policies that affect the future of our wild lands and hunting tradition. Bill insisted that we would now be recognized, not as individuals for our contributions, but as individual members who are the Boone and Crockett Club. Only by that collective relationship can we be truly effective. Jack Parker, Steve Adams, Tim Hixon, and Dan Pedrotti saw the wisdom of Bill's vision and seized the opportunity to make the Club relevant and vital again to the hunter-conservation community. I know that Bill is watching us and smiling. He would be most pleased with the steps we are now taking.

In closing, we are leading the hunter-conservation community in part by the creation of the American Wildlife Conservation Partners. I thank Dan Pedrotti for his vision; my thanks also to Steve Mealey, Jack Ward Thomas, and Kathleen Thomas for making sure that the AWCP, in its infancy, did not fail. Today, as we celebrate the wonderful trophies collected and displayed in Kansas City, not only is our records program healthy, our leadership in ethics is secure. In the 21st century, we are the leaders, just as we were at the beginning of the 20th century.

Robert Model, age 62, was born in Greenwich, CT. He is owner and President of Mooncrest Ranch in Cody, WY. Mr. Model attended The Browning School and Elon College. Mr. Model is currently Vice President of Stillrock Management and Vice President of Elmrock Capital, both based in New York. He is a past director of the National Forest Foundation; current Chairman of the American Wildlife Conservation Partners; board member for the Theodore Roosevelt Conservation Partners. He has previously served as a Director on the boards of CapMAC, Overhills, Inc., Piggly Wiggly.

Mr. Model is currently President of the Boone and Crockett Club, as well as a member of the following organizations: The Rocky Mountain Elk Foundation, Izaak Walton League, Safari Club International, FNAWS, Quail Unlimited, Clove Valley Rod & Gun Club, Philadelphia Gun Club, Theodore Roosevelt Conservation Partners. In addition to his involvement in national organizations, Mr. Model actively supports many local groups and organizations in Wyoming.

Mr. Model is married and has three children.

RECORDS OF NORTH AMERICAN BIG GAME COMMITTEE

Eldon L. "Buck" Buckner, Chair
Baker City, Oregon

Gilbert T. Adams
Beaumont, Texas

Lee M. Bass
Fort Worth, Texas

Marcus T. Barrett III
San Antonio, Texas

Jack E. Beal
Ft. Lauderdale, Florida

Herman A. Bennett
Brownwood, Texas

George A. Bettas
Stevensville, Montana

Joe Bishop
Steamboat Springs, Colorado

Tommy L. Caruthers
Denton, Texas

Craig Cook
Anchorage, Alaska

John O. Cook III
North Bend, Washington

Ernie Davis
Cotulla, Texas

H. Hudson DeCray
Bishop, California

Patrick J. Gilligan
Hillsborough, California

Richard T. Hale
Ottawa, Kansas

Robert H. Hanson
Wapiti, Wyoming

Vernon D. Holleman
Temple, Texas

Frederick J. King
Bozeman, Montana

William C. MacCarty III
South Boston, Virginia

Butch Marita
High Bridge, Wisconsin

Earl Morgenroth
Reno, Nevada

Jack S. Parker
Carefree, Arizona

Marie Pavlik
Fort Lauderdale, Florida

John D. Pearson
Sheldon, South Carolina

James M. Peek
Viola, Idaho

Arthur C. Popham, Jr.
Kansas City, Missouri

John P. Poston
Helena, Montana

Richard D. Reeve
Anchorage, Alaska

Jack Reneau
Missoula, Montana

Glenn A. St. Charles
Seattle, Washington

Mark B. Steffen
Hutchinson, Kansas

Wayne C. van Zwoll
Bridgeport, Washington

Paul D. Webster III
Wayzata, Minnesota

TABLE OF CONTENTS

Award-Winning Trophy Stories continued

Award-Winning Trophy Stories continued

Tabulations of Recorded Trophies in the 25th Awards Program 471

Tabulations of Trophies Accepted in the 25th Awards Program continued

ILLUSTRATIONS

Field Photographs of Award-Winning Trophies continued

Field Photographs of Award-Winning Trophies continued

25th Awards Field Photos

25th Awards Field Photos continued

25TH NORTH AMERICAN BIG GAME AWARDS

PANEL OF JUDGES
KANSAS CITY, KANSAS
2004

Paul D. Webster, Chair
Wayzata, Minnesota

Mark O. Bara
Georgetown, South Carolina

William L. Cooper
Tifton, Georgia

Richard C. Berreth
Prince George, British Columbia

Albert C. England
Lloydminster, Alberta

John T. Caid
Pinetop, Arizona

Robert H. Hanson
Wapiti, Wyoming

Larry R. Carey
Spokane, Washington

Homer Saye
Cypres, Texas

Daniel R. Caughey
La Honda, California

Timothy D. Walmsley
Fowler, Illinois

CONSULTANTS

Eldon L. "Buck" Buckner
Baker City, Oregon

Jack Graham
Edmonton, Alberta

L. Victor Clark
Verdi, Nevada

Glenn E. Hisey
Chatfield, Minnesota

Frederick J. King
Gallatin Gateway, Montana

Sagamore Hill was the home of Theodore Roosevelt, 26th President of the United States and Founder of the Boone and Crockett Club, from 1885 until his death in 1919. Pictured above is the trophy room at Sagamore Hill. The Sagamore Hill Medal (inset) was created in 1948 and may be awarded by a Big Game Awards Program Judges Panel, if in their opinion there is an outstanding trophy worthy of such distinction.

INTRODUCTION

▼ ▼ ▼ ▼ ▼ ▼ ▼ ▼ ▼

GEORGE A. BETTAS ED.D.

Executive Director of the Boone and Crockett Club

The Boone and Crockett Club's 20th Big Game Awards, held in Albuquerque, New Mexico, on June 8-10, 1989, was my introduction to the Club's awards program. Although it was 15 years ago, I remember the event as if it were yesterday. What I remember most from that event was the presentation of the Sagamore Hill Medal to Gene Alford of Kamiah, Idaho, but I also remember the enthusiasm surrounding the presentation of each award by Dr. Phil Wright and the sage comments by Club president, Red Duke. My fond memories of the 20th Awards, coupled with the vision of Eldon "Buck" Buckner, Chair of the North American Big Game Records Committee, the members of the Records Committee, the Judges Panel, and our Boone and Crockett Club's professional staff provided the overarching vision and spirit which our Boone and Crockett team brought to the 25th Big Game Awards Program in Kansas City, Missouri, on June 17-19, 2004. The 25th Awards Program was the zenith of the Club's Awards Programs to date and included the recognition of eight new World's Records in seven different categories and was one of our best ever attended. The overall excellence of the event for the trophy owners and guests was simply "the best" and will provide a benchmark for all future awards events.

As I introduced each trophy owner, read their hunting stories, and each of them received their medals and plaques I kept thinking of how the culture of hunting in North America has changed and how rapidly it continues to change. I was also thinking about the Sagamore Hill medal and the fact that at the 25th Big Game Awards Program in Kansas City, even though there were eight new World's Records and many fine trophies and associated hunting adventures, the Sagamore Hill medal was absent.

For me, Gene Alford's story symbolized the very essence of the Sagamore Hill Medal. As I think about Gene and his experiences afield, it is clear to me that in today's fast-paced society, the far majority of hunters will never have the opportunity to achieve Gene's level of experience with the land and its animals.

It's been said that a journey of a thousand miles must begin with a single step. The Boone and Crockett Club took that step more than 117 years ago when our founders embarked on a remarkable journey that established the major elements of our North American model of wildlife conservation, which is largely responsible for the abundance of places to hunt and the wildlife we currently enjoy. Today, we continue on that journey, step by step, and in doing so we face more challenges than ever before in achieving our mission of conservation leadership. Over one hundred years have passed since sportsmen first adopted an ethical code of conduct. Today, technology, society, and we have changed. What was once a predominately rural society is now predominately urban, wherein fewer and fewer people have routine contact with the land and its wildlife.

We live in a democracy wherein the rules we live by are determined by majority vote. For those who value hunting, it is fortunate that the majority of the population who do not hunt tolerate or accept hunting. If hunting is to survive, to be practiced by our children and future generations, we must preserve, enhance, and protect the image of hunting and hunters as a positive force in wildlife conservation.

The human pressures on our land and the wildlife it supports have increased steadily throughout the period of human habitation. As the human population grows, so does our collective need for food, water, land, and fuels. Stepping forward and accepting responsibility for the land and its wildlife made hunters, trappers, and fishermen North America's first modern conservationists. As such we are acclaimed by many for the recovery of hunted wildlife species and the creatures of the most effective system of conservation in the world. This system of wildlife stewardship worked because those individuals and groups who cared the most stepped forward and took responsibility for these resources. The Boone and Crockett Club's Big Game Awards Program celebrates our success in conservation and the importance of hunters in the ongoing conservation movement.

We are living in a culture that is changing at a very rapid pace. The shrinking American day, the connectedness craze, the maturation and diversity of our society, globalization, the information-based economy, the willingness of individuals to pay to save time, and the rapid changes in technology are driving much of what most Americans do today. These changes are altering the face of hunting in North America and the world. All of these changes are impacting "how" we hunt and "what" constitutes hunting. In the marketplace consumers dictate style and product. As hunters are impacted by changes in our society so will be the changes in what constitutes ethical hunting and fair chase. The Boone and Crockett Club and its members have always taken the high road when it comes to conservation, fair chase, and outdoor ethics. As our society changes we will be constantly challenged to define, reaffirm and, at times, modify our position.

As our society continues to grow and change, and our lifestyles become more and more distant from the land, replicating Gene Alford's hunting experiences will become more and more difficult. Gene Alford's story was unique as his life was unique when compared to today's common lifestyles. Even so, there exists the potential today for hunters to equal Gene's example of fair chase, pursuit of excellence in trophy quality, personal sacrifice, and sufficient focus and drive to hunt one on one for an outstanding big game animal. The hunter of today and tomorrow may not have the same opportunities to develop the outdoor and hunting skills that Gene Alford had, but there will always exist the opportunity for hunters to practice ethical hunting methods, develop the necessary hunting and outdoor skills, and have hunting experiences that will be worthy of the Sagamore Hill Medal in the future. This will be true as long as we have hunting in North America.

As we celebrate our 25th Big Game Awards Program and the conservation system that produced these animals, let's reflect on Gene Alford's hunting experiences as we think about hunting in the 21st Century. When it comes to hunting, the legacy left by our hunting heroes who have gone before us provides the foundation for us to build the future. Gene's approach to hunting and the common values that guided his hunting experiences are an integral part of our hunting heritage.

Let's all toast Gene and the best of trophy hunting. Gene passed away at his home in Kooskia, Idaho this past month. Let's wish him dogs with good noses, gentle mules, and good tracking snow in that special place where he is now.

GENE ALFORD, 1924-2004

Editor's Note: Much of the following article was originally written by Harold Nesbitt in 1989 when he was editor of the Boone & Crockett Associate's Newsletter. *Since the story of the Alford cougar is so unique, the author has updated, edited, and added to Nesbitt's original work in this article.*

For only the fourteenth time, the Boone and Crockett Club awarded its highest award, the Sagamore Hill Award, to a trophy representing the highest attainment of sportsmanship and Fair Chase at the 20th North American Big Game Awards on June 10, 1989. The award was presented to Gene Alford of Kamiah, Idaho, for his cougar scoring 16-3/16 points that is second only to the World's Record in the category. Alford's story embodied the best of the sporting tradition that the Boone and Crockett Club has always encouraged and recognized with its records keeping for native big game of North America.

I met Gene Alford for the first time on June 8, 1989, at the 20th North American Big Game Awards in Albuquerque, New Mexico. He was very reserved and on the bashful side, but I found him to be a tremendously interesting and knowledgeable person as I engaged him in a number of discussions about everything from cougar hunting to packing into the back country with horses and mules. As a result of our meeting in Albuquerque I became well enough acquainted with Gene that he invited me to bring my horses and mules and join him for two different 100 mile pack trips into Idaho's Selway-Bitterroot Wilderness. I made the first trip with Gene in August 1989 and the second trip two years later with Gene and my two daughters. These trips afforded me the opportunity to engage in many wonderful conversations with Gene, but most of all I got to know him as a person and developed a great appreciation for Gene as a hunter, woodsman and outdoorsman.

Gene Alford moved to Idaho in 1959 to work for an outfitter, guiding hunters in the Selway River area. He had always loved hounds and cougars, and had spent many years

Photograph from B&C Archive

Buck Buckner (right) and his wife, Hope, were instrumental in arranging for Gene Alford (left) to attend the 20th Awards Program in Albuquerque, New Mexico. They had to convince Gene to attend without making him aware that he would be the recipient of the Club's highest award, the Sagamore Hill Medal.

hunting cougars with his strike dogs in California. The cougar hunting skills he had perfected in California served him well when he moved to Idaho's Selway Country. Before long Gene discovered that he had found a pretty close approximation to "cougar paradise." Idaho is great cougar country, with plentiful food (deer, elk, and other game) and great cover provided by mountainous areas with limited access for motorized vehicles. Before long he took up residence in Kooskia, (pronounced Koos-kee), nestled amid protective hills at the confluence of the Southfork and Middlefork of the Clearwater River at the gateway to the Selway-Bitterroot Wilderness. While living there and guiding in the backcountry, Gene soon found a great way to spend a month each winter, hunting cougar with his dogs. Gene's annual cougar hunt evolved into a regular feature of his yearly calendar.

Each February, he would hire a local pilot to fly him, with his dogs and gear, into a campsite along the Selway River in the Selway-Bitterroot Wilderness. There, he would set up camp and let each day's agenda be determined by the cougar sign he and his dogs found on his daily hunting routes. Gene chose the month of February because, in his experience, he had learned that during February there were concentrations of big game animals, especially whitetail deer, along the Selway River, which attracted good numbers of cougar. The weather along the river during February was generally better than the earlier months and facilitated more days of hunting.

You should understand that Gene Alford was no spring chicken when he took his record-book cougar. He was 66 years old at the time. A lot of folks at that age are concerned about a trip to the library on a snowy day, let alone being put out on their own in a wilderness area, with only two dogs for companionship, for a month. But, at the time of his hunt Gene was more than up to the task. He was in excellent physical condition, with a wiry build and the slight squint of the Westerner who has spent a great many days afield under the blazing sun. And he had been chasing big cougar in this fashion for nearly 30 years.

Interestingly, Gene felt that the weather conditions are the most serious health hazards to be faced on his winter outings. With the ever-present snow and ice, a fall resulting in broken limbs and severe impairment of function could be fatal. So, Gene exercised caution and good sense, including using ice cramp-ons on his boots to avoid slipping on icy surfaces.

Gene brought some big cougar to bay in his years of hunting in this fashion. In 1961, he killed two big toms that were entered in the Boone and Crockett Club's Records Program with the same score, 15-12/16 points, both equal to the score of the then World's Record. The scores of both were found to be slightly smaller by the Awards Judges Panel, but both were given the same final score, 15-11/16 points, and entered into the 1964 records book as tied (with two others at the same score) for number three for the category. A lesser hunter might well have hung-up the ice cleats and gun after this accomplishment, but not Gene Alford. He continued his yearly hunts, treeing a great many cougar and simply photographing or looking at most of them before letting them go; he was after a really big one.

Part of Gene's resolve to continue after a big one was disappointment in his two cougars ending up as only number three for the category after the initial entry score indicated they would tie the long-standing record (which incidentally was Theodore Roosevelt's cougar taken in 1901 near Meeker, Colorado).

At that same competition (as the Awards were called in those days), a cougar entered by Ed Burton and taken in 1954 scoring 15-12/16 points, tied the World's Record. In those days, communications were not as good as today. Gene did not attend the competition, and he had to rely on information relayed to him with the return of his skulls. Apparently that information failed to properly settle questions in Gene's mind as to how his two skulls dropped in score and in potential rank, giving him additional incentive to find another, bigger tom.

Interestingly, Burton's cougar may have been even larger had not a sloppy field-dressing job with an ax removed an estimated 2/16 inch from the skull length.

Similarly, one of Gene's cougars was missing a portion of the back of its skull as well. At the time Gene hunted with a .38 pistol and accidentally shot one of these record cats at the base of the skull, destroying part of the skull resulting in a significant loss of skull material and a lesser skull length. Thereafter, Gene hunted with a Smith and Wesson Model 19 .357 revolver and did not have to worry about an errant bullet hitting a cougar in the wrong place.

Of course, both then and now, only the material present and unaltered on a trophy can be officially measured. So, Burton's trophy simply tied the World's Record instead of setting a new standard. Gene's damaged cougar skull was similarly scored and his trophy likewise scored lower than it would have if all of the skull material had been present. In any event the harvesting of these exceptional cougars certainly did indicate that there were some big toms out there.

Gene found what may well be his ultimate cougar on February 26, 1988. His hound, Scratch, struck the tom's trail at 8 a.m. that morning. Gene's hunting technique is different from what most cougar hunters are used to in areas where cougar are hunted during the winter when snow is present. Gene described the dogs and the technique used by most hunters as "turn in" hounds/hunting. What he means is that the hunters locate a cougar track by driving a vehicle or snowmobile along backcountry roads until they locate a cougar track. When they find a track they assess the "freshness" of the track and attempt to determine the size of the cat by the size of the track. When a suitably fresh and sizeable track is found the hunters "turn in" their dogs on the track, making sure that the dogs follow the track in the direction in which the cat is traveling.

Gene hunted with a "strike dog" and believes this method of hunting is more challenging and demanding since the hunter is on foot and the dog is allowed to range ahead of the hunter as the hunter courses through the country. Gene perfected this method of hunting cougar while he was in California where there was seldom any tracking snow and cougar were hunted on dry ground. Gene would also tell you that hunting cougar in snow is much easier than hunting on bare ground, requiring more highly trained dogs with excellent noses. The other interesting aspect of Gene's hunting technique on this hunt is that his second dog was not a hound. His second dog was Kelly, Gene's constant companion.

Kelly is a Kelpie, a stock dog much more often found on a ranch than on cougar hunts. When Scratch struck a cougar track, Kelly was right on his heels during the chase with all the enthusiasm for chasing the cat that she would have for chasing a rank old range bull out of the brush on a hot summer day.

Gene's hunting involved hiking through deer winter ranges at elevations ranging from 2,000 feet to more than 7,000 feet. When the dog "strikes" a cougar track the dog pursues the track, and sometimes follows the track in the wrong direction because the dog is not under the immediate control of the hunter who can see what direction the cat is traveling. On other occasions the strike dog will pick up a cougar track on ice or frozen ground where no tracks are visible. In either case the strike dog pursues the cat and the hunter follows until the cat is treed, the scent lost or until the hunter can get the dog turned around if it is backtracking.

Gene knew the crossing points of the cougar in the area he hunted and noted that the old toms travel in circles, making the circuit in about two weeks. The cats do this so as to continually be hunting undisturbed game and not push the game from the area.

In the case of Gene's record cougar he, Scratch, and Kelly picked up the track in a saddle at about 3,500 feet in elevation. Scratch began cold trailing the track with Kelly in pursuit as well. After an hour of cold trailing and a considerable amount of gain in elevation Gene found one of the cougar's tracks in a patch of soft snow under a fir tree. The dogs were headed in the right direction, but they were still cold trailing! Three hours after the trail had been cut, Gene found himself on top of a 6,000 foot ridge with the dogs following the cat's trail down the other side. Just a short distance down the back side of the mountain the dogs jumped the cougar. Fortunately for a tired Gene and his dogs, the cougar only went about halfway down the mountain before in Gene's words, "stepping up the first tree it came to." A very tired Gene rested before taking some pictures and then using his .357 pistol to shoot the huge tom. It was when he started to skin the cat that he realized just how big-bodied this cougar was. It was so heavy that Gene couldn't lift the hindquarters to aid his skinning. It was obviously heavier than the normal 200 pounds of a really big tom cougar.

It was estimated by Gene and others that the big tom must have weighed about 225 pounds — a real monster cat. Gene recalled quite vividly just how heavy the skin and skull were; they weighed 42 pounds when he got back to his camp, a real load under the weather conditions and after the day's long and tiring chase.

After the required 60-day drying period, Gene had the skull measured officially for entry into the Boone and Crockett Club's 20th Awards Program. Just as in 1961, the entry score tied the current World's Record score. Would this be history repeating itself? Yes it would, but with a much more pleasant ending.

The score for entry was 16-4/16 points, placing it in an apparent tie with the World's Record taken by Douglas E. Schuk in 1979. The 20th Awards Final Judges Panel scored Gene Alford's trophy as 16-3/16 points, not a tie for the World's Record but clearly the new All-time number 2 for the category. As fate would have it, Gene's number 2 cougar had an old injury to its face and all of its nasal had been crushed and healed back in a snub nosed position, losing at least a quarter of an inch in overall skull length. Without this injury Gene's cougar would have easily been a World's Record!

In view of the great number of years of hunting by Alford with a lofty goal of trophy quality, the personal sacrifice to hunt with just his dogs each year, and the details of an

Top, Gene Alford accepts his Sagamore Hill Medal from past president of the Boone and Crockett Club, Red Duke, at the 20th Big Game Awards Program, in 1989. Bottom, Gene's cougar skull (front and center in case) measured 16-3/16, just 1/16 of an inch shy of the World's Record. Gene took the cougar after spending years in pursuit of a big cat.

excellent, Fair Chase hunt and kill, this trophy was a top contender for the coveted Sagamore Hill Award. This time Gene would not have any questions about the process and the recognition for his trophy. However he would tell you that a question still lingers in his mind, he boiled the skull to clean it and may have boiled it longer than he needed to, thereby causing the skull to shrink more than it would have if beetles or a maceration chamber had been used to clean it.

There was some stiff competition for the Sagamore Hill Award. The 20th NABG Awards recognized six new World's Records (barren ground caribou, Central Canada barren ground caribou, Sitka blacktail deer, Coues' non-typical whitetail deer, muskox, and the new category of non-typical American elk) and a number of other fine, high-ranking trophies, most with fine hunting stories. Still, there was something about Gene's story and his obvious love affair with big cougar and wilderness hunting with strike dogs that tugged at the Judges Panel members' hearts. Gene's determination to hunt 29 years to get a big cougar piqued the interest of the Panel of Judges and the panel asked Buck Buckner to personally go to see Gene and get all the details. Tracking Gene down and getting this accomplished took some doing as Gene had no telephone and lived on some acreage high above the Clearwater River in north central Idaho. Buck finally contacted Gene and flew his plane to Idaho where he landed in a horse pasture and recorded Gene's story. Buck reported back to Walter White, Chairman of the Records of North American Big Game Committee and sent him a copy of the tape. Upon receipt of Buck's report the Panel of Judges recommended Gene for the Sagamore Hill medal.

The Sagamore Hill Medal is the highest award of the Boone and Crockett Club. It is named after the favorite home of the Club's founder, Theodore Roosevelt, and it is given in memory of him and his two sons, Theodore Jr. and Kermit.

Stipulations for the award state that it cannot be given more than a single time in an Awards Program, and it can only be awarded for a trophy that embodies both trophy quality and the essence of Fair Chase hunting. It is not necessarily given in every Awards, with its absence indicating the Judges Panel's conclusion that no trophy truly worthy of this highest award had been presented to them. The Sagamore Hill Medal may also be presented for exceptional service by an individual to the Club and its goals. Prior to the 20th Big Game Awards, the Sagamore Hill Medal had been presented 13 times for trophies and four times for individuals for service to the Club.

After long and detailed discussions of all suitable candidates for the Sagamore Hill Medal, the Judges Panel voted to recommend Gene Alford's cougar trophy for the award. The Panel's recommendation was presented to the Executive Committee of the Boone and Crockett Club who could either accept the recommendation and prepare the medal, or reject the recommendation and thus end the matter. The Executive Committee heartily agreed with the Judges Panel and directed that the award be prepared for Alford's fine trophy.

Photograph courtesy of George A. Bettas

Gene Alford and his faithful hunting companions, Scratch and Kelly, in the Selway-Bitterroot Wilderness where they spent countless months together tracking cougars.

It has always been tradition for the Sagamore Hill Award to be a surprise ending to the Awards Banquet. The awards other than a possible Sagamore Hill Award are made known on the day of the banquet at Press Day when the working press is convened with the trophy owners in the trophy display so that stories and photos can be obtained first-hand. It has also been tradition for the recipient to be present to receive the Sagamore Hill Medal, if at all possible. But Gene Alford lived in a small Idaho town and didn't care a lot for big-city lights and formal dinners.

Help would have to be recruited to get him there. Buck was a member of the Judges Panel who was acquainted with Gene. Walter White, Chairman of the Club's Records Committee, asked Buck to try to get Gene to the Awards Banquet without telling him of the Sagamore Hill Award. Buck did his job in fine fashion. Buck and Gene spoke the same language; both were lean, taciturn Westerners who loved the outdoors and hunting. With help from Buck's wife, Hope, Buck had Gene present for the activities. Since Gene had never flown on a commercial airplane, Buck had a few challenges in getting Gene to Albuquerque for the 20th Awards Program. When Buck told Gene he wanted him to come to Albuquerque, Gene asked Buck if it would be if it was alright for him to wear his cowboy hat. "Of course," Buck assured him! Next Gene asked Buck about dress for the occasion. Buck suggested he buy an inexpensive western sport coat and that would be just fine.

Buck arranged to have Dick Humphries fly Buck's plane to Kooskia and pick up Gene in the same cow pasture where Buck had landed before. Dick picked Gene up and flew him to Boise where he boarded the plane destined for Albuquerque with one stop in Denver. Gene missed his connecting flight in Denver, but finally made it to Albuquerque and the Awards Program. The evening of the Awards Banquet Gene asked Buck for assistance in tying his tie. He said, "Buck, I have been messing with this knot for an hour and with this bobbed off thumb I need some help with this tie. Buck was unsure just how Gene had lost half of his thumb, but took care of the one last detail for Gene before the Awards banquet. During the awards ceremony it was evident that Gene was enjoying each minute, with only one question in his mind as to why it was so essential that he be present.

Of course, as June 10 wore on, Gene got to wondering if maybe there was a chance that his cougar would receive the Sagamore Hill Award. He heard the other trophy owners and writers talking about the possibilities, and his trophy was mentioned in the group. He really didn't want to think about it for fear it might not come true. In fact, at the banquet, with a program in front of him listing all the awards to be made, including the Sagamore Hill Award, Gene refused to look at the pages. By the time the regular awards had ended and Gene was called to receive the Sagamore Hill Medal, you could tell by the wide grin on his face and moist eyes that it was a dream come true for Gene.

As Gene remarked to Buck on the return flight home, "I never thought 27 years ago when I started trailing cougar that the trail would lead to here." Gene Alford's long odyssey on the trail of a big tom cougar embodies a great deal of the mystique of all hunters, and trophy hunters in particular. It also has the happy ending of the highest award of the Boone and Crockett Club, one of those all-too-rare moments in this life when the guy in the white hat wins big.

George A. Bettas, Ed.D., Stevensville, Montana, is the Boone and Crockett Club's Executive Director. He became a Regular Member of the Boone and Crockett Club in 1989 and has served as the Club's Vice-President of Administration, Vice-President of Communications, Chairman of the Associates Committee, and Editor of *Fair Chase* magazine. He has been an Official Measurer and member of the Records Committee since 1990. He is a founder and Past President of the Mule Deer Foundation and retired Vice-Provost - Student Life and Dean of Students at Washington State University, Pullman, WA.

BOONE AND CROCKETT CLUB'S

25th Big Game Awards
2001-2003

▼   ▼   ▼   ▼   ▼   ▼   ▼

Photographs courtesy of B&C Staff and Cliff White

Clockwise from top left: Buck Buckner and Jack Reneau verifying scores; The sheep display at Cabela's was one of the best ever; Members of the 25th Awards Judges Panel Standing (l.–r.) Mark B. Steffen (KS), Mark O. Bara (SC), Robert H. Hanson (WY), Richard T. Hale (KS), Eldon L. "Buck" Buckner (OR – Records Committee Chair), Albert C. England (AB), Paul D. Webster (MN – Judges Panel Chair), Homer Saye (TX), Jack Graham (AB), William L. Cooper (GA), L. Victor Clark (NV), Timothy D. Walmsley (IL), Larry R. Carey (WA). Kneeling (l.-r.) Richard C. Berreth (BC), Jack Reneau (MT), Daniel R. Caughey (CA), Frederick J. King (MT), John T. Caid (AZ) and Glenn E. Hisey (MN – P&Y Records Chairman).

REVIEW OF THE 25TH AWARDS PROGRAM

▼ ▼ ▼ ▼ ▼ ▼ ▼ ▼ ▼

ELDON L. "BUCK" BUCKNER

Records of North American Big Game Commmittee, Chair

and

JACK RENEAU

Big Game Records, Director

The Boone and Crockett Club's 25th Awards Program will go down in history as one that broke many records. Nine new World's Record trophies, representing eight categories, were among the 117 trophies on display at Cabela's in Kansas City, Kansas, during May 5 through June 19, 2004. This was the largest number of trophies on display since 1995 when 105 were on exhibit for the 22nd Awards Program at the Dallas Museum of Natural History in Dallas, Texas. A record number of 4,220 entries were received during the 25th Awards Program Entry Period, which started on January 1, 2001, and ended December 31, 2003, all of which is testimony to both outstanding big game management and increased knowledge and effort by today's hunter/conservationists.

Although the Judges Panel reviewed more trophies than ever before, fewer score changes occurred because of a shrinkage allowance policy implemented by the Club's Records Committee in 1992. This policy was adopted because of concerns with normal shrinkage that occurs from the time a trophy is officially scored and accepted in B&C until it is re-scored by an Awards Program Judges Panel. The scores of 87 trophies (74%) seen by the 25th Awards Program Judges Panel remained the same, while 15 trophies (13%) experienced higher scores than originally entered, and 15 (13%) received somewhat lower scores. The drop in scores for the latter trophies was greater than the shrinkage allowances for their respective categories and therefore attributed to factors other than natural shrinkage.

These results are just the opposite of what happened prior to implementation of the shrinkage allowance policy at the 20th Awards Program in 1989. Prior to implementation of this policy the scores of approximately 80 percent of the trophies reviewed by the previous Awards Program Judges Panels dropped. The remaining 20% either stayed the same or went up.

The 25th Awards marked the first time awards were presented in two new categories: Columbia blacktail, non-typical, and Sitka blacktail, non-typical. Obviously two of the new World's Records fell in these categories. New World's Records were also announced for bighorn sheep, non-typical Coues' deer, muskox, pronghorn (two-way tie), Roosevelt's elk, and tule elk. Some observations of broad entry categories follow.

For the first time, two pronghorn trophies both taken in Arizona two years apart, tied with a new World's Record score of 95 points. The top photograph features David Meyer, right, and his guide, John Caid, with David's buck and in the bottom photograph Dylan M. Woods, right, is congratulated by fellow award recipient and well-known outdoor writer, Chuck Adams. Dylan's buck can be seen in the background.

HORNED BIG GAME

PRONGHORN

It is appropriate that Hayden Lambson's pronghorn painting was chosen for this book's dust jacket. For the first time, two pronghorn trophies, both taken in Arizona two years apart, tied with a new World's Record score of 95 points, edging out Michael J. O'Haco's Arizona buck by an impressive 1-4/8 inches. O'Haco's pronghorn had been recognized as the World's Record since 1985. David Meyer took his buck on the Arizona Strip in 2002, a year after taking another outstanding trophy in Yavapai County that also received an Honorable Mention from the 25th Awards Program Judges Panel. Dr. Meyer's trophy was confirmed as a new World's Record in 2003 by a Special Judges Panel, which was specifically convened to verify the World's Record status of his trophy and the new World's Record Roosevelt's elk

Dylan Woods took his exceptional buck in Coconino County two years before Meyer, but his entry was not submitted until much later. Both of these trophies were confirmed as tying for World's Record status at their original entry scores.

SHEEP

Unlike the 24th Awards, the 25th Awards boasted an outstanding sheep exhibit, highlighted by Guinn Crousen's two life-size Alberta bighorns, scoring 208-3/8 and 202-1/8, closely followed by Jack Greenwood's and David Nygard's Montana rams, both scoring over 200 points. Crousen's big ram, taken on Luscar Mountain, Alberta, in 2000, displaced one of the oldest World's Records in the book — Fred Weiller's 208-1/8 Alberta ram taken in 1911 by 2/8ths of an inch!

James Schneider's aged and broomed New Mexico desert ram, scoring 179-3/8, received the First Place Award in its category. Four other desert sheep, including three scoring in the 180s, were also invited but not sent in, so they will appear in the records listings with asterisks, subject to further confirmation.

Dall's sheep were well represented by four Alaska trophies. William Dunbar's two rams, both over 40 inches and both from the Chugach Mountains, taken over 10 years ago, received First and Third Place Awards with respective scores of 177 and 172-2/8.

Donald Mann's beautiful life-size Stone's Sheep, taken near Muncho Lake, British Columbia, in 2000 and scoring 174-6/8, was an attention-getter at the Awards and garnered First Place, closely followed by Ronald Selby's 174-1/8 ram from Yukon Territory. All sheep sent to the Judges Panel were confirmed at their original entry scores.

MUSKOX

Muskox records continue to spiral upwards at every Awards Program it seems. At the 24th Awards in Springfield, Missouri, three years ago, Vicente S. Sanchez-Valdepenas' potential World's Record failed to arrive in time for panel scoring, but was subsequently verified by a Special Judges Panel convened in 2001 during the 25th Awards Program as a new World's Record at 127-2/8. Mr. Sanchez-Valdepenas' muskox was on display at the 25th Awards.

However, Craig Scott's big bull, taken near Norman Wells, Northwest Territories, in 2002, was scored and verified by the Judges Panel as the new World's Record at 129 points.

ROCKY MOUNTAIN GOAT

Four great billies were submitted, including a beautiful life-size mount taken by a lady hunter, Dora Hetzel, who assured us that she earned her trophy! Dora took her goat, scoring 53-6/8, along Del Creek in British Columbia in 2003. According to the records books, her billy is the second largest ever taken by a woman.

BISON

Two bison trophies added a distinctive touch to the trophy display. Duane Richardson's Pope and Young Club World's Record bull, scoring 131-6/8, was taken with a bow during a tough hunt in Arizona's House Rock Valley in 2002. Duane's bull took the First Place Award. Terry Mathes' Wyoming bull, which was taken in Teton County in 1998 and scores 124-2/8, received Honorable Mention.

DEER

COUES' WHITETAIL

One trophy that is likely to stand as a World's Record for some time is an incredible non-typical buck, scoring 196-2/8, that was taken on the San Carlos Indian Reservation some 35 years ago by a tribal member. It replaces the former World's Record established at the 24th Awards Program three years ago in Springfield, Missouri, by 10-1/8 points! This massive buck is currently owned by antler collectors Dana J. Hollinger and Bob Howard. The top typical head entered was taken by Sergio Orozco with a bow and is the Pope & Young Club's current World's Record. Its entry score was 132-7/8, but it was not sent in for judging, leaving Bradley Johns' 125 point buck to take the First Place Award. Bradley's trophy was taken in Graham County, Arizona, in 2000. Mr. Orozco's buck will be asterisked and unranked in future records books until its score is verified by submission to the Club's big game records committee of two additional scorings.

WHITETAIL

The number of whitetail entered in the 25th Awards Program remained essentially unchanged over the 24th Awards Program. Eight hundred and seventy-six typical whitetails were received during the 25th Awards Program, compared to 881 during the previous three years. While there were no contenders for World's Record status, Hubert Collins' 2003 Saskatchewan buck took the First Place Award at 203-3/8, confirming that it is the seventh largest typical whitetail ever recorded by B&C. Among non-typical entries, Tony Lovstuen's great Iowa buck taken in 2003 was panel scored at 307-5/8 and is now recognized as the largest recorded whitetail ever taken by a modern-day hunter. It ranks in third place in the non-typical category because of two larger deer that were found dead in the woods. Jerry Bryant's Illinois monster, scoring 304-3/8 took the Second Place Award. Bryant's buck is

Photographs from B&C Archives

Clockwise from top left: There were a total of 42 deer trophies on display at the 25th
Awards Program including Jerry Bryant's non-typical whitetail scoring 304-3/8, being
measured here by Richard C. Berreth and William L. Cooper; the non-typical whitetail deer
display was impressive with the two highest scoring hunter-taken trophies every; plus
Lavonne Bucey-Bredehoeft, right, who received a Second Place Award for her non-typical
mule deer taken in 1961. She is pictured here with her family and friends.

the second largest non-typical buck ever recorded by B&C for a modern-day hunter. Mike Beatty's massive non-typical buck, which unofficially scores 304-6/8, was noteworthy because of its absence. Beatty was invited to send his highly touted non-typical buck to have the score verified by the 25th Awards Program Judges Panel, but he declined the invitation. His buck is not accepted in B&C and cannot be accepted until serious concerns with the procedure for scoring it are resolved by a Judges Panel.

MULE DEER

During the 25th Awards 147 typical entries were received at the All-time minimum score of 190 points or more, showing a slight trend upward. Approximately another 120 more specimens were received scoring below the All-time minimum, but above the Awards minimum. One of the more interesting stories of the mule deer recognized in Kansas City is that of Lavonne Bucey-Bredehoeft who was present to receive the Second Place Award for her non-typical buck, scoring 269 points, which she shot 43 years earlier in Wyoming as a young girl. Be sure to read her complete hunting story which appears on page 144 of this book.

COLUMBIA BLACKTAIL

The non-typical Columbia blacktail category was established at the start of the 25th Awards Program to recognize exceptional deer that were not eligible for entry in any other category. A total of 25 entries were received in this new category. Ten were invited to be recognized by the 25th Awards Judges Panel, as is customary with newly established categories. The first World's Record recorded for this new category was taken by Frank S. Foldi in 1962 in Polk Co., Oregon, and scores 208-1/8. Nine of the top ten trophies invited were sent in for Judges Panel scoring — all but one being older trophies taken prior to the current Awards period.

SITKA BLACKTAIL

There were 29 trophies accepted in the typical Sitka blacktail category during the 25th Awards Program and four in the newly established non-typical category. The creation of the non-typical category presented the Club with one of its most unique situations since the first Awards Program was conducted in 1947. One of the Club's longest standing policies governing the Awards Programs is that a trophy can be submitted for listing in only one entry period. However, since the non-typical Sitka blacktail deer is a new category, a massive buck taken by William B. Steele in 1987, and accepted in the 21st Awards Program in 1988 as a typical buck at 126-6/8 suddenly became eligible for entry in the non-typical category at 134 points because of a single abnormal point on its left antler. Mr. Steele's trophy didn't need to be re-scored by the 25th Awards Program Judges Panel since its measurements were already verified by a previous Judges Panel. The only thing necessary to reclassify Mr. Steele's trophy was to transfer the measurements from his typical score chart to a non-typical one and recalculate the final score. As a result of this procedure, Mr. Steele's trophy, which received the Second Place Award at the 20th Awards Program in 1989, also received the First Place Award in Kansas City at the 25th Awards Program and was declared the World's Record. Mr. Steele's trophy is the only trophy ever to receive a Place Award at two different Awards Programs.

ELK

AMERICAN ELK

While standing World's Records were not challenged in either American elk category, two heads were especially notable. The first is a magnificent typical bull, scoring 411-3/8, taken by Chuck Adams with a bow in Rosebud County, Montana, in 2000. This incredible bull, which is also Pope and Young Club's World's Record, received the First Place Award in Kansas City. The second is a massive non-typical bull that was taken in 1888 by William D. Deweese in Rio Blanco Co., Colorado. This latter head scores 430-2/8 and is tied for 13th place in the All-time records book, illustrating that there are still some great old trophies out there waiting to be discovered. It is currently owned by the Royal Gorge Regional Museum and Historical Center, which was formerly known as the Canon City Municipal Museum.

ROOSEVELT'S ELK

Jason S. Ballard's Oregon entry established a new World's Record at a score of 404-6/8. This bull replaces the one taken by Karl Minor on Vancouver Island, British Columbia, in 1997. Mr. Minor's bull was declared the World's Record at the 24th Awards Program in 2001 with a score of 396-5/8.

TULE ELK

Although on display at the 25th Awards, Bryce Evans' new World's Record scoring 365 points was an entry in the 24th Awards, but it was not sent in so the 24th Awards Program Judges could certify it as the World's Record. Only an Awards Program Judges Panel or a Special Judges Panel, which is convened between Awards Programs, can certify a trophy as a new World's Record. Thus the 25th Awards Program Judges Panel re-scored and certified Mr. Evan's bull as the World's Record though it remained an entry in the 24th Awards Program. Noted bowhunter Chuck Adams received First Award for his 309-7/8 bull taken in Monterey County, California, back in 1990.

CARIBOU

Unlike the 24th Awards Program, where new World's Records were established in barren ground and mountain caribou categories, there were no new contenders for such titles this time, although all categories were well represented. The caribou category receiving the most entries during the 25th Awards was the Quebec-Labrador category with 46 trophies meeting or exceeding the Awards minimum. The next two most popular categories were the barren ground caribou and the Central Canada barren ground caribou categories with 44 entries in each.

Brian Williams' awesome life-size mount of his huge tom cougar was one of the first and most impressive sights to greet visitors to the Awards display at Cabelas. When Brian recounts his story about the hunt, he says, "The lion snarled at me, not like any old lion would snarl at you, but like the fourth largest lion in the world would snarl at you."

MOOSE

Those who saw the display of moose trophies will remember it as an impressive one. It included a huge Canada moose specimen taken by Doug Frank near Kinaskan Lake, British Columbia, in 2002 that now ranks in second place with a score of 240-6/8. Another memorable moose was Mark Rose's Alaska-Yukon bull, with its unusual accordion pleated palms and the third widest spread in B&C records at 80-3/8 inches! Mr. Rose took his exceptional bull, which scores 247-7/8 and ranks 15th in its category, near Rapid Creek, Alaska, in 2003.

BEARS and COUGAR

Black Bear entries were headed by John Bathke's Manitoba bruin with a score of 22-14/16, which now ranks in sixth place in the All-time records. Another top ranking bear trophy is Eugene Williams' grizzly, scoring 26-14/16, from Kala Creek, Alaska, which now shares the number four slot with two other bears. A first at the 25th Awards was a three-way tie for the First Place Award in the Alaska brown bear category. Robert Ortiz, Steve Rakes, and Gene White all took bears scoring 29-3/16!

Brian Williams' awesome life-size mount of his huge tom cougar was one of the first and most impressive sights to greet visitors to the Awards display at Cabelas. This cat, taken in Archuleta County, Colorado, in 2001 scores 16 points and ranks in fourth place in the All-time records book with two other trophies.

In summary, the 25th Awards with its outstanding big game trophies gave testimony to the effectiveness of modern game and habitat management that started with the effort of Boone and Crockett Club's founder, Theodore Roosevelt, some 117 years ago. May we hunter/conservationists have the courage and wisdom to face the challenges that lie ahead if such success is to continue.

Eldon L. "Buck" Buckner is the current Chairman of the Boone and Crockett Club's Records of North American Big Game Committee. First appointed an Official Measurer in 1968 while serving as a U.S. Forest Service range conservationist in Arizona. He has served as Judges Panel Chairman, Consultant, and Judge for Boone and Crockett Club Awards Programs since 1990.

Jack Reneau is a certified wildlife biologist who has been Director of Big Game Records for the Boone and Crockett Club since 1983. He was responsible for the day-to-day paperwork of the Boone and Crockett Club's records-keeping activities from 1976 to 1979 as an information specialist for the Hunter Services Division of the National Rifle Association (NRA) when NRA and Boone and Crockett Club cosponsored the B&C Awards Program. Jack earned a M.S. in Wildlife Management from Eastern Kentucky University and a B.S. in Wildlife Management from Colorado State University.

AWARD WINNING TROPHY STORIES

TROPHY STATS

▼ ▼ ▼ ▼ ▼

Category
black bear

Score
$22^{14}/_{16}$

Location
McCreary, Manitoba — 1998

Hunter
John J. Bathke

Length of Skull
$14^{5}/_{16}$

Width of Skull
$8^{9}/_{16}$

BLACK BEAR
First Award – 22 $^{14}/_{16}$

▼ ▼ ▼ ▼ ▼ ▼ ▼ ▼ ▼

JOHN J. BATHKE

As we had been doing for almost 30 years, several friends and I again went to Manitoba to hunt ducks and geese in late September. This year it was 1998. We have stayed in McCreary for the last 15 years or more, finding that it is well situated for the areas we like to hunt.

We like to socialize in the pub after hunting, having gotten to know quite a few local people over the years. Saturday evening I was having a beer with a local man named Rick, who was maybe only just old enough to drink.

Rick knew we were from "the States" and that we were there to hunt. As he likes to hunt, too, we were discussing all kinds

Unplanned Hunt – A Bear Story

of hunting when he asked me if I hunt bears. I said that I did. He said, "We have bears."

I said, "I know Manitoba has tons of bears."

He said, "No, on our farm. You should come shoot one of our bears".

I told him I would try. I also told him that many things would have to fall into place first, for this to work.

Having been coming to the area for so many years, I knew local outfitter and guide Terry LaDoux well. I called to see if he had a tag available for the specific area of Rick's farm. He said he did have one left and that he would sell it to me, since it was well into the bear hunting season and he felt he would not need it for another hunter.

I had one chance, one time, to hunt bears. That was Monday afternoon. We were scheduled to hunt ducks and geese on Monday and Tuesday morning and then return to Minnesota. Luckily, Terry was available.

I needed to borrow a gun, since all I had were shotguns for the ducks and geese. Rick loaned me his gun, which was a very old bolt action .270. He said it was right on at 100 yards. I trusted him, since I did not have an opportunity for target practice.

We got to the farm in early afternoon and set up near 18 beehives that were on the east edge of some grazed woods. We were across a fence in a grazed pasture, with benches set up behind a six-foot high pile of manure, facing west. The weather was perfect and warm, with some high clouds and a light breeze from the west. There was nothing more to do but wait.

Later, we started to hear noises in the woods. It was more than one animal. There was a wolf pack in the area and we thought maybe the wolves were coming around. Then, as the noise came closer, we started hearing low grunts and decided it was bears. Later, we did hear the wolves about a half a mile to the south.

Finally, a bear stepped out of the woods and walked toward the beehives. I looked through the scope. The cross hairs in the scope were black and so was the bear. Since I could not see the cross hairs, I centered the bear in the scope and waited. It sat down near the beehives facing us. I took a moment to be sure it was really centered in the scope and then fired at 70 yards.

The bear ran into the woods for a ways and then stopped. Since its noise stopped instead of fading into the distance, we assumed it was down, or had at least stopped running. Then it groaned. We picked up everything, loaded into the truck, and headed down the fence. We had to go a quarter of a mile to a gate, go through, close the gate, and come back.

When we got back to the beehives, light was fading. We started looking for blood and found very little. I had a small flashlight and even with that we found only the little bit of blood and tracks going into the woods. I stayed while Terry went to the farmhouse a half a mile away for more flashlights.

I walked into the woods. I had the flashlight, and the woods were open from grazing, so I could see pretty far. I took my time with the rifle ready and walked on. I found the bear about 50 yards in, lying still. I slowly approached. There was no movement at all; it was dead.

Terry returned with help from the farm. It took several of us and some engineering to get the bear into the truck. When we did, it filled the truck box. I had shot it in the middle of the chest and the bullet exited behind its left shoulder.

We went to the farm for supper and then took the bear to town. Terry is a taxidermist and agreed to process the bear and make a rug. While working on the skull, he realized how big it was and called to tell me about it. He wanted to present it to the Manitoba Big Game Trophy Association, and I thought that was a good idea. He called again later to say that he thought it might be the biggest for the year and that maybe we would want to come to the banquet in the spring.

My wife, Sue, and I did attend the banquet. We found out that it was a new Provincial record black bear, and we had a wonderful time. We picked up the bear rug, skull, and meat that same weekend.

The bear weighed 625 pounds, and was not fat! It stood about five feet high (its back was even with the tops of the beehives), and the rug squared out at 8 feet 3 inches. The bear also had very long legs. The rug is too big for our walls, so it is folded and covers our concert grand piano in the living room. After it was officially scored by the Boone and Crockett Club, I found out that it is the sixth largest black bear ever recorded.

Award Winning Moments...

Photograph by Jack Reneau

Thousands of visitors viewed the 25th Awards Trophy Display at Cabela's while it was open to the public during May through June. Above is a group of young school kids admiring the mule deer trophies and the bear skulls.

Photograph by Cliff White

TROPHY STATS

▼ ▼ ▼ ▼ ▼

Category
black bear

Score
$22^{10}/_{16}$

Location
Lincoln County, Wisconsin — 2002

Hunter
Daniel J. Kufahl

Length of Skull
$13^{14}/_{16}$

Width of Skull
$8^{12}/_{16}$

Photograph by Jack Renea

Daniel J. Kufahl accepting his plaque and
medal from Buck Buckner, Chair of the Big
Game Records Committee.

BLACK BEAR
Second Award – 22 $^{10}/_{16}$

▼ ▼ ▼ ▼ ▼ ▼ ▼ ▼ ▼

DANIEL J. KUFAHL

My hunt actually began back in March 2002, when some of my hunting buddies and I came across a bear in its den while walking runways looking for deer antlers. My hunting area is located near Merrill, Wisconsin, in the Newood Wildlife Area. My primary stand was in a thick, wet, swampy area surrounded by a heavy concentration of oak ridges.

We started baiting in early April, hoping to attract that same bear we saw while looking for antlers. The intent was also to attract any other additional bears. So, from early April to the middle of June, we put out bait, which included outdated bread and bakery mixed with cherry juice and strawberry jam, in a hollowed stump every Saturday. Then from the middle of June until the season opened in September, we baited every Wednesday afternoon and Saturday morning.

As the season approached, I kept picturing that bear we saw in the den earlier that spring. Some of the markings on the trees and the tracks left on the ground during the summer led me to believe that the same bear or a different decent-sized bear was in the area.

The season opened on Wednesday, September 4, 2002. I took three days of vacation so I could begin hunting as soon as the season started. In past experiences, it seemed like the chances of getting a big bear, or seeing one for that matter, decreased daily because of all the activity. With other bear hunters around, and the bird and archery deer seasons approaching, I knew my hunting days were limited.

The first three days were long and uneventful. On the first day, I began my hunt at my backup stand, which was on the side of a hill along a huge swamp through which the Copper River runs. This stand was about a mile away from my primary stand. My cousin, Tom, came along with his video camera to tape any action that might take place. About half an hour before daylight, we saw a decent bear going through the woods. Unfortunately, that was about as exciting as it got.

Around 10 a.m., we moved to my primary stand and sat there until dark. The afternoon was sunny and fairly warm, and the mosquitoes were thick. Around 5:30 p.m., two young fishers came prancing through the woods looking for any leftover snacks. Then, at dusk, three smaller bears came into the bait. They all strolled in from different directions within five minutes of each other. We thought the first one was a circus bear, as it wasn't able to tip the stump over, but just climbed on top of the stump, knocked off the cover, and reached down the hole to get some food, barely keeping its balance.

The next morning was damp, cool, and pretty uneventful, so my cousin went back to the shack, but he returned to the stand later in the afternoon. Once again, around dusk, along came the same three young bears. This time they seemed quite antsy about something. However, dusk settled, and nothing came of it.

Day three was rainy so we waited it out, sleeping, back at the shack. It cleared up later that morning, but it was so hot and humid that we waited until late afternoon to go hunting. That evening we didn't see anything except a lot of mosquitoes.

Saturday was a day off because of a friend's wedding so I didn't put out any bait, which made it the first Saturday I hadn't set out bait all summer long.

The next day, after a previous long night out, we wandered into the stand around 4:30 p.m. and brought a nice chunk of wedding cake for the bears to snack on. About an hour after sitting down, we had a very nice bear come up from behind us and walk to a spot directly below us. Unfortunately, it suddenly ran back the way it came, never giving me a chance for a shot. I'm pretty sure the bear was well over 200 pounds. After another hour passed, I was starting to feel disappointed because I hadn't been able to get a shot at that earlier bear, and had only seen those three smaller bears during our first three days out.

Then, at about 6:40 p.m., a huge raccoon appeared at the stump. Moments later, the raccoon took off. I looked at Tom and said, "Get ready, something is coming."

About 200 yards away, we could see a big bear sneaking through the underbrush, just catching a glimpse of it every once in a while. After we finally got a good look at the bear, I told Tom, "You do the best you can to get it on video. I'm going to take the first good shot I get."After seeing how fast the earlier bear had come and gone that evening, I wasn't going to take any chances on missing the opportunity with this one. Finally, after about 10 minutes, the bear was about 10 yards behind and to the left of the stump and about 80 yards from the stand. I heard Tom turn on the camera. As the bear approached the stump, I slowly raised my gun, got it in my sights, and pulled the trigger on my .280 bolt-action. The bear fell instantly, kicking on its back. It got up and took off in the direction it came from.

We waited excitedly for about 15 minutes then climbed down from the stands and went to look for blood on the trail. After finding a fair amount of blood, we were confident I had hit the bear well and that it hadn't gone far. We started tracking slowly. Twenty minutes later, we found the big bear 40 yards away.

It was unbelievable how big it looked lying there. Tom had the camera rolling as I put the tag on it. Realizing how big the bear was (380 pounds when it was field dressed), we left it to go back to the shack to get some help. After rounding up a few extra helpers, we headed back out to the woods, and the work began. Once we were back in the woods by the stand, it was kind of spooky because during the time we were gone to get some help, the stump had been tipped over and quite a bit of the bait had been eaten. There were bears still in the area. It took several of us to field dress the bear and haul it to the truck. Once back at the shack, it was picture time and then to town to register the bear.

The next day it was off to the taxidermist. Initially, I didn't realize the bear's Boone and Crockett potential. The taxidermist actually brought it to my attention. When I found this out, I was even more excited about what I already thought was the most exciting hunt of my life! After the skull sat for the required drying time, I took it to Steve Sirianni, an official B&C measurer from Wausau, Wisconsin. Immediately after seeing the skull, he said, "This is going to be the biggest black bear skull I ever scored." The bear officially scored 22-10/16 B&C points. I guess you could say the rest is history.

BLACK BEAR
Second Award – 22 $^{10}/_{16}$

▼ ▼ ▼ ▼ ▼

DANIEL J. KUFAHL

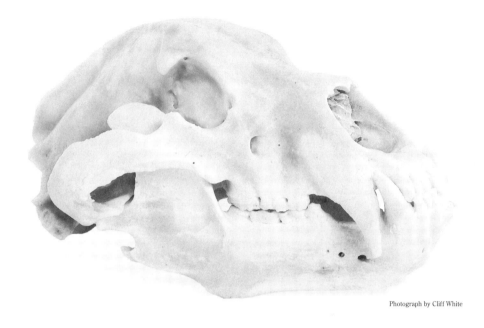

TROPHY STATS

▼ ▼ ▼ ▼ ▼

Category
   grizzly bear

Score
   $26^{14}/_{16}$

Location
   Kala Creek, Alaska — 2001

Hunter
   Eugene C. Williams

Length of Skull
   $16^{11}/_{16}$

Width of Skull
   $10^{3}/_{16}$

Eugene C. Williams accepting his plaque
and medal from Buck Buckner, Chair of
the Big Game Records Committee.

GRIZZLY BEAR
First Award – 26 ¹⁴/₁₆

▼ ▼ ▼ ▼ ▼ ▼ ▼ ▼

EUGENE C. WILLIAMS

Looking into the forest shadows, I could see a form that looked out of place against a backdrop of thick spruce. I shouldered my rifle and peered through the scope. The image observed through the riflescope electrified me as I realized I was only yards from the monster grizzly — and I was clearly the focal point of its attention.

Dark Timber Grizzly

This hunt started days before, on April 28, 2001, when local area Alaska Department of Fish and Game biologist Glenn Stout and I went on a snow machine ride into the Kaiyuh Mountains south of Galena. Our day's adventure was driven by the notion that we wanted to see some new country. Spring thaws had settled the heavy mountain snow pack, opening up some backcountry that is rarely visited.

We each carried rifles with us on this occasion, just in case we spotted a distant wolf or possibly a bear, though it was a bit early for bears to be emerging from hibernation.

Breaking out above the line of timber and onto the open alpine tundra, we were met with snow flurries and low clouds that blanketed our intended destination with a thick carpet of white — so dense that to press on would risk getting us lost or driving off a cliff.

Backtracking to lower elevations near the upper tree line, we came across a several-days-old track of a large grizzly bear. The bear had moved up out of the timber of one drainage and slipped down into the head of another. We guessed the bear's destination to be the bottomlands along the Yukon River, approximately seven miles to the northeast, where the monster would likely stalk and pull down a moose to feed what had to be a ravenous post-hibernation appetite.

Photograph courtesy of Eugene C. Williams

Tracks of the author's grizzly, disappearing into a wooded area.

As the day's plan was no longer workable, we elected to satisfy our immediate curiosity in the enormous track by following it a short distance into the heavy timber. Glenn joked that he would defer any bear shooting that day to me, as I was carrying a .30-06 and he was packing his .223 varmint rifle. The direction taken by the bear put it on an intersecting course with the Yukon River. Curiosity in the tracks quickly vanished as the deeper, unsettled snows of the steep timbered slopes caused our snow machines to bog down and us to perspire freely and often in digging out mired machines. With the excitement of this game now gone, we retreated back the way we had come.

Thoughts of the monster bear haunted me for the next two days. On the evening of April 30, I gave Glenn a call to see if he was up for another trip to the bush to look for the bear. He declined, electing not to waste a day of his vacation time to pursue my fanciful notion of finding a large bear in the thousands of square miles of roadless wilderness south of Galena, Alaska, where we lived.

My wife was reluctant to allow me to go on my own, fully understanding the risks of snow machine failure, weather, and terrain — not to mention risks associated with confrontations with bears. What probably worried her more than anything was the notion of me crossing the Yukon River on a snow machine this time of year. It was spring. Snow pack was melting. River ice had to be thawing. She signed off on my plan for the solo trip, but only after I promised to wear a life jacket while on the river and grilling me as to the contents of my day pack in case I had to spend a night in the woods. I left her a topographic map, on which I defined the area where to look for me should I not return. She was also advised that Glenn would know where to begin to look for me if need be.

I left the house at 6 a.m. on May 1. The temperature was 10°F. With six extra gallons of fuel and a pair of snowshoes, I headed out on my snowmobile. My plan was a simple one. I would follow an abandoned, decades-old dozer trail that started on the south bank of the Yukon River upstream from the village of Galena. One branch of the trail led through the hills and then cut down to and across Kala Creek, about two miles off the Yukon, and terminated at an old military radar site on Ketlkede Mountain. The other branch led up to and across the Kaiyuh Mountains to an inactive mining claim. As Glenn and I had taken the west fork to access the Kaiyuh Mountains on the earlier trip, I decided to travel the east fork of the dozer trail down into Kala Creek. This was new country I hadn't been in. I reasoned, too, that this course had the potential to put me in a position to intercept the trail of the bear discovered earlier, or at least possibly into the country where the bear might be.

It didn't take long, once leaving the south bank of the Yukon River, to travel the two miles of old dozer trail into the bottom of Kala Creek. To my amazement and delight, there in the frozen slush atop the creek ice was a lone set of very large bear tracks headed away from the Yukon and back up into the mountains.

There was no way to gauge the age of these tracks. The slush, or "overflow" as it is called locally, could have been the result of any of the freeze/thaw cycles of the several previous days. Overflow can be a trap for unsuspecting snow machiners or dog mushers. The condition typically is hidden under an undisturbed surface crust of snow, where seepage from snow melt, springs, or adjacent wetlands collects. Breaking through the surface crust into several inches (or several feet) of slush/water can ruin your day, particularly if aboard a 600-pound snow machine. As temper-

GRIZZLY BEAR
First Award – 26 $^{14}/_{16}$

▼ ▼ ▼ ▼ ▼

EUGENE C. WILLIAMS

atures had dropped into the single digits the previous night, and coupled with settling from the recent warm weather, the overflow here was frozen hard clear to the creek's surface ice in most places.

I followed the bear's trail up the creek on the snow machine out of curiosity, with little thought about the possibility of a bear in the last tracks on the other end. But after 200 yards of following the creek, with open water peeking through and gurgling sounds below, I thought more about cold wet feet and the dreadful notion of pulling a waterlogged snow machine out of a hole in the creek ice. I retreated.

Returning to the first point of intersect with the tracks, I headed off on the old dozer trail toward Ketlkede Mountain in search of more tracks. The run to the mountain top didn't take long and no other tracks were discovered.

I returned to the creek, electing to follow the bear track on foot as a form of morning entertainment. The weather was crisp and the skies clear. Winds were light and variable. I was intrigued by the meandering course the bear had taken upstream. It was interesting to note, as I followed its path, what objects or odors caught its attention. Occasionally, the bear would turn at 90° angles and moving off a few feet to investigate something in its surroundings. At one point, its nose told it there was a shed moose antler buried under two feet of snow, which the bear dug up and bit into. The heavy print of the bear was obvious and easily discernable well ahead along the creek's course. Occasionally, it broke through the crust into the intermittent overflow or soft snow beneath. In contrast, I was leaving little evidence of where I had been.

After two hours of fanciful pursuit on foot, I decided I should return to the snow machine, as going overland with the machine to this point on the creek was an easy option. I would also be that much closer to a ride home when I elected to call it quits. I returned with the machine, and struck off again on foot on the tracks of the grizzly.

The bear was still sticking to the creek bottom. I told myself that if it stayed in the bottom or turned east into the tundra/open scrub black spruce stands, I would follow. That was, of course, providing the snow crust would carry me. If the bear turned west into the timbered slopes of the Kaiyuh Mountains, where snow was deep and soft, I would give up the pursuit.

The grizzly regularly cut across the points of land in the creek's many meanders, but sometimes would stick to the creek channel and follow it around the bend. If the bear took the shortcut and I could see through the timber to the other side, I would follow. If it took a shortcut through the trees and visibility was poor, I would follow the meandering channel around and pick up the track on the other side.

The author crossed paths with this award-winning grizzly while on a day hunt when he was living in Alaska. The bear scores 26-14/16 points and received a First Place Award at the 25th Awards Banquet in Kansas City.

Over the course of the morning's trek, it became apparent to me that the grizzly's trail here had been made since the temperature had plummeted late the previous evening. Where the animal had walked on snow-free southern bank exposures, it had tracked dirt and spruce needles out onto the clean snow. Had the dirt been tracked out onto the creek the day before, the tracks would have been melted out by the sun's warm rays being absorbed by the dark material. These tracks were not. I now knew I had a chance for this bear.

I removed my shooting glove, checked my weapon, and ensured myself that my scope was on low power. I was carrying a .300 Mag Browning BBR, a companion on countless previous hunting trips.

The game of simply following a track in the snow had transformed into a cautious pursuit. The pursuit remained much the same as the previous three hours — in and out of the timber along the course of Kala Creek, going upstream. The sun was still low in the clear eastern sky and morning shadows were long. Once more, I followed the grizzly's shortcut across a narrow point of land at the bend in the creek channel. I had broken with the morning's discipline of not following the track into the timber when I couldn't see bear tracks in the snow in the creek on the far side. The point of land here, though narrow, was of higher elevation. There was very little plant understory.

I felt secure, and assumed the bear had simply returned to the open channel on the upstream side. The giant bear had not! Once in the trees, the grizzly had come across a maze of moose tracks along the far bank and elected to follow them — and travel by stepping into the tracks left by the moose!

I no longer had a clear picture of where the bear was. I scanned the creek channel upstream and downstream — no bear tracks. My attention turned to the moose tracks at my feet. I couldn't discern which direction the bear had gone. I looked to my left and spotted a form that didn't fit with its surroundings. I shouldered the rifle and peered through the scope at the strange form. It was a grizzly! The bear was facing me head-on, while standing with front feet atop a downed tree. It was huge! The bear's intent stare told me it had seen me before I saw it. The grizzly was too close! I knew full well it was a mere few seconds away. A charging, running bear can out run anything afoot in these parts.

As the safety came off and my finger found the trigger, my mind was asking the question of what would happen next. Would the bear turn and run at the shot, or would it come for me? The rifle fired and I quickly worked the bolt to chamber a fresh round. As if in slow motion, the bear reared up, roared, threw its head back with front paws high in the air and tumbled over backwards. Then all was quiet. The grizzly got up momentarily behind the blowdown timber and then sank out of sight. It remained quiet!

As it turned out, the bear had been napping behind some blow-down timber along the creek bank, in a bed it had prepared for itself by scratching away the two feet of snow and ice down to bare earth. Remaining hidden through my approach, it had heard me approaching, or possibly caught my scent in the variable breeze that was blowing, and got up.

I looked at my watch. It was 11:45 a.m. I waited a full 10 minutes before walking in a big semicircle around the bear on the creek side. The grizzly had tumbled backwards down the bank into the creek channel. I approached cautiously. When close enough to lob in some tree branch projectiles, I did so, to ensure the animal was dead. As I got close enough to use the gun barrel, I poked the grizzly with it to ensure no life was left. The bullet had struck the bear at the midpoint of its sternum and traveled the length of the body, stopping just under the hide of its right hip. The 200-grain bullet had done its job.

The animal was in excellent physical condition, but with very little body fat remaining. It was an old bear with some long-ago healed dental problems, likely created by an encounter with a flying moose hoof. I had been on the track since 8:00 a.m., having followed it for over five miles on foot.

There was a healthy bounce in my step as I returned to where I had last parked the snow machine. I carefully guided the snowmobile up the Creek from where it was parked and was able to maneuver to where the grizzly lay. Skinning the animal was easy, other than the two feet of soft snow, which made it difficult to turn animal.

It was an interesting ride for the two of us on the snow machine during the trip home. The distance to my home's back door from where the bear fell was 35 miles.

This was my first grizzly. At this point, I knew I had harvested a nice trophy, but had no idea how big the bear really was!

I called a taxidermist in North Pole to tell him what I had. Charlie Livingston of Alaska Wilderness Arts and Taxidermy was skeptical, at best, as I described the size of the animal to him. "How big? You have to be kidding!" he said.

Mr. Livingston had worked with scores of grizzly trophies and had not seen anything like I described. Green-scored by Glenn Stout, and subsequently by Mr. Livingston, it was pointed out that it may be within a few points of the World's Record grizzly.

The news that I had taken a big grizzly passed through Galena quickly. Galena, a traditional Native Athabaskan community, consists of about 650 people. Though half white now in cultural mix, many Natives still adhere to a lifestyle dependent upon natural resources. The interior grizzly is respected and typically not hunted alone. Many were in awe of the notion that I went out on a solo bear hunt.

I returned to the kill site the following weekend to reflect on the last moments of this hunt. I collected the moose antler the grizzly had dug up and chewed on. I measured the distance from where I was standing when I shot to where the bear was located at point of bullet impact. It was only 38 yards!

I am certain that it was this bear that had left the large tracks Glenn and I had spotted earlier. There aren't that many big grizzlies out there. Most larger interior Alaska grizzlies taken by hunters measure six to seven feet in length. This one measured 8'3"! This animal clearly is a trophy of 10 lifetimes.

To be able to step out and hunt from one's back door and do a day-trip grizzly hunt is easy enough to do when living in rural "bush" Alaska. To cross paths with a Boone and Crockett bear is an entirely different matter. Mr. Livingston advised me, "My friend, you will not out do this monster ever again."

Gene Williams, the author/hunter, currently resides in Aberdeen, South Dakota. He is the Manager of the Sand Lake National Wildlife Refuge Complex. The Complex is part of the National Wildlife Refuge System administered by the United States Fish and Wildlife Service. In 2001, Gene resided in Galena, Alaska where he served as Manager of the Koyukuk/Nowitna National Wildlife Refuge Complex, the largest land-based Complex in the National Wildlife Refuge System.

Award Winning Moments...

Photograph by Jack Reneau

From left to right, Richard E. Jobe (grizzly bear), Larry A. Meyer (grizzly bear), Daniel J. Kufahl (black bear), and Eugene C. Williams (grizzly bear) pose together in front of the bear skull display during the Press Day for trophy owners at Cabela's in Kansas City.

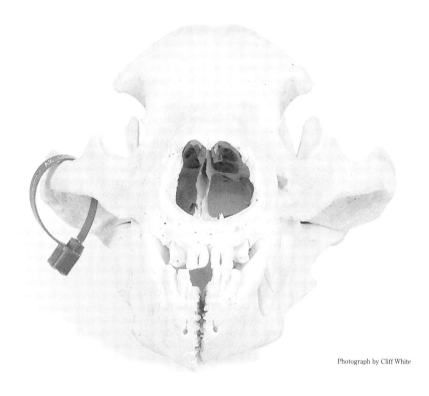

Photograph by Cliff White

TROPHY STATS

▼ ▼ ▼ ▼ ▼

Category
grizzly bear

Score
$26^{12}/_{16}$

Location
Kuskokwim River, Alaska — 2001

Hunter
Richard E. Jobe

Length of Skull
$16^{6}/_{16}$

Width of Skull
$10^{6}/_{16}$

Photograph by Jack Rene

Richard E. Jobe accepting his plaque and
medal from Buck Buckner, Chair of the Big
Game Records Committee.

GRIZZLY BEAR
Second Award – 26 ¹²/₁₆

▼ ▼ ▼ ▼ ▼ ▼ ▼ ▼ ▼

RICHARD E. JOBE

In May 2001, my brother, George, and I were going to help Richard Wilmarth with his gold mining operation in the Flat area. Incidentally, as a side note, Richard won the first Iditarod race ever run in 1973. He called my brother and told him to get a bear tag because the bears were breaking into the gold mining camps.

Richard picked us up in Palmer. He dropped us off at his gold mine and left because there was too much snow, and it was too cold to run the equipment and pumps in order to mine the gold. A couple of days later he returned with Piper, a black Labrador, to keep us company. He talked to us for a little while then returned to his residence in Red Devil where he lives with his wife, Shirley, and their four kids.

A couple of days after Richard left, we came across a huge bear track along the edge of the woods, about 125 yards away from camp. Days later I turned in early and my brother stayed up to read. All of a sudden George yelled, "Bear!" I jumped out of bed and pulled on my pants and shoes, then he handed me the binoculars. I took a look and handed them back. There was no question this was a good bear!

Since George got a grizzly a couple of years earlier, it was my turn. I grabbed his .338 and we stepped out on the small porch of the wanigan in which we were sleeping. The bear didn't know there was anyone in the camp. I asked George where I should shoot from. He said, "Right here!"

I shot the bear broadside through both lungs. It made a semi-circle away from us and disappeared into the brush. My brother and I went over and found it piled up about 40 yards from where I shot it. We approached with caution, but it was dead.

The bear has everything going for it — its size, its fur, and its claws (the longest being over three inches long) are all exceptional. Boone and Crockett Club Official Measurer, Wayne DiSarro, measured the skull at 26-12/16 B&C points. Dan Foster, a taxidermist from Wasilla did a full mount with a habitat base. The bear is on display at my restaurant in Pennsylvania enclosed in a glass case. It sure is a beautiful bear and it gets quite a bit of attention from our customers.

Photograph courtesy of Richard E. Jobe

Richard E. Jobe's grizzly bear was taken on a hunt with his brother George at gold mine.

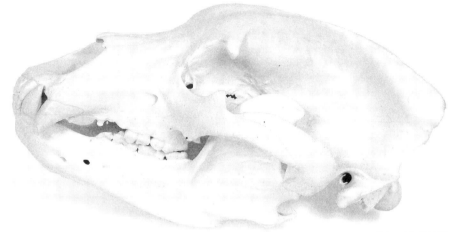

Photograph by Cliff White

TROPHY STATS

▼ ▼ ▼ ▼ ▼

Category
grizzly bear

Score
$26^{10}/_{16}$

Location
Windy Creek, Alaska — 2001

Hunter
Kyle R. Moffat

Length of Skull
$16^{9}/_{16}$

Width of Skull
$10^{1}/_{16}$

Photograph by Jack Rene

Kyle R. Moffat accepting his plaque and
medal from Buck Buckner, Chair of the Bi
Game Records Committee.

GRIZZLY BEAR
Third Award – 26 ^{10}/$_{16}$

▼ ▼ ▼ ▼ ▼ ▼ ▼ ▼ ▼

KYLE R. MOFFAT

Sitting in Wasilla in mid-afternoon of September 21, 2001, my brother Luke (17 at the time) and I (15 at the time) were itching to get back to Cantwell to get some big bull moose on video. Our freezer was already full from a moose Luke had shot a few days before, and moose season had just closed, so hunting moose was out of the question. What we had planned instead was to call in some moose and see if we could get them on video raking the brush and strutting their stuff. Living in Cantwell, you can't be too careful with the amount of bears roaming the area, so we brought firearms in case we saw one that we wanted to harvest and also for protection.

After we got home, we packed our things then headed out for our afternoon outdoor adventure. It was easy to enjoy the calm, sunny afternoon.

After about 45 minutes of riding four-wheelers, we arrived in the Windy Creek drainage area,which lies northeast of the Denali Highway.

We started to walk back to an ideal location where we were going to call and glass. Carefully topping the last knob, I instantly spotted a grizzly milling around in the brush! It was only 80 yards from where we sat. We went back over the knob out of sight and I put a round into my Savage .30-06.

We crept back up over the knob. The bear was obviously still unaware that we were there. I sat down, rested my elbows on my knees, and squeezed a round off behind the boar's front shoulder. After I hit the animal, it started to tear up the tundra in a cloud of fury, which lasted until it caught another 180 grains of lead.

We waited for awhile before we went down to the animal, just to make sure it was dead. When we had it scored, I learned that not only did it make the Boone and Crockett Club's records book, but also ranked as the fourteenth largest grizzly ever recorded.

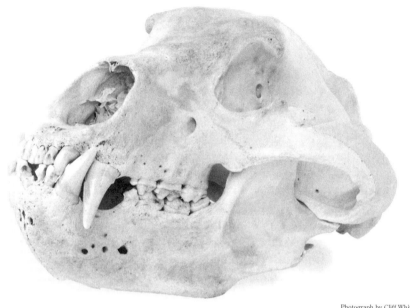

TROPHY STATS

▼ ▼ ▼ ▼ ▼

Category
grizzly bear

Score
$26^6/_{16}$

Location
Nulato Hills, Alaska — 2002

Hunter
Larry A. Meyer

Length of Skull
$15^{14}/_{16}$

Width of Skull
$10^8/_{16}$

Larry A. Meyer accepting his plaque and medal from Buck Buckner, Chair of the Bi Game Records Committee.

GRIZZLY BEAR
Fourth Award (Tie) - 26⁶/₁₆

▼ ▼ ▼ ▼ ▼ ▼ ▼ ▼ ▼

LARRY A. MEYER

I booked my grizzly hunt with Vance Grishkowsky of Unalakleet, Alaska, in early 2000. He has a great area for bear and has harvested a number of records-book bears over the years. Vance guides a number of bowhunters, but my choice was a rifle hunt.

My 12-day hunt started on September 1, 2002. The two Honda ATVs were packed for a four-day trip with food, water, tent, and hunting gear. We had a 28-mile ride back to a location where Vance had great success in the past. Just as we were getting close, the weather started to close in fast. By 4 p.m., we couldn't see 25 feet in any direction because the fog was so thick. We set up our first spike camp and stayed in that spot for three days. It reminded me of looking through a milk bottle as I tried to look out at the surroundings.

We managed to save water run-off from our tent for coffee, tang, and our dehydrated dinners. We did not hunt the first three days, but on the fourth day, we did get about a one-hour break to do a little glassing. We saw one huge bear, but it was on the other side of a large drainage, and we could not get to it. Just as the weather cleared, it started to fog us in again. We decided to try and get back to our home base in Unalakleet to get supplies and hope for better weather.

The fog persisted in the high country. Vance and I went up the Unalakleet River to check on his two bowhunters and a few new locations. The boat trip was 65 miles to where we couldn't get the jet motor to take us any farther. The bowhunters hadn't had much action and we didn't see any fresh sign.

We headed back to our home base. The ride back was somewhat faster, but 12 hours in a boat is a long day. We did stop and talk with some native friends. They had their gill nets out and were drying the trout they had caught.

Days six and seven brought more heavy fog. Once again, we were locked down to our base camp. Our plan was to move south when there was a break in the weather. Time was moving too slow and too fast all at the same time.

Days eight and nine saw the first clear weather of the trip. We headed south along the Bering Sea for 30 miles, right along the beach. Travel is only possible at low tide, but we finally ended up in the high country with clear skies and lots of berries!

After two full days of hiking across many miles of rough terrain, we never saw a bear. It was already time to move again. That night we waited for low tide and headed back to base camp. We were going to head back to the first area and hope for clear skies.

On day 10, we began our trip back. The trail was very rough because of all the rain and snow. It took almost an entire day to do what we had done in half a day before. Our two-man

Larry A. Meyer's grizzly bear went down with simultaneous shots at 15 feet from Larry and his guide, just as it was making its move to ambush them.

tent was up just before darkness set in. Vance wanted to return to where we had seen the big bear on day four.

Our trek began at daybreak, glassing and moving. At about 9 a.m., we finally caught a break. We spotted a big grizzly feeding on berries about half a mile away. We shed all the gear we didn't need as fast as we could. That bear would only be feeding a short time before finding some dark hole for the rest of the day.

As we crested the last big hill in the tundra, we saw our bear. Vance set up the spotting scope for a quick look and I pulled out the range finder. Vance said, "It's a big bear. Take it."

I said, "It's 507 yards; too far for my 7mm."

After a quick discussion, we tried to move closer. It was a big risk to take. One wrong move and the bear would be gone.

Luckily, the bear was still feeding when we got to the next ridge. It was now 303 yards away. I set up the shot off of a small spruce tree and then fired. The bear stood up on its hind legs and bit at its shoulder. I knew then that I had hit it. Two more quick shots as the bear dove into heavy cover and it was gone. I'm sure my guide and I were both thinking the same thing ... a wounded grizzly in some of the thickest cover one could ever imagine. I reloaded and Vance pushed all our gear back into the backpacks.

When we got to the berry patch where the bear had been eating, we tried to find signs of blood, but found nothing. There was no blood, no hair, nothing, but a few tracks where the bear had taken off. After about 20 minutes, we found some blood right on the edge of a spruce thicket. We knew it was hit.

We began to follow as this bear took us deeper and deeper into dense cover. Our visibility was 10 to 20 feet, sometimes less. The big grizzly was now bleeding very heavily on both sides. We were sure we would find it dead with that much blood.

A quarter of a mile into our tracking, the grizzly found a mud hole, did a little patchwork, and stopped bleeding completely. Vance and I stood there in disbelief. How could it go from dumping blood to nothing that fast? We made a few circles around the spot where we lost the track. This search was too dangerous with a wounded grizzly, so we had to come up with a new plan. We were depressed and just sat there in silence for several minutes. Just as I was going to ask about our next move, I sensed that Vance could hear something that I could not. As he motioned for me to be still, I waited until he said, "Larry, I can hear your bear and it's not far away! Check your gun. Make sure you have one in the hole. We'll move toward the sound. Be ready to shoot at close range. When we see the bear, we will be right on top of it."

The next 15 minutes gave me the biggest adrenaline rush I've experienced in 40 years of hunting. As we moved closer to the sound, I could slowly hear it. I would describe it as deep breathing and digging with a few unknown noises mixed in. It seemed as if this huge grizzly was ready to kill whatever was after it. It was apparent that it wasn't moving anymore. I thought I spotted it 10 different times, but finally there it was, only 15 feet away. The bear's two beady eyes were fixed right on us. All you could see was its monster head and neck. We both shot at the same time, just as the bear was making its move. It never made it out of the two-foot deep hole it had dug for its ambush.

Things could have gone terribly wrong in those last few seconds, but luckily we got this big fellow before it made its charge. No bullet would have stopped this 9-foot charging bear at 15 feet. Vance and I just stood there with the cross hairs on its neck, waiting for any movement, but this bear was now mine.

We slowly walked over. What we saw took my breath away. Not only was this bear a magnificent trophy with a beautiful cape, but it had definitely been ready for us. This grizzly had dug a sizable hole in the frozen ground and was set to make a major charge. Its hind legs were locked into the rear of its mud wall, ready to charge out like a cannon ball. It was sick of being followed and had made its last stand.

We marked our way back to our packs with small strips of my handkerchief. This was the only way we could relocate the bear in the thick cover. It took two complete handkerchiefs before we got to a place that was recognizable. We gathered our gear and made our way back.

It took an entire day to skin the bear and remove the skull. Rolling and moving a 9-foot grizzly will take the energy right out of you. I sure was glad that Vance took the cape and I hauled the skull. Late that night we returned to our spike camp feeling like two lucky, happy, and very tired hunters.

The next day, back at base camp, we got the skull clean enough to measure. We knew it was high in the book. I remember thinking how lucky I was to be in the right spot at the right time. This was the best trophy I had harvested in my hunting career. When we got around to measuring the cape, it squared at 9-feet 5-inches without stretching it.

This massive bear is displayed next to my brown bear and a black bear in what I call my "bear den." Someday, I hope to collect a polar bear to complete my bear slam.

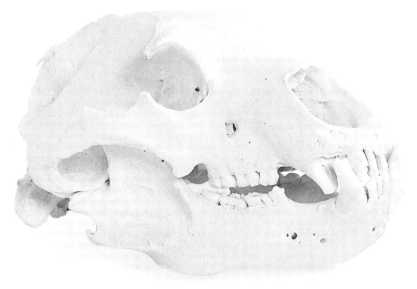

TROPHY STATS

▼ ▼ ▼ ▼ ▼

Category
grizzly bear

Score
$26^6/_{16}$

Location
Kuskokwim River, Alaska — 2003

Hunter
William G. Farley

Length of Skull
$16^3/_{16}$

Width of Skull
$10^3/_{16}$

Photograph by Jack Rene

William G. Farley accepting his plaque and medal from Buck Buckner, Chair of the Big Game Records Committee.

GRIZZLY BEAR
Fourth Award (Tie) - 26⁶/₁₆

▼ ▼ ▼ ▼ ▼ ▼ ▼ ▼ ▼

WILLIAM G. FARLEY

I sat back in the seat, my weary body sinking into the soft cushion of the small aircraft. I was heading toward Anchorage and a much-anticipated date with a plate full of fresh halibut. Fourteen days of freeze-dried food will do that to you. I closed my eyes and replayed the previous two weeks "in the bush" as the locals call it.

It was the third week of September 2002, and I had just arrived in camp and met my guide, Mark. I explained to him I had a tag for a grizzly, caribou, and wolf. I was most interested in the grizzly. Mark explained that he had been in an area on two previous hunts in the year with other clients and had seen a monster grizzly — by far bigger than any of the other bears. One of the packers had also seen it in the valley on two different occasions. It was a difficult valley to hunt, but this bear would be worth it if we could locate it. Mark had hoped another client would come in who was hunting grizzly and opt to venture back into this valley. I told him I was up to it and possibly we could get lucky. Mark mentioned they had also seen some other bears that were beautiful trophies, just because of the colors.

The first three days were raining as hard as it always does in Alaska, with 40 mile-per-hour winds, all day and night. Our tent was inside of a patch of seven-foot high alders and it still sounded like a flag in a windstorm.

We were finally able to get out on day four and start glassing. We spotted a huge white wolf that bedded down. We put on a stalk and got to 150 yards. It had a wound on its neck and haunch, showing a big, red, bloody blotch, but a wolf is a wolf, especially a white one. While waiting for it to stand up after about an hour, I caught movement out of the corner of my eye. In came a huge gray male trotting by, stopping to look at the white wolf. Mark said, "Take it. It has a better coat."

So I swung to the left and killed the wolf with one shot. It turned out to be a huge 125-pound male with a fantastic coat — a once-in-a-lifetime trophy and a great beginning to a long awaited trip.

We glassed two different grizzlies the next day, but both were at the other end of the valley. This was a long and arduous hike that I would learn like the back of my hand. We kept hoping to spot the huge boar that we had come into the valley for, but all of the bears we saw were smaller, blond, or silver bears with cubs.

Finally, on the morning of day five, I spotted a large dark spot that looked out of place. Then it moved. I believed it was the big boar, but we only saw it for about five seconds before it was enveloped in fog, and gone. We never saw that boar again in 2002. We continued to glass and spot bears each day.

Two different years, many hikes, and much different weather flashed in William G. Farley's mind when he took this grizzly. The big boar scores 26-6/16 points.

On day eight, we spotted a huge blond with chocolate legs, hump, and head. It was early in the afternoon, but we decided it probably wouldn't stay long enough for the three-hour hike to that end of the valley. Four hours later the bear was still there! We opted to start making the hike every day to be at the end of the valley where we were seeing all of the bear activity. We made the hike three days, seeing smaller bears, but not the big boar.

On day 12, we were making our usual trek, which by now was becoming a chore. We had no longer sat down when we spotted the big blond bear from four days earlier. It was about one mile away and running down a valley, looking back over its shoulder. We suspected it might be the large boar chasing this big blond, but we did not see it. We glassed the blond and decided it was an absolutely beautiful trophy and would probably measure eight feet. It was blond and chocolate, my perception of the ideal mountain grizzly.

We chose the route for the stalk, while the bear was feeding in a berry patch. I mentioned to Mark how unpredictable the winds can be below these mountain ridges and valleys. He assured me our crosswind was consistent. However, I had wind indicators that confirmed my fears; the wind was swirling. We continued on, but the wind would occasionally hit me in the back of the neck. We were about 500 yards from the bear and thinking about a shot, when we looked into the berry patch one more time and the bear was gone. We looked for it and then my stomach sank as I saw the bear running away as fast as it could go. The wind had betrayed us. It was one of the most disappointing moments of my hunting career. I took off running, trying to loop around the alder patch and possibly get another glimpse, but it was not meant to be, no matter all our hard work.

GRIZZLY BEAR
Fourth Award (Tie) – 26⁶/₁₆

▼ ▼ ▼ ▼ ▼

WILLIAM G. FARLEY

The hike back to camp was extremely long and quiet. The next day was the last day of the hunt. We woke to a cold, wet morning and once again made the long journey to the end of the valley. I opted to leave my rain gear to avoid carrying any more than necessary. Big mistake! We chose to sit up on the side of the hill and watch the valley where we had seen the blond the day before and hopefully find the big boar. The weather turned more than miserable. I had a big black trash bag, cut a hole in the top and pulled it over me. My new plastic Alaskan fleece did not help. By now it was raining and blowing snow, with a sleet combination, all at the same time. Mark couldn't sit still, and had to walk around to try and stay warm. We both finally agreed it was futile and nothing would be out in this weather except us.

I always hate to give up, and always feel that anything can still happen. On the way back to camp, low and behold we spotted a bear down in the creek. We watched the animal and it eventually came out of the creek and spotted us. That bear came to within 35 yards of us. It was a smaller bear, so I decided to go home without and come back next year.

Soon it was August 31, 2003, and I was coming back to try it again, hunting the same valley — just return and maybe get lucky and spot that big boar. I was hunting with Mark again. I was excited to be back in the same valley to try again to find that big bear, but at the same time questioning whether we should have tried a different area. We both decided it would prove to be okay, as nothing in the area had changed.

I had my good luck charm with me on this trip — my hunting buddy, Tim Moore, of Parkersburg, West Virginia, who had brought me good fortune on many other trips. Tim had a caribou and black bear tag.

We glassed the first evening, though we could not hunt because we had just flown in that day and the season did not open until the next day. The familiar valley seemed like an old friend. This year the weather was hopefully a good omen, as it was the best I have ever experienced in Alaska. We spotted game everywhere. We saw three black bears on the face of one mountain, several groups of caribou and two grizzlies, both blond, but one almost white.

The next day, we started out by spotting the two blonds again, and after an hour of glassing and deliberation, we decided the white bear was too unusual a trophy to pass up. So we took off on a stalk. After two hours, we came out onto the mountain we had seen them on. Unfortunately, they were gone.

We sat almost half an hour and enjoyed the balmy 70° Alaska weather. I picked up my glasses and looked up into our valley where all of the action had taken place last year and there it was! The boar was out grazing on berries in the same patch we had seen the blond last year. There was no mistaking it; this bear was a monster. Even over a mile away, it looked like a black Volkswagen.

We took off at a renewed pace. We approached the valley and it was still out in the berries, but drifting toward the alders. Being mindful of the wind because of the blown stalk last year, I suggested we stay back a distance and see where it went.

The bear had disappeared about 15 minutes earlier and we were sitting looking for it, when all of a sudden it appeared, moving through the alders down the creek we were sitting beside. We moved back and angled closer to the creek. The boar was coming right down the creek to us. The light color on its head and hump glowed in the sunlight. It looked like a huge African lion. As the boar made its way down the creek toward us, it came to a fork, and our fork had no place for it to go. Tim hit it with the range finder at 251 yards. I decided with the .340 Weatherby Magnum and 250-grain bullets it was time. Two different years, many hikes, and much different weather flashed before me as the gun bucked against my shoulder.

We made our way down and were disappointed not to find it lying there. The boar had gone into a thick stand of alders about one acre in size. Mark went in looking for it and came out, no luck. He went back in, bringing tension to a higher level. No luck! We went back to where it was standing when I shot and found blood and lung. All three of us started following a very good blood trail and came upon one of my most memorable trophies of my hunting career.

The most impressive thing that stood out about it was how big its head was, and the size of its paws and claws. The bear's head was too large to pick up and hold for pictures. The relief I felt after finally taking my mountain grizzly was immeasurable. I had taken the big boar we had come into this valley to find a year ago. He squared 9 feet 9 inches and its skull scored 26-6/16 B&C points.

Award Winning Moments...

Photograph by Jack Reneau

Kyle Moffat, left, was just 15 years old when he took his award-winning grizzly bear. He and his brother, Luke, who was also along on the hunt, traveled from Alaska to attend the 25th Awards Program in Kansas City. Kyle is pictured here with well-known outdoor writer and B&C Member, Chuck Adams, who had two award-winning elk at the 25th Awards Program.

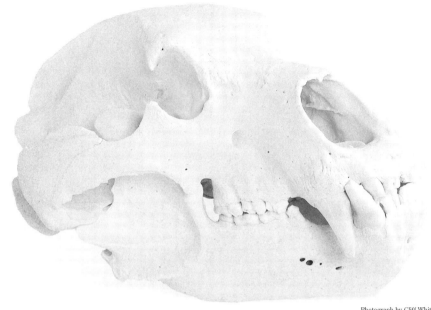

Photograph by Cliff White

TROPHY STATS

▼ ▼ ▼ ▼ ▼

Category
   Alaska brown bear

Score
   $29^3/_{16}$

Location
   Deadman Bay, Alaska — 2001

Hunter
   Robert M. Ortiz

Length of Skull
   $17^9/_{16}$

Width of Skull
   $11^{10}/_{16}$

Photograph by Jack Ren

Robert M. Ortiz accepting his plaque and
medal from Buck Buckner, Chair of the Bi
Game Records Committee.

BOONE AND CROCKETT CLUB'S

ALASKA BROWN BEAR
First Award (Tie) – 29³/₁₆
▼ ▼ ▼ ▼ ▼ ▼ ▼ ▼ ▼

ROBERT M. ORTIZ

I spent many evenings admiring the photos of the magnificent trophies and reading through the recorded entries that were in the 11th Edition of the Boone and Crockett Club's *Records of North American Big Game*. After awhile, I told myself, "I'm going to hunt Alaska, and I think I'll start by hunting the biggest and meanest bears around."

It was the fall of 2000, and I set my sights on an area in the southwestern part of Kodiak Island called Deadman Bay. After a few phone calls, I got in touch with Alaskan Guide Tom Kirstein to inquire about hunting Deadman Bay for Alaska brown bears. Tom caught me off guard by responding, "Well, I actually have an opening for this coming spring. You interested?"

I guess I must have been. On April 29 of the following spring, my companion, Tonya Buxton, and I found ourselves in Kodiak, Alaska, some several thousand miles away from our home state of New Mexico.

The next day, and after several hours in the air just above Kodiak's rugged snow-capped peaks, we landed via floatplane at the headwaters of Deadman Bay. Upon our arrival we were greeted by guide Tom Kirstein, assistant guide Jeff Poor, videographer Doyle Moss, and hunters Jim and Angie Ryan. Everyone was very courteous and sincere in welcoming us to the great hunt. After the formal greetings and so forth, our gear was carried over to the bear camp, which sat nestled in the thick alders several hundred yards away.

The camp consisted of three aged wooden structures. The largest of the three was considered the main cabin and it had two rooms. One room contained a kerosene stove, sink, dining table, and some shelving, while the other contained a few sets of bunks for sleeping. The main cabin was a place that lent warmth to our bodies at the beginning and at the end of each hunt day. It was also the place where we enjoyed our early morning breakfasts and our end-of-the-day dinners, not as guides and hunters, but as newly-made friends.

Photograph courtesy of Robert M. Ortiz

Base camp was located on the banks of Deadman Bay in the southwestern part of Kodiak Island, Alaska.

The two other cabins were small 7'x7' wooden structures. Each contained a set of bunks, two shelves, and a small heater. Tonya and I would house in one cabin for the next several weeks. Jim and Angie would house in the other. For some odd reason, Tonya was not buying my "It doesn't get any better than this" story.

After unpacking our gear, I proceeded to check the accuracy of my rifle one last time. Several shots later, I was confident that my rifle would perform if and when it was summoned to do so. On this particular hunt I was using my .30-378 Weatherby, equipped with a 3.5-14x52mm Leupold scope, and shooting my favorite bullet, the 180-grain Barnes X. As always, my rifle was set to shoot dead-on at 300 yards. This setting is one that had proven to be deadly accurate in the past, and one that would ultimately have the chance to prove itself again.

Word was that Tom Kirstein ran a good bear camp, especially with the assistance of folks like professional hunting guide Jeff Poor. Tom was very outspoken and there was no doubt that he knew most all there was to know about bear hunting. On the other hand, Jeff was very quiet and kept to himself most of the time. Nonetheless, Jeff proved to be one of the best guides and hunters with whom I have ever had the pleasure of hunting. It was agreed early on that Tom would guide Jim and Angie, and that Jeff would guide Tonya and me.

During the early evening of the first day we arrived at camp, I sat alone on the shale-covered shoreline looking westward at the majestic snow-capped mountains that sheltered the bay and its inhabitants from the rest of the world. As the sun's rays pierced down through the clouds and onto the bay's waters, I immediately felt God's grace and blessings. I knew that I was in a very special place. It was at that moment that I bowed my head and thanked God for granting me the opportunity to bear witness to the magnificence of the grand creation that stood before me.

Following dinner that first evening, Tom shared some of his bear hunting adventures with us. He also told us a little about the history of the island and of Deadman Bay. He went on to mention that there was a good book on the cabin's shelf titled, *Monarch of Deadman Bay*, and that it told the story of a mighty Kodiak brown bear that once roamed and ruled in Deadman Bay. Before closing for the night, I chose the faded brown-colored book from the many that lay on the cabin's shelf. I decided to make it my evening read for the next several days.

The *Monarch of Deadman Bay* was indeed a book that shared an early tale of a mighty Kodiak brown bear that once roamed and ruled in Deadman Bay. In the story, the Mighty Monarch inhabited and ruled the area for many years, and it did so despite the fact that one-half of its right front paw had been bitten off in a battle to the death with another great, but less fortunate, Kodiak bear. As I eagerly read page after page of the tale, I could only imagine what it might have been like to hunt a creature as great as the Mighty Monarch. As fate would have it, however, I soon too would cross paths with the mighty half-pawed Monarch, who had returned once again to roam and rule in Deadman's Bay.

During the springtime, the bears on Kodiak prefer the hillsides and the cover of the alder and willow bushes. As such, hunting them requires many hours of glassing and spotting. Luckily, we came prepared with 10x50 Swarovski binoculars and a 20x60 Swarovski spotting scope and a lightweight tripod. Additionally, hunting the drainages on Kodiak during springtime also means snow melt,

ALASKA BROWN BEAR
First Award (Tie) – 29 ³/₁₆

▼ ▼ ▼ ▼ ▼

ROBERT M. ORTIZ

deep rivers, and fast running water. To deal with these obstacles, we equipped ourselves with waist-high Gore-Tex waders, as well as wading boots that could be utilized both in the water and on land hiking comfortably for many miles over the rough terrain.

The weather changes on Kodiak are phenomenal. I can recall leaving camp one morning under a clear blue sky, bright sun, and warm weather. Two hours later, it rained cats and dogs. Then about an hour after that, the sky turned deep black and the winds blew hard enough to easily capsize a medium-sized boat. Then about an hour after that, it calmed, started snowing for a while, and then the sun came out again. No doubt, we were pleased that we had the proper all-purpose weather-proof clothing, a definite "must have" on Kodiak.

On the first day of the hunt, we spotted two bears that were approximately two miles away from us on the other side of the bay, and near the top of a 4,000 foot snow-covered hillside. We stayed watching the bears until they disappeared into a deep drainage. We also spotted a group of mountain goats on the same hillside and just below the area where we had initially spotted the two bears. The second day of hunting was dreadfully windy, making it very difficult to hold our binoculars steady enough to glass any particular area meaningfully. Nevertheless, we were able to spot several different bears that were hanging out just below a rock-faced hillside about a mile away. The circular blowing wind, however, rendered the thought of any stalk on these bears null and void.

The third day of the hunt proved worse than the second. I swore that I had never been in wind so fierce in all my life. So much for our "all-purpose" clothing on that particular day, as it seemed as though we had none at all.

The fourth day, however, started off like a gem. The skies were clear blue, the sun was shining bright, and the weather was nice and warm. Needless-to-say, that was the day that I learned that the weather on Kodiak can instantly change, that is, from one extreme to the next. Despite the nasty weather, we did spot two medium-sized bears that particular evening. Neither one, however, was the type of bear we were after.

It wasn't until breakfast on the morning of the fifth day that our luck changed for the best. The past four days we had hunted down-bay and Tonya couldn't bear the thought of spending another one just sitting and glassing. She was eager to exercise and suggested that we hike upstream. Jeff seemed favorable to the idea, so we decided to hike to an area upstream where several of the rivers commenced their journey down to the bay. After about a six-mile hike and crossing several deep and fast-running rivers, we elected to stop and glass for awhile. It was no surprise that the wind proved once again just how relentless it could be.

Robert M. Ortiz (right) and his guide, Jeff Poor, pictured here with the mighty half-pawed Monarch of Deadman Bay. The bear, scoring 29-3/16 points, received a First Place Award at the 25th Big Game Awards Banquet in Kansas City.

We glassed on and off for about two hours, when Tonya and I decided to take some shelter from the cold wind. We were just over the hill from Jeff when he came running frantically over the top shouting, "Bear!"

Jeff had spotted a bear on the other side of the drainage about 600 yards away. The bear had been sunning out of the wind in an area that made it almost impossible to see it. We studied the 9-footer for about 25 minutes, when for some reason, the bear quickly got up from where it was lying and commenced to travel up the draw. That particular draw ultimately led to a deep canyon. It was then that we realized why it was rapidly moving out of the area. About 100 yards behind it in the brush moved a very large dark brown-colored creature. When the creature became visible, it was without a doubt the largest and most impressive bear that I had ever seen, dead or alive!

The enormous creature was most likely pursuing the 9-footer for an afternoon challenge to the death, or for its next meal, or maybe both. Whichever it was, the next thing I heard was Jeff saying, "Let's get a movin'!"

It immediately became apparent to me that the bear was headed straight for the canyon, and that we only had a couple of minutes to try and get to a point that would enable us to get a shot. Within seconds we had our packs and rifles slung over our backs and we were traveling through the brush as if it never existed. Somehow during our run, I was able to reach over to the top of my barrel and remove the balloon I had placed over it to keep it free from debris. Nothing, and I mean nothing, was going to stop my shot at this bear. But, maybe I spoke too soon. As we were proceeding in the direction of our would-be vantage point, we ran out of mountain. Two feet in front of us was a 60-foot straight down drop. I knew that this was it; I could either shoot from there, or let the bear get away.

Off came the packs. I immediately piled them in front of me to create a shooting rest. I then turned the adjustable objective on my scope to somewhere between 300 and 400 yards, and loaded one in the chamber hoping that the big brown bear would give us a shot. Fortunately for us, the 9-footer had traveled to the corner of the drainage which was 350 yards away, and then traveled down and into the canyon. We could only hope the large creature that followed would do the same. Just then, out of the brush came the big brown following its predecessor's trail over to the same drop-off point. Jeff quickly ranged the point at 350 yards.

When the big brown reached the edge of the rim, it looked down and then picked up its nose in the air attempting to scent its prey. All I kept thinking was, "What a Monster!"

It was then that I laid the cross hairs on the bear's right-front vitals and pulled the trigger. I knew it was a hit, as the bear had picked up its right front leg off the ground, turned around, and started back in the direction of the brush. Then, in mid-stride, the bear turned to its right and ran in a direction directly away from us. As everyone who hunts big bears knows, follow-up shots are highly recommended, so a few more were taken to make sure the job was finished. This time it slowly made its way about 20 yards into the brush and collapsed. We waited for about 45 minutes, as this was not a wounded bear that we wanted to meet up with in the brush on that day, the next day, or on any day for that matter.

After convincing ourselves that the big brown had expired, we proceeded to find a way to get to the bottom of the canyon, cross the waist-high ice-cold river, and then climb up the other side and over to where the bear had last lain. As we cautiously neared the big brown, I began to realize how incredibly big this bear truly was. Its head was so massive that I couldn't wrap my arms around the sides of it. The widths of its forearms were an easy 26 inches. Its coat was long and a beautiful chocolate-brown color with cinnamon highlights, and not a single rubbed area.

After the excitement of the handshakes and picture-taking, we began the tenuous skinning process. When I lifted the bear's right arm, my eyes froze in amazement as I stared at the bear's paw. At that moment, I could not believe what I was seeing. One-half of the bear's right-front paw was missing, just like in the story of the Mighty Monarch. Suddenly, the same special feeling of that first evening's sit on the shale-covered shoreline ran through my body. Upon realizing what had just happened, I bowed my head and thanked God for bringing back the Mighty Monarch, to once again roam and rule in Deadman Bay.

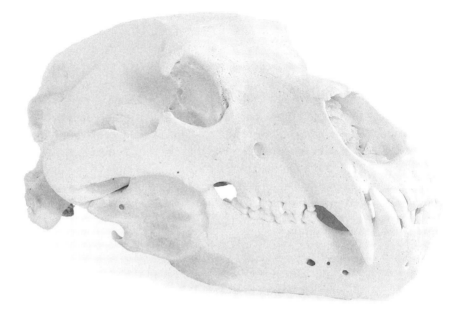

Photograph by Cliff White

TROPHY STATS

▼ ▼ ▼ ▼ ▼

Category
    Alaska brown bear

Score
    $29\,^3/_{16}$

Location
    Cold Bay, Alaska — 2001

Hunter
    Gene White

Length of Skull
    $18\,^{10}/_{16}$

Width of Skull
    $10\,^9/_{16}$

Photograph by Jack Renea

Gene White accepting his plaque and medal from Buck Buckner, Chair of the Big Game Records Committee.

50

ALASKA BROWN BEAR
First Award (Tie) – 29³/₁₆

▼ ▼ ▼ ▼ ▼ ▼ ▼ ▼ ▼

GENE WHITE

My guide, Mark Mitchell, and I had been perched on a high hillside about 50 feet above the normally level tundra for 13 hours near Cold Bay, Alaska, on opening day in 2001. We could see a lot of country from that great height.

The weather was nicer than I had anticipated. It was in the mid-40s and rainy, windy, and cold. I had expected it to be a nightmare of blizzards, whiteouts, and unbearable conditions, based on all the horror stories I had read as a boy in *Outdoor Life*, *Field and Stream*, or *Sports Afield* — the popular magazines of the day. But, being from Florida, I was still freezing! Even wearing all the clothes I brought didn't keep me warm. That fear of a really bad front moving in and my being holed up in my small tent we used as shelter was in the back of my mind. We only had to hike about 400 yards to our lookout point from our tent. That short of a walk didn't get my body heat up.

Dick Gunlogson had dropped us off two days earlier. He gave us the warning, "Stay here and glass the area, don't go and stink up the valley."

Mark and I did as instructed. The first day we had seen two nice bears on the open terrain, but they were downwind and had caught our scent before we got within a mile of them. I then understood what Dick was telling us. These bears have an unbelievable nose; you must approach them from where they can't smell you.

After we got to our hillside lookout on the second day, I searched for a spot out of the wind, to stay warm and still see some country. We hadn't been there half an hour before Mark, crouched over, came running over toward me from the other side of our perch and looking wild-eyed. "You don't have a gun big enough for what's coming at us," he whispered excitedly.

From the look in his eyes, I assumed it was a bear. He took me to where he had

Photograph courtesy of Gene White

Gene had time to catch this silver salmon. Notice the rifle he is packing — he saw four bears while his was fishing.

Gene White had a great year in 2001. He took a cougar that made the records book and also harvested this award-winning Alaska brown bear. Gene was hunting in Cold Bay, Alaska, when he took this boar scoring 29-3/16 points.

been glassing, and there, coming at us, was a bear as big as a tank. My arsenal was a .334 Sako rifle loaded with 225-grain Swift A-frame bullets. Mark was backing me up with his .375.

We didn't even discuss not trying for the bear. I assumed he was just telling me this is our bear and it is big, or at least that was what I was hoping he was telling me. We knew we didn't have much time because the bear was going to reach a spot where it would soon pick up our scent.

Mark instructed me to get my gear and follow him. I did, but not as fast as he could move. He pleaded with me to hurry, and I wanted to. Stuff was coming out of my pack, littering the valley. Mark had been a linebacker at Iowa a few years earlier and was in good shape. It had been many moons since I played fullback on my college's soccer team — a position I selected because I wouldn't have to run the entire length of the field. My oxygen-starved lungs were yelling at me to slow down.

We made it to the spot where Mark felt we could ambush our prey, but there was no bear. Had it gotten there before we did? Had it smelled us and taken off? If so, we would have been able to see it in that open country.

Mark knew exactly what to do. The bear had to be in the shallow ravine that ran toward the hillside we had just come around. We began backtracking along the top of the ravine we had just skirted. That depression was upwind from our position and realistically the only place the bear could be. We could see every place else.

We eased ahead along the ridge about 100 yards. Then I could see the top of its shoulders, lumbering along and appearing unaware of our presence. At the same instance I saw the bear, it suspected something was wrong and stood up on its hind legs to see what was following it. The bear looked at me and I looked at it from only 80 yards. In hindsight, it being below me kept me from gasping at its enormous size.

The bear dropped down on all fours and took off. It was either shoot now or go back and sit on that freezing hillside. I shot, and then I shot again. This time the bear went down.

My rifle did a great job. I tried to pick its head up to get a picture, but it took all my strength to lift it. The bear was so heavy it took both of us college athletes to roll it over.

My whole life I had dreamed of making the Boone and Crockett records book, probably thinking that if it was to be, it would be with a whitetail or elk, which I hunt often. Earlier, in January 2001, I had taken a mountain lion with some friends in Montana that made the book with a 15-4/16 score. Now this bear....WOW! What a great year. I should have bought a lot of lottery tickets in 2001.

ALASKA BROWN BEAR
First Award (Tie) – 29³/₁₆
▼ ▼ ▼ ▼ ▼
GENE WHITE

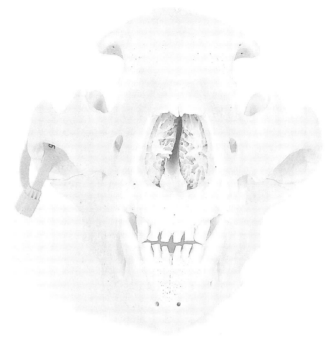

Photograph by Cliff White

TROPHY STATS

▼ ▼ ▼ ▼ ▼

Category
   Alaska brown bear

Score
   $29^3/_{16}$

Location
   Egegik Bay, Alaska — 2003

Hunter
   Steve Rakes

Length of Skull
   $18^{11}/_{16}$

Width of Skull
   $10^8/_{16}$

Photograph by Jack Rene

Steve Rakes accepting his plaque and medal from Buck Buckner, Chair of the B[i] Game Records Committee.

ALASKA BROWN BEAR
First Award (Tie) – 29³/₁₆

▼ ▼ ▼ ▼ ▼ ▼ ▼ ▼ ▼

STEVE RAKES

Every other year along the Alaska Peninsula is a time eagerly awaited for by those lucky and fortunate enough to hunt brown bear. I had contracted with Becharof Lodge of Egigik, Alaska, just a short flight South of King Salmon, for the October 2003 hunt.

I arrived in camp a couple of days early to settle in and get acquainted. The Cessna landed on Becharof's private runway at 5 p.m. on September 29. The Lodge's owner, Bruce Hallingstad, greeted me with a "Nice to see ya; eat some grub, and get ready... You're leaving now."

"Now?" I asked.

"Within 20 minutes. The tide is right; tomorrow's weather's not. Now!" he said.

Once I took a breath, I was okay with the commotion. After all, I was here because this is where the brown bears were. If Bruce had arranged for me to spike out two days early, well...who was I to question?

My guide, Mark Wagner, and I jumped aboard an 18-foot aluminum skiff and made our way across the wide Egigik River to an abandoned set-netter's cabin. These homesteads were used in years past for the long summer runs of silver and king salmon. This "spike" camp had cots, head, and elbowroom, and sure beat the tented spike camps to which I've become accustomed. The setting was beautiful, literally right on the Bering Sea. I spent each night listening to the waves crash in from the west and watching the orange sun settle in behind them.

The wind howled all night and into the next day. We spent this pre-opener getting organized, securing the homestead, blowing up our raft that would be used if we spotted a bear across the many sloughs, lakes, and inlets, and basically swapping stories. As it turned out, Bruce was right on in getting us over there early. The river had large swells and solid white caps all day. We would have never made it across in that kind of weather. It rained and blew hard all day long and well into the night. It slowed enough for a quick four-mile beach scout, which turned up a buried seal kill with plenty of fresh bear sign all around. I couldn't wait for the first light of October 1. Needless-to-say, I barely slept a wink.

Our set-netter had installed an old antenna tower, which worked perfectly as a look-out. The terrain is mostly flat and rolling tundra, so we could see quite a distance from atop the tower. Almost immediately, we spotted a large lone bear across the inlet to our east. We boarded our two-man raft and headed for the other side. We were approaching an area where we thought we could get a better look when we noticed two other smaller bears with the bear. It was exciting to watch for awhile, but we, of course, left this lady alone.

Photograph courtesy of Steve Rakes

Steve and his guide, Mark, had to pack in a raft to cross the lake to get to Steve's Alaska brown bear. The skull measured 20-3/16 inches and received a First Place Award at the 25th Awards Program in Kansas City.

We decided to head down the beach to check out our seal kill site. We had just stepped on to the beach, when we noticed two sets of tracks that literally walked right behind where we slept. As we approached the kill, it was obvious that these two bears had devoured what was left during the night.

We continued south a few miles and later came across an extremely large fresh track. We followed along the beach for a couple more miles until the bruin turned inland. We walked along the beach and climbed the sandy ridgeline every few hundred yards to see if we could spot the bear.

After a number of these look-sees, Mark spotted the brute about a mile inland and still nearly another mile to our south. The lone bear was in a slough that surrounded a freshwater lake. We stayed along the beach until we could make a straight line inland toward it. Once above the shoreline, the lay of the land was flat. There was zero cover; we literally had to belly-crawl though the tall grass and tundra to get a closer look.

As we approached, we could now tell that the big bruin was on the other side of the lake. We inched our way the mile or so through the wet terrain and were soaked when we made it to the lake's west edge. I set up my spotting scope and we decided the bear would go nine feet. I had really hoped for a little bigger boar, but after spending 13 days on the Alaska

Peninsula in 1999 and going home with just great memories, I tried my best to make it grow. As I studied though the scope, the bear turned away, and it had the biggest backside I'd ever seen. I was confident it'd push over nine feet and decided to take the shot.

ALASKA BROWN BEAR
First Award (Tie) – 29³/₁₆

▼ ▼ ▼ ▼ ▼

STEVE RAKES

It was 225 yards with a 30-mph crosswind. This lake had white caps and the wind had the tall grass lying on its side. I set up my shooting sticks and was comfortable enough to take this long shot. I had always felt that 100 yards is really a max when shooting at dangerous game, but this bear was big, and this was as close as we could get.

The bruin was slowly feeding along and broadside. I laid the cross hairs in front of its shoulder, allowing for the wind. The first shot hit two feet back from where I'd aimed and broke its spine. The next sight I can see as clearly now as I could then. It would take both front arms and throw them high into the air as it continued on. I couldn't tell from our vantage point, but it was in about 18 inches of water. With each thrust, water would splash eight feet into the air. This obviously slowed it enough for another couple of quick rounds and it was finished.

The high fives flew and then we started thinking about how in the heck we were going to get to the downed bear. I stayed put to mark our spot in this flat terrain while Mark made his way around the lake. An hour later, he was back. The "lake" never ended. He decided to head back to camp, deflate the raft, and pack it back to our shot site. We inflated the raft and made it to the bruin over three hours after the first shot.

We carefully circled the bear wide on opposite sides to be sure it was dead. It lay motionless with its nose beneath the water. As I circled about ankle deep, my next step took me to my waist. I was completely stuck in muck, with water pouring over my hip-waders, and all this with the largest animal I'd ever approached only a few feet away. I remember thinking, "Oh, I hope it's dead! I hope it's dead!"

Thankfully it was. Mark made his way around and pulled me free, and with every second this bear grew. There was no ground shrinkage here, and we began to think it might even be a 10-footer. We caped it in the 18 inches of water where it lay and managed to get all 197 pounds of skull and wet cape in our raft, along with both of us. We then made our slow paddle back across.

We made it back to camp at dark, radioed in our success, and then the celebration began. The next morning the skiff arrived, and I was taken back to the main lodge. My hunt portion had lasted all of one day, but this memory will last my lifetime.

When we spread out the hide, it squared just over 10 feet 9 inches before it'd been fleshed; it would finish just over 11 feet. On December 2, after the official Boone and Crockett drying period of 60 days, the skull measured an incredible 29-3/16, which currently places the bear in the top-100 of All-time.

My fall of 2003 is one I won't soon forget. I sincerely thank Mark and Bruce for their help in making this a great year.

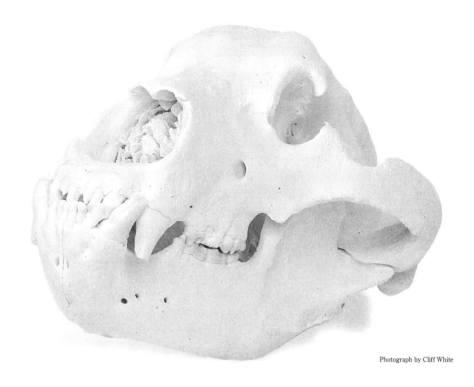

Photograph by Cliff White

TROPHY STATS

▼ ▼ ▼ ▼ ▼

Category
Alaska brown bear

Score
$28^{15}/_{16}$

Location
Terror Bay, Alaska — 2003

Hunter
Terry A. Monson

Length of Skull
$17^{10}/_{16}$

Width of Skull
$11^{5}/_{16}$

BOONE AND CROCKETT CLUB'S

ALASKA BROWN BEAR
Second Award – 28^{15}/$_{16}$

▼ ▼ ▼ ▼ ▼ ▼ ▼ ▼ ▼

TERRY A. MONSON

I was hunting for Alaska brown bear on Kodiak Island in the spring of 2003 in the area of Terror Bay. It was Sunday, May 11, and the twelfth day of my grueling quest.

We glassed the mountainside until 9:30 p.m. Then the four of us, with all of our gear, headed back toward base camp. Shortly afterward, we spotted a bear coming down through a ravine. We scoped it, but couldn't tell how large the bear was. We soon realized just how large it was when it stood and rubbed its back against a tree.

Day Twelve at Terror Bay

I squeezed off the shot and hit the bear just behind the shoulder. The bear dropped straight down. Dennis yelled out, "Good Shot!"

But then the bear got up. As I ejected my shell, my guides Dennis and Phil each fired. The sound from the report of each rifle was incredible. These big bears can take a lot, so we fired until it no longer moved.

They determined it was an older bear, 15 years of age or more, because it had white claws and worn teeth. They thought it probably weighed over 1,300 pounds. The next day, the guides and packers fleshed the bear. Once that job was finished, they measured the unstretched hide, and we all were amazed when it squared out at 10 feet 2 inches. They measured the skull and found it to be 28-15/16 inches, one of the largest for the 2003 season.

Photograph courtesy of Terry A. Monson

Terry A. Monson took this award-winning Alaska brown bear in 2003. The skull measures 28-15/16 inches.

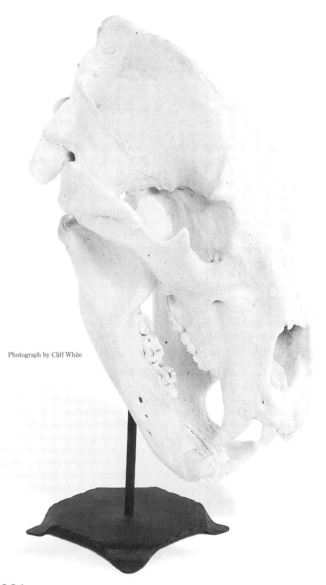

Photograph by Cliff White

TROPHY STATS

▼ ▼ ▼ ▼ ▼

Category
Alaska brown bear

Score
$28^{14}/_{16}$

Location
Afognak Island, Alaska — 2001

Hunter
Ricardo E. Longoria

Length of Skull
$17^{11}/_{16}$

Width of Skull
$11^{3}/_{16}$

BOONE AND CROCKETT CLUB'S

ALASKA BROWN BEAR
Third Award (Tie) – 28 $^{14}/_{16}$

▼ ▼ ▼ ▼ ▼ ▼ ▼ ▼ ▼

RICARDO E. LONGORIA

Texas is a very long way from Afognak Island, Alaska, but for a chance at a legendary Alaska brown bear, Ricardo Longoria knew it was well worth the trip. After months of planning, April 2001 would bring the culmination of all the waiting and anticipation.

Ricardo flew to Kodiak Island, and then boarded a floatplane for the short island hop to Afognak. There he met his guide for this lifetime adventure, a man named Roy Randall.

Afognak Island, Kodiak's smaller sister, is a beautiful island with varying terrain. Small inlets and bays create many nooks and hidden places, both for wildlife and for fishing boats seeking refuge from the Gulf's often wicked temperament. The island is alternately open and timbered, with a monoculture of Sitka spruce providing cover for Sitka blacktails, Roosevelt's elk, and giant brown bears.

Other than humans, bears on Afognak Island lead a comparatively luxurious life. The relentless salmon runs provide limitless protein and vitamins. On top of that and just for good measure (and a good dessert) salmonberries cover the landscape.

The flight to Afognak occurred on April 25. Hunting in this wet, dreary landscape actually began on April 27. In typical coastal Alaska fashion, it was very overcast with a steady, light rain.

At 8:30 p.m., on his first day of the hunt, Ricardo found the bear of his dreams. It was a true monster in every sense of the word, but full of beauty at the same time. Its head was enormous, as was the rest of the body on this overgrown predator. At a distance of 50 yards, Ricardo fired a bullet from his .375 H&H and quickly ended his quest for the world's largest omnivore.

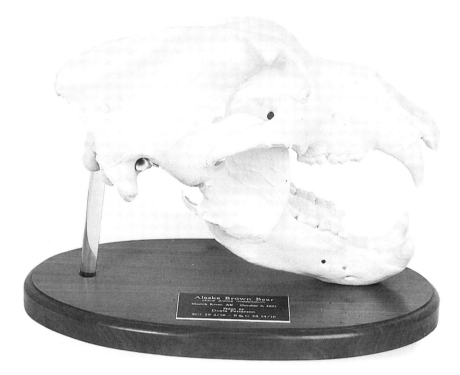

Photograph by Cliff White

TROPHY STATS

▼ ▼ ▼ ▼ ▼

Category
    Alaska brown bear

Score
    $28^{14}/_{16}$

Location
    Meshik River, Alaska — 2001

Hunter
    Doyle D. Patterson

Length of Skull
    $17^{12}/_{16}$

Width of Skull
    $11^{2}/_{16}$

ALASKA BROWN BEAR
Third Award (Tie) - 28^{14}/$_{16}$

▼ ▼ ▼ ▼ ▼ ▼ ▼ ▼ ▼

DOYLE D. PATTERSON

When push comes to shove, I like to think the good guys always win. On October 6, 2001, I was surrounded by good guys and it was my day.

My hunting partner, Jim Weatherly, and I had spent six rain-soaked days glassing for bears. We were with our guide, Todd Walton of Alaska Trophy Adventures, in the vast tundra of the Alaska Peninsula.

Late on the sixth day of our hunt, Jim, Todd, and I spotted a large bear far off on the tundra, miles away. I was the designated shooter for the day, and we decided this bear was going to be worth going after. We had been glassing bears for nearly a week, and we had a good feeling about this one.

Bristol Bay Bruin

After traveling several miles in this hummock-laden land, we took a high point to glass for the old boy that we hoped to cut off. An eternity seemed to pass by, yet we hadn't spotted it again. I had pretty much given up on the bear and decided to go to the next high spot and glass once more.

As if out of nowhere, there it was! The bear was coming straight at us at about 400 yards. Then it started to angle away from us and was rapidly covering ground. Todd and I were off to attempt to cut it off again. Todd ranged it at 104 yards and I dropped prone on a three-foot hump of blueberry bush. I let go with a 225-grain .338. "Ol' One Ear," as it became known, dropped like a rock. Great! Then it got up and was really mad. Another shot to the boiler room, a miss, and then this bear absorbed everything we owned and never winced. It was over after the first two shots, but neither the bear nor I knew this. Had it been necessary to go another 25 yards, I know I would not have gotten this bear if it weren't for Todd and Jim, I'd still be out there dreaming about how I was going to get this giant's hide and skull five miles back to camp.

My bear now occupies a prominent place in my living room. Everyday it reminds me of one really great hunt!

Photograph courtesy of Doyle D. Patterson

Ol' One Ear dropped to a shot from Doyle D. Patterson's .338 near Meshik River, Alaska, in 2001. The bear scores 28-14/16.

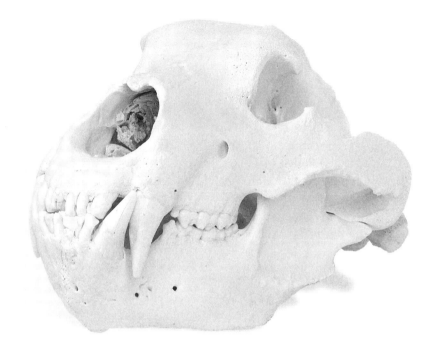

Photograph by Cliff White

TROPHY STATS
▼ ▼ ▼ ▼ ▼

Category
Alaska brown bear

Score
$28^{14}/_{16}$

Location
Pumice Creek, Alaska — 2001

Hunter
Larry F. O'Brian

Length of Skull
18

Width of Skull
$10^{14}/_{16}$

Photograph by Jack Ren

Larry F. O'Brian accepting his plaque and
medal from Buck Buckner, Chair of the B
Game Records Committee.

ALASKA BROWN BEAR
Third Award (Tie) – 28 ^{14}/$_{16}$

▼ ▼ ▼ ▼ ▼ ▼ ▼ ▼ ▼

LARRY F. O'BRIAN

A short time after returning to South Florida from a Montana big-game hunt in the fall of 1998 we, like most hunters, needed to make plans for our next hunt. My hunting partner of 13-plus years, Glenn Cavalier, and I got together to make our plans. We decided, after a very short time, to make our next hunt for Alaska brown bear.

Once we made our decision, we began the research for our outfitter and hunt dates. We were planning to book our hunts as one-on-one, and I decided to call my close friend Ross Gull, an elk guide in Utah, to see if he would like to accompany me on this great adventure. After a few days of contemplation, he decided to join me as a non-hunter. We contacted our favorite agent who we had used several times in past years and learned that his choice of outfitters was booked for fall 1999, but not for fall 2001. We then made our decision to book our hunt for fall 2001. On our agent's recommendation, we chose LaRose Guide Service of Anchorage, Alaska, and booked our hunt in January, 2000.

I spent the next 21 months preparing and anticipating my departure for Alaska to experience my dream hunt/adventure. I viewed hunting the Alaska brown bear as such a great honor and privilege. It greatly helped me endure the seemingly slow passing of time, as did my intense, physical preparation, rifle range visits, etc. I did anything and everything I could to make sure I would be fully prepared, including keeping in touch with our agent and guide service. I viewed this as a once-in-a-lifetime opportunity.

Finally, our long wait was over and on September 26, 2001, we left home for our flight to Anchorage. Glenn and I, along with Ross, spent three days in Anchorage, relaxing and anticipating our hunt. On September 29, 2001, we left Anchorage on our Pen Air flight to Gary LaRose's Pumice Creek Camp, with a stop on the way at King Salmon. Glenn and I were able to shoot a couple of rounds

Photograph courtesy of Larry F. O'Brian

Larry O'Brian's good friend, Ross Gull, accompanied him on the 2001 Alaska brown bear hunt near Pumice Creek.

from our rifles in camp after we arrived to ensure nothing had been altered on our flight. A guide was assigned to Ross and me. A second guide was assigned to Glenn. We had a very nice dinner and stayed in the main camp overnight.

The following day, Ross and I, along with our gear, were transported by tundra aircraft to our spike hunting camp near Olds Creek drainage. Our hunt would start the next morning on October 1 and would continue through October 10, if necessary.

Days one, two, and three consisted of an early breakfast and a hike of one to two hours over rolling, uneven tundra, with steady rain and temperatures in the teens. We then had to climb a knob, some 300 yards high, from which we glassed for approximately eight to ten hours a day. We saw two very nice Alaska Peninsula moose, both bulls, but despite our very dedicated efforts, we did not see one bear. Not seeing any bears for three days tends to make you a little concerned, but little did we know things were about to look up.

On day four after our hike, when we were just about ready to climb the knob, we saw a bear just to the north of us. It was within 200 yards and walking in our direction. My guide and I immediately went to the ground and assumed the prone position. By the time the bear was within 125 yards my guide advised me not to shoot. He then said we would hold out for a specimen that he could judge to be eight and a half feet or larger. Fortunately the bear never spotted us. It slowly walked away out of our view. What a thrill! Having my cross hairs on the first Alaska brown bear I had ever seen in the wild was a very exciting moment. It certainly made the climb up the knob to glass for the balance of the day much easier. As we headed down the knob to return to camp in late evening, I was still upbeat from seeing my first ever Alaska brown bear in the wild. Our fourth evening in camp consisted of dinner, a small amount of talk, and early to bed.

Day five was our usual trek to the knob and up for more glassing. Even though the weather for the four previous days was typically harsh, the fifth day seemed to be my real test. It was very cold, raining, with steady winds gusting at times upward to 40 mph. I sure was glad I had Ross with me. Being from Utah, he wasn't struggling with the conditions. Without his encouragement I would not have made it. I felt I was very near hypothermia and just could not rid myself of the chill. Just when I was about to give, we saw a very large, light colored sow with two cubs in the Olds Creek Drainage below. We were able to watch them for about 30 minutes. This was all I needed. It was as if I had been warm and comfortable all day. I suddenly felt totally recharged.

Later in the day, we saw a dark colored bear traveling towards us, parallel to the creek below. It appeared to be a boar by the way it carried itself. As it walked and came closer, my guide and I decided to descend the knob toward the creek to prepare for a shot if presented the opportunity. We stopped within 50 yards of the bottom of the knob. I had already decided if I was able to place the cross hairs in my scope on this bear and the guide gave me the go ahead, I was going to take full advantage of my opportunity. I was convinced I would make the necessary shots. As we sat and waited for what seemed like hours, it finally appeared below, coming from the south and to my right. I had it in my cross hairs by the time my guide placed it with a range finder at 130 yards. After my guide glassed it one last time with his binoculars, he advised me not to shoot as he was confident we could find a larger bear.

ALASKA BROWN BEAR
Third Award (Tie) – 28 ^{14}/$_{16}$

▼ ▼ ▼ ▼ ▼

LARRY F. O'BRIAN

We climbed back up the knob and glassed until just before dark and headed back for camp. We had dinner, discussed the events of our day and were confident the bear action was picking up. We didn't feel it would be in our best interest to change our camp location, even though our outfitter, Gary LaRose, had given us the option. With half of my hunt over I decided to go to bed, as daylight came very early.

On day six, even though I felt that I had done all I could, I silently committed to myself that I would do anything and everything necessary to ensure my success with this adventure for the balance of our trip. We had been glassing all day with no sightings until approximately 4 p.m. My guide spotted what he felt was a very large bear grazing across the creek below and up on a ridge. He felt the bear was large because he could see it so clearly at such a great distance. We made the decision to pursue. After a little more than two hours we crossed the creek and arrived at our destination. We crawled the last 50 yards or so on our bellies, took our first look at the field we thought it would be in, but the bear was nowhere to be found.

After an hour or so, we were convinced the bear had re-entered the brush. We decided to start our return. If we didn't cross the creek before dark we would be forced to spend the night away from our camp in extreme conditions and make the cross at sunrise. We decided to step up the pace and try to cross the creek before dark. Responding to this sense of urgency, Ross and I, even with due diligence, filled our hip waders with icy waters during our trip across the creek. We just made it across by dark. At our first opportunity we sat down with our Maglites and removed the water from our hip waders.

By the time we arrived at camp it was after 10 p.m. Even though our day had been very tiring, I was grateful that I had now seen six bears and had an opportunity to harvest two of them. Being totally exhausted, we ate dinner and went straight to our tents for a good night's sleep.

Days seven and eight were very exciting days, even though we spent a total of 16 to 18 hours glassing from our same knob on both days. We saw 17 different bears. This really had me excited; I was gaining confidence that I would soon get my chance. This brought our total to 23 bears seen, but for various reasons we could not pursue any one of them. They were either sows with cubs, too far to stalk, or the wind was not in our favor. On our return to camp in darkness on the seventh day, my guide thought he heard a bear in the brush we were passing through, which made the three of us uneasy for the final hour or so before we arrived in camp.

Both nights we had dinner and decided to go to bed immediately thereafter. Ross and I talked for a while after slipping into our sleeping bags. He kept reassuring me that even though I had only two days left on my hunt that, more times than not, success comes late in

Photograph courtesy of Larry F. O'Brian

Larry F. O'Brian harvested this award-winning Alaska brown bear on the ninth day of a 10-day hunt. The bear scores 28-14/16 points.

the hunt. He told me to stay positive, confident, and ready. All of his encouragement really seemed to help and inspire me.

Just before I fell asleep, I realized that with only two hunting days left, going home without a bear was now beginning to look like a possibility. However, I committed myself to staying positive through the final days and hours, especially after listening to Ross, whom I totally respected and in whom I had the utmost confidence. I also decided if the worst should happen, and I was unable to harvest a bear, I would forever be grateful for having had the privilege of pursuing such a magnificent creature. I had what I believe to be my best night's sleep, not knowing the happiest moment of my life was just around the corner.

On day nine, we had our breakfast and started our journey to the knob. All the way out I was being told not to worry, that something good was going to happen, and that one of those bears out there was going to make a mistake. It really lifted my spirits. I was convinced this would be the day and I had better be ready.

After climbing the knob and glassing until approximately 11 a.m., I hung my binoculars on a tree limb and decided to walk to the north, across the knob about 10 yards or so, just to stretch and give my eyes a rest. Even though I was resting my eyes, I was instinctively looking at the creek in front and to the north of me, when I saw a very dark bear in the creek. It was eating salmon and lumbering in our direction. It looked very large, even though it was almost a mile away. I went to retrieve my binoculars and also notified my guide that he should bring his spotting scope. When we returned to the spot, after taking one look, my guide said to me, "Get your rifle, we are going to run down this knob. If you follow me, I will head for a spot in the creek to intercept it. Let's just hope it keeps eating and coming."

When we made it down the knob, we ran toward the creek, which was another 200 yards away. We were in hopes of arriving at the creek with the bear coming in our direction, eating salmon, but maybe 100 to 200 yards north of us. We were totally in shock when the bear appeared broadside, approximately 50 feet directly in front of us, and winding us. I looked to my guide. Just his expression was telling me it was time to shoot.

I had already learned when hunting the Alaska brown bear to place the first shot in the boiler room, and don't stop shooting until you unload your rifle, which I did. With the bear walking south, I sent the first shot through its right shoulder. The bear immediately turned its body and head, one-quarter turn and came charging. When it was finally lying dead, it was five steps, or approximately 15 feet from where I was standing. The complete encounter lasted somewhere between four and seven seconds.

Even with a steady rain, fog, and temperatures in the teens, I was so thrilled that even the harsh Alaska weather conditions were no longer a concern. For me, nothing could ever top this. It was now time for my guide to cape my bear and prepare for the trip back to our spike camp. The caping process was finished around 5 p.m.

We loaded the full cape on my guide's back and started toward camp. After we climbed up the creek bank and hiked a short distance, my guide decided he was too exhausted to continue. Concerned the hide might be used for food during the night; we buried the hide, covered it with leaves and branches, and headed back for camp. After a nice meal, a good night's sleep and breakfast the following morning, my guide was able to pack the full hide back to our spike camp.

After the hide was flown from spike camp back to the main Pumice Creek Camp, Rod Arno, one of the guides at the main camp, told me the hide would measure 10 feet square or better. The skull was officially measured several weeks later by an Official Measurer of the Boone and Crockett Club and was certified to have a B&C score of 28-14/16. The hide was later measured and determined to be 10 feet, 2 inches square.

Harvesting an Alaska brown bear is truly my dream come true, by far my greatest adventure. My sincerest thanks to Gary R. LaRose, Registered Guide of Anchorage, Alaska, for all his help in making my dream hunt such an outstanding success. His knowledge, honesty, dedication, and hard work will always be remembered and appreciated. Also, I would like to thank my good friend, Ross Gull, for all his encouragement and for being there to share my greatest moments ever. Having him along to share my harvesting of an Alaska brown bear, especially one accepted by the Boone and Crockett Club, was certainly a great privilege for me and made my adventure that much more special and memorable.

Photograph by Cliff White

TROPHY STATS

▼ ▼ ▼ ▼ ▼

Category
   cougar

Score
   16

Location
   Archuleta County, Colorado — 2001

Hunter
   Brian K. Williams

Length of Skull
   9 $^4/_{16}$

Width of Skull
   6 $^{12}/_{16}$

Photograph by Jack Rene

Brian K. Williams accepting his plaque an
medal from Buck Buckner, Chair of the B
Game Records Committee.

COUGAR
First Award – 16

▼ ▼ ▼ ▼ ▼ ▼ ▼ ▼ ▼

BRIAN K. WILLIAMS

My mountain lion story began a long time ago when I was just a boy. I grew up in southern Oklahoma where I hunted coons, bobcats, squirrels, and rabbits with my dad, David K. Williams, our friend, Charles "Cotton" Russell, and my uncle, Mark Gillham, who were all houndsmen.

My family moved to Colorado in 1979. My dad raised and hunted with a few bear hounds the first couple of years we lived in Pagosa Springs, until he became a government trapper near Grand Junction. He hunted with Larry Sanders and Jeff Brent, the state bear and mountain lion men, for a couple of years. I accompanied them a few times in the summer after problem bears that were killing the local ranchers' sheep.

The lion snarled at me, not like any old lion would snarl at you, but like the fourth biggest lion in the world would snarl at you.

I attended high school in Pagosa Springs where I met Mike Ray, his dad, Dick Ray, and Dick's brother, Sam (owner and operator of Bear Paw Outfitters), and Dick and Sam's brother, Rodney. I started guiding for Dick, owner and operator of Lobo Outfitters, just after I finished high school.

The Rays had a lot of good dogs then, as they do now. About four years after I began working for Dick, I went to work for his brother Sam. I acquired some dogs from Sam; I even traded him a crazy old horse for one. I hunted bear and lion with him for several years; those were the best years of my life. I raised my own hounds for a little better than 10 years, then the constant barking of eight hound dogs started to wear on my neighbors, so I reluctantly decided to sell them. I called Mike, and he and Dick agreed to buy my dogs. Four of my dogs were really proven. Charlie, Andy, and Pebbles I got from Sam. Doozie, a female, I bought from my old friend, Cotton, in Oklahoma. I also had a few pups. I told Mike that Snoopy, one of the females, was going to be a good hound.

After that I didn't lion hunt much until I booked a hunt with Lobo Outfitters in January 2001. This would be the hunt I would never forget. A little before daylight on the morning of the first day of my hunt, Mike and I took off on snowmobiles in search of a big tom track that Mike believed was in the area. We had gone about two miles when Mike stopped dead in his tracks, and as sure as the nose on your face, there was a huge track in the two-day old snow. We tried to cut the track again by circling the area. Not finding it again, we knew it had to be in that area.

Brian K. Williams and his hunting partner, Mike Ray, went through some of the roughest country as they followed the hounds in search of the big tom.

We went back and picked up the dogs, but by then it had warmed up and the dogs could only cold trail. But to hear my old dogs, Andy and Pebbles, trailing again was music to my ears. I was kind of glad that they didn't tree a cat that day because my hunt would have been over too soon.

We hunted a few more times in February and also in March, but I was unsuccessful during those times. Other hunters with Lobo Outfitters, however, took a good many lions that season. Some were huge, with one scoring 15-6/16 Boone and Crockett points.

It was a long summer and fall. Then, on December 1, 2001, after a good six-inch snowfall, I resumed my hunt with Lobo Outfitters. Harold Thompson, a local dentist and a good friend of the Rays, was my guide that day. Harold went out early to beat the rush of other lion hunters in our area. I had overslept that morning and was rushing around trying to find my tire chains. By the time I arrived at Mike's, he was loading dogs in the truck. He said that Harold had gone ahead of me. Mike told me to take Andy, Jube (a dog Mike and Dick had raised), and Snoopy. Mike was taking a hunter to a different area. I was glad to hear that I would find Harold in the same place that Mike and I had spotted the big tom track nearly a year before.

When I found Harold, he had already found a track not far up the road, so by the time we figured out that it was a female, the other lion hunters had hit the other roads in the area. Harold and I made a different plan. He was going to go to the end of the road and I was going to make sure the other hunters hadn't missed anything.

I called Mike on his cell phone and he told me they had found a good tom and all but had it treed. I told him where Harold had gone, and Mike said that it was a bad area and Harold was probably stuck. We hung up and I

COUGAR
First Award – 16
▼ ▼ ▼ ▼ ▼
BRIAN K. WILLIAMS

went to check on Harold. To my surprise, he wasn't stuck. He informed me that he had found a dandy track near the end of the road. He had already called Dick, and Dick told Harold that we might as well try it. We went back to where Harold had found the track and turned the dogs out. It was 11:30 a.m., and my thermometer read 26°. We had a chance!

Harold and I got our packs together and added extra food and supplies, knowing that we might have to spend the night. We were going into some of the roughest country I knew of, and we were also off to a late start. I turned the three dogs loose, and they were out of ear shot in a hurry. I cannot speak for Harold, but I was excited in a scary kind of way, knowing we had some dangerous cliffs and ledges to climb through. In some places we even had to take off our packs and crawl through narrow ledges.

About 3 p.m., we could hear the faint sound of dogs in the distance. The going got a little easier and we could see that the big tom knew exactly how to maneuver through the rough terrain. We had two pistols; mine was a 9mm and Harold had a .357. I asked Harold if he wanted to take the tom. He had taken a huge tom a few years back, so he declined my offer, saying he just loved the chase. I was wondering how big the cat was because I had already killed three lions in the past, two of which had skulls 14 inches in size. I thought to myself that I couldn't believe I was actually the hunter this time, and not the guide. We found scrapes in the trail along the way, indicating that this was a large tom, but its track didn't seem overly large. I did note that the tom had an extra-long stride.

We eventually made our way to where the dogs had the cougar treed. We saw the back half of the lion in the tree first. Harold asked, "What do you think?"

I gave him a thumbs up. I was grinning when I saw the front half of the lion. Harold tied up the dogs while I readied for the shot. I took aim and jerked the trigger like a greenhorn, not knowing the pistol was on safety. Realizing just how excited I really was, it was a struggle to stay calm. I took a deep breath and squeezed the trigger. This time the result was a good lung shot.

When the mammoth tom hit the ground, it ran down the side of the mountain about 25 yards. I followed right behind it. When I whizzed by Harold, I asked if I could borrow his .357. He handed me the pistol while continuing to hold Andy. Unfortunately, we had only taken two leashes. I rounded the brush and rocks, thinking the tom had gone quite a ways, but to my surprise, it was sitting on its hind end in some boulders not 10 yards away. The tom turned and faced me. It couldn't go through the boulders, and its only escape was to go through me.

Now, I have been in some tough spots with lions before. I have seen a lion crush a dog's jaw and legs. An angry lion on the ground can do a lot of damage to a pack of dogs, not to mention what this tom could do to me. I had a pistol in each hand ready for the battle.

The lion snarled at me, not like any old lion would snarl at you, but like the fourth biggest lion in the world would snarl at you. As the legendary Ben Lily would say, I got the "lock tail" and ran backwards as fast as my cowardly body would carry me. For those of you who don't savvy "lock tail," it's when a dog is in the scared retreat mode and has its tail tucked tight between its legs against its belly.

Well, I made it back to Harold and the ecstatic hounds. We decided to just let the fatal shot take its toll and wait a few minutes. It worked; when we went back, the monster had perished. I wanted to move it to a rock to take some pictures so Harold grabbed a front leg and I grabbed the other front leg. Failing to pull in sync, the lion didn't budge. We had to put our backs into it and pull together to get it to the rock. I told Harold I was going to try to lift it for a picture. He chuckled. I guess I still had a little adrenaline left, because I managed to barely hold it up for a couple of quick shots. I was still so excited; I had no idea the trophy I had.

Mike and his hunter had taken a good tom, also. Later, Mike came looking for us. He could hear the dogs and cut across the canyon. It was an easier route than what we had taken, except that he had to cross a deep and frigid river. He had taken some small logs and made a footbridge. I was glad to see him as he walked up to us. He said that my cougar was the biggest lion he had ever seen. Mike is very conservative when it comes to judging the size of an animal, so I thought he was teasing me. When we arrived back at Mike's house, Dick said that the lion was the widest he had ever seen. I realized that Mike hadn't been teasing me.

Mike and Dick very conservatively measured the huge skull. It was well over 16 inches. After the 60-day drying period, it officially scored 16 B&C points. It is now the new Colorado state record. The prior record had been held by President Theodore Roosevelt since 1901. His cougar scores 15-12/16.

I would like to thank Mike and Dick Ray of Lobo Outfitters and Harold Thompson for giving me the hunt-of-a-lifetime. I thank God for watching out for us lion hunters out in such treacherous country. I want to give a special thanks to the dogs, Andy, who is about 10 years old now, Snoopy, who is in her prime, and Jube, one of the best young dogs I've ever seen.

Photograph courtesy of Brian K. Williams

Brian holding his award-winning cougar that scores 16 inches. The big tom went down with one shot from Brian's 9mm.

Award Winning Moments...

Photograph by Jack Reneau

For the first time ever, three Alaska brown bears tied for First Award. Pictured above are two of the hunters, Gene White, left, and Steve Rakes, right.

Photograph by Cliff White

TROPHY STATS

▼ ▼ ▼ ▼ ▼

Category
  cougar

Score
  $15^{13}/_{16}$

Location
  Jefferson County, Washington — 2002

Hunter
  David Medley

Length of Skull
  $9^{5}/_{16}$

Width of Skull
  $6^{8}/_{16}$

COUGAR
Second Award – 15 ^{13}/$_{16}$

▼ ▼ ▼ ▼ ▼ ▼ ▼ ▼ ▼

DAVID MEDLEY

David Medley had seen a big cougar track the previous year; one big enough that he didn't forget it. Some hunters David encountered had tried to track it, but to no avail. The big cat was too agile and elusive.

The next year, a friend approached him and said he had seen something that he thought David might be looking for. David went up and checked it out. Sure enough, it was that huge cougar track. David tracked it for awhile, but knowing he had only a pistol, he backtracked and decided to try again the next day with a rifle.

The next day, he was back on the track. He had packed a lunch and was prepared to spend the day after the great cat. He finally found the track again and could see it was headed toward a lake and a place they called the "Coppermine Bottom."

He walked about halfway around the lake and was on a small boardwalk when he noticed a cluster of birds acting up on the other side of the lake. He kept looking to see what was making the ruckus, when he noticed something in the tree, long like a snake, and moving back and forth. He brought up his binoculars and saw at once that it was a cougar. David instantly surveyed the situation and knew he would never be able to get around the lake without the cougar seeing him. He knew his best opportunity was going to be to take the shot from there.

As he peered through the cross hairs, he could hardly believe that he finally had the big cat in his scope. The cougar was lying down facing him, and David placed the shot so that if he missed the head he would hit the body. He figured the distance at about 130 yards and slowly squeezed the trigger on his .270.

After the shot, David knew he could never get around the lake and properly check everything out before it got too late, so he elected to come back the next morning. He called a friend that night and told him about his encounter. He was fairly confident in the shot and felt that the cat was probably "the big one."

He and his friend went out the next morning and looked around, but could find no sign of a hit. He even casually surveyed the lake surface. David was a bit perplexed because he felt really confident in the shot. He started up the tree to investigate and found blood. As they looked around, David began to wonder if the big cat might have fallen out of the tree and into the pond. He peered into the depths, and after a good while, thought he could make out a tooth and part of its nose. Sure enough, David's trophy cougar was lying on the bottom of the lake in seven feet of water!

This was a definite predicament. It was way too cold to even think about stripping down and going in the water after it. It might even be borderline suicidal.

Instead, they found a small boat and a long pole with a hook on the end of it. Eventually they were able to slowly maneuver the big cat to shore. After they got it to town they weighed the huge tom. Its field-dressed weight was 186 pounds! This huge cat is also the second largest cougar ever taken in the state of Washington.

As told to the Boone and Crockett Club by David Medley.

Award Winning Moments...

Photograph by Jack Reneau

Craig Boddington, right, accepts the Plaque of Appreciation on behalf of Leupold recognizing them as an official sponsor of the Boone and Crockett Club's 25th Awards Program in Kansas City.

Photograph by Cliff White

TROPHY STATS

▼ ▼ ▼ ▼ ▼

Category
American elk - typical antlers

Score
411^3/$_8$

Location
Rosebud County, Montana — 2000

Hunter
Chuck Adams

Length of Main Beam
Right: 55^5/$_8$ Left: 56^5/$_8$

Circumference Between First and Second Points
Right: 9^6/$_8$ Left: 9^5/$_8$

Number of Points
Right: 6   Left: 7

Inside Spread Measurement
52^3/$_8$

Photograph by Jack Rene

Chuck Adams accepting his plaque and
medal from Buck Buckner, Chair of the Bi
Game Records Committee.

AMERICAN ELK
Typical Antlers
First Award – 411³/₈

▼ ▼ ▼ ▼ ▼ ▼ ▼ ▼ ▼

CHUCK ADAMS

The huge elk caught me by surprise. I was hunting mule deer with my guide when a bull bugled 200 yards away. I say "bugle," but that's really not the word. "Growl" would better describe the sound.

Seconds later, a line of cow elk streamed from the timber, fanned across a clearing, and dropped their heads to feed. I locked my binoculars to my eyes.

I'll never forget what happened next. A very large 6x6 galloped into view, scattering cows as it charged headlong through the herd. And right on its tail was the biggest, gnarliest bull elk my guide and I had ever seen.

Montana Mega Bull

There was a deer tag in my pocket, but I had bagged my Montana elk four days earlier. That bull was also a stunner, with massive 6x6 antlers. Incredibly, the bull in front of me dwarfed my 6x6 in every sort of way.

The monster had heavy, deeply arching beams and seven long points per side. The spread was impossibly wide, and every point was long. Even the seventh tines would easily measure a foot. The third points (normally shortest on an elk) looked to be 17 or 18 inches long. Brow tines stretched forward beyond the nose, a sure sign of exceptional length. Main beams dropped downward over the bull's rump, making the huge "whale tail" back forks look even bigger.

We watched that elk until nightfall, and during those two final hours, I inspected the bull from every possible angle. I carefully compared it with the elk I'd already taken, and reached an astonishing conclusion. With main beams pushing 60 inches, an inside spread at least 50 inches, and long points all around, I decided this elk would

Photograph courtesy of Chuck Adams

Research with records books and topographic maps helped Chuck Adams locate his award-winning bull taken in Montana.

Photograph courtesy of Chuck Adams

Chuck Adams took this archery bull in 2000. The bull scores 411-3/8 points and received a First Award at the 25th Awards Program in Kansas City.

score at least 50 inches more than mine! That meant we were looking at a bull that would score well over 400 points!

I shot a decent mule deer a few days later, and headed home with the image of that huge elk permanently burned in my brain. I told a few friends about it, and thought about that bull every day and every night for the next 11-1/2 months.

September 14, 2000, found me hiking the same drainage where the giant bull had been the year before. My trusty guide, a good friend of mine, was across the canyon glassing and listening for the bull. My pal prefers not be mentioned by name because he's afraid people will zero in on his elk hot spots. I don't blame him a bit.

I knew from past experience that mature elk often rut in the same place year after year. "Please, God," I thought. "Let that theory be true!"

I felt my neck hairs prickle as a familiar, single-note bugle rolled down the draw. The gravel-voiced monarch was back, less than half a mile from where we'd seen it in 1999. There was no mistaking the sound.

Half an hour later, I caught the herd as they crossed the last opening below a dog-hair-thick bedding hillside. Weather was beastly hot — already 80 degrees — and animals were racing for shade.

My view was not a good one, but I instantly recognized the bull as it trudged between two trees. It looked a bit smaller than I remembered. It had the same wide and downward-curving beams, and the same very long points, but only six tines on the right and a shorter seventh on the left. Yet, it was still a huge elk.

I believe it's always a mistake to pressure elk in their bedding areas. If you do, you risk running them away for good. We called it a morning, and went back to camp for lemonade and a snooze.

Elk move around a lot and don't bugle consistently when weather is warm. It was very warm in mid-September 2000. My guide and I heard and saw nothing that evening. We located only ten cows and one small bull the following day. The country was steep, remote, and densely overgrown — just the place for a giant herd bull to feed and breed silently without being detected.

I was certain the bull was still nearby. I could feel it in my bones.

Pale pink arrows shot upward across the sky as we hiked uphill at dawn on the third morning. Hot yellow light soon oozed over the mountains, followed by a blazing sun. I could barely see to shoot, and it was already 75 degrees!

AMERICAN ELK
Typical Antlers
First Award – 411³/₈
▼ ▼ ▼ ▼ ▼
CHUCK ADAMS

We split to look and listen from opposite ridgelines. A cow elk popped into view 300 yards ahead followed by another and another. Soon more than 30 cows and calves were feeding in front of me, slipping in and out of the trees like ghosts.

I saw only one antler at first, but I recognized the rack as the animal came into view. The colossal bull crossed an opening and nudged a cow with its rack. Its left seven-point side flashed clearly before the bull disappeared, showing the dramatic down-sweep of the beam.

My heart was doing handsprings as I trotted crosswind and closed in on the herd. I knew my guide had seen them too and would be close behind. We'd hunted together like a well-oiled machine. As always, I'd hunt and he'd hang back to watch.

The elk were moving rapidly toward the same hillside where they'd vanished two days before. I veered away and loped uphill in a huge half-circle, well hidden by trees. With luck, I just might get a shot.

The big bull pushed its herd up a densely wooded draw. Cows chirped now and then, and the bull growled once. From past experience, I knew the ravine took a 45-degree bend half a mile ahead. I eased around a hill, chugged up a draw, and hooked back over the top at the most likely ambush point.

Good Lord! Elk were streaming past as I peeked above the ridge. A split-instant later, the giant bull appeared 50 yards below, strutting along the same trail as its cows. I grabbed my range finder, swung the reticule on the nearest elk, and punched the distance button — 39 yards.

I ducked down, drew the bow, and eased back up to shoot. I had to crouch, twist, and lean to clear a low-growing branch.

The bull came broadside, and I let go a single cow chirp with the diaphragm call I always clench in my teeth during an elk stalk. The monster stopped and whipped its head to stare. My 40-yard pin found its heart. Thirty minutes later I wrapped both hands around the biggest elk antlers I had ever seen. The animal had gone less than 75 yards before dropping.

The giant 6x7 rack spread 60 inches, weighed 39-1/2 pounds, and scored 411-3/8 official B&C points, making it one of the largest typical American elk ever measured by that fine organization. My bull was also declared a new Pope and Young Club's World's Record. In 2001, I was presented the Ishi Award, Pope and Young Club's top honor and only the 14th given in the Club's 40-year history, for taking this extraordinary elk. This bull stands as the second largest typical elk taken by bow or gun in Montana. Taking this elk is a high point in my bowhunting life.

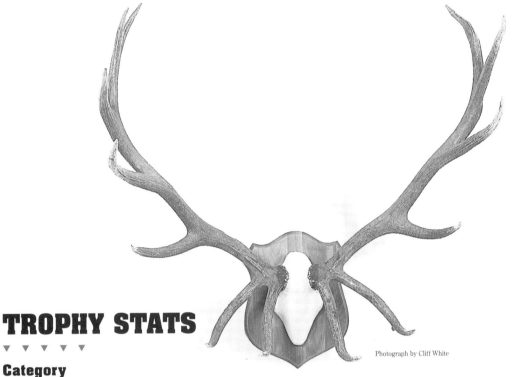

Photograph by Cliff White

TROPHY STATS
▼ ▼ ▼ ▼ ▼

Category
American elk - typical antlers

Score
$394^2/_8$

Location
Utah County, Utah — 2003

Hunter
Lynn O. Grant

Length of Main Beam
Right: $52^3/_8$ Left: $52^1/_8$

Circumference Between First and Second Points
Right: $9^2/_8$ Left: $8^6/_8$

Number of Points
Right: 7   Left: 7

Inside Spread Measurement
49

Photograph by Jack Renea

Lynn O. Grant accepting his plaque and medal from Buck Buckner, Chair of the Big Game Records Committee.

AMERICAN ELK
Typical Antlers
Second Award – 394 $^2/_8$

▼ ▼ ▼ ▼ ▼ ▼ ▼ ▼ ▼

LYNN O. GRANT

It started nine years ago when Thane Campbell and I applied for a Utah Limited Entry Elk tag. Every year after that, we researched areas, applied, and every year we thought this might be the year, but it wasn't. Finally, in 2003, we figured we had about a 50/50 shot at the tag we wanted. On April 30, 2003, we received notice that after nine years of trying we had finally drawn a Utah elk tag in the zone we wanted to hunt. We were fired up to say the least. We had hunted all around the area, but had not actually hunted this area before.

We started making phone calls to anybody who might be able to give us information about the area. Craig Clyde, a Utah wildlife biologist, was particularly helpful. He gave us some great information about some areas to start looking at. A few days before the season opened, we started scouting an area he had told us about. Over the next couple of days, we saw several nice bulls. We also met a few archery hunters who were on the last days of their hunt; they were nice enough to give us some good information. One was Steve Tibbals. He said he had horses and if we needed help packing out an animal to give him a call.

As opening day approached, we were really excited. The day before the season started, we spotted what I thought was the biggest bull I had ever seen. It was up a draw about a mile and a half from any road. We came up with a plan; Thane would hunt from the top, and I'd come up from the bottom.

On opening day, I left the truck about an hour and a half before daylight. I brought enough food and drink to spend the day up the draw where we had seen the big bull. I found a good vantage point and stayed there all day glassing. I spotted several nice bulls, but not the one we were looking for. With about one hour of daylight left, I figured if the bull had been there I would have seen it. So I started heading back to the road, slowly hunting on the way out.

When I was roughly a mile from the road, I spotted the bull about 800 yards south of me. It didn't take but one quick look through the binoculars to know that this was the bull we were looking for. The sun was

Photograph courtesy of Lynn O. Grant

Longtime hunting partners, Thane Campbell, and Lynn O. Grant are pictured above with their elk from the 2003 season.

Lynn O. Grant dropped this typical American elk scoring 394-2/8 points with his .300 Winchester Magnum. Levi Tibbals, pictured above, and his brother Steve brought their horses in the following day to help Lynn pack the elk out.

going to go down soon, so I knew I had to work fast. I dropped into a ravine and came out about 400 yards from the bull.

I knew I couldn't do any better, so I steadied my .300 Winchester Magnum and fired. The bull started into a ravine, so I fired again. It spun and ran my direction into a clearing. Finally, the elk went down. Walking up to it, I knew I had just taken a big bull, but until I got up close I didn't realize how big it really was. I knew I didn't have much daylight left so, after a prayer of thanks, I filled out my tag and hung it on the bull.

I arrived at the truck well after dark. Thane had heard the shooting and wanted to hear all the details. It was awesome telling him what had just happened. On the way back to camp we called Steve Tibbals. He said he'd be there at daylight with horses to help us. That night, I might as well have packed up my bedroll and headed back up to where the elk was because I didn't sleep a wink.

The next morning Steve, his brother Levi, and three horses arrived to help us. What a welcome sight. I had left before daylight and was at the elk as Thane, Steve, and Levi arrived. It was something to see the looks on their faces as they saw the bull for the first time. After snapping some pictures, we quartered up the meat, caped out the head, and were able to get everything out in one trip. Later, at camp, Thane put a tape on the antlers and figured the bull would score close to 400 B&C points. I couldn't believe after all these years of applying that I had killed a bull of this size on opening day.

Thane continued hunting and seeing nice bulls but nothing he wanted to shoot. On the fifth day of the hunt, Thane got a nice 6x6 just two canyons from where I had gotten mine. Unfortunately Steve wasn't available so we boned out the meat and packed it out on our backs.

AMERICAN ELK
Typical Antlers
Second Award – 394²/₈
▼ ▼ ▼ ▼ ▼
LYNN O. GRANT

We met so many good people on this hunt; it really added to the great success we were fortunate enough to have. After the 60-day drying time, the antlers officially scored 394-2/8 points. Looking back on this hunt, there are many things I'll remember — having a great hunting buddy to share the experience with, meeting great people who helped us out, finding the best Mexican food restaurant in the world, and how God blessed me with such a magnificent animal.

Photograph by Cliff White

TROPHY STATS

▼ ▼ ▼ ▼ ▼

Category
American elk - non-typical antlers

Score
$444^4/_8$

Location
Coconino County, Arizona — 2003

Hunter
Ronald N. Franklin

Length of Main Beam
Right: $54^6/_8$ Left: $52^6/_8$

Circumference Between First and Second Points
Right: $9^4/_8$ Left: $9^4/_8$

Number of Points
Right: 9   Left: 10

Inside Spread Measurement
$52^2/_8$

Photograph by Jack Renea

Ronald N. Franklin accepting his plaque and medal from Buck Buckner, Chair of the Big Game Records Committee.

AMERICAN ELK
Non-typical Antlers
First Award – 444⁴/₈

▼ ▼ ▼ ▼ ▼ ▼ ▼ ▼ ▼

RONALD N. FRANKLIN

I had just received the news I had been drawn for one of the toughest units to get a tag in the Arizona draw. I called everyone I knew to pass on my good fortune. Everyone was so excited and ready to help on the hunt. The sleepless nights then started, dreaming of big bulls screaming and rutting. A few weeks later, though, I found out that I had drawn my second choice and not the unit I originally thought.

I started scouting, going every weekend and any chance I had some time to slip up to my unit. My brother Charlie, who also had a tag, was getting information from co-workers since he worked in the area we would be hunting. That information really came back to pay off in the long run.

No really big bulls materialized during my scouting, but as it got closer to the season they started to rut. Some really nice bulls started to show and I could tell from the antler growth on even the young bulls that this was going to be a great year to have a tag.

The season started uneventfully. We were seeing nice bulls everyday, just nothing I thought was worth taking so early in the season. It's amazing how each year it seems the elk change. One year it's all about bugling for a response, the next year it seems that cow call was the ticket, but this year it definitely was the cow call I had. That call seemed to be the only one that got a positive response without sending the elk out of the country.

About a week into the hunt it got really interesting. My buddy, Travis Mast, was supposed to join us, but got held up at work for a couple of days. I was excited because the last time we hunted together we had an opportunity at a huge 375-class 6x7 bull. That year my shot didn't connect somehow. Since I was hunting alone for a few days, I tried an area that Charlie and I had heard about. Supposedly, a really big bull had been shot at and missed earlier. I ran into another hunter who had heard of this bull, but said he hadn't seen it. He seemed to say it with a gleam in his eye. Ha! I thought to myself that he wasn't giving it to me straight. The bull had to be around. The stage was set to find the bull of a lifetime.

That night, Travis showed up around 3:30 a.m. after driving all night to get there. When my lantern kicked on at 4 a.m., he said he might skip the morning hunt and get some rest. Then he jumped up and said he didn't want to miss anything. Driving out, I told Travis about the encounter with the other hunter. I also told him that I knew this big bull was still around.

What unfolded over the next several hours took teamwork. We arrived at our area about an hour before daylight. We sat in the predawn silence and heard only one faint bugle way

Photograph courtesy of Ronald N. Franklin

Ronald N. Franklin took this elk during the 2003 season in Coconino County, Arizona, with the help of us hunting partner, Travis Mast. The bull scored 444-4/8 points and received a First Award at the 25th Big Game Awards Program in Kansas City.

off. We moved up the ridge, where I had patterned the elk and their crossing each morning. We decided to wait near a water hole until something got stirred up. As the dark turned gray, we heard a bugle way off. We both pointed about 90 degrees off from one another, so we split the difference and off we went!

As it started to get light we heard the bull bugle several more times, which helped us to pin down the direction. We knew we had to get there before they started to feed off, so we ran to intercept it. Eventually, we stopped to catch our breath. Just then, Travis said, "Stop. Did you hear that?"

We crouched down just in time to let two satellite bulls walk right by us at a short distance. As we started to get closer we saw very fresh sign. This was getting really serious, really fast. Just then we caught movement. Another satellite bull walked within 15 yards of us. As we moved up, we saw a few cows and heard a big smash as two bulls were crashing and fighting. Then Travis whispered, "Oh, my gosh! It's huge! I'm counting 10 or 12 points!"

Just then another bull bugled behind us, which worked to our advantage. It brought the huge bull around to our side of the cows at 80 yards. The bull then started to rake some trees. Finally, I decided every time it put its head down to rake, I would move up. This cat and mouse game went fast when I finally realized I was within range.

AMERICAN ELK
Non-typical Antlers
First Award – 444⁴/₈

▼ ▼ ▼ ▼ ▼

RONALD N. FRANKLIN

Everything was perfect. The bull had its head down, and I drew and released. Time froze, everything stood still, and the bull just turned and looked the other way where the arrow had blown through and bounced into the trees behind it. The broadhead had done its job. It took like what seemed forever before anything happened. I had already removed another arrow from my quiver when the bull started to run. It was almost like a dream. The bull went 40 yards and then it was over.

Travis charged me and started hugging me as I just stood there in shock. It was like it was meant to be. I would like to thank all the people who made this hunt possible: Steve Sherwood of TNT Taxidermists who was a great help and went above and beyond; to my friends and brother who helped with the hunt and scouting; and most of all to my wife and son who understood my passion for hunting and allowed me to chase those dreams I had of a summer of big bulls screaming and rutting.

Photograph by Cliff White

TROPHY STATS

▼ ▼ ▼ ▼ ▼

Category
American elk - non-typical antlers

Score
$442^3/_8$

Location
Gila County, Arizona — 2001

Hunter
Dan J. Agnew

Length of Main Beam
Right: $53^7/_8$ Left: $49^7/_8$

Circumference Between First and Second Points
Right: $8^7/_8$ Left: $9^2/_8$

Number of Points
Right: 7   Left: 8

Inside Spread Measurement
44

Photograph by Jack Rene

Dan J. Agnew accepting his plaque and medal from Buck Buckner, Chair of the Bi Game Records Committee.

AMERICAN ELK
Non-typical Antlers
Second Award – 442³/₈

▼ ▼ ▼ ▼ ▼ ▼ ▼ ▼ ▼

DAN J. AGNEW

It was a three-mile drive and another one-mile hike across the valley floor to get to the rutting area where Mark Stevens and his dad, Jess, had spotted the big non-typical bull several days before my arrival on Arizona's San Carlos Indian Reservation for the start of my September Dry Lake Unit elk hunt. John McClendon, an Arizona outfitter who has guided me on many successful elk hunts, had told me he'd heard a rumor there was a big bull on the San Carlos. Since I'd also killed a big bull on the reservation in 1997, I bought a Dry Lake tag hoping to get a chance at a monster bull.

In Search of Mr. Big

After a three-hour drive from the Phoenix airport, I arrived at Jess' camp late on Monday, September 3. Mark and Jess shared with me the results of their scouting activities. After listening, I knew the big non-typical they'd spotted (which they'd nick-named Mr. Big) was definitely the one I'd heard the rumor about. My tag was good for 14 days, but I'd hoped to be back home in less than 10 to get my 3 teenagers packed and off to college. Mark said "We've got to be up early and walk in while it's still dark. It's been over 90 degrees every day and the elk are heading for the cool of the timber bedding areas right after daylight." With those words, I unpacked my gear and settled into my sleeping bag for what I knew would be a short night's sleep.

When the alarm went off at 3:30 a.m., Jess and Mark were already up and drinking their coffee. I hadn't slept much. But then I never did on the night before the first day of a September elk hunt... just too much anticipation. The three of us got into my rented SUV and after a 45-minute drive, we parked in the cover of a cedar grove. We were about a mile from where Mark and Jess had seen elk feeding and rutting during the prior week. I grabbed my binoculars and my .30-378, and we began our hike in the dark. It wasn't long before I began to hear the greatest sound in the world to an early-fall elk hunter... bugles coming from several different directions. We approached as silently and cautiously as we could because there were only a few small gullies and minimal ground cover to mask our stalk. The wind was favorable and after getting as close as we dared, I finally hunkered down waiting for enough light to see if one of the bugling bulls was the rumored Mr. Big.

As it slowly became light enough to see, Mark spotted the big non-typical about 1,000 yards away with a group of over 80 cows, grazing and already lazily moving toward one of the several draws that led back into the steep, timbered hillsides. As I focused my binocu-

Dan J. Agnew pictured here with his 2001 non-typical American elk. Dan purchased a September Dry Lake Unit elk tag in Arizona's San Carlos Indian Reservation after hearing rumors about this big bull. It scores 442-3/8 points.

lars, I knew this animal was the kind of which bull dreams are made. Unfortunately, between us and the big bull were another half dozen bulls and a smattering of cows. They were strung out for several hundred yards feeding toward the cooler bedding areas of the hillsides. We silently waited. The country was so wide open we knew we'd be seen and spook all or part of the herd if we tried to get closer. I decided to wait for a try later that afternoon.

That afternoon we set up early and waited patiently for the big bull and its harem to come out of the timber on the steep hillsides to feed and water on the valley floor. Just before dark, Mark again saw the big bull. It had walked out of some timber and then bedded again on the hillside under a large juniper about 800 yards away. With lots of cows feeding between us and the bedded bull, Jess got out his spotting scope and I finally got a good look at Mr. Big. What a monster! I'd seen a lot of big bulls in my years of hunting, but none quite like this one. After glassing the big non-typical for a good five minutes, I guessed it would score around 420 B&C points. Mark said, "It'll score better than that." Unfortunately, any stalk was problematic as there were too many other elk between us and the bull. We were also quickly running out of daylight. We patiently waited, but the bull never got up from under that juniper before dark. We headed back to camp anxious for the next morning's hunt.

We made it in the next morning without being seen and were perfectly set up. All the big bull had to do was show. I knew I could get a clean shot given good daylight and the right opening. As luck would have it, we saw approximately 40 cows and 10 bulls that morning, but no Mr. Big. We spent some time cautiously following the elk into the timbered hillsides at a safe distance, but our bull was nowhere to be found. We went back into the same area the next several days and it was as if Mr. Big simply disappeared. I was

getting worried. Had it spooked and ran off? Had it gathered its cows and gone to another area? Was it feeding and rutting only during the night? We were at a loss as to where the bull was or if it would return, but I knew that I had to be patient and just wait.

The following morning came and went the same way. We watched numerous elk go to water and feed. We cautiously followed several of the bulls into the canyons as they headed to the sanctuary of their timbered bedding areas. But again, the big bull had simply disappeared. Mark's brother, Homer Stevens, came to camp after breakfast, and we told him of our travails and uncertainty about where the big bull was located. Homer said, "Unless it's become totally nocturnal, it's got to be getting pretty thirsty. There's not much water around so maybe it will come to water late this afternoon while it's still daylight."

I was desperate and six days into my hunt. It sounded like as good a plan as any. Homer and I found a spot in the valley where we could watch near the water without being seen. This also afforded us a good view of several drainages the elk had been coming out of in the late afternoons as they headed for water and the lush feed on the valley floor. After sitting and glassing the hillsides for about three hours and with only a half-hour of daylight left, we hadn't seen or heard any elk. As we decided to move about a quarter mile to the east, Homer said, "Here come some elk." As Homer and I raised our binoculars in unison, Homer said, "That's it!"

Homer and I froze. We watched the big bull and about 20 cows head straight for the water. When they crossed the top of the earthen dam and disappeared, we moved. He and I had about 700 yards of ground to cover, hopefully before the elk watered and were on their way. As we closed the distance, I was soaked with sweat and my heart and lungs were gasping for air. Trying to run quietly for a half-mile in 80 degree heat at an elevation of 6,000 feet was not something I was used to doing. As I tried to catch my breath and collect myself, I chambered a round and flipped up the covers on my riflescope. Seeing that bull stand on the water's edge only a hundred yards away was incredible. Fortunately, the wind was calm and neither the bull nor the cows had seen us or heard us coming. I squeezed the trigger and watched the Mr. Big fall. After waiting for the mandatory 60-day drying period, the 8x7 bull officially scored 442-3/8 B&C points.

It was a hunt I'll remember forever. My thanks go to God for creating this incredible game animal and to my tribal guides, the hard-working Stevens family, for the time and effort they spent in helping me find this trophy-of-a-lifetime. I'm fortunate it was my turn to find the right bull in the right place at the right time. I stayed in San Carlos for a few more days and flew home on September 10, 2001. The next day would change the world forever.

Photograph by Cliff White

TROPHY STATS

▼ ▼ ▼ ▼ ▼

Category
American elk - non-typical antlers

Score
434³/₈

Location
Colfax County, New Mexico — 1962

Hunter/Owner
Lawrence Sanchez/Ed Sanchez

Length of Main Beam
Right: 48⁴/₈   Left: 47

**Circumference Between
First and Second Points**
Right: 9²/₈   Left: 9¹/₈

Number of Points
Right: 8   Left: 9

Inside Spread Measurement
35³/₈

Photograph by Jack Ren

Ed Sanchez accepting his plaque and
medal from Buck Buckner, Chair of the B
Game Records Committee.

AMERICAN ELK
Non-typical Antlers
Third Award – 434³/₈

▼ ▼ ▼ ▼ ▼ ▼ ▼ ▼ ▼

LAWRENCE SANCHEZ – HUNTER   ED SANCHEZ – OWNER

Written by Ed Sanchez as told by his father, Lawrence "Boss" Sanchez

Lawrence "Boss" Sanchez was a cowboy, ranch hand, and avid hunter. He was a great family man, and enjoyed telling the story of the huge bull elk he killed on Elkhorn Ridge on the Philmont Scout Ranch. The ranch is located near the small village of Cimarron, New Mexico.

On a crisp, cool October morning in 1962 (the first Saturday of elk season), Boss shut the alarm clock off at 3:30 a.m. He scrambled out of bed and cooked a hearty breakfast of eggs, bacon, and toast. He also made a lunch to carry along. His 4x4 Ford, which had been running for 15 minutes, was now warm and ready to roll.

He drove over to pick up his great friend and co-worker, Leo Martinez. They briefly discussed their hunting plans and decided to try the north end of the ranch. Their trip took them through the village of Cimarron and onto the northwest end of the ranch. The next part of their trip through Ponil Canyon and over the ridge to Dean Canyon was uneventful. Traveling northwest in Dean Canyon, the hunters noticed fresh elk sign in the area. Daylight was approaching as they headed toward Elkhorn Ridge, where they parked the pickup.

Boss was hunting with a 6mm Remington rifle. His old friend, Jack Garrett, a Remington representative, had given it to him three years earlier. Leo was carrying his hexagonal-barreled .30-30 Winchester that he had hunted with for many years.

At daylight, the two old friends parted company and began hunting in their

Photograph courtesy of Ed Sanchez

Lawrence "Boss" Sanchez and his son, Ed, pictured here with the non-typical elk that Boss took in 1962. The rifle is the original 6mm Remington that he used on the hunt.

respective areas. Boss set out on foot to the west and Leo headed east. The plan was to meet back at the truck at noon.

Boss had walked a mile when he caught sight of a huge bull elk grazing in a small meadow. He knew that all his best hunting strategies and skills needed to be utilized. His first instinct was to take a long shot at 400 yards. Boss, being a "crack" shot, knew that it would be too long of a shot for his 6mm to be effective, so he decided to put the sneak on and attempt to get a closer shot. Boss knew that a bull this huge was extremely smart and could detect even the slightest scent or noise. Using his finest skills, he stalked his quarry and was able to get within 250 yards of the giant.

Carefully, he raised his rifle and placed the cross hairs on the elk's heart area. Boss knew that one good shot would be his only chance. Being extremely careful, he took aim, pulled the trigger, and the trophy bull elk went to the ground. Loading another round, Boss proceeded toward the elk. At 20 feet, he placed the cross hairs on the elk again, waiting about 5 minutes. Then, noticing no movement, he walked closer and touched the animal with his rifle. There was no reaction from the elk. Boss said aloud, *"Gracias a Dios.* This is my trophy."

He admired the giant bull elk and again said a short prayer. He then field-dressed the massive bull and tied his game tag to the antlers.

Boss met Leo back at their vehicle and told him he had killed an 8x9 down the ridge from where they stood. Both men hugged and rejoiced about their whole hunting experience — the experience of a lifetime. After a great deal of work, they were finally able to load the elk on to the vehicle and head back home.

The story was out about how Lawrence "Boss" Sanchez had killed a 17-point bull elk. There were no measurements taken and very few photographs in those days. Dad sawed the scalp off with a carpenter's saw and stored the antlers in the basement of our home.

Approximately five years later, Arabella B. Sanchez, Boss's oldest daughter, was given the antlers. She hauled them to California, where they were kept indoors in her study room. Every year she would use the antlers for her Christmas tree. After her retirement from the school system, she sold her house, loaded her belongings (elk antlers included), and headed back to her favorite state of New Mexico.

In August 2003, Arabella presented me with a gift-of-a-lifetime. In a birthday card to me, she stated, "I would like for you to have the elk antlers Dad gave me years ago." I graciously thanked her and took my birthday gift home.

In 2003, I took the trophy antlers to a Boone and Crockett Club Official Measurer who scored them at 434-3/8 points!

Rob Arnaud, of Arnaud Outfitting, Inc. of Gallatin Gateway, Montana, introduced me and a picture of my trophy to Dennis "Shoe" Shoemaker, of the Rocky Mountain Elk Foundation. The unselfish, exhausting work of Shoe, Tom Waddell, and the Rocky Mountain Elk Foundation made it all come together. The exceptional bull was shoulder mounted by Shoe, who found a cape similar to the first picture taken of the antlers and hide. The trophy is now on the Rocky Mountain Elk Foundations's 2004 Great Elk Tour.

Award Winning Moments...

Photograph by Jack Reneau

**Both Ron Franklin (second from the right) and Clay Heuett (second from the left)
received awards for their outstanding non-typical American elk taken in Arizona.
Outfitter and guide, Shane Koury (left) and guide, Dwayne Adams (right) made the trip
to Kansas City to celebrate with Clay.**

Photograph by Cliff White

TROPHY STATS

▼ ▼ ▼ ▼ ▼

Category
American elk - non-typical antlers

Score
429⁶/₈

Location
Navajo County, Arizona — 2003

Hunter
Clay R. Heuett

Length of Main Beam
Right: 49¹/₈   Left: 49⁶/₈

Circumference Between First and Second Points
Right: 9⁷/₈   Left: 10¹/₈

Number of Points
Right: 9   Left: 9

Inside Spread Measurement
40

Photograph by Jack Rene[

Clay R. Heuett accepting his plaque and medal from Buck Buckner, Chair of the Bi[
Game Records Committee.

AMERICAN ELK
Non-typical Antlers
Fourth Award – 429$^6/_8$

▼ ▼ ▼ ▼ ▼ ▼ ▼ ▼ ▼

CLAY R. HEUETT

Tom Groves, my hunting partner of 20 years, and I had our hunting dreams come true. It took 12 years, but we had finally been drawn for an elk hunt in our favorite unit in Arizona. Tom, Dwayne Adams, my son Brian, and I started scouting a couple of weeks before the hunt. We saw some quality bulls and knew this was going to be a special year. Dwayne is a guide for Koury Guide Service and grew up in the area, so we had an excellent chance of killing a big bull.

Opening morning, September 12, 2003, came and Tom went to an area that held some good bulls. One hour into the hunt, Tom had killed a 6x7, 350-class bull at 20 yards — a great bull.

Dwayne and I, scented up with Carlton Scents, opened with a 340-class bull at approximately 45 yards. It was a "non-shooter" according to Dwayne, something I would hear a lot during this hunt. We moved areas and got right on another bull. It was a 6x7, 350-class, again at 45 yards and again a non-shooter. As the morning hunt came to an end, we had passed up chances at a couple of quality-sized bulls, along with a few satellite bulls. We decided to head back to camp and regroup for the evening hunt.

That evening, Brian joined us to help videotape the rest of the hunt. We returned to the same area and found two different 350-class bulls that we videotaped. We agreed that they were non-shooters. As day one came to an end, we decided to change areas and look for the next class of bulls.

As the next few days of the hunt went by, we videotaped many bulls in the 320-360 class, but nothing we wanted to take this early in the hunt.

Monday's hunt proved to be eventful. We got right on a 370-class bull that we called "Broken Sword" because of a broken fourth point. We decided to put a stalk on it, and we fought our way through five or six satellite bulls. I had a quick 60-yard shot, which ended up low underneath its chest. As we continued to trail the Broken Sword bull, we had many opportunities to take a quality satellite bull, but never got another chance for the Broken Sword bull.

Missing that shot, though, was a blessing in disguise. After the morning hunt, Dave and Shane Koury alerted us of a 400-plus monster bull, so we opted to hunt that bull. The next morning, we sat in the area where Dave saw the bull, but the only elk that came in was a tall 360-class 7x7.

Clay R. Heuett, right, with his son, Brian, center, and guide, Shane Koury, pictured with Clay's award-winning non-typical American elk. The bull scores 429-6/8 points and received a Fourth Award at the 25th Awards Program in Kansas City.

For the evening hunt, Shane Koury joined us. We chose to chase bugles instead of sitting. This proved to be a good plan because we ended up seeing the 400-class bull for the first time with our own eyes. After finding it, we attempted to put on an aggressive stalk. Before I could draw back for a 50-yard shot, the cows busted us. As the herd jumped the fence line, we picked a shooting lane and waited for the bull to pass through. Unfortunately, we underestimated the yardage and I shot low — another missed opportunity.

Saturday morning, September 20, we were disappointed to hear that Dwayne had been hospitalized with pneumonia. Our thoughts were with Dwayne as we decided to hunt the same area and came across numerous satellite bulls, but not our 400 bull.

September 21, Sunday morning, we found ourselves among the herd before dawn. From a distance, we heard the crack of antlers and immediately figured this was our bull. We slowly worked our way toward the fighting. In the process, the fighting and bugling ceased. We quickly caught a glimpse of our bull as it moved away. For half an hour, we were mislead by another bull. We realized our mistake when we faintly heard our bull's distinct bugle, and promptly turned and headed in its direction.

As we approached within 150 yards, we heard our bull fighting again. Seizing the opportunity, we sprinted to within 20 yards. The energy of these two bulls fighting was extremely

intense. Dust and the sound of crack-
ing antlers filled the air. As I drew
back, Shane glassed the bulls and
instructed me that our bull was the
back one.

I released the arrow and made
contact, but my bull was so full of

adrenaline that it kept on fighting. As the bulls continued to fight, I nocked another Easton
arrow equipped with Thunderhead 100-grain broadheads. The second shot also hit. The bull
continued to fight as I prepared for a third shot. Several seconds later, the bull finally noticed
it was hurt.

As it disengaged from fighting, the other bull charged at it. My bull spun and ran right
at us, passing within a few yards, and knocking one of the arrows to the ground right at our
feet. Knowing that I had hit it twice, we decided to wait 30 minutes before tracking. I must
admit that this was the longest 30 minutes of my life. Once we started tracking, we discovered blood right away. We didn't have to go far as our bull was lying dead 80 yards away. This
big, beautiful non-typical 9x9 was bigger than we ever could have imagined.

After celebrating, we loaded the bull in the truck and headed toward town. But first we
had a stop to make. That was at the hospital to show Dwayne our prized bull, since he could
not be with us at the time of the kill.

I have many people to thank for the help they provided. Thank you, Brian, for spending
your entire vacation and all your spare time with good ol' Dad. Thank you also to Will
Heuett, Kevin Van Driel, Dwayne Adams, and Shane and Dave Koury for all your help.

TROPHY STATS

▼ ▼ ▼ ▼ ▼

Photograph by Cliff White

Category
American elk - non-typical antlers

Score
430²/₈

Location
Rio Blanco County, Colorado — 1888

Hunter
William D. Deweese/Royal Gorge Regional Museum and Historical Center

Length of Main Beam
Right: 56   Left: 55⁷/₈

Circumference Between First and Second Points
Right: 7⁷/₈   Left: 8²/₈

Number of Points
Right: 8   Left: 9

Inside Spread Measurement
49⁷/₈

AMERICAN ELK
Non-typical Antlers
Certificate of Merit – 430 ²/₈

▼ ▼ ▼ ▼ ▼ ▼ ▼ ▼ ▼

WILLIAM D. DEWEESE – HUNTER
ROYAL GORGE REGIONAL MUSEUM AND HISTORICAL CENTER – OWNER

The story on the following pages was written by William Dallas "Dall" DeWeese in 1888, over 115 years before his elk was ever scored for the Boone and Crockett records book. It is not simply a recounting of the story of his hunt. It is also a priceless look into the past of our hunting heritage. Everything in this story tells a tale, whether it's the hunting slang of the day, the things they saw, or what common thoughts and acceptable practices were in that era.

The year 1888 was amidst the infancy of conservation. The roots of the Boone and Crockett Club (North America's oldest conservation organization) had been planted only one year previous. Game laws were noticeably absent, as were general public concerns for the future of our wildlife populations and welfare. Very few people in that era thought about "fair chase" or ethics in the field. Those concepts were all but non-existent. Hunting was a simple act – reduce to possession, cook, and eat.

The fact that Dall DeWeese even took the time to write of his adventure is amazing in itself. It also shows, however, that even in that day, people still had appreciation for wild things and places. There are also references in this story that show evidence of the beginnings of people's changing views. At points in the story, he references the fact that they waited for a clear shot, as to not wound cows and calves. He also mentions, "We saw dozens of fine fat deer at close range but killed none, as we were not out to see how much game we could slaughter and let lay in the mountains – as is too often done." This exact sentiment is one of the founding principles of why the Boone and Crockett Club was established, as well as North American wildlife management as a whole.

Some of the content of this story would be, by today's standards, unethical and irresponsible. Back then it was not only acceptable, it was commonplace. We have chosen not to sanitize the story, nor correct the grammar. This story is an education, as well as a glimpse into past realities. It also shows that even in 1888, there was a true romanticism of wild places. The original words and language leave these pages authentic. Dall DeWeese's story appeared in the Canon City Clipper on October 31, 1888.

Successful Hunters!

Ten Days Among The Elk, Bear, and Deer.

A Former Tipp Boy's Successful Hunt After Big Game in The Rockies.
Camp Big Horns, Colo., Sept. 1888.
Messrs. Bowman, Clark Bros., Williamson, Hawver, and Huber: —

My Dear Nimrods – Your letters were received in due time stating that it was impossible for you to join me this fall in an elk hunt in the Rocky Mountains. I regretted much to receive this word and think you "tender-feet" will regret sending it after reading of our grand time.

Mr. J. E. Brown, Mr. L. E. Franck (county treasurer), both "old-timers" here, and myself took train September 3d, crossed the Rockies to the mouth of Eagle River where I had saddle horses and pack animals (jacks) awaiting us. There are no toll pikes in this country but simply a jack trail leading here and there up into the cedars and pinons, then up to the quakenasps, thence higher to the spruce-covered mountain tops and timber line peaks, and into the very heart of the Rocky Mountains. We soon packed our bedding and supplies on our jacks and took the trail leading up Sweetwater (Turret Creek.) We reached Sweetwater Lake the same evening and camped for the night. The lake is one mile long and half a mile wide, located in a canon between two great mountains; its waters are full of the beautiful speckled trout and our jointed rods, lines, leaders and flies were quickly adjusted and seventeen of the speckled beauties were landed and prepared for supper.

The next morning the bright face of Old Sol found us in the saddle and two miles up the steep ascending trail. What fresh invigorating atmosphere and how grand the scenery of this forenoon ride! We climbed higher through groves of quakenasp and the grassy mountainsides until noon when we reached the "flat tops," or summit of the range. I wish I could picture this landscape for you so you could imagine the grand surroundings of our camp, but I can only say that these flat tops are timbered with dense groves of the stately spruce and are broken here and there with open parks which are covered with a luxuriant growth of the tall gramma grass. Notwithstanding the altitude is 10,000 feet, fine springs, small streams and lakes are everywhere. Turret Peak and Shingle Peak tower up to 12,000 feet – 1000 feet above timber line – and on their North sides lays perpetual snow. From these peaks you can see forever! You can see into Egeria Park, the head waters of the Grand, Piney, Eagle, Roaring Fork, Muddy and Bear Rivers, and at their base heads the great White River. This was the Ute Indians' paradise for summer and fall hunting, and here is the home of the elk, mountain sheep, silver tip grizzly and cinnamon bear, and the gamey black tail [mule] deer. Three o'clock p.m. found our jacks and horses unpacked and picketed out in the rich grass, dinner over, tents up, hunting equipments in place, and then we started out after fresh meat for supper, although we had a goodly supper of bacon.

Sundown found us all back in camp with three deer packed in and hung on the spruce [in] back of the tent. I killed a big buck that weighed 260 pounds, fat an inch thick over the rump, horns in the velvet which makes for a fine trophy.

Having all the camp meat necessary the next day was spent in looking for elk sign through the spruce forests on the North and shady sides of the breaks on the flat tops. Our notes compared favorably on our return at night, and after camp-fire stories we retired fully convinced that we were in the land of the "wapiti," and believing that our desire to kill a bull elk would soon be gratified.

The next day we discovered quite a chain of small lakes about six miles Northward, with no end to elk and bear sign in their vicinity. We saw dozens of fine fat deer at close range but killed none as we were not out to see how much game we could slaughter and let lay in the mountains – as is too often done. We returned to camp early that day, boned our meat, salted it down in the hides under the spruce trees where the sun never shines and covered it up with boughs. Then we folded our bedding, packed some supplies on our jacks, saddled our horses and made a branch camp at one of the newly discovered lakes by 8 o'clock the same evening.

After we had retired we heard a bull elk "bugle" – probably a half mile distant – and he came nearer and nearer until he was within 200 yards of the camp. Here he bugled and repeated, striking every note in the staff in a loud, clear, shrill, whistling tone that echoed from park to woodland. It was indeed a grand serenade, but we were so eager for a crack at his elkship that we did not await its conclusion. Hastily kicking aside the blankets we hurriedly dressed and tried to steal a march on him. There being no moon it was quite dark, and we stole along the edge of the spruce near the open park that he was crossing. We could hear him coming and down we crouched near a clump of willows. All was still as death save the rustle of the tall grass at his feet and occasionally a musical bugle, but he was going at right angles from us and passed within 80 yards – close enough to hear him breathe. But alas! We could not make out the outline of his "darned old carcass," and he gained the shelter of the spruce and bugled again. I tired to answer him but my "bugle" was evidently a sad failure, or else he heard one from a more congenial mate, for he bugled us a loud "good-bye" or "some other evening" that grew fainter and fainter, and shivering with cold we crept back to bed muttering an emphatic good-night to bull elks.

In the morning we were out early and all keeping together we followed along a high ridge near the lakes. Fresh sign was seen on all favorable ground and we kept a sharp lookout. Presently the splashing of water near at hand attracted our attention and looking down we discovered a band of elk in a little lake just beyond a grove of spruce. The wind was against us, and silently we stole around to the opposite edge of the timber. Here a grand sight met our eyes – a band of forty elk, all cows and calves except on fair sized bull. Some were in the water and others were in an open park. The distance was 300 yards and it was impossible to get a shot at the bull to kill. However we chanced it, and, taking care not to hit the cows and calves, we singled him out and fired together. Off they went like a flash under cover of the spruce, and we followed, finding blood on the trail. After following the trail half a mile we concluded it was a flesh wound and returned to camp – thinking we might have done better and feeling like shooting eight or ten deer we saw while coming back.

Next morning before sun up we were off in different directions. At this season of the year the elk are beginning to band together, the velvet has just shed from the antlers of the bulls, and the bark can frequently be seen off of spruce trees eight feet from the ground where they have been rubbing their antlers. I made a long trip and struck the fresh trail of a band of elk, mostly bulls as the tracks were large. I followed the trail a mile or more some-what toward camp and saw they were headed for a large body of spruce timber. As it was about noon and being close to camp I concluded to go in, get something to eat and then ride my horse over to the location of the elk and take my evening hunt, for one hour at sun down is worth the balance of the day in elk hunting. On reaching camp I was joined by Mr. Brown who asked if I had moved the jacks from where he had picketed them out in the morning. I had not and went to the park where they should have been. Gone? Yes, gone! Our Rocky Mountain Mocking Birds had "broke" camp and struck out for home, their pace doubtless accelerated by the scent of a gray silver tip. Mr. Franck and myself, after lunch, saddled our horses and rode over in the direction I had tracked the elk. After going a mile we rode out of the spruce on a point to look over the country. The sun was half an hour high and the shadows of the spruce groves were stretching out over the parks – and this is the hour for the elk to come from the forests and feed in the parks. Sitting quietly in the saddle, our gaze roving over the beautiful landscape, we sighted a band of elk a mile away just emerging from the spruce. We counted eleven; all were large, one in particular, and we remarked that there was an "Old Towser." He stopped and looked square at us – then moved on. Now was our opportunity. Slipping away from our saddles and leaving the horses for a "blind," we start-ed on a run through the spruce groves, open parks, up, then down the ravines, across anoth-er park and finally reached the last spruce grove that separated us from the game. Stealing quietly through this we reached the edge that fringed the park. Peeping out I saw a great bull elk lying down in the tall grass 140 yards away and looking right at us. I saw he was a monster, and we gave him a double shot. Over he went – then he was up and off into the spruce like a flash! The others fled to the top of the hill and were gone in a second. We fol-lowed their trail in a forest of spruce twenty miles wide, found no blood, and the sun went down. We stared blankly into each others faces and wondered if it was possible to miss such a monster. Finally we decided to return to camp and pick up the trail early the next morn-ing. We kicked ourselves back to camp and declared that if we had really missed that ele-phant we would fold our blankets, go to Canon City and never say elk again.

The next morning we were up with the stars and rode over to where we had left the trail. Staking our horses we were soon tracking the "Monarch of the Glen." Although the dense spruce forest was tracked by elk, we could easily follow the right one as it was almost an inch

SUCCESSFUL HUNTERS !

Ten Days Among The Elk, Bear And Deer.

A Former Tipp Boy's Successful Hunt After Big Game In The Rockies.

CAMP BIG HORNS, Colo., Sept. 1888.

Messrs. Bowman, Clark Bros., Williamson, Hawver and Huber :—

MY DEAR NIMRODS—Your letters were received in due time stating that it was impossible for you to join me this fall in an elk hunt in the Rocky Mountains. I regretted much to receive this word and think you "tender-feet" will regret sending it after reading of our grand time.

Mr. J. E. Brown, Mr. L. E. Franck. (county treasurer,) both "old-timers" here, and myself took train September 3d, crossed the Rockies to the mouth of Eagle River where I had saddle horses and pack animals (jacks) awaiting us. There are no toll pikes in this country but simply a jack trail leading here and there up into the cedars and pinons, then up to the quaken-asps, thence higher to the spruce covered mountain tops and timber line peaks, and into the very heart of the Rocky Mountains. We soon packed our bedding and supplies on our jacks and took the trail leading up Sweetwater (Turret Creek.) We reached Sweetwater Lake the same evening and camped for the night. The Lake is one mile long and half a mile wide; located in a cañon between two great mountains; its waters are full of the beautiful speckled trout and our jointed rods, lines, leaders and flies were quickly adjusted and

morning. I had not and went to the park where they should have been. Gone? Yes, "bugle"—probably a half mile distant—and he came nearer and nearer until he was within 200 yards of the camp. Here he bugled and repeated, striking every note in the staff in a loud, clear, shrill, whistling tone that echoed from park to woodland. It was indeed a grand serenade, but we were so eager for a crack at his elkship that we did not await its conclusion. Hastily kicking aside the blankets we hurriedly dressed and tried to steal a march on him. There being no moon it was quite dark, and we stole along the edge of the spruce near the open park that he was crossing. We could hear him coming and down we crouched near a clump of willows. All was still as death save the rustle of the tall grass at his feet and occasionally a musical bugle, but he was going at right angles from us and passed within 80 yards—close enough to hear him breathe. But alas ! we could not make out the outline of his "darned old carcass," and he gained the shelter of the spruce and bugled again. I tried to answer him but my "bugle" was evidently a sad failure, or else he heard one from a more congenial mate, for he bugled us a long "good-bye" or "some other evening" that grew fainter and fainter, and shivering with cold we crept back to bed muttering an emphatic good-night to bull elks.

In the morning we were out early and all keeping together we followed along a high ridge near the lakes. Fresh sign was seen on all favorable ground and we kept a sharp lookout. Presently the splashing of water near at hand attracted our attention and looking down we discovered a band of elk in a little lake just beyond a

Courtesy of Royal Gorge Regional Museum and Historical Center

The article written by William D. Deweese about his hunt for this great non-typical American elk first appeared in an 1888 edition of the *Canon City Clipper*. The story is reprinted in its original context to give readers an idea what hunting was like more than a century ago.

deeper and much larger than the other tracks. After tracking 200 yards we saw that one of us had our brand on him for occasionally we found a drop of blood. He kept in the heaviest timber, and I knew that was a good sign for the Indians say, "Heap hurt when go through heap brush!" We tracked him a mile into the heart of the forest to where the ground and logs were covered with a rich, green, velvet-like moss, and where the sun never penetrates. Here we "jumped" him and away he went; we fired five shots after him, and then I ran to the left about forty yards and gained a higher spot of ground from where I got a broadside shot, the ball breaking his left shoulder and down he went! We rushed up to him; he still struggled, shook those massive antlers and eyed us with vengeance. A merciful shot through the heart ended his career. We then gazed in astonishment at his gigantic size. He measured 15 feet and 4 inches from the point of horn to the hind hoof, and girted 9 feet. His antlers are the largest I ever saw; the beams are six feet long and are five feet between the points, having nine perfect points on one beam and eight on the other – hence the name of our camp, "Big Horns." Old hunters came to see him and they say he is the biggest elk ever killed in this country. He dressed over 700 lbs. of meat. We found that one of us had hit him in the neck the evening before, and on cutting out the bullet, which was imbedded in the neck-bone, it proved to be a Winchester – and my comrade used a Sharps.

After dressing him we returned to camp, taking some of his meat with us for supper, and as we kindled our camp-fire that night we gave three cheers for the Monarch Bull Elk, Harrison and Morton, and the boys of Tippecanoe.

The next day Mr. Brown returned with our "mocking birds" and we packed in our elk and boned the meat. The next morning we started to move camp again; our animals were packed and we were in the saddle at daylight. We struck a trail and had only gone half a mile when I caught a glimpse of three silver tip bears on the opposite side of an open park we were just entering. Hastily notifying Mr. Brown, who was just behind me, we slipped out of our saddles and started for the game. I gained a bunch of willows between the bears and myself, and Mr. B. kept to the right along the trees. I opened fire and down went a bear. I advanced and continued firing to keep him down. Mr. B. got into position and began shooting, while the other two bears slowly retreated up the hill snarling and stopping occasionally to snap viciously at us. I expected them to come at us, for the one I had shot lay kicking on the ground and squalling terribly; and so I filled the magazine of my gun with cartridges as I ran, expecting a dozen more bears to appear at any moment (I am glad they did not for I was out in the open park with no trees handy.) Mr. Franck, who was some 300 yards behind us fixing his saddle when the rumpus started, came riding into the fight on the dead run, and the first shot from his old Sharps rifle hit a bear in the neck and silenced him forever. The other bear carried off our lead and escaped. I tell you there was music in the air for a few minutes, the constant bang! bang! bang! of our rifles, the snapping and squalling of the bears, the bray of our jacks as they rushed terror-stricken from the scene, and our shouts to each other to "stand your ground and give 'em h—l!" made up a scene at once exhilaratingly exciting. But it was over in half the time it takes to write it. We came out without a scratch and got two bears out of the three. Their robes are fine and we will have them made into rugs to keep as mementos of a most thrilling experience.

After a close search for an hour we found our jacks huddled together with a part of their packs off and frightened nearly to death. We were soon on the move again and came down to our first camp, satisfied with our day's sport.

AMERICAN ELK
Non-typical Antlers
Certificate of Merit – 430 $^2/_8$

▼ ▼ ▼ ▼ ▼

HUNTER - WILLIAM D. DEWEESE

In the early morning we were up early and rode six miles to another locality, and then swung around to a "salt lick" where we had seen a band of mountain sheep several days before. It was sundown when we reached the ridge in front of the "licks," and we dismounted and quietly crept to the top. Three hundred yards distant was a band of eleven elk standing around the lick. It was too dark to see the antlers, but we were satisfied several of the larger ones were bulls, and singling out our targets we fired. At the first round they rushed up the mountain which was very steep. This gave us an advantage, although we were firing a distance of over three hundred yards. We continued firing until each of us succeeded in killing an elk – Mr. Brown bringing down a fine bull. We dressed them and returned to camp, arriving at 11:30, where we prepared a meal from the fat of the land.

In the morning we decided that the swelling was out of our necks, broke camp and started for home. We reached the railroad on the 16th and sent eight pack animals and two packers back to camp to bring out the balance of our game. Reached home on the 17th ready for business and feeling that we have a new lease on life which could not be had only through an elk hunt in the Rocky Mountains.

Dall DeWeese.

Canon City, Colorado.

New World's Record

TROPHY STATS
▼ ▼ ▼ ▼ ▼

Category
Roosevelt's elk

Score
404^6/$_8$

Location
Benton County, Oregon — 2002

Hunter
Jason S. Ballard

Length of Main Beam
Right: 54^1/$_8$ Left: 57^5/$_8$

Circumference Between First and Second Points
Right: 8^2/$_8$ Left: 9^4/$_8$

Number of Points
Right: 9   Left: 8

Inside Spread Measurement
40^6/$_8$

Photograph by Cliff White

112

ROOSEVELT'S ELK
First Award – 404⁶/₈

▼ ▼ ▼ ▼ ▼ ▼ ▼ ▼ ▼

JASON S. BALLARD

It was spring break, 1988, and I was getting a vacation from my college classes by helping fertilize the grass seed fields on the farm that had employed me since childhood. The old Chevy truck — heavy laden with fertilizer power bins — whined and groaned its way up the very steep stretch of road just past the old Feichter house. Suddenly, there ahead of me were nine elk; a rag-horned four-point, two massive cows and an assortment of yearlings and calves. Quickly, I radioed Frank and

Sunday's Best

Brad, and they caught up just in time to see the tan rumps bounce over the hill to the West of us. I knew then that I would hunt Roosevelt's elk in earnest when my education was complete and time would allow it.

There is an old cliché that time has a way of getting away from us — and we know it does. The past 12 years have been good to the elk in the Willamette Valley of Western Oregon, with the herd approaching 200 animals. The original nine probably stumbled into the Valley by accident. They soon learned that the valley floor offers thousands of acres of ryegrass, fescue, corn, and millet, while oak and ash forests along the Muddy Creek ensure ample cover for these noble creatures. Safety from hunters is also available when the animals retreat to the local wildlife refuge. Working as a high school shop teacher offers many great perks, but ample time to hunt in the fall is NOT one of them. Deer hunting from my home (literally) has always been a blessing for me. A few hours here and there yields a buck during most years. But elk are different. They demand more time and effort.

It was summer break, 2002, and I was back on the farm working as a maintenance mechanic during harvest. I had drawn a Willamette Unit elk tag and was planning to hunt during the last of summer break. The

Photograph courtesy of Jason S. Ballard

Jason S. Ballard pictured here with his Willamette Valley Roosevelt's elk. The bull scores 404-6/8 points and is the new World's Record.

area that I could hunt was limited to a few hundred acres, but the hunt was long and it was just a matter of time before some animals ventured onto my path. While I was hoping for a nice bull, I knew in my heart that it would be difficult to pass on a spike or a big cow—just like those first ones I'd spotted 12 years before.

Frank drove up to my service rig just after 6 a.m. to tell me my dad had spotted five bulls in an un-thrashed ryegrass field, which was less than a mile from where I was working. We hopped in his pickup and drove down to get a look, but they had vanished into heavy cover before we arrived. My hunt was to start the next week and it was exciting to have five branched bulls right where I was planning to hunt. Further scouting showed that these animals were frequenting an old fruit orchard, and by the varying sign, it appeared as though they had been in there multiple times in the past few weeks. Poor wind conditions, large expanses of open fields, and bulls feeding nocturnally would prove to make my hunt a challenge. I set out to capitalize on any opportunities that should arise.

It became clear that the bulls were crossing into the orchard and surrounding ash grove through open fields at night, and retreating back to heavy brush and timber before first light . . . except for that one morning when my dad spotted them.

In the days before the hunt, I agonized over the best approach to get at one of these nighttime monsters. I decided to revert back to my archery hunting tactics, minimizing scent and visibility, and created a situation where I would be shooting unseen from known distances. A dip in the landscape beside a small creek on the downwind side of the elk crossing offered an ideal location for a ground blind. Berry vines were trimmed, and yardages were marked from the blind in 100-yard increments out to 500 yards. Barnes X-bullets were loaded for my .30-06 and test fired at 100, 200, 300, and 400 yards to ensure exact shooting precision at known ranges.

The first few days of the hunt yielded a close encounter with a large three-point black-tail, a family of raccoons, a coyote, and a beaver. Both my seven-year-old and five-year-old boys had accompanied me on these first outings, but no elk were spotted.

On the ninth day of the hunt, Benjamin, my 7-year-old son, spotted what he described as "hay bales" moving at about 400 yards to the north of us. Like any good dad, I scolded him for talking while we were sneaking into our ground blind and told him to stop being ridiculous. Upon closer inspection, we discovered that the big "hay bales" were four massive bulls heading for the heavy brush, but it was about eight minutes before legal shooting hours. I attempted a makeshift stalk with nothing between the bulls and me, but clear morning air. By the time legal light arrived, the four big boys were 600-plus yards away, trotting into the brush. The two largest bulls were immense, and Brutus (the bigger of the two) was unlike anything I'd ever seen. Never before had my cross hairs been on an elk like this one and I was amazed at the sheer mass of this creature. It was time to reassess the game plan.

After second-guessing my blind location, I decided to stick with the original strategy as there was no way I could cover the entire area. I had to bank on what seemed most probable, which was that the bulls would use their preferred path of travel again. They did.

Most Sundays are a day of praise and worship for our family. Church service was in the park on that August morning, and I looked forward to attending when I returned from my morning hunt. As it turned out, my morning plans were radically changed.

ROOSEVELT'S ELK
First Award – 404 6/8
▼ ▼ ▼ ▼ ▼
JASON S. BALLARD

It was 12 minutes before shooting hours when two six-points and a massive bull stepped out of the ash grove into the field, followed a few minutes later by a massive eight by nine-point Roosevelt's bull. My cousin, Randy, had come along for the morning hunt, and he spotted the first bull out at about 450 yards. When the third bull appeared we were certain it was the one we wanted, as it appeared to be half again bigger than the nice six-point bulls. I knew there was another one to come, but was shocked to see it was even bigger than the previous bull!

It quickly became apparent that these bulls would be out of the area in less than 10 minutes. I do believe that God's grace was upon me this crisp August morning. For some reason, the two six-points locked antlers and began to fight. They pushed, shoved, rattled, and clanked horns for the next 12 to14 minutes, and the big bulls stopped to watch, thus buying precious time. The fighting bulls shoved each other nearly 200 yards across the field, and while they were still sparring, I had decided to shoot the No. 2 bull since Brutus was in the brush at 500-plus yards shredding trees in an effort to shine up his impressive rack. All of the elk were within 100 yards of my hunt boundary and I dared not wait too long because everyone knows that a bull in the hand is worth more than a monster bull in the bush . . .

As the fighting went on, bull No. 2 offered a constant full broadside shot at slightly less than 400 yards, and Brutus was still out of range shredding trees. The time was now. I eased the safety off, adjusted myself in the prone shooting rest built from straw and topped with an old wool army blanket. As I began to squeeze the trigger, No. 2 whirled and faced us. The bull was staring right at us; I could feel its burning glare. "Safety back on. Breathe deep, and wait . . . I cannot take this long of a shot with a mere .30.06 unless it's standing broadside," I said to myself.

The fighting continued. Big bull No. 2 was still staring intently at us, and then into my field of view stepped Brutus. The bull stopped broadside at 450 yards. I turned the safety off, took a deep breath, aimed the rifle, and squeezed the trigger. The shot clipped the edge of the shoulder blade and the bullet lodged in the spine, and Brutus dropped without a step taken.

As we slowly walked up on Brutus, we realized that we were looking at a once-in-a-lifetime world-class Roosevelt's bull. The work started soon thereafter. But all in all it was a good Sunday, and I remembered to give thanks to the Creator of this magnificent animal, even if I wasn't wearing my Sunday's best.

Photograph by Cliff White

TROPHY STATS

▼ ▼ ▼ ▼ ▼

Category
Roosevelt's elk

Score
374 $^3/_8$

Location
Bonanza Lake, British Columbia — 2002

Hunter
Ronald K. Bridge

Length of Main Beam
Right: 50   Left: 47

Circumference Between First and Second Points
Right: 9 $^2/_8$ Left: 8 $^5/_8$

Number of Points
Right: 8   Left: 8

Inside Spread Measurement
42

Photograph by Jack René

Ronald K. Bridge accepting his plaque and medal from Buck Buckner, Chair of the Big Game Records Committee.

ROOSEVELT'S ELK
Second Award – 374 $^3/_8$

▼ ▼ ▼ ▼ ▼ ▼ ▼ ▼ ▼

RONALD K. BRIDGE

At 1 a.m., I was awakened by the ringing phone. It must be an emergency, I thought. Anyone who knows me would not have called at this time, being aware that I always started my day at about 4 a.m.

The voice on the other end of the line sounded vaguely familiar. I sat up on the edge of the bed and shook my head in an effort to clear it from the clouds of sleep from which I had just been awakened.

It was the voice of a guide working with outfitter Eugene Eugler. Immediately, I was fully awake and listening intently. This was the same man who had been my guide during a hunt for sheep along the Stikine River eight years previous.

It was during this hunt that I had fulfilled my lifelong dream of hunting for Roosevelt's elk. My successful experiences with hunting moose, caribou, elk, grizzly, and sheep had all been exciting, but they did not replace my desire to hunt Roosevelt's elk. What a beautiful animal, so graceful in movement and proud in its stance.

My excitement began to mount as he began to inform me that he had contacted an experienced outfitter, Dave Fyfe, of North Island Guide Outfitters in British Columbia. Better yet, Dave informed him that he had one permit left for the upcoming season on Roosevelt's elk. I immediately called Dave to reserve and confirm my desire to obtain this hunt under his last available permit for the season.

October 10, 1998, was my first hunt for the Roosevelt's elk, and I was able to take a great bull. This hunt began a very long and rewarding relationship with not only Dave Fyfe, but also Doug Rippingale, my guide. It also had just wet my appetite. I wanted this hunt again.

I scheduled another hunt for October 10, 2000. On this hunt, I was accompanied by two other avid hunters — my son, Larry Bridge, and my brother, Glynn Bridge. We all had a very successful hunt, each taking excellent elk. Again, the outfitter and guides were top notch, and we all had a wonderful time. Not surprisingly, we all scheduled the same hunt again for October 10, 2002.

As our plane began its descent into Campbell River, once again I felt my excitement beginning to mount. I anticipated a great hunt, yet there was also another feeling I just couldn't quite put a finger on. While I was happy with my prior success, I still wanted "the one." I had pretty well decided, however, that this was going to be my last hunting trip for Roosevelt's elk. We arrived in British Columbia on October 8, 2002, which allowed us two days prior to our hunt to rest and to look over the hunting area with our guides. Once again,

Ronald K. Bridge (kneeling left) pictured with his hunting partners (from left) Travis Trace, Morris Trace, Dave Frye, and Doug Rippingale. Ronald's elk scores 374-3/8 points and received a Second Place Award at the 25th Awards Program in Kansas City.

Doug Rippingale was my guide. Doug had been out scouting for several days prior to our arrival and thought he had found a favorable place for me to hunt. I also liked the area he had chosen and we decided this would be where we would start on opening morning.

We left well before daylight for the three-hour drive to our starting place. Upon arriving at our destination, we were dismayed to discover that our plans had been foiled. Apparently, other hunters also thought this was a favorable place to hunt and had beaten us there. We had no other choice but to retreat and find another strategic location. Both, my son Larry, and brother Glynn had a successful day, each taking nice elk.

After three days, Larry and Glynn both decided they were bored and ready to go home. We all agreed that there was no need for them to stay and I certainly didn't mind being left behind. Doug and I had been hunting hard, but the unseasonably hot and dry climate for this time of year on the island was making it difficult. I had spotted two or three small bulls, but these were of little interest to me. If I couldn't take one larger than what I already had from past hunts, I was going to go home with nothing. I was waiting for "the one."

Doug had remained very patient and diligent in his efforts to help locate the animal he knew I wanted. Our mutual respect for each other's experience definitely played a key role here. Days four, five, and six had gone by. Due to the extreme weather conditions this year and the fact that I'm not as young and fit as I used to be (I'm over 60), the long, hard hunt was starting to take a toll on me. Finally, on day seven, it was time to relocate to another area.

ROOSEVELT'S ELK
Second Award – 374 ³/₈

▼ ▼ ▼ ▼ ▼

RONALD K. BRIDGE

Doug recruited the assistance of two other guides, Morris and Travis Trace (father and son), as well as outfitter Dave Fyfe to help spot.

Around 3 p.m. the same day, Morris spotted two elk sparring. Morris picked up his binoculars and studied them for awhile. He decided that one of them was exactly what I was looking for and headed back to find Doug and me.

My excitement began to mount again and all of a sudden I had a newfound burst of energy. We followed Morris for approximately 25 minutes as he led us to the area where he had spotted the elk. Upon arriving, we found that one of the elk had moved into a thicket. The only things visible were its antlers and just a part of its body. From what I could see, this bull's antlers were magnificent.

We sat and studied its movements for awhile. It appeared as though it had no immediate plans to move from the thicket. As we began to study the thicket and surrounding terrain, we noticed an old logging road surrounding the entire thicket area. Doug and Dave agreed on a plan. Dave decided to place me at a point where I could see almost all the way across the thicket. Dave then traveled down one side of the logging road and came into the head of the thicket. He continued toward the middle of the thicket, heading in my direction. This minor disruption in its environment caused the elk to move toward the very edge of the upper road.

I was now in position. My faithful companion .270 was by my side. Blood was racing through my veins and suddenly everything seemed quiet except for the sound of my own heart pounding. The feeling was intense. This was what I had been waiting and working for. All eyes were watching. As if this wasn't enough, what did Doug lean over and say? "The pressure is all on you now."

Gee, thanks, I thought. My shot followed. The distance measured 350 yards. The best part was that we didn't know just how large the bull was until we climbed up to it. The rack was an 8x8 and became one of the top ten Roosevelt's elk in the Boone and Crockett records book.

Photograph by Cliff White

TROPHY STATS

▼ ▼ ▼ ▼ ▼

Category
 tule elk

Score
 309$^7/_8$

Location
 Monterey County, California — 1990

Hunter
 Chuck Adams

Length of Main Beam
 Right: 40$^1/_8$ Left: 41$^2/_8$

**Circumference Between
First and Second Points**
 Right: 7$^5/_8$ Left: 7$^4/_8$

Number of Points
 Right: 7   Left: 6

Inside Spread Measurement
 40$^7/_8$

Photograph by Jack Re

Chuck Adams accepting his plaque and
medal from Buck Buckner, Chair of the F
Game Records Committee.

TULE ELK
First Award – 309⁷/₈

▼ ▼ ▼ ▼ ▼ ▼ ▼ ▼ ▼

CHUCK ADAMS

I heard the elk before I saw it — a raspy, two-note shriek that nearly blew the hat off my head. Seconds later, a massive 7x7 swaggered into view. It stopped to pulverize a tree, staring belligerently around. The distance was less than 100 yards.

I blinked my eyes and fought the feeling that something was very wrong. This animal sounded like any other elk and acted like a herd bull in the rut. But the critter was standing in sun-blasted grass with poison

Tule Elk on a Griddle

oak bushes behind it and a live oak tree in front. Heat waves rippled and a searing summer breeze whipped dandelion puffs past my face. The animal seemed normal, but the country and weather were bizarre.

Another elk bugled nearby. The 7x7 stretched its neck and galloped away with antlers laid across its back. In two blinks of an eye, a canyon gobbled it up.

I rubbed a sweaty palm across my face and went after the elk. My tee shirt was soaking wet and oak leaves crunched underfoot. Wild oats rustled my pant legs and my boot soles burned like hotplates through my thin, cotton socks. It was 95 degrees in the shade, and I had trouble believing there were rutting elk in front of me.

The date was August 1, 1990; the place was northern California's Pacific Coast foothills. For the first time in almost a hundred years, a hunter with a bow-and-arrow was stalking massive-antlered tule elk across sun-blasted, rattlesnake-infested terrain. I felt fortunate to be that hunter and grateful to the Golden State's game department for making the opportunity a reality.

Most American hunters had never heard of tule (pronounced too-lee) elk. These unique animals thrived in a few isolated habitats within driving distance of San Francisco, California. At the coming of white man, thousands of tule elk roamed the mountains, foothills, and valley floors of this state. Sadly, encroaching human population and poaching eroded these animals to small remnant herds.

Tule elk were protected in California for many years. Thanks to transplant programs and smart management by state biologists, populations have mushroomed. As elk approached maximum carrying capacity on public and private property, officials made plans to open the hunting season, making the recovery of the elk another conservation success story for hunters.

When California announced its first tule elk season in the late 1980s, I was living in Montana. To my disappointment, I discovered the lottery drawing for elk was limited to

Chuck Adams was the first bow hunter in over a hundred years to hunt the majestic tule elk. The bull he harvested scores 309-7/8 points.

California residents. After years of fantasizing about a hunt for these unique animals, it seemed I was out of luck.

I was no stranger to tule elk. I was born and raised in northern California, and saw my first tule bulls as a kid hunting jackrabbits and ground squirrels. As a teenager, I watched a magnificent bull tear an oak tree to shreds with its 8x8 antlers. One of my favorite blacktail deer areas overlapped with tule elk habitat, and my mouth watered each time I encountered a heavy-antlered bull.

The tule is a small elk, but its antlers are a sight to behold. They resemble those of a red deer, with widely palmated main beams and breathtaking crown points on top. It is not uncommon for tule elk to carry seven or eight tines per side. Biologists say the tule elk is a kissing cousin to the much larger Roosevelt's elk, with the same antler configuration and same West Coast orientation.

Antler tips appeared above a rock pile dead ahead. I dropped to my knees and raised my binoculars to look. The tines were thin and short. I crouched in dismay as a juvenile 5x5 strolled out, nibbled a clump of grass, and circled downwind. The bull smelled me and fled in a cloud of dust, taking the rest of the herd with it on hammering hooves. There must have been 25 animals in the bunch.

I did not see nor hear another elk that day, despite hours of hiking over hill and dale. As I poked along, I considered my good fortune at being able to hunt elk I had always dreamed about. My big break had come five months earlier, when my good friend and well-known outfitter, Larry Heathington, called me out of the blue. He had an excited edge to his voice.

"Have you heard of California's Landowner 580 Program?" Larry asked. Before I could answer, he continued.

"The state lets a few ranches sell big-game permits on a first-come, first-served basis. If a landowner agrees to improve habitat and help state-owned herds to grow, the state tries to make it worth his trouble. Wildlife wins, the landowner wins, and game populations expand across public and private land."

"I understand all that," I told Larry. "So what?"

"Guess who just got asked to guide six of California's first 580 tule elk permits!" Larry answered gleefully. "You wouldn't be interested in one, would you?" I could almost see him grinning over the phone.

Larry outfitted hunts in Arizona, Idaho, Colorado, and California. He had personally guided me to the last sheep in my 1986 bow-and-arrow Grand Slam—a beautiful desert ram.

TULE ELK
First Award – 309 7/8
▼ ▼ ▼ ▼ ▼
CHUCK ADAMS

He had also suggested the area where I bagged Pope and Young Club's new archery World's Record Coues' deer in 1989. When Larry recommended a hunt, I listened. In the case of tule elk, I listened twice as hard.

Larry's pitch was simple. He had access to a ranch near Monterey, California. He had scouted the elk. The landowner had directed him to sell six tule tags, and Larry said there were dozens of trophy bulls. He had seen one 9x9, one 7x8, and a number of 7x7s and 6x6s. He did not need to twist my arm.

So here I was with a coveted tule elk tag in my pocket and the bowhunt-of-a-lifetime to look forward to. The elk had beaten me on the first day, but I had more than a week left to match wits with these animals.

I was surprised that tule elk were so skittish. After all, they had not been hunted in decades. The problem was mountain lions. California's non-hunting public had voted to ban lion hunting several years before. Fresh cougar tracks marked every road on the ranch, and I saw two cow elk with fresh wounds on their sides from mountain lion attacks. The big felines often stalked and killed tule elk, making these animals watchful and wary.

My task as an archer was complicated by noisy terrain and a tule elk's preference for semi-open habitat. In spite of soft camo clothing and my sneakiest foot-hunting tactics, these animals continued to give me the slip.

Take August 2, for example. The day dawned with coastal fog blanketing the foothills. I shrugged into a warm jacket and tugged my stocking cap around my ears. I shivered in the morning air, but I knew cool conditions would be short-lived.

Larry and I glassed from a hilltop as the mist burned away. We spotted a big bull at the same time. The animal was bedded with two juvenile bulls a half mile away. One look through the spotting scope was enough for me. This elk was spectacular, with nine tines on each main beam. The top of the rack looked like a Christmas tree!

I dropped off the hill, crossed a swamp below a stock pond, and circled to approach from downwind. I noticed elk rubs on oak trees and fresh tracks along the swamp. In one place, a bull had rolled in the mud. When tule elk rut, they follow the same rituals as American and Roosevelt's elk.

I was 200 yards away when the big bull rose, tossed back its head, and let go a ferocious bugle. Tule bulls rut in early to mid-August, a month and a half before other elk. They chase cows in the stifling heat.

I had an elk call, but I decided not to use it. Larry had warned me that tule bulls were slow to approach a call because the country was so open. If they could not see a rival bull, they were likely to circle wide and catch the hunter's scent.

My stalk was not meant to be. The 9x9 and its buddies were 75 yards away when I peered around an oak tree and realized there was no more cover between us. All I could do was wait. Then the wind fanned my back. The bulls turned and fled. A minute later, they were a half mile away and still running.

That evening, footing ruined another chance. A bull bugled in scattered oaks. I spotted it and planned a stalk. It was huge, with classic 7x7 antlers plus "cheater" tines on both sides.

The bull stayed in the oaks, bird-dogging three cows along a slope. Air currents were perfect, but the ground was covered with dry leaves. I was forced to scoop out a place for each step with my hand. At dead dark, I was still 80 or 90 yards from the bull, with no quick way to move forward.

On the morning of August 3, Larry's glassing talent paid off.

"A great bull just walked in that draw!" my guide exclaimed, jabbing his finger for emphasis. "You can't see it now, but it's headed toward that open ridge."

I decided to circle the canyon where the bull had disappeared. With luck, it might show itself before bedding for the day.

I hiked up a long yellow slope. The bull was somewhere to my right, surrounded by trees and open stretches of grass. If it didn't bed right away, I might have a chance.

Something flickered in the oaks a hundred yards ahead. The bull was feeding below a knob, its ears and antlers shining in the hot summer sunlight. I counted seven tines on the right and eight on the left. The beams were massive and long, the antler spread incredible. This was the best bull I had seen, even more impressive than yesterday's 9x9.

I crouched and pussyfooted ahead. I dropped to my knees and then to my stomach. The top of the rack was still in view, the bull's head safely below the ridge. Perfect.

Suddenly, the elk disappeared. The ridgeline was close, so I slithered forward on my belly. The antlers reappeared, pointing directly at me above the grass. The elk was lying down, its rack bobbing as it chewed its cud. My range finder said 55 yards. I nocked an arrow and settled down to wait. If I tried to draw now, the bull would catch the movement and run.

Thirty hot minutes later, the elk stood up, stretched, and looked the other way. I drew as I rolled to my knees, planted the 50-yard sight high behind its shoulder, and let the bowstring go. The arrow hissed on its way and cracked like a hardball against a bat. The bull lunged downhill, stumbled across a ravine, and collapsed.

My California tule elk was the first ever bagged by a modern bowhunter. It was also a giant of its kind, with an official B&C score of 309-7/8 — some 25 points above the B&C minimum.

I had dreamed about hunting tule elk most of my life, but the experience was more exciting than I could ever have imagined. Whether you draw a lottery permit for California tule elk or purchase a Landowner Tag, this is a worthwhile hunt.

Award Winning Moments...

Photograph by Jack Reneau

Chuck Adams, right, accepts the Plaque of Appreciation on behalf of Swarovski Optik recognizing them as an official sponsor of the Boone and Crockett Club's 25th Awards Program

Photograph by Cliff White

TROPHY
STATS

▼ ▼ ▼ ▼ ▼

Category
  tule elk

Score
  292

Location
  San Luis Obispo County,
  California — 2003

Hunter
  Lee M. Wahlund

Length of Main Beam
  Right: $40^1/_8$ Left: $36^5/_8$

**Circumference Between
  First and Second Points**
  Right: $8^2/_8$ Left: $7^1/_8$

Number of Points
  Right: 6   Left: 7

Inside Spread Measurement
  $43^2/_8$

Photograph by Jack Re

Lee M. Wahlund accepting his plaque an
medal from Buck Buckner, Chair of the I
Game Records Committee.

TULE ELK
Second Award - 292

▼ ▼ ▼ ▼ ▼ ▼ ▼ ▼ ▼

Lee M. Wahlund

I started to do some research into hunting tule elk about four years ago, when I met Jon Fischer in the California Game & Fish booth at a show in Reno. He is the senior biologist for the elk program. With his help, I obtained a list of the ranches in California that are in the Private Land Management Program. These ranches are issued tule elk permits that can be obtained by non-resident hunters. I then contacted each of the ranches and began talking to past clients to narrow down my list of ranches. One of these was a new ranch that was coming into the program and had not been hunted before. This fact caught my interest and after talking to the ranch owner, I decided to hunt there if we could make the arrangements.

The ranch owner had me contact an outfitter who would be handling the hunts, and we soon came to an agreement for a hunt in 2002. Shortly before the scheduled hunt, the outfitter started giving me reasons why he wouldn't be able to take me that year. After the season was done, I again contacted the ranch owner directly and found that the first outfitter had been deceptive and was not going to be handling the hunts for the year 2003. I explained what had happened and the rancher assured me that he would make sure I had an opportunity to hunt if I wanted.

Finally at the end of July, I flew into Los Angeles and drove to the ranch near Paso Robles for my long-awaited hunt. That evening, I met with the son of the ranch owner and we took a drive around the ranch to look for elk. After seeing a couple of small bulls by themselves, we found that most of the elk were in one group. Since the rut was in full swing, we found one herd bull had gathered about 60 cows in its herd, and had 7 other bulls hanging around the fringe of the group. Our hunt didn't start until the next day, so we set up the spotting scopes to watch the show.

As we watched the herd bull, I learned some history on this elk. This bull had the nickname "Charger," which seemed appropriate since it was constantly chasing one smaller bull after another. It had been the main herd bull on the ranch the year before, but was not taken by any hunter since it had broken off one side of its antler before any hunter had arrived for the season. I hadn't been able to hunt the ranch the year before, so the thought flashed through my mind that maybe this bull and I were destined to meet.

The following morning, I met the outfitter and his assistant to complete the paperwork. Then along with the rancher's son, we set out to find the herd again. We quickly found them feeding in the same large, rolling barley field. We set up the spotting scopes from about a mile away, and watched about half of the elk start to bed down. We felt that

Photograph courtesy of Lee M. Wahlund

Lee M. Wahlund pictured above with his tule elk scoring 292 points that received a Second Place Award at the 25th Big Game Awards Program in Kansas City. Lee obtained a tag for a ranch in San Luis Obispo County through California's Private Land Management Program.

they probably wouldn't move much and were within range of a hill that would give us a good approach from the downwind side. It was time to make our move, and now the anticipation went to a new level as we started to make our stalk.

Soon we were making our slow approach to the hill, with all eyes straining for the first glimpse of elk. We found the herd was located more to our right, so we backed off to make another approach about 200 yards further up the hill. This time the approach put us in the best position for a shot. As I crawled to the crest of the hill, I could see the big bull in the herd with the other bulls bedded off to one side. I quickly got into a seated position as the cows started to get up and move off. The big bull was on the far side of the herd and was moving around trying to keep its cows together. The next minute was totally nerve racking as I tracked it in the riflescope waiting for it to give me a clear shot. The bull would start to clear, only to have a cow or calf create a potential problem for the shot. Finally, the opportunity came with a quartering away shot, which told me that I had to take it now. At the shot, I thought I heard a hit as I chambered another round. It wasn't needed as I saw the bull start to stumble and go down. Everyone had a big smile as we approached because we knew this was a great bull.

Then I found myself smiling for the camera with a records-book tule elk and knowing that I had now taken a Super Slam, all 29 species of North American big game. This endeavor has involved 20 years of hunting that started without any specific plan, but with just the thought that "I haven't been there or I haven't hunted that."

I want to thank my wife, Lorraine, for knowing the enjoyment I find in hunting and always encouraging me. Also, thank you to the hard working, honest outfitters and guides who have given me all those great memories. I hope you all will enjoy and share our great hunting heritage.

TULE ELK
Second Award – 292
▼ ▼ ▼ ▼ ▼
LEE M. WAHLUND

Photograph by Cliff White

TROPHY STATS

▼ ▼ ▼ ▼ ▼

Category
mule deer - typical antlers

Score
206$^1/_8$

Location
Summit County, Colorado — 2002

Hunter
Robb R. Rishor

Length of Main Beam
Right: 24$^5/_8$ Left: 24$^5/_8$

**Circumference Between
Burr and First Point**
Right: 5   Left: 5$^1/_8$

Number of Points
Right: 5   Left: 5

Inside Spread Measurement
25$^2/_8$

MULE DEER
Typical Antlers
First Award – 206¹/₈

▼ ▼ ▼ ▼ ▼ ▼ ▼ ▼ ▼

ROBB R. RISHOR

By Heidi Leavitt

This all started when I got a job in Colorado as a packer. Pulling my pack string, I would encounter some very nice bucks, much bigger than the ones I had seen in my home state of Idaho! So I suggested to Robb Rishor to put in for the late rifle hunt. A few years went by, and Robb finally drew a tag. I had an idea where to hunt.

Hunting time came around. We gathered our camp gear, packed the bow, threw in the rifle (just in case), and headed south for Colorado. We arrived a day early to get the scoop on the local gossip and hunting news. It's always good to see my buddies, Wade and Dave. We talked of old times and new, where the deer might be, who's been successful, how are the neighbors, etc.

The boys at the ranch informed us they were going into the backcountry to pull an empty elk camp out the following day and would pack our gear up there if we would like. You bet!

There was quite a bit of snow on the ground and the weather was cold. We all got an early start the next morning, and helped the boys saddle up. We packed our stuff on a mule and headed out. Robb and I hiked behind. We made it to the camp, helped Dave and Wade pull the tents down, packed the animals up, and then said our good-byes.

We were in the big deer country and the season started the next day. We pitched our little tent, gathered some wood, ate some dinner, and snuggled in for the night. Geez, what a long night! The temperature dropped, the wind ripped through the trees, and it snowed! I thought the tent was going to blow over!

In the morning, the wind had finally died down and all was quiet. We brewed a quick cup of coffee and headed out to hunt in six inches of fresh snow. Unfortunately, the deer knew something because on this side of the mountain we didn't see a track all morning and we were soaking wet!

We needed deer, so we pulled our camp, threw it on the sled, and headed down off the mountain. Dave and Wade saw us coming; they laughed and wondered how the night went. Fortunately for us, Dave put us up in the barn where we could dry out and regroup.

While drying out our gear, we watched the mountain to the east hoping to spot a nice buck. We could see a few herds of does running around. There had to be a buck near. Snow squalls continued the whole afternoon. It was difficult to glass for deer, but we had spotted a

Photograph courtesy of Robb R. Rishor

Robb R. Rishor's typical mule deer scores 206-1/8 points and received a First Place Award at the 25th Awards Banquet in Kansas City. Robb took this buck with the help of his girl-friend, Heidi Leavitt, in Summit County, Colorado, during the 2002 season.

few bucks before the light faded.

On this hunt, you could use either a bow or rifle. Robb had always wanted to kill a nice buck with his bow, so the plan for the following morning was to archery hunt.

While Robb was checking his gear, I spotted a pretty nice buck chasing a few does. I'm not very good at determining if the buck is a "170" or a "190," but I thought this one might be good. I hollered over to Robb to check out the buck. Robb did, and said it was big. He grabbed the big magoos, which are these huge 16x70 binoculars. Robb started jumping around like a six-year-old kid. He had never seen a buck this big!

I was thinking about how we were going hunt this buck with a bow and whether we would even find it in the morning. Then the plans changed. Robb wanted this deer. He didn't want to take the chance and lose this buck, so we threw his bow back in the case. We glassed until dark and watched the buck disappear in the canyon.

Finally, when morning came, it was cold. Robb grabbed his rifle and daypack. Pulling the trusty sled, which now contained our packs and the waders needed to cross the river, we headed across the meadow. We were hoping to forge the river by daylight. Crossing the meadow turned out to be a big job. With every other step, we busted through the crusted old snow. To make matters worse, the bottom of the sled was full of ice so it was a real bear to pull. We made it two-thirds of the way across the meadow by daybreak. As we stopped to catch our breath, Robb spotted the big buck in the early light. Now fully excited, we plowed harder through the snow, finally got to the river, and quickly changed into the waders.

Crossing the river wasn't too bad, and we left the waders on the far side for our return trip. We were in pretty thick brush and snow was starting to fall. If the big buck hadn't gone too far, it should only be 1,500 yards away. Robb rummaged through his pack to get the range finder. Then he loaded his gun and handed me a few bullets in case things got "western."

Robb expected to see the buck in a little draw just ahead of us. We climbed out of the creek bed ready to shoot, but the buck wasn't there. Where did it go?

Ahead of me, Robb was creeping along the wide draw, trying to stay covered. He saw the big buck moving toward him. The buck was in some cover so Robb moved to get a clearer shot, not noticing a few does watching him. Suddenly, deer were blasting out everywhere! Robb threw his pack on the ground and tried to get a shot, but his scope was full of snow. We had been tagged big time! Robb looked at me disgustedly. He had spooked the buck of a lifetime to who knows where. Robb was sick!

What now? We needed to regroup. There had been a heavy 4x4 buck to the northeast of us so we headed that way, up the mountain. Besides, the deer we spooked needed to settle down awhile. Robb was really being hard on himself. He was sick and frustrated, and couldn't quit thinking about the fact that it was the biggest buck he had ever seen. It was at least 30 inches wide and would definitely make the book! On and on...

The heavy-horned buck never showed itself, but while we were hiking up the mountain we did come across a smoking hot mountain lion track headed south toward this big bluff across the draw. I like lion hunting so that was exciting to me!!

Anyway, we decided to head for the big bluff, hoping to find a vantage point and locate the big buck. Hiking down into the ravine then up slowly, we reached the bluff by early afternoon. We bellied down and snuck to the edge to look down into the canyon. There was the big herd of deer. Some were bedded; some were feeding; some were scattered in the timber and sage. But at the bottom edge of the bluff, we could see lion tracks in the snow heading to the deer. I still hadn't seen the big buck, so when I spotted another nice buck and pointed it out to Robb, he just shook his head. It wasn't "the one."

Pretty quickly all the deer were looking up in alert. Surely they weren't looking at us. The wind was in our faces, and we had been pretty cautious. So, we watched. They all were focused on something at the bottom of the bluff. Suddenly the deer bolted! We glassed the whole bunch as they scattered, but our big buck wasn't there. Why had the deer run? The lion track we had seen earlier meant the lion was right below us. It must have been stalking the deer that just blew out of the canyon. So where was the big guy?

Now we knew the big buck wasn't under the bluff. We decided to loop around the canyon and then head above the river's edge, hunting in a big circle. We saw another buck across the draw and tried the grunt tube on it. That was fun. It turned and looked at us for quite a while. Eventually, we hiked across the draw below it and continued to search for the big guy. We cut through the thick timber to the river's edge.

By now, it was late afternoon. We peeked over another draw toward the river and saw 11 does bedded in the sage. Robb headed down the ridge to glass, but stopped. He had forgotten his rifle, which he had leaned against a tree. He returned to retrieve his gun and had only taken two steps, when all of the sudden there was the buck! It was 160 yards away in the junipers looking at us and ready to head out. Robb whispered, "Don't move."

He quickly dropped down on the ridge, got the cross hairs of his rifle on the buck, and made the shot with no time to spare. One jump and the buck would have been gone again!

Wow! It all happened so fast! Excitedly, we high-fived. The snow was coming down hard and the mountain was quiet. Twenty-five minutes passed, then we headed down to find Robb's big buck. What a beauty! All we could see was one antler sticking out of the snow. Holy smokes, it was big! A perfect five-pointer. We knew right away that the buck would make the records book. It was hard to imagine; what a lucky day. Come to think of it, we owed a lot to that lion. If it hadn't blown the deer out of the canyon earlier, we would still be watching and waiting for the big buck to show itself.

The following morning, a few locals had already heard about the "big buck." We all gathered around, drank coffee with our friends, and retold our story several times. What a hunt!

On the way home, it was hard to imagine what had transpired the last few days. We had an enormous buck in the back of the truck, and we knew it was big. When we returned to Idaho, we ran into the wife of the local Boone and Crockett scorer, Dick Wenger. She sent us to Dick's workplace. He was excited when he saw the buck.

December passed and after 60 days of waiting to officially score the buck, the day finally arrived. Robb called Dick to get the official score. After hours of checking and rechecking, adding and re-adding, the final tally was 206-1/8 points. Wow! We just looked at each other in awe, then we looked back at the buck.

In December 2003, Robb received a call from his buddy, Skeet. Skeet had been on the Internet at a chat room when he noticed a guy by the name of Mike was asking if anyone knew Robb Rishor. Well, Skeet e-mailed Mike back and indicated he knew Robb. Mike had been looking for Robb ever since the *Fair Chase* issue came out with Robb's buck listed in it. Mike had been collecting the sheds off this deer for two seasons he had also filmed this buck in its wintering grounds not far from where the buck was killed. When the big buck didn't show up the winter of 2003 - 2004, Mike wondered if it had been harvested. He wanted to know if the buck he had been filming in the winter grounds for the past two years was the same buck that had been harvested by Robb. So Skeet e-mailed Mike a photo of the buck; it was a match!!

Robb eventually connected with Mike to discuss the now famous deer. How exciting to know someone had been filming and observing this same buck! Another story in itself. Not long after Mike and Robb's conversation, Robb received his invitation to the Boone and Crockett Club's 25th Awards Program.

Note from the hunter: This was a truly special experience and a once-in-a-lifetime hunt. Special thanks to a mountain lion, Ted Thebirt (a good friend), and Heidi, my girlfriend, my guide, and author of this story.

Award Winning Moments...

Photograph by Jack Reneau

Trophy owners had time to swap stories and enjoy each others' company during Press Day. Pictured above are Lee M. Wahlund (tule elk), Lavonne Bucey-Bredehoeft (mule deer, non-typical), and Larry F. O'Brian (Alaska brown bear).

Photograph by Cliff White

TROPHY STATS

▼ ▼ ▼ ▼ ▼

Category
mule deer - typical antlers

Score
$203^4/_8$

Location
Utah County, Utah — 2000

Hunter
Carl B. Webb

Length of Main Beam
Right: $28^6/_8$ Left: $28^1/_8$

**Circumference Between
Burr and First Point**
Right: 5   Left: $5^1/_8$

Number of Points
Right: 6   Left: 5

Inside Spread Measurement
$29^4/_8$

MULE DEER
Typical Antlers
Honorable Mention – 203⁴/₈

▼ ▼ ▼ ▼ ▼ ▼ ▼ ▼ ▼

CARL B. WEBB

Utah's annual auction for the Governor's mule deer tag always brings much interest. The person with the winning bid has the luxury of hunting in any open unit within the entire state of Utah, from September 16th – December 31st. One thing is for sure, though; the rights that come with that tag do not come cheap. The intense bidding that ensues will, in turn, generate tens of thousands of dollars that are used to benefit Utah's wildlife programs and sportsmen's groups.

Carl Webb was the successful bidder for the 2000 tag. He quickly enlisted the services of Mayben Crane to guide him on the hunt. Several people were part of the process, scouring many areas in Utah in an attempt to find Carl the buck he so desired.

Footage was eventually gathered of a great typical in Utah County, east of Spanish Fork. The buck had beautiful long tines, a great inside spread, and looked like it would score high in the records book.

Carl was quickly notified and came into Utah from San Francisco, California, on November 29th. On December 2nd, long after most other hunters in Utah are already looking back on the results of their fall's work, Carl and his guides encountered the big buck. It was about 8 a.m., sunny and clear, with a light skiff of snow on the ground when the tag was finally filled.

When Carl raised his .300 Winchester Magnum and filled the scope with that magnificent typical mule deer, it was the culmination of much work on the part of many people. Carl Webb's 2000 Governor's tag typical now ranks as the 18th largest typical mule deer ever taken in Utah.

Photograph courtesy of Carl B. Webb

Carl B. Webb pictured behind his typical mule deer with Doyle Moss, left, and Mayben Crane, right. The buck scores 203-4/8 points.

Photograph by Cliff White

TROPHY STATS

▼ ▼ ▼ ▼ ▼

Category
  mule deer - typical antlers

Score
  $201^4/_8$

Location
  Franklin County, Idaho — 2000

Hunter
  Forrest Christensen

Length of Main Beam
  Right: $29^2/_8$ Left: $28^5/_8$

**Circumference Between
  Burr and First Point**
  Right: $5^6/_8$ Left: $5^4/_8$

Number of Points
  Right: 9   Left: 6

Inside Spread Measurement
  28

MULE DEER
Typical Antlers
Honorable Mention – 201⁴/₈

▼ ▼ ▼ ▼ ▼ ▼ ▼ ▼ ▼

FORREST CHRISTENSEN

My buck was taken near my home. On that particular day, about 10 of us decided to ride around on top of a nearby mountain. Eventually, we all headed down over the edge, toward the creek. Some of us took open ridges and some of us took the timber on the way down.

It was the second day of the season and nice out. Part way down, I was lagging behind while watching an area. Nothing showed, so I cut over to a timbered ridge that a couple of guys had already gone down 10 minutes earlier.

As I was breaking out onto the ridge, I spotted a buck headed right at me. I glimpsed the buck as it whirled and headed back. I pulled my .243 from my shoulder and ran to see if I could see where it went. I saw the buck up the hill, almost buried in brush. I swung my scope around and just as it came into view, I saw it start to move out. I lowered my gun slightly and fired once. The brush against the rifle barrel blew back as the shot went off and the deer disappeared.

I ran back into the timber to see if I could see or hear anything. I thought I heard something, so I ran another 30 yards to where it was more open. I didn't find anything. Ten minutes later, I worked back over the ridge and looked around. Still nothing. Finally, I went back to where I had shot and was about ready to give up, believing I had missed.

I decided to look once more and finally found some blood. Incredibly, there the buck was, lying only five yards from where I shot it. I had hit the buck in the lungs. It was only then that I saw the rack. I couldn't believe how big the buck was.

*Story courtesy of **Idaho's Greatest Mule Deer** —www.idahobiggame.com*

Photograph by Cliff White

TROPHY STATS

▼ ▼ ▼ ▼ ▼

Category
mule deer - non-typical antlers

Score
$274^2/_8$

Location
Shackleton, Saskatchewan — 2003

Hunter
Glen A. Miller

Length of Main Beam
Right: $25^7/_8$ Left: $25^6/_8$

Circumference Between Burr and First Point
Right: 6   Left: $5^5/_8$

Number of Points
Right: 15   Left: 12

Inside Spread Measurement
$25^3/_8$

Photograph by Jack Ren

Glen A. Miller accepting his plaque and medal from Buck Buckner, Chair of the B Game Records Committee.

MULE DEER
Non-typical Antlers
First Award – 274^2/$_8$

▼ ▼ ▼ ▼ ▼ ▼ ▼ ▼ ▼

GLEN A. MILLER

One of my greatest loves is bowhunting for big mule deer bucks. My son, Chad, takes a week off every year so we can experience the great outdoors together. It is so invigorating to be with nature and away from everything else. There is nothing like keying in on each stalk and matching your intelligence with another species' superior wit.

It was on October 22, 2003, that I encountered this incredible mule deer during my fif-teen day of hunting in southwestern Saskatchewan, Canada. It was this day that luck, patience, and determination to hold out for a big deer paid me back in spades. I was given the chance at the biggest deer I had seen since hunting season started.

Glassing to see where this deer bedded and carefully planning the ensuing stalk into where it lay were the keys to this successful hunt. There were so many variables to con-sider. A perfect plan had to be envisioned and meticulously carried out. Wind direc-tion, terrain, and the direction the deer was facing were all very critical factors to be weighed.

As you can see, it ended up being a day when everything went 100-percent my way. "Life is good."

Photograph courtesy of Glen A. Miller

Luck, patience, and determination to hold out for the big deer paid Glen A. Miller back when he took this award-winning buck in Saskatchewan during the 2003 season.

Photograph by Cliff White

TROPHY STATS

▼ ▼ ▼ ▼ ▼

Category
mule deer - non-typical antlers

Score
269

Location
Weston County,
Wyoming — 1961

Hunter
Lavonne M. Bucey-Bredehoeft

Length of Main Beam
Right: $25^4/_8$ Left: $26^5/_8$

**Circumference Between
Burr and First Point**
Right: $5^4/_8$ Left: $5^4/_8$

Number of Points
Right: 13   Left: 14

Inside Spread Measurement
$17^4/_8$

Photograph by Jack Rene

Lavonne M. Bucey-Bredehoeft accepting
her plaque and medal from Buck Buckner
Chair of the Big Game Records Committee

MULE DEER
Non-typical Antlers
Second Award – 269

▼ ▼ ▼ ▼ ▼ ▼ ▼ ▼ ▼

LAVONNE M. BUCEY-BREDEHOEFT

Nearly 43 years ago, Dad took our family on what became the hunt-of-my-life. I was 12 at the time and there was not a single moment that was not an adventure.

You might say the "hunt" began when I was born. My dad, George R. Bucey, was sure that he was going to have all sons, so along with my brother, Erich, I received knives, rifles, and gear for all of the spe-

Thanks Dad

cial occasions. I learned to hunt small game at an early age and was ready for deer in the fall of 1961.

Loaded in the pickup, with a homemade camper that Dad had made in about two days, we were off for Newcastle, Wyoming, and the 30,000-acre ranch of Vic Lesselo. We were prepared to rough it in the teepee that would sleep 12, with a fire in the center. My mom,

Marie, had spent weeks sewing it on her Singer Sewing Machine and we all took turns holding the canvas to keep it straight as she sewed. Even though my sister, Marcie, did not hunt, she was involved. All we would need were the 24 lodge poles that we would cut when we got to the ranch. The drive out was non-stop; it was the only way Dad ever took a trip. The sooner we got there, the more time we had to hunt.

The first day was spent catching up on what everyone in camp had done the past year, setting up our teepee, and planning strategies for the next day's hunt. The result of the pow-wow around the fire was that Joe, a family friend who drove out with us, and his son would go together, Dad would take my brother, and I would go with Bob, Vic's son-in-law. He lived on the ranch and knew where the best hunting was. That was my advantage.

Photograph courtesy of Lavonne M. Bucey-Bredehoeft

Lavonne and her father, George, pictured with her deer taken 41 years previously.

Lavonne took this award-winning non-typical mule deer when she was 12-years old. The buck scores 269 points.

At first light, we drove a long distance from the ranch house. We parked the truck and each set of hunters went in a different direction, with a designated time to meet. It was a cold, sunny day in October. Bob and I walked for awhile and then paused by some trees. The noises of nature were all around, but no deer. It was nearing 10 a.m., and finally we spotted three. They winded us in time to run directly away from us, giving me nothing good at which to aim. We slowly and quietly followed.

We were at the edge of a wooded area when we spotted my deer. It seemed too far away. I looked at Bob; he nodded and mouthed, "Shoot."

I aimed, exhaled half of my breath, and fired. The deer stumbled and then bolted. We ran after it. The buck moved down a slope and dropped behind a log. All we could see was the rack. It got bigger the closer we got to it. Bob patted me on the shoulder and said, "You got it!"

Bob and I studied the buck for a long time. It was huge. All the way back to the truck we talked about what Dad would say and decided to cook up a story that I had shot a little spike buck.

It was late afternoon when we retrieved my deer. I will never forget Dad's face when he actually saw it. Expecting a spike, the closer he got, the slower he walked. He turned and said, "Are you sure you didn't shoot a small elk?"

Excitement erupted. Dad crushed me with hugs, as did my brother, who had taken a very respectable buck with a typical 5x5 rack.

Word spread quickly. Bob said that hunters had known of this buck for many years, so when Dad took me (with the guys) to the local coffee shop, I was the center of attention. I remember when we walked in, a gruff voice from the back said, "Is she the one?"

Since I was the only female in the place, I knew that meant me. I took two steps behind Dad, hoping to disappear. Dad then proceeded to tell everyone about teaching me to shoot the Rock Island .30-06 with peep sights (the same rifle with which he took his first deer). "I took her to the targets beside the barn and told her the rifle would kick. I pushed her shoulder hard with the heel of my hand to simulate the kick. She took the shot, hit dead on, and was nearly knocked off her feet. Her eyes got big and before she could react, I asked her if she was hurt. She said, 'no' and I told her to do it again. She did. Each time she was kicked and each time she went back and did it again. After she shot the buck, she was anxious to

tell me that the rifle didn't kick anymore. I was afraid she would get buck
fever and that she was just dreading
the kick from the rifle."

For 41 years, the "39-point buck"
(points we could hang a ring on) hung
majestically on the wall overseeing the

MULE DEER
Non-typical Antlers
Second Award – 269
▼ ▼ ▼ ▼ ▼
LAVONNE M. BUCEY-BREDEHOEFT

active life of my family. The buck became the silent member who was introduced to guests
and silently acknowledged by friends who would come and go. It was never officially scored.

Just as Dad had introduced me to hunting, he introduced me to woodcarving. I took
a class with Kirt Curtis, well known for his animal carvings. The project was to carve two
mule deer heads and capes. I asked if I could carve the non-typical rack from the deer I
shot when I was 12. He agreed. As the carving progressed, everyone wanted to know
what it had scored. I decided that I would have it done so I no longer had to say, "It has
never been scored."

Dale Ream, Official Measurer for Boone and Crockett Club and Director of Records for
Missouri Show-Me Big Bucks Club scored it at 269. The actual number of points is 27 and
the greatest spread is 33 inches. I received the official acceptance certificate from Boone
and Crockett Club. And so, the hunt continues. Thanks, Dad!

Photograph by Cliff White

TROPHY STATS

▼ ▼ ▼ ▼ ▼

Category
mule deer - non-typical antlers

Score
259⁵/₈

Location
Sublette County, Wyoming — 1973

Hunter
H. Duane Hermon

Length of Main Beam
Right: 25¹/₈   Left: 25⁴/₈

Circumference Between Burr and First Point
Right: 5²/₈   Left: 5²/₈

Number of Points
Right: 10   Left: 11

Inside Spread Measurement
20⁷/₈

Photograph by Jack Rene

H. Duane Hermon accepting his plaque and medal from Buck Buckner, Chair of the Big Game Records Committee.

MULE DEER
Non-typical Antlers
Third Award – 259⁵/₈

▼ ▼ ▼ ▼ ▼ ▼ ▼ ▼ ▼

H. Duane Hermon

The year was 1973. A group of us from northern California headed out to our favorite hunting place out of Big Piney, Wyoming, for a week of deer hunting. The weather that year was pretty darned cold and the north wind was making it tough to hunt. That's not even counting all the snow around the area west of Big Piney.

Four members of the group had gotten their bucks during the week of October 15. That left Bob Rodgers and me to fill our tags by Saturday, October 20, the day we planned to head home. On that day, three of us decided to go out one more time to see if we could locate bucks for the remaining two of us. Bob went out to start his pickup to warm it up and wait for me and Fred Mazzoni. Fred was the oldest member of the group and my father-in-law. When Bob stepped on the gas to leave the motel, his truck would not move. We discovered the tire was frozen to the ground.

We switched vehicles, and after getting into Fred's jeep, headed out to Riley Ridge and Deadline to look for deer. In town at the motel it was 0° F. When we arrived out at one of the spots to hunt, I was dropped off first on the side of a hill. Bob was then taken out to the north side of the hill. When Bob got out of the jeep and started to walk, the bitter cold north wind was taking his breath away. He couldn't breathe, so he started to climb back into the jeep. That's when he heard a rifle shot from the area where I had been dropped off. Bob jumped back out of the jeep and took off for the other side of the hill to see what I was shooting at.

When he got to the top and looked down, he was shocked to see a big buck running below him on a ledge. He didn't waste any time. He raised his rifle and brought the buck down, followed by a finishing shot.

When I met up with Bob, I told him that I was pretty sure that my first shot had hit the deer. After the buck was field dressed, we found my .243 bullet where I had first shot it. The way it was in our camp was that first blood claims the deer, so that meant the buck was mine. Bob got a big 3x3 buck not long after.

While we were taking care of my buck, another buck was spotted far away trying to get through the deep snow. It was a monster 4x4 that was wider and bigger-bodied than my big non-typical, but all of our party had by then filled their tags. However, the determination of Bob and me to fill our tags against the cold weather conditions can't be forgotten; it is something I will always remember.

Photograph by Cliff White

TROPHY STATS

▼ ▼ ▼ ▼ ▼

Category
mule deer - non-typical antlers

Score
$252^7/_8$

Location
South Saskatchewan River, Saskatchewan — 2001

Hunter
Glenn A. Vestre

Length of Main Beam
Right: $21^7/_8$ Left: $22^6/_8$

Circumference Between Burr and First Point
Right: $5^4/_8$ Left: $5^5/_8$

Number of Points
Right: 15   Left: 11

Inside Spread Measurement
$26^6/_8$

BOONE AND CROCKETT CLUB'S

MULE DEER
Non-typical Antlers
Fourth Award – 252⁷/₈

▼ ▼ ▼ ▼ ▼ ▼ ▼ ▼ ▼

GLENN A. VESTRE

As an avid big game hunter, I had always entered my name for the mule deer draw. The year 2001 was no exception. There is always that long anxious waiting period from the time of the entry until the letter finally arrives telling you whether or not you have been chosen. I distinctly remember that it was a scorching hot day in July on the Saskatchewan prairies when my friend, Dan Mattock, and I found out we were successfully drawn for mule deer that fall.

It had been four long years since we had a tag for these prairie monsters. The draw for the hunt was in Zone 23, which is a very large zone and is bordered on the west by the South Saskatchewan River. The area that my friend and I chose to hunt was along the river. It was familiar hunting ground for both of us, as we lived nearby.

Doubled

Hunting for any type of deer in this area is a challenge, as there is a certain amount of determination by every hunter who wants the big one. As we sat there and pondered at our luck of being drawn for that area, we also wondered if we would also be lucky in our hunt in the fall, one could only hope! The summer went quickly and soon it was time to shine up the firearms and gather up the ammunition for the big hunt.

We had spotted a big non-typical mule deer on our hunts in previous years and wondered if it still existed. Dan and I had named the buck "Double D" because it had two great drop tines protruding off its main beams.

At last the hunting season arrived. It was Monday, November 5, and we were ready to go. We packed up the truck and headed to the area along the river where we had seen the big buck once before. The river flows northward and is banked by high rolling hills and ravines with thick brush and trees, making walking very difficult. Because of the terrain, it also made it easy for wildlife to escape from our sight. Dan and I had pushed a lot of brush and deep draws that first morning. Both of us had seen some very nice bucks, but we held our fire, hoping to find that most-wanted trophy deer. After the first tiring day of trudging through rough terrain, we still found ourselves eagerly anticipating the following morning. Maybe, just maybe, this would be the day!

Before we went out the next day, we discussed our strategy and where we would start the hunt. It was early Tuesday morning, and we decided to head to a large hayfield located just up from the river's edge a short distance. As the sun rose, we noticed several other hunters working the hills and draws where we had been the day before and had no luck. We opted to move further north and work our way down to the river, where there was less pressure from other hunters.

After an hour or more of scouting and intense anticipation of the hunt, we decided that my friend would move along the top of the river bank while I would push the thick brush below and along the river's edge. As I plodded along, I noticed that in one spot I could actually make my way across the riverbed via a sandbar to an island in the middle of the river. The chunk of habitat, which was the island itself, was not very big and had only a small amount of brush on it.

As I was pushing my way through the brush, a big doe jumped up and crashed out of the thicket, taking me by surprise. I continued on, making a lot of noise to rouse up any wildlife that may have been resting on this quiet, secluded, and supposedly safe haven for wildlife. Suddenly, I heard a crash in front of me that sure sounded like a heavy animal. In an instant, I thought to myself, "What is it? Could it be the big one? Will I be able to set my sight and shoot?"

Many thoughts and questions flew through my mind in just seconds. I soon found myself running about 20 feet to the edge of the island.

I was shocked at what appeared in front of me. It was that gigantic non-typical mule deer! My heart raced as I prepared to shoot. As if it were a dream, the monster buck stopped and looked toward the riverbank where Dan was situated. The mule deer forgot all about me at that moment, as it was concentrating on what it had seen or heard.

The buck was approximately 275 yards away and my 760 Remington .30-06 rose to the occasion. The shot echoed down the river and over the thickets and the buck folded up and hit the ground. I sat a few moments to be sure it did not get up. Again there were many thoughts and questions that crossed my mind as I approached the fallen animal. "Was it the 'big one'? Did I really get it, or was it all a dream?"

As Dan and I reached its side, we realized that it was "Double D." My dream had come true! Needless to say I was overwhelmed by my good fortune.

The excitement of the hunt and the actual kill is always followed by field dressing. Luckily, there was a trail down the bank to the river's edge where the deer fell, making it easily accessible by truck.

Dan and I, along with some other hunting buddies, met at the neighbor's shop to celebrate the harvest that afternoon.

Later I had the deer aged by the Department of Natural Resources. The buck was thought to be eight or nine years old. My 15x11 scored 252-7/8 points and was the highest scoring mule deer in that category for 2001 in Saskatchewan. It also ranks as the eleventh-largest ever taken in the province of Saskatchewan. Giant mule deer like this are rare in North America. The brow-tines on this rack are above average at 6-5/8 and 5-4/8 inches. Now add 68-3/8, total of the lengths of the abnormal points, and this buck enters into an elite group of non-typical mule deer.

Photograph by Cliff White

TROPHY STATS

▼ ▼ ▼ ▼ ▼

Category
    mule deer -
    non-typical antlers

Score
    248 $^4/_8$

Location
    Lincoln County, Nevada — 2001

Hunter
    Alan B. Shepherd

Length of Main Beam
    Right: 22 $^6/_8$ Left: 26 $^3/_8$

Circumference Between Burr and First Point
    Right: 5 $^4/_8$ Left: 5

Number of Points
    Right: 9   Left: 6

Inside Spread Measurement
    26 $^6/_8$

Photograph by Jack Rene

Alan B. Shepherd accepting his plaque an medal from Buck Buckner, Chair of the B Game Records Committee.

MULE DEER
Non-typical Antlers
Fifth Award - 248⁴/₈

▼ ▼ ▼ ▼ ▼ ▼ ▼ ▼ ▼

ALAN B. SHEPHERD

The 2001 hunting season started the same as every other year — applying in April and waiting until June to find out if you were successful or not. This year I was pleased to find out that I had drawn the best area in southern Nevada for trophy mule deer. My hunting partner, Kyle, and brother-in-law, John, also drew the same unit.

As it seems with every deer tag that I have drawn, the season came in with a full moon, high temperatures, and little cool weather in the forecast. This usually means that the deer are going to bed for the day with-

Blind Luck

in an hour of sunrise and not coming out again until near dark. After 10 days of hunting in good deer areas, I had nothing to show for my efforts. I had seen a number of bucks, but not the right one to fill my tag. My brother-in-law, John, had harvested his first mule deer — a nice 22-inch 4x3. Kyle was persistent enough to fill his tag with a 27-inch three-point.

On the last Tuesday afternoon of the season, I decided to take my wife and two girls on an afternoon hunt. The warm weather had finally decided to break and it gave us some scattered showers and cooler temperatures. We headed for a prescribed burn area that the BLM completed a few years back in the Clover Mountains. The trip produced no deer, but the girls got a nap out of it. On the trip home that night, my wife asked why I didn't go back to the same areas we had previously hunted. I said that we try different areas in the hope of finding a good deer.

A conversation with Kyle later that night set the stage for the hunt on Halloween. Kyle suggested we hunt the prescribed burn area in the Clover Mountains as my wife had suggested. I thought we should go back to the Delamar Mountains where he harvested his deer. Kyle won, and we settled on the Clovers.

Maybe the rain and cooler temperatures kept the buck out longer than normal. Maybe it was just blind luck, but there it was. I wish that I could say we had scouted this buck the whole summer, spent endless hours learning its hiding spots and its favorite feeding areas, had miles of video of it, or had spotted it miles away and spent the rest of the day stalking it, but I can't. We hadn't been hunting long when I caught a glimpse of what appeared to be a deer standing in the burnt trees. As I prepared for a shot, if presented, Kyle was sizing up the deer through his binoculars. He informed me that it was a buck with antlers that were at least past its ears and appeared to be a four-pointer.

Alan B. Shepherd was pleasantly surprised when he found out he drew a tag in one of southern Nevada's best areas. He capitalized on the opportunity by taking this award-winning, non-typical mule deer during the last week of the season.

The buck was standing quartering away and looking over its rump when I took my first shot. I watched the buck duck as I missed. I quickly shot again and saw a quick flash of white in the scope. Scared that I missed again, I was wondering where it had gone. Kyle informed me that the deer was on the ground.

Making our way through the burnt trees, I was expecting to find a nice four-pointer. When I finally saw it, I got one of the biggest thrills of my life. Rounding the last burnt tree, we got our first good look at the buck and realized it was more than just a four-pointer. The buck just seemed to keep growing, getting even bigger when we rolled it over. The buck had nine tall tines on the right side and six on the left. Its antlers were thicker than baseball bats and carried this mass clear to the tips. We spent the next half-hour dressing it out and taking pictures.

I had the buck measured by some friends who are scorers for the Boone and Crockett Club, as well as the Nevada Records book. The non-typical score was 248-4/8. It was almost 33 inches wide and had over 20 inches of circumference measurements on each side. My deer received a Kit Carson Award from the Nevada Wildlife Trophy Association as the largest non-typical harvested in the State of Nevada during 2001. It is the largest non-typical harvested during the past 36 years in Nevada. This buck ranks in the top ten largest non-typicals ever harvested in Nevada according to Boone and Crockett Club's records book.

Since I was fortunate enough to harvest this deer, it has been featured in *Eastmans' Hunting Journal*, *King's World's Hunting Illustrated*, and National Rifle Association's *American Hunter*. I am very appreciative of these magazines for their support of our hunting heritage and showing that the average guy can have a chance to harvest an animal like this.

I would like to thank my wife, Beth, for putting up with my desire to hunt. She enjoys hunting and fishing, and we are able to share the outdoors with our two daughters, Amanda and Brooklin. I would also like to thank Kyle Teel for being my hunting partner and taxidermist for without him this story wouldn't have the ending it does.

MULE DEER
Non-typical Antlers
Fifth Award – 248 4/8

▼ ▼ ▼ ▼ ▼

ALAN B. SHEPHERD

Photograph by Cliff White

TROPHY STATS
▼ ▼ ▼ ▼ ▼

Category
Columbia blacktail -
typical antlers

Score
170$^1/_8$

Location
Trinity County, California — 2000

Hunter
Eric Helms

Length of Main Beam
Right: 26   Left: 24$^5/_8$

**Circumference Between
Burr and First Point**
Right: 4$^4/_8$ Left: 4$^4/_8$

Number of Points
Right: 5   Left: 6

Inside Spread Measurement
17$^2/_8$

COLUMBIA BLACKTAIL
Typical Antlers
First Award – 170¹/₈

▼ ▼ ▼ ▼ ▼ ▼ ▼ ▼ ▼

ERIC HELMS

When Eric Helms was trying to decide where to go hunting the next day, he gave little thought to huge blacktails. After all, it was just a general season. He was just looking for something with antlers. He decided on Hayfork Summit.

The next morning, he was up by 4 a.m. for the two-hour drive to one of his favorite hunting areas. As the day dawned, he was greeted by fog and overcast skies. It didn't matter; he was hunting.

He unloaded his four-wheeler from his pickup and headed out toward a burned area. It was fairly open country for blacktails, but it wasn't lacking in steepness. After the 15-minute ride, he parked. He then hiked out to one of his favorite ridges, hoping to spy a decent buck.

It was only about 8:30 a.m. when he found what he came for. There, 50 yards away and looking at him, stood a nice buck! Eric never even hesitated. One well-placed shot in the neck and the buck was down.

Eric hiked back up and got his four-wheeler. Luck was with him all day that day. Not only had he taken a great buck, but he was able to get right to the deer, making for an easy pack out.

Being only 27 years old at the time, he really didn't know what he had, other than it was a pretty decent buck. Following his 1st Place Award at Boone and Crockett Club's 25th Awards Ceremonies, Eric finally has a pretty good idea of what he accomplished that day on Hayfork Summit.

As told to the Boone and Crockett Club by Eric Helms.

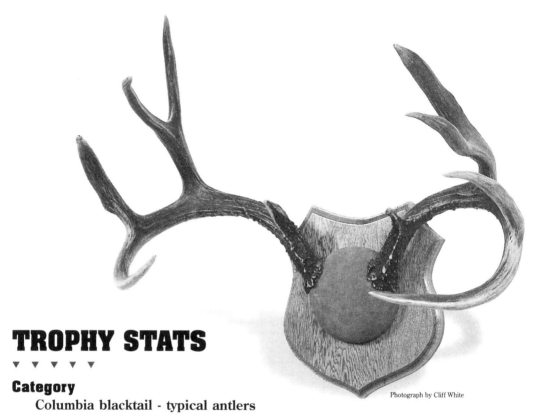

Photograph by Cliff White

TROPHY STATS
▼ ▼ ▼ ▼ ▼

Category
Columbia blacktail - typical antlers

Score
$166^2/_8$

Location
Polk County, Oregon — 1959

Hunter
Earl Starks

Length of Main Beam
Right: $25^5/_8$ Left: $25^3/_8$

Circumference Between Burr and First Point
Right: $4^2/_8$ Left: $4^1/_8$

Number of Points
Right: 5   Left: 5

Inside Spread Measurement
$21^6/_8$

COLUMBIA BLACKTAIL
Typical Antlers
Second Award – 166 $^2/_8$

▼ ▼ ▼ ▼ ▼ ▼ ▼ ▼ ▼

EARL STARKS

In the early part of November 1959, I was hunting with my partner, Bob, in an area called Fishback Ridge. This is a spot located about seven miles southwest of Monmouth, Oregon. It's actually in the northwest corner of the Camp Adair firing range. During World War II, from 1942-1945, many farms in this area were sold and the land vacated so that Camp Adair could be established. It was subsequently opened to hunting in 1947 and has reverted to mostly timber and farmland now on about one thousand acres.

The area was ideal for all wildlife. There were apple orchards, grapes, wild flowers, rose bushes with rose hips, and a variety of grasses. Many fir trees and large oaks provided shelter, and altogether there was very good eating for the many animals there. Squirrels, chipmunks, pheasants, quail, and deer could be frequently seen at the site, and I often saw hawks flying overhead.

It was a clear, frosty morning, shortly before sunup. I had hiked up the ridge alone and looked down across abandoned farmland. As I stood there admiring the view, two does stepped out of the nearby oak wood lot. They were about 200 yards away. The sun was at my back and the wind was in my favor.

I stood absolutely still, watching the deer. Just then, a big four-point Columbia blacktail buck strolled out of the woods behind them. They all started feeding on wild rosehips, gradually munching their way towards me. I knelt down so as to remain undetected. As I waited, the two does kept coming closer; the buck followed close behind. At one point, I cautiously raised my head to see what was happening. One of the does lifted its head just then, too, and looked right at me. However, because the wind was not blowing toward the doe, it didn't smell my presence. Placidly, it lowered its head and resumed munching the wild rosehips.

I continued kneeling there in the deep grasses, watching the buck's progression as it sauntered out from behind the does. It, too, was chomping on the rosehips as it leisurely moved along.

When the buck lifted its head, I raised my sights, took aim for the neck, and fired. It went down, but as I approached the buck, it moved, so I fired a finishing shot.

After field dressing it, I placed the buck under a small fir tree near the road. Then I hiked down from the ridge to retrieve my car and locate my hunting partner. Together, we loaded the buck into the car trunk for the triumphant trip back home. My family was really amazed when they saw the rack of antlers on that animal.

Photograph by Cliff White

TROPHY STATS

▼ ▼ ▼ ▼ ▼

Category
Columbia blacktail - typical antlers

Score
164$^6/_8$

Location
Clackamas County, Oregon — 2003

Hunter
Howard D. Bunnell

Length of Main Beam
Right: 23$^4/_8$ Left: 23$^6/_8$

Circumference Between Burr and First Point
Right: 5$^1/_8$ Left: 5$^2/_8$

Number of Points
Right: 5   Left: 5

Inside Spread Measurement
17$^4/_8$

Photograph by Jack Ren

Howard D. Bunnell accepting his plaque
and medal from Buck Buckner, Chair of
the Big Game Records Committee.

BOONE AND CROCKETT CLUB'S

COLUMBIA BLACKTAIL
Typical Antlers
Third Award – 164⁶/₈

▼ ▼ ▼ ▼ ▼ ▼ ▼ ▼ ▼

HOWARD D. BUNNELL

My big buck was one that I and other people had seen during the previous three years. Most of the time, it was late at night or early in the morning when I would catch the deer sneaking around our farm. The buck never stood around long enough for me to get a good look, but it appeared to be a four-pointer every year I saw it. The buck's antlers were so nice that I would shake just looking at them!

On the afternoon I got my chance — its last chance — I was sitting in my outdoor nursery, using some doe scent, a doe bleat, and rattling antlers. I am not sure which worked because the buck wasn't with any does. It was traveling with a forked-horn that was really heavily horned. Maybe the forked-horn will be around next year!

When I saw the "big guy," the forked-horn was ahead of it. There is not a lot of room in a nursery full of Japanese maple trees in full fall color to get a good look, but it was enough to see that it was "the one."

I was using a Savage Model 24 in .223 caliber with hand-loaded Speer bullets. One shot was all it took; it was down.

I have spent 50 years of hunting all over the state for deer. I suppose it is with more than a little irony that I get my "big one" on my own farm! What a day!

Photograph by Cliff White

TROPHY STATS

▼ ▼ ▼ ▼ ▼

Category
Columbia blacktail -
typical antlers

Score
$163^5/_8$

Location
Lake County, California — 1976

Hunter
Bill Conn

Length of Main Beam
Right: $21^6/_8$ Left: $22^1/_8$

Circumference Between Burr and First Point
Right: $4^3/_8$ Left: $4^3/_8$

Number of Points
Right: 4   Left: 5

Inside Spread Measurement
$20^3/_8$

Photograph by Jack Ren

Bill Conn accepting his plaque and meda
from Buck Buckner, Chair of the Big Gam
Records Committee.

COLUMBIA BLACKTAIL
Typical Antlers
Fourth Award – 163⁵/₈

▼ ▼ ▼ ▼ ▼ ▼ ▼ ▼ ▼

BILL CONN

Being born and raised in northern California, I guess it was my calling to become a blacktail hunter. That's about all I did from 1967 to 1976. From time to time, I would also hunt inland for mule deer, pronghorn, and bear. I was a guide and outfitter from 1969 to 1977, which kept me really busy most of the time. But I always managed to take some time off so my wife Judy and I could hunt blacktails .

Usually we hunted Mendocino County, where I've taken some really nice blacktails over the years, but this time we decided on Lake County. I knew some great country in Mendocino National Forest that ranges from 5,000 to 7,500 feet. And I mean rough country!

We went up the day before the season. We decided not to take the horses and mules, as it takes so much more of your time and we would be bowhunting. So we went in on foot.

I had a place in mind for Judy It was about one-quarter of the way down this canyon, and it had a small spring coming out of the hillside. The spring is well-used by deer and bear, and Judy had tags for both. I set her up and then went on down toward the bottom of the canyon. I had hunted this canyon the year before and missed a chance at a 150-class blacktail. That buck was just a little smarter than I was.

As I got to the bottom, it was just turning light. I was on a great deer trail that went up the other hillside. There was quite a bit of running water in the stream and green grass on the floor of the canyon. I had made a ground blind the year before at this site, so since I knew what the yardage was to the deer trail, I used my old blind.

The first hour nothing happened. Then I heard something coming down the trail. The sound was coming from some really thick stuff that thinned out the last 50 feet before the creek bottom. I prepared myself, but it turned out to be a sow with two cubs. They drank water and ate grass, and the cubs played for what seemed like an hour. When they went up the other hillside, it was pushing 10 a.m. I decided I'd give it another half hour or so. It was only 10 minutes later when I heard what I thought was a cow coming down the hill that the bears had just gone up.

My back was killing me from being on my knees so long, so I stood up. Just as I did, a huge 4x4 blacktail came out of the brush. It took about four steps, stopped, and looked back at the trail for what seemed like three or four minutes. The buck then came toward the creek following the deer trail. It had to get to at least the creek for me to have a good shot. Finally, the buck stopped and drank from the creek at a spot I knew was about 35 yards from

Bill L. Conn standing in front of his barn with several records-book Columbia blacktail deer, including the award-winning buck, top center, that he donated to the Club's National Collection of Heads and Horns after the 25th Awards Program in Kansas City.

my blind. It stood broadside, so I let the arrow fly and hit it in the chest. The buck went 25 yards and dropped for good.

When I got to the buck I couldn't believe it. I've seen a lot of blacktails, but this was the biggest deer I'd ever seen. It was well over 250 pounds on the hoof. I didn't have a tape measure on me, but I could tell by one of my arrows that it was 26-27 inches wide. I got it cleaned it out, caped and skinned it, covered it with brush, and went back up the hill to Judy. She had taken a shot at a 3x3, but missed.

When I told her what happened to me, the first thing out of her mouth was, "Damn you for killing that buck down in the bottom of that canyon!" She's done this before.

It took us until noon the next day to get it back to our camp. That's after boning it out and making four trips with our meat packs. We were beat!

At camp, I was salting the cape and had the antlers on the pickup hood. A Forest Ranger stopped to see the antlers; he couldn't believe it. When he saw the size of the antlers and cape, he said in his 28 years, he'd never seen such a big animal. He took a picture for himself, and I had him validate my tag (in those days you had your tag validated.) After he left, I told my wife, "You know, we didn't even bring a camera!"

You want to kill big blacktail? Get to those places that are hard to get to. If you don't have horses, walk in. There is still good blacktail hunting today; just do it! Good luck.

Moments in Measuring...

Photograph by Ryan Hatfield

Paul D. Webster, left, served as the Chairman of the 25th Awards Judges Panel. He worked closely with Jack Reneau, Director of Big Game Records, to verify all of the final scores.

Photograph by Cliff White

TROPHY STATS

▼ ▼ ▼ ▼ ▼

Category
Columbia blacktail - typical antlers

Score
$172^5/_8$

Location
Washington County, Oregon — 1919

Hunter/Owner
Fred Wolford/Gary A. French

Length of Main Beam
Right: $23^6/_8$ Left: $23^1/_8$

**Circumference Between
Burr and First Point**
Right: $4^7/_8$ Left: $4^6/_8$

Number of Points
Right: 6   Left: 5

Inside Spread Measurement
21

COLUMBIA BLACKTAIL
Typical Antlers
Certificate of Merit – 172⁵/₈

▼ ▼ ▼ ▼ ▼ ▼ ▼ ▼ ▼

FRED WOLFORD - HUNTER   GARY A. FRENCH - OWNER

By Gary French

This tremendous typical Columbia blacktail was taken by Fred Wolford in 1919 near Castor Creek, in Washington County, Oregon. It was most likely along the Pacific Railway and Navigation Company (P.R. & N. Co.) line, known today as the Port of Tillamook Bay Railroad.

My grandfather, Burr French, was a neighbor of Fred Wolford. They were living in Banks, Oregon, and worked together for the Hillsboro Division of the P. R. & N. Co. that ran from Hillsboro to the mouth of the Salmonberry River.

Burr was with Mr. Wolford when he killed the buck. When Mr. Wolford passed away in the '30s or '40s, my grandfather asked Mr. Wolford's widow if he could have the antlers and his request was granted.

My earliest recollection of the antlers is seeing them nailed to a wooden shield and hanging in our garage at our home in Banks. Whenever the subject of the antlers was brought up, it was always mentioned that the buck was killed along the railroad near the "tunnel." The tunnel was a local landmark on U.S. highway 26 near the head of Castor Creek.

Photograph by Cliff White

TROPHY STATS

▼ ▼ ▼ ▼ ▼

Category
Columbia blacktail - non-typical antlers

Score
188$^6/_8$

Location
Shasta County, California — 1981

Hunter
Brad E. Wittner

Length of Main Beam
Right: 23$^4/_8$ Left: 19$^7/_8$

Circumference Between Burr and First Point
Right: 4$^3/_8$ Left: 5$^1/_8$

Number of Points
Right: 7   Left: 9

Inside Spread Measurement
17$^4/_8$

Photograph by Jack Rene

Brad E. Wittner accepting his plaque and medal from Buck Buckner, Chair of the B Game Records Committee.

COLUMBIA BLACKTAIL
Non-typical Antlers
First Award – 188⁶/₈

▼ ▼ ▼ ▼ ▼ ▼ ▼ ▼ ▼

BRAD E. WITTNER

It was early Friday evening when my dad, Rex, and I were driving out to deer camp at Buck Fever Lodge. After we started down the dirt road, I mentioned to my dad, "You know, I've only harvested two deer in my life, and I've never really taken one that was completely mine. The first one was just standing in the road, and I was given first shot. The second one Scott Ferguson and I both shot at the same time, and we never could decide who downed it, so we shared. I know hunting is more about the camaraderie (or "camadrey" as my dad says) than the shooting, but still, it sure would be nice to have a deer where I spotted it, and I made the shot alone."

He was understanding, but said not to worry; my time would come. He also said that we should just enjoy ourselves and let the shooting take care of itself.

I was 23 years old at the time and had been hunting since I was 13. My older brother, Paul, had taken many more deer by that time and even some of the younger guys had more under their belt than me. It wasn't a concern over volume, mind you; it was just the fact that I hadn't harvested one that I could call my own.

Dad bought into a deer camp back in the '50s, along with childhood friends, Dave Smith and Ed Ferguson. It included of seven sections of land encompassing about 4,500 acres. Paul and I had hunted exclusively out there since we came of age at 13. Dave's sons, Robbie Dishman and Derek Smith, and Ed's sons, Scott and Jon also followed suit. Several of the guys used to camp and fish out of the little stream that ran by the cabin in the off-season. It was always a magical place to me.

We had 11 guys at the cabin that weekend — definitely an overflow crowd. So, I slept in the camper shell of Paul's truck. The next morning, Honey Bear (Scott Powell) woke me and said, "Let's get moving; it's already daylight!"

Of course, we managed to oversleep. Needless to say, with the sun rising on a beautiful northern California morning (in other words, terrible hunting weather), I felt like our chances for seeing anything were pretty slim. We decided to hunt an area called Cutthroat, where we would move all these guys we had down the ridges to scare something up.

As our merry band drove down through the culvert and started up Cutthroat ridge, we must have looked like quite a sight. Eleven guys, a couple of ice chests, and our weapons all crowded into two CJ-5 Jeeps.

As the hunt began, most of the guys were talking and laughing and only half-heartedly looking. Honey Bear urged me to be on the lookout. To see something before him would be a real challenge as he was an excellent spotter.

Suddenly, I spotted what was obviously a buck. It was about 200 yards away on the next ridge. I hollered, "There's a buck!"

I got into a prone position. I evidently waited just a moment too long for Honey Bear to get set as my backup, because he said, "Are you gonna shoot, or wait for it to bed down?"

I shot and it immediately dropped. We then saw the buck get back up and disappear — or was it another deer? I was positive I hit it right in the neck with my .300 Savage (a gift handed down from my grandfather to Dad to me.) It is very accurate, but does not possess a lot of knockdown power. So, with the rest of the guys spotting for us, Honey Bear, Paul, and I made our way to the spot where I had shot to start the tracking process.

Honey Bear was a big burly logger with a full beard. He looked like Grizzly Adams from the old TV show. He was also in great shape. He therefore moved ahead of us quickly as we headed for the spot. I first heard, "I see the buck; it's a great big four-pointer."

After a brief pause it became, "Hey you guys, you don't need to go to Idaho for big deer, this here's a five-pointer!" Finally, he shouted "Six. It's a six pointer."

Our faithful crew across the ravine thought he was pulling our leg. It seemed as if the closer he got, the more points the buck grew.

As I broke into a small clearing, I saw Honey Bear hunched over an enormous Columbia blacktail deer. He turned and looked at me with a huge grin. "Brad, it's a seven-pointer!" I could see the entry hole in the base of the neck. It hadn't made it very far; it was about 20 yards from where it had originally been standing.

I couldn't believe it. As far as I knew, we had only had a handful of bucks larger than a four-pointer in the history of Deer Camp, and certainly never a seven-point. We didn't even bother to shout over to the guys of our new count. Officially it is scored as a 7x9, but that includes the unusual two eye guards on one side.

We were so excited that we started dragging this monster whole up the extremely steep ravine. Fortunately, there was a road up the hill. The Ferguson boys realized our foolhardiness and brought a winch cable down to us, meeting us about a third of the way up the hill. Once we reached the road, we were met by the rest of our crew — Dad, Dave Smith, Ed Ferguson, and Ed's dad Vern, who's still hunting at age 80.

You know, it seems like the old-timers always have the best timing. After most of the hootin' and hollerin' settled down and we had counted and recounted the points, Vern said "Brad, I've been huntin' out here for nigh onta 50 years, and I aint never seen a buck that big."

Well, I didn't think it was possible for me to be more ecstatic until he said that. We headed back to the cabin and commenced an outstanding skinning party. The buck dressed out at 180 pounds, which was a good 50-60 pounds heavier than normal. I don't think I'll ever forget that adventure. And although I greatly appreciated all the help in retrieving my kill, I was especially pleased to finally have a buck I could call my own. I don't know if there's a word to describe it, but I always thought it was cool that the conversation Dad and I had the previous night actually came true and in such spectacular fashion.

Photograph by Cliff White

TROPHY STATS

▼ ▼ ▼ ▼ ▼

Category
   Columbia blacktail - non-typical antlers

Score
   187

Location
   Douglas County, Oregon — 1967

Hunter
   Alva J. Flock

Length of Main Beam
   Right: $21^5/_8$ Left: $22^6/_8$

**Circumference Between
   Burr and First Point**
   Right: $4^2/_8$ Left: $4^2/_8$

Number of Points
   Right: 6   Left: 6

Inside Spread Measurement
   $17^2/_8$

Photograph by Jack Rene

Alva J. Flock accepting his plaque and
medal from Buck Buckner, Chair of the B
Game Records Committee.

BOONE AND CROCKETT CLUB'S

COLUMBIA BLACKTAIL
Non-typical Antlers
Second Award – 187

▼ ▼ ▼ ▼ ▼ ▼ ▼ ▼ ▼

ALVA J. FLOCK

In September 1967, while visiting with my father and brother, Dad asked me if we should hunt whitetail deer with our muzzleloaders that year. We all agreed on a weekend to meet at our friend Don Wright's place at Glide, Oregon, during general deer season.

All of my previous hunting experiences were family affairs — Mom and Dad, my brother, his wife and kids, my sister, her husband and kids, my wife, and me. We all lived, cooked, and slept in a large wall tent that measured 16 ft. x 32 ft. x 5 ft. We stayed for up to a month at a time during hunting season.

The three of us met at Don's place on Friday night. The next morning was overcast with a slight wind. My brother with a .45 Kentucky Flintlock, Dad with a .45 Hawken rifle, Don with a .45 Hawken rifle, and me with a .45 Hopkins & Allen caplock, started out around my friend's cleared pasture at about 100 yard intervals. Don was about 100 yards from the cleared land, Dad was next, then me, then my brother at about 400 yards from the pasture. The timber was Douglas-fir and Oregon white oak with some scattered vine maple patches.

I had gone about 500 yards and just skirted a patch of vine maple when I looked up and saw a buck standing directly in front of me about 100 yards away. I slowly raised my .45 Hopkins and Allen, aimed just above its brisket, and pulled the trigger. The deer turned a somersault, landing on its back with head and antlers under some brush.

As I approached the buck, I started to reload my rifle when my brother came up. He asked if he could shoot it, rather than me hav-

Alva and Margine Garrett Flock pictured with the buck in 1967.

ing to reload and shoot. He then placed the finishing shot in the neck. The deer was a black-tail — my first and only.

We dragged the buck back the way I had come, across the pasture, and hung it in a tree next to Don's house. We hunted the next day, but didn't take any more deer. We left Sunday afternoon.

Mom and Dad came to my place the next weekend to help butcher, cut, and wrap the meat. Mom took a photo of me, the deer, and the gun I used for hunting. I put the antlers in a cardboard box and stored them in my father's shop. In 2001, the deer was entered at the Spring Sportsmen's Show in Redmond, Oregon. It took first place, and I won a new ATV.

Award Winning Moments...

Photograph by Keith Balfourd

Alva J. Flock, right, and his brother, Mike Flock, enjoyed press day together. They are shown standing here next to Alva's award-winning non-typical Columbia blacktail deer.

Photograph by Cliff White

TROPHY STATS

▼ ▼ ▼ ▼ ▼

Category
Columbia blacktail - non-typical antlers

Score
$178^4/_8$

Location
Mendocino County, California — 2002

Hunter
Russel F. Roach

Length of Main Beam
Right: $23^2/_8$ Left: $22^5/_8$

Circumference Between Burr and First Point
Right: $5^2/_8$ Left: $5^1/_8$

Number of Points
Right: 6   Left: 12

Inside Spread Measurement
$22^2/_8$

Photograph by Jack Rene

Russel F. Roach accepting his plaque and medal from Buck Buckner, Chair of the Bi Game Records Committee.

COLUMBIA BLACKTAIL
Non-typical Antlers
Third Award – 178 $^4/_8$

▼ ▼ ▼ ▼ ▼ ▼ ▼ ▼ ▼

RUSSEL F. ROACH

Mendocino County, California, has long been famed as a haven for large, records-book blacktails. On October 27, 2002, it once again lived up to its billing.

Russel Roach left his home in Ft. Bragg, California, on October 22 for a week-long deer hunt. He no doubt had visions of finding a great buck, but rarely are those dreams as realized as they were for Russel.

On October 27, Russel was in the middle of a late afternoon hunt. Suddenly, before his eyes, there stood a huge blacktail buck. The antlers were exceptionally tall and seemed to have points all over! Russel quickly grabbed his .270 Weatherby Magnum and made a fine 220-yard shot to bring it down.

As he approached the animal, his heart was racing. It was a true giant of its species. The beams spread wide like two outstretched arms, and it was a true non-typical. What a gift! This great buck has a total of 18 points and is currently the fifth-largest non-typical Columbia blacktail ever accepted and verified by Boone and Crockett Club.

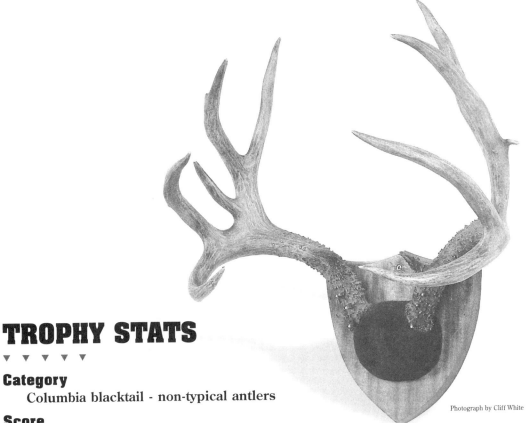

Photograph by Cliff White

TROPHY STATS

▼ ▼ ▼ ▼ ▼

Category
Columbia blacktail - non-typical antlers

Score
$177^4/_8$

Location
Washington County, Oregon — 1954

Hunter/Owner
John Susee/Randal P. Olsen

Length of Main Beam
Right: $22^7/_8$ Left: $23^5/_8$

**Circumference Between
Burr and First Point**
Right: $4^6/_8$ Left: $4^7/_8$

Number of Points
Right: 6   Left: 6

Inside Spread Measurement
$17^2/_8$

COLUMBIA BLACKTAIL
Non-typical Antlers
Fourth Award – 177 ⁴/₈

▼ ▼ ▼ ▼ ▼ ▼ ▼ ▼ ▼

JOHN SUSEE - HUNTER   RANDAL P. OLSEN - OWNER

The massive, long-tined Columbia blacktail that hangs on Randal Olsen's wall is not just a family heirloom. It is also a tribute, both to the breath-taking animal and to Randal's grandpa, John Susee, who killed it in 1954.

Randal knows little of his grandpa, who died not long after Randal was born in 1954. He knows even less of the deer, only that it met its end with a bullet from Grandpa John's rifle near the town of Banks. He has imagined many times the events and the way they may have unfolded.

The story may be gone, but respect and admiration live on. John may be gone, but Randal's favorite memory of his grandpa will always be there to look at and daydream about the day that Grandpa John brought down one of Oregon's greatest blacktails.

TROPHY STATS

▼ ▼ ▼ ▼ ▼

Category
Columbia blacktail - non-typical antlers

Score
176⁵/₈

Location
Clackamas County, Oregon — 1970

Hunter
Ronald G. Searls

Length of Main Beam
Right: 21⁴/₈   Left: 22

Circumference Between Burr and First Point
Right: 4²/₈   Left: 4³/₈

Number of Points
Right: 8   Left: 8

Inside Spread Measurement
16⁵/₈

COLUMBIA BLACKTAIL
Non-typical Antlers
Fifth Award – 176⁵/₈

▼ ▼ ▼ ▼ ▼ ▼ ▼ ▼ ▼

RONALD G. SEARLS

For those who have never chased the elusive blacktail, it is hard to imagine the complexities that can be presented while hunting this great animal on its home terrain. Near constant rain, extremely dense foliage (often 10 feet high), poison oak, the most rugged of landscapes – all mix together to provide the hunter with the most punishing, but rewarding of experiences.

It was November 1970 when Ronald Searls and his younger brother Steve went into this unforgiving realm in search of blacktails. Clackamas County would be the place of choice, and Ronald would be packing his 8mm Mauser.

As usual, the rain was coming down hard. To add to it, no game had been seen. Yes, it was turning out to be a typical day of blacktail hunting in western Oregon.

Then, as if the sun had burned through the clouds and changed the weather, something happened that would change their day's luck. Ronald heard something. It sounded a heck of a lot like a deer's snort. Ronald turned around to investigate, and there stood the largest blacktail he had ever seen – and it was standing only a few feet away!

Instinct then took over. The deer was so close that aiming was, for all practical purposes, unnecessary. Ronald literally almost reached out and touched the buck with the barrel. Just as fast as it had begun, it was now over. All Ronald knew was this blessing from out of nowhere had somehow made that rain and brush-choked hunt much more pleasant than before, and the one-mile drag back to their vehicle was a piece of cake.

Photograph by Cliff White

TROPHY STATS

▼ ▼ ▼ ▼ ▼

Category
Columbia blacktail - non-typical antlers

Score
$173^7/_8$

Location
Clark County, Washington — 1976

Hunter
James D. Gipe

Length of Main Beam
Right: $20^6/_8$ Left: $21^3/_8$

**Circumference Between
Burr and First Point**
Right: $5^2/_8$ Left: $5^1/_8$

Number of Points
Right: 6   Left: 8

Inside Spread Measurement
$18^6/_8$

Photograph by Jack Rene

James D. Gipe accepting his plaque and medal from Buck Buckner, Chair of the Bi Game Records Committee.

COLUMBIA BLACKTAIL
Non-typical Antlers
Sixth Award – 173 $^7/_8$

▼ ▼ ▼ ▼ ▼ ▼ ▼ ▼ ▼

JAMES D. GIPE

It was cold and windy on November 18, 1976, so windy that I had to get in behind some rocks to glass across the big canyon in front of me. This was the high country in eastern Clark County, Washington, an area where the huge old growth timber had been burned off in a series of fires that started in the early 1900s. After the fires, this country turned into fine game habitat, very thick with brush of all kinds. The hillside I was glassing was steep, but it had some open places to watch and hopefully see a deer move.

After maybe 30 minutes or so I observed several deer in one of the openings. As they

passed by one of the old burnt snags, I could actually see branched antlers on a buck. That quickly caught my attention, as anyone who has spent much time hunting blacktail deer will understand. Now I needed to make a plan to cross the canyon and try to stalk these deer. The wind was from the left, so my route had to cross up to the right and get above them. There were some fir trees on a flat that was right above the area where the deer were, and it was a big enough landmark to easily find.

Like most plans, this one had some kinks; it was much farther and thicker than it looked. It took me about an hour to cross the canyon and find the fir trees. I knew the chance of the buck still being there was slim at best. Once through the trees, I stopped to look around and decide what to do next.

This was one of those situations where I was in the right place at the right time. As I stood there, two big bucks were coming up through the brush toward me. No time

Photograph courtesy of James D. Gipe

Original photograph from 1976 showing James D. Gipe with his award-winning non-typical Columbia blacktail, which scores 173-7/8 points.

to think! I shot the first one as he passed to my left at about 20 yards, and could only watch as the other monster blacktail went up past me to the right.

All of the sudden, it was really quiet. Was the big buck gone or had I hit it? There was a trail going down the hill so I followed it for 50 yards and found the buck. It had come to a stop by one of the old logs that was on the hillside. I had to pull its head around to see just what I had shot. What a buck! It was bigger than any blacktail I had ever seen or heard of.

Sitting there beside the buck, I thought back on the last couple of hours. How lucky was I to have even seen him in the first place? Then to find it again after crossing the canyon was unbelievable. The thing I gave thanks for most was being able to get in close and make a clean, one-shot kill.

After awhile, it was time to get to work caping and caring for the meat. I covered the meat to keep the birds from bothering it until I came back with my packboard. There was a tall sapling that I pulled over and tied my white t-shirt to, hopefully to help find my way back the next day. What a neat trophy to carry! Its double drop points on each main beam were like handles to hold onto.

After getting to the truck, all I could think of was showing the buck to my friends and family. I knew the county road to my house was closed, so my first stop was at the local fire station. My friends, Don Brakey and Bill Miller, worked there and were thrilled to see my buck. A call to my wife confirmed the road was still closed, so I told her about the buck and said I'd be home as soon as I could. Next was a call to Ray Croswell, a long-time blacktail hunter who would really appreciate this buck. We had a great time showing the buck to everyone who stopped by.

I finally got home in the evening to show it to my family. Ray, Don, and Bill went with me the next morning to pack out the meat. My white shirt was still there and led us right to the kill site. We boned out the meat and had an easy pack. We decided this old boy must have been a scrapper; the buck had scars on its neck and we found where two ribs had been broken sometime and healed up. The Washington Department of Fish and Wildlife aged the buck at 7-1/2, years and its final B&C score is 173-7/8 points.

Now, 28 years later as I write this, every detail is sharp in my memory. What a pleasure it has been to show this buck and tell the story over the years. The recent letter from the Boone and Crockett Club inviting me to bring the deer to Kansas City for the 25th Awards Program finally gave it the recognition it deserves, and I proudly accepted their offer to display it.

Award Winning Moments...

Photograph by Julie T. Houk

The 25th Awards Program activities in Kansas City were the most successful of all the Awards Programs the Club has ever conducted. Nearly 300 trophy owners, guests, associates, and club members gathered to celebrate.

New World's Record

TROPHY STATS
▼ ▼ ▼ ▼ ▼

Category
Columbia blacktail - non-typical antlers

Score
208$^1/_8$

Location
Polk County, Oregon — 1962

Hunter/Owner
Frank S. Foldi/Steve D. Crossley

Length of Main Beam
Right: 21$^7/_8$ Left: 20$^4/_8$

**Circumference Between
Burr and First Point**
Right: 4$^2/_8$ Left: 4$^3/_8$

Number of Points
Right: 9   Left: 9

Inside Spread Measurement
17$^5/_8$

BOONE AND CROCKETT CLUB'S

COLUMBIA BLACKTAIL
Non-typical Antlers
Certificate of Merit – 208¹/₈

▼ ▼ ▼ ▼ ▼ ▼ ▼ ▼ ▼

FRANK S. FOLDI - HUNTER   STEVE D. CROSSLEY - OWNER

By Frank S. Foldi

I started hunting near a town called Valsetz in the Black Rock Mountain area when I first moved to Oregon from Washington. A logging friend of mine had hunted there for years, had always had success, and had taken some nice bucks. I hunted there the first year just to check it out. It was as great as advertised.

The area was about an hour's drive, so I'd go down for the weekend. I went down three times the first season and always saw deer. I took a nice three-pointer the first year and saw a couple of dandies.

My second year was very stormy, but as it was the last part of the season, I hunted hard despite the weather. Even though the visibility was bad, I still-hunted. I slowly walked on some fairly open deer trails.

After awhile, I spotted a couple of does approximately 65 yards in front of me. They didn't see or scent me, so I knelt down to watch them. They seemed nervous. At first I thought it was because of me, but then I noticed they were looking uphill to the right. It must have been 10 or 15 minutes before they started moving away from me.

Almost immediately a tremendous buck came into view, walking down to the trail. It stopped, looked at the does, and that's when I shot. The buck walked a few yards to the trail and collapsed.

This deer is the biggest buck I have ever shot in approximately 50 years of hunting blacktail deer. I hung its rack on my garage for two or three years until someone told me that might not be wise. It has since been officially scored and is now the largest non-typical blacktail ever scored by Boone and Crockett.

Photograph by Cliff White

TROPHY STATS

▼ ▼ ▼ ▼ ▼

Category
Columbia blacktail - non-typical antlers

Score
197 $^4/_8$

Location
Trinity County, California — 1955

Hunter/Owner
Newt Boren/Richard Shepard

Length of Main Beam
Right: 23 $^7/_8$ Left: 22 $^6/_8$

**Circumference Between
Burr and First Point**
Right: 4 $^1/_8$ Left: 4 $^1/_8$

Number of Points
Right: 11   Left: 11

Inside Spread Measurement
19 $^1/_8$

COLUMBIA BLACKTAIL
Non-typical Antlers
Certificate of Merit – 197⁴/₈

▼ ▼ ▼ ▼ ▼ ▼ ▼ ▼ ▼

NEWT BOREN - HUNTER   RICHARD SHEPARD - OWNER

My stepdad, Newton "Newt" Boren, was a simple man. A plumber by trade and a darn good one I might add. He was also a great hunter. He loved to get out with "the guys" and hunt. His group even purchased their own hunting camp to use whenever the time came to bring the meat home. They loved to hunt in Northern California and in particular along the Mad River in Trinity County.

We don't know a whole lot about the trip that Newt took on this particular occasion, but we do know by the picture that he bagged himself a really nice buck! He was very proud of his kill on this trip, and I am sure he held all the bragging rights in camp that night. I would imagine he was very disappointed when he got his deer back to camp and realized that the right drop tine had broken off in the process of bringing it back to camp. The whole lot of them went back to the place where Newt shot the buck to try and locate the missing tine. To their dismay, they were not able to find it. All the same, Newt did really well that day!

Photograph courtesy of Richard Shepard

Original 1955 photograph of Richard Shepard's stepdad, Newton Boren, with Newt's non-typical Columbia blacktail deer scoring 197-4/8 points.

Newt was so proud of his deer that he had it mounted and placed above his fireplace in his home. The head mount was surrounded on the wall by a real-life scene painted onto the fireplace. It was really nice. When my wife and I moved to Montana, Newt blessed us by giving us his prize, which we then had remounted by the late Larry Jensen, a B&C Official Measurer. Larry was a world class taxidermist and scored it while it was in his care. It was at that time we realized what an extra precious thing Newt had placed in our care. We lost Newt to Alzheimers a few years back but his hunt lives on in our home. We won't ever forget it!

Photograph by Cliff White

TROPHY STATS

▼ ▼ ▼ ▼ ▼

Category
Columbia blacktail - non-typical antlers

Score
$176\,^5/_8$

Location
Trinity County, California — 1947

Hunter/Owner
Harland C. Moore, Sr./James A. Swortzel

Length of Main Beam
Right: $20\,^4/_8$ Left: $20\,^3/_8$

Circumference Between Burr and First Point
Right: $4\,^7/_8$ Left: $4\,^6/_8$

Number of Points
Right: 8   Left: 10

Inside Spread Measurement
$13\,^4/_8$

190

COLUMBIA BLACKTAIL
Non-typical Antlers
Certificate of Merit – 176⁵/₈

▼ ▼ ▼ ▼ ▼ ▼ ▼ ▼ ▼

HARLAND C. MOORE, SR. - HUNTER   JAMES A. SWORTZEL - OWNER

By James A. Swortzel (Nephew)

This hunt took place between the Van Duzen River and the Mad River in Trinity County, California. The year was somewhere in the 1940s. Harland Moore was 14 years old. Although he had grown up with a rifle, he was a novice hunter who was excited to be along on the hunt. The hunting party consisted of Harland, his parents, Alex and Mabel Moore, and his brother-in-law, Joe Whitlow.

Harland was hunting the thick oaks above what is now Ruth Lake on the Old Coach Ranch. When he jumped this exceptional buck, he was not given much time to make the shot. But make it he did, using his old octagon-barreled Winchester .30-30. The buck **The Manzanita Buck** humped up and ran through the thick oaks, disappearing over the hill.

When Harland reached the spot and found the blood trail, he knew the shot was good. After tracking for about 80 yards, he looked up to see the buck standing about 70 yards away in a Manzanita bush. Up came the .30-30. BOOM! Nothing happened. BOOM! Again nothing happened. Two more attempts failed to yield any different results. Unable to believe he had missed four standing shots after having hit it on the run, he thumbed more shells into his rifle. Taking a rest on a nearby tree, he shot it one last time with no reaction.

As he cautiously approached the buck with rifle at the ready, Harland could see blood on the shoulder and chest. The buck had been dead the whole time, but was being held up by the Manzanita bush it had run into. Upon closer inspection, the deer had been hit with all six shots — any of which would have been fatal.

Photograph by Cliff White

TROPHY STATS

▼ ▼ ▼ ▼ ▼

Category
Sitka blacktail - typical antlers

Score
120⁶/₈

Location
Kizhuyak Bay, Alaska — 2001

Hunter
Walter W. Woodward

Length of Main Beam
Right: 18⁷/₈   Left: 18²/₈

**Circumference Between
Burr and First Point**
Right: 3⁶/₈   Left: 4

Number of Points
Right: 6   Left: 5

Inside Spread Measurement
15⁴/₈

Photograph by Jack Rem

Walter W. Woodward accepting his plaque
and medal from Buck Buckner, Chair of
the Big Game Records Committee.

BOONE AND CROCKETT CLUB'S

SITKA BLACKTAIL
Typical Antlers
First Award – 120⁶/₈

▼ ▼ ▼ ▼ ▼ ▼ ▼ ▼ ▼

WALTER W. WOODWARD

On the day after Thanksgiving 2001, my brother-in-law, Bruce Nelson, my nephew, Lars Ursin, and I set off on our annual deer hunt from Port Lions, Alaska. My wife, Victoria, was raised in Port Lions, where most of her family still lives. We try to be with her family for Thanksgiving dinner and to hunt deer the day after. Port Lions is a village of about 250 people and is located about 10 minutes by air or one hour by skiff from the city of Kodiak.

We left the house before daylight on four-wheelers. It was a very cold and clear November morning, but there was not yet any snow on the ground. We rode about half an hour before it started getting daylight. It took about another half-hour before we arrived at our hunting spot — a total of about eight miles from Port Lions. The terrain was quite rugged, with patches of alders and Sitka spruce, but otherwise quite open.

We started to glass, and shortly thereafter, spotted a buck and some does going over a hill at about 200 yards. We ran to the top of the hill and the deer were an easy shot at about 100 yards. I was shooting a .243 Winchester Model 70 Featherweight with a Leupold scope. I was using hand-loaded ammunition with 1OO-grain Nosler partition bullets. Bruce and Lars were not carrying rifles, as they had already taken their quota of deer for the year. That left me. I aimed at the buck and shot it behind the front shoulder. It went about 100 feet before going down. The buck was a sterile deer with spindly, very sharp antlers still in the velvet. It was very large and fat as these deer don't rut. For some reason yet to be determined, these sterile deer are becoming more and more common on Kodiak Island.

Photograph courtesy of Walter W. Woodward

Walter W. Woodward with his "Thanksgiving" Sitka blacktail deer taken in 2001. The buck scores 120-6/8 points.

We dressed out the deer, keeping an eye out for hungry brown bears in the area. We were headed for home, when Lars spotted another buck with some does off in the distance. I had my deer for the day and was only mildly interested, but after looking through my scope I became very interested! The buck seemed quite far away for a .243, but Bruce determined with his range finder that the deer was at 286 yards. Because it was open between us and the deer, we could not find a way to get closer. I decided to shoot. The deer was facing us, so I took a good rest, aimed at the top of its head, and fired. To my surprise it dropped in its tracks.

After seeing the buck up close, I knew it was big, but I didn't realize how big. I was used to hunting whitetail and mule deer in Idaho and Washington and didn't know how big Sitka blacktail deer got. After field dressing it, we headed for home again.

Just for fun I entered the rack in the Big Buck contest at Mack's Sporting Goods in Kodiak. After the contest was over, Tom Merriman (the owner of Mack's) called and said, "Congratulations! You won the Big Buck contest." It has since been officially scored 120-6/8 B&C points.

Award Winning Moments...

Photograph by Jack Reneau

The three typical mule deer at the 25th Awards Program trophy display all scored over 200 points, and all three came from different states – Colorado, Utah, and Idaho. These three states have historically been the top records-book mule deer producers. Robb R. Rishor's 206-1/8 Colorado buck (top center) was taken on a November controlled hunt. Carl B. Webb's 203-4/8 Utah typical (lower left) was taken on a Governor's tag. Forrest Christensen's 201-4/8 Idaho buck (lower right) was a modern-day rarity; it was taken during an October general season hunt.

Photograph by Cliff White

TROPHY STATS

▼ ▼ ▼ ▼ ▼

Category
Sitka blacktail - typical antlers

Score
116⁷/₈

Location
Prince of Wales Island, Alaska — 2003

Hunter
James W. Bauers

Length of Main Beam
Right: 16⁶/₈   Left: 16⁷/₈

Circumference Between Burr and First Point
Right: 4¹/₈   Left: 3⁷/₈

Number of Points
Right: 5   Left: 5

Inside Spread Measurement
13³/₈

Photograph by Jack Ren...

James W. Bauers accepting his plaque and medal from Buck Buckner, Chair of the B... Game Records Committee.

SITKA BLACKTAIL
Typical Antlers
Second Award – 116 ⁷/₈

▼ ▼ ▼ ▼ ▼ ▼ ▼ ▼ ▼

JAMES W. BAUERS

I parked my truck at the end of an alder-over logging road on the afternoon of August 2, 2003. After strapping on my backpack and grabbing my handgun, I started through the dense old-growth forest for a thousand-foot climb to the alpine. I had hunted this mountain on Prince of Wales Island, Alaska, several times in past years and was familiar with the route. The last section of the climb was made easier with a piece of rope left tied to the base of a tree at the top of a small cliff. I reached my camping spot about two hours before dark and set up my small tent. After setting it up I glassed a few average bucks while taking in a gorgeous sunset.

I was out of the tent the next morning as soon as there was enough daylight to spot deer. This alpine consisted of small rolling hills and several rocky outcroppings. There was no one vantage point that would allow me to glass the whole area from one location so I made a slow circle around the hill on which I was camping.

Stopping often to glass, I spotted two small bachelor groups of bucks on the far side of my hill. Their red summer coats made them easy to see in the early morning sun. None were in the class I was looking for and after about a third of a mile I made it back to my starting point.

After stopping briefly to take a photo of a three-pointer standing next to my tent, I decided to make the same circle again as it was still early. Even though the deer are easy to spot with the red coats, I reminded myself to use my binoculars more on this circuit. While still standing 20 yards from my tent I focused my 10x32s on a rock outcropping a quarter-mile away. Right in the middle of my field of view, silhouetted against the blue sky, was a good buck. The decision of whether or not it was a shooter took about one second.

I had the sun behind me, but had to wait

Photograph courtesy of Richard J. Shepard

If you look closely, you will see the three-point buck on the left edge of the photo. James spotted this buck near his tent on the first full day of his hunt.

James W. Bauers pictured here high atop a mountain on Prince of Wales Island in Alaska. After removing the velvet, the buck scored 116-7/8 points.

until the buck moved a few yards into some brush below the rocks before attempting to get closer. We were at about the same elevation, so as soon as it and a companion buck disappeared, I hustled down across the valley that separated us. The bucks were traveling broadside to me along a ridgetop. I angled toward a point 200 yards ahead of them. When I reached the top of the ridge they were on, I turned toward them, walking slowly. The low brush on the ridge limited visibility to about 100 yards.

After going only a short distance we spotted each other at the same time. They froze and so did I. Both bucks were at about 100 yards, broadside, and quartering a bit toward me. I put my glasses on the second buck for a quick look, since it was much wider than the buck I was after. It wasn't as tall though, and I decided to take the first buck.

I rested the .44 on my monopod, held the cross hairs on its shoulder, and touched off a bullet. Both bucks remained statues. I just wasn't steady enough after crossing the valley in such a hurry and had put the shot over its back. Rather than try that again, I slowly slid my pack off and put it on the ground in front of me. I got into a prone position, with the revolver resting on top of the pack. Since the buck had not moved yet, I shot it first with my range finder at 108 yards. I had shot several three-inch 100 yard groups with my pistol only a few days earlier. This time when the gun bucked, I heard the slap of the bullet hitting the buck's shoulder. It was behind some rocks in about three jumps, but I was sure of the shot this time and found it only 30 yards from where it was hit.

Photograph by Cliff White

TROPHY STATS

▼ ▼ ▼ ▼ ▼

Category
Sitka blacktail - typical antlers

Score
$114^4/_8$

Location
Kodiak Island, Alaska — 2001

Hunter
Danny J. Lee

Length of Main Beam
Right: $17^4/_8$ Left: 17

Circumference Between Burr and First Point
Right: $3^5/_8$ Left: $3^6/_8$

Number of Points
Right: 5   Left: 5

Inside Spread Measurement
$14^6/_8$

SITKA BLACKTAIL
Typical Antlers
Third Award – 114⁴/₈

▼ ▼ ▼ ▼ ▼ ▼ ▼ ▼ ▼

DANNY J. LEE

On November 7, 2001, my hunting partner, Colin Roth, and I flew to Kodiak Island from Anchorage via an Alaska Airlines jet. We then hopped on a Widgeon from Kodiak to camp. Upon our arrival, Wayne, our host and transporter, greeted us with a four-wheeler and helped carry our gear to camp. As soon as we were unpacked and into our field gear, we headed up a mountain behind camp. Sitka blacktail deer would be the object of our affection on this trip.

The next day we spotted a few deer that were relatively close to camp. The rest of our search was less than productive, other than seeing one very large brown bear. We spotted it on the opposite side of the strait from Sitkalidak Island. It displayed speed and power that left us speechless. That afternoon we returned to camp and set out on foot along the side of the mountains behind camp, looking for the deer we had seen earlier. Our effort on that wet afternoon yielded nothing more than bear sign.

The third day was draped in the kind of weather that gives the Gulf of Alaska a bad name. After much discussion, our strategy for this day's hunt was to go across the bay from where our camp was located, around a point, out into open water, and back up the next bay to the south. As we rounded the point it was apparent that we needed to rethink our goal. We were in six to eight foot seas and it was getting worse. The weather front coming at us from the Gulf created a solid black wall that started at the water's surface and seemed to extend upward to heaven. It was headed toward our position, and it was becoming apparent that the storm would eventually close in around us. The skiff was taking a beating and so were we. As we pressed on, a growing sense of "venison is great, but it's not worth dying for" soon became the dominant thought and the decision to turn back was made.

Photograph courtesy of Danny J. Lee

Danny J. Lee, right, and his hunting partner, Colin Roth pictured here at base camp on Kodiak Island during their 2001 hunt.

Photograph courtesy of Danny J. Lee

Danny J. Lee took this award-winning buck on the last morning of his hunt on Kodiak Island, Alaska. The 5x5 typical Sitka blacktail deer scores 114-4/8 points.

Once back in the protection of the bay we quickly opted to hunt the hillsides across the bay from camp. As we got out of the skiff, I thought we might as well jump in the water since we couldn't be any wetter. The wind was carrying wet snow at a 45 degree angle and our gear was beginning to fail. As we worked our way through the alder thickets, I realized that we were the only animals moving around out there. The rest were smart enough to stay out of this weather. That day ended just as the last two had — hunters zero.

The fourth day was a different matter. The weather turned and Kodiak put on one of her best dresses. It was a beautiful day and we were only a couple miles across and up one of the mountains behind our camp when I took the first deer of our hunt. After taking that deer down to the beach and field dressing it, I returned to a high ridge on one of the nearby mountains. The rest of the afternoon was spent glassing the surrounding mountains.

Later that day my partner showed up a couple hundred feet below my position. He was returning from his hunt up the next valley to the north. I watched as he stood still for an extended period and then I heard the report of his rifle. We felt pretty good as the following day we were scheduled to be picked up by the plane, and we had finally scored.

The fifth morning was the last we'd spend on Kodiak during this hunt. It was a beautiful morning, the water was as smooth as glass, and the sky was clear. The temperature had dropped the night before and winter was in the air. These conditions were sure to set off the signal to rut. This would bring all the deer further down the mountains. We couldn't resist making one more run. Travel in the boat was easy

SITKA BLACKTAIL
Typical Antlers
Third Award – 114⁴/₈

▼ ▼ ▼ ▼ ▼

DANNY J. LEE

now, although very cold at the speed with which we were now able to move across the bay. The first hour or so of our hunt produced only a fox sighting. We became so cold that we quit for awhile to warm up and take a few pictures of the awesome scenery that lay before us. After we were partially thawed, we proceeded to a point on the west end of the bay and into a little cove.

As we approached our hunting area, we could see deer immediately. We started a stalk around a knoll and up the side of a hill that was a couple hundred feet high. As we rounded the knoll, Colin spotted a buck and took a shot. We lost sight of that deer and began looking for it in the island grass that they blend in with so well. Colin went around the back of the knoll and into the alders and I went high.

By the time I reached the top, I was starting to get winded. I stopped before cresting the top to catch my breath and check my readiness. I approached the crest of the ridge cautiously. I strained to see into the grass and was taking very short steps as more of the valley between the knoll and hill became visible.

It was then that I spotted a doe. It was staring right at me and I froze. I could see its eyes, but I could only make out part of its head as the rest blended into the landscape. My next thought was, "I wonder if it has company this morning?"

At that moment Colin stepped out of an alder thicket just across the knoll and to the left of me. I pointed to my eyes and then toward the deer to signal the fact that I had spotted something. He froze as I slowly shouldered my rifle and began taking those few last steps to the top. There, standing on the opposite side of the valley, I saw one of the most majestic sights I've ever seen. The buck's chest caught my eye first; it was black and broad. I put the scope on the black spot and determined it was a deer. I moved up, spotted its eye guards, dropped the cross hairs, and took the shot. It never moved. I turned to Colin and said something to the effect of "I think we just took one fine buck."

We later found the deer Colin had shot. They blend in so well we had walked right by it earlier.

I'll never forget that trip. The camaraderie, Kodiak Island's beauty, and the taking of "Stinky" as we affectionately call the buck now, made the trip unforgettable. As handsome as the buck was you'd understand that nickname if you had been in the back of the Beaver with it on the return trip.

I had entered a Big Buck Contest sponsored by Boondock Sporting Goods in Eagle River, Alaska, before returning home. My second buck placed first and I was the proud owner of a new Remington 700 Titanium rifle.

New World's Record

TROPHY STATS

▼ ▼ ▼ ▼ ▼

Category
Sitka blacktail - non-typical antlers

Score
134

Location
Control Lake, Alaska — 1987

Hunter
William B. Steele, Jr.

Length of Main Beam
Right: $19^6/_8$ Left: $20^3/_8$

Circumference Between Burr and First Point
Right: $4^5/_8$ Left: $4^4/_8$

Number of Points
Right: 5   Left: 6

Inside Spread Measurement
$16^3/_8$

Photograph by Jack Rene

William B. Steele, Jr. accepting his plaque and medal from Buck Buckner, Chair of the Big Game Records Committee.

SITKA BLACKTAIL
Non-typical Antlers
First Award – 134

▼ ▼ ▼ ▼ ▼ ▼ ▼ ▼ ▼

WILLIAM B. STEELE, JR.

It was 4 a.m. on a foggy August Friday morning as I drove the 20 miles of gravel road to reach my hunting area. I had chosen a large unnamed mountain with an area of about 10 square miles. The closer I got to the trailhead the thicker the fog got.

I parked the truck and grabbed my loaded pack frame. I was following a creek that would lead me to the top of a 1,500-foot ridge. The total elevation of the mountain is around 2,400 feet. It was a mile hike to the ridge top and on several occasions I almost turned around. The fog was getting so thick you could only see a few feet. To be

The Hunt That Almost Wasn't

able to hunt deer this time of the year in the alpine, you need to be able to glass. There is nothing worse than sitting on a mountain top in the fog, hearing deer walk around you, and not being able to see them. The wind was lightly blowing and moving the fog around, but mostly it was just bringing it in off the ocean and pushing it up the ridge. I trudged on hoping the sun would burn the fog off soon. Anyway, there are a lot worse places to be than on a damp mountain in southeast Alaska chasing Sitka blacktail deer.

An hour later, I reached a pass on the ridge. The fog was just pouring through. As I picked my way around the stunted trees, I jumped a few deer and heard them bound off without being seen. Again I began thinking about how ridiculous this was. All I was doing was spooking deer, but then the fog would part briefly and I would get a glimpse of a forked horn or doe.

I continued on, dropping into a large bowl. It was now obvious that I wasn't going to make it to the top of the mountain. During the first couple months of deer season here, the deer like to hang out in the alpine away from the bugs. The best way to hunt them is to move around from one vantage point to another, glassing for a shooter and then figuring out how to get within rifle range of it. This wasn't turning out to be that type of a hunt. As I dropped into the bowl, I noticed that once the fog came through the pass it stayed at that elevation. Many of the lower parts of the bowl were clear. The bad thing about this area was that I was still well below tree line. There were quite a few sub-alpine muskegs in the bowl to hunt. A muskeg is the Alaskan version of a meadow, only wetter.

I decided to take a break, have a snack, and try to do some glassing. As I munched on a peanut butter and jelly sandwich, I noticed a group of deer. They were 1,200 yards away across the valley in a muskeg at the base of the mountain. Glassing through streamers of fog, I picked out what looked to be a heavy-antlered deer. It was difficult to really make out what it was other than a buck. The deer at this time of the year were still in velvet. Add to that the dreary day and all I could see was brown on top of the buck's head.

I decided to work my way across and get closer. I made a mental note of where they were in the muskeg, took a compass bearing, and headed off down through the brush. When I reached the creek, I figured I was within a few hundred yards of where I thought they should be. I left my pack frame at the creek so I could sneak better.

I began to pick my way through the thick alder and conifers toward what I hoped was the muskeg. Finally, I worked myself up to the base of the mountain. From there I could see the muskeg where the deer were 20 minutes earlier, but it was empty. I took a few deep breaths to slow down my pulse after the walk across the valley.

After a quick breather, I pulled out my camo bandana and tied it around my face. The wind was light and swirling, but mostly in my face. I started to creep up the edge of the timber toward where I thought the deer should be. The brush inside the timber was too thick for me sneak in, so I was stuck out on the edge. I would take a step and look all around for deer eyes and then take another. It seemed like this went on forever.

Eventually the timber edge ran out and I was forced out into the mostly open muskeg. My pace slowed even more. I was trying to make sure I didn't miss any deer or worse yet have them see me first. I had to make sure I rolled my feet as I took each step. That way I wouldn't make that slurping sound when my heel came out of the ground, like when you walk across the tidal flats. The only cover now was scraggly four-foot shore pine. I hunkered down and kept on sneaking.

All of the sudden, I saw the bucks through stand of pines between us. They were two of the largest bucks I had ever seen. Both of them were large-framed four-pointers. That was when time slowed to a crawl. I didn't have a shot where I was, so my plan was to continue on to the pines. Those pines were about 75 feet away, and the bucks were another 50 feet further. I continued on painfully slow for another 30 feet.

The bucks were feeding and moving off to my right toward the timber. That's when I noticed the doe off to my left. It had me pegged, staring straight at me. I just froze. The doe knew something was wrong, but wasn't sure what. I glanced at the bucks and one had fed almost into view. I looked back at the doe, moving only my eyes, and saw it was starting to do that stiff-legged walk they do just before they bolt.

I knew my time was running out. I looked back at the buck, slowly started to raise my rifle, and leaned to my right as far as I could without tipping over. At the same time I tried to keep an eye on the doe. With this additional movement, the doe was getting anxious. By then, I had the .30-06 to my shoulder, and I could see most of the buck past the tree. I put the cross hairs on its shoulder, held my breath, clicked the safety off, and squeezed the trigger. The buck jumped and then raced out of sight down through the muskeg. At the sound of the shot, deer were running everywhere. There were at least five or six more bounding away that I hadn't seen.

I pulled the bandana off my face, took a deep breath, and looked at my watch. It was 11 a.m., on August 7, 1987. I walked back to the creek to get my pack and let the buck have some time to itself. I felt good about my shot, which appeared to be a double-lung hit.

SITKA BLACKTAIL
Non-typical Antlers
First Award – 134

▼ ▼ ▼ ▼ ▼

WILLIAM B. STEELE, JR.

After walking back up to the muskeg, I followed its trail down through the grass and found the buck no more than 150 feet away. That's when I realized just what a nice buck it was. I didn't have a camera with me then, as I didn't like carrying the extra weight. It was the largest-bodied Sitka blacktail I had ever seen. I cut my tag and began to field dress it. After quartering and boning out the meat, I loaded the pack frame and started the long pack out. On the way back to the truck, I kept thinking about what a nice buck it was.

It wasn't until I was in the truck driving home that I realized just how big a rack I had. I was sitting in a pilot car line waiting to get through some road construction when the dump truck driver behind me blew his horn and motioned me over. I got out, and he asked if he could look at my deer. I pulled it out, and he said that he bet it would make Boone and Crockett Club's records book. He told me that he had shot a deer the week before on the mountain across the road from where I was today. He had seen my truck parked there this morning. So much for secret hunting spots! Anyway, the guy had a taxidermist friend who had scored his rack in the 125-class and he thought that mine looked to be as big. After I removed the velvet and let the antlers dry, it officially scored at 126-2/8 points. I guess that's not bad for a hunting trip that almost got canceled due to weather.

Editor's Note: When William B. Steele's Sitka blacktail was originally measured, it was scored as a typical because there wasn't a non-typical category. When the non-typical Sitka blacktail category was created at the beginning of the 25th Awards Period, the score on William B. Steele's great trophy was changed to 134 points. It was recognized as the World's Record non-typical Sitka blacktail at the Boone and Crockett Club's 25th Awards Program in Kansas City, on June 19, 2004.

Photograph by Cliff White

TROPHY STATS
▼ ▼ ▼ ▼ ▼

Category
   Sitka blacktail - non-typical antlers

Score
   126⁷/₈

Location
   Prince of Wales Island, Alaska — 1984

Hunter/Owner
   Dan L. Hayes/B&C National Collection

Length of Main Beam
   Right: 17   Left: 17⁵/₈

**Circumference Between
Burr and First Point**
   Right: 4²/₈   Left: 4⁴/₈

Number of Points
   Right: 6   Left: 8

Inside Spread Measurement
   13⁷/₈

SITKA BLACKTAIL
Non-typical Antlers
Second Award – 126 7/8

▼ ▼ ▼ ▼ ▼ ▼ ▼ ▼ ▼

DAN L. HAYES - HUNTER   B&C NATIONAL COLLECTION - OWNER

It was a typical day in coastal Alaska on August 15, 1984. A steady drizzle set the tone, with a nice rolling fog added just for good measure. This is the norm when hunting Sitka blacktail, and Dan Hayes was no stranger to hunting in southeast Alaska.

Dan Hayes was hunting on Prince of Wales Island, long famed for its trophy Sitka blacktails. At 10 a.m., Dan saw the biggest Sitka blacktail he had ever seen. He promptly dispatched the giant of its species with a .243 at 130 yards.

Dan's giant Sitka blacktail now stands as the second-largest ever recorded by the Boone and Crockett Club. Dan was generous enough to donate this fine set of antlers to the Boone and Crockett Club's National Collection of Heads and Horns, which is located at the Buffalo Bill Historical Center in Cody, Wyoming. Through Dan's generosity, a quarter million people a year will have the opportunity to view his incredible trophy along with all the other magnificent trophies in the collection.

Photograph by Cliff White

TROPHY STATS

▼ ▼ ▼ ▼ ▼

Category
   whitetail deer - typical antlers

Score
   $203^3/_8$

Location
   Sturgeon River, Saskatchewan — 2003

Hunter
   Hubert Collins

Length of Main Beam
   Right: $25^7/_8$ Left: $27^2/_8$

Circumference Between Burr and First Point
   Right: $5^7/_8$ Left: $5^5/_8$

Number of Points
   Right: 6   Left: 6

Inside Spread Measurement
   $19^3/_8$

BOONE AND CROCKETT CLUB'S

WHITETAIL DEER
Typical Antlers
First Award - 203³/₈

▼ ▼ ▼ ▼ ▼ ▼ ▼ ▼ ▼

HUBERT COLLINS

I've been hunting with a bow for eight years now. I wish I had taken it up sooner! I like the challenge.

On October 24, 2003, I was out scouting around Sturgeon River. I had two stands set up on the property of a friend who was generous enough to let me hunt his land. There was a lot of sign that deer were using the area.

I knew my son, Robert, wanted to fill his tag, so I decided to bring him out the next day. On October 25, we set up in our stands by 3 p.m. I put Robert in the area that looked like it would have the most action.

It was a typically cold and windy fall day with a gray, overcast sky drizzling rain with the odd snowflake falling now and then. By 5 p.m., I hadn't seen any game. I was thinking to myself that I should've dressed warmer and decided to pack up and go home.

Just as I stood up, a movement caught my eye. Standing under a spruce tree was a nice buck at a distance I judged at about 25 yards. The deer stood there for a while and I could see it was casing the area. Like all mature whitetail deer, this buck was very cautious. I was sure it would spot me, but luck was with me. It came in and began feeding. Every few seconds its head would come up, and it would check everything out again.

After the deer did this about five or six times, I was set up to draw. The next time its head went down, I drew. When it lifted its head again, I let go. It dropped on the spot.

I climbed down and went to check the buck out. I thought it was a fairly nice buck, guessing it would score around 160-170 B&C points.

I picked up Robert and told him I had taken a nice deer. We then picked up a friend to help us load the buck. It took us three tries to get it on the rack of the quad.

I had the antlers at home for 11 days before my curiosity got the best of me. I phoned Ron Johnson in Big River, who I knew did scoring. When Ron put the tape to it, we couldn't believe it. The green score of this buck was 206-1/8 points! You can imagine the excitement.

The 60-day drying period fell on Christmas Day, so we set the measuring date for Dec. 29, 2003. My buck's official score ended up being 203-3/8 points! It has been thrilling. This is one hunt I will never forget.

I want to thank the wildlife, which have been a great source of entertainment for me. I've sat there many times and just watched the show. I also want to thank the local landowners for allowing me to hunt on their land. Without their generosity, my experiences outdoors wouldn't be as rewarding. Last, I thank my family for their patience and support.

TROPHY STATS

▼ ▼ ▼ ▼ ▼

Category
whitetail deer - typical antlers

Score
$198^6/_8$

Location
Lewis County, Missouri — 2002

Hunter
Daryl L. Blum

Length of Main Beam
Right: $26^6/_8$ Left: $26^6/_8$

Circumference Between Burr and First Point
Right: $4^1/_8$ Left: $4^1/_8$

Number of Points
Right: 6   Left: 5

Inside Spread Measurement
$21^5/_8$

Photograph by Cliff White

BOONE AND CROCKETT CLUB'S

WHITETAIL DEER
Typical Antlers
Second Award – 198 $^6/_8$

▼ ▼ ▼ ▼ ▼ ▼ ▼ ▼ ▼

DARYL L. BLUM

I began hunting at a very young age and finally shot my first deer, a button buck, at the age of 13. My dad, Forrest, who passed away in September 2002, could not have been prouder of me or my first deer. As far as my dad was concerned, it could have been the new World's Record. My dad drove me around town in his truck with the deer in the back, tailgate down, showing it off to family and friends. That was in 1973. A lot has changed in the deer hunting world since then.

The 2002 season did not start out much different than past deer seasons. I did my usual preseason scouting to keep tabs on where the does had been bedding and feeding. Other than the early fall scouting, I like to keep a low profile as I believe scouting too much just before the season will only educate the deer. Also, I have hunted the same 300-plus acre farm in Lewis County near Williamstown, Missouri, for the past 26 years. I know the location of every tree and rock, so there is no need to continually scout the area.

I have several stands on the farm, and in my opinion, the homemade ladder stand I put up about six years ago is the best. I've taken a couple of nice bucks out of this stand, including a 140-inch 10 point on opening day 2000. What makes this stand so great is the location. It sits along a creek bottom that parallels a steep bluff on one side and tall grass and sprouts on the other side. There is only one place for the deer to cross from in the bedding area to their feeding area. On the other side of the feeding area is big, hardwood timber.

Opening day was November 16, 2002. I was up at 4:30 a.m., in the homemade ladder stand by 5:30 a.m., and settled in for a

Photograph courtesy of Daryl L. Blum

Daryl L. Blum with his typical whitetail deer scoring 198-6/8 points. He took the buck on opening day of the 2002 season from his favorite stand.

beautiful, clear, cool morning of deer hunting. At first light, a few deer were starting to move through the corn field and eating a few acorns as they headed to the bedding area. All together, 10 or 12 does and a yearling passed by my stand. By 8 a.m., I could have filled one of my doe tags, but I was holding out for a buck, since Missouri offers bonus antlerless tags that I could fill later.

Around 8:30 a.m., I spotted two more does. They were 100 yards away along the edge of the grass field close to the creek heading west. I noticed they were acting differently than the rest of the deer I had seen earlier in the morning. The wind was coming out of the northeast that November morning and I was downwind, so I knew they could not smell me. I then saw another movement out of the corner of my eye. I focused in on it and saw antler tips bobbing along through the tall grass behind the does. Suddenly, a buck came into full view. I said to myself, "Look at that big buck."

Even though the rut was on, the buck didn't seem to be chasing the does. It appeared it was comfortable just following them. The deer continued on a slow walk and stopped to look around.

Rather than getting wrapped up in the antlers, I focused on getting a clear shooting lane. As the buck was coming into the opening, I raised my Remington .30-06 and found the buck's shoulder in the cross hairs. When the buck stepped into the opening, I squeezed the trigger and was expecting to hear a loud bang. I only heard a click! I could not believe it; I forgot to put a shell in the chamber after climbing up into the stand!

The buck stood there for a second before running toward the does. I quickly chambered a "real" round and once again found the buck in the scope. When the deer reached the does, it stopped to look back. Big mistake! That allowed me to get the cross hairs on its neck. At nearly the instant that the rifle roared, the buck collapsed in a heap!

I was so excited at this point, my heart was racing. I stood there for awhile watching to make sure it was down for good and to calm myself. I then unloaded my rifle, climbed down from my stand, and started walking toward the buck. I've heard of ground shrinkage, but as I got closer the antlers just kept getting bigger.

As I stood there looking at the biggest deer I had ever seen, I thanked God for a great day and a great hunt. Suddenly, a strange, but warm feeling came over me. My mind drifted back to that first button buck I killed 30 years earlier, and it felt as though my dad was standing beside me. I still believe that somehow my dad pushed that buck toward me.

After field dressing and tagging the deer, I walked out of the hunting area and retrieved my ATV. After getting the buck into the wagon and hauling it out of the timber, I still struggled getting the brute into the truck even with all the adrenaline flowing.

I drove to the check station, where there were many nice deer being checked in that morning. When I checked mine in, all eyes turned toward my buck. I thought my deer was big, but it wasn't until then that I realized how big it was. Everyone had started to comment on my buck.

Once the deer was checked in, I spent the next few hours showing it to family and friends. I now wish I would have taken the time to take more pictures, as I have very few from that day.

In February, after the official 60-day drying period, I took the rack to Bear Creek Bow Works in Fairmont, Missouri, to have it officially measured. Dale Ream measured the deer for entry into the Boone and Crockett Club's Awards Program and Missouri Show-Me Big Bucks Club. I was greatly surprised when Dale came up with a net score of 198-6/8, and only 3-4/8 inches of deductions, making it an almost perfect "10."

WHITETAIL DEER
Typical Antlers
Second Award – 198 ⁶/₈

▼ ▼ ▼ ▼ ▼

DARYL L. BLUM

TROPHY STATS

▼ ▼ ▼ ▼ ▼

Category
  whitetail deer - typical antlers

Score
  196 $^6/_8$

Location
  Kane County, Illinois — 2000

Hunter
  Ray Schremp

Length of Main Beam
  Right: 29 $^6/_8$ Left: 29

**Circumference Between
Burr and First Point**
  Right: 5 $^2/_8$ Left: 5 $^6/_8$

Number of Points
  Right: 6   Left: 8

Inside Spread Measurement
  21

Photograph by Cliff White

WHITETAIL DEER
Typical Antlers
Third Award – 196 $^6/_8$

▼ ▼ ▼ ▼ ▼ ▼ ▼ ▼ ▼

RAY SCHREMP

November 21, 2000, for most people, was just like any other day. But for a few people in Kane County, Illinois, it was history in the making.

Ray Schremp was out enjoying the cold, windy November day, hoping to run across a big whitetail. Of course, a lot of people have that same vision, but very few get to realize it and see what Ray was about to see.

He waited patiently as the wind continued to test his resolve. At 4:15 in the afternoon, his life was about to change. All of a sudden, the buck of his dreams stepped into his field of view. It was a monster typical whitetail It had six points on the right antler, eight on the left, and the longest main beams he had ever seen.

Ray drew his PSE bow, focused on his target, and released the 125-grain broadhead. That simple motion would rewrite records books. Ray's beautiful 2000 whitetail would soon become the biggest typical whitetail ever taken in Kane County, and the fourth-largest to ever come from the whitetail heaven of Illinois.

Photograph courtesy of Ray Schremp

Ray Schremp with his award-winning typical whitetail deer. Ray took this deer during the 2000 season in Illinois. The buck scores 196-6/8 points.

Photograph by Cliff White

TROPHY STATS

▼ ▼ ▼ ▼ ▼

Category
whitetail deer - typical antlers

Score
194

Location
Kent County, Maryland — 2002

Hunter
Kevin C. Miller

Length of Main Beam
Right: $28^4/_8$ Left: $28^6/_8$

Circumference Between Burr and First Point
Right: 5   Left: 5

Number of Points
Right: 6   Left: 6

Inside Spread Measurement
$22^2/_8$

Photograph by Jack Re

Kevin C. Miller accepting his plaque and medal from Buck Buckner, Chair of the F Game Records Committee.

WHITETAIL DEER
Typical Antlers
Fourth Award – 194

▼　▼　▼　▼　▼　▼　▼　▼　▼

KEVIN C. MILLER

It was a cold first Saturday in the 2000-2001 firearms season. I left the barn and headed across the 14-acre alfalfa field planted just for deer forage. As I walked across the frosted field, I spotted a group of deer shadows grazing. One snorted; then they ran into the woods by my tree stand. I was able to sneak in without being seen or heard as the slight breeze was in my favor.

The sun began to break over the horizon, so I could see the group on the far hill. Lucky for me, the deer didn't run and scare any of the other deer in the area. As far as I could tell they were all does. Slowly, they eased out of sight.

A half hour after sunup, a four-point buck entered into the woods. It surveyed the woods and started to walk toward my stand. Then it stopped at an uprooted tree. While there, it was paying special attention to one spot. I decided to scope it to see what was going on.

Through the scope, I could see some ivory in the branches. My legs started to shake. It was the right side of a rack. Wow! It was the most impressive antler I had ever seen. For the next hour I watched the buck move, but it never showed me its left side. I knew the right side had six long and heavy points.

A small group of does entered into the woods. I looked up at them just as the buck headed up the hill. Instinctively, I jumped up and shot for its shoulder. The buck dropped like a rock, disappearing into the brush.

Usually I wait for an hour or so to give the deer a chance to die, but I knew there was no need today. I unloaded my shotgun and made my way to the buck. My shot had entered high in the left rib cage and exited through the right shoulder. I could not believe what I was seeing. The buck was a perfect 12-pointer. I knew it was special, but I did not realize at the time that it would become the new Maryland State Record.

Once everyone saw the buck, we realized it was the same deer that had left three years' worth of sheds in a 200 yard radius. The first one I found was when it was three years old. This set was a complete set dropped in a soybean field. The next year's antler was found by my brother Brad, when the deer was four years old. The third antler was found by my Uncle Charlie when the deer was six. Uncle Charlie also has a trail camera photo of the buck before the season.

Even though we knew it was there, no one had ever seen the buck while hunting. It has been an honor for me to share in this magnificent deer's eight-year history. Maybe one day I will meet its offspring.

Photograph by Cliff White

TROPHY STATS

▼ ▼ ▼ ▼ ▼

Category
whitetail deer -
non-typical antlers

Score
307 $^5/_8$

Location
Monroe County, Iowa — 2003

Hunter/Owner
Tony W. Lovstuen/Bass Pro Shops

Length of Main Beam
Right: 26$^3/_8$ Left: 23$^5/_8$

Circumference Between Burr and First Point
Right: 8   Left: 6$^4/_8$

Number of Points
Right: 21   Left: 17

Inside Spread Measurement
22

Photograph by Jack R

Eric Volmer of Bass Pro Shops acceptin
the plaque and medal on behalf of Tony
Lovstuen from Buck Buckner, Chair of th
Big Game Records Committee.

WHITETAIL DEER
Non-typical Antlers
First Award – 307⁵/₈

▼ ▼ ▼ ▼ ▼ ▼ ▼ ▼ ▼

TONY W. LOVSTUEN - HUNTER   BASS PRO SHOPS - OWNER

No animal on earth is either as hunted, harvested, or sought after as often as whitetail deer. To think of how many whitetail bucks have been taken by hunters over the last 150 years is a staggering and mind-boggling statistic. So, when 15-year-old Tony Lovstuen squeezed the trigger on his .50-caliber Knight muzzleloader, the proverbial "shockwave" that went through the whitetail hunting world was not substantial; it was unparalleled.

The Lovstuen family had known that a monster-sized whitetail buck was in the vicinity for some time. They had tried without success to outwit the reclusive giant. Several family members were involved over a several year span in finding sheds, attempting to pattern the buck, and gathering all the information they could on how it lived.

In 2002, the entire whitetail world found out about the existence of a potential record-breaker. *North American Whitetail* magazine published several pictures that had been taken of the giant, touting him as "Iowa's Walking World's Record." Regardless of what this huge buck might score, no one doubted that it was one of the greatest whitetails to have ever walked.

On September 29, 2003, all of the hard work and effort was finally realized. A special youth season was in progress that preceded Iowa's general hunting season. It was 6:50 p.m. on a sunny and clear Iowa day in Monroe County. As Tony peered through the sights at one of the world's greatest whitetails 70 yards away, he squeezed the trigger. When the buck went down, both a whitetail's life and a family's quest were over.

Even though Tony did not know at the time exactly what he had done, he would soon find out. Tony had not just taken a great whitetail. Millions of hunters over hundreds of years had taken tens of millions of whitetails, but Tony Lovstuen had just taken the biggest whitetail buck ever bagged by a hunter. It was also the third-largest ever recorded, with both entries above it being found dead. Tony had just personally fulfilled the dream that every whitetail hunter has had.

The buck's final Boone and Crockett score, after panel judging, was a staggering 307-5/8 points. It is one of only four deer to officially score over 300 B&C points. While the deer has only an eight-point typical frame that scores 155-2/8, it has a total of 152-3/8 inches of abnormal points! It has a total of 38 points (21 on the right and 17 on the left.) The weight of the massive, gnarled rack of bone is 11 pounds, 8 ounces.

While the indescribable set of antlers is not what many would call "pretty," it is easily one of the most remarkable deer racks anyone could ever witness. This buck is a testament to hard work, good modern conservation values and practices, and the pursuit of dreams.

Photograph by Cliff White

TROPHY STATS

▼ ▼ ▼ ▼ ▼

Category
   whitetail deer -
      typical antlers

Score
   304³/₈

Location
   Fulton County, Illinois — 2001

Hunter
   Jerry D. Bryant

Length of Main Beam
   Right: 27³/₈   Left: 27²/₈

Circumference Between Burr and First Point
   Right: 5¹/₈   Left: 5⁷/₈

Number of Points
   Right: 17   Left: 20

Inside Spread Measurement
   23¹/₈

Photograph by Jack Re

Jerry D. Bryant accepting his plaque an
medal from Buck Buckner, Chair of the I
Game Records Committee.

WHITETAIL DEER
Non-typical Antlers
Second Award – 304³/₈

▼ ▼ ▼ ▼ ▼ ▼ ▼ ▼

JERRY D. BRYANT

The morning of November 15, 2001 was clear and cool with temperatures around freezing. A friend had invited me to go turkey hunting near Canton, Illinois, the day before. This 120-acre farm was well-known for both a plentiful turkey population and also a well-managed deer herd.

At 3:30 a.m., we packed all of our hunting equipment into his van and started our journey for a day's hunt. At about 4 a.m., we set up my turkey blind and headed back to the farm house. With two cups of coffee downed and all of the hunting equipment ready, we headed for the woods.

Fred went to a deer stand, and I went to my turkey blind. It was a beautiful morning as the sunlight began to outline the trees. I could hear the creek gurgling below my blind and thought to myself, "It just doesn't get any better than this."

The morning was uneventful. Around 10 a.m., I decided to go back to the farmhouse. As I stepped out of my turkey blind, I noticed a nice scrape on the ground about 10 feet away. My friend and I decided to set a deer stand over the scrape, and by 2:45 p.m., I was back in the stand with my crossbow and backpack handy.

Around 4 p.m., I ate a Twinkie and popped the top of a Mountain Dew. I hung my crossbow on a small limb while I enjoyed the beautiful scenery while eating my snack. Fifteen minutes later five turkeys walked over the hill. I moved ever so slightly, and, to my amazement, the turkeys went over the backside of the hill.

At about 4:30 p.m., I saw a big doe heading down the trail. It stopped 15 yards from my deer stand, and as I raised my crossbow,

Photograph courtesy of Jerry D. Bryant

Jerry D. Bryant's non-typical whitetail deer is the second largest hunter-taken whitetail in the records book. Its final score of 304-3/8 ranks it number four on the All-time list.

it looked back over its shoulder. It made me think that something was coming. All of a sudden, the doe bolted and ran down the hill. I thought to myself, "Well, that's the end of that."

Then, out of nowhere, I heard a thrashing and tree limbs rattling. I looked in time to see a monstrous buck coming down the same trail as the doe. It stopped in the same spot the doe had. As I held the soda can between my knees, I put the cross hairs on its heart/lung area and pulled the trigger. The buck raised and lowered its head several times.

I stood up and spilled the Mountain Dew all over my legs as the can fell to the ground. I thought, "I missed! How could I miss?" The buck turned and stumbled as it walked about 15 yards before it fell.

I got down from my stand about 20 minutes later and walked over to this huge deer. I dropped down by its side and thanked God for giving me the opportunity to harvest such a magnificent animal. I really believe that it was simply the buck's day to be harvested, and I feel privileged to have been the one to do it.

Moments in Measuring...

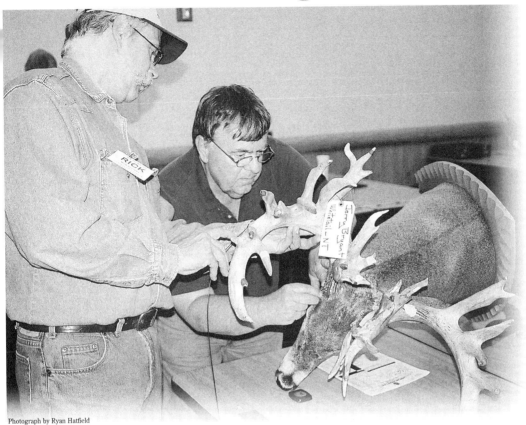

Photograph by Ryan Hatfield

Awards Panel Judges, Rick Berreth and Bill Cooper measure the length of the main beam on Jerry Bryant's non-typical whitetail deer. The buck's final score is 304-3/8 points.

Photograph by Cliff White

TROPHY STATS

▼ ▼ ▼ ▼ ▼

Category
   whitetail deer - non-typical antlers

Score
   $260^1/_8$

Location
   Garrard County, Kentucky — 2002

Hunter/Owner
   Benjamin J. Brogle/Bass Pro Shops

Length of Main Beam
   Right: $24^1/_8$ Left: $24^1/_8$

Circumference Between Burr and First Point
   Right: $5^5/_8$ Left: $5^5/_8$

Number of Points
   Right: 18   Left: 17

Inside Spread Measurement
   $23^4/_8$

Photograph by Jack Re

Eric Volmer of Bass Pro Shops accepting
the plaque and medal on behalf of
Benjamin J. Brogle from Buck Buckner
Chair of the Big Game Records Committe

WHITETAIL DEER
Non-typical Antlers
Third Award – 260¹/₈

▼ ▼ ▼ ▼ ▼ ▼ ▼ ▼ ▼

BENJAMIN J. BROGLE - HUNTER   BASS PRO SHOPS - OWNER

By Bill Cooper

On the afternoon of November 14, 2002, Ben Brogle, a dairy farmer in Garrard County, Kentucky, drove to a section of the county where his cousin had reportedly spotted a big buck earlier that morning. The farm where the deer had been sighted included a wooded hollow slightly over a half mile long that was surrounded by cultivated fields and pasture-land. Referred to locally as the "thicket," the hollow includes hardwoods, pockets of cedars, and small feeder ravines all choked with a dense understory of saplings, vines, and briars.

"It wasn't unusual to sight deer there from time to time, but for the most part, the thicket was an area deer moved in and out of as opposed to staying throughout the year," Ben noted. "Considering the rut was going on, I was concerned the big buck my cousin spotted was merely passing through the hollow, searching for does.

"My idea that evening was to simply look the area over and, if I saw anything promising, return the following morning," the hunter explained. "The first thing I did was stop by my cousin's house to find out exactly where he had seen the deer. I also asked him about the size of the buck's rack, and his response was to spread his hands about two feet apart."

Overlooking the thicket from just below his cousin's house, Ben could tell the wind direction dictated that he hunt on the opposite side. Directly across the hollow, a cornfield bordered the tree line, and he decided that would probably be the best place for an evening stand.

However, just as he reached the other side and was about to park the truck, Ben spotted a big buck hightailing it over a nearby ridgetop. Grabbing his rifle, he jumped from the truck and began running across the cornfield. Fortunately, the corn had been picked which made the going a little easier; however, he still had to cover a considerable distance before reaching the top of the hill.

"I was hoping to get an idea of which direction the deer had gone," Ben said. "As I approached the crest of the hill I slowed down and eased forward until I could see over the top. Amazingly, the buck was still in sight, slowly walking through the field approximately 275 to 300 yards away."

Out of breath from the long run, Ben couldn't begin to hold the rifle still enough for such a long off-hand shot. Thinking he might have a chance at the deer with a solid rest, he quickly dropped into shooting position on the ground. However, the slightly rolling ter-

Ben Brogle followed a tip from his cousin who had previously spotted a big buck in the thicket near his dairy farm. Ben happend upon this buck that afternoon. It scores 260-1/8 points and received a Third Place Award at the 25th Awards Program in Kansas City.

rain of the field made it impossible to see over the corn stubble.

After the hunter got back to his feet, a combination of nerves, excitement, and frustration, got the better of him, and he fired at the distant deer. The shot missed badly.

"The second I pulled the trigger I knew it was a mistake," the hunter related. "I thought to myself, 'You idiot; you know better than to try something like that!'"

But Ben had little time to contemplate his error in judgment. At the shot, the buck whirled around and began running directly at him.

Ben said, "After a short distance the deer spotted me and turned, which is hardly surprising, considering I was a big orange blob standing completely in the open. Looking back on the situation, I feel confident the buck was heading back to the thicket. Had I been lying on the ground, he probably would have continued coming straight to me."

Ben watched the giant whitetail circle out through the corn field, jump a fence into an adjoining field, and eventually disappear into the thick bottom. On the way back to his truck, the hunter began experiencing a roller coaster ride of emotions.

"Only another deer hunter can relate to my feelings at that time," he said. "I was frustrated, mad, and disappointed to the point of tears; I literally felt sick. When I got back in the truck I called my wife and told her I'd just missed the biggest deer I'd ever seen. I also asked her to say a little prayer that I'd get another chance at him."

To Ben's credit, being upset didn't keep him from making what will undoubtedly be the most profound decision of his hunting career.

"When I was younger, I believed any big buck that was jumped would probably run a mile or two before stopping," Ben noted. "However, over the years I've found that simply isn't always the case. I can recall one instance where a large buck that a hunting buddy and I jumped returned to nearly the same spot within an hour.

"In this particular situation, there had been no prior hunting or disturbance on the farm, and despite having just been shot at, the buck didn't appear to be terribly spooked," Ben pointed out. "When I last saw the deer, it was heading toward the far end of the hollow. While I realized it might keep right on going, I thought there was a good possibility that eventually the buck would circle back to where I had jumped it near the corn field. The only problem was I needed to be on the opposite side of the hollow, and the wind was blowing in the wrong direction for that to work."

Ben drove back across the bottom and parked his truck at a barn on top of the hill. Then, as he contemplated his next move, the wind suddenly shifted and began blowing out of the north.

"I remembered the forecast had mentioned a cold front moving in, but I couldn't believe the timing," Ben laughed. "I immediately set out walking, and after going about 400 to 500 yards farther down the hollow, I picked out a good vantage point and sat down."

Perhaps 30 minutes after getting situated, the hunter spotted the giant deer slowly making its way back up the hollow. This time the distance was only 125 yards, the buck was broadside, and Ben was sitting in a comfortable shooting position.

"Believe me, I was totally focused on the deer and not its rack," he said. "I kept telling myself, 'Whatever you do, don't miss this shot!'"

When Ben finally squeezed the trigger, there was no doubt the bullet found its mark, but the buck turned and started running. At this point, the hunter wasn't about to make any assumptions or take unnecessary chances. He continued shooting until the big deer went down.

As Ben began walking toward the downed buck, relief flooded over him. But there was also heartfelt thankfulness for having been given a second chance, along with an upwelling of excitement over having taken such a big deer.

However, the evening still held one additional surprise for the hunter. During his entire afternoon adventure, he'd had only brief distant glimpses of the buck's antlers. Now, for the first time, he was about to see the rack up close.

"I knew the buck was big and wide, and I was fairly certain I'd seen a couple of drop tines, but that was all," Ben noted. "Because of the deer's size, I just assumed it was probably a 10 or 12-pointer. When I got to where the buck was lying, the sight of the antlers was literally overwhelming. I honestly had no idea there were so many points on the rack."

After catching his breath, Ben called home to tell his wife the good news. Then he phoned his brother-in-law to request assistance with moving the deer.

During the latter conversation, the question of the buck's size came up. Ben's response was, "About 35 or 36 points!"

There was immediate laughter over the phone, followed by "Yeah, right! How big is it really?"

"I repeated the same thing at least two more times, and he never believed me," Ben laughed. "I finally told him to come on down and do the counting himself."

Other than sheer size, possibly the most outstanding feature of this great buck's rack is the amazing balance between the right and left antlers. Except for two drop tines, most of the abnormal points are contained within the 6x6 typical frame. This is especially unusual for a giant non-typical, where it is not uncommon to see growth patterns that produce points sticking in every conceivable direction.

For Ben and his family, the whole experience surrounding this trophy buck has been like a ride on a magic carpet. They can't begin to estimate the number of individuals who have called or dropped by to see his outstanding whitetail. At times it's been a bit of an ordeal, but they wouldn't change a thing.

"I just want to thank the Good Lord for allowing me to be part of this," Ben says. "It has truly been beyond my wildest dreams."

Award Winning Moments...

Photograph by Keith Balfourd

Four impressive non-typical whitetail deer were on display at Cabela's for the 25th Awards Program. Two of the bucks rank as the top two ever taken by a hunter – Jerry D. Bryant's buck scoring 304-3/8 points (far left) and Tony W. Lovstuen's buck scoring 307-5/8 points (far right). Benjamin J. Brogle's buck (bottom left) scores 260-1/8 points and Howard G. Pauls' buck (bottom right) scores 259-2/8 points.

Photograph by Cliff White

TROPHY STATS
▼ ▼ ▼ ▼ ▼

Category
whitetail deer - non-typical antlers

Score
$259^2/_8$

Location
Souris River, Manitoba — 2001

Hunter/Owner
Howard G. Pauls/Bass Pro Shops

Length of Main Beam
Right: $24^4/_8$ Left: $23^3/_8$

Circumference Between Burr and First Point
Right: $5^3/_8$ Left: $5^6/_8$

Number of Points
Right: 12   Left: 14

Inside Spread Measurement
$21^7/_8$

Photograph by Jack Ren

Eric Volmer of Bass Pro Shops accepting the plaque and medal on behalf of Howar G. Pauls from Buck Buckner, Chair of th Big Game Records Committee.

BOONE AND CROCKETT CLUB'S

WHITETAIL DEER
Non-typical Antlers
Fourth Award – 259^2/$_8$

▼ ▼ ▼ ▼ ▼ ▼ ▼ ▼ ▼

HOWARD G. PAULS - HUNTER   BASS PRO SHOPS - OWNER

It was an exciting time after my brother Richard shot his 245-6/8 B&C non-typical white-tail. It filled the rest of our group with anticipation for the balance of the muzzleloader season and the coming rifle season. We had always dreamed about shooting a deer bigger than the 232 non-typical sheds Richard and John had found. In fact, the senior philosopher of the group, cousin John, said we would have to change how big we dreamed after Richard shot his deer. For me, that dream came true three weeks to the day after Richard shot his amazing deer.

What Dreams are Made of

The whole 2000 muzzleloader season had been an exercise in frustration. I never saw a buck that scored higher than 110. Needless to say I was happy for the rifle season to start and hoped to see some good bucks.

We started hunting on the fourth day of the opening week and conditions were good, with 10 inches of snow on the ground and temperatures in the -5° to -10° Celsius range. The first day of the hunt, I decided to go to one of my portable tree stands, which is located on a heavily wooded ridge overlooking a thick draw about 150 yards wide. I thought I would try to rattle something in. After a couple hours and no deer, Richard, who had been still-hunting, came along so I dropped my rattling antlers out of the tree and crawled down to meet him. We talked for a couple minutes and then left to meet the guys for coffee. Because of that little chat, I forgot my rattling antlers at the base of the tree. Little did I know at the time, that particular move was going to put me in a position to shoot a deer-of-a-lifetime.

With the rut in full swing, the group as a whole had seen a fair number of bucks, but only a couple in the 140-150 point range. Unfortunately, no one could connect. On the other hand, I only saw one deer all day. The second day of the hunt ended much the same as the first, and frustration was starting to set in.

That night we discussed what we would do on our last day, as only four of us were left with tags to fill. We decided to start out in the morning sitting in tree stands. My plan was to go to a deer stand I had not sat in so far in either season.

The next morning, Cory, one of my hunting partners, said he was going to a stand that was about 300 yards from the stand where I had left my rattling antlers a couple of days earlier. We were about an hour late getting out there, so I decided to stay in the same area, pick up my rattling antlers, and sit in the same stand I did the first day. While walking to the

The Souris River region of Manitoba produced two monster non-typical whitetail deer during the 2000 season. Howard G. Pauls took this tremendous buck just three weeks after his brother took a buck that scores 245-6/8 points. Howard's buck ended up with a final score of 259-2/8 points and received a Fourth Place Award at the 25th Big Game Awards Program.

stand, I was grumbling to myself about how dumb it was to go back to the stand where I had only seen one deer in the four times I had used it.

Upon arriving, I picked up the antlers, climbed up the tree, and proceeded to drop the antlers just as I was crawling into the stand. Now I was really ticked off. I never bothered to climb down and get them as I figured no deer were around anyway so what's the sense!

After a few minutes of feeling sorry for myself, I started thinking about what a nice place this was to be in, and that it sure beat working. Slowly, I started to cheer up. After about an hour, it started to snow pretty hard. I can remember thinking that this is what you see in some of the hunting videos; the only thing missing is the big buck coming toward me.

All of a sudden, out of the corner of my eye, I saw movement to my left in the heavy brush. I raised my rifle to look through the scope and saw it was a doe. It was in a hurry and kept looking back, so I continued scanning behind the doe. I caught a glimpse of another deer moving through the thick brush. At first I thought it was just another doe. However, I kept watching to get a look at the head. When it crossed through an opening, I got a split second look at it. I could tell right away that it was indeed a buck, with good beam length and good tine length. This deer was only 125 yards away. I was having a hard time seeing the buck, though, much less shooting it, due to the extremely dense brush cover.

At this point, I looked up to see where the doe was going and saw it moving across in front of me in fairly good view. I figured the buck would

WHITETAIL DEER
Non-typical Antlers
Fourth Award – 259²/₈

▼ ▼ ▼ ▼ ▼

BASS PRO SHOPS - OWNER

follow so I kept tracking it in my scope, waiting until I saw the front shoulder through the trees. At that instant, I pulled the trigger on my Browning Stainless A-bolt and sent a hand-loaded .270 round on its way. When the bullet hit, the buck reared up on its back legs, fell over backwards, then got up and scrambled into some heavy brush about a 100 yards away.

I couldn't see my buck again until I got to within 50 yards of where it lay. I got into a position where I could get another shot if it decided to get up. Sure enough, at 25 yards, the buck scrambled up. I did, however, manage to get away a good shot to finish it off as it was running away.

When I walked up to the buck and saw how big it was, I let out a yell to Cory 300 yards away. "What a buck!" I shouted.

My first thought was that this buck might be close to or as big as my brother Richard's big buck. As soon as we got the deer out of the bush, I put a tape to it. As I was measuring, I was getting more and more excited. Once we were done calling out the measurements, Rick started adding up the numbers and said he was having a tough time adding because the totals were getting too big! The buck's final B&C score was 259-2/8.

Whoever would have thought that two non-typical Manitoba monarchs could come out of the same brush a half mile apart? I guess dreams do come true; just make sure you dream big enough. Special thanks to Henry, Cory, and Rick, who gave up the rest of their hunting day to help me with my deer.

Photograph by Cliff White

TROPHY STATS

▼ ▼ ▼ ▼ ▼

Category
Coues' whitetail - typical antlers

Score
125

Location
Graham County, Arizona — 2000

Hunter
Bradley Johns

Length of Main Beam
Right: $19^6/_8$ Left: $19^5/_8$

Circumference Between Burr and First Point
Right: $4^1/_8$ Left: $4^3/_8$

Number of Points
Right: 7   Left: 6

Inside Spread Measurement
$15^4/_8$

Photograph by Jack Rene

Bradley Johns accepting his plaque and medal from Buck Buckner, Chair of the Big Game Records Committee.

236

COUES' WHITETAIL
Typical Antlers
First Award – 125

▼ ▼ ▼ ▼ ▼ ▼ ▼ ▼ ▼

BRADLEY JOHNS

It is a seven-hour drive to one of my favorite places in the world. While driving back roads through the hills of the Sonoran Desert and crossing snow-covered mountain passes, I wondered with each ascending ridgeline which saddle or rock bluff held the biggest Coues' bucks. "Dad, will you stop looking for deer! That mountain is five miles away! You're going to drive us into a canyon," complained Keith, my 14-year-old son.

Growing up with the woods of upstate New York in my backyard helped to build a **Another Coues' Hunt** foundation for the passion I have today. As a boy, hunting filled my days. It kept me out of trouble and taught me to have goals as a young adult. I feel lucky to have such a passion.

I moved to Arizona in 1978 as a young man of 22 years. I quickly fell in love with the Southwest and all its diversity. It didn't take me long to meet Dennis McAdams, an Arizona hunter who knew his way around and awarded me with many quality hunting opportunities. Spending all of our time scouting, shooting, and hunting, our techniques evolved. We started hunting Coues' deer in 1984, quickly learning that by not tagging out early you could have a chance at a bigger-racked buck. By 1985 we were glassing mile-wide canyons with tripod-held 15x binoculars, and that changed everything. I've spent the last 18 years trophy hunting.

Finally, while going through the last pass, I could see my mountain. No more pavement! "It's 10 a.m., and I'm in great shape," I thought to myself.

With every turn, a new angle and view of the area appeared. There was just enough snow on the north slopes. Southern Arizona has magical places that hold just the right environment and genetics to grow the biggest Coues' whitetail bucks. "I'm back!" I exclaimed to myself.

It was December 26, and I had four and a half days left to hunt. It was my third trip of the 2000 hunt, a time when I have the ridges to myself. Wanting to spend the last two days in my best area, I chose to start at another set of ridges that run off of the same mountain peak in the other direction.

It was noon when we arrived at camp. Keith and I quickly threw on our packs, grabbed our rifles, and went in separate directions without so much as a goodbye or good luck. He walked down the ridgeline to a flat to call coyotes, and I headed toward the top of a large bowl. I had hoped to walk for an hour and top out to glass for the afternoon, but I spotted deer rutting below the ridgeline ahead of me. It was dead calm, and as cold as I wanted it to be, with light snow flurries quietly floating down. I spent the afternoon watching several smaller bucks work the area.

The dominant buck, a juvenile with modest antlers, stayed busy pushing off the smaller bucks. Noticing the random sounds of sparring and sticks breaking below kept me entertained as I sat and glassed. At last light I tossed a few rocks, hoping to push the deer from their hidden arena, standing and listening between each rock. I had to laugh as the intensity of the fight increased despite the bombardment. "How am I not hitting them on the head?" I wondered.

I decided to bypass them the next morning by hiking to the upper ridges before first light. It was breezy this morning, with periods of snow that intensified as I glassed my way up from saddle to saddle. As I crossed the last steep rock slide before topping out, I was thinking of a large-racked buck that got away from me two years earlier in the next canyon. After arriving at the top, I spotted activity just below me. I glassed two small bucks pushing a doe. Then I saw another larger, darker deer up on the ridge. When I set up my tripod and examined the larger deer, I quickly realized that I needed to set up. My scope was on the buck and the safety was off, but the deer was at 200 yards, and its head was just behind a juniper tree. Just as I realized the main beam that I thought I was looking at through the branches was its G-2, the buck bounded over the edge, showing all it had. Another memory…

After topping out at only mid-morning, I started working the main ridgeline, but didn't see many deer. With wind blowing snow right through me and glassing being tough, I decided to quickly make my way down the ridgeline and glass a large slope I had passed by in the dark. I dropped off to the north midway down the ridge and found a break in the juniper trees to set up out of the wind. There was enough activity to keep me interested for about 30 minutes, while a decent three-pointer worked a doe across from me in a saddle 500 yards up from my truck.

Since I had decided to move camp, I headed straight at the buck. With the wind blowing hard in my face, I walked to within 40 yards before the doe and the buck took off over the edge. Keith was in camp when I returned, so we picked up and headed for the other ridge.

We made camp at the base of the new ridge and again parted company. It was about 1 p.m. when I reached the top. The wind completely stopped as the sun came out, and I decided to reach a high point between two saddles and glass the other side for the afternoon. Looking straight across the canyon and about one mile away was a pyramid-shaped peak with saddles on both sides — usually the hub of activity in this large area. Talk about a panoramic view — the glassing was endless from this vantage point. The huge slope was covered in tall grass and spotted with oaks and juniper, with some thicker areas. After panning for activity, I started to concentrate on the main saddle and trails that skirted the ridgeline.

While bracketing an area near the second saddle, I noticed movement in the thick oaks just under the peak. It was a doe moving slowly in and out of view. Then another figure behind it came into view. It was a rack — a huge rack — at 1,500 yards. I strained to keep the buck in view as it sporadically appeared through the oak branches. Both deer weaved their way through the thicket, slowly heading downhill toward me. The buck stayed just out of sight for the most part, so I concentrated on keeping the doe in view.

COUES' WHITETAIL
Typical Antlers
First Award – 125

▼ ▼ ▼ ▼ ▼

BRADLEY JOHNS

The doe teased the buck for a half hour by letting it get close then running away. I caught glimpses of the rack behind the doe every once in a while. I picked up and moved downhill 40 yards at a time, but only when I had the doe in plain view. As the doe finally moved out into the sun, I pleaded to the elusive buck, "Come on, just let me see you one time."

My eyes were watering as I strained to keep in focus, waiting for a good look at the buck. I kept going back to the doe for reference.

They were at 1,000 yards as the doe continued feeding well into the opening. I could make out the silhouette of the large deer at the edge of the thicket, where it stood alert like a bronze statue not willing to let the sun touch its body. "Okay, there's the doe, it's starting to move again," I thought.

Looking back, the buck was gone, so I started scanning the area. Finally, there the buck was, moving out of the trees just above the doe. I've seen some big bucks in this area, but this deer was awesome!

For the next half hour, they slowly worked their way down and to the right. Having them in view, I moved down the ridge and kept pace. It was very steep with rock slides, and I used as much cover as possible while trying not to roll rocks or fall. "I may get a chance at this buck," I thought, as my heart started to pound and my teeth chattered in the cold.

I set up on a bluff to glass. "This is it; I can't go any lower. Where am I going to shoot from?" I wondered.

The deer were still moving to the right and stopped to feed in an opening. They were straight across from me now. Lying down behind my rifle, I clicked off the safety and concentrated on cross-hair placement. Putting pressure on the trigger, I started to tremble. My rest was terrible. "I think that I can control it and take the buck right now… no."

The angle was bad, and I was very uncomfortable. I put the safety back on and sat up behind my tripod. I knew I had to get a better rest, but felt that this could be my only chance. They were feeding next to a large thicket of small trees, and if they went in there I may never see them again.

Just as I got the cross hairs on the big buck again, the doe went into the thicket. "I had better shoot," I told myself.

Lying downhill and trying to hold my barrel up, I clicked off the safety and slowly squeezed, then stopped. Just as I sat up behind my tripod again, the buck bedded down and continued looking in the direction of the doe. I was sure the doe had also bedded down. Looking around for a better rest, I decided to move up 30 yards and to the right, where there was a rock bluff and a perfect spot to set up.

Photograph courtesy of Bradley Johns

Bradley Johns took this award-winning typical Coues' whitetail while on an Arizona hunt in 2000 with his son, Keith. The buck scores 125 points.

Again trying not to roll rocks, I reached the spot and set up my tripod. The buck was still there, so I set my rifle on my pack, dug in, clicked off the safety, and began to squeeze. I thought to myself, "Yes, this is better. No, wait until it stands up, I can't chance it."

Breathing deeply and trying to get my composure, I waited the buck out. It stayed there for a half hour, always looking up to make sure that doe was still there. Then it stood up. I quickly got ready, put pressure on the trigger, and s-q-u-e-e-z-e-d.

Just as I had almost enough pressure on to break the trigger, the buck started walking toward the thicket. I groaned inwardly, and then it stopped. I squeezed; it moved again; I squeezed; it disappeared into the thicket. As I released the pressure off the trigger, I sighed. Then I sat up and glassed the perimeter of the thicket for the next 45 minutes trying to figure out where the deer might come out. With only an hour of shooting light remaining, it didn't feel good.

Straining to find them again, I finally saw a deer. It was the doe! My heart started pounding again as I frantically panned the area for the buck. Suddenly I saw it, standing on a rock outcropping 350 yards away. As I tried to get my scope on the buck, it vanished. I sat back up to glass and found the doe again, but no sign of the buck. The doe was working its way to my right, getting farther away with every step. Keeping tabs on the doe, I panned the trail behind and spotted the buck's rack moving toward the doe through the trees. Looking back, the doe walked into the middle of the last opening and squatted to urinate before it dropped out of sight for good. I thought, "This is my last chance. The buck will surely stop in the

BOONE AND CROCKETT CLUB'S

same spot, drop its head and smell the ground."

I found the distant opening in my scope and waited. I saw its rack appear through the trees as it slowly approached. The buck stopped on cue, looked to the left, then to the right, and put its nose to the ground. I squeezed the trigger. After the recoil and the sound of the bullet hitting its target, I saw all four legs rolling over as it tumbled. Sitting up, I looked through my binoculars and thought to myself, "I was calm! That was a perfect shot."

I picked up my gear, folded my tripod, and brought my binoculars up to my eyes and looked at the opening. Completely drained I reached the grassy opening and found the buck neatly folded in a small hole, topped by its massive rack.

It was 10 p.m. before I made it back to camp with the caped trophy securely strapped to the top of my pack. Keith, in total surprise, said, "Is that a whitetail?"

"Yes, it is," I replied.

COUES' WHITETAIL
Typical Antlers
First Award – 125

▼ ▼ ▼ ▼ ▼

BRADLEY JOHNS

Photograph by Cliff White

TROPHY STATS

▼ ▼ ▼ ▼ ▼

Category
Coues' whitetail - typical antlers

Score
128³/₈

Location
Sonora, Mexico — Picked up in 2002

Owner
Kirk Kelso

Length of Main Beam
Right: 20¹/₈   Left: 20³/₈

Circumference Between Burr and First Point
Right: 4¹/₈   Left: 4¹/₈

Number of Points
Right: 5   Left: 5

Inside Spread Measurement
16⁷/₈

Photograph by Jack Rene[e]

Kirk Kelso accepting his plaque from
Buck Buckner, Chair of the Big Game
Records Committee.

COUES' WHITETAIL
Typical Antlers
Certificate of Merit – 128 $^3/_8$

▼ ▼ ▼ ▼ ▼ ▼ ▼ ▼ ▼

KIRK KELSO - OWNER

This set of antlers was purchased in October 2002 by Kirk Kelso. The circumstances regarding this deer's demise are not known. It was purchased by a ranch owner who had a ranch approximately 40 miles south of Puerto Libertad in northern Sonora, Mexico. It is the eighth largest typical Coues' deer ever recorded by the Boone and Crockett Club.

Photograph by Cliff White

TROPHY STATS

▼ ▼ ▼ ▼ ▼

Category
Coues' whitetail - typical antlers

Score
127 $4/8$

Location
Sonora, Mexico — Picked up in 2003

Owner
Kirk Kelso

Length of Main Beam
Right: 19 $5/8$ Left: 20 $3/8$

Circumference Between Burr and First Point
Right: 3 $6/8$ Left: 4

Number of Points
Right: 6   Left: 5

Inside Spread Measurement
12 $6/8$

Photograph by Jack Rene

Kirk Kelso accepting his plaque from Buck Buckner, Chair of the Big Game Records Committee.

COUES' WHITETAIL
Typical Antlers
Certificate of Merit – 127⁴/₈

▼ ▼ ▼ ▼ ▼ ▼ ▼ ▼ ▼ ▼

KIRK KELSO - OWNER

The fateful events of how this big Coues' deer met its end are unknown. It was found dead on a ranch in northern Sonora, Mexico, by a cowboy who worked on the ranch. This elusive buck, too smart to be taken by a hunter, ranks as one of the finest typical Coues' deer ever recorded.

TROPHY STATS

▼ ▼ ▼ ▼ ▼

Photograph by Cliff White

Category
   Coues' whitetail - non-typical antlers

Score
   138⁵/₈

Location
   Sonora, Mexico — 2000

Hunter
   Glenn Hall

Length of Main Beam
   Right: 16⁶/₈   Left: 16⁶/₈

**Circumference Between
Burr and First Point**
   Right: 4³/₈   Left: 4³/₈

Number of Points
   Right: 9   Left: 6

Inside Spread Measurement
   11⁵/₈

COUES' WHITETAIL
Non-typical Antlers
First Award – 138 ⁵/₈

▼ ▼ ▼ ▼ ▼ ▼ ▼ ▼ ▼

GLENN HALL

It was the first day of December and I was in Sonora, Mexico, with my good friend Jay Scott. We were positioned on a glassing point we had located during a scouting trip in mid-November. The place we were hunting was a large ranch south of Aqua Prieta.

This was a do-it-yourself hunt. There was no comfy ranch house, no fancy guide, just Jay, me, and our ambition to find a big buck. Our morning had already been quite eventful. First, we took the wrong two-track road. Then we got the truck stuck in a boulder-strewn ravine. Frustration was mounting as we got out of our jam and back on the road. We reached our spot on the windy side of the point and started glassing to the west.

The hillside was just starting to glow in the early morning light. We were scanning two big canyons full of oak trees and yellow grass when Jay spotted a female mountain lion and its half-grown kittens. The adult lion was sneaking along, but the two youngsters were more interested in playing than hunting.

We watched the lions for awhile before returning to the task at hand. We glassed hard, but only found a lone doe way up the canyon. Suspecting the lions had something to do with the absence of deer, we were about to move spots. It was then that I saw two deer three ridges over. Out came the spotting scope, which soon revealed two bucks. One would probably score about 85 B&C points and had a very distinctive tan-colored body; the other buck looked really big. It had drop tines hanging off of both main beams between its G-2s and G-3s.

This buck was worth pursuing, so we packed up our gear and started the long hike. Two hours later, we were at the bottom of the ridge. We decided that the bucks had probably slipped off the backside into the shade. We worked our way up a canyon, following a small stream, and gained some altitude across from where we thought the deer would be.

Jay soon spotted a deer feeding in the open. It was a small buck, not one of the two we had seen earlier. I continued glassing and noticed some movement through the trees. Out stepped a nice 3x3, followed by a buck with many points. Jay set up the spotting scope, and we were pleasantly surprised to see a buck with 5-inch eye guards and points going every-where. Since it was our first day hunting, I wanted to make certain this was the buck for me. Jay thought it would score around 118 B&C points, but wasn't sure because of the non-typi-cal rack. That was all I needed to hear and decided to give it a try. The distance was 400 yards, but the hill we were on was really steep, making it hard to get a steady rest for the

Photograph courtesy of Glenn Hall

Glenn Hall and his good friend and hunting partner, Jay Scott, were on a self-guided hunt in Sonora, Mexico, when Glenn took this non-typical Coues' whitetail. The buck scores 138-5/8 points and received a First Place Award at the 25th Awards Program in Kansas City.

shot. Jay stacked some rocks up for a rest, but I wasn't comfortable with this and decided to try and get closer. During all of this, the buck was bedded on a small flat under some trees. Jay stayed and watched the buck as I started my stalk.

It was about noon and starting to get hot. I worked my way around a big rock and heard the familiar buzz from a rattlesnake letting me know I was in its comfort zone. Skirting the snake, I continued my climb up the hill. When I reached a high point, I started looking for the bedded buck. It was already up, walking slowly in the shadows. I ranged it at just under 300 yards, set my pack up as a rest, and readied for the shot. The buck was walking in and out of the thick stuff.

When it stopped, I pulled the trigger. Dust flew from the ground just over its back and it took off running. I jumped up, chambered another round and ran closer to the canyon's edge searching for the buck. I looked where I thought it should be, but found nothing. Then something caught my eye; there was the buck sneaking down the canyon directly below me! This time I held a little low, squeezed the trigger, and down it went. I watched it through the scope and yelled to Jay that the buck was down. We met at the buck and admired this great Coues' deer that had given me a second chance.

Moments in Measuring

Photograph by Jack Reneau

Chairman of the Big Game Records Committee, Buck Buckner (right), reviews the scoring procedure of the new World's Record non-typical Coues' whitetail deer with John Caid, one of the members of the Judges Panel. Each trophy that is sent to a Judges' Panel is scored independently by two teams of two judges each and their scores are compared with the original entry score.

New World's Record

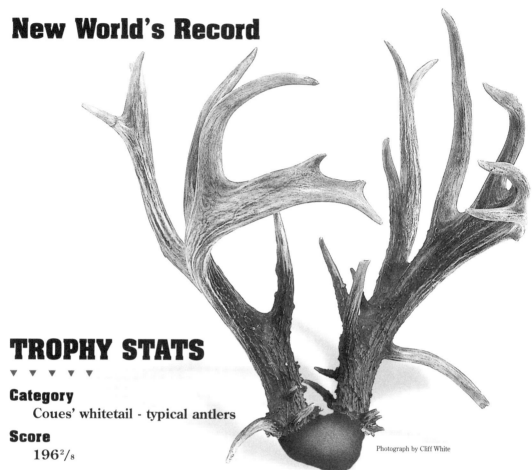

Photograph by Cliff White

TROPHY STATS

▼ ▼ ▼ ▼ ▼

Category
Coues' whitetail - typical antlers

Score
$196^2/_8$

Location
Graham County, Arizona — 1971

Owners
D.J. Hollinger & B. Howard

Length of Main Beam
Right: $20^4/_8$ Left: $19^3/_8$

Circumference Between Burr and First Point
Right: $4^6/_8$ Left: $4^6/_8$

Number of Points
Right: 11   Left: 15

Inside Spread Measurement
$12^3/_8$

Photograph by Jack Rer

Dana Hollinger accepting his plaque from Buck Buckner, Chair of the Big Game Records Committee.

COUES' WHITETAIL
Non-typical Antlers
Certificate of Merit – 196 $^2/_8$

▼ ▼ ▼ ▼ ▼ ▼ ▼ ▼ ▼

NATIVE AMERICAN - HUNTER
D.J. HOLLINGER & B. HOWARD - OWNERS

Not much is known about the circumstances of the hunt on the day that the largest-ever recorded Coues' deer was taken. That information passed away with the now deceased hunter. Undoubtedly, he must have been in awe of his tremendous trophy.

This phenomenal deer was taken in the late 1960s on the San Carlos Indian Reservation by a tribal member. It was taken south of Highway 70, possibly in the Mt. Turnbull area.

The 11x15 rack sports a 152-3/8 typical frame and an incredible 43-7/8 inches of abnormal points. This outstanding Coues' deer was originally sold to an antler dealer many years ago. It is now owned by Dana J. Hollinger and Bob Howard.

Photograph by Cliff White

TROPHY STATS

▼ ▼ ▼ ▼ ▼

Category
    Coues' whitetail - non-typical antlers

Score
    133 $^4/_8$

Location
    Sonora, Mexico — Picked up n 2002

Owner
    Kirk Kelso

Length of Main Beam
    Right: 19 $^4/_8$ Left: 19 $^5/_8$

**Circumference Between
Burr and First Point**
    Right: 3 $^2/_8$ Left: 3 $^3/_8$

Number of Points
    Right: 5   Left: 7

Inside Spread Measurement
    15 $^3/_8$

Photograph by Jack Re

Kirk Kelso accepting his plaque from
Buck Buckner, Chair of the Big Game
Records Committee.

BOONE AND CROCKETT CLUB'S

COUES' WHITETAIL
Non-typical Antlers
Certificate of Merit – 133⁴/₈

▼ ▼ ▼ ▼ ▼ ▼ ▼ ▼ ▼

KIRK KELSO - OWNER

This deer was found on January 16, 2002, on a ranch we had under contract in Northern Sonora, Mexico. It was found by me and my guide, Raphael Jaime, while hunting for deer.

Raphael had just slid down a steep bank to cross a dry creek bed and stumbled onto the skull and antlers lying in the sand. Needless to say we were both quite shocked at the size of this deer, which had either been taken by a mountain lion or had died from natural causes.

Photograph by Cliff White

TROPHY STATS

▼ ▼ ▼ ▼ ▼

Category
   Coues' whitetail - non-typical antlers

Score
   121$^1/_8$

Location
   Sonora, Mexico — 2000

Hunter
   Michael L. Braegelmann

Length of Main Beam
   Right: 19   Left: 19$^2/_8$

**Circumference Between
   Burr and First Point**
   Right: 3$^3/_8$ Left: 3$^3/_8$

Number of Points
   Right: 7   Left: 8

Inside Spread Measurement
   13

Photograph by Jack Re

Michael L. Braegelmann accepting his
plaque from Buck Buckner, Chair of the
Big Game Records Committee.

COUES' WHITETAIL
Non-typical Antlers
Honorable Mention – 121$^1/_8$

▼ ▼ ▼ ▼ ▼ ▼ ▼ ▼ ▼

MICHAEL L. BRAEGELMANN

Our Mexico Coues' deer hunt began as a result of receiving a large pile of "pink rejection slips" from the Arizona Game and Fish Department. My wife, Zona, and I had applied for a total of 10 permits in Arizona, plus others in New Mexico, and were unsuccessful on all counts. Most hunters can understand the sense of despair and frustration we were feeling at having nothing to hunt.

The day after the Arizona draw, I called Kirk Kelso of Pusch Ridge Outfitters to see if he had any openings in Mexico. Unfortunately, he was fully booked. Low and behold, a few days later, Kirk called me with good news. He had two clients cancel on an early December Coues' deer hunt in Mexico. I quickly grabbed the opportunity and the paperwork began.

Our hunt preparation consisted of several outings to the Tucson Rifle Club for some much-needed long range practice. I had recently purchased a new Weatherby Accumark in .300 Weatherby Magnum and wanted to use it on this hunt. Kirk suggested I purchase a 6.5x20 Leupold scope that was modified with extra stadia wires to help with long-range shooting.

I gave my rifle to Kirk so that he could mount the scope on it. He even worked up a very accurate handload for me! Now that's above and beyond the norm for an outfitter! The rifle was shooting very accurately, and I had cross hairs for 300, 400, and 500 yards.

In December, we flew from Tucson to Hermosillo, Sonora, without a hitch. Kirk met us at the airport and helped us through customs. In no time, we were loaded in the Suburban and heading for the ranch. Although the ranch was very remote, the accommodations were comfortable.

Joining us on the hunt were Skip Donau and Bert Vargas from Tucson, Fred Daum from Oregon, and Gary Wood from California. More about their success later.

The first morning, Zona and I were glassing with our guides Jim Reynolds and Alex Valencia. Since our only Coues' deer hunting was in Arizona, we were not prepared for the quantity and quality of the bucks we were seeing! In the first hour, we saw four bucks that were in the 100 B&C point range! One buck gave us the slip into a forest of ocotillo cactus, and two others gave us the slip after an exciting stalk. What a first morning.

After a short lunch break, we headed to higher country for some more glassing. Once again, the quality and quantity of bucks was shocking! Late in the day, we were watching three different bucks scattered across a far hillside when Alex whispered, *"Muy Grande!"*

After being unsuccessful in the drawing a Coues' deer permit in Arizona and New Mexico, Michael Braegelmann and his wife Zona booked a hunt in Sonora, Mexico. Michael took this non-typical Coues' whitetail deer, which scores 121-1/8 points.

He pointed across the canyon. I wasn't impressed with this buck, as I had been looking at it for some time through my binoculars. After a minute or two of my broken Spanish and his broken English, I discovered he was looking at a different deer bedded in the shade on a closer hillside. After finding the buck in the binoculars, I agreed that this truly was a *"MUY GRANDE!"*

We were at least 1,200 yards across the canyon from the buck, and light was fading fast, so the quiet stalk wasn't so quiet! Jim, Alex, and I moved (or should I say slid) down the hill with Zona following close behind. I guess we were making more noise than we thought, because the buck stood from its bed and began working its way to the top of the ridge. When we were as close as we could get, we began frantically searching with our binoculars to try to relocate this bruiser. Jim found the buck standing behind an oak tree. We used my laser ranger finder and determined the oak tree was 503 yards away. I quickly set up for the shot and waited for the buck to step out. Then Jim said, "It's moving uphill!"

I was prepared for the deer to move around the tree and show itself, but with the tree between us, it moved up and straight away. Finally, it stepped into our view at the top of the ridge and stood quartering away from me. Jim took a laser reading at 551 yards. The shot was going to be at a steep uphill angle, so I laid the 500 stadia line on its shoulder and

BOONE AND CROCKETT CLUB'S

squeezed the trigger. No one saw the buck run off or go down. We had no idea what had happened to it so we made the hike across the canyon to search for the buck. Not five yards from where it had stood lay my deer! We were stunned with the size of its rack! The antlers were officially scored for Boone and Crockett at 121-1/8, and that was with approximately 11 inches of antler broken off!

COUES' WHITETAIL
Non-typical Antlers
Honorable Mention – 121¹/₈

▼ ▼ ▼ ▼ ▼

MICHAEL L. BRAEGELMANN

We spent the next three days looking for a big buck for Zona. On the fourth day, Kirk joined us. We decided to try to locate the buck that had given us the slip on the first day. We worked our way to the same hill, set up our equipment, and believe it or not, found it bedded under the same tree. We decided to not make the same mistake we did the first day of trying to get too close. Kirk, Zona, and Alex hiked out to a vantage point that Kirk felt would present a shot. Jim and I stayed behind, keeping the deer in our binoculars.

It seemed like an eternity passed as we waited for Zona to get in position to shoot. We were watching the bedded buck when it suddenly lurched forward and the report from the rifle echoed down the canyon toward us. Kirk decided that since Zona was shooting his rifle, she could kill this buck from a different position. Zona made an incredible 494-yard, one-shot kill on this magnificent 109-7/8 inch non-typical buck!

This type of hunting requires the best in optics and equipment. You need quality binoculars and spotting scopes, as well as the ability and patience to sit behind them for hours. You also need a rifle and ammunition capable of accurately shooting at long distances. That equipment, coupled with lots of range time with Kirk, practicing at 300, 400, and 500 yards, resulted in a very successful hunt for us.

The hunt was a great success for all of us in camp. Skip Donau took a 114-1/8 B&C buck, Fred Daum took a 109-4/8 buck, Bert Vargas shot a 100-class deer, and Gary Woods' buck scored 112 points!

Since taking this buck in December 2000, I've returned to Sonora, Mexico, to hunt Coues' deer with Pusch Ridge Outfitters four more times. I've been fortunate to take Coues' deer scoring 103-1/8 points typical, 122-4/8 points non-typical, 104 points typical, and my most recent buck scored 111-7/8 points typical. I'm looking forward to my next Coues' deer hunt in Sonora, Mexico!

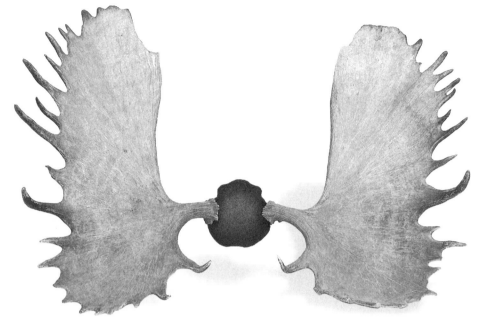

TROPHY STATS

▼ ▼ ▼ ▼ ▼

Category
Canada moose

Score
$240^6/_8$

Location
Kinaskan Lake, British Columbia — 2002

Hunter
Doug E. Frank

Greatset Spread Measurement
$63^4/_8$

Length of Palm
Right: $48^7/_8$ Left: $47^2/_8$

Width of Palm
Right: 18   Left: $19^4/_8$

Number of Normal Points
Right: 16   Left: 16

Doug E. Frank accepting his plaque an
medal from Buck Buckner, Chair of th
Big Game Records Committee.

CANADA MOOSE
First Award - 240⁶/₈

▼ ▼ ▼ ▼ ▼ ▼ ▼ ▼ ▼

DOUG E. FRANK

The hunt we had planned for a year almost didn't happen for me. A month before I was to go moose hunting with Jon Swenson and Dewayne Larue, I was playing in a softball game and injured my knee. I completely tore my PCL and partially tore my ACL. With the help of a knee brace and plenty of exercise, I was able to get enough strength back to go on the hunt.

The trip didn't start out very well. Power problems at our airport nearly made us miss our flight. We then got to Vancouver, British Columbia, and encountered more flight problems. The next morning, when we were on our flight to Smithers, British Columbia, the plane had to turn around due to fog. We had to return to Vancouver just to board another plane and try again, not knowing if this plane would also be unwilling to land in fog .

Another problem was that this delay made us three hours late for our next flight! Luckily, they held up the connecting plane just for us three hunters, otherwise, we would have had to wait two more days. There were a few people on that plane ride who were upset with us. When we finally arrived at our destination, our outfitter, Leonard Creyke, had been waiting for us for five hours. We spent the night at Leonard's place, which was a nice cabin with a fireplace and a generator.

The next morning we flew by floatplane to Buckley Lake, where Leonard had his base camp. We unpacked our gear and got our bunks ready for the night.

We awoke to the smell of bacon on the fire and the sounds of our guides getting our horses ready. This was the first time I met my guide, Charlie. I could tell he was experienced just by the thorough way he was getting things ready.

The three of us went with Dewey's guide, Chris, up to the top camp. On the way up, we saw a nice moose run into the brush. Chris and Dewey took to higher ground to see if they could get another look.

While they were gone, I had my first encounter with a moose. This bull was hot on the trail of the first moose. All of the sudden, all hell broke loose. It sounded like someone was slapping 2x4s together. The two bulls were fighting only 100 yards from us! We couldn't see them, but they were sure going at it, knocking down small trees, thrashing branches, and grunting. This lasted nearly half an hour.

After listening to the two bulls, we finished our ride to the top camp and put up our tents. By the time that was done, Kitty, the camp cook, had our food ready. We sat around the campfire that night and talked about what we had seen and heard.

The sight of his moose rack on the pack horse made Doug E. Frank forget about time and the long ride back to camp in the dark. His Canada moose scores 240-6/8 points and received a First Place Award at the 25th Awards Program in Kansas City.

At first light, Charlie woke me up. Our horses had wandered off during the night, even though they were hobbled. We started hunting as we followed the tracks of the horses. Charlie eventually went on ahead and rounded them up while I continued hunting.

Once Charlie came back with the horses, we saddled up and rode to the top of a place called Moose Mountain. From there, we could see far in every direction. There were valleys and timber below us, with meadows and another area with six-foot high willow shrubs. We saw only one small moose as we glassed.

That afternoon we spotted about 10 different bulls and some cows, but no big bulls. We saw a grizzly walking through the timber below us, and we also heard a wolf howling in the timber. As the sun started to go down so did the temperature. The 45-minute ride back to camp seemed to take 2 hours. It was nice to finally see the light of the campfire.

The next day, the weather really changed. It went from being in the 50s to snowing. The snow was so thick that visibility was limited to a few hundred yards. Charlie decided to take me near timberline, where he thought we would see some bulls.

We sat under some trees to stay out of the wet snow while Charlie called for a moose. It didn't take long for him to call in a small bull. It was within 75 yards before we could see it wasn't the one, so we let it walk back into the timber. We stayed there for five hours before both of us had enough of the wet and cold. We then decided to head back to camp to warm up and dry off.

BOONE AND CROCKETT CLUB'S

The next day the weather was the same. We took a four-hour ride into an area where Charlie had seen some bigger bulls two years earlier. As we arrived, we could see two bulls and three cows about 300 yards away.

CANADA MOOSE
First Award - 240 ⁶/₈

▼ ▼ ▼ ▼ ▼

DOUG E. FRANK

Charlie started calling and the bigger bull started toward us. The smaller bull then started pushing the cows into the timber. The big bull didn't seem to care because it liked the sounds Charlie was making. The moose came within 100 yards. Charlie said it had a 55-inch spread or better, but we would have to be patient if I wanted a bigger one. I said that was fine.

The snow never let up, so we decided to head back. Four hours later, I was glad to be back at camp. I was sore, tired, and hungry. It was nice to sit by the warmth of the fire, listening to the stories of the day and past hunts.

Sunday was sunny and without wind. Charlie wanted to go back where we had been, but I was reluctant because of the four-hour ride. He said there were 60-inch moose there and that this time we would spend the night out under the stars. So, Kitty packed us a few things for the trip while we prepared the horses. Kitty, who is not only camp cook, but also Charlie's girlfriend, went with us.

The weather warmed up to about 45 degrees as we rode on. We rode back in even further than we had on Saturday. We arrived at a glassing point about 1 p.m., where we glassed and ate lunch. Three bulls and several cows appeared in a meadow below us. One bull looked considerably bigger than the rest. As I watched these moose, Charlie was off looking at another area. When he returned, he said that he had spotted a really nice moose across the canyon. He looked at my moose and said that he thought this other one was bigger. The only problem was that it was clear across the canyon.

After some discussion, we all decided to go after the big moose. After a while, we left Kitty with the horses and took off on foot. When we got to where the moose should have been, we couldn't locate it, so we decided to go back where we had been glassing and make camp.

When we got back, Charlie took the horses to graze while I did some glassing. I saw some cows feeding in the meadow below me. That's when the moose stepped out from behind some trees. I knew instantly this was the bull I wanted. I found Charlie and asked him to check it out, just to make sure. When Charlie got there, he said it was definitely a good bull.

The only problem was the moose was 700 yards away. We had to work our way down the mountain to a rocky ledge. At this point, we were still 500 yards away. With legal shooting light coming to a close, we had to decide whether to take the bull now or wait until morning. We decided to try our shot from there, using the rocks as a rest.

With Charlie looking through his binoculars, I put the cross hairs on its back and fired at the moose. The bullet hit something solid, but the moose never moved. Charlie said to shoot again. I did, and again the moose never moved. I was starting to wonder if I was judging the distance correctly. Charlie said to shoot again so this time I took a deep breath and let it out. On this shot, the moose flinched, but now the cows were running into the timber. I was worried the bull would soon do the same. Just as I was set to pull the trigger again, it lifted its nose straight in the air and then tipped over.

Neither of us realized exactly how big the bull was until we saw it up close. It was the bull of a lifetime! It ended up weighing 1,600 pounds. We field dressed it that night and skinned it in the morning. While skinning the bull, we found three bullet holes behind its front shoulder, in a grouping about the size of a coffee can. This time the ride back to camp didn't seem to take as long. The sight of those moose antlers on the packhorse in front of me made me forget time. As we rode into camp, Dewey was there. He also was all smiles as he had taken a 58-inch moose.

We rode back to the base camp to wait for Jon to get his moose. When we arrived, we found the cooking tent all torn up. There had been a bear in camp looking for food.

Jon finally shot a 48-inch moose during a snowstorm in the area where I had shot mine. When it was time to go, we were all happy to leave. We were, however, excited about coming back again to a place where not many people can say they have been to hunt for a trophy animal. Hopefully we will have some more stories to tell in the future.

Moments in Measuring...

Photograph by Ryan Hatfield

Glenn Hisey, a member of the 25th Awards Judges Panel, begins preliminary work to determine the correct line for measuring the length of the palm on Mark Rose's Alaska-Yukon moose. Glenn is Chairman of Pope and Young Club's Record Committee.

Photograph by Cliff White

TROPHY STATS

▼ ▼ ▼ ▼ ▼

Category
Canada moose

Score
220³/₈

Location
Hancock County, Maine — 2002

Hunter
James T. Robertson

Greatest Spread Measurement
61³/₈

Length of Palm
Right: 43⁷/₈   Left: 43⁴/₈

Width of Palm
Right: 14⁴/₈   Left: 17³/₈

Number of Normal Points
Right: 16   Left: 14

Photograph by Jack R

James T. Robertson accepting his plaq
and medal from Buck Buckner, Chair
the Big Game Records Committee.

CANADA MOOSE
Second Award – 220³/₈

▼ ▼ ▼ ▼ ▼ ▼ ▼ ▼ ▼

JAMES T. ROBERTSON

I have always loved to hunt and fish. I have also been trapping since the age of 10. For many years, I have wanted to go on a hunt for something big, such as a moose, elk, or caribou. That finally happened in October 2002.

A co-worker named Tom Pittenger, whose daughter Angela lives in Maine, sent me an application for the moose hunt. I filled it out and drew the tag on my third year of trying. I made Zone 28 my first choice. The reason behind my choice was that it had only been open one year previous, so there should have been time for a moose to grow big in that zone.

I surfed on the Internet for camps, and for some reason, Eagle Lodge and Camps caught my eye. I booked my hunt with them.

I had a five-hour flight, with a changeover in Cincinnati. I flew into Bangor on Sunday, October 6, and was picked up at the airport by lodge owner John Rogers. Upon arriving, I settled in and met with the three guides and two other hunters that night. My guide was Marcus Rogers, John's brother. The two other hunters were from New York and Pennsylvania. The regulations were explained to us as well as what was required of each of us and what we could expect during the week. The journey was about to begin.

I'll be honest, I figured I wouldn't see a moose, much less kill the biggest of the year. We rode an hour and a half each day to Aurora, hunting hard for three days. We called, rode to different locations, tried canoe rides, and walked a lot. All of this took place in the most beautiful scenery I could imagine. Marcus cooked breakfast in the woods every morning and packed a lunch. We never left the woods and hunted all day long, every day, for nearly 12 hours a day. Whenever it was legal shooting time, we were hunting.

The New York hunter killed his moose on Tuesday in Zone 18. The Pennsylvania hunter got his moose on Wednesday in Zone 10. I was getting tired and a little discouraged, but Marcus promised he would find me a moose. I talked to my wife back in South Carolina each night and she kept telling me it was going to happen. When we left camp Thursday, Marcus was so confident. He said he didn't even pack a lunch because today was the day and it would happen quickly. I slept most of the trip that morning.

When we were several miles from the location we were going to hunt, Marcus told me to look in the road. Running in front of the truck was the biggest animal I had ever seen — a big bull moose. It was 30 minutes before legal shooting time and I just watched it disappear into the woods. Marcus said that it was about a 55-inch moose and asked if I wanted to try for it or go hunt the place he had picked out the night before. Now if any-

James Robertson's Canada moose collapsed in this creek after one shot from his .30-06. The moose scores 220-3/8 points and received a Second Place Award in Kansas City at the 25th Awards Program.

one wouldn't have tracked this moose for a little while, then I would worry for it was the first moose I had seen after hunting for several days.

We waited until legal hunting time, but things just didn't work out. We tracked the bull for several miles, and I guess it's probably still running. At least I had now seen a moose, and if I flew 1,200 miles from the house just to see one, I was happy. Things were improving!

We then decided to go to our original destination and try our luck. When we left the truck, Marcus said we were going to walk for a couple of miles toward a heath where he had spotted moose on several occasions. He had saved this place for later in the week because of the distance for packing out the moose if we were lucky enough to get one.

Marcus took a reading on his GPS and marked the truck's location. It was 9 a.m. when we headed into the woods. He kept calling every several hundred yards on his homemade coffee can call. After approximately 30 minutes, Marcus said he heard a cow in the distance and thought it was in the heath that he had told me about. "If there's a cow, there's probably a bull," he said.

He checked the wind and we tried to get a little closer on the downwind side. Quietly, we approached the heath. Marcus crawled and took a peek. He looked back over his shoulder and nodded his head that he saw a moose. It had its head down feeding. At this point, Marcus couldn't tell whether this was a bull or cow. After a minute, its head came up. That was the first time all week that Marcus got excited. He froze for a moment in amazement, then turned to me and whispered, "My God! It looks like two sheets of plywood!"

CANADA MOOSE
Second Award – 220 ³/₈
▼ ▼ ▼ ▼ ▼
JAMES T. ROBERTSON

I had to look. I crawled a few feet to him and looked. The moose's head was down again feeding. When the bull raised its head, I looked to Marcus and smiled. My words were, "That's what I came here for."

We were about 200 yards away and needed to crawl about 80 more to get in an opening for a shot. It seemed like the longest 10 minutes of my life. When we crawled to the opening, Marcus asked me if I could take it. I looked, and only 20 yards away was a dead tree for a good rest. I decided to make that little crawl. We took turns making sure the bull's head was down and we wouldn't be seen. The bull was at a great disadvantage, because its antlers were so huge you could tell easily when it was going to look up. Upon reaching the tree, I raised my rifle. I told myself to make the first one count.

At about 10:30 a.m., I put the cross hairs right behind the shoulder blade and squeezed. I heard the blast, and then the bull gave out a grunt as the 180-grain .30-06 bullet hit. The bull collapsed right out of sight. I looked back at Marcus. He said, "Darn! They usually don't just fall like that and disappear."

We stood up and could only see the tip of one antler moving a little. I asked Marcus, "Do you think I got it?"

The best words I heard on the entire hunt were the next. Marcus smiled, shook my hand, and said, "It's done."

We carefully walked over to the huge bull. I could only stand and shake my head in disbelief. The bull had fallen in the small stream where it was feeding. Marcus jumped in the water and started counting points. At first count he said 33. He looked at me and said, "You don't really realize what you have just done."

All I knew was that I had killed a moose. He then told me he had been guiding for 20 years and never seen anything close to this. This could be the new state record. I really just kind of blew this off. I was excited, but I wasn't even thinking about anything like that. I was just ecstatic to kill a moose. A life-long dream that most people never achieve had now come true for me.

Now the hard part was yet to come, or at least we thought. Marcus set our location on his GPS and we headed to the truck. We had to drive about a mile to the top of a hill with the cell phone to get a signal. He called back to the lodge and told his brother, John, to bring a trailer and some help. Marcus then let me make a phone call to my wife back home. I told her the story and what was ahead for the rest of the day. She was crying with joy and ready to tell my kids, who were in school.

Marcus and I went back and started flagging a trail to the moose, for what we thought would be an all day pack out. After two hours, John, his father, and the two other hunters arrived. They were all anxiously waiting to see this giant that Marcus had described (all skeptical of course).

As luck would have it, John heard a logging skidder in the far distance. He said, "Hold everything until I get back."

When John came back in about 30 minutes, he yelled that the skidder was coming, I think everyone felt relief. We tied a rope on the moose and dragged it about 100 yards and then carefully lifted it with the skidder. The logger drove the moose all the way to the vehicle and set it down on John's trailer. What luck! Then the trailer tires went flat and we had to get air for the tires.

Marcus field-dressed the bull and then we headed back to the lodge. The trip back to Lincoln seemed shorter than the previous three days. It was comical looking at all the thumbs up, chins dropping, and people shaking their heads in disbelief. We arrived back at camp too late to check the bull at the check station.

The next morning, the bull was transferred into a full-size Chevy truck for the ride to the check station. The trophy was then ready to be delivered to the taxidermist. The first words he said were, "Boone and Crockett."

He did a preliminary scoring, and at the time it would have been the new state record. After the drying period of 60 days, it was learned that the bull is the new number 2 All-time in Maine, falling short of the state record by less than an inch. Its final score is 220-3/8 points. It had a 61-3/8-inch spread and 30 points. It field-dressed 1,130 pounds.

The moose head was delivered to me on April 19 by Marcus. I might add that moose meat is delicious. Now my house has regular visitors to see the moose. The year 2002 was a great one for me. My eight-year old son, Jamie, also killed his first two deer (a doe and a six-point buck.)

I thank my dad, who passed away in 1985, for introducing me to the great heritage of hunting. I am now carrying on the family tradition. But most of all, I thank God for the experience of a lifetime. I don't intend to apply for a moose hunt in the future, but my son is already eager for a chance. Who knows, a big bull elk or caribou may be out there in the years ahead.

Award Winning Moments...

Photograph by Jack Reneau

Outdoor writer, Jim Zumbo accepts the Plaque of Appreciation on behalf of Mossy Oak Brand Camo recognizing them as an official sponsor of the Boone and Crockett Club's 25th Awards Program in Kansas City.

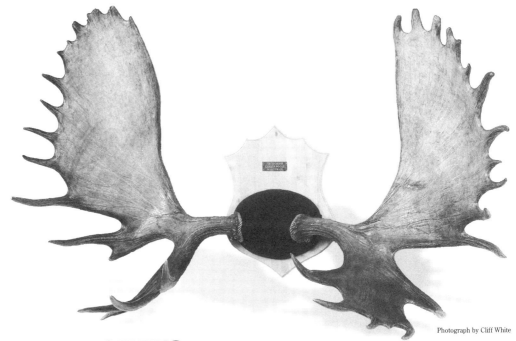

Photograph by Cliff White

TROPHY STATS

▼ ▼ ▼ ▼ ▼

Category
Canada moose

Score
217⁵/₈

Location
Buffalo River, Alberta — 2001

Hunter
Abe Teichroeb

Greatest Spread Measurement
64³/₈

Length of Palm
Right: 44³/₈   Left: 42⁷/₈

Width of Palm
Right: 16³/₈   Left: 15⁴/₈

Number of Normal Points
Right: 11   Left: 16

Photograph by Jack Re

Abe Teichroeb accepting his plaque and
medal from Buck Buckner, Chair of the
Big Game Records Committee.

CANADA MOOSE
Third Award – 217 5/8

▼ ▼ ▼ ▼ ▼ ▼ ▼ ▼ ▼

ABE TEICHROEB

In late September 2001, our family had our annual moose hunt. We left home at 6 a.m. Monday morning. There were 50 miles to travel with truck and trailer, and then another 20 miles with our quads. Our hunting area is located around and near the Buffalo River that runs into the mighty Peace River. This year our hunting group included me, Bill, John, and Willy Teichroeb.

On the way to our camp, we had some trouble getting through the swamps, but finally managed to get to our campground at 1:30 p.m. We prepared lunch, fried some burgers, and geared up for the evening hunt.

John got his moose, which green-scored around 150 B&C, on Wednesday morning. The last three days of the week, I spent time calling about a mile north from camp. I heard a moose answer every day. It seemed to be a very smart moose because it never came out into the opening.

Saturday morning, we made our way to where I had been calling. There before us stood this moose with an enormous rack. It instantly started walking away from us, so we decided to take the shot. The moose was around 450 yards away, and we didn't know if we had hit it or not. My son, Bill, and I followed the moose through the brush, where I got another shot at it. The moose stumbled and continued on. When Bill and I came out of the bush onto the detour trail, Willy and Bill followed the detour while John and I looked for a sign of blood. We found blood and managed to track it down into a valley, where we found it. We then field-dressed it and hauled the bull to a cooler in town.

In April 2002, I made a trip to Grande Prairie to get the antlers scored by Brent Watson, who is an official measurer for the Boone and Crockett Club. The final score turned out to be 217-5/8 points.

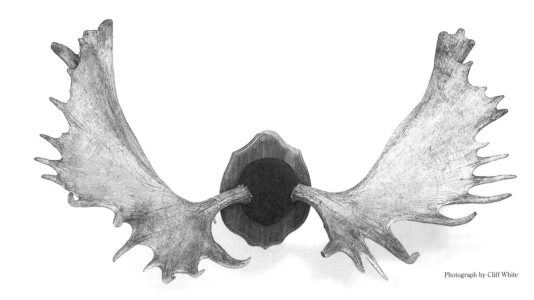

Photograph by Cliff White

TROPHY STATS

▼ ▼ ▼ ▼ ▼

Category
Alaska-Yukon moose

Score
247⁷/₈

Location
Rapid Creek, Alaska — 2003

Hunter
Mark S. Rose

Greatest Spread Measurement
80³/₈

Length of Palm
Right: 45⁶/₈   Left: 46²/₈

Width of Palm
Right: 21²/₈   Left: 18⁵/₈

Number of Normal Points
Right: 11   Left: 11

Photograph by Jack Ren

Mark S. Rose accepting his plaque and
medal from Buck Buckner, Chair of the
Big Game Records Committee.

ALASKA-YUKON MOOSE
First Award - 247⁷/₈

▼ ▼ ▼ ▼ ▼ ▼ ▼ ▼ ▼

MARK S. ROSE

"Mark, you need to take your hunting to the next level," urged my big brother, Gary. I knew I should listen to him. I have hunted whitetails in my home state of Texas all my life and have shot a pronghorn in New Mexico; my brother, however, has hunted all over the world. I finally agreed, and Gary made all the arrangements for my moose hunt on the Alaska Peninsula. Even after all the preparations had been made, I had a difficult time being comfortable with the trip, which would be a big deal for me, and also being away from my business for two weeks.

I arrived at Wildman Lake Lodge with several other hunters in early September, the day before moose season opened. The following day, my guide, Bill Burwell, and I waited our turn for the bush plane to take us to a spike camp. We were the last group to go. By afternoon, the weather had turned for the worse and we had to stay at the lodge another day. This seemed to be a bad break. I had really wanted to be in the field for opening day.

The next day we flew out and set up spike camp at the base of a frozen volcano. We had several hours of daylight left after setting up camp, so we decided to glass. We made our way through thick alders to a spot overlooking Rapid Creek Valley. I learned at this point the terrain was terribly rough and the hunt was going to be very physically demanding — much more so than anything I had faced on previous hunts — but I was ready for the challenge.

From our vantage point we could see probably two miles in either direction. As we began glassing the valley, we saw the flash of an antlered palm belonging to a moose that was lying on the edge of the alders. We continued to watch the bull, which was about 800 yards away. When the moose stood up, we almost died. Bill said it was the biggest bull he had ever seen (and he had seen plenty of moose in his long career of guiding) and guessed that the bull's rack had an 80-inch spread. I knew the moose was a monster, but I did not know how good Bill's long range judging was. I couldn't legally shoot the moose on the same day that we arrived in spike camp, so we returned to camp and waited for tomorrow.

The next morning, we went back to the same overlook and were shocked to find the monster moose in the same spot as before. With the help of a spotting scope, we counted 34 points. Bill insisted the moose was 80 inches wide with a bell about 30 inches long. We proceeded down the mountain across the raging stream and battled our way through the woven alders to the grassy area where we had located the bull . . . but it had vanished. It had probably heard us thrashing through the alders. We found a 20-foot circle where the moose had been bedding down, and waited for it to return. We never saw the moose again that day.

Mark S. Rose with his First-Award Alaska-Yukon moose taken near Rapid Creek, Alaska. Mark took this moose after spotting it several days earlier. His patience paid off when he connected with this bull, which scores 247-7/8 points.

The next morning we returned to our overlook and saw a smaller bull with a cow. "He's about 70 inches," Bill said, "You might consider going for it. He's definitely a shooter." I told Bill that I had six more days in the field and we were going for the big one! The next day we saw the huge bull back in the exact spot where we had first spotted it. Bill and I discussed what went wrong with our previous stalk and came up with a plan so the moose would not hear our approach. We hiked about 300 yards downwind before cutting into the alders to work our way back toward the animal along an old game trail.

I was ready! We walked up the trail until the giant moose stood up in front of us. It was looking straight us at about 100 yards. I shot it twice behind the front shoulder. Bill yelled to keep shooting. He was afraid that the moose would run into the alders, making the task of skinning and quartering much more difficult. I took two more shots and then saw the moose collapse in the grass.

Bill field-measured the antlers with a string and told me the rack was close to 81 inches wide. We spent the rest of the day taking photos, skinning and quartering the huge moose. It got late in the day and since we were three hours from spike camp, we pitched a tent right next to the carcass. I will always remember Bill telling me to make sure I had a bullet in the chamber and to turn the scope all the way down. "If we have some action tonight it's going to be really close," he warned me. It rained all night long, but fortunately, the bears stayed away.

ALASKA-YUKON MOOSE
First Award – 247 4/8

▼ ▼ ▼ ▼ ▼

MARK S. ROSE

The trophy is the largest Alaska-Yukon moose entered in the Boone and Crockett Club's 25th Awards Program. With a score of 247-7/8 B&C points, it places fourteenth in the all-time records book. The moose rack has a spread of 80-3/8 inches, making it the third largest spread ever recorded.

Photograph by Cliff White

TROPHY STATS

▼ ▼ ▼ ▼ ▼

Category
Alaska-Yukon moose

Score
238

Location
Kenai Peninsula, Alaska — 2002

Hunter
Richard K. Mayer

Greatest Spread Measurement
$70^4/_8$

Length of Palm
Right: $49^2/_8$ Left: $46^4/_8$

Width of Palm
Right: 15   Left: $15^4/_8$

Number of Normal Points
Right: 14   Left: 16

Photograph by Jack Renea

Richard K. Mayer accepting his plaque
and medal from Buck Buckner, Chair of
the Big Game Records Committee.

ALASKA-YUKON MOOSE
Second Award – 238

▼ ▼ ▼ ▼ ▼ ▼ ▼ ▼ ▼

RICHARD K. MAYER

My hunt started in Kenai, Alaska, with my good friend and hunting buddy of many years, Jim Sobol. I booked my 14-day moose hunt through Cabela's with Alaska Saddle Safari's Outfitters for September 2002. My guide was Laine Lahndt, a registered guide with many years of experience calling and hunting moose. I was trying for my moose grand slam since I had already killed a Canada and Wyoming (Shiras) moose.

We started the hunt by taking a float plane to Border Lake in the National Moose Range. Then we rode horses for three hours to our wilderness tent camp in an area we would be hunting that has size restrictions on moose. In order to be legal, the moose antlers must have three eye guard tines or be 50 inches wide.

We started hunting every day by walking miles in different directions, glassing, and looking for moose. I was not trophy hunting; I just wanted any legal bull.

I hunted hard for days, seeing only black bears, a few cow moose, one small forked horn bull, and a brown bear. The weather was warm, about 60°F to 70°F with rain every day. We needed a cold night with a hard frost to make the moose move and start their rut. Jim, my hunting partner, hadn't seen much either. On the seventh day, Jim did shoot a nice black bear at close range (10 feet) while it stood up on its hind legs.

It was on the tenth day of the hunt that I got my moose. It was raining on and off all day. Late that afternoon, I was watching a beautiful rainbow to the northeast, when up on a hill I thought I saw something. With my binoculars, I saw what looked like a big bull moose about a mile away. My guide started calling to the moose by rattling and hitting trees with his homemade paddle (an oil can taped to a stick.) He also grunt-called with a moose magnet.

We did not see the moose on the hill anymore, as it had started to walk down the hill heading in our direction. Waiting for over an hour, I was standing there thinking I'm cold, hungry, and wanting to start the long walk back to camp. I never thought the moose would hear the calling and come to us from

Photograph courtesy of Richard K. Mayer

Richard K. Mayer, right, and his good friend and hunting buddy, Jim Sobol, pictured together with Richard's award-winning Alaska-Yukon moose.

Richard took his Alaska-Yukon moose on the tenth day of his hunt on Alaska's Kenai Peninsula with a Browning A-Bolt Stainless Stalker .300 Win. Mag. The bull scores 238 points and has a total of 30 points.

that far away. Just then Laine turned to me, pointed, and yelled, "Moose!"

The bull was coming on the ridge right at us. It must have heard the calling. At about 85 yards, it turned and started to go down the ridge away from us. Laine made some cow calls and said not to shoot until he stopped the moose. I thought maybe Laine was trying to see if it was legal, but he knew it was a large moose! The bull stopped at about 135 yards, and Laine said, "Shoot!"

Everything seemed to go in slow motion. I had turned to get my Browning A-Bolt Stainless Stalker .300 Win. Mag., which was leaning against a tree. I had to pop up the scope covers and rack a shell in the chamber to get ready for the shot.

I shot once, hitting the moose. It was a big animal, and even the .300 was not enough to bring it down with one shot. I sent some more rounds its way, connecting on all but one. Eventually, the big animal fell dead in its tracks.

Laine and I said our congratulations and took some pictures. He had a measuring tape with him that went to 62 inches, so we measured the antlers and saw that they were still about 10 inches wider! What a moose!

By this point, it was starting to get dark. It was also starting to rain again, and we still had a long walk back to camp. That night I did not sleep because I was so excited. All I could think about was my moose, and that a brown bear might get to it before we got back in the morning.

Early the next morning several of us from camp went back to cut and pack out my moose. We didn't know just how large it was until we saw it in the morning light. After taking lots of pictures, we measured my moose. It was just over 70 inches wide, had 30 points, and green scored about 244.

ALASKA-YUKON MOOSE
Second Award – 238
▼ ▼ ▼ ▼ ▼
RICHARD K. MAYER

It took seven horses to pack the meat and antlers out to the float plane. Once there, the pilot had to tie the antlers to the plane's floats because they were so large. The pilot said this was the first time ever that he could not fit the antlers of a moose inside the plane.

We kept some moose meat in camp, even the moose heart that the guides were going to cook up for us. Maybe the fresh meat smell is what attracted the bear, as later that night we had a large black bear come to camp and into our tent. It was just a few feet from Jim's head! After the bear walked out, it started to bite and drink our soda. Jim tried to wake me to shoot it because I still had a black bear tag. During the scramble to get my gun and shoot the bear, however, it ran off in the darkness. Before the bear left, he managed to drink our soda and even stole the moose heart from inside the outfitters tent. The bear bit right through their tent screen to get it.

After 14 days in the woods, my moose was the only legal bull we ever saw. What a way to make my moose grand slam! The only really nice sunny day we had on the whole trip was the day we left camp. It made for a beautiful horse ride to get on the float plane.

Thanks again to Lou Albrant, outfitter of Alaska Saddle Safaris and my guide, Laine Lahndt, for memories of a lifetime and a real Alaskan moose adventure.

TROPHY STATS

▼ ▼ ▼ ▼ ▼

Category
Wyoming moose

Score
193

Location
Bingham County, Idaho — 2000

Hunter
Richard K. Smith

Greatest Spread Measurement
51

Length of Palm
Right: $40^4/_8$ Left: $42^2/_8$

Width of Palm
Right: $14^1/_8$ Left: $11^7/_8$

Number of Normal Points
Right: 12   Left: 14

Richard K. Smith accepting his plaque
and medal from Buck Buckner, Chair of
the Big Game Records Committee.

BOONE AND CROCKETT CLUB'S

WYOMING MOOSE
First Award – 193

▼ ▼ ▼ ▼ ▼ ▼ ▼ ▼ ▼

RICHARD K. SMITH

The moose hunt in my part of Idaho lasts nearly three months, from September until November. It is a once-in-a-lifetime draw for Idaho residents, and that's about how long it took me to draw it. I started trying in 1969, and finally received my permit in the summer of 2000! My hunting partners on this particular hunt were my 13-year-old son, Russell, Brian Cammack, and Kay Martin.

It was a good time to draw this tag. We had spotted, during the previous two seasons, a huge moose in the hunting area for which we were applying. On October 6, Kay Martin spotted the bull once again. We knew right away that it was the one we were looking for.

I shot it with a .45-70 at a distance of about 200 yards. The moose was killed in the Blackfoot Mountains, which is only about 30 miles east of my home.

This moose was worth the wait. According to Boone and Crockett, it is the second-largest moose ever taken in my home state of Idaho.

Photograph by Cliff White

TROPHY STATS

▼ ▼ ▼ ▼ ▼

Category
Wyoming moose

Score
$187^3/_8$

Location
Bonneville County, Idaho — 2000

Hunter
Robin R. Pearson

Greatest Spread Measurement
$50^3/_8$

Length of Palm
Right: $42^4/_8$ Left: $42^7/_8$

Width of Palm
Right: $12^7/_8$ Left: $12^4/_8$

Number of Normal Points
Right: 13   Left: 7

WYOMING MOOSE
Second Award - 187³/₈

▼ ▼ ▼ ▼ ▼ ▼ ▼ ▼ ▼

ROBIN R. PEARSON

My best friend, Les, called me one day in the summer of 2000. He said he had been on the Idaho Fish and Game web site to see if we had drawn a moose tag and had called to let me know that our names had been chosen. The excitement began.

We immediately started to make plans. Most of the hunting area that we had drawn was on private ground, so we started to make calls to the landowners to get permission to hunt on their land. We also called people who would have information about moose in the area. We then started to scout and become familiar with our hunt unit. My personal goal on this hunt was to harvest a 50-inch moose. I also decided that I wanted to shoot it with my bow.

The anticipation continued to grow as the season neared. We finally made the decision to hunt in the Wolverine area. On the opening weekend, August 30, it was hot and dry. We saw a lot of sign but no bulls. We continued to hunt on the weekends through both August and September. We saw a lot of moose, but no bulls with the size that I wanted.

Toward the first of October, the weather had started to cool off. At this point, the bigger bulls started to appear. Finally, my buddy harvested a nice bull in the first part of October. I wasn't able to go with him that day because I had to work.

We then planned a week-long hunt for the last week of October in a new area where we had permission to hunt on a big ranch. We got up to a cool, rainy day. We did a lot of spotting and glassing, finding a great deal of moose. One particular herd had about seven bulls in it, but they were about three miles away.

We worked our way closer and glassed them again discovering that there were some really nice bulls in this herd. After deciding to stalk the herd, we worked our way up through some cows and calves. There wasn't much cover, just a few quaking aspens and brush. We got within about 500 yards of the herd, but then they took off.

We glassed them again. They were just too far away to harvest with a rifle. I had decided earlier to harvest my moose with my bow, but had my rifle with me just in case I changed my mind. While glassing the moose, we could see that there were some nice bulls. We watched them as they went over the top of the ridge, then we circled around, hoping to find them on the other side. As we got up on top and tried to stay in the brush, we saw several bunches of moose. None of them, however, were the ones we had spooked over the top.

As we worked our way around to a rock outcropping that looked into some brush down below us, we tried to stay in the brush as much as we could until we were up on top. These brush patches were comprised of aspen, alders, and other types of brush, most of which were about three inches in diameter. They were also as thick and tangled as hair on a dog's back, and almost impossible to walk through.

We could finally see the group about 30 yards below us, but the brush was so thick that it was difficult to make them out well. It was impossible to shoot one with a rifle, let alone a bow. What was probably only several minutes of waiting seemed like an eternity.

We had to devise a plan. Because there was a clearing to the right side of us, Les would work his way down and to the left. I stayed where I was. When Les got closer the bulls started moving to the right, just like we had hoped they would. As the bulls started to move out of the brush to where I could see them, I realized that they were going to be too far away for the bow. I left the pack and the bow and took my rifle.

There was one bull that kept hanging back, and it was difficult to see which one was the big bull that I had glassed. I began frantically glassing again to see if I could tell which one was the biggest bull. From what I could see, it was the one hanging back. My gut instinct agreed, telling me that the biggest bull was the one hanging back and letting the younger ones come out first.

I watched as the first bulls began to walk out of sight. At this point, I committed myself to concentrating on the one that was hanging back. I felt strongly that it was the biggest. After studying the moose in the binoculars, I became certain that it was a nice bull. I also knew that I would never know which one was really the biggest because the others were gone now.

I looked through my range finder and saw that it was at 137 yards. I knew the bull was going to get the heck out of there as soon as I shot so I found a good rest, picked a spot in the vitals, and shot. It went down right in its tracks. I watched the bull closely through the scope to see if it would get up, but it never did.

About then, Les yelled to see if I had killed my moose. I didn't answer him. I wanted to watch the bull a little longer, just to make sure it didn't get up. Eventually, I yelled back to Les to let him know that I had it down.

I approached the bull, excited to see how big it was. When I got there, I found that the moose was more than big enough to meet the goal I had set for myself. Several of my friends said I should have it measured, so I did. Not only was the bull 50 inches, it also made the records book! It was on October 27, 2000, that my life-long dream to shoot a trophy bull moose became a reality

Award Winning Moments...

Photograph by Keith Balfourd

Trophy owners, guests, Club members, and associates gathered at the trophy display in Cabela's on the first night of the 25th Awards Program to kick off the event.

Photograph by Cliff White

TROPHY STATS

▼ ▼ ▼ ▼ ▼

Category
Wyoming moose

Score
181

Location
Jackson County, Colorado — 2001

Hunter
Dennis Pahlisch

Greatest Spread Measurement
$52^4/_8$

Length of Palm
Right: $35^4/_8$ Left: $35^6/_8$

Width of Palm
Right: $11^3/_8$ Left: $11^6/_8$

Number of Normal Points
Right: 11   Left: 12

WYOMING MOOSE
Third Award - 181

▼ ▼ ▼ ▼ ▼ ▼ ▼ ▼ ▼

DENNIS PAHLISCH

A lot of today's trophy hunts begin with drawing the tag. I was very excited in April, 2001 to realize that I had drawn a Wyoming moose tag in Area 7 of Colorado. I got busy and started checking out outfitters that had hunted this area in the past. I booked a hunt with Scott Limmer of Comanche Creek Outfitters and Co-outfitter Red Feather Guide Service near Waldon, Colorado. My wife was able to join me on the trip; it was an extra bonus to have her near when a trophy-of-a-lifetime like this could be harvested.

We started hunting national forest the first two days of the hunt, seeing several cow moose and a few small bulls. We walked 10 to 15 miles per day, calling many times during the day, trying to find that special bull, On the third day of the hunt, we received permission from a local rancher to enter the forest through private property. We arrived at the ranch that morning right at sunup because we did not want to disturb the rancher any earlier. We confirmed the permission and proceeded up the ranch road to the national forest.

We had only been hunting about 10 minutes when to our surprise we saw a bull and two cow moose standing about 300 yards ahead. We continued to sneak and crawl closer until

we could get a view of the moose again. At once we noticed the immense spread and the many points on the bull's antlers. We patiently advanced inches at a time until we were within 250 yards of the moose.

The first shot sunk home and I knew in my mind that even though the mammoth animal did not fall, it was mine. After two quick follow-up shots, the moose lay dead, and the excitement and celebration began.

This is definitely not the most difficult trophy taken that hangs on the wall in my den, but by far it is the best trophy as far as ranking in the Boone and Crockett Club. I would like to give thanks again first to my wife for putting up with my passion and joining me in my past hunts and future hunts. And next, thanks to Scott and Todd, the outfitters, for the much enjoyed hunt.

Photograph courtesy of Dennis Pahlisch

Dennis Pahlisch drew a Wyoming moose tag in Area 7 of Colorado for the 2001 season. He took this award-winning moose, which scores 181 points.

Photograph by Cliff White

TROPHY STATS

▼ ▼ ▼ ▼ ▼

Category
mountain caribou

Score
440$^7/_8$

Location
Nisling River, Yukon Territory — 2003

Hunter
Larry D. Merillat

Inside Spread Measurement
42$^6/_8$

Length of Main Beam
Right: 57$^2/_8$ Left: 55$^3/_8$

Width of Brow Palm
Right: 11$^2/_8$ Left: 9

Number of Points
Right: 16   Left: 16

Photograph by Jack Ren[...]

Larry D. Merillat accepting his plaque an[d]
medal from Buck Buckner, Chair of the
Big Game Records Committee.

MOUNTAIN CARIBOU
First Award – 440 7/8

▼ ▼ ▼ ▼ ▼ ▼ ▼ ▼ ▼

LARRY D. MERILLAT

This hunting story began in the spring of 2001. I was getting ready to retire from my job after 42 years. I had commented that instead of a fancy watch at retirement I would rather have a nice hunting trip to the Yukon or South Africa.

My retirement party was scheduled for the end of March 2001. A couple of weeks before then, my wife asked me what it would cost to take one of these trips. I told her that from what I had checked out it would be about $15,000 or more. She told me later that someone from the company had called to see if she could get that info from me without letting on that they were asking.

At the retirement party, I received a check from the president for the total amount, to be applied to whichever hunt I chose. This started the process of checking out outfitters in the Yukon, which is the place I picked to go.

After looking over four or five, I narrowed it down to two. Then I made some phone calls to speak in person to the owners. My main goal was to get a 60 inch or better moose, within an area that also allowed me to hunt mountain caribou and grizzly. I already had a barren ground caribou and a woodland caribou. These were nice trophies, but not in the records book. It was the same with moose. I had one from Newfoundland and one from Wyoming, but they were only 34 inches wide or smaller, hence the goal for a 60-incher.

I talked with Tim and Jen Mervyn, of Mervyn's Yukon Outfitting, about what they could offer. I then called five of the hunting references to check out their experiences. All had had good hunts and seen many animals. I was hooked. I called Tim back and booked a hunt for the 2003 season to get the best hunting 15 days in September.

Then the planning began of which rifle and load to use. I have both the .338 Winchester Mag. and the .340 Weatherby Mag. I do my own hand-loading, so I tried some loads in each. In the end, I decided on the .340 Weatherby and a 250-grain Nosler

The main camp on the Kltaz River for Larry Merillat's 2003 mountain caribou hunt.

Partition bullet sighted in 1-1/2 inch high at 100 yards. This is basically the same load I had used on my caribou hunt in Newfoundland.

I had decided to drive my pickup and pull a small trailer to Whitehorse, Yukon. I wanted to bring back the meat, and if I did get a good moose and caribou I wanted the room to haul them without any problems. However, now I had another problem because my wife didn't want me to drive that far all by myself. So she started asking different people if they knew of anyone who might want to go with me.

It didn't take very long before I heard from a friend of mine I used to work with named Dick Anspaugh. He had retired three years before me. He came by and asked if he could go with me. He had never gone on any kind of hunt like this before. He had hunted white-tail deer for many years, but that was about it. I agreed and began going over with him what he needed to take for the hunting trip. He would be using a .30-06 with 180-grain Nosler Partition bullets.

We spent the next year shooting our rifles and doing a lot of walking to get in shape for the hunt. Then, three months before the hunt, he twisted his leg and hurt his knee. After a call to Tim, he said he felt that Dick could still hunt because we would be using horses for the long hauls.

We left for the Yukon on September 4, 2003, taking turns driving and going for 10 hours or more each day. We arrived in Whitehorse on September 9, checked into the motel and gave Tim a call to tell him we had arrived. His wife Jen answered and said he was out at one of the hunting camps, but was expected back later that day and would have him call us. A couple hours later he called and wanted us to come to his home for a talk about the hunt, and to see how Dick was walking with his bad leg. We talked about the hunting season so far, which Tim said was going very well. They had already taken some really nice animals. After he saw Dick walk around some, he said that there was a camp called Willows Camp that would let him hunt all three animals with only short horseback rides and stalks.

Then he told me I wasn't going to be so lucky. Where he was sending me would require some long horseback rides to cover all the ground necessary while looking for the type of game we wanted to hunt. He said there were some really big caribou that had been seen in that area the week or so before. It was called the Klatz River Camp, and asked if I could leave for camp that day. Since he had so many hunters to take out the next day, he wanted to take me part way and stay overnight at the Nesling River Camp. When the plane brought the other hunter in on September 11, I would be picked up and taken on to the Klatz River Camp. I agreed, and we did it.

When the plane landed as close to the camp as it could get, we actually landed on top of a mountain. The pilot said the camp was a half-hour ride by horseback from where he had to land. We had barely got out and started unloading my gear when my guide, Mark Greenlee, and the horse wrangler, Mike Schroeder, came up over the edge of the mountain with the horses to pack us back to the camp.

We were in camp by 2 p.m., but since we could not hunt that day, we just went through gear and got acquainted. Mark talked about what to expect the next day. He said that we

would ride back to the top of the
mountain and then go to the northwest on the high ridges.

The next day, we saw a few cow
caribou, followed by a nice big bull.
We watched it for about 20 minutes,

MOUNTAIN CARIBOU
First Award – 440⁷/₈

▼ ▼ ▼ ▼ ▼
Larry D. Merillat

but Mark said that we could do better. I said I would trust his judgment, so we let it pass.
We didn't see any larger bulls the rest of the day, so we went back to camp. We spent about
three hours on horseback that day. The following day we saw only cows and small bulls.

The next day started out about the same, with a little snow and strong winds up on the
high ridges. We saw a few cows and small bulls again about noon, and decided to go a little farther. We then stopped to eat our lunch and use the spotting scope for a while.

As we came around the next mountain, we were about 100 yards below the top. Mark
quickly pulled up and told me to get off the horse. He had seen some caribou along the
mountain. He took a quick look through his spotting scope and said that there was a really nice one we should get a better look at. By the time we reached the top of the mountain,
we were tuckered out. It was about 80 feet across the top and we could see over both sides
when we stood up.

On the left side there were about a dozen cows and two bulls. The smaller bull was
about the size of the one we spotted the day before. The other one was a lot bigger than
the first, but we didn't realize how big it truly was. Mark had me get down and use my
backpack as a rest for my rifle. We kept watching as the group of animals got closer. At
about 150 yards, we could see they were angling down the mountain away from us.

I told Mark I was going to take my shot. I shot, and it was a clean miss; I still don't know
what happened. They turned and started running back the way they had come from. I tried
another shot and shot right under the bull. Then they went out of sight around the shoulder of the mountain. Mark said, "Well, that's that. Let's watch and see where they go."

In just a few minutes they came into sight on the right side of the mountain, so we
moved over and set up to watch them again. They had stopped running, but were moving
at a fast walk and coming right at us about 50 yards from the top. After reloading and trying to get calmed down, I was all set up again and waiting. Mark and Mike were both
watching with me and saying to just calm down and to breathe deeply a few times. The
caribou stopped at 80 yards and milled around, with some looking back the way they had
come from. They still didn't know what had happened. Mark said, "When the bull is clear
of the other cows, go ahead and take a shot."

I did. The big bull took about three steps and went down, with the others just milling
around and unsure of what the danger was. After watching a short time, we stood up at
the edge of the mountain. Then the other caribou saw us and started walking on, watching us as they moved away. As they got far enough south they got wind of us and started
running to the east and the next mountain. The closer we got to the downed bull, the more
Mark kept saying, "Boy, it is big."

Larry Merillat and his good friend, Dick Anspaugh, drove to the Yukon for the 2003 hunt. Larry took this award-winning bull scoring 440-7/8 points.

After we took some pictures and congratulated each other on a good hunt, we all began to realize how big it actually was. After skinning and bagging meat in some mesh meat bags, we went back to camp for the night.

That night we called Tim on the radio phone to tell him we were ready to have the meat and antlers picked up the next day. The next morning we brought everything back to the airstrip on top of the mountain with all the pack horses. Tim flew in and picked everything up, taking the load back to Whitehorse to the meat locker for processing.

Over the next few days, Dick and I were able to take some more fine animals. I fulfilled my dream of getting a 60-inch moose, by taking a 65-incher! Dick also had great success. His caribou scored around 404 and his moose was 61 inches wide. And to top it off, he got a seven-foot blond grizzly; all this on his very first hunting trip. He was 69 years old and said he couldn't have asked for a better hunt-of-a-lifetime.

We left the next day for home with our meat, skins, and antlers. We sure were glad we had taken the trailer. By the time we arrived home, it was October 4, we had driven 7,069 miles round trip, and had been gone a whole month. After waiting the 60 days for drying, my caribou scored 440-7/8. What a very nice surprise when I wasn't really set on anything that big when I started out! I really appreciated how Tim and Jen of Mervyn's Yukon Outfitters took care of us. They are a class act in my book.

Photograph by Cliff White

TROPHY STATS

▼ ▼ ▼ ▼ ▼

Category
mountain caribou

Score
$416^7/_8$

Location
Arctic Red River, Northwest
Territories — 2002

Hunter
Garth W. Peterson

Inside Spread Measurement
$45^2/_8$

Length of Main Beam
Right: $50^3/_8$ Left: $49^5/_8$

Width of Brow Palm
Right: 10   Left: 5

Number of Points
Right: 18   Left: 21

Photograph by Jack Renea

Garth W. Peterson accepting his plaque
and medal from Buck Buckner, Chair of
the Big Game Records Committee.

MOUNTAIN CARIBOU
Second Award – 416 ⁷/₈

▼ ▼ ▼ ▼ ▼ ▼ ▼ ▼ ▼

GARTH W. PETERSON

This hunt began to take shape at the 2000 Rocky Mountain Elk Foundation convention. Kelly Hougen, owner of Arctic Red River Outfitters Ltd. (Northwest Territories) and I have had booths at this show for a number of years. We had discussed the possibility of a Dall's sheep and mountain caribou hunt on numerous occasions.

Since this hunt would be a 10-day backpack hunt and I wasn't getting any younger, I booked with Kelly for August 27 through September 7, 2002. It would be my retirement present. My son, Matt Peterson, would be my hunting partner.

Two years passed quickly, with time spent operating our own outfitting business in northern Colorado. Many days

The Arctic Red and a Trophy Caribou

were spent trying to get my body into shape to carry 50-60 pounds of backpack up and down the Mckenzie Mountains. Many more hours were spent trying to picture this magnificent country in my mind. I have been to northern Canada many times over the years, but never to this area.

August 25, 2002, saw us boarding our flight in Denver for Edmonton, Alberta. There was an overnight stay in Edmonton, then on to a Canadian North B737 for our flight through to Yellowknife, N.W.T., then to Norman Wells, N.W.T. Here we met the other hunters who would be our companions for the next 10 to 12 days.

August 27 dawned to reveal fog along the McKenzie River that would delay our departure for base camp on the Arctic Red River. Around mid-morning, the fog began to burn off and our group boarded a North Wright Airways Twin Otter for the one-hour flight northwest from Norman Wells to base camp. As the wheels left the runway, I looked over at my son and could see the same feeling of adventure, anticipation, and excitement mirrored in his eyes that I was feeling. Spectacular country with rivers, lakes, and muskeg slipped beneath us; all the while the Mckenzies grew larger. This was truly wilderness. This was why we had come north.

With a couple of short detours to take a look at a good bull moose or some sheep on a barren slope, we were soon on our downwind leg for landing on Arctic Red's gravel airstrip. Soon, we were all out greeting Kelly, his staff, and a group of hunters who were waiting to depart with their trophies. As the Twin Otter departed, Kelly instructed all of us to climb aboard the four-wheelers for the short ride from the airstrip to the lodge. Here, Matt and I found out that we would have about three hours to do a final sort of our gear.

Then we would be flying out to meet our respective guides. They had flown out earlier that day to the areas we planned to hunt.

A few hours later we were back at the airstrip. I was to fly out first as I had the longest flight. Matt would follow, but to a different location. I did not realize it at the time, but I would not see him again, except briefly from the air for the next 10 days.

With my backpack in the baggage area, me in the back seat, and Kelly at the controls of the Super Cub, we headed west up the Arctic Red. Forty-five minutes of flying over the most beautiful country I had ever seen brought us to the point where Kelly pointed out a small improvised landing strip marked out with blaze orange tape on a gravel bar in the Arctic Red. The tundra tires smoothly touched down on the gravel, we rolled to a stop, and I had my first meeting with the young man who would be my guide and companion for the next 10 days, Mr. Tavis Molnar.

Kelly headed back to base. Tavis, with a slight grin said, "I hope you saved enough room in your pack to carry half the food and camp gear."

I grimaced and replied that I had. Since the gravel bar the landing strip was on was not suitable for an overnight camp, we struck out to wade part of the river and find a spot to set up our first night's camp. Wading the river with a 70-pound pack is not one of my most enjoyable endeavors, but with the aid of a walking stick and some instruction from Tavis, we selected a spot that was suitable and set up camp. This consisted of a four-man back-pack tent large enough to accommodate both of us, some clothing, and our rifles in relative comfort. This is grizzly country, and it is standard operating procedure to have your rifle handy at all times.

Tavis' plan was to reach a drainage that, to his knowledge, had not been hunted before. He had 13 years of guiding experience in this area and still had not seen it all. I do not know how to describe the immensity of this beautiful land. This would require one more move of camp, which was accomplished the next day. I might add that our first priority was to find a good Dall's ram. From this camp we could glass a number of sheep, but nothing that appeared to be mature full-curl rams.

Day three found us climbing the mountain next to camp to try and glass the drainage on the other side. It was a hard climb and I realized that I wasn't nearly as well-conditioned as I thought. After a number of hours glassing and looking over about five rams, Tavis quietly said, "There's the one we want."

Even though it was a long ways away, you could tell it was a beautiful animal. Back at camp that night, plans were laid to try and find an easier way into the valley the ram and its smaller partner were using. I knew it would be a tough day. After working our way literally up the stream bed coming out of the basin, we managed to get into position in the valley at a spot we could glass the rams we'd seen the day before. They were still located on a ledge that was not possible for us to reach. Tavis finally said, "We'll just have to wait and see if they move."

And move they did. After a few hours of lying on the ground through periods of sleet, snow, and sunshine, the rams were up and moving down the mountain. We were off, with the hope that they would come far enough down for us to make a stalk. Reaching a point where we believed we were directly below them, we started inching up over a scree pile when suddenly Tavis exclaimed, "There they are!"

MOUNTAIN CARIBOU
Second Award – 416 7/8
▼ ▼ ▼ ▼ ▼
GARTH W. PETERSON

He was pointing down to the creek bottom not 150 yards below us. Tavis was glassing the rams. I asked, "How does the ram look?"

As Tavis answered, "It's a dandy," I took the shot.

As we worked our way down to the ram, I was filled with such an array of emotion. Sitting beside the ram— even now, two years later, the tears come— the sadness, the joy, the reverence and so much more overcame me. We arrived back at camp that night at 11 p.m., two very tired and happy hunters with cape, horns, and boned out meat.. The next day was spent preparing the cape and making arrangements to be picked up and flown to a caribou spot. This all went well with the exception of having to create a landing strip for the Super Cub to land on, which took a little time. This done, two Cubs arrived. One took the horns, cape, and meat to base camp; the other took Tavis and me caribou hunting.

The new location was spectacular. It was an area Tavis had hunted often with good success, but not yet this year. After two days of glassing for caribou and seeing only grizzlies and wolves (a wonderful way to spend two days) the decision was made to move to another area. We landed at Caleb's Camp, crawled out of the Cub, and immediately began seeing caribou. Caleb's Camp is named after Tavis' younger brother, who is also a guide with Kelly. As with most camps used for any length of time in this country, this one also had its share of grizzly stories.

The terrain here was quite different from the steep mountains we had just visited. This landscape consisted more of rolling mountains and little cover. The next morning found us glassing from a spot Tavis liked. We soon located a group of five bulls, with one that required a closer look. The bull was hard to judge, because it seemed to have exceptional length on the main beams and points with a double shovel, but very little palmation. It had a very good spread, almost elk-looking. The bull looked great to me and Tavis thought it might go 370-380 B&C, so I said, "Let's go!"

Now I'm not an experienced caribou hunter, but the next five hours had me wondering why the bulls did what they did — first up one mountain, then back down to where we started, then off on another hike, never slowing enough to close the distance for a shot. Finally, they topped a rounded peak. I thought that was going to be the end of that bull, but Tavis knew better. He said, "Let's go; I think they might stay put up there."

By this time, I was dragging. We finally reached a spot just below the crest, when Tavis said, "Get your rifle out of your pack. I think they're just over the top."

I had no sooner done this than he exclaimed, "Here it comes!"

All I could see was a rack coming over the crest directly at us. There wasn't a thing

With the help of his guide, Tavis Molnar, Garth W. Peterson was able to connect with this mountain caribou in the Arctic Red River area of Northwest Territories. The bull has a total of 39 points and scores 416-7/8 points.

taller than lichen growing around us, so both of us were sitting there like rocks. Finally, at 60 yards, the bull turned enough to give me a quartering shot. That was all it took, and it was over.

The bull was a tremendous animal. We began now to suspect that it might be better than we had hoped for. I was humbled. I could not believe the blessings that were given to me on this hunt and I took a few moments to say, "Thank you."

The caping and boning of the meat was quickly handled by Tavis. We then shouldered our loads (I can't believe the weight that Tavis time and again carried) and head for camp. We arrived late that afternoon to find that Kelly and his father-in-law were there doing some maintenance, so the meat and antlers went back to base camp that evening. It was quite a sight to see that rack strapped to the strut of the Super Cub as they climbed away.

The next morning we were picked up and flown to base camp. A hot shower certainly hit the spot. Matt would not be in until the next day. Unfortunately, he had not had an opportunity to harvest an animal up to this point so I was hoping this last day of his hunt would produce some luck. I could see in his face when he climbed out of the Super Cub that that had not been the case. But, as he shared later, he had a wonderful guide and they spent some precious time in country and with wildlife the likes of which neither of us could have possibly imagined before this hunt.

To Kelly and Heather Hougen, all the staff, and especially to Tavis Molnar, my guide and now friend, I wish to say, "Thank you." It seems like such an infinitesimally small thing to say in return for such a monumentally wonderful two weeks. I have tried time and again to put into words my feelings — just how much this experience means to me, and I can't. So I'll just say thank you to those mentioned and to my Lord, for it was through his Grace that I was there.

Photograph by Cliff White

TROPHY STATS

▼ ▼ ▼ ▼ ▼

Category
woodland caribou

Score
329²/₈

Location
Parsons Pond, Newfoundland — 2000

Hunter
Donald L. Strickler

Inside Spread Measurement
40⁷/₈

Length of Main Beam
Right: 40³/₈   Left: 40²/₈

Width of Brow Palm
Right: 13³/₈   Left: 11¹/₈

Number of Points
Right: 10   Left: 13

Photograph by Jack René

Donald L. Strickler accepting his plaque
and medal from Buck Buckner, Chair of
the Big Game Records Committee.

BOONE AND CROCKETT CLUB'S

WOODLAND CARIBOU
First Award – 329²/₈
▼ ▼ ▼ ▼ ▼ ▼ ▼ ▼ ▼
DONALD L. STRICKLER

I arrived in Deer Lake, Newfoundland, on November 5, 2000. I was met at the airport by Roger Keough and his wife, Sharon, from Parson's Pond Outfitters. This was my fourth hunting trip with Parson's Pond Outfitters; two previous trips in 1998 and 1999 garnered Boone and Crockett records-book caribou. I was eager this year to take a double shovel bull on this outing, as well as reunite with friends I had made on previous trips.

Parson's Pond is located north of the Gros Mourne National Park, on the West shore of Newfoundland's Northern Peninsula. I was staying at Roger Keough's home in Parson's Pond while on this trip, which is a great place to view the November migration of caribou from the Long Range Mountains to the coastal plains. We had viewed several small herds of caribou on our way from Deer Lake to Parson's Pond.

The first day of my hunt was November 6, 2000. Roger, his brother, Lewis, (a previous hunting companion), and I traveled north. We saw several small herds, stalking one herd from approximately a half mile that had a nice bull. I chose not to take this bull since it did not have double shovels, but did manage to take several pictures at a distance of 75 yards.

On November 7, 2000, the second day of my hunt, Roger, Lewis, and I left Roger's home and once again headed north. Just a few miles north of Parson's Pond, Lewis spotted a small herd of caribou approximately one and half miles away and noticed a nice bull in the herd.

We stopped for a closer look and decided to stalk. The weather was beautiful for this time of year in Newfoundland, making it a great day for a walk in the bogs. We walked about one mile, seeing several other small herds of caribou with some small bulls. As we were making our way around one of the many small ponds, Lewis spotted another herd at about 400 yards. We made our way toward them using what cover we had. We were able to get within 75 to 80 yards. We

It was at this point I found the bull I had been looking for. It had all of the characteristics I was in search of, including a beautiful pair of double shovels. I was behind a small spruce tree and was able to take a shot using my .300 Weatherby with 180-grain Nosler Partitions, which I knew would do the job. My first shot was a little too far back. After this first shot, the caribou herd ran a short distance, and then stopped. The herd did not spot us. After a long minute, the few caribou that had been blocking my targeted bull moved and I was able to take my second shot, which finished the job.

I had just taken my third, and largest, Boone and Crockett records book caribou. After taking pictures, Roger and Lewis made quick work of caping and quartering. We were all packed out and back to Roger Keough's home in time to enjoy another great lunch prepared by Sharon Keough.

Photograph courtesy of Donald L. Strickler

Donald L. Strickler took his third, and largest, woodland caribou on a 2000 season near Parsons Pond in Newfoundland. The bull, which scores 329-2/8 points, received a First Place Award at the 25th Big Game Awards Program in Kansas City.

With my hunt over, I spent the next couple of days visiting with friends, including the parents of Roger and Lewis. They were a wonderful older couple who had raised 10 children. They were staying with Lewis and his wife, Nan. I also visited with Sharon's parents, Mr. and Mrs. James Hancock, who were visiting from Labrador. During this time I was able to enjoy my favorite Newfoundland cod fish and baked goodies prepared by Sharon and Nan. But, by far, the greatest reward of the whole trip was receiving a quilt made for me by Roger and Lewis' Mother, who has since passed away.

On my flight back to Harrisburg, Pennsylvania, I could not help to think I was the luckiest person in the world. Good friends, good health, my son, Mark, who has made me proud, three Boone and Crockett records book caribou in three years, and a wonderful wife of 35 years, Barbara, who would be waiting for me at the airport. At the age of 63, I have very much to thank God for.

Award Winning Moments...

Photograph by Julie T. Houk

25th Awards Program trophy owners, Donald L. Strickler (woodland caribou), Francis N. George (Central Canada barren ground caribou) and his wife Diana, and Eugene C. Williams (grizzly bear) enjoy the award-winning moose on display during the Thursday Welcoming Reception at Cabela's.

Photograph by Cliff White

TROPHY STATS

▼ ▼ ▼ ▼ ▼

Category
woodland caribou

Score
327$^3/_8$

Location
Caribou Lake,
Newfoundland — 2002

Hunter
Robert Sparks

Inside Spread Measurement
32$^3/_8$

Length of Main Beam
Right: 33$^5/_8$ Left: 36$^3/_8$

Width of Brow Palm
Right: 12$^2/_8$ Left: 13$^6/_8$

Number of Points
Right: 19   Left: 18

Photograph by Jack Reneau

Robert Sparks accepting his plaque and
medal from Buck Buckner, Chair of the
Big Game Records Committee.

WOODLAND CARIBOU
Second Award – 327³/₈

▼ ▼ ▼ ▼ ▼ ▼ ▼ ▼ ▼

ROBERT SPARKS

The planning for my October 2002 hunt started back in 1999, when I went to Newfoundland on my first combination moose and caribou hunt. While driving the 2,400 miles to get there, hurricane Floyd hit the east coast. This made travel very difficult.

I arrived at Caribou Pond Outfitting in Glenwood, Newfoundland, just in time to go to one of their spike camps. While there, I shot a moose on the second day of the hunt — not a big moose, but my moose.

They then moved me to another spike camp to hunt for caribou. Just after lunch one day, we went to scout out the area before the afternoon hunt. We saw a nice bull out on one of the bogs. I decided to take it.

That evening, after quartering the caribou and before we could cape the bull out, hurricane Gert hit. We ran for cover. When we came out in the morning, my caribou cape and rack were gone. They were taken by a bear in the night, during the storm, and we didn't hear a thing. It was then that I started to make plans to come back, as soon as I could save up the funds for another hunt.

In the spring of 2000, I asked friends Steve Zigman and Barry Hohol if they wanted to go along. They both excitedly said yes. I called Baxter Slade of Caribou Pond Outfitting in January 2001 to set up a hunt for the week of October 6, 2002.

In April 2001, my left hip started to collapse from disease. My right one was also going bad and I thought my hunting days were over. I had surgery in July 2001 with the hope of fixing my hip so I could make the hunt. It didn't work! I almost died in October, and spent 24 days in the hospital. I had another surgery in February, and finally a hip replacement in April. I was determined to go, even if on crutches. After much physical therapy, I was ready to give it a try.

We packed my cargo trailer with a freezer, generator, a very large homemade cooler, and several others to haul the meat back. We packed all our hunting gear and were ready

Photograph courtesy of Robert Sparks

Robert Sparks and his guide had to walk through several bogs like this one during the hunt.

Robert Sparks took his award-winning bull with the assistance of his guide, Kevin Thompson. Robert's bull scores 327-3/8 points and received a Second Place Award at the 25th Awards Program in Kansas City.

to set out the next morning.

That night, three tornados hit our area. We had to delay our start until power was back on and people had water. At 2:30 p.m., we were finally able to leave Wisconsin for the four-day, 2,400-mile trip to Glenwood, Newfoundland.

Baxter Slade, owner of Caribou Pond Outfitting, was at the helicopter hanger to meet us at noon on Sunday, October 5. After introductions, we boarded one of his helicopters and he flew us 30 minutes to the lodge. What a nice surprise, as I thought we were going to the spike camps that I went to in 1999. The lodge was a very nice place, with wood heat, generator, satellite TV, full-time singing cook (Walter), and a beautiful view of the lake. It was a first-class operation all the way around.

We had some time to kill before the guides arrived, so we went to the target range on the beach to check our rifles before the hunt. I was shooting a Browning A-Bolt Stainless Stalker in .270 Winchester caliber.

Soon, the guides showed up. What a great bunch of guys! We drew names to see who would be going with whom the next day. I drew Kevin Thompson. We talked about the hunt the next day, and as Steve was only doing a moose hunt, he would go with Barry on his caribou hunt the first day.

On Monday, we got up at 5 a.m. and had a large breakfast. We were on the trail on the ATVs about 6:30 a.m. After a 30-minute trip, the walking started. A three-hour hike in alders and on the bog is something most of us Wisconsin hunters are not in shape for. Being on crutches only two months earlier made it even worse! I had just about had it walking and was thinking about shooting a small caribou bull we were watching, when we noticed something white moving about a mile away. When Kevin said he could see the rack even at this distance, we forgot the small bull. Off we went with a lot more energy.

WOODLAND CARIBOU
Second Award – 327³/₈

▼ ▼ ▼ ▼ ▼

ROBERT SPARKS

We walked across a couple of bogs and through some thick spruce and alder thickets to get to the bog where we had spotted the big bull. It was gone. It was very disheartening, as it took us almost an hour to get there.

My guide then motioned for me to get down and move up toward him. There, lying next to some bushes on the bog, we could see one antler tip when the bull moved its head. It was about 300 yards away.

We tried to get closer, but as soon as we started moving, some cows bedded with the bull saw us. They jumped up when we got to within 150 yards. The bull got up, but was shielded by the cows. I didn't have a shot. The bull finally moved forward enough so I could see its head and neck clearly. Kevin said to take the shot before they ran. I shot and the bull dropped right in its tracks.

As I walked toward him a total of 10 cows got up and ran off. Neither Kevin nor I had seen them until that point.

There was no ground shrinkage here, as the rack seemed to grow the closer we got to it. What a magnificent animal!

After field-dressing it, Kevin said we had about a two-hour, five-mile walk back to the ATV. I told him that was good, because I was staying with my caribou so I didn't lose this one to a bear like in 1999. Also, he could go faster without me.

It was a beautiful, sunny, crisp day. I had water, my lunch, and a raincoat to sit on. I didn't mind the three-hour wait. I just sat with my caribou, going over the hunt. It sure beat walking the bog!

The helicopter came and picked us up, dropping the caribou right on the dock back at the lodge. We quartered it and sent it to the butcher before 8 a.m. on the second day. The four hunters in camp had harvested three caribou and two moose. You can't beat that!

Later, I had it scored for the Boone and Crockett Club's records book. Its final score is 327-3/8 points.

Photograph by Cliff White

TROPHY STATS

▼ ▼ ▼ ▼ ▼

Category
woodland caribou

Score
$313^3/_8$

Location
Hinds Lake,
Newfoundland — 2002

Hunter
William D. Graham

Inside Spread Measurement
$30^7/_8$

Length of Main Beam
Right: $37^4/_8$ Left: $34^7/_8$

Width of Brow Palm
Right: 9   Left: $7^1/_8$

Number of Points
Right: 23   Left: 13

Photograph by Jack Renea

William D. Graham accepting his plaque
from Buck Buckner, Chair of the Big
Game Records Committee.

BOONE AND CROCKETT CLUB'S

WOODLAND CARIBOU
Honorable Mention – 313³/₈

▼ ▼ ▼ ▼ ▼ ▼ ▼ ▼ ▼

WILLIAM D. GRAHAM

It was the third week of October 2002 when we landed in Newfoundland for a moose and caribou combination hunt. My friend and hunting partner, Vern Middleton, and I had decided to book a hunt with Ray's Hunting and Fishing Lodge in Howley, for a week's challenge in territory we had never ventured into before. The accommodations and food were outstanding, as were our guides and cooks, which made our stay truly enjoyable.

Our camp consisted of six other hunters from different parts of the U.S., all looking for either moose, caribou, or a combination of both. Each morning after breakfast, our guides would roll in with pick-ups and RVs for the day's journey. Our hunting range was located outside of Howley near Hinds Lake, an area consisting of small mountain ranges, vast logging areas, and marshy bogs (if you left your knee-highs at home, you might as well stay on the plane.)

The hunt was rough; areas of flat dry ground were few and far between, with occasional river and cliff obstacles added in for character. Sunshine was a bit of folklore around there during these fall hunts, but when it did come out, you could see for 20 miles. Our guides didn't have any reservations about walking long distances. Our first morning's walk consisted of 11 miles before lunch. The skies were gloomy for most of the first part of the week. I had seen several small herds and single caribou milling around, but nothing I wanted to take.

On day four, it snowed three inches, which made the roads and slopes that much more slippery. Fortunately, even though a little more miserable, the white background made the moose stand out like a blaze orange hunting suit in the middle of a flock of sheep. I took full advantage of the conditions to harvest a moose that we had located at the bottom of a brushy draw. Newfoundland moose, in general, are not notorious for huge racks, but the steaks they yield are notorious for those who have huge appetites. I feel truly lucky to have taken this animal and frequently reminisce about the hunting conditions and my mount.

The week was coming to an end and I still had a tag to fill. The morning of the 18th was mushy and dreary. The snow had melted, but the fog made visibility approximately the distance of a cheap whitetail grunt call.

Around 11:00 a.m., it started to lift in layers and we began to see ghostly silhouettes of caribou ahead. We crept a little closer and glassed a group of around 20 head of cows and one small bull. As much as we wanted to, we could not see anything of honest size, so we turned around and started walking away.

Fortunately, I looked back over my shoulder one last time. There stood the largest caribou I had seen on the entire trip. The bull raised its head up from behind a boggy

A last chance look over his shoulder rewarded William D. Graham with a chance at this woodland caribou. The hunt took place near Hinds Lake in Newfoundland. The bull scores 313-3/8 points.

depression and was now looming four feet above the entire herd. Calmly, I suggested to my guide that maybe we should take a better look at this one. Judging from the look in his eyes and the unbuckling of his backpack, I figured we were going to start covering ground. We closed the distance down from 200 yards to around 150 yards and I crawled the remaining 25 yards. The ground was wet and covered with short ground brush; I made my way to a small hump. I had already chambered my .308 and was ready to shoot.

As I peered over the mound through my scope, it was easy to see the beast. Trouble was, all of the 22 cows were intermingled with the bull. I glanced back at Perry, my guide, as he is silently screaming to me, "Don't shoot a cow!"

Nervously, I held my position, until the blur of tan fur melted away to only one with antlers. I pulled the trigger (too nervous to squeeze.) Much to my surprise, very little happened. The entire herd slowly started to walk away from me. I took a second shot, with basically the same response as the first shot. The herd started walking straight away from me. I settle down a bit and took a third shot. This time the bull reared its head straight up into the air and shook its rack.

The distance widened and I needed to get closer. There was one small tree between me and the group, so I crouched down and headed directly for the tree. It made a perfect rest, helping to steady my aim during this frazzling experience. I knew I needed to make this shot count as I squeezed the trigger. This time the results were different. Peering through my scope, I witnessed the frozen stance, followed shortly by two staggering steps, and the disappearance of its rack from the horizon. All four shots were direct hits, but the bull barely flinched. The memory of its endurance and the excitement of this hunt is something I will remember forever.

WOODLAND CARIBOU
Honorable Mention – 313 $^3/_8$

▼ ▼ ▼ ▼ ▼

WILLIAM D. GRAHAM

Photograph by Cliff White

TROPHY STATS

▼ ▼ ▼ ▼ ▼

Category
 barren ground caribou

Score
 426$^6/_8$

Location
 Shagak Bay, Alaska — 2002

Hunter
 James A. McIntosh

Inside Spread Measurement
 34$^1/_8$

Length of Main Beam
 Right: 55$^3/_8$ Left: 54$^2/_8$

Width of Brow Palm
 Right: 6$^4/_8$ Left: 9$^2/_8$

Number of Points
 Right: 19   Left: 16

Photograph by Jack Renea

Brian McIntosh accepting his son, James'
plaque and medal from Buck Buckner,
Chair of the Big Game Records Committee.

BOONE AND CROCKETT CLUB'S

BARREN GROUND CARIBOU
First Award – 426 $^6/_8$

▼ ▼ ▼ ▼ ▼ ▼ ▼ ▼ ▼

JAMES A. MCINTOSH

After six eleven-hour days in a row, our work was coming to an end, leaving me and three of my friends tired of work and ready to hunt. Jessica Cheatwood, Eric White, Adam Maier, and I rushed back to our living quarters, grabbed our gear, and proceeded to the Shagak Bay trailhead, which was a 15 minute drive from town. We only had two and a half hours to hike to the north spit of Shagak Bay before darkness fell. I had spotted some caribou in that area during the past weekend, and noticed a huge herd bull keeping track of the cows.

Once we reached the trailhead, I parked the truck, and we started unloading our gear. I realized I had forgotten my lucky walking staff, which I had made from a piece of bamboo that I had found on the beach two years earlier. I have taken it on every caribou hunt since and almost called off this hunting expedition, but continued unloading the gear.

We started down the small trail that led to Shagak Bay. I had been on this trail many times before, but this time it was for a different purpose, and the trail seemed to flow quickly under my feet. We made it to the bottom and started skirting the shoreline through the long grass and soggy muskeg. As we approached the first of many hills, the sun was starting to set and the evening chill was beginning to settle in. It was the end of September. The time when the coats of the caribou were changing, getting ready for the long winter, and the bull manes would be perfect.

While making our first ascent on one of the many hills, Adam stopped to take a picture of an eagle perched on a bluff overlooking one of the streams that emptied into Shagak Bay. The stream still had some pink salmon making their last run upstream to breed; the smell of fish lingered in the air. We kept moving while he took his pictures and told him we would wait for him at the next descent back to the beach. As the others continued on, I stopped about 200 yards before the descent to glass the area and could make out ten animals high up on the next mountain. I wished I had had my lucky walking staff because it also made a great rest for my 10x binoculars. Since we had another 40 minutes of solid hiking to get to our camping area, I kept moving.

Adam had joined Eric and Jessica. They were waiting for me at the descent point, and upon my arrival informed me that Adam had lost his sleeping bag somewhere along the way. Earlier during the hike, Adam had stepped into a "tundra hole" filled with water and fell, soaking himself. Unknown to us at the time, his fall had loosened the ties that held his sleeping bag on his pack. We decided it must have fallen off his pack when he stopped to take pictures of the eagle. Since it was getting dark, we decided to pitch camp there as walking around the dark was dangerous.

While Eric and Adam went back for his sleeping bag, Jessica and I moved up the mountain to find a good campsite. We found one about 300 meters up the mountain in an area that was flat and had plenty of soft moss that would keep us dry and comfortable. If you have never slept in a bed of tundra moss you are truly missing out.

There was also a small stream close by for water that was fortunately free of rotting salmon. We started unloading our gear, and I realized that we were missing the tent poles. After discussing this with Jessica, we decided to make a lean-to out of the Alaska pack frames. It didn't look too bad when completed, and once everyone was inside it would be comfortable. We did not have a way to keep the middle of the tent up, so I made sure my weapon was cleared and used it as the center pole. It was my grandfather's 1903 Springfield .30-06, which my father had given to me years before. The original stock was in my gun safe at home. The composite stock I replaced it with made the weapon a little lighter, but kicked a little harder. A friend of mine who lives in Homer, with whom I have been on many hunting trips, nicknamed it "Ole Painful."

That evening, we broke out some food and enjoyed a clear Alaska evening where millions of stars glistened overhead. It was one of the nicest skies I have ever seen, and being in the company of good friends made it even more enjoyable. Eric, Adam, and Jessica were all in top physical condition and had packed out animals before. Fresh meat was hard to come by, and packing out and processing an animal is a good way to get some.

The wind picked up around 3 a.m., and our little lean-to was taking a beating. I was on the windward side and wrapped the edge of the tent underneath my sleeping bag to keep our tent from blowing away. Around 5 a.m. the wind died down and I laid there in the darkness wondering about the coming day's events, how the hunt would go, and if the conditions would be right for a good stalk. It was beginning to get light outside so I got out of my sleeping bag. The air was chilly and I was glad to have my polar fleece tops and bottoms on. After putting on my boots, I went outside to stretch and get the coffee going. I looked up at the mountain and was very disappointed to see the entire area where I wanted to hunt socked in with fog. I knew there was no chance in that thick fog and decided to wait for it to lift. If it did not, I would cancel the hunt.

My friends were still in the tent sleeping and I started over to the stove to make some coffee. Looking one more time at the mountain, I saw antlers moving down the mountain towards us below the fog line. I ran to the tent and pulled the weapon from the center, collapsing the tent on Eric, Adam, and Jessica. Reaching in my bag, I grabbed one round and loaded my weapon. I loudly whispered at Jessica, saying, "Jess get up, there are caribou coming down the mountain. I am heading up toward them."

I had taken Jessica on her first caribou hunt and we had crept to within 100 yards of her first bull. It was something that I will never forget.

I looked once more at the mountain to see if I could tell which way the caribou were going. It looked as if they were skirting the cliff line about 400 yards above us. The winds were right, blowing to the south, and I started off in a semi-jog to get into a position I could fire from.

There was a small draw that had been beaten down from previous animal movement and I guessed that would be where they would cross. I laid down in the prone position and flipped out my bipod. My heart was beating fast due to the sprint up the hill. I took a deep breath and settled into a good shooting posture. Knowing I only had one round didn't help with my rapid pulse. I tried to breathe slowly and wondered where the animals would appear.

BARREN GROUND CARIBOU
First Award - 426 6/8

▼ ▼ ▼ ▼ ▼

JAMES A. MCINTOSH

Then I saw the first one. It was a young bull that stopped to graze on the tundra. Another young bull came up beside it and they started to jump around in a playful manner. I estimated that they were about 150 yards out. Both looked back the way they had come and then I saw what caught their attention. A huge bull was raking the tundra as it walked and stopped in a small depression just beyond the two young bulls. I could see the top of its back and the moss being thrown up in the air as it continually beat up the tundra heads. I moved the scope back to the two young bulls and they were staring directly at me. Slowly, I turned my head and saw Jessica coming towards me. She was still wearing her pajamas and was barefoot, but moved slow and kept low. The two young bulls moved up the mountain about 25 yards from where the big bull had been trashing the tundra.

I kept my cross hairs on the big bull. It was still unaware of the alert from the two young bulls and continued to rake the tundra, but I didn't have a shot. I had to wait until it moved from the depression for a good shot. After what seemed like an eternity, the big bull took one leap and gave me the shot. I squeezed the trigger, taking the mule kick in the shoulder, and did not see the big bull anymore. The two young bulls were still watching me from the ridge, but did not seem to be spooked. Had I missed the bull? Had it gone back into the ravine? I didn't think so because I knew the shot was good, so I decided to just wait for a few minutes before going to check.

When we decided to go check, the young bulls ran. I saw the antlers before I saw the body. I started to get that feeling you get when you're overwhelmed with excitement and happiness. Jessica and I hiked up to the bull. It was a clean kill, right behind the front shoulder. Eric and Adam, who had watched the whole thing from the lean-to, came up to see the bull. We admired the beautiful animal and the massive antlers for awhile knowing that now the real work would begin soon.

Returning to camp, we made breakfast and discussed the best way to transport the meat out. Over a cup of coffee and some oatmeal, it was decided that Jessica and Eric would pack out the gear to the truck and then return with the empty frame packs, while Adam and I started dressing out the bull. Finishing breakfast, we packed up everything into the two packs that Eric and Jessica would transport back to the truck. Adam and I grabbed our gear and proceeded back to the bull while Jessica and Eric started hiking the four miles back to

Photograph courtesy of James A. McIntosh

James A. McIntosh took this award-winning bull while on a hunt with three of his close friends in Alaska's Shagak Bay area. The tremendous barren ground caribou scores 426-6/8 points and received a First Award at the 25th Awards Program.

the truck. By the time Jessica and Eric had returned, we were almost finished preparing the meat for long hike back to the trailhead. The packs were large enough that we tied the hindquarters and front shoulders to the frame packs. The neck meat, rib meat, back straps, and tenderloins were put in bags and tied to the frame or in the pack itself. Each pack weighed at least 100 pounds. The hike back to the truck would be a long one.

We debated about leaving the head and cape for another trip, but the ravens and eagles perched on the ridge made the decision for us. If left, the birds would fly down, pick apart the head, and ruin the cape. Therefore, we tied the head and cape to my pack after redistributing the weight, keeping it as high up as possible. The hike back was long and painful, but I wouldn't have traded it for anything. It was the price of taking such a nice bull and the experience is one that I will never forget. I would have never even attempted a hunt like that without having my friends there, and I thank them for making one of my dreams possible.

My bull officially scored 426-6/8 points and received a First Award at the 25th Big Game Awards Program in Kansas City. My father, Brian, received my plaque and medal on my behalf. I regret that I couldn't accept it myself, but I am currently working as a civilian in Iraq.

316　　　　　　　　　　　　　　　　　　　　BOONE AND CROCKETT CLUB'S

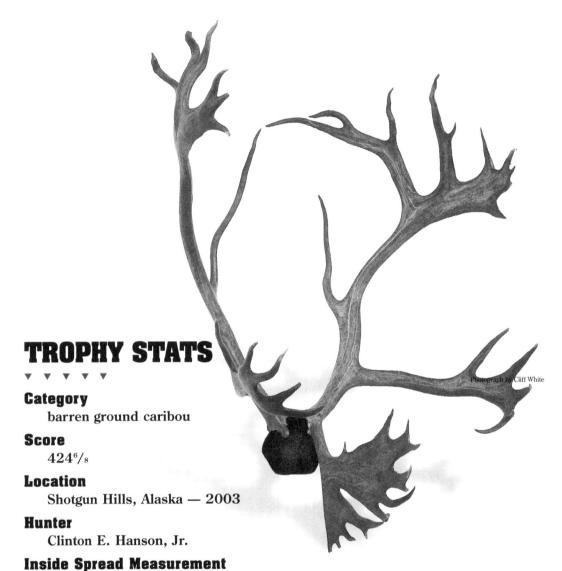

Photograph by Cliff White

TROPHY STATS

▼ ▼ ▼ ▼ ▼

Category
 barren ground caribou

Score
 $424^{6}/_{8}$

Location
 Shotgun Hills, Alaska — 2003

Hunter
 Clinton E. Hanson, Jr.

Inside Spread Measurement
 $34^{5}/_{8}$

Length of Main Beam
 Right: 48   Left: $46^{5}/_{8}$

Width of Brow Palm
 Right: 1   Left: $19^{2}/_{8}$

Number of Points
 Right: 13   Left: 30

BARREN GROUND CARIBOU
Second Award – 424⁶/₈

▼ ▼ ▼ ▼ ▼ ▼ ▼ ▼ ▼

CLINTON E. HANSON, JR.

Since moving to Alaska in the spring of 1991, I have enjoyed numerous great hunting and fishing experiences. Most years, I have been able to go on two fly-in hunts. For 2003, I had a caribou hunt planned north of Dillingham and a Sitka deer hunt on one of the islands in Prince William Sound. One of my hunting partners on previous hunts (Dave Stimson) and I decided to hunt the Mulchatna caribou herd in late September because the bigger bulls start showing up as the rut gets near. The bulls' manes are longer and white by then and make beautiful mounts if you are fortunate enough to harvest a trophy bull.

We had contacted Tikchik Airventures, owned by Rick and Denise Grant, in Dillingham earlier in the year and arranged for a date to fly in. We both had flown with Tikchik on other hunts and were pleased with the service. As the day neared, Dave shipped most of our gear out on Northern Air Cargo. When the day finally came, we flew a commercial air carrier to Dillingham and were picked up by Denise at the airport. We gathered a few more supplies and went over to Shannon's Pond where Tikchik Airventures had its Beaver airplane on

floats. After a little more time loading gear, we were off on what would prove to be another great adventure.

As we flew north over seemingly endless birch and spruce forests, wet meadows, lakes, and ponds, we spotted a few moose and a lot of old caribou trails made from past years' migrations. After more than an hour in the air, we were over wide open country with occasional small lakes scattered between low hills and valleys. We saw several small bunches of caribou near some of the lakes, but no big concentrations.

Rick, our pilot, was a bit concerned about leaving us on one of these small lakes this late in the year as it was possible it could freeze before our scheduled pickup eight days later. We decided to fly over to a big

Photograph courtesy of Clinton E. Hanson, Jr.

After a stormy night, the successful hunters experienced an uneventful flight back from camp to Dillingham.

lake that would not freeze for some time even if it did turn cold. I had hunted off this lake two years earlier with my son, so I was familiar with the area. On that trip, we had harvested four nice caribou bulls. As always at the beginning of a hunt, we were filled with anticipation as we set up our tents and camp.

The next morning, we set off for the top of a big ridge a couple miles distant. On the previous hunt, I had spotted good numbers of caribou there. It was pretty tough going, busting through brush and around beaver ponds, but we finally got to the top. Unfortunately, there was not a caribou within walking distance anywhere in sight, nor had we seen any indication of any caribou sign on the way up. We made a big five-mile loop down the ridge with similar results and by then the day was about over. Dave said a couple times as we headed back to camp, "I can't believe you carried four caribou this far through this stuff and were still willing to hunt here again."

I had some of the same thoughts myself. The next day we headed off in the opposite and easier direction, at least as far as the terrain goes. We saw a lone calf and several hours later, a single yearling cow. Dave harvested the cow as he wanted the meat. The limit was five caribou, so it wouldn't prevent his hunting for a bull later. It was about two miles back, but the cow was small, so it wasn't a hard pack with half a caribou each.

We decided this location was not going to work and called Rick on the satellite phone for a move the next day. Rick came early the next afternoon in the Beaver and moved us about 15 miles. As we were setting up camp, we saw a herd of about 60 caribou. There were several nice bulls browsing along the lake. However, since state law prohibits hunting the same day you are airborne, we could only watch and hope they would be around the next day.

During the night, the rain and wind started. By daylight it was raining hard with wind and poor visibility. We left camp late and made a small loop in the area near camp without seeing any caribou. After lunch, the rain had slowed down, so we made another jaunt in hopes something had moved in.

We split up, with Dave on the other side of the ridge from me. Shortly after, I heard a shot. It was followed by a second shot. I went over the top and saw a herd of about 20 caribou. They were within rifle range, but none of the bulls were what I was looking for. I saw Dave a few hundred yards off and he had a nice bull down. We butchered the bull together. By then it was windy and raining hard again as we carried half of the caribou back to camp. We made a second trip for the rest of the caribou and antlers and were extremely happy to get into a dry tent out of the rain and wind. Gore-Tex may be 100-percent waterproof under normal conditions, but something had failed. I was as wet on the inside as if I had taken a dive in the lake.

The rest of the night was windy and the rain continued non-stop. There was so much noise from the rain beating on the tent, the wind flapping the tent fabric, and the waves breaking on the shore 30 feet away; it was hard to get any sleep. Every year, some hunters have their tent fail in these type conditions. Luckily, our tent withstood the storm with no difficulties.

When morning finally came, it was still windy, but the rain had stopped. We headed out beyond where Dave had harvested his bull. There were small bunches of caribou scattered around, mostly cows and calves. We observed a couple single bulls, but

BARREN GROUND CARIBOU
Second Award - 424⁶/₈

▼ ▼ ▼ ▼ ▼

Clinton E. Hanson, Jr.

nothing that I wanted to try for. After watching a while, we observed a bunch coming off the hill. They were followed by a second bunch with several bulls, including the two very big bulls. I knew these two were shooters, but I told Dave that we better watch and see where they were headed before we made a move.

Caribou browsing across the tundra are usually impossible to catch, so the best strategy is to see which direction they are headed and cut a diagonal to get ahead of them. As we watched, the second bunch continued on a direct line toward us. The bigger of the bulls was herding the cows and making certain that the satellite bull stayed a hundred yards or so away. It paid little attention to the other half-dozen smaller bulls in the herd as they must not have been a threat.

When they were about half a mile away, the cows decided to lie down. The big bull got some of the cows up a few times, but they would lie back down as soon as they got a chance. The big bull continued to monitor the satellite bull, but finally gave up and laid down.

I was now faced with a dilemma. Should I wait until they got up and started moving, hopefully in our direction? Or should I try to stalk them and get close enough for a shot? Unfortunately, they were in the open tundra. No cover or topography was provided to get behind and stalk them. The herd seemed very settled where they were. Some were also out of sight when they laid down. All the rest were facing the opposite direction, so I decided to amble slowly toward them. If I could gain a few hundred yards, it looked like there was a little swale that would hide me for a good distance before I would be in the open again. Everything went well and none of the caribou ever looked at me.

As I got into the swale, I was out of sight and made it another couple hundred yards closer. Once again, I was in the open, but the caribou still had not noticed me. I walked slowly in a bent over position and covered another hundred yards or so. I figured I was pressing my luck, so I crawled another 50 yards to a hummock where I could rest my rifle. I was now a little more than 200 yards away and figured it was a relatively sure shot. I have done most of my hunting in Alaska with a Leupold scope on a .338 Winchester Magnum. You don't really need that kind of power for caribou, but this was brown bear country and I always have a tag in case the opportunity for a bear comes up.

I was prone on the ground, looking at the bull through the riflescope. It was still lying down, resting its head on the ground, and facing the opposite direction. From the prone position, it didn't present that large of a target. I didn't feel it was that difficult a shot, but I remember thinking not to blow it; this is the biggest caribou I had ever had in my scope. I squeezed the trigger and heard the bullet hit. Two more shots for insurance and it was

Clinton E. Hanson, Jr., left, and his hunting partner, Dave Stimpson, pictured here with Clinton's award-winning barren ground caribou. Clinton's bull scores 424-6/8 points and was taken near Shotgun Hills in Alaska.

down for good. I went back 50 yards, picked up my pack, and walked over to the bull.

Sometimes when you walk up to an animal, they seem to shrink in size. Not this bull. It grew and was even bigger than I thought. Dave came down and we were both amazed at the mass and the length of the bez points and back tines. We were certain it would place well up into the Boone and Crockett Club's records book, but there were more pressing matters at hand. We then took care of the field-dressing, caping, and packing it back to camp.

We took a number of pictures with both our cameras only to learn later that many didn't turn out because of moisture. Fortunately, the weather was good as we loaded our packs. We stashed the rest of the meat and antlers, then set off for camp, which was about one and a quarter miles away. We arrived back at camp at 6:30 p.m. and decided to get the rest in the morning. That night was worse than the night before. The winds were stronger and the waves bigger.

The next morning we faced the decision of whether to carry a rifle for bear protection or go without and have an easier time packing. Since the country was open and we had not seen any bear sign, we decided lighter was better. As we neared the site of Dave's caribou kill, we saw that something had moved the rib cage. We glassed the area, but saw no signs of life or that any vegetation had been raked over the rib cage like a bear usually does. We cautiously approached. Upon examining the carcass remains, we concluded that it was a wolverine that had been feeding on the remains. We headed on. As we approached the stashed meat and antlers of my bull, we again carefully glassed the area for bears, but fortunately the stash was intact. We loaded up our packs and before we got back, it was raining hard again. We still had some neck meat and the antlers so it was back for another trip. Like before, the rain gear wasn't working very well. I was as wet inside as outside, but at least we had the whole bull in camp. All we had left to do was wait for Rick and the Beaver to come for the scheduled pickup the next day.

After another stormy night, Rick arrived about noon to somewhat improved weather. The flight back was uneventful, observing a few caribou and moose along the way. Once back to Dillingham, it was a few hurried hours getting meat and antlers to Northern Air Cargo, changing our airline tickets, and flying back to Anchorage. The meat and antlers arrived a day later. Dave and I green scored it and came up with 424-4/8 points. It officially scored 424-6/8 after the 60-day drying period. Regardless of the score, this bull is the trophy-of-a-lifetime.

TROPHY STATS

▼ ▼ ▼ ▼ ▼

Category
Central Canada barren
ground caribou

Score
404

Location
Courageous Lake, Northwest Territories — 2001

Hunter/Owner
Gordon A. Welke/Doris Welke

Inside Spread Measurement
$42^7/_8$

Length of Main Beam
Right: $51^3/_8$ Left: $54^2/_8$

Width of Brow Palm
Right: $^1/_8$ Left: $15^3/_8$

Number of Points
Right: 12   Left: 16

Photograph by Cliff White

CENTRAL CANADA BARREN GROUND CARIBOU
First Award – 404

▼ ▼ ▼ ▼ ▼ ▼ ▼ ▼ ▼

GORDON A. WELKE – HUNTER   DORIS WELKE – OWNER

I'm a lucky man! I have been lucky in life, love, and the pursuit of adventure; my hunting trip to Courageous Lake, Northwest Territories, was no exception.

In August 2001, I arrived at Yellowknife. The day was blustery and overcast, and I was somewhat depressed that my friend, James Morrell, wasn't on the hunting trip with me. I left my room to explore the city, which had a wonderful downtown and a beautiful museum. On the walk back to the hotel I met Bruce Lawrence, with whom I would share my next hunting adventure. In the days to follow, Bruce would become known as "Titanic" due to the swamping of his boat and his trek across the tundra.

The next morning, we flew to Courageous Lake. I met my guide, Terry Rock, who previously was a wildlife biologist in Saskatchewan. We had immediate camaraderie, as I had worked as a fisheries biologist in the same province.

On our hunt the following day, I spooked a very nice caribou. Terry told me to wait as he felt I could find a better animal. The next morning we found another animal, which he encouraged me to shoot, but I declined. As we traveled along, I spotted a group of caribou with two large bulls. Terry suggested we look further down the lake, but I convinced him to let me pursue the animals while he checked out the other area. His last words were, "You can't catch up to a caribou." Oh Ye of little faith!

I climbed the hill only to find the caribou had split into two groups – one bull and several cows going along a ridge, and the other three bulls grazing while moving rapidly in the meadow below. I decided to follow the group on the ridge, but they disappeared. Perhaps Terry was right! You can never catch up with a caribou.

On my return, I found the three bulls had bedded down in the meadow below about a half mile away. I assessed the situation and felt if I crossed over some muskeg I would be out of sight most of the way.

The stalk began. First, I laboriously crossed the muskeg to get behind a small knoll. I was tired, panting, out of breath, and excited. My chest heaved with every breath and I rested for a while. I thought, "What would my guide tell me to do?"

I crawled on my hands and knees for another quarter of a mile and then began to crawl on my belly for the last 200 yards. Suddenly, the two small bulls got up. I rose to my knees, ready to shoot. The large bull lay still, so I crawled on my belly to a rock to steady my .300 Winchester Magnum.

After a crawling on his hands and knees for a quarter of a mile, followed by another 200 yard belly crawl, Gordon A. Welke took this award-winning Central Canada barren ground caribou. The bull scores 404 points and received a First Award.

While viewing the bull through the scope, the cross hairs moved up and down over its back with each breath I took. I thought, "Should I scare it up?"

I tried to time the oscillation of the cross hairs with my breath and pulled the trigger. I heard a thud; then its head fell directly back. Its eyes didn't close, and it didn't move.

On my 266-yard run to the caribou, I knew I had shot a big one, but I didn't realize how big it really was. My guide returned, completely oblivious to what had happened. "Let's go to supper," he said.

"No," I responded. "I've got a caribou down and it's big."

We moved across the tundra. He looked at the bull and said, "You're a lucky man."

The next day, my guide Terry lost his glasses in the tundra. We had gone several miles before we realized it. I told him, "I'm a lucky man. Let's go back and find them."

He laughed. "You've got to be kidding," he said.

We drove back to the spot where we had taken off in the boat. I walked out into the tundra and reached down and picked up his glasses. "Now do you believe me?'

Some people believe in luck, but the reality is you have to have confidence and faith in yourself and no fear of the unknown to be a lucky man. I regret not being able to share this hunting experience with my old hunting buddy, Captain James Morrell, but I was lucky enough to make a new friend, "Titanic."

Photograph by Cliff White

TROPHY STATS
▼ ▼ ▼ ▼ ▼

Category
Central Canada barren
ground caribou

Score
402^6/$_8$

Location
MacKay Lake, Northwest Territories — 2001

Hunter
Gordon Carpenter

Inside Spread Measurement
46^7/$_8$

Length of Main Beam
Right: 49^7/$_8$ Left: 49^4/$_8$

Width of Brow Palm
Right: 13^6/$_8$ Left: 14^5/$_8$

Number of Points
Right: 23   Left: 17

Photograph by Jack Rene

Gordon Carpenter accepting his plaque
and medal from Buck Buckner, Chair of
the Big Game Records Committee.

CENTRAL CANADA
BARREN GROUND CARIBOU
Second Award – 402 $^6/_8$

▼ ▼ ▼ ▼ ▼ ▼ ▼ ▼ ▼

GORDON CARPENTER

We booked the hunt with True North Safaris the year before, when my hunting and fishing partner, Greg Powell, and I were at an SCI Convention. After a long year of anticipation, we finally arrived at MacKay Lake Lodge in the Northwest Territories, just a short flight north of Yellowknife.

As we unloaded from the twin Otter, Gary Jaeb and his staff from True North Safaris greeted us and directed everyone to their cabin. After settling in, we met in the lodge to be assigned guides and begin a rundown on what we could expect on our hunt. Our guide, Eddy Doggie, was a member of the Dog Rib Tribe.

The date was Monday, September 10, 2001, and Greg and I were excited about our new adventure. After having lunch, Greg and I made a quick check on our rifles to make sure they were still zeroed. Satisfied with our lodging and the accuracy of our rifles, we relaxed, surveyed the landscape, and waited impatiently for the next day.

Tuesday morning after breakfast, we met up with Eddy and made our way down to the boat landing. We layered on the clothes, knowing not only that it would be a mighty brisk boat ride in a 16-ft. aluminum boat, but we also had the possibility of getting a little wet. We headed up the lake. It turned out go be very cold and wet, but that didn't matter because we were looking for caribou.

Being on my first caribou hunt, I was expecting to see thousands of caribou running over us, but that wasn't the case. We saw small herds of cows, calves, and small bulls, but the larger bulls seemed to hang around in small groups of four or five. We glassed the countryside for hours it seemed. My guide then said we should take a closer look at what looked like four good bulls.

Photograph courtesy of Gordon Carpenter

Gordon Carpenter and his hunting partner, Greg Powell, pictured above, and their guide, Eddie Doggie, make their way across the bay in a 16-foot aluminum boat.

Photograph courtesy of Gordon Carpenter

Gordon Carpenter took this award-winning Central Canada barren ground caribou on the first day of his first caribou hunt. The bull scores 402-6/8 points and received a Second Award at the 25th Awards Program in Kansas City.

We started out after them, hoping we could stalk within range before being spotted. Greg and I had already flipped a coin to see who would get the first shot, and I was the lucky one. The country was fairly easy walking, and we must have trailed them close to a mile. We finally came to an area with tall grass and the only stunted trees for miles around.

There at 150 yards stood the four bulls. After about two seconds of glassing them, my guide said the one on the right was a good one and that I should take it. We had heard stories about guides wanting hunters to take the first one and hurry back to camp, and I was not an expert on judging caribou racks. I did know that I should check the tops and shovels. This one had good double shovels, good tops, and the part I really like, a very good spread. Taking careful aim, I let go with my Model 70 .300 Magnum. The bull dropped instantly.

What a relief! It was a good clean kill, and all the pressure was lifted. I had the rest of the week to fill my second tag. We took all the normal pictures, caped it, quartered it, and hauled it back to the boat. We spent the rest of the day on another bull for Greg that he got late in the afternoon.

On our rough ride back to camp, we talked about our successful day in the wilderness and looked forward to a nice cold one back at the lodge. As we beached the boat, one of the camp taxidermists met us and started telling us about the tragic event of 9/11. That did a pretty good job of taking the wind out of our sails. We were the last to come in, so when we unloaded and went to the lodge, everyone was glued to the TV.

The rest of the week we made the best out of a bad situation. Greg took his second bull Thursday and I took my second one on Saturday. In between, we fished for lake trout and took a few ptarmigan. When it was all said and done, my first bull was the largest of 40 caribou taken on this hunt. I hadn't thought much about putting it into "the book" until one of the men in camp, who was an Official Measurer, put the tape on it. It green scored approximately 408 points, minus a few deductions.

We were anticipating it being a big hassle traveling back home, so we decided to leave the heads there and have them mounted in Canada and shipped back complete. Some time in August 2002 the crate arrived at my house, and I could finally hang my big bull beside my other trophies.

CENTRAL CANADA BARREN GROUND CARIBOU
Second Award – 402 6/8
▼ ▼ ▼ ▼ ▼
GORDON CARPENTER

Photograph by Cliff White

TROPHY STATS

▼ ▼ ▼ ▼ ▼

Category
   Central Canada barren
   ground caribou

Score
   $400^3/_8$

Location
   Little Marten Lake,
   Northwest Territories — 2001

Hunter
   Joel C. Garner

Inside Spread Measurement
   $40^6/_8$

Length of Main Beam
   Right: $53^6/_8$ Left: 57

Width of Brow Palm
   Right: $19^1/_8$ Left: $6^7/_8$

Number of Points
   Right: 18   Left: 17

Photograph by Jack Renea

Joel C. Garner accepting his plaque and
medal from Buck Buckner, Chair of the
Big Game Records Committee.

BOONE AND CROCKETT CLUB'S

CENTRAL CANADA
BARREN GROUND CARIBOU
Third Award – 400³/₈

▼ ▼ ▼ ▼ ▼ ▼ ▼ ▼ ▼

JOEL C. GARNER

My caribou hunt took place at Little Marten Lake, 160 miles North of Yellowknife, Northwest Territories. The hunt was hosted by Americana Adventures out of Yellowknife. The day after we arrived at camp on Little Marten Lake, the hunt began. The weather was very mild, but windy, as would be expected.

The hunt started out well, with me getting my first caribou within the first hour. The bull was very nice, scoring 326. I would have been very proud to leave with that trophy alone, but I had another tag to fill. My wife, who is my regular hunting partner, also had a tag to fill.

For the next three days, we spent time moving from area to area glassing for caribou. Not many were seen, as the migration had not quite started. On the fifth day, we moved to an area north of camp called the Hidden Lake area. The trek to this area required us to leave our main boat, hike over a short distance to another smaller lake, and proceed up that lake in a boat that was of questionable seaworthiness. A little bit of water bailing was required.

We proceeded up a small river into an area we had glassed days earlier from several miles away. We had seen several nice bulls there. At times during our move up the river, we had to beach the boat and walk along the riverbank so we could float the boat over shallow areas where large boulders made it impossible to clear otherwise. Andy, our guide, was very adept at maneuvering the boat over these areas so we could continue our trip up river.

As we hiked along the riverbank we sighted a few caribou on a ridge just north of us. We climbed a hill to glass the valley beyond and were finally able to see our first large herd, maybe 400 caribou. We backed off to come in from a better angle.

We were near a bend in the river when we spotted three good bulls in a meadow moving slowly away at about 350 yards. It was Patty's turn to shoot. We were able to make a good sneak to within 200 yards of the bulls. Patty chambered a round in her .270, steadied herself on a willow branch, and touched it off. A perfect spine shot put the bull down where it stood. As we approached the downed bull Andy remarked, "Now we're seeing some good bulls."

Andy dressed the bull out in the tradition of his Inuit ancestors, with only a small knife, until it was easily packed back to the boat and back to camp. Patty's bull green scored at 351-3/8.

It was now my turn to fill my second tag. The next morning, September 11, 2001, we had no idea the events that would take place on that day. After a foggy start to the day, we boated straight north across the lake to see what we could find. After beaching the boat we set off on foot, moving farther north about two-and-a-half miles.

We started to see caribou about 11 a.m., spotting a herd with some nice bulls. We began the stalk. After 30 minutes of crawling on our bellies, we found ourselves on a sandy ridge looking over a herd of about 50 head, including several bulls. Andy picked out one very nice bull at 200 yards. He told me to get ready as this one was pretty good. I used my backpack for a rest and got ready for the shot. The camera was ready. Five minutes passed. The bull was feeding across the ridge and wasn't getting any closer. "Andy, should I shoot?" I asked.

"It looks good, probably 360," Andy said.

Click. My safety came off. "Ok?"

He paused. "No. I think we can find a better."

"You have got to be kidding!" I said. "This one is great!"

"No, there's bigger."

We walked back to the boat and I wondered if we had made a big mistake. It was getting late so we started back to camp. As we approached camp, we decided we had time to make a quick side trip to the back of the bay not far from camp. As we moved that way, we noticed two bulls at about 1,000 yards standing on a point of land directly in front of us. I commented that one of the bulls looked really nice. Andy said the bull was okay, but he didn't seem to think it was the bull we were looking for. We continued on for another 500 yards, just to get a closer look. Andy's binoculars came up and he said, "It's pretty nice and it has double shovels."

We exited the boat and as I got close, I saw the bull run over a small ridge. I ran to cut it off. By that time, Patty and Andy were there and the camera was rolling. I crossed the ridge 150 yards above where the bull had disappeared. There it was, still on the point. The caribou spooked, and now I was between it and escape. The bull turned and came full bore at 50 yards and broadside to where I was standing.

My first shot exploded on the surface of the lake, half an inch above its back. The bull passed me as it headed for safety. I fired the second round, which dropped it instantly. It was over. I knew the bull was very nice, but I had no idea how nice until we got it back to camp and green scored it at over 400 B&C.

After the excitement was over, we went to the mess tent for dinner. That was where we heard what had happened at home on the fateful day of September 11, 2001. We were anxious to get back home, but had to stay an additional day because of planes being grounded. We were able to take advantage of the great fishing at Little Marten Lake during this time and that helped take our minds off of what was happening.

We had a wonderful experience at Little Marten Lake. Americana Adventures, the staff in camp, the guides, and food are first rate and my hunting partner and I plan to return. Thank God for these moments in our lives.

Award Winning Moments...

Photograph by Jack Reneau

Linda Powell accepts the Plaque of Appreciation for Remington Arms recognizing them as an official sponsor of the Boone and Crockett Club's 25th Awards Program in Kansas City.

Photograph by Cliff White

TROPHY STATS

▼ ▼ ▼ ▼ ▼

Category
Central Canada barren
ground caribou

Score
399$^6/_8$

Location
Nicholson Lake, Manitoba — 2001

Hunter
Francis N. George

Inside Spread Measurement
42$^5/_8$

Length of Main Beam
Right: 50$^3/_8$ Left: 54$^7/_8$

Width of Brow Palm
Right: 13   Left: 11

Number of Points
Right: 32   Left: 17

Photograph by Jack Reneau

Francis N. George accepting his plaque
and medal from Buck Buckner, Chair of
the Big Game Records Committee.

CENTRAL CANADA
BARREN GROUND CARIBOU
Fourth Award – 399 6/8

▼ ▼ ▼ ▼ ▼ ▼ ▼ ▼ ▼

FRANCIS N. GEORGE

My dream hunt for Central Canada barren ground caribou was about to begin. Four of us, Norm George, John Moore, Bob Porter, and myself, had driven from Buffalo, New York, a few days earlier. We were waking up from an overnight stay in Thompson, Manitoba, taking turns showering, sipping coffee, and watching the morning news. It was Sept 11, 2001!

Unspeakable horror unfolded before us. Coffee cups, half empty, dangled from our fingers as we witnessed images of the second plane. Who could commit such an atrocity?

We learned that all flights had been suspended, which ended our chances of being flown into camp that day. We spent the day idly in Thompson, not knowing what the future held for us, our hunt or our nation.

On day two, word came to us that northern bush planes could fly if they had hunters in camps. After filing a manifest with the Canadian military at Churchville, Manitoba, we were flown to the hunting camp on Nickelson Lake. Ted Jowett, our outfitter, had a well set up camp with all of the needed comforts. The guides, camp staff, and cook took excellent care of us during our stay.

The days were sunny and relatively warm, but extremely windy. Nights turned cold and still, with the Aurora Borealis entertaining us most evenings.

We hunted hard, but saw only a few caribou in the far distance. Arctic wolves occasionally revealed themselves as they searched the tundra for food.

Day four of our hunt found us waking to the sound of a plane landing on the lake. Because of the lack of caribou, Ted had arranged for a Cessna to fly us north to where the caribou herds were probably gathered.

Our guide Omer, John, and I were on the first flight out. The pilot found a small lake approximately one and a half miles from Northwest Territories, just large enough to land on and dropped us off.

The next day, we left the cedar and spruce cover surrounding the lake and started across the open tundra. As we hiked, we saw more and more caribou, mostly cows and small bulls. Continuing our search for a respectable bull took us further onto the flat, featureless tundra, which gradually gave way to a small rise. We could see caribou bedded on the crest to our right. Glassing the herd found no suitable bull.

Still glassing through my binoculars, I panned left and spotted several good bulls bedded a short distance from the herd. Commenting with enthusiasm, I asked Omer to check

Using a rock as cover on the flat tundra, Francis N. George crawled within shooting distance to take this Central Canada barren ground caribou with his Ruger .270. The bull scores 399-6/8 points and received a Fourth Place Award at the 25th Awards Program.

out these bulls. Not knowing if he heard me over the wind, I glanced his way just as he was finding the bulls in his binoculars. He stopped turning with a sudden jerk and exclaimed, "That's the one you want."

We had a problem. The bull was too far for a shot and there was nothing to conceal our approach. Spotting a fairly large rock halfway between us, and a bit to our left, we circled to get in line with the rock. If we could make it to that rock, I'd have a shot. Belly crawling, we reached it as the bulls stood up and began milling about. Omer said that they probably thought we were wolves and that I should hurry. The rock provided a steady rest for my Ruger .270. I asked Omer the distance, took a deep breath, squeezed the trigger, and completely missed! It was so windy, I believe the caribou didn't even hear the shot and stayed put. I pulled my thoughts together, chambered another round, compensated for the wind and shot true. Quickly, John took my position on the rock and took another nice bull before they ran off.

Approaching the downed bull, we began to realize what an amazing trophy I had. Majestic and still in velvet, with plenty of mass, long and numerous points, it was an awesome sight.

After much congratulations and picture taking, we caped and boned the meat from both caribou. Making several trips to the lake we landed on left us tired, but all was on shore. Having no communication with the plane, we sat in the sunshine, waited, and marveled at our good fortune.

When the plane did arrive, we loaded the meat first, then discovered that my antlers would not fit through the door. Rejecting the pilot's joking remark to cut off a few antler points, we removed the planes door and back seat, barely allowing the antlers on board. It was a cramped flight back to camp, but smiles were found all around.

As we unloaded the largest caribou ever taken from this camp, I was intoxicated by the fanfare from the staff and the other hunters. We celebrated into the night. Who could sleep anyway?

CENTRAL CANADA BARREN GROUND CARIBOU
Fourth Award – 399 $6/8$
▼ ▼ ▼ ▼ ▼
FRANCIS N. GEORGE

Photograph by Cliff White

TROPHY STATS

▼ ▼ ▼ ▼ ▼

Category
   Quebec-Labrador caribou

Score
   $423^6/_8$

Location
   Helluva Lake, Quebec — 2001

Hunter
   Jeff C. Wright

Inside Spread Measurement
   $52^5/_8$

Length of Main Beam
   Right: $50^2/_8$ Left: $49^1/_8$

Width of Brow Palm
   Right: $7^4/_8$ Left: $16^2/_8$

Number of Points
   Right: 26   Left: 24

BOONE AND CROCKETT CLUB'S

QUEBEC-LABRADOR CARIBOU
First Award – 423⁶/₈

▼ ▼ ▼ ▼ ▼ ▼ ▼ ▼ ▼

JEFF C. WRIGHT

In the fall of 2001, Jeff Wright decided to take his 11-year old son, Adam, on his first big game hunt. They would be going after caribou near Schefferville, Quebec. They would share everything from the new memories they were making to the .243 rifle they were using.

They made the drive from Maine to Montreal, and then boarded a plane to Schefferville. Shortly thereafter, they were able to embark on their first hunting adventure together in the north country.

On September 9, they hunted, but saw only beautiful scenery. September 10 was not much different. They tried to hunt, but after getting caught in a deluge of rain, they spent the entire afternoon just trying to get dry.

September 11 brought tragedy to the world. Being somewhat isolated from the events by their primitive location, Jeff and Adam went about the day as normal. While that day has left its mark for millions of people, Adam will likely remember the day as much for encountering his first caribou in the wild. While looking over the countryside, they found a nice group of bulls and cows. They took off, in hopes of cutting the group off at a pass. They did, but it was so windy and variable that Jeff elected not to take the 300-yard shot.

Adam took off with the guide and was able to get into a better shooting situation. One pull of the trigger later, Adam had taken his first big game trophy.

The next day, they went back to the same area, but didn't see any game. They had resigned themselves to being skunked when Jeff saw a lone bull on the way back to camp. He made a perfect 450-yard shot on his first animal of the trip, bringing it down with the ever-dependable .243.

The next day, they selected a location where they could watch two main ridges in the open country. Before long, they saw a large group of caribou on an open hillside. Soon after, they spotted another group. They continued to watch for over an hour as the caribou worked their way toward them.

The waiting hunters figured where the herd would cross the river, so they moved to take a position. After a 45-minute wait, the herd began to appear. It was Adam's turn to shoot and, as bulls started showing, Adam's good aim had once again brought down a nice Quebec-Labrador bull. He quickly handed the rifle to Jeff.

At that point, there were nearly 20 bulls together, all of which were nice. More bulls were constantly showing up over the rise as the herd poured forward. Jeff had so many to choose from it became difficult. In the end, he selected a particular bull simply because it was the only animal that presented a clean broadside shot. He doesn't honestly know if it was the largest in the magnificent band of animals. There were two other exceptional trophies in the bunch, but both hunters were now tagged out. Instead, after making a 60-yard shot on the bull of a lifetime, they had the pleasure of slowly watching the herd walk away and continue on their meandering path.

Award Winning Moments...

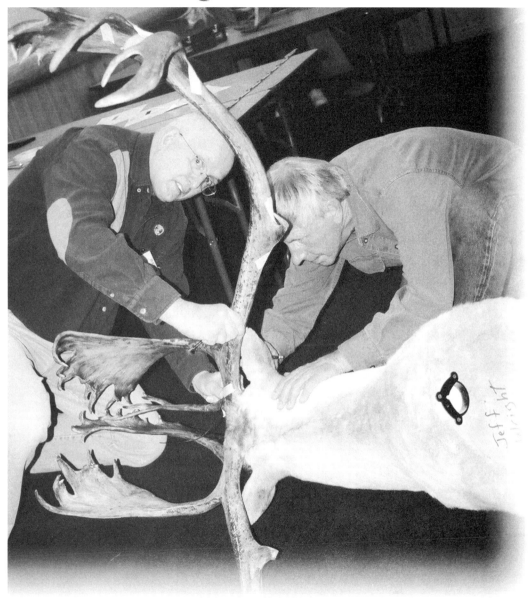

Photograph by Ryan Hatfield

25th Awards Judges Panel team, Ab England, left, and Fred King, right, mark the starting point for the length of main beam measurement on Jeff Wright's Quebec-Labrador caribou.

Photograph by Cliff White

TROPHY STATS

▼ ▼ ▼ ▼ ▼

Category
Quebec-
Labrador
caribou

Score
402^6/$_8$

Location
Mollet Lake, Quebec — 2001

Hunter
James C. Johnson

Inside Spread Measurement
45^5/$_8$

Length of Main Beam
Right: 56^5/$_8$ Left: 53^4/$_8$

Width of Brow Palm
Right: 13^3/$_8$ Left: 15^5/$_8$

Number of Points
Right: 22   Left: 21

QUEBEC-LABRADOR CARIBOU
Second Award – 402⁶/₈

▼ ▼ ▼ ▼ ▼ ▼ ▼ ▼ ▼

James C. Johnson

My quest to collect all of the North American big game species recognized by Boone and Crockett (excluding polar bear, Pacific walrus, and Atlantic walrus) led me to a hunt for Quebec-Labrador Caribou. In 1999, I arranged for a two-week hunt out of Kuujjuac, Quebec. Due to "wrong place, wrong time" and unpredictable migration patterns, I did not see a live caribou for the entire hunt. That's hunting.

In 2001, I chose to hunt with Nunami Outfitters at Mollet Lake, 130 miles inland from Hudson Bay. My trip to the Nunami Outfitter's lodge took me 800 miles north from Montreal to the native town of Kuujjuarapik, Quebec. I traveled to Kuujjuarapik on a Dash 8 Turbo plane and then transferred to a Twin Otter for the 130 air-mile trip.

This was a case of "right place, right time." Thousands of caribou from the Leaf River herd were crossing at the upper end of the lake, which was 15 miles by boat. The influences of the Hudson Bay waters allow trophy caribou hunting until late October, whereas hunting in eastern Quebec is frozen out in late September, before the rutting season starts. An October hunt makes for outstanding hunting during the rut and migration. At this time of year the Leaf River Herd, which is 250,000 to 300,000 animals strong, is migrating to winter grounds. This herd winters approximately 200 miles south of Mollet Lake in central Quebec.

Dion, our guide with Nunami Outfitters, has been guiding at Mollet Lake for the four years the lodge has been open. He was extremely knowledgeable of the lake, river, and rapids system. The first morning of my hunt Dion, Jim Gehr, and I traveled to the Rapids '8' crossing. Jim, the other hunter I was paired with, won the coin flip to see who got to shoot first. He had a Boone and Crockett-class bull down in no time. Fifteen minutes later, I collected my fine caribou at 150 yards.

Nunami Outfitters is owned by the Inuit/Eskimo natives and was established at a hydro-exploration camp as a means of natural resource harvest to help support the native people. The unique landscape and location make this area perfect for migrating caribou.

The caribou herd was plentiful and close to camp at times. The weather in October was mild due to the Hudson Bay effect, with temperatures during the day reaching upper 30s to mid-40s and the nights barely reaching freezing.

As for my quest for the five species of Boone and Crockett recognized caribou, I collected a Boone and Crockett woodland caribou in Newfoundland in 2003, which completed my "caribou slam."

TROPHY STATS

▼ ▼ ▼ ▼ ▼

Category
Quebec-Labrador caribou

Score
$397^3/_8$

Location
Fel Lake, Quebec — 2001

Hunter
Roscoe Blaisdell

Inside Spread Measurement
$45^2/_8$

Length of Main Beam
Right: 53   Left: $51^6/_8$

Width of Brow Palm
Right: 13   Left: 4

Number of Points
Right: 21   Left: 20

Photograph by Cliff White

Photograph by Jack Renee

Roscoe Blaisdell accepting his plaque and medal from Buck Buckner, Chair of the Big Game Records Committee.

QUEBEC-LABRADOR CARIBOU
Third Award – 397 $^3/_8$

▼ ▼ ▼ ▼ ▼ ▼ ▼ ▼ ▼

ROSCOE BLAISDELL

I have been hunting since I was seven years old and have always been facinated by antlers. When I was 10, I read a book on measuring antlers and have been measuring ever since. I must have measured my father's big New York buck five times. I became a Boone and Crockett Official Measurer about 10 years ago, and am now president of the New Hampshire Antler & Skull Trophy Club. It's a great feeling to meet successful hunters and to give recognition to them, the trophy, and the states in which the animals were taken.

Ever since I was young, I dreamed of hunting caribou. I would picture herds of bulls with tremendous antlers of all configurations walking past me and me having to choose which one to shoot. I finally got to go on my first caribou hunt in Alaska a few years after graduating from college. On this self-guided trip, I managed to take a caribou that missed the Boone and Crockett minimum by only two inches. I also shot a great moose that does qualify for the records book.

I have now been on 6 caribou hunts over the 1ast 15 years. I find the area these animals live in to be fascinating, which helps to draw me back every few years. It's almost like being on another planet. On my last few hunts, I have used my muzzleloader to add to the challenge. Also, I had a goal to get an animal that would qualify for the *Longhunter Muzzleloading Record Book* – the official records book for animals taken by muzzleloader. It is compiled and published by the National Muzzle Loading Rifle Association. If I was very selective and really lucky, I could hope to get another Boone and Crockett animal as well.

I come from a hunting family and generally accompanied by my father, Edwin, on big game hunts throughout North America. On this trip, not only did my father join me, but also my mother Katherine, brother Carl, his teenage son Cedric, and daughter Jessica. We, along with other friends and relatives, all hunt whitetails on our woodlot in Vermont together, and do our best to help each other get his or her deer.

After having several hunts in we saw only 2 to 75 animals per week, Paul suggested trying out a new outfitter he was booking for called Labrador Outdoors. I told him we were willing to give it a try, but we had better have an improvement on numbers of animals seen. As any caribou hunter knows, the migration is hit or miss.

Our hunt took place in Quebec, 50 miles due north of Schefferville, Quebec, and within 20 miles of the Labrador border. We drove to Montreal with food and supplies on August 22, 2001. We needed to start the hunt on this date so my niece and nephew could be back hom

Boone and Crockett Club Official Measurer, Roscoe Blaisdell, nearly passed up this bull as he was engrossed in videotaping it along with two other bulls. He ultimately put the camera down and took this bull, which ended up receiving a Third Place Award at the 25th Awards Program in Kansas City.

ein time for school. Early the next morning, we flew to Schefferville, then later that day continued on to the hunting camp by floatplane.

We had the whole camp to ourselves. Everyone was anxious to explore the territory so after unpacking we all went our separate ways. I soon saw some good bulls and got them on video and camera. I normally take videos of my trips so I can relive the hunt years after the adventure.

The area we were hunting was on the edge of thick spruce timber and open tundra. Amazingly there were very few mosquitos or black flies, even though it was quite warm. On all of my previous hunts in the tundra, we suffered from the insects.

The next morning, I was up at 5 a.m. ready to hunt. Even though the camp manager said it wasn't necessary to get up so early as the caribou travel all day, I wanted to get in every possible minute of hunting. The previous day, I had found a bottleneck between the edge of a lake and a steep area that funneled many of the caribou. As I was nearing a place to overlook this area, I noticed three nice bulls about 200 yards away and coming in my direction. As usual, I got out my camcorder and camera and took film of them. Soon the bulls, all similar in antler size, were getting very close to me, but I hadn't considered shooting any of them yet.

As an Official Measurer used to handling quite a few nice caribou, I should have immediately realized that all three were real trophies. However,

QUEBEC-LABRADOR CARIBOU
Third Award – 397 3/8
▼ ▼ ▼ ▼ ▼
ROSCOE BLAISDELL

when you are in the mode of passing up animals and having overly high expectations sometimes you can make mistakes and pass on a good animal. When the bulls were about 60 yards away, I put my camera down. I realized that one of them was very heavily palmated on the tops, besides having all of the other things necessary to score high. I knew I had a second tag and could be really selective for the next one.

It was an easy shot. The bull went down and then got up, so I quickly reloaded and finished the job. I filmed the other bulls walking slowly away. I did not realize at the time that they were also of Boone and Crockett size. Each time I see my video, I cringe at seeing what I let go. When I walked up to my bull, I saw it indeed was a very nice animal and proceeded to take plenty of photos. I then boned it out and started the long haul to camp with half a caribou on my back.

On the way back to camp, I met my mother and father. They each had taken bulls that morning and were in the process of quartering their animals. Both my parents are veterinarians in their mid-70s and are very capable in the outdoors. My mother has in the past had to help adult men field-dress their deer, as they had no idea what to do. The camp manager was very generous in helping them pack out their animals while I finished packing out my bull.

The rest of the week went well. There was great trout fishing and everyone took two animals, some of them quite large. One that my niece, Jessica, shot probably qualifies for Boone and Crockett, but I haven't had the opportunity to measure it yet. On the last day, I shot another bull that also ranks very high in the Longhunter Record Book, even after a neighbor's dog ate part of the rack! I saw at least 200 caribou that week and we all had a great trip.

When I got home, I measured the rack and couldn't believe it scored close to 400 points! This is when I first realized what a great trophy it was.

About six months after shooting the caribou, I took it to my good friend Ron Boucher of Vermont to have it officially measured. Ron was one of the Boone and Crockett panel measurers to score the famous World's Record Hanson buck. He kidded me for waiting so long to get it measured and we were both happy with the resulting score.

New World's Record

TROPHY STATS
▼ ▼ ▼ ▼ ▼

Category
pronghorn

Score
95

Location
Coconino County, Arizona — 2000

Hunter
Dylan M. Woods

Length of Horn
Right: $19^3/8$ Left: $18^5/8$

Circumference of Base
Right: $7^2/8$ Left: 7

Length of Prong
Right: $6^7/8$ Left: 7

Photograph by Jack Renea

Dylan M. Woods accepting his plaque and
medal from Buck Buckner, Chair of the
Big Game Records Committee.

PRONGHORN
First Award (Tie) – 95

▼ ▼ ▼ ▼ ▼ ▼ ▼ ▼ ▼

DYLAN M. WOODS

It was finally time to find out what I was going to be able to hunt for in the fall of 2000. After having an archery bull elk tag in 1998 I was not expecting to get another very soon, so I had my hopes on getting a deer tag for that year. I never even expected to get a pronghorn tag in famous Unit 9 after only five years of applying! I was only 20 years old and did not see a pronghorn tag in my near future. I just kept applying for the tag year after year with no hope of being drawn anytime soon. I called Game and Fish, hitting the redial button dozens of times (just like every year), until it was finally my turn to listen to the recording. When the computer told me I had not been drawn for deer I thought I was done for. Boy was I surprised when I heard I had a pronghorn tag. I was so surprised, in fact, that I had to hit the redial button a few dozen more times just to call and double check.

Neither I nor any of my friends had ever hunted pronghorn before, so I knew I had some work ahead of me. Being in college at the time, I knew I had to set my priorities straight. All schoolwork was instantly set aside and the real work began. I had never hunted the unit before, so my first few weekends were devoted to staring at maps and driving every road I could find. Many of these trips were with my friend, Scott Ellis, and his father, Ken.

We found some pronghorn as we drove around. In the weekends to come, we found several more in the areas we decided to concentrate on. We kept track of all of the bucks we found and where they were from largest to smallest. I'm not going to lie. At the time, none of us even knew what was big or small; we just compared everything we saw. Once we had located a few bucks, we kept an eye on them during the rest of our scouting.

As opening day approached, we decided where we were going to be on opening morning. Finally, it was Thursday, September 28, and Scott, Ken, my other friend, Nathan Schreiber, and I were on our way to set up camp. By mid-afternoon, camp was set and there was nothing left to do but relax a little, eat some dinner, and enjoy the warm evening with good company. Then came the night of no sleep, awaiting whatever the morning had in store.

We woke up extra early to be sure we were the first ones to our hunting spot. We had decided to hunt an area where there were two bucks that hung around with some does in front of a hill in the mornings. The plan was for Nathan and Ken to drive around the front of the hill and watch the show from a distance, while Scott and I approached the hill from the back to spot the bucks and then move down on them. Boy were we disappointed when we arrived well before light and found that someone had beaten us there.

Off we went to find Ken and Nathan. When we found them they had good news. On the

When their first choice of hunting spots was already taken on opening morning, Dylan M. Woods, left, and his hunting partners, Nathan Schreiber and Scott Ellis, moved to another area, which resulted in finding the new World's Record pronghorn. The buck officially scores 95 points.

drive in, the bucks and does ran across the road in front of them in the opposite direction of the other hunters. The hunt was back on!

Scott, Nathan, and I headed out after them while Ken stayed at the truck. By this time the sun was just coming up and the perfectly clear sky was already getting warm. The three of us just walked slowly, keeping an eye ahead of us as well as down the small gullies to our left that were just deep enough to hide feeding pronghorn. Every few steps we would stop as much as possible and scour the areas hiding behind trees.

During one of these stops, I motioned to the other guys that I saw something. As I looked, I did not see the animals we were looking for. Instead, I saw one buck feeding by itself 300 yards away. The buck had no idea we were there.

As soon as I saw horns through my binoculars, I started to tremble. The buck was much bigger than the two we were looking for. We had one problem though. There were plenty of trees around, but the one we were hiding behind was the only one between the buck and us. My Remington 7mm Mag. had no problem with those 300 yards, but there was just enough of a rise between us that I could not shoot lying down.

Nathan and Scott stayed put while I crawled another 30 or so yards to lie under a tree. I decided to wait there. I could see its head sticking out of the gully. If it walked away or came closer I could shoot. I only had to wait a few minutes, but it was enough to calm myself.

Then the buck walked straight toward me. When I could see its body, I looked at it through my scope and lost it again; the trembling was back. I put my cross hairs on it and squeezed the trigger. Before the gun even fired,

PRONGHORN
First Award (Tie) – 95
▼ ▼ ▼ ▼ ▼
DYLAN M. WOODS

I knew I had missed. But somehow that calmed me, and a second later my second shot had the buck on the ground.

The next thing I knew, the three of us were giving high fives and hugs. As we walked up to it, we knew it was big, but we had no idea what we were really looking at. The fun part was over by 7:30 a.m. opening morning. Scott went to get his dad and the truck, as Nathan and I hurried to clean the big buck. It was only 7:30 a.m., but it was getting hot fast.

We arrived in camp, and after skinning and caping the buck; we decided we would try to measure it. We were measuring up the back of the horns and got about 16 inches. We were way off! The horns actually measured 19-3/8 and 18-5/8 long.

On the way home, everyone we showed it to was amazed. That was when I realized I had more than I thought. I had the taxidermist rough score it for me and that is when I knew I had taken an incredible trophy. After the drying period, I had it officially scored by Mike Cupell in Phoenix. I was in shock when he told me it beat the current World's Record with a score of 95 Boone and Crockett points! I had a great time, and I am glad that my friends got to share something this magnificent with me. Since then people have told me, "I guess you don't need to put in for pronghorn anymore."

I am just getting started. My next goal is archery pronghorn!

New World's Record

Photograph by Cliff White

TROPHY STATS

▼ ▼ ▼ ▼ ▼

Category
  pronghorn

Score
  95

Location
  Mohave County, Arizona — 2002

Hunter
  David Meyer

Length of Horn
  Right: 17$^2/_8$ Left: 17$^2/_8$

Circumference of Base
  Right: 7$^2/_8$ Left: 7$^2/_8$

Length of Prong
  Right: 7   Left: 6$^1/_8$

Photograph by Jack René

David Meyer accepting his plaque and
medal from Buck Buckner, Chair of the
Big Game Records Committee.

PRONGHORN
First Award (Tie) - 95

▼ ▼ ▼ ▼ ▼ ▼ ▼ ▼ ▼

DAVID MEYER

When life gives you a second chance, you better take it. Being able to hunt at all in 2002 was miraculous; to be able to harvest a World's Record pronghorn was extraordinary.

Several years ago I underwent very serious surgery to remove a large mass in my chest, followed by a long recovery period that kept me from working, hunting, climbing stairs, or even moving from a chair for quite some time. During this forced period of inactivity, I began thinking of a hunt for pronghorn. I extensively researched pronghorn, including their history and taxonomy. During this time I was able to review the Boone and Crockett Club's *Measuring and Scoring North American Big Game Trophies* along with the Club's records books, where I learned that the

A Hunt to Remember

genetics of Arizona pronghorn dominate the elite group of trophy-class pronghorn with trophies such as the exceptional heads harvested by O'Haco and Wetzler, and the more recent Barry buck. This led to our focus on Arizona as the location for my hunt.

After securing a pronghorn tag at the Rocky Mountain Elk Foundation auction in the spring, my scouting team in early June had observed and followed an exceptional pronghorn in area 13B. We reviewed film of this buck throughout the summer of 2002 and could not believe the estimated mass measurements of this antelope, which neared 50 inches [D1, 2, 3, 4].With the homerange of the buck established, there was great anticipation as our August hunt approached, but even with the increased intensity and multiple stalks during the first day of our hunt, we could not overcome the wariness of this large buck, and when open to view could not close the distance.

We began our second day of hunting at daybreak through an opening in Hurricane Cliffs. There were four different small elevations in the terrain that allowed us to crawl undetected and locate a small group of pronghorn (six does and two young bucks), which the large buck had joined. Our prone crawling on the shale did not improve our position, and our second stalk into the valley only allowed continued wayward movement of the herd. We could not close the distance to less than 1,000 yards. We made more aggressive stalks that afternoon, but a doe's alarm protected our buck and we lost contact with it. John Caid, my guide, and I decided we should return to the outer part of the cliff, climbing to the top and glassing at each interval to view the valley, and then fixing our course by the direction and movement of the does.

We circled the cliff and then dropped down toward Square Pond, believing their movement could be back to water. As it began to rain, we saw the movement of the lead doe over

Photograph courtesy of David Meyer

David Meyer, right, and his guide, John Caid, with the new World's Record pronghorn. David took the buck in Mohave County, Arizona.

the next ridge where the group, including the large buck, had bedded down. It had now been 12 hours of stalking, and we felt we were close. We carefully moved to the next small ridge of elevation, and then the big buck was there, moving toward us!

The pronghorn came closer than I would have believed. I could not control my breathing, and I was standing without a rest. I have always been able to shoot well, with or without a rest, as I had been privileged to hunt whitetail deer, and had equally great experiences (without success) for Coues' deer in the past. As it came closer and caught us by sight, its white rump elevated as the buck paced and turned slightly. I shot, and it disappeared into the sage. I knew I had missed.

It was not the physical exhaustion, but the feeling that I had failed all the wonderful people who had helped me get this far. I kept replaying the site pictures and shot in my mind in slow motion. "I should have waited until he stopped; I should have been in a sitting position with a rest; I should not have shot at all until he was closer; I should have controlled my breathing; I should have…" I wondered if I would ever see or have the opportunity to be that close again.

On August 9, eight days following our initial stalk, we had planned a new approach. There were a series of serpentine-like washes that were bone dry from the drought. It seemed that morning slowed forever, as we arose from each gully to sight the empty green sagebrush of the plateaus.

After the fourth of these attempts, there was movement beyond the clay as it blended into the sage. I sighted a prominent bush, near which there was movement. One smaller buck moved, but I could not see the larger buck. It

PRONGHORN
First Award (Tie) – 95
▼ ▼ ▼ ▼ ▼
DAVID MEYER

seemed that I had stared at that bush forever, though it had actually been less than an hour. At first only the protrusion of two horns appeared above the boundary between clay and grass. Finally, the large buck appeared. It had moved considerably toward us, and John quietly ranged the buck at 178 yards. Then the pronghorn stopped moving. I wondered whether the buck could see us, but it appeared that it was looking beyond us. It turned, giving me a quartering-away shot, and did not move. Before hearing the shot, it went down, and the herd that was bedded down came up and was gone. We waited, but there was no movement above the grass. We did not move for a few minutes and silently observed with respect this wonderful buck. After caping the animal and dividing the meat for our families, we measured the antelope's horns. I had estimated the size of these horns so many times since the films of June that I could not believe the actual field measurements were accurate. They were staggering, and the heaviness of its horns appeared massive.

Based on an incisor sent to a laboratory, the age of the animal was determined to be three years, five months, approximating half the age estimated by Arizona Game and Fish, who had trapped this pronghorn in January 2000 in the Prescott Valley area [19A] and transplanted it within the genetic relocation program into the 13B area. A Boone and Crockett Official Measurer scored the horns, and his office guided the completion of our application for the 25th Awards Program. A Boone and Crockett Special Judges Panel was convened in May 2003, and verified the score and certified my buck as a new World's Record pronghorn. We have been privileged to be invited to the Awards Program in 2004, and this trophy was on display at Cabela's with other new World's Records at the 25th Awards Program in Kansas City.

I hope the genes of this animal will remain viable and strong. There are recent reports of an even more significant pronghorn in this area, and certainly in the future a higher score will be recorded. But for me, there will be no greater thrill than that morning of August 9, 2002, and no hunting experience that will equal that day. From the first reference I read on pronghorn during my recovery, to being able to review the scouting of our group, the stalking, the failure, and then the success of the harvest of this pronghorn, has been an exciting process. All those who helped me along the path will always be remembered. And finally, this most memorable experience allows me to think back to some words written a long time ago by Robert Drake in The Delta Review:

"But it's joy that somehow takes you outside yourself, maybe even for a minute lets you forget all about yourself and care only for something else . . . And you rejoice simply that some things can be . . . And that is the most wonderful thing in the world and it don't happen often, 'I can tell you.'"

This was truly a time and a hunt to remember.

Photograph by Cliff White

TROPHY STATS
▼ ▼ ▼ ▼ ▼

Category
pronghorn

Score
89

Location
Humboldt County, Nevada — 2002

Hunter
Chris R. Winkel

Length of Horn
Right: 16   Left: $16^1/_8$

Circumference of Base
Right: $7^5/_8$ Left: $7^5/_8$

Length of Prong
Right: $6^3/_8$ Left: $6^4/_8$

PRONGHORN
Honorable Mention – 89

▼ ▼ ▼ ▼ ▼ ▼ ▼ ▼ ▼

CHRIS R. WINKEL

On the morning of August 24, 2002, Chris Winkel squeezed the trigger and cemented his place in history. When the stately pronghorn fell, Chris had just taken the eighth-largest pronghorn to come from the great state of Nevada.

As with most open-country pronghorn hunting in the west, it all starts with putting in for a controlled hunt application followed most often by years of waiting. The year 2002 would be the year for Chris, and he wanted to make the most of it. He scouted the area and eventually was able to make the most out of a lifetime opportunity.

At 6:28 a.m., the sound of Chris' .270 shattered the beautiful Nevada morning. The 305-yard shot was true as an arrow, and ended his season and his quest for a trophy pronghorn. As the slight morning breeze continued to blow, the sense of accomplishment and beauty of the day would be something he would never forget.

TROPHY STATS

▼ ▼ ▼ ▼ ▼

Category
pronghorn

Score
85 $^4/_8$

Location
Yavapai County, Arizona — 2001

Hunter
David Meyer

Length of Horn
Right: 18 $^1/_8$ Left: 17 $^6/_8$

Circumference of Base
Right: 6 $^7/_8$ Left: 6 $^6/_8$

Length of Prong
Right: 5 $^4/_8$ Left: 5 $^6/_8$

Photograph by Jack Rene

David Meyer accepting his plaque from
Buck Buckner, Chair of the Big Game
Records Committee.

PRONGHORN
Honorable Mention – 85⁴/₈

▼ ▼ ▼ ▼ ▼ ▼ ▼ ▼ ▼

DAVID MEYER

I had to think back only for a moment about what led me to the hunt and the harvest of the my pronghorn in August 2001. I had been diagnosed and treated for a malignancy in 2000. After my family knew that I was on the mend I began to be occupied by the thoughts of what hunt I could plan. I was not able to draw a bow or shoot with good accuracy with my primitive weapon. Yet one evening late, as my sleep was interrupted by forced inactivity, I began thinking of a pronghorn hunt.

My hunting first began in Tennessee when I started trapping at eight years of age. I would plan with my dad, Henry, how the traps would be set. My mom, who is still so very active at 92, had just last year sent to me a diagram of the initial creek bed in which these traps were set in location and in the manner that I had learned from my dad, who had always roamed the woods.

I was taken by my friend, Arky, on my first big game hunt in 1988. From then, I was privileged to experience many hunts for whitetail deer, rocky mountain elk, and bear. I have also had equally great experiences without success for mountain goat, Coues' deer, and barren ground caribou.

When I began to plan my pronghorn hunt, I would read and talk to anyone who would speak to me. I spoke to so many people who were so very kind during this period, such as Kim Bonnett. And though they could not go with me as their quotas were filled, they were so instrumental in my continued interest.

With my limitations, my spirits were greatly encouraged when we had the privilege of speaking to supervisor Greg Medina of the Taos District and officer Dan Brooks (both of the New Mexico Department of Game and Fish.) They were both very helpful and supportive. Also very helpful and kind were Ms. Tori Whitaker and Ms. Louise Gonzalez, within the same department. I do not know how anyone could have been any kinder. I had called this office initially because I remembered hunting above Segundo, Colorado, on my first elk hunt and seeing pronghorn during that period on our visit to Vermejo Park.

Following this support, I spoke to my old friends from White Mountain, John Caid and Roland Eghelbah, and asked if they could help with the hunt for pronghorn if I did obtain a permit. I then spoke to my old friend from Utah, Stan Meholchick, and he continued to search for a tag while encouraging me to continue my rehabilitation program. I later was referred to Don Johnson in Arizona and he informed me about the auction of a pronghorn tag at the Desert Bighorn Sheep Society fundraiser. John and I were so encouraged, and

I was on the phone with him during the auction. We quickly buried ourselves in the exciting bidding that ensued.

Though our disappointment was noted, I was encouraged a few weeks later to find that there was an auction for a second permit by the Rocky Mountain Elk Foundation, of which I am a life member. We were successful in our bidding on this pronghorn tag and received a call from Cookie Nicoson, who is one of the volunteers with the Phoenix Chapter, RMEF. This time the bidding had stopped and had not, as before, eliminated us. I could not believe it when I received the call.

Through the kindness of Jimmy Savoini and his family, we would be allowed to hunt on their ranch near Prescott, Arizona, in Yavapai County and the gentle and rolling hills would be a good, but kind, first test of hunting after my recovery. The Savoini family had spotted on two occasions a fine pronghorn buck on their ranch. This is the buck we would be going after. My friend Roland had seen this buck about two weeks previous to the hunt, so we were hopeful it was still in the area.

I was still recovering from my illness, so the somewhat gentle rolling hills and terrain were a welcome sight. The beautiful Arizona countryside made for a spectacular hunt, regardless of what we would encounter on our quest.

We hadn't been hunting long when we saw a great pronghorn buck and a doe in the bottom of a ravine. We did our best to use the wind and approach them from the best possible angle. When John, Roland, and I crested the hill, the buck was 325 yards away.

The buck had not seen us, but the doe was acting of nervous. The buck soon began to notice these signs itself, and we knew our time was limited. There was really nothing to use as a rest on, so I would be forced to take the long shot off-hand. I raised my lifelong companion 7mm and squeezed the trigger. It was a perfect hit and the buck was down instantly.

This hunt was one of the most rewarding of my life. Good friends, helpful and friendly people, and overcoming adversity all helped to make this a hunt I will forever remember as the hunt-of-a-lifetime.

Award Winning Moments...

Photograph by Jack Reneau

Dwaine Knouse accepts the Plaque of Appreciation for Cabela's recognizing them as an official sponsor of the Boone and Crockett Club's 25th Awards Program in Kansas City.

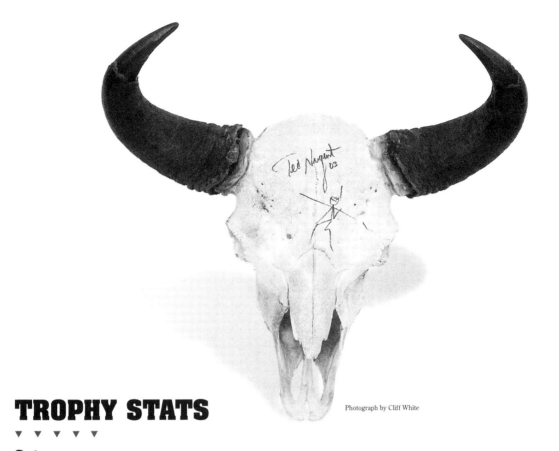

Photograph by Cliff White

TROPHY STATS

▼ ▼ ▼ ▼ ▼

Category
bison

Score
$131^6/_8$

Location
Coconino County, Arizona — 2002

Hunter
Duane R. Richardson

Length of Horn
Right: $21^5/_8$ Left: $21^4/_8$

Circumference of Base
Right: 16   Left: $15^1/_8$

Greatest Spread
$19^5/_8$

Photograph by Jack Reneau

Duane R. Richardson accepting his plaque and medal from Buck Buckner, Chair of the Big Game Records Committee.

BOONE AND CROCKETT CLUB'S

BISON
First Award – 131 $^6/_8$

▼ ▼ ▼ ▼ ▼ ▼ ▼ ▼ ▼

Duane R. Richardson

I woke up my son, Russ, the morning after he had just played and come up short for the Arizona State Championships in football. I told him I had some good news and needed him to verify what I was looking at. He wandered in and looked at the computer screen in my office and confirmed my findings of having the number one of four bison tags for the House Rock Ranch hunt in northern Arizona. My excitement was shared by him and everyone else I could call at that early hour who might be interested in my glory.

My son wanted me to do the hunt with my bow. The tag allows you to hunt with any legal weapon, but I agreed with my son. My choice would be that of the stick and string.

My Last Bull

Scouting started in January before the season to get the lay of the land, and possibly find a few big bulls in some out of the way places. The Ranch manager stated that he had not seen nor heard of any bison since the first part of September. He also said that we would really have our work cut out for us. That sentiment went right along with the video tape that the Game and Fish sends successful applicants. It basically says, "Congratulations but get ready for the hardest hunt in the world."

I was never one to forego a challenge, so I put together a team of people who had expertise in each area needed. We were able to execute a wonderful game plan. I am blessed to have a family and group of friends who are without a doubt some of the best hunters in the entire west.

I would start my hunt in a very remote spot separated from the other hunters by many miles and an entire mountain range. I had the pleasure of meeting two of the other hunters on previous scouting trips, and they were really nice people who were going to be fun to hunt with. I told them of my plans to pursue with stick and string and they thought I was either crazy or just not really fond of bison steaks.

Orientation day was now here. Two weeks earlier, I had located in the area I wanted to hunt four bulls I believed would push the state record. After orientation, I drove back to camp in a blinding snowstorm that stopped around 3 a.m. "Perfect," I thought to myself.

We really needed to cover some ground and look for tracks in the area where I last saw the four bulls. At the end of day one, my dad, George, and Bill Bolt were able to come up with some signs we determined were three days old. Phil Dalrymple and I decided to track around and see what we could come up with on the next day. My uncle Bob and Craig Thornton would try to eliminate other areas where we might have missed the bulls from the day before.

Day two panned out nothing but cold, wet feet and sore leg muscles. Day three was pretty much the same thing. We would leave camp well before sunrise and return with headlights, covering literally hundreds of miles between us and not so much as a track found.

On day four, our excitement level soared to a new high. Phil had found some huge tracks leading east toward the plateau. I had already had visions of two huge bulls traveling together and just hanging out away from the rest of the herd. The further we tracked, the deeper the snow got, to the point where we guessed it to be 36-inches deep. We finally reached the time of day where we were running out of light and the tracks were still heading up the plateau. We decided to back off and come back the next morning.

While en route to where we had cut tracks the day before, we cut one single set of tracks headed out of the deep snow to the west. We tracked them over 10 miles, taking up most of the day, only to find they belonged to the biggest bull I had ever seen! The problem was the bull was a stray cow from a cattle herd. The tracks of a cow and a bison are identical, and cannot be told apart by even the most seasoned hunter or rancher; however after day five it was pretty depressing to say the least.

We determined that we needed to change location, and day six was spent moving the camp a hundred miles away, closer to the "House Rock Ranch." Arriving at the ranch, we learned that two of the four hunters were finished. One hunter remained and had taken his horses back to Phoenix for some fresh stock.

Several years ago, the first archery bison hunt on the north Kaibab was undertaken by my father. He was able to connect on a bull the first day of a 30-day hunt. Dad's experiences on the Kaibab for those many years were invaluable when it came to planning the rest of our hunt. There was an area above the ranch that we knew would hold some big bulls. We spent the afternoon of the seventh day trying to figure out a way to access that area. Phil had some commitments; he needed to get back for on the seventh day, so he left around noon.

While looking for an access point across a huge canyon, my dad, Craig, and I came across two very large sets of tracks. Dad was elated at the freshness and size of the tracks. He told me, "Corky, this is a huge bison."

I remember telling him (after spending day five tracking down a cow), "No, Dad, those are just rogue cattle."

He answered back, "If these are rogue cattle, then they are carrying around bison hair and fur with 'em because I found enough to stuff a volleyball with."

He was right! After seven days, we finally had a track that was under two days old. I grabbed my pack, bow, and quiver and began tracking. The bison seemed to be spending most of their time in an open field that provided good feed. I cut some tracks that had very sharp edges on them. They had to have been made that morning. The bison chips were extremely fresh. The tracks headed down a pinion-juniper point that is half a mile long and half a mile wide — a good bedding area, heavy with shade.

A light snow had fallen and I decided to check around the bedding area to see if I could find tracks leading out. I made a circle around the point without finding any tracks leading out. It was around 4 p.m., so I decided to start at the end of the point and work my way back to the feeding fields to the west. Four hundred yards into the point, I found two fresh beds still warm. What really got me excited and had me nock an arrow on my string was when I found foamy urine with the bubbles popping on a flat rock.

BISON
First Award – 131⁶/₈
▼ ▼ ▼ ▼ ▼
Duane R. Richardson

The wind was perfect, blowing from west to east as I entered the feeding area. All of a sudden, the ground began to shake as two bulls came running from the south and headed toward a small draw. What went wrong? The wind was perfect, and I knew they had not heard me. Something or someone had spooked them.

After spending seven days looking for the quarry, I was just thankful and praising God that I had seen bison — running or not. I hurried over to the edge of the draw where they had disappeared, only to find the biggest one had stopped across a small draw. I remembered thinking to myself, "If that bull would just turn and come back to the feeding grounds I will be in good shape."

As if on cue, the bull (not knowing what had spooked it) turned and headed back uphill to the west of me. I hurriedly took off my boots to do the shoeless dance one more time. I ran 200 yards while quartering towards the bull in order to get a lane where I could get a good shot.

The bull stopped in an opening 35 yards away, with only its head entering the opening. I could see its right side and knew it was something special. If it would only stop for a minute to give me a good shot. I was already at full draw for about 15 seconds, waiting for it to move. The bull finally stepped forward and I released the arrow. The arrow got there faster than I anticipated. I hit it square in the front shoulder, just up from the leg, with my first shot.

I immediately grabbed another arrow and ran up the hill to cut the bull off in order to get another shot at it. I was uncertain how much penetration I had made from my first arrow. To my amazement, the bull had already begun to weave and was having a hard time standing up. The arrow had penetrated to the opposite shoulder and only my fletch remained visible.

I followed it about 150 yards before it stopped for the first time. This time the arrow penetrated dead middle and dead center. The bull walked away and I pursued it, grabbing for arrow number three.

While in pursuit I was locked in and focused on getting shot three away. Then I heard a sound. "Psst."

"Psst," I think I heard something again.

"Corky," I hear, in a loud whisper. Standing on a small rim, above where the bull had just stopped, stood Dad and Craig. They went on to tell me how they had found these two bulls in the feeding area that they had spooked after catching sight of them. They felt about as high as a wart on a snakes belly after running off the only two bulls we had seen in a seven day period, especially without being able to find me They explained that they were just following the tracks where the buffalo had spooked, when all of the sudden, they saw the largest of the two coming toward them. Unbeknownst to me, the bull had stopped no further than 10 yards below them. My dad was wondering where I was, when all of the sudden he heard the sound of an arrow. The next thing he saw was an arrow sticking out of the bull in the ten-zone. He kept telling me that I needed to slow down on my pursuit, but the view he had of the bison was of its left side and he didn't know that I had a well-placed arrow on the right side. The bull went down no more than 75 yards from our conversation.

Kaibab is laced with wilderness area from one end to the other, but this bison chose to die on a two-track logging road; packing would not be a problem. Once we approached the bison, my dad knew right away that he had never seen a picture nor heard of one with this size of horns. The bull expired with one side of the horn down in the dirt, and it took all three of us to turn its head around and see if we had two sides that matched; indeed we did!

I was able to get a hold of Phil before he had made his trip back to Tucson. He had traveled halfway when he heard part of a broken up cell phone message from me. He determined that one of two things had happened: either I needed help or I had gotten a bison. Either way, he was headed back. He found us around midnight.

I drove down to the game manager's house to get him to confirm a bow kill before any field-dressing took place. He couldn't believe that I had actually killed one with a bow on one of Arizona's most difficult hunts. When he saw the bison, he said that to his knowledge, he had not seen that particular bull. He aged the bull according to the jaw age charts, aging the bull at over 16 years.

God had blessed me way beyond my wildest dreams with an exceptional animal and extraordinary friends and family that will remain with me for a lifetime and an eternity. Did I mention that he died on an old road? If you have ever skinned and quartered a 2,000-pound animal then you know how truly blessed I was.

Award Winning Moments...

Photograph by Keith Balfourd

On Press Day, several members of the outdoor media interviewed, filmed, and photographed the trophy owners. Pictured above is well-known outdoor writer and MC of the Welcoming Dinner, Craig Boddington (left) talking with Guinn Crousen about this new World's Record bighorn sheep.

TROPHY STATS

▼ ▼ ▼ ▼ ▼

Category
bison

Score
124 $^2/_8$

Location
Teton County, Wyoming — 1998

Hunter
Terry Mathes

Length of Horn
Right: 18 $^1/_8$ Left: 18 $^1/_8$

Circumference of Base
Right: 15 $^6/_8$ Left: 15 $^1/_8$

Greatest Spread
28 $^1/_8$

BOONE AND CROCKETT CLUB'S

BISON
Honorable Mention – 124²/₈

▼ ▼ ▼ ▼ ▼ ▼ ▼ ▼ ▼

TERRY MATHES

In 1998, I applied to the Wyoming Game and Fish Department bison draw. Shortly thereafter I learned I had drawn for the second shoot. The first time I was called to go after my bison, I was ready to leave when I received a phone call from the Game and Fish. An animal rights group stopped the hunt with an injunction.

Shortly after the first time, I was called a second time to go for my bison hunt. I left for Jackson Hole and, once again, the hunt was stopped by the same group.

The third time I was called, there were only three days left to hunt that season. If it didn't work out this time, my hunt would probably be over.

I arrived in Jackson and was required to do a composition and oral test. The Game and Fish wants to make sure you know the difference between male and female bison before you begin your hunt. My license was only good for male bison.

First thing on the morning of October 29, I was able to hunt for my bison. My friend, Jeff O'Brien, arrived at the hunt area, which was on U.S. Forest Service land, not on the national elk refuge. We spotted a bison that fit all the descriptions I was given to identify a male buffalo. The bison spotted us as well, and ran over a hill.

We put on our fluorescent orange and I pulled out my .300 with my 3x9 scope and started hunting. We spotted the bison in some aspens that were close to the closed area, which was the refuge. We searched for the boundary markers and found that the animal was legal to shoot. I used a rest in the "V" of a tree and made a clean kill.

Jeff and I walked over to the animal and found that it was absolutely huge. I didn't know it was a record-class bison as I wasn't thinking of a trophy hunt. I was just excited to even draw a license. We field-dressed the animal and the Game and Fish biologist took samples for disease testing.

I feel very lucky to have been able to take this trophy animal. Later, on the same day as I harvested it, there was another injunction put on the area we hunted. I was one of only two people able to take a bison on the hunt.

Photograph courtesy of Terry Mathes

After his third attempt, Terry Mathes, was finally able to take this tremendous bison that scores 124-2/8 points.

TROPHY STATS

▼ ▼ ▼ ▼ ▼

Category
Rocky Mountain goat

Score
$54^6/_8$

Location
Vixen Inlet, Alaska — 2001

Hunter
Ross M. Groben

Length of Horn
Right: $11^4/_8$ Left: $11^4/_8$

Circumference of Base
Right: $5^6/_8$ Left: $5^6/_8$

Greatest Spread
$6^1/_8$

BOONE AND CROCKETT CLUB'S

ROCKY MOUNTAIN GOAT
First Award – 54 ⁶/₈

▼ ▼ ▼ ▼ ▼ ▼ ▼ ▼ ▼

ROSS M. GROBEN

It was October of 2001 when my friend and guide, Ed Toribio, called me from Ketchikan, Alaska. I had met Ed years ago in college and our interests in forestry and hunting had kept us in regular contact over the years. I have hunted with Ed every three or four years since then. Our earlier professions in forestry had kept us both in the outdoors and in excellent physical condition. We have made some grueling hunts together in the mountains of southeast Alaska. Ed is an extremely tough and competent woodsman and outdoorsman, and together we have weathered many severe conditions hunting in the late season.

On this expedition I was looking for a great goat. I appreciate competition taxidermy and wanted a beautiful, long-haired goat to mount life-size in a natural setting. I also appreciate a trophy-quality animal that exemplifies mass and evenness in addition to overall size. When I hunt with Ed, we are able to access some very tough areas where the "big boys" hang out and very few hunters ever tread. We do this hunting other game in other states as well. Trophy hunting in this manner, with these things in mind, has allowed me

to see many quality animals and enjoy lengthened hunting experiences by not ending a hunt early. To watch and learn from these animals that I have chosen not to shoot has taught me valuable lessons and helped me be successful in getting the wary, older, and challenging animals.

I arrived in Ketchikan less than 24 hours after Ed contacted me at my home in Oregon. Ed has been a registered guide in Alaska for many years now, specializing in trophy goats. He has guided his hunters to as many as three B&C goats in a year with his limited clientele. He knows his business well. Ed had enlisted his friend, Aaron Worthy, a young tough guy, to hunt with us. That way we could pack the proper gear in and hopefully pack a goat out in

Photograph courtesy of Ed Toribio

A bush plane taxis towards the hunting group on a remote lake on the Cleveland Peninsula to pick them up to take them home.

one trip. This was not a hunt for the timid, and we would have heavy packs in steep, brushy country.

As our bush plane floated out of the sky and down to a lake on the Cleveland Peninsula, I anticipated the long hike through the big timber and thick brush of southeast Alaska. It would culminate in a spike camp somewhere about timberline. Ed had the plan well thought out. We knew the weather could turn nasty at any moment this time of year. It did, but we were prepared and experienced.

After hiking nearly 3,000 feet in elevation and most of the day, we arrived at Ed's predetermined spike camp location in a high saddle between two mountains, and just below timberline. The wind was blowing through the saddle, along with the usual driving rain. We were in for a storm that night.

We set up camp, stacked some wood, and started a fire. We were cold and wet after a long day of hiking from the lake near sea level. Ed brewed up some hot tang and some freeze-dried dinners. The hot food and drink hit the spot, and we were soon in the three-man tent to get some sleep.

In the morning, after hot oatmeal and coffee, we ascended from the saddle on the east mountain just high enough to spot a billy through the fog, but only for an instant. It was blowing again and raining along with mixed snow. Ed rigged up a tarp in the rocks for some protection from the elements, allowing us to set up and use a spotting scope. We were hoping to see the billy if the fog cleared again. We found some scattered wood here and there and started a warming fire. Then we settled in for a long wait.

Late in the day, the wind blew open a hole in the fog just long enough for us to see that the billy was still there. Although we determined it to have 8-1/2 to 9 inch horns, we were looking for a bigger and older billy.

It was late afternoon so we headed back down the mountain to spike camp where we were in for a dramatic night of wind and more nasty weather. In the middle of the night we listened in awe as the wind howled through the trees. During one intense gust some of the grommets finally gave way under the pressure of the wind and one of the tarps ripped free. Then another tarp string snapped and it sounded like all the tarps were being torn to shreds. We reluctantly crawled out of the tent with our headlamps, illuminating the ferocious storm. We were shivering within seconds, but managed to make some quick makeshift repairs and crawled back into our bags, hoping everything would hold together the remainder of the night. We really hoped the big hemlock adjacent to out tent would not decide to let go in the storm. I can remember dozing off and on, only to be awakened by each blast of wind, each time sounding as if a jet were passing by at tree top level. We later got the weather report indicating the wind had been blowing over 100 miles per hour. Not even Ed's expertise in survival-type weather could hold up against Mother Nature that night.

When daylight came, and without any breakfast or much sleep, I immediately pulled on my boots and headed back up the east mountain. Ed and Aaron agreed to reassemble camp. There was no time to waste as I was in a hurry to beat the fog that always seems to blow in not long after daylight.

ROCKY MOUNTAIN GOAT
First Award – 54⁶/₈

▼ ▼ ▼ ▼ ▼

Ross M. Groben

My plan was to traverse a very long ridge at the top of the east mountain and look back to a rugged steep face on the westerly sister mountain a mile away. Like any "bruiser" of big game animals, they often live in the roughest, most inaccessible areas of their home range. In this case, there was protection for a big billy from wolves and grizzlies on these steep precipices. They guard these places even from other billies and hide out there for great lengths of time during the winter months.

After a couple hours, I reached the end of the ridge, fighting the wind, rain, and sleet. I stopped several times on the leeward side of large boulders the size of trucks so I could hold steady to glass the long distance and try to see through the weather. The fog and sleet were blowing horizontally in the gale force wind. It was interesting to see it being sucked through the saddle far below and to my left.

Finally, there was an opening for a brief moment, just long enough for me to spot a goat bedded on the rock face across and to my left.. I could just make out its front leg bent up as it braced itself against the wind as it lay bedded. The goat's body was huge. I knew from experience that most likely this was the billy I wanted. Generally, most animals take to the leeward areas for protection from weather, but not this big billy. I have seen this before hunting other trophy animals. The big ones are the toughest and the smartest.

I grabbed my gear and high-tailed it off the east mountain, and down to the saddle and spike camp. As I approached, Ed and Aaron were still fixing camp. I shouted to them to grab their gear and follow me up out of the saddle and onto the west side of the other mountain. I was still traveling light with only a fanny pack. I'm glad Ed and Aaron grabbed their packs and some food as they followed me.

It took an hour to reach a point that I could begin to peer over the edge and locate ourselves in relation to where the billy had been bedded. I had marked several outcroppings from the east mountain, but the fog and rain and snow blowing sideways allowed only moments to pierce its cover. It made me wonder if I had it right when there was no billy in sight. I had the area pegged, but it took another full hour of stealth and repeated mock crawls to try and locate the billy. Finally, we had covered the area thoroughly with no luck.

We decided to hike over the top, above tree line, to look for tracks and ensure our goat had not given us the slip. While Ed and Aaron were covering the top of the ridge, I headed down a small finger ridge around the back side of the rock face where the goat had been bedded . I immediately found day-old tracks. As I descended down the grassy finger, the sign became fresher and fresher. I knew I was now in the billy's hidey-hole. I headed for a timbered ridge that hooked back to the right and below where I had spotted the goat early that morning. This was the only other angle to see the face, the draws, and rocky brush-covered ridges. Hopefully, I could find the goat. This face had a cliff below that dropped off over 1,000 feet straight down. The brush was so thick anything could successfully hide

Ross M. Groben, Ed Toribio, and Aaron Worthy pose for a picture with Ross' award-winning Rocky Mountain goat. The billy scores 54-6/8 points and received a First Place Award at the 25th Awards Program in Kansas City.

there, but I felt it in my blood that the billy was close. I knew I would find it no matter how long it took.

As I was heading for the big timber and hopefully a place to see, I noticed a small hole in brush and trees. I could see part of the rock face covered with green vegetation. I turned to my right and crept up to the small opening realizing it was a game trail. As I came to the edge, there it was. The billy was only 40 yards from me, feeding along the steep sidehill. The wind was still perfect.

This goat was huge in both body and horn, but I needed Ed to make sure. I only saw it momentarily and then instantly headed back up the hill to look for Ed. He was heading my way with Aaron right behind him. Ed and I know how to hunt together, and he knows me well. I knew he would be coming. When we separate and he doesn't see me for a while he knows I am usually onto something. He was already looking for me.

We hurried to the opening to size up the billy. We didn't just want a B&C goat, we wanted a exceptional B&C goat with good hair and one we could harvest for a life-size mount. This was the billy.

It was almost facing us and feeding our way, 40 yards out and slightly below our level. I had to place the shot just to the left of its right horn and into its body at the base of the neck and in front of the right shoulder. The shot had to kill the goat instantly or we would lose it over the 1,000 foot waterfall and cliff below. Even then it was risky. Once Ed informed me that its horns were extremely long and had mass that carried far up the horn, I decided to take the shot. Ed knew this billy was exceptional.

At the shot, the billy disappeared. It was dead before it hit the ground, as there was really no ground to hit, it was so steep. The goat had been feeding across a small headwall and instantly dropped out of our sight. We heard it for only a second and then nothing but the sound of rain and wind.

Ed headed over the steep face of slick green vegetation with me close on his heels. Ed went right for the cliff, contemplating the worst. Part way down to that edge, I headed across to the small chute where we lost sight of it at the shot. And there the billy was right above me, caught sideways with its head buried underneath its huge body. The goat was positioned at right angle to the chute. Its head had helped pin it in the chute, but ready to dislodge at any moment and slide by me over the cliff. As we worked up to it, Ed told me that we had one big goat. And as we all tugged and pulled and situated the goat to get its head uncovered and its body stabilized, we all realized just how exceptional this goat was.

It was exciting to have accomplished our search for an exceptional B&C goat. The stalk, the chase, and the hunt for it were satisfying as we looked at it and appreciated everything it was. We guessed the billy's body size at 400 pounds and felt its 11-1/2-inch horns smoothly in our hands. Its hooves were a mess with huge chunks missing, caused from the rocky conditions and its age. The billy was eight years old and had exceptional horn growth its first year on that mountain.

The three of us skinned it and boned out the meat. The full skin and the meat were all we could pack in one trip back to camp. We all wear cork boots, as without them the wet, slippery, vegetated cliffs would be fatal. Even the bare rocks can be climbed with sharp, pointed corks.

We arrived in camp at dark and enjoyed retelling each part of the day's events in detail as we celebrated by the fire. The rain, snow, and wind had finally let up a little. Hunting with Ed and Primo Expeditions is what great hunting is all about. The rough weather, the woodsmanship, the trophy goats, and the success make memories that are not forgotten and are what brings us back to the outdoors for more.

Photograph by Cliff White

TROPHY STATS

▼ ▼ ▼ ▼ ▼

Category
   Rocky Mountain goat

Score
   54

Location
   Stikine River, British Columbia — 2003

Hunter
   Shawn K. MacFarlane

Length of Horn
   Right: $10^3/_8$ Left: $10^2/_8$

Circumference of Base
   Right: $6^1/_8$ Left: 6

Greatest Spread
   $7^6/_8$

378

ROCKY MOUNTAIN GOAT
Second Award – 54

▼ ▼ ▼ ▼ ▼ ▼ ▼ ▼ ▼

Shawn K. MacFarlane

I have wanted to hunt mountain goats for as long as I can remember. Though not as glamorous as other North American big game, goats possess a rugged, indestructible beauty that has appealed to me since I was old enough to pull a trigger. The harsh, unforgiving environment that mountain goats call home only added fuel to my romantic notions. I spent many winter evenings dreaming of backpacking adventures into remote places, glassing the billy of my dreams from some high perch or across a rocky canyon, and then executing the perfect stalk, overcoming difficult odds to finally collect my prize.

So, in the late 1970s, in my home state of Washington, I began applying for

The 25-Year Wait

a goat tag. Now, it's important to note that in those days, Washington issued a lot of goat tags. A lot. "Just not my turn yet," I told myself. "Your luck will change."

But as each year rolled by, and the number of available tags grew fewer and fewer, my luck did not change. In 1996, Washington introduced a point system and I thought that now, surely my luck would change. My luck did not change.

By the time I received my annual notification in August 2003 that, once again, I had not drawn a goat tag. I was one frustrated goat hunter. Taking the only course of action left available to me, I booked a hunt with Heidi Gutfrucht, owner of Northwest Ranching and Outfitting. Come October 2003, the itch would be scratched.

I arrived in Dease Lake on October 8, for what was to be an eight-day backpack hunt in some of the most productive mountain goat country British Columbia has to offer. After a short and scenic floatplane ride, we touched down at our destination. In the fading evening light, as I unpacked and organized my gear, I was treated to the sight of moose feeding on the other side of the small lake, which had served as our landing strip. I took the sighting of any wild game to be a sign of good things to come and was anxious to get an early start the next day.

Anticipation was high the next morning as Heidi, her guide, Shawn Dennis, and I motored our way across the Stikine River by jet boat while a steady rain fell from the sky. The Stikine flowed high and fast, stained by glacial silt, and from the first moment I looked at her, that river had my respect.

Once we were on the other side, we donned our packs and began the climb that would eventually lead us into prime goat country. I wish I could say that the three-hour climb was

Shawn K. MacFarlane ended his hunt of a lifetime on the first day when he took this award-winning Rocky Mountain goat. Shawn, center, is pictured here with guide Shawn Dennis, left, and outfitter Heidi Gutfrucht.

easy, but I'd be leaving out the part about the blisters I raised on my heels and the cramping in my thighs and calves. Heidi and Shawn are both in top shape and had me outclassed in the hiking department. Upon arriving at our spike camp we dropped our packs, watered up, and continued up the trail as the ceiling began to lift and the sun broke through the clouds.

Easing our way out onto the open rocky cliffs, glassing the breaks ahead, it didn't take long for our guide to spot the first goats. What a sight. It was just like I had always imagined it. Rugged, solitary animals bedded in a rugged inaccessible place. Too far away to field judge, we began closing the distance. As we made our way along the top of the breaks, we began to see more goats. Each time we gained a new vantage point, we spotted new goats. The only problem was all the animals that we saw were across the canyon or in places that mere mortals dare not tread.

We were standing on the edge of a shear rock cliff, taking another look at the first goats we had spotted when our guide, Shawn, leaned out and peeked over the edge. His eyes got as big as silver dollars as he nearly leaped back from the lip of the shear rock face. There, bedded 70 yards straight below us was a lone billy. We could tell that it had great mass at its bases, but really had no idea how long its horns were because we were looking straight down at

ROCKY MOUNTAIN GOAT
Second Award – 54

▼ ▼ ▼ ▼ ▼

SHAWN K. MACFARLANE

them. Heidi put the spotting scope on the billy, counted its growth rings, and estimated it to be at least five and a half years old, but still was not able to get any idea of its length. It was decision time.

I had waited a lifetime for this hunt. Did I really want to end it on the first day? Ultimately, the decision to shoot had more to do with the fact that it was in a place we could get to than because we thought the billy was a good animal. In fact we were so uncertain of exactly how big the billy was that I considered passing it up. I knew my guides wanted me to take it, but like true professionals, they never pressured me.

Finally, I looked out across the canyon at the sharp gray cliffs that fell hundreds of feet straight down to the little creek below. I saw goats bedded out on the edge of impossible places. Places that we had no chance of getting to. I looked straight down at the billy laying only 70 yards below, and made my decision. "Let's take it."

After a brief disagreement with Shawn regarding how low to hold on a straight downhill shot, I belly crawled out to the edge, hung over the lip of the cliff, and promptly shot twice over the billy's back. Lesson number one, always listen to your guide! Now, holding a foot below its brisket, my third shot found its mark just as the billy disappeared behind the contour of the cliff.

Nervous moments passed before it reappeared. The goat was walking normally and did not appear to be hit. It was out at about 150 yards now and heading for the safety of the river breaks. Heidi had warned me that sometimes a wounded goat will leap over the edge of the breaks in an effort to escape, never to be recovered. We could hear the thwack of the 180-grain bullet hitting home, but the billy never flinched. At about 250 yards, the billy paused in a big jumble of rocks, stood motionless a moment, and then collapsed. It was finally down.

We had to backtrack around the rim of the canyon to find a safe route to get down to the billy. It seemed like it took forever. After handshakes and bear hugs, Shawn dug a tape measure out of his pack. "Ten and three-eighths inches," he announced.

Heidi and Shawn began to laugh out loud. I knew by their reaction that the billy I had almost passed on was in fact, the billy of a lifetime.

TROPHY STATS

▼ ▼ ▼ ▼ ▼

Category
Rocky Mountain
goat

Score
$53^6/_8$

Location
Del Creek, British Columbia — 2003

Hunter
Dora L. Hetzel

Length of Horn
Right: $10^2/_8$ Left: $10^2/_8$

Circumference of Base
Right: $6^1/_8$ Left: $6^1/_8$

Greatest Spread
$7^6/_8$

Photograph by Jack Renez

Dora L. Hetzel accepting her plaque and
medal from Buck Buckner, Chair of the
Big Game Records Committee.

ROCKY MOUNTAIN GOAT
Third Award – 53 $^6/_8$

▼ ▼ ▼ ▼ ▼ ▼ ▼ ▼ ▼

Dora L. Hetzel

I was excited and a little nervous about heading to Canada again. I had accompanied my husband, Bob, on his first attempt at hunting a mountain goat two years earlier. That hunt proved to be an unsuccessful, very grueling, and exhausting trip — not one that I was ready to repeat. This time, however, we were both hunting. The thought of harvesting my own goat was the fuel that kept me going.

Bob and I left Chicago for Kyllo Brothers Outfitters on August 25, 2003. We stayed over night in Prince George at a bed and breakfast with owners, Jackie and Lutz Klaar. A lot of hunters heading for Kyllo's stay there, and it was enjoyable hearing stories of the hunters before us. The following morning we headed for the airport where a small plane would take us to camp.

Camp was located northwest of Prince George, British Columbia, near Del Creek and Finlay River. As we landed on the dirt runway, we could see the log cabin main house, horse corrals, and other small buildings that housed the staff. We were greeted by Scott Kyllo, owner and operator. After settling in, we met the staff and our guide, Bill Chapman. At the time, Bob and I were the only hunters in camp. The main house was an impressive log cabin building with trophies proudly displayed on the walls.

And so our hunt began. Early in the mornings we would travel by truck on logging trails to the base of the mountains or to the tops of the valleys where we could glass. Bob and I both had tags for black bear, elk, caribou, wolf, and mountain goat. We had seen many black bear, grizzly, and moose, but elk, caribou, and wolf were a little harder to find that time of year. We did see, however, a lot of mountain goats. Once we decided to go after an animal, it was then we faced a long, rigorous climb to get close enough for a shot. The days were long and very tiring, but seeing so many animals kept our spirits high.

Bob was the first to harvest his goat — a billy with 9-1/2-inch horns and a great white coat. His hunt was a two-day event, up one side of a mountain, down the other, and half way up yet another. We camped overnight on the mountain and packed out his goat the next day. This experience had about done me in. I told our guide, Bill, that I didn't think I could handle climbing another mountain for my goat. Bill assured me that I had it in me to complete the hunt.

The weather had been great for August. The morning we set out for my goat was no exception. We loaded up the truck that would take us to the base of the mountain. Bill had

Dora L. Hetzel gathered up enough strength to take her own Rocky Mountain goat after hiking along with her husband, Bob, for his. Dora's billy measures 53-6/8 points and received a Third Place Award at the 25th Awards Program in Kansas City.

explained the night before about an area in which he had seen goats, and that's where we were headed. As we slowed to a stop, Bill pointed out the spot where he had spotted the goats once before. I glanced up and thought to myself, those mountains don't seem so bad. First impressions can be tricky. We climbed out of the truck and put our packs on our backs. Ready for anything, we had food, tents, and all the necessities for an overnight stay.

We started our hike across a clearcut, then into the woods. Soon we came upon some rocky gorges. As we ventured further into the woods we came upon grizzly sign and a grizzly bedding area. I had an eerie feeling about being in the quiet woods knowing that a very large bear was probably watching. Finally, we approached an outcropping where we could see across a very large ravine to the side of the next mountain. There they were! Two large-bodied billies feeding in the bright sunlight.

Bob was quick to point out the larger of the two and excitedly told me to get ready. Sizing up the goat in the binoculars was difficult, as I could not stop shaking. Bill whispered to me that it was a very large billy. I took a firm grip on the .300 and laid down on the rocky outcropping.

Trying to calm myself, I breathed deep. After a few moments, when the goat turned broadside, I squeezed the trigger. Boom! I was so nervous I couldn't tell if my shot had hit its mark, but my husband's reaction told me it did. "Great shot! Great shot!" he exclaimed.

Trying to find the goat in the scope to make another shot was almost impossible. Finally, there it was, standing as if nothing was wrong. I let off another shot but missed; I was shaking so bad I

ROCKY MOUNTAIN GOAT
Third Award – 53^6/$_8$

▼ ▼ ▼ ▼ ▼

Dora L. Hetzel

could hardly hold the gun. Just then the goat stepped down into the tree line out of sight. I waited to see if it would show itself again, but it didn't. My stomach turned at the thought that I may have lost such a great trophy. Bill, thinking the goat had for sure been hit, decided we would go after it.

Bob stayed behind on the outcropping to watch from a distance. Bill and I set off to what I thought would be a quick hike up the side of the mountain. Boy was I wrong! The valley between the outcropping where we stood and the opposite mountainside proved to be more than challenging. We struggled down the valley and up the other side trying to get above where the goat was. After a two-hour climb, we finally got there. Bill crept up and peeked over a large rock and quickly sunk back down. He motioned that the goat was just over the rock. I prepared myself and slowly climbed over to where I could see it.

As I peered over the rock, I saw the large beast 15 yards away staring right at me. Strangely enough, the billy just stood there. I brought my gun up and steadied myself. I waited and watched though the scope as the goat just stared at me. Then, as if in slow motion, it turned to go down the hill. I let off a shot that landed behind the shoulder. It disappeared into the trees once again. I heard a loud crash in the trees and knew the goat was down. Through my binoculars, I looked to see if Bob had caught the action. He signaled "touchdown" which told me he had.

Bill and I sat down exhausted from both fatigue and excitement. By the time we headed down to find my goat, Bob had made his way to us. The three of us searched to find where the goat had landed on the steep mountainside. As I approached the goat, I could hardly stand my legs were shaking so much. I didn't realize at the time just how massive the animal was. Bob and Bill both commented that it was the largest goat either had seen before. I felt very fortunate to have successfully taken my mountain goat.

Luckily, I was able to complete the hunt early enough in the day that we were able to pack out the meat and hide and just make it back to the truck as it got dark. Later that night we cleaned the hide and green scored the goat. Scott Kyllo and other guides at camp couldn't believe the mass of the horns and were more amazed at how old my billy was. Scott estimated 11 years or better. The green score was 52-6/8 points, which won my guide, Bill Chapman, the Silver Buckle, a Canadian guide's award.

After returning to the U.S., I took my horns to a B&C measurer to get an official score. The final measurement turned out to be 53-6/8 inches, scoring high enough to be invited to the 25th Awards Program where my goat received a Third Place Award. Looking back on my hunt, I am grateful that my husband and I both harvested great mountain goats, but I'm even more grateful that we were able to experience our hunts together.

TROPHY STATS

▼ ▼ ▼ ▼ ▼

Category
Rocky Mountain goat

Score
$53^4/_8$

Location
Elko County, Nevada — 2002

Hunter
R. Dean Conley

Length of Horn
Right: $10^4/_8$ Left: $10^6/_8$

Circumference of Base
Right: 6   Left: 6

Greatest Spread
$7^4/_8$

ROCKY MOUNTAIN GOAT

Fourth Award – 53⁴/₈

▼ ▼ ▼ ▼ ▼ ▼ ▼ ▼ ▼

R. Dean Conley

By Christa Conley

On October 6, 2002, my father Dean Conley, family friend Jerry Vega, Uncle Travis Myers, and myself, Christa Conley, arrived at the bottom of the beautiful Ruby Mountains sometime around 5:30 a.m. After loading all our packs and discussing a plan, we started up the north side of Lamoille Canyon. The trip to the top of this 10,000 foot peak would take somewhere around three to four hours.

Prior to this, we had been on several scouting trips. My dad and a few of his friends had been to the top several times; I had only been there once. We knew the goats were there; between the 4 of us we had seen approximately 50 head in the area where we were preparing to hunt.

When we were about halfway up the mountain we spotted a large herd off to our right. They had gathered there from a previous snow. This herd was mostly ewes and lambs, and maybe a couple of young billies. We had stopped to watch the herd move slowly around to the other side, when a nice billy appeared above us over the skyline. We immediately set out the spotting scope, watched its every move, and debated whether it was worth pursuing. We agreed this goat was definitely what we had been looking for. Soon, it bedded down in a large cluster of rocks. We instantly noticed it would be unable to see us come in from below.

We carefully put the spotting scope away and began our ambush. Slowly, but surely, we made our way to the top, being careful not to make any noise. When we got there, we saw the billy had moved to the left and was standing on a large boulder with surrounding rocks. My dad had to aim carefully to hit it, as only its head and shoulders were visible. Jerry and I waited patiently as Dad took his time aiming. Dad shot once and the rocks scattered around the goat.

Jerry and I hollered in excitement thinking Dad had just taken a beautiful goat. We walked over to where the goat had been standing and there were no signs of blood or anything. We soon realized Dad must have shot directly below it. Knowing the hunt was over for the day, we relaxed and ate lunch at the top of the mountain. While taking a nice break before we started down the mountain, we spotted a couple of goats across the mountain to our left. We discussed going up that peak and agreed on a good plan. On our way down the mountain we saw a ewe and lamb, and also a small group of young billies.

On October 7, we decided to take a day off to give ourselves a well-deserved break. That night I spotted about eight head with the spotting scope. They were grazing on the peak we were planning to climb.

R. Dean Conley, second from right, sits proudly next to his daughter Christa, and hunting partners Travis Meyer and Jerry Vega. Dean's Rocky Mountain goat scores 53-4/8 points and received a Fourth Place Award at the 25th Awards Program in Kansas City.

The following morning, we arrived in the canyon about 5:30 a.m. We had dropped off Travis on the west side of the peak to be a lookout. We told him to start up the peak and meet us at the top once he knew Dad had shot. We headed up the south side of the mountain, reaching the top within three hours. We then headed west to where we had located the goats the previous night.

About three-quarters of the way up the peak, we spotted a decent billy lying alongside a ridge we needed to cross. So as not to spook it, the three of us decided to go below and around the goat. That took quite awhile because the mountainside we crossed was nothing but loose rocks and boulders. Finally, we reached some solid ground with a few dead trees. Dad and I stayed below the trees, while Jerry went up higher to scout. We were now very close to the peak we had been striving to reach, while Jerry very slowly crawled to the top of a clump of rocks.

Dad and I took out the spotting scope and were glassing when we spotted a gorgeous, large billy. Jerry saw the billy about 900 yards away and remained frozen, for fear of scaring it away. Dad and I looked it over for quite some time. The billy must have known something was not right, because it remained still over the ridge for about 20 minutes. We decided this is what we had come for; this was the one.

The billy must have thought there was no apparent danger, because it slowly turned away and walked around to the opposite side of the peak. Dad and I crawled up the rocks after

Jerry's all-clear signal. Jerry said he thought that billy was definitely worth going after. After all agreeing, we headed for the goat, now along the front side. We were coming in from the back and moving down the side so we could get a clear view of where it was, when we once again spotted the goat. It was looking to the southeast, down into the canyon. We quietly discussed whether it was the same goat we were after for about three minutes. The billy was about 200 yards away and situated such that if it was to be shot, it would not roll all the way down the peak to the bottom. Dad then asked me, "Christa, is that the same goat?"

ROCKY MOUNTAIN GOAT
Fourth Award – 53⁴/₈

▼ ▼ ▼ ▼ ▼

R. DEAN CONLEY

Reassuringly I said, "Yeah, that's it Dad; that's the one!"

He confidently pulled out his Ruger 7mm, rested it carefully on one of our sweatshirts, and aimed. He had to be patient, so he would not make any mistakes. He then pulled the trigger. "Boom!" The goat went down! We all stood up breathless, then looked at one another. We shouted out knowing that Dad had taken it with one shot!

Quickly, we gathered our gear and eagerly headed toward the downed goat. I was in front and so anxious to see this wonderful beast we all worked so hard to get. After walking to where I thought the goat was, I started to worry as I did not see it. I climbed about 10 feet to the very top of a rock gathering, and looked down. I saw a goat lying there. I screamed, "It's still alive!"

My dad angrily yelled at me, "Quiet! You're going to scare it!"

The goat got up and started down the ridge with a slight gimp. My dad hurriedly ran to where he could see the goat. As soon as he saw it, he knew it was not the billy he had shot. He looked around and saw his goat lying motionless, right where it had been shot. He stated, "Christa, it's right here."

I let out a deep sigh of relief for fear I had just let our goat get away. Suddenly, about 15 goats ran down the south side of the ledge. Not one of them had moved after my dad fired his rifle!

Jerry, Dad, and I climbed up the rocks to where the goat lay. Dad picked up the billy's head and was elated! The goat was so big! We knew whatever the measurements were going to be, this billy would make it into the records book. We started skinning and quartering right away. My Uncle Travis arrived at this time to help quarter. Once we finished, we all took a heavy load and headed down the mountain.

The walk down seemed like it took forever! I didn't think we were ever going to get to the bottom! We struggled the whole way down and my Uncle Travis was getting exhausted. Being so anxious, I was the first one to the truck. Jerry followed, then my dad. Poor Uncle Travis was last. When he finally reached the bottom, sweat was caked on Uncle Travis' face; he could barely move!

This hunt was the most memorable hunt I had ever been on. Dad's goat ranks third in the state with a score of 53-4/8 and took the Kit Carson first place award for the year of 2002. Without the help of Jerry Vega, Uncle Travis Myers, Carey MacDonald, Enos Vega, Tim Murphy, and Gary German, this hunt wouldn't have been possible. Thank you all very much!

New World's Record

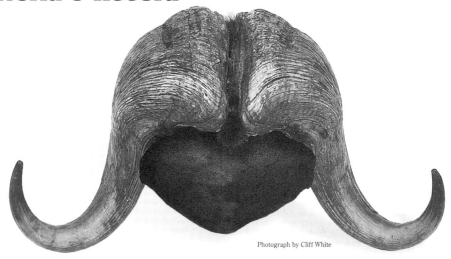

Photograph by Cliff White

TROPHY STATS

▼ ▼ ▼ ▼ ▼

Category
muskox

Score
129

Location
Norman Wells, Northwest
Territories — 2002

Hunter
Craig D. Scott

Length of Horn
Right: 29^5/$_8$ Left: 28^3/$_8$

Width of Boss
Right: 11   Left: 11

Greatest Spread
29^1/$_8$

Photograph by Jack Renea

Craig D. Scott accepting his plaque and
medal from Buck Buckner, Chair of the
Big Game Records Committee.

MUSKOX
First Award – 129

▼ ▼ ▼ ▼ ▼ ▼ ▼ ▼ ▼

CRAIG D. SCOTT

It's a long way from the rocky, windswept, often fogbound island of Newfoundland on Canada's east coast to the heart of the Northwest Territories' small town of Norman Wells on the Mackenzie River just south of the Arctic Circle. Craig Scott is one of the many hundreds of Newfoundlanders who has made the journey from "the Rock" to the Northwest Territories. For Craig, one of the appeals of living "north of sixty" was the wonderful big game hunting opportunities promised by a life in the western Arctic.

Muskox populations in the Northwest Territories have been doing very well over the last few decades, after having been virtually eliminated during the early part of the last century. They have rebounded in both numbers and distribution to the point where trophy hunting by both resident and non-resident hunters is again possible across a wide portion of the huge territory. In the Sahtu region of the central Northwest Territories, resident hunters have been able to apply for one (1992/93 - 2000/01) or two tags (since 2001/02) on a limited-entry draw system. Craig eagerly entered the resident draw for each of the five years prior to his name being selected for the 2001/02 hunting year — the first year in which resident hunters had two tags available in the draw. This was a chance to participate in a

truly exciting and quite unique big game hunting opportunity. Craig was absolutely delighted when he found out his name had been drawn in May 2001.

Craig had no previous experience with muskox. He'd never even seen one in the wild, since muskox do not live on the island of Newfoundland. Yet he now held a precious tag for one of these shaggy, quintessential Arctic animals. So, he enlisted the help of a friend in Norman Wells, Garth Hummelle, to go along with him when the time came for his planned muskox hunt in March. Garth has a growing taxidermy business in Norman Wells and has worked for many years as a guide for Dall's sheep and mountain caribou for non-resident hunters in the Mackenzie Mountains. Garth was to

Photograph courtesy of Craig D. Scott

Craig D. Scott, right, took this World's Record muskox on the first day of his one and only muskox hunt. The bull scores 129 points.

prove a valuable asset to Craig's muskox hunt. In addition to enlisting the assistance of Garth, Craig also decided to visit the local wildlife biologists with the Department of Resources, Wildlife, & Economic Development (DRWED) - the government agency that shares responsibility for managing muskox and other big game species within the Sahtu Settlement Area.

On one of the bitterly cold winter February days that are common in the Sahtu, Craig visited the DRWED office in Norman Wells where he talked with Wildlife Technician Richard Popko about muskox and what he should be looking for in an animal. Craig's primary focus for this hunt was simply to finally taste muskox meat and to put a good supply of meat in his freezer. He wasn't particularly looking for a trophy. In his time in the eastern Arctic, Richard had many years of experience with muskox. He had been an assistant on a famous study of the animals at Polar Bear Pass in what is now the territory of Nunavut. Richard talked with Craig about the animals, and then showed him a large, framed picture of a massive bull muskox that had been taken by a professional wildlife photographer not far from Norman Wells a year or so earlier. Richard had even accompanied the photographer on the trip during which this picture had been taken. Richard said to Craig, "This is what you want to look for," then showed Craig the muskox section of the 11th Edition of the Boone and Crockett Club's *Records of North American Big Game* — just for his further edification. When Craig got home later that evening and was talking to his wife Molly, he said to her, "Well, at least now I know what one looks like!"

On March 22, 2002, Craig, Garth, and their friend Mark Kelly, were finally out on their hunt in a series of rocky hills near Kelly Lake, about 18 miles northwest of Norman Wells. These hills are covered in alpine tundra and surrounded by thick boreal forest. They are a favorite habitat for the Sahtu's muskox throughout the year, but particularly in late winter when snow depths in lower-lying areas can make movement and feeding a little more difficult for the animals. It was a bright, sunny day and quite warm by Sahtu standards, -25°F and with a good six inches of fresh snow draped over the hilltops. A perfect day for hunting!

Craig was carrying a 7mm Remington Magnum and 150-grain shells. After walking about a mile and a half, the trio spied four animals in the distance over a couple of smaller plateaus. It was a little too far to see just how big the animals were, but there was good opportunity for using the plateaus for moving in on them without being detected. The hunt was on! They snuck around the plateaus until they were about 150 yards away. Garth, with the practiced eye of a seasoned hunting guide, told Craig that there was at least one big one in the group after glassing them thoroughly with his binoculars. The men waited and watched the group for another 20 minutes without moving. They were above the small group by about 15 feet; there were no trees in the way, and the shooting conditions were excellent.

The time had come for Craig to take the muskox that Garth had so clearly identified. The foursome was feeding, so their heads were down. Craig took careful aim and his first shot hit the animal square in the chest and lungs. The big bull took the shot, but then turned and ran. Muskox, particularly big old bulls, are amazingly tough animals — as Craig was about to find out. He had

MUSKOX
First Award – 129
▼ ▼ ▼ ▼ ▼
CRAIG D. SCOTT

to follow the animal through the snow, but at least it was relatively easy to follow the sign because of the snow. He worked hard to catch up to it again and managed to finish off the animal. Or so he thought. The valiant old bull managed to find the reserves to get back to its feet, turn, and chase Craig for about 20 feet before falling for the last time not far from where Craig stood, who by now was a little shaky on his own legs!

Garth and Mark made their way over to Craig and his bull. Garth is a man of few words, but excellent big game judgment. Garth's first words to Craig were, "Yup, it's big."

The three carefully caped the animal for Garth, who would later do a front shoulder mount. Then they bagged the tasty meat and made for home in Norman Wells. They wholeheartedly agreed they'd had one very exciting first-ever day of muskox hunting in Northwest Territories!

On April 8, after having let the horns dry in his shed for almost three weeks, Craig again visited the DRWED Wildlife Office to pick up some maps and to shoot the breeze about his muskox hunting experience with the biologists. Craig was describing the size of his horns when the biologists asked him to return home, pick up the horns, and bring them back to the lab. The Regional Wildlife Biologist, Alasdair Veitch, scored the horns out at 128-6/8 points. Then, the Boone and Crockett book was again taken down off the shelf. The current World's Record for a muskox was at 127. Alasdair told Craig repeatedly that since he was not a Boone and Crockett Official Measurer, Craig shouldn't get too excited about having a potential new World's Record. What was certain was that Craig's bull was an extraordinary specimen of the species!

While Alasdair was measuring the horns on a table in the lab, Richard disappeared for a few minutes and returned with the framed print of the big bull he'd shown Craig earlier in February. The shape of the horns and a suite of distinctive scars/cracks on them showed that Craig had taken Richard's advice to heart. He'd shot the bull in the photograph!

After the requisite 60-day drying period was over, Craig took his muskox horns to the capital of the Northwest Territories in Yellowknife where he met with Warren St. Germaine — a Boone and Crockett Official Measurer. Warren took Craig's horns and gave them the treatment. When it was over, Craig Scott's muskox was scored higher than any other muskox in history.

It is indeed a long way from the rocky, windswept, fogbound island of Newfoundland to the heart of Northwest Territories. For one fortunate Newfoundlander, that long trek has culminated in fulfilling any big-game hunter's dream with the taking of a World's Record trophy. However, Craig says that his bull will definitely be the only muskox he ever takes because "it's just too darned much work!"

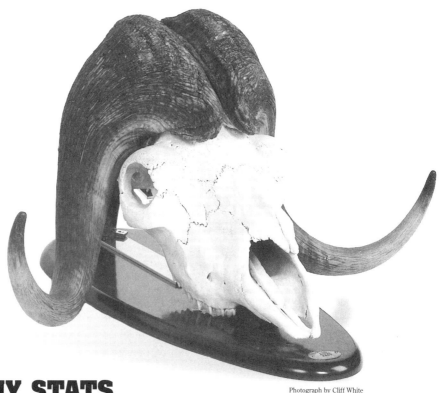

TROPHY STATS

▼ ▼ ▼ ▼ ▼

Category
   muskox

Score
   $127^2/_8$

Location
   Kugluktuk, Nunavut — 1999

Hunter
   Vicente S. Sanchez-Valdepenas

Length of Horn
   Right: $29^2/_8$ Left: $29^7/_8$

Width of Boss
   Right: $10^6/_8$ Left: $10^6/_8$

Greatest Spread
   $29^6/_8$

MUSKOX
Second Award – 127²/₈
▼ ▼ ▼ ▼ ▼ ▼ ▼ ▼ ▼
Vicente S. Sanchez-Valdepenas

There they were! In a far off sea of snow and ice, at the bottom on the other side of the open arctic valley, was a group of 30 muskox napping placidly with the temperature close to -60°F.

Although frigid, the day was shining; a soft sun veiled by scudding clouds slightly blurred the sky. It was the best possible weather that could be hoped for in that latitude exceeding 70° north.

A very thick layer of wool and hair that covered these animals from the upper part of their backs fell in a cascade over their bod-ies, reaching the ground. An escapee from **Hunting the Muskox** pre-history. They looked like direct descen-dants of the extinct woolly mammoths — hairy elephants from the some pre-historic peri-od. Although the wooly mammoths disappeared long ago, their bodies have been found intact as if hibernating in the Arctic ice. They are silent witnesses of an evolving history, living witnesses of their past, gestating in the glacial ice.

Charlie, my Inuit guide, was leading the operation. It had taken us several days to reach the area. We had traveled by sleigh to Kugluktuk in the Coronation Gulf from Yellowknife, Northwest Territories and before that, from Benavente (Zamora), Spain.

Charlie tracked the herd and finally found them. We got closer in an attempt to stalk, but it was impossible to hide in that snowy valley. The herd reacted quickly as we approached, creating a circle of defense with the females and young toward the center and the large, powerful males lining the outer part of the circle.

Charlie and I were trying to locate a good trophy. The males, very uneasy and nervous, thought we were bears. They are not afraid of man because they don't know him. They are rightly afraid of bears, and man is the only predator in addition to the bear that stands on two legs. It would have been impossible to shoot in those circumstances; it was a very compact group and the bullet might hurt another animal after passing through the first.

Suddenly, the nervousness culminated in a stampede. And even though it was the first time that I had seen a muskox, I focused on a large male whose wool was lighter and who was lingering behind the rest of the group. It had been unable to maintain the pace of the escape. After retreating about a mile, the herd regrouped.

We managed to get within 200 yards of them, but they were very nervous and excited. They quickly ran away once again. That same animal with the lighter hair once again fell behind the herd.

Against his guide's wishes, Vicente S. Sanchez-Valdepenas chose to take this light-colored old bull from the herd. It was declared the World's Record by a Boone and Crockett Club Special Judges Panel that met in Missoula, Montana, during August 2001. The bull scores 127-2/8 points.

Charlie was trying to locate a good trophy, and I continued to insist, "Charlie, excuse me, I don't know anything about muskox, but that animal that falls behind, it is either sick or the oldest one in the herd. Since these animals don't lose their horns, and if it is the oldest it must be a good trophy."

"Yes, Vicente," Charlie replied, "but I am going to see if I can spot a really good one."

Stuffed in that marvelous arctic gear, I was about to start boiling. These suits protect you from intensely cold temperatures, but when you walk long distances, the suit turns into an oven. I was not prepared to run any further.

The herd again traveled about less than a mile and regrouped, placing themselves on a rocky hilltop where the wind had swept the snow away. The snow was very fine, like dust or sugar.

Once again they formed a circle, and once again they stampeded when we got closer. They were about 170 yards away from us when they started to run again. Charlie was once again trying to locate a good trophy with enormous difficulty due to the increasing nervousness of the herd. My light-colored and old muskox once again fell behind the stampede by a good margin.

I could not resist the temptation. I took off my right mitten since it limited my capacity to handle the rifle. I aimed my dear and powerful .30-378. Without Charlie's permission, I centered the reticule on the body of that powerful

MUSKOX
Second Award – 127²/₈

▼ ▼ ▼ ▼ ▼

VICENTE S. SANCHEZ-VALDEPENAS

animal, trying to avoid the mistakes of localization caused by so much wool above and below the animal. I softly pressed the trigger. Even now, I can remember the scene — an imaginary movie in slow motion. A vision of slow movement seen through my rifle scope.

Suddenly, my dream was finished, awakened by the powerful recoil and the roaring of my rifle. That marvelous instant that was marching in slow motion disappeared before my surprised eyes.

The stumbling animal remained still while the herd moved away. With quick and automatic movements acquired from many years of hunting in Spain, I placed a second bullet in the marvelous specimen. The hunt was over.

The muskox was large and beautiful, a relic from the past. I didn't feel like a Cro-Magnon, but rather like a Neanderthal in Atapuerca. I had the sensation, the experience, and the feelings that might have been felt by those ancient hunters of millenniums past.

Editor's Note: Vicente's muskox was declared the World's Record by a Special Judges Panel that met in Missoula, Montana, during August 2001. Special Judges Panels are called together during an Awards Program to certify potential World's Records that are accepted by Boone and Crockett Club. Vicente's muskox remained the World's Record until the 25th Awards Program Judges Panel declared Craig Scott's muskox, scoring 129 points, the World's Record in Kansas City on June 19, 2004.

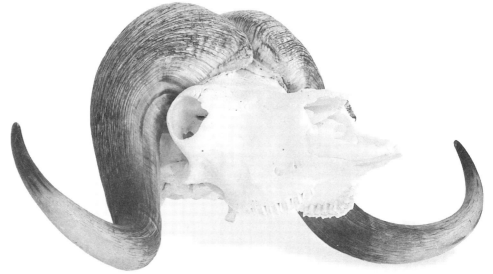

Photograph by Cliff White

TROPHY STATS

▼ ▼ ▼ ▼ ▼

Category
muskox

Score
126 $^4/_8$

Location
Coppermine River, Nunavut — 2003

Hunter
Robert M. Ortiz

Length of Horn
Right: 30 $^6/_8$ Left: 30 $^7/_8$

Width of Boss
Right: 10 $^3/_8$ Left: 10 $^5/_8$

Greatest Spread
29 $^7/_8$

Photograph by Jack Renee

Robert M. Ortiz accepting his plaque and
medal from Buck Buckner, Chair of the
Big Game Records Committee.

BOONE AND CROCKETT CLUB'S

MUSKOX
Third Award – 126⁴/₈

▼ ▼ ▼ ▼ ▼ ▼ ▼ ▼ ▼

ROBERT M. ORTIZ

Most of the major record-book entries listed Fred Webb's name when it came to giant muskox. My first meeting with Fred regarding my desire to hunt these awesome animals took place in 2002 at a hunting convention in Reno. At that time Fred warned me that the hunt was akin to "An Arctic Expedition," and that daily temperatures would range between minus 25°F and minus 45°F. Such temperatures were hard for me to imagine after living in sunny New Mexico for the past 38 years. Despite the warnings, I made arrangements to arrive in Kugluktuk, Nunavut, on March 17 to hunt muskox.

Prior to the hunt, I spent a good amount of time selecting hunting gear for the Arctic's extreme sub-zero conditions. At the end of this task, I ended up taking all new gear except for my binoculars, spotting scope, and muzzleloader. I elected to take my .54 caliber Knight (MK 85) muzzleloader for the hunt. I would utilize a 275-grain Barnes X bullet (with sabot), powered by 110 grains of GOEX FFg black powder.

I met with Fred and Martin Webb at the Kugluktuk Airport on March 17 as planned. Upon my arrival, I came to find that four other hunters would be joining me on the same expedition. We were transported from the airport to a small cabin where we were advised to change into our sub-zero suits and be prepared to leave in an hour. After that, we proceeded with our gear over to a frozen lake where six snowmobiles sat parked, each pulling behind it an attached home-made wooden sled. Loaded on the fronts of each sled were a tent, caribou hides, a Coleman stove, and a few fuel containers. The backs were loaded with a couple of duffels that were stuffed with our sleeping bags. We then were advised to take a seat as best we could on the duffels. Those were our seats for the remainder of the trip.

Our expedition began around mid-day, traveling miles upon miles on an endless blanket of ice and hardened snow. Riding on the back of the sled seemed okay at first. After awhile, however, the constant and endless pulling and jerking of the sled over the rugged terrain were taking their toll on me, as was the minus 35°F temperature. We stopped to make camp for the evening after some 75 miles. I remember thinking to myself at that time, "I and everybody around me must be nuts!"

The camp consisted of canvas tents staked to the ice with caribou hides placed inside them for flooring. Our drinking water was obtained by melting large blocks of ice that were cut with an axe from the same frozen body of water that we camped on. Needless-to-say, warm soup from a package and frozen bannock (Eskimo bread) never tasted so good. On that first night and on every night thereafter we slept with our Coleman stove on full throt-

Robert M. Ortiz took this massive muskox with one shot from his muzzleloader. The great bull scores 126-4/8 points and was taken in 2003 near the Coppermine River in Nunavut.

tle.

We broke camp early the next morning and journeyed farther away from civilization and into the white abyss that lay before us. We had traveled around 30 miles when suddenly our snowmobile quit running. We tried everything to get it started, but nothing worked. So there we stood, alone, stranded in the middle of absolutely nowhere. Lucky for us, several of the other party members found us when they backtracked to investigate why we weren't following.

The snowmobile had overheated and cooked the engine's rings. A search of everyone's tool box produced several spare parts, but not what we needed. Nevertheless, the Eskimos worked non-stop in the freezing cold. They cut, bent, filed and fitted the old parts with the spares until they made it work again. After witnessing them repair the engine under those conditions, any fears and doubts that I had were laid to rest. I was in good hands, and as far as I was concerned, the muskox were in lots of trouble.

After the engine was fixed, we were on our way again. The farther we traveled toward our targeted hunting destination, the rockier the terrain became. Our travel became slower as we skated through and around the jagged rocks that protruded through the moonscape-like terrain. Later in the day, we spotted a small herd of caribou. Seeing the herd lent credence to the tale that animals actually did inhabit this frozen and desolate place we were in.

MUSKOX
Third Award – 126⁴/₈
▼ ▼ ▼ ▼ ▼
Robert M. Ortiz

It was late in the day when we decided to stop and make camp again. After dinner that evening, my guide, Ron Elgok, brought to my attention the Northern Lights that filled the sky above our camp. It was an awesome sight. The Lights were like green, blue, and red-colored banners of florescent mist dancing back and forth across the sky. I remember looking at the moon through it all and telling Ron, "There's blood on the moon. That means we're going to kill a big one tomorrow."

I then laughed. He just looked at me and shook his head, implying that maybe I was as crazy as he was.

We left camp early the next morning and split up. Two of the hunters hunted south and three of us hunted north. Several hours later, we spotted our first herd of muskox on a rock-covered hillside. It was difficult to glass them in the bitterly cold conditions. The slightest amount of breath or heat from our eyes caused the lenses to ice instantly. I avoided this problem by bringing the binoculars close enough to my eyes to where I could see through them, but not to where any type of heat could transfer to the glass. In any event, there were no shooters in the herd. We continued our search.

Around mid-day we caught sight of six running muskox just before they topped the horizon about 400 yards away. We pursued their tracks up the hill. When we reached the top, they were at the bottom about 300 yards away. The six had joined a herd that totaled about 30 animals. Seeing that there were several good bulls in the herd, we commenced our stalk. Some two hours later, my companion hunters had two fine bulls on the ground. However, I still hadn't spotted the bull I was looking for.

I continued to glass the herd and watched in amazement as two bulls repeatedly rammed heads until they were bleeding profusely from their heads and noses. I wondered if it was their way of telling me to back off. If it was, I didn't allow myself to be intimidated. I was committed to finding "the one."

After we watched them for about 15 minutes, the herd got nervous and bolted. I pursued them for quite a distance. An hour later, I caught up with the herd. They had traveled to the side of a small ravine where they felt some protection from the threat that was upon them. I distanced myself about 200 yards on top and away from the side of the ravine where they were. However, they knew I was there. Their apparent curiosity and nervousness caused them to top the ravine sporadically in an attempt to see me and my whereabouts. In doing so, they allowed me to fully glass their bosses. About 20 minutes later, the big herd bull wanted to know where I was. It came just high enough up the ravine to a point where I could see it. Immediately, I knew the bull was "the one" I wanted to shoot.

Unfortunately, the big bull went back down and out of sight. This was my chance, however, to get closer and in a position for a better shot. I had closed the range to about

75 yards when several other bulls topped the ravine and were looking straight at me. My greatest fear was them bolting and taking the rest of the herd with them. I stayed completely still, not knowing what else to do.

Then it happened. The big herd bull topped the ravine again to see what was going on. In doing so, it took one step to its right, exposing its left vitals to be exposed. From my standing position, I placed my sights on the exposed vitals and squeezed the trigger. The 275-grain Barnes X bullet screeched from the bore with authority and struck the massive prehistoric-looking animal. There was no doubt the giant muskox was hit, as it staggered several steps to its right and then fell over, crashing into the snow-packed earth.

I walked over to the where the giant rested. Its bosses were wide and perfectly symmetrical, and its horns curled deep and then hooked up and past its nose. I remember being excited about it all, shaking hands, and taking pictures. We then caped the animal and quickly removed the meat from its bones before it froze. In doing so, we located the perfectly mushroomed bullet just inside the hide on the opposite side.

We then returned back to camp where we enjoyed some fresh muskox loin as we recounted the day's great events. A quick green-scoring of the giant bull placed it well above the current muzzleloader World's Record. After the 60-day drying period, the my bull was officially confirmed to be the largest recorded muskox ever to be taken with a muzzleloader. My gratitude is extended to all those who made my hunt the hunt-of-a-lifetime.

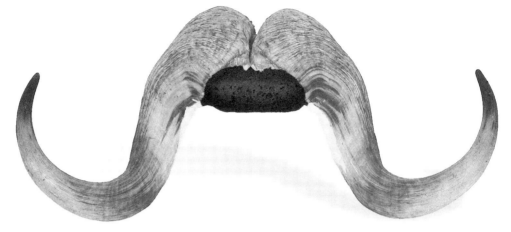

Photograph by Cliff White

TROPHY STATS

▼ ▼ ▼ ▼ ▼

Category
    muskox

Score
    125$^6/_8$

Location
    Kugluktuk River, Nunavut — 2002

Hunter
    William J. Smith

Length of Horn
    Right: 29$^7/_8$ Left: 29$^3/_8$

Width of Boss
    Right: 10$^3/_8$ Left: 10$^5/_8$

Greatest Spread
    28$^7/_8$

Photograph by Jack Reneau

William J. Smith accepting his plaque and
medal from Buck Buckner, Chair of the
Big Game Records Committee.

MUSKOX
Fourth Award – 125⁶/₈

▼ ▼ ▼ ▼ ▼ ▼ ▼ ▼ ▼

William J. Smith

After having spent the better part of the last 25 years hunting the various recognized species of North American big game animals, I now find my personal hunting goals nearly fulfilled. Today my hunts are more than ever governed by quality rather than quantity. Such was my mental state when I decided to book my second hunt for muskox.

My desire to make yet another hunting adventure to the Arctic was originally kindled by the chance to once again experience the lifestyle of the Inuit people. Always happy and a genuine race of people, they have an ability to function as efficient hunters and trappers under some of the harshest extremes Mother Nature has to offer. They have won my total respect.

My original muskox hunt took place in February 1981 on Banks Island, Northwest Territories, Canada. I was a young man entering a world I had never seen before. It was a short, whirlwind hunt, and I successfully harvested an excellent representative of the species. As subsequent years passed by, I realized that with muskox, as with most other big game species throughout North America, trophy quality may vary with different geographic locations and genetic influences. There is a distinct difference in body size and trophy quality from the animals living throughout the Arctic islands versus those on the mainland. I decided while finalizing my plans for this hunt that my main objective was to enjoy my Arctic experience to the fullest and set my sights high in an attempt to harvest a bull that would qualify for the All-time Boone and Crockett records book. With this in mind, I booked my hunt through Webb Outfitting, Ltd. for March 2002 out of Kugluktuk, Nunavut.

I arrived at the Arctic community as planned with a high level of anxiety for the upcoming hunt, yet somewhat apprehensive regarding my ability to cope with the extremely cold temperatures. My goal to harvest a record-book animal was firm in my mind, and I knew this would probably require me to stick it out for multiple days in order to look over several bulls.

Upon my arrival, I met my guide, John Avaligak. Sleds and snow machines were quickly packed, and from the community of Kugluktuk we were soon heading east across the sea ice of the Arctic Ocean. The five-hour trip to where camp would be established was warm and comfortable. Midway into the journey, we stopped at a fishing camp along the shoreline for the traditional hot tea and snacks. Finally, we proceeded inland along the Kugaryuak River for about another hour until we reached our final destination.

The white, obscure landscape soon became an outpost of civilization as wall tents were erected for the guides, me, and one other hunter from Georgia. Soon dinner was cooking inside the tents over Coleman stoves. To my surprise, wire antennae were suspended outside the tents and radio communication was established with surrounding villages miles away. With

William J. Smith backtracked to take this bull after first underestimating the width of its boss. This was William's second muskox and its score of 125-6/8 points made it an award-winning bull at the 25th Awards Program in Kansas City.

the tents reduced in height for maximum heat retention and caribou hides spread on the tent floor covering the underlying snow, we were comfortably resting within, totally protected from the elements outside. As we finally turned in for the night, both of my apprehensions were put to rest because I knew I was fully prepared for the low temperatures and John, my guide, understood my desire to look at several bulls in pursuit of a real trophy.

The following day found us traveling in broken hills of snow and black boulders. From the highest vantage points, we would carefully glass for animals in the distance. Several stalks were made to check prospective bulls closely, but none were what I was looking for. Finally, about midday, we found a group of nine bulls with four mature older males. There were two bulls that really stood out. We stalked them for quite a distance to get a closer look. In this area of hills and ravines, it was easy to get up close and personal to evaluate these bulls.

One bull in particular caught my attention. Its bosses were very white in color and the respective mass carried way out along the length of its horns as they dropped along the sides of its face. Horn length was very impressive as the curvature dropped slightly below the jaw line and then easily back up to the eye sockets. We spent a long time looking at this group of bulls. They would stand facing us in their defensive posture and finally trot off in distrust of what we were about. By staying down wind of the animals and keeping a low profile, I'm sure these animals feared we were wolves or arctic grizzlies. After several encounters with this group of bulls, I just could not make up my mind on this one tremendous animal. The width of the boss would measure only 8" to 8-1/2" based on my estimates. I looked at my guide and told him it's the first day; I wanted to keep looking. Unexpectedly, we heard the report of a rifle from the other hunter about two miles away. I suggested we head in that direction to see what caliber of bull he had harvested. This single suggestion would prove to totally change the outcome of this hunt.

MUSKOX
Fourth Award – 125⁶/₈

▼ ▼ ▼ ▼ ▼

WILLIAM J. SMITH

We followed tracks in the snow in the direction of the rifle shot and soon came upon the happy hunter from Georgia and his trophy bull. I walked up to the bull in admiration and offered my congratulations to the successful hunter. As I ran my hands over the magnificent horns, one thing immediately caught my eye. The thing I overlooked when trying to evaluate the previous group of nine bulls was that the rear part of the boss extends further backward and is covered by hair. The bull that I estimated having 8 to 8-1/2-inch wide bosses most likely had an additional 2 to 2-1/2" of horn that was hidden by hair. This would make its measurement closer to 11" — a measurement I knew I would need to reach my goal. I looked at my guide and told him we needed to try to find that group of bulls again. With a look of confidence he said we'd give it a try.

After an intensive search, we did indeed relocate the bulls. It was surprising how far they had wandered off from where we last studied them. Once again, that one outstanding bull caught my attention. Now I felt confident that this bull had all the qualifications to meet the B&C minimum requirements. The last haunting thought left my mind that this was only day one of my hunt. I knew that no matter what the final outcome, I would be extremely pleased with this animal.

As stated earlier, within this group of nine bulls there were four that were truly of a more mature, trophy caliber. I shot my bull through the chest, and as it staggered and trotted off a short distance, the other three bulls whirled and drove it into the ground with their horns. As they stood hovering over the downed animal, I sensed that the lead animal had been taken down and I was witnessing pure animal instinctive behavior as the pecking order was about to be re-established to determine dominance amongst the bulls.

As I approached my trophy bull, mixed feelings of admiration and fulfillment overwhelmed me. After pictures were taken, we began the task of caping the hide for a life-size mount and loading up the meat for the long ride back to camp.

Two days later, we were back in the community of Kugluktuk. I knew it would be just a matter of time before I would be heading back to the bustling world of business as usual in the "Lower 48." Upon leaving the Inuit community and once again having been fortunate to experience firsthand their hunting traditions, I was sad. I wondered if yet another trip would some day bring me this far north.

I thank Fred and Martin Webb for their organization and tightly run ship. Anyone who knows these fine gentlemen can identify with my statement that to make a hunt with their outfit is worth the planning, just to deal with Fred. My hat goes off to John Avaligak. At times, I'm sure he must have thought I was crazy to study and turn down so many fine bulls — his tolerance paid off in the end. When the tale of the tape computed the final numbers, I realized my goal and much more. This bull is truly one for the book!

Photograph by Cliff White

TROPHY STATS

▼ ▼ ▼ ▼ ▼

Category
   muskox

Score
   125

Location
   Kugluktuk, Nunavut — 2001

Hunter
   Anton Gossein

Length of Horn
   Right: $28^3/_8$ Left: $28^7/_8$

Width of Boss
   Right: $10^6/_8$ Left: $11^2/_8$

Greatest Spread
   $30^5/_8$

MUSKOX
Fifth Award – 125

▼ ▼ ▼ ▼ ▼ ▼ ▼ ▼ ▼

ANTON GOSSEIN

My muskox adventure began at the 2000 SCI Convention in Las Vegas where Mike Ferrari, a long-time hunting buddy, introduced me to Fred of Webb & Sons Outfitting. Mike had successfully hunted for muskox and caribou and spoke highly of Fred Webb and his outfitting business. He especially praised the guides he had on his hunt. After some discussion with Fred, I booked a muskox hunt for March of 2001.

I spent the next few months preparing for my upcoming hunt, reading all I could find on "Oomingmak" or the bearded one (as the Inuit call the muskox). Muskox are true survivors of the glacial period that covered North America. They are covered with a short underlayer of wool of exceptional warmth, and a second much longer outer coat of shaggy hair up to 62 cm long. Because of their shaggy coats and massiveness, muskox appear to be extremely large animals. Needless to say, they are extremely adapted to survive in their frigid environment. Muskox horns begin to grow when a calf is four to five weeks old, and continue to grow until the muskox is about six years old. The large and sweeping horns of an adult bull merge at the bases to form massive, heavily-ridged, and furrowed bosses.

My friend, Mike Ferrari, and I are about the same build and size, and I was fortunate in that he loaned me his arctic clothing and boots. In preparation for the hunt, I degreased my .300 Winchester magnum and practiced shooting wearing heavy clothing. It is imperative that one has the correct clothing for an arctic hunt, for the temperatures are very low and the chill factor can become extreme!

On March 18, 2001, I left San Diego (where it was nice and sunny) for my hunt. We arrived in Yellowknife that evening where it was snowing and extremely cold. There was a blizzard coming our way, and the weather front was predicted to hit the area in the next 24 hours. The next morning, I left Yellowknife and flew to Kugluktuk (Coppermine) to begin my muskox hunt. After a brief introduction and a visit with the Fish and Game officer to get the necessary license and tag, I met my guide, Stanley Carpenter, and my assistant guide, John Avilingak. I also met two other hunters who would be hunting in the same area as I, Bill Keebler from Phoenix, and his guide left first. Bob Merkle from El Dorado, Arkansas, and I left to hunt in an area close to Bill soon after.

Bob Merkle and I were each loaded onto snowmobile-pulled wooden sleds (komatiks) and were off toward the muskox hunting grounds, trying to stay ahead of the oncoming blizzard. We traveled about 50 miles and had to set up camp, for the weather turned very bad, and the visibility was next to zero. The blowing snow crystals made navigation next to impossible. Traveling on a komatik was as bad as I had read; I was, however, still surprised

The hunters traveled about 50 miles and then set up camp in a blinding snowstorm. Anton Gossein and his hunting partners withstood one of the most severe blizzards in recent years.

at the beating one takes in the wooden sled. Later, I learned that a small wheel-barrow inner tube, inflated and placed under one's rear, helps greatly to soften the ride.

Bob Merkle, our guides, and I spent the next two days in our tents, for we had whiteout conditions and could not see off in the distance far enough to locate any animals. We did see a wolverine and a fox while traveling from Kugluktuk to camp. We spent the two days sharing stories and conversing with our guides. This type of hunt is definitely different from others I have experienced over the years, but the camaraderie enjoyed by hunters goes a long way when stuck in camp waiting for the weather to change.

On March 22, the sky was blue and the entire area, as far as one could see, was a sparkling, twinkling landscape. It definitely required one to wear sunglasses or goggles. The guides took Bob and me up to a vantage point to glass for muskox while they left us to look over another area. The guides shortly returned and informed us that they had located some muskox off in the distance and that we would have to get closer to see exactly how big they were. As we traveled toward the muskox it became obvious that these were a group of females and small bulls. We studied them and Stanley Carpenter said that there had to be a bachelor herd around here somewhere.

We had no sooner left this group of animals when Stanley located another group just behind a hill that blocked our view from the previous group of animals. We stopped and studied the animals. Most of them were mature bulls. Bob and his guide circled to the left and my guide and I circled wide to the right. We got behind a small rise and waited for the herd to move closer. I heard Bob Merkle shoot and the bulls ran toward us, slowed down, stopped, and just stood around. Stanley pointed

MUSKOX
Fifth Award – 125
▼ ▼ ▼ ▼ ▼
ANTON GOSSEIN

out the largest one and I immediately shot the bull. It dropped instantly as the others ran off. The taking of the bull was somewhat anticlimactic, but walking up to the bull and listening to my guide's excitement was exhilarating. Stanley kept reiterating, "It's a big one!"

After all the high fives and picture taking, the work began! We had -40° Fahrenheit temperatures and the animal had to be dressed and skinned quickly, before we had a frozen-solid animal. Both Stanley and his assistant guide went to work and made short order of the skinning and butchering of the animal. We loaded the meat on two sleds and retuned to camp, where Bob and I shared our experiences and the guides finished caping the heads of our bull muskox inside one of their tents.

That night we learned, via short-wave radio, that Bill Keebler had also taken a nice muskox using his muzzleloader. The next morning, we all returned to Kugluktuk and met up en route to meet with Fish and Game to acquire the proper tags and seals for exporting or trophies back to the U.S.

This hunt is one I will never forget. I survived -40° temperatures with 40 mile per hour winds (-125° wind-chill factor). Fred Webb met us at Kugluktuk and informed us that we experienced one of the most severe blizzards in recent years and that we all took exceptional trophies.

I cannot say enough about my guides, Stanley Carpenter and John Avilingak. These men made my hunt safe. It is only with professionals like them that such a hunt is possible. I have made arrangements to hunt the Arctic one more time in 2005 and will be hunting for polar bear. This land up north is stark, but the frozen tundra and ice have a beauty of their own. Hunting in the Arctic is definitely fair chase and is a test of fortitude and stamina. It tests one's will to survive in what I believe is the toughest environment on earth.

New World's Record

Photograph by Cliff White

TROPHY STATS

▼ ▼ ▼ ▼ ▼

Category
  bighorn sheep

Score
  $208^{3}/_{8}$

Location
  Luscar Mountain, Alberta — 2000

Hunter
  Guinn D. Crousen

Length of Horn
  Right: $47^{4}/_{8}$ Left: $46^{5}/_{8}$

Circumference of Base
  Right: $15^{7}/_{8}$ Left: $15^{7}/_{8}$

Greatest Spread
  $23^{1}/_{8}$

Photograph by Jack Renea

Guinn D. Crousen accepting his plaque
and medal from Buck Buckner, Chair of
the Big Game Records Committee.

BIGHORN SHEEP
First Award - 208³/₈

▼ ▼ ▼ ▼ ▼ ▼ ▼ ▼ ▼

GUINN D. CROUSEN

By Craig Boddington

It was late in the afternoon on November 28, 2000, on Luscar Mountain in Alberta's Rockies. The echoes of Guinn Crousen's .270 Weatherby Magnum had died away and the great ram was down. Many men would have run forward to see their prize up close. But Guinn Crousen is both patient and practical. He'd waited more than a dozen years to finish his Grand Slam with a Rocky Mountain bighorn — not just any bighorn, but the right one. He'd tried to obtain this particular tag for four years, believing that Alberta offered the best opportunity for the kind of ram he wanted. With the right tag finally in hand, he'd tried for 15 days to get a shot at this particular ram. Now it was getting dark and cold in the Alberta mountains. He was tired and his bad knees hurt. The ram could wait a little bit longer. So while his hunting partners sprang forward, Crousen turned back to retrieve his pack and jacket, dropped during the final moments of the stalk.

A few minutes later, moving more slowly with adrenaline levels dropping, Crousen approached his ram. His hunting team — Randy Babala, Ron McKenzie, and Lyle Moberly — were sitting quietly, looking at the downed monarch. Crousen approached from the rear, seeing the full curl of the ram's horns. "My gosh, boys, he's big," he said.

Randy Babala looked up and spoke quietly in the silence of the moment. "Guinn, you may have a new World's Record." And Guinn Crousen sat down and cried a little.

Few among us have the dream of taking a World's Record of any species, and even fewer come to believe that it might actually happen to them. Guinn Crousen of Dallas, Texas, was not among either group. His father was a retired Marine Gunnery Sergeant who saw service from Nicaragua to the island campaigns of World War II. Guinn grew up with his Dad kicking his tail in true Marine Corps fashion — and teaching him a strong sense of ethics extending from the field to the work place. As a hunter, Guinn Crousen learned to hunt hard and hunt fair. Like most hunters, he dreamed of someday taking a really great trophy — which meant, as it does to most of us, an animal that would make the minimum in the All-time records book *Records of North American Big Game*. As a businessman, he built up a successful corporation, which in time allowed him to expand his hunting horizons.

In 1985 his friend, Don Harold, persuaded him to attend the Foundation for North American Wild Sheep convention. As a result he booked his first sheep hunt, taking a nice Stone's ram with Myles Bradford in northern B.C. He followed up with a Dall's sheep with Stan Stevens in the Mackenzie Mountains of Northwest Territories. Then, in 1989, he took a desert sheep in Baja Norte. Now he had three-fourths of a Grand Slam, all nice sheep but no record-class trophies. He got to thinking that he'd like to close out his Slam with a really big ram, one that would make the book and stay there.

As a measure of Guinn Crousen's patience and persistence, he didn't just book a bighorn sheep hunt. He did his homework, deciding that western Alberta, near Jasper Park, offered the best available opportunity for the kind of ram he was looking for. And he booked four hunts simultaneously, four years in a row, with Gordon Utri's Whispering Pines Outfitters.

He only hunted two of the four years, allowing friends to take his other two bookings. He was hunting Unit 438, and during those two lengthy hunts he never saw a good ram in his hunting area. But from a favored vantage point he could see the Cardinal River Mine, an area closed to hunting, and in that promised land he frequently glassed good sheep.

When the Alberta auction tag first came out he recognized the opportunity. Six of the ten largest bighorns in the record book and half the top twenty came out of Alberta. Crousen was sure Alberta offered the best opportunity for a really big ram. Starting in 1995 he bid on the Alberta tag for four out of the next six years, losing the bid three times. In 2000, at the Rocky Mountain Elk Foundation gathering in Denver, after dreaming of a good bighorn for a decade, he walked away with the Alberta sheep tag.

What to do with it? Crousen knew he wanted to hunt Unit 438, between Jasper Park and Cardinal River Mine. He also knew that no human being knew the area better than veteran sheep outfitter Randy Babala. Babala grew up in nearby Cadomin, Alberta, roaming the hills as a youngster and eventually guiding in the area for his uncle, Jim Babala. After guiding and outfitting Alberta bighorns for years Randy Babala eventually sold out, relocating to sheep country in the Yukon, but he still knew the area better than anyone.

Crousen called him to ask him to guide the hunt. After the preliminaries Babala, bluntly asked him, "What do you want with the tag?"

Without hesitation Crousen answered, "I want to join the '200 Club'."

Babala didn't know what that meant, so Crousen explained that he wanted to join the tiny group of sheep hunters who had taken rams that achieved a final score — "net and dry" — of 200 points or better.

Long silence, then Babala said, "There are thousands of sheep hunters who have died, and thousands more that are gonna die, without ever seeing a ram that big — let alone connecting. But if you want to try, come on up and let's go hunting!"

Crousen's team would consist of Randy Babala, assisted by Ron McKenzie and Lyle Moberly, with Lenore Vinson acting as camp cook. "Camp" and headquarters would be Babala's house in Cadomin. Crousen set aside the whole month of November for the hunt, but the agreement was that there was no point beginning until the rams started to move. Interestingly, they did no scouting; everyone involved knew there were big rams on the old mine, or across the area in Jasper Park. With rutting activity the rams would move — and maybe a really big ram would show. On about the seventh of November Babala called Crousen, telling him the rams were starting to move a bit. It was time.

BIGHORN SHEEP
First Award – 208 ³/₈
▼ ▼ ▼ ▼ ▼
GUINN D. CROUSEN

Crousen arrived on the 9th of November, and from that evening onward they hunted all day, every day except Sundays, dawn to dark. The weather was cold, with highs in the teens, occasionally reaching above freezing, but strangely dry. Early on they got seven or eight inches of snow, but for most of the hunt it remained clear and cold, with occasional snow flurries and periods of high winds. Crousen remembers one day when "nickel-sized rocks were blowing through a drainage."

On the third day, late in the evening, they glassed a very big ram, unique and recognizable because of his exceptional length, but much too far away to see clearly. It was too late to move closer that evening, but the next morning they picked the ram up again on the old mine. Crousen knew instantly this was the largest ram he had ever seen. Babala was non-committal; he simply said, "He'll net/dry 200." From that moment this ram became the quest, but they never again attempted to precisely call its measurements.

On the fifth day they lost the ram and didn't see it again for six long days. During this period they separated, going in different directions to glass, then meeting back up to discuss what they had seen. Ron McKenzie and Lyle Moberly went up to Mystery Lake, while the rest of the team took up different vantage points along Luscar Mountain, glassing down into the mine and west toward Jasper.

By now the rut was in full swing, with rams moving everywhere. Rams from the mine area seemed to have extremely dark horns, almost certainly because of the coal dust. Jasper Park was only four or five miles away, but the Park rams were identifiable because of golden-colored horns.

Eventually, about the 19th of November, they found the long-horned ram again, still in its sanctuary on the old mine. The rams were fighting heavily, and Crousen was afraid to look through the spotting scope. He would ask Randy, "Has he broken anything?" No, it had not. The ram was still pretty, was still the "net/dry 200" they sought — and it was still as safe as if he'd been on the moon.

Early on Crousen had told Babala, "Randy, consider this tag yours. Tell me when you would shoot a ram."

One afternoon they worked in behind some cedars, coming up just 35 or 40 yards above three ewes. A big ram came out of the draw below and stopped just 40 yards below them. Randy Babala whispered, "I'd shoot that ram."

Crousen just looked at him, so Babala went on, "You told me to tell you when I would shoot a ram. I would shoot that ram."

"How big is he?"

"He's 196 or 197, no deducts, a gorgeous ram. I would shoot him."

Crousen passed it, with Babala saying, "Gosh, that ram sure is pretty!"

By November 27th, with time growing short, they had the long-horned ram pretty well located — but it was staying well within the sanctuary. After they came off the mountain

Guinn D. Crousen waited for days to take the new World's Record bighorn sheep. The award-winning ram scores 208-3/8 points and received a First Place Award at the 25th Awards Program in Kansas City.

Crousen took a shower, then came into the main room. Nobody was saying anything, so Babala broke the silence. "Guinn, we better have a talk. Maybe that ram isn't gonna come out. We should start thinking of a different ram or you might be going home in four days with nothing."

Crousen thought about it for a moment, then replied, "Well, that's all right. It's going to be that big ram or nothin'."

"Okay, let's have supper," said Babala, and that was that.

The ram was still there that morning. Crousen and his crew spread out on the backside of Luscar Mountain, glassing down along the mine's sawtoothed boundary. In the late afternoon a pack of coyotes — at least three, maybe more — dashed into the herd of sheep down on the mine's flat, reclaimed meadows. Suddenly sheep were running everywhere, moving out of the flat and up into the rough rocks. Babala appeared at Crousen's side. "He's coming out. Let's go!"

They left their gear and ran, pulling up short as Babala said, "There's the ram, there's the boundary stake. He's out. Take him!" It was a going-away shot at just about 70 yards, and the ram that would become the new World's Record bighorn belonged to Guinn Crousen, his team, and all of us who care about such things.

In 1911, in Blind Canyon, Alberta, Fred Weiller took a ram that stood as the World's Record for 90 years. Among all of Boone and Crockett Club's categories for North American big game only the World's Record woodland caribou has stood for a longer period. As Guinn Crousen and his ram have proven, records are made to be broken, but few of us who have studied the record book ever believed that Fred Weiller's ram would be beaten.

The reasons for this are obvious. Our bighorns have made a wonderful comeback in many areas, so it isn't necessarily clear that there are fewer bighorns today than there were in 1911. But in today's well-managed herds the permits are carefully allocated for a sustainable yield, not necessarily to allow the maximum growth potential. Few herds have the genetics and the feed and minerals to produce "net/dry 200-point rams," and among those that do very few rams escape predators, hunters, hard winters, and other natural calamities long enough to reach their maximum potential. Were I a betting man, I would have bet that Fred Weiller's Blind Canyon ram would stand forever as the largest-horned bighorn sheep known to have ever lived. I would have been wrong. Guinn Crousen's Luscar Mountain ram, taken on November 28, 2000, officially scored on August 15, 2001, in Missoula, Montana, by a B&C Panel of Judges at 208-3/8 points, is the new World's Record bighorn by two eighths of a point.

It's interesting to note that Crousen's ram achieves its fabulous score in unusual fashion. With bases of 15-7/8 inches, it is not particularly heavy-based as bighorns go. Crousen and his team were absolutely correct when they recognized its incredible length; at 47-4/8 inches on the right and 46-5/8 inches on the left its horns average the second longest of any bighorn sheep in the All-time records book. And while the bases are not huge by bighorn standards, it carries the mass very well into the first, second, and third quarter measurements. It is a great ram, well-judged, well-hunted, and well-taken. Now it's a part of hunting history, and I think I would have cried a little on that mountain as well.

Photograph by Cliff White

TROPHY
STATS

▼ ▼ ▼ ▼ ▼

Category
  bighorn sheep

Score
  202 $^1/_8$

Location
  Leyland Mountain, Alberta — 2001

Hunter
  Guinn D. Crousen

Length of Horn
  Right: 45   Left: 44$^7/_8$

Circumference of Base
  Right: 15$^6/_8$ Left: 15$^6/_8$

Greatest Spread
  24$^6/_8$

Photograph by Jack Rene

Guinn D. Crousen accepting his plaque
and medal from Buck Buckner, Chair of
the Big Game Records Committee.

BIGHORN SHEEP
Second Award - 202¹/₈

▼ ▼ ▼ ▼ ▼ ▼ ▼ ▼ ▼

GUINN D. CROUSEN

When Guinn Crousen fired the bullet in 2000 that brought down the new World's Record bighorn ram, it bested a mark that many thought would never be beaten. For eighty-nine years, Fred Weiller's former World's Record, taken in Blind Canyon, Alberta in 1911, was the biggest North American sheep ever recorded. Guinn, along with guide Randy Babala, had shocked the sheep hunting world.

The following year, 2001, found Guinn and Randy hunting together again. They were hunting "Section 438," located a mere 1-1/2 miles from Jasper National Park in Alberta, Canada. Guinn was adamant that he would be as selective this year as the last. He would rather go home empty-handed than take any ram that scored less than 200 B&C. It was a tall order; only a few more than 20 rams in the history of records keeping had ever topped that mark.

Unlike the previous year, which had tested the resolve of both men, this hunt would unfold in a more reasonable time frame. The hunt started on November 10. On November 11, Randy saw a huge ram in his spotting scope. It was going around a mountain and out of sight, but they could see horn sticking out on both sides of its body. They both knew instantly that it was a good one. They gave chase, but soon saw that it was futile. Darkness descended upon them and both men retreated, ready to try harder again the next day.

On the morning of November 12, with a night full of thoughts on the big ram, Guinn and Randy set off after king-sized quarry. The ram hadn't gone far, and they soon located him again. The hunters came around from the backside of the mountain, hoping for a better angle, and knew they might be close. After talking it over, we was decided that Randy would hike up to the top and take a peek. Guinn could tell from Randy's body language that they were right on top of the ram.

Randy came back down, and Guinn asked, "Is he over 200?"

Randy replied, "I don't know. Shoot him. He's big."

Guinn, then and now, felt that Randy was as good a judge of score as anyone he knew, and fully trusted his guide's decision. He listened to the words and did just as instructed. He hiked up and was surprised to see the ram no more than 40 yards away! A thunderous BOOM echoed through the canyon walls, and Guinn had just taken yet another breathtaking ram. Randy would later be proven correct, as the final score of the huge ram would be 202-1/8 points.

Guinn's 202-1/8 B&C ram may not be the World's Record but, to him, this gorgeous sheep is every bit as honored and loved in his heart. The symmetry, classic look of the horns, and handsome stature of the ram will always make this hunt one of Guinn's favorites.

TROPHY STATS

▼ ▼ ▼ ▼ ▼

Category
　bighorn sheep

Score
　200$^7/_8$

Location
　Sanders County, Montana — 2001

Hunter
　Jack M. Greenwood

Length of Horn
　Right: 44　Left: 44$^7/_8$

Circumference of Base
　Right: 17　Left: 16$^7/_8$

Greatest Spread
　26$^1/_8$

BIGHORN SHEEP
Third Award – 200⁷/₈

▼ ▼ ▼ ▼ ▼ ▼ ▼ ▼ ▼

JACK M. GREENWOOD

The summer of 2001 found me working in Alaska. On one of my weekend phone calls, I heard, "You will never guess what you got in the mail."

After several wrong guesses, I refused to guess any more and made my teenagers tell me. This is how my bighorn sheep hunting season started. It was a combination of surprise and excitement that erupted from my mouth. After 17 years of getting refunds, this was truly a dream come true.

In August, I was able to get a week off from work. Back to Montana I went to do some preseason scouting. Not being familiar with the hunting district, my first stop was the Forest Service office to buy a map of the area. My second stop was the Montana Department of Fish, Wildlife, and Parks office where they gave me the name of the local biologist to call for more information.

Finally, my dad and I were off to do some leg work. The morning was spent driving the back roads to get the lay of the land; the afternoon found us hiking a trail and doing a little glassing of the steep, rocky terrain. No sheep were sighted, but we were still excited. My time was up, however, and I had to fly back to Alaska.

On September 6, I was once again in the air, this time home for the fall and winter. I was anxious to get to my hunting district as soon as possible. On September 10, my wife and I drove the 90 miles from our home to the hunting district, with the plan of me doing some hiking and her picking me up at a prearranged destination. Everything went according to plan, except that, once again, I was not able to locate any sheep. There was a lot of sign, but the weather was hot and all the animals were moving as little as possible.

Saturday, the 15th of September, was

Photograph courtesy of Jack M. Greenwood

Jack M. Greenwoods' son Jerry, and his wife, met him the day after he took the award-winning ram and helped him pack it out of the mountains.

opening day. My 15-year-old son, Jerry, was able to go with me and we were expecting a great day. Using binoculars, we were able to locate some sheep at first light. It looked like they were returning from the river and climbing back to their daytime haunts. Using some landmarks, we determined where they bedded and also the best route for us to approach.

Donning our backpacks and my Ruger .30-06 rifle and Leupold scope, we were off. A couple of hours later, we found a good vantage point and began to glass the opposing rock-slide. My son found three sheep, all rams. Now we were really excited! We set up the spotting scope for a better look. The rams turned out to be little guys — one yearling and two not quite 3/4-curls. We were able to watch them for five hours undisturbed at a distance of 345 yards.

Toward evening, I asked Jerry whether or not I should try for the largest ram (my tag was good for either sex.) Due to school and sports, this would be the only time he would be able to hunt with me. He looked the ram over again and said "I wouldn't shoot a ram that little on opening day."

I took his advice, and we began to load up our gear. As we were getting ready to leave, a clatter in the rocks got our attention. We watched as a band of ewes and lambs came around the hillside. It was a nice finish to a great day.

I wasn't able to make it back to hunting for 10 anxious days, but my calendar was now open for as long as it took. I loaded my backpack with five days worth of food and gear, grabbed my rifle, told my family good-bye, and off I went.

The morning of the 25th, I hiked down an overgrown road. After a couple of hours of fruitless glassing, I decided to return to the drainage where my son and I had observed the rams on opening day. It was near evening when I reached the area and set up to glass. Almost immediately, I was able to locate 23 ewes and lambs working their way down the mountain toward the river. It was fun to watch them fearlessly jump from rock to ledge. Just at dark, I found a group of seven sheep high on the mountain. However, the light was too poor for a good look. I went to sleep that night wondering what they were.

On the dawn of the 26th, I was searching the mountains for sheep. The ewes and lambs were still there, but where were the rams? I moved to glass another spot and movement caught my eye; it was a bunch of rams! The spotting scope revealed three rams. Two were little guys, but one needed a closer look.

I headed back to the exact spot where my son and I had watched the rams on opening day. As I was climbing up the now familiar mountain, I paused for a breather. I happened to glance up at the mountain that was at my back. On opening day, my son had brought to my attention some large, white boulders on this particular mountain. As I looked up at them, one of those boulders ran down the mountain a little ways.

I grabbed my binoculars and instantly found the ram of my dreams! It was in a group of four rams and was lying down apart from the others. I quickly changed plans, abandoning my backpack for my fanny pack. I shouldered my rifle and began to climb.

It was 11:30 a.m. when I first saw the rams. It took a little over an hour to gain the necessary elevation to begin the stalk. In my haste to get to the ram, I neglected to get a good

landmark for reference. Due to the
wind, I had circled around the back of
the mountain. I was now attempting to
come around and locate the rams. I
crept around the mountainside with
my eyes peeled.

BIGHORN SHEEP
Third Award – 200 ⁷/₈

▼ ▼ ▼ ▼ ▼

JACK M. GREENWOOD

After a short distance, a patch of white caught my eye. I dropped to the ground and
maneuvered to get a better look. It was a ram, lying down under a big fir tree. It was facing
away from me, chewing its cud with not a care in the world. I retrieved my laser range finder from my fanny pack and focused; it was 142 yards. I looked the ram over thoroughly. It
was nice, but I didn't think it was the big one.

Suddenly, the ram was on its feet. It stretched and wandered out of sight. While I was
wondering what to do, another smaller ram appeared and bedded down in the first ram's
vacated bed. This second ram was facing me. I was able to watch it doze at such close distance that I could literally watch the ram open and close its eyes. This ram was also undisturbed by my presence. But just like the other ram, this one decided it was time to move.
It got up and followed the exact route of the first ram. I had now been on the mountain for
nearly two hours, viewing two rams for most of that time at less than 150 yards. It was
truly incredible.

For the moment, there were no rams in sight. I was confident, however, that the rams
were close and that my presence was undetected. I looked at my watch, which said it was
2 p.m., and debated what would be the best course of action. Should I move and try to find
the rams and thereby run the risk of spooking them? Or sit tight and wait for them to move?
I opted for the latter and spent the next two hours second-guessing my decision.

At 4 p.m., a clatter of rocks brought me to full attention. Through the brush and trees, I
could make out the rams as they began to feed. I was able to identify three rams momentarily; two were smaller rams, a third was a nice ram (the one I had watched earlier) but the
fourth had its head down and was facing away from me. It seemed liked 10 minutes before
it picked up its head. When it did, I said, "That's the one."

The rams continued to feed, wandering in and out of view. I sat tight, hoping for a shot.
The second-largest ram began to feed directly toward me. I figured it would come out in the
open in about five more steps, and I decided I would take it. I thought to myself that it was
too good of a ram to pass up at 120 yards. But for some unknown reason, the ram turned in
its tracks and went back the other way. My opportunity was gone. I watched and listened for
several minutes, but the rams seemed to have moved.

Cautiously, I began to make my way across the rocks to the point where I had last seen
the rams. Peeking over the edge, I noticed that I had a good field of view, but that there
weren't any rams in sight. I kept scanning closely.

All of a sudden, out of a little fold in the hillside, the rams bolted into view. They were
above me and running away. I had my rifle up, trying to find the big one. It was up front, followed by the others. They bunched up together behind a big Ponderosa pine tree, hesitat-

ing a moment before emerging on the other side. The big ram was once again in the lead, but they were now quartering away. I don't remember taking my safety off; it was like second nature. The ram was in my cross hairs, and then I remember the recoil and looking for the ram, which was now rolling down the mountain. I reloaded, picked up my empty, and watched as the ram came to rest against a small tree. Then I noticed the other three rams. I quickly looked them over and then focused my attention on the downed ram. I made my way over to it and when I approached the ram, I said, "It's a monster."

I had to maneuver the ram down the mountain to a flat piece of ground, 400 yards through the rocks and shale, trying to be as careful as possible. It took nearly 45 minutes. Now light was fading fast, and I needed to get it caped and field dressed. I worked both fast and furious. When I finished, I thought about taking some pictures. Unfortunately, in my hurry that morning, I had left my camera in my backpack. Oh, well. I hung the head and cape up in a tree as high as I could and made my way toward my pack. I was able to hike back to my truck, arriving about an hour after dark.

I called my family on my cell phone and made plans for my wife and son to come the next day and help me bone and pack out the ram. It took most of the day for us to get the job done. By the time we got to a Montana Fish, Wildlife, and Parks office for the necessary check-in, it was past quitting time. Luckily, someone was still there and was able to check it in. This was the first time that a tape was placed on the ram. The bases measured 16-7/8 inches and 17 inches, and the horn length were both 44 inches or greater.

It is hard to describe how I felt because I do not consider myself a trophy hunter. I had hoped to harvest a nice ram, but this was beyond my dreams. After the 60-day drying period, I had the ram officially scored. It ended up scoring 200-7/8 B&C points.

I had always felt that bighorn sheep hunting was a dream — something other hunters got to do. I was grateful just for the opportunity to hunt such a magnificent animal. To harvest such a trophy was the culmination of my dreams.

Award Winning Moments...

Photograph by Keith Balfourd

The 25th Awards Program trophy display included 118 incredible specimens representing 34 of the 38 categories of North American big game recognized by the Boone and Crockett Club. Included in the display was this collection of outstanding sheep specimens, which included the new World's Record bighorn sheep (not pictured).

Photograph by Cliff White

TROPHY STATS

▼ ▼ ▼ ▼ ▼

Category
  bighorn sheep

Score
  $200^1/_8$

Location
  Fergus County, Montana — 2003

Hunter
  David J. Nygard

Length of Horn
  Right: $44^3/_8$ Left: $41^6/_8$

Circumference of Base
  Right: $16^3/_8$ Left: $16^5/_8$

Greatest Spread
  $26^6/_8$

Photograph by Jack Renea

David J. Nygard accepting his plaque and
medal from Buck Buckner, Chair of the
Big Game Records Committee.

426

BIGHORN SHEEP
Fourth Award – 200¹/₈

▼ ▼ ▼ ▼ ▼ ▼ ▼ ▼ ▼

DAVID J. NYGARD

My wife and I had just returned from a camping trip last July 2002. I was unpacking the truck when she called out that I had received a tag from Montana Fish, Wildlife, and Parks. I had drawn a moose tag in 1998, so I thought that the tag was for mountain goat, due to the better odds than the almost impossible-to-draw tag for bighorn sheep. I almost fell over when she handed me the envelope and I saw that, indeed, I had hit the hunting lottery and now had a sheep tag in my hands.

After I settled down a little, I called my best friend and hunting buddy, Joe Weigand, in Helena. His wife answered and I told her the news and asked if I could kidnap her husband this fall. She laughed and said that even she wouldn't be able to stop him from hunting with me for sheep. He was happy for me, like only a true friend would be. We had been putting in for sheep tags for years and were just waiting for one of us or a family member to draw. From that moment on, I read every magazine article and book I could get my hands on regarding sheep judging and hunting. I watched as many videos as I could, to learn how to really judge a good ram and understand its habits and ways. I made calls to the area biologist in Lewistown regarding sheep numbers, trophy ram potential, and harvest data. Needless to say, I had sheep fever.

About this time, I had another stroke of luck. It came in the form of a co-worker giving me the name of a guy who hunted the same area in 1998. He had taken a good ram with his bow. I called Kim Latterell and after several conversations, he accepted my offer to accompany Joe and me on this hunt. Kim had spent a lot of time in that area and knew it well. He also had some video footage of some rams that he had filmed during his hunt.

We all put in for the time off from our jobs and planned an opening day hunt in mid-September. We debated whether or not to hunt from the river by boat or go in with a camp on foot. We contacted a landowner and were granted access to public land across his land as long as it was by foot. We decided to go this route since none of us had the proper boat needed, and we figured it would be less crowded that way. We borrowed two game carts from friends and family and poured over maps until a game plan was in place. The days seemed to drag by, but September 13 finally came; we loaded up the trucks and took off.

We met a good friend of mine in Lewistown and had a nice lunch with him and his family. We topped off the trucks with fuel and headed up to the wild Missouri Breaks country. About 1:30 p.m., we met with the landowner and visited for awhile. We had to make a slight change in plans as the landowner had some people already in the area we had originally intended to hunt. We checked maps to make sure he knew where we would be and that we were in the right spot.

As we drove on in to the locked gate, we noted how dry everything was. The landowner said that there had been no measurable precipitation for 81 days or so. With that in mind, we were very careful of where we drove and parked the vehicles. We scouted our way into the hunting area late that afternoon with two objectives: 1) find some rams if we could, and 2) find a place to set up camp. We did locate a band of seven rams, but they were all young. We watched them for a good while and then hiked back out to camp by the trucks for the night.

I was very impressed with the ruggedness in this area of the Breaks. It was much steeper and more unforgiving than the area of the Breaks where I bowhunt for elk. We had a cold camp that night, but anticipation was high. On Sunday morning, we decided to scout an area nearby that we might use as a plan B. After glassing for hours, all we had found were two young rams.

We went back to the locked gates and started loading up the game carts with all of our gear, food, and water. It turned out to be quite an engineering feat, but with ropes and several bungee cords, we finally headed in the three-plus miles to where we wanted to set up camp. With quite a bit of grunting, we finally made it to the dry coulee bed and set up camp on a nice, sandy spot. This proved later to be a very fortunate spot to place the tents. We were too tired to look for sheep that night, so we retired early to get a good rest for opening day.

Monday, September 15 was a day I am likely to never forget. We left camp with the sun up and sky partly cloudy. It was very mild still, probably in the 50s. As we hiked in, we stopped constantly to glass the country that seemed to change with every footstep. We were sure that we must be missing some sheep, but the country is so vast and deep that we just kept on looking.

We finally found some rams at about 8:00 a.m. There were five small rams together feeding and one ram bedded on a knife ridge. It quickly became obvious that getting in bow range undetected would be a challenge. We moved on and looked back the way we had come. We saw four more rams lined out feeding at a good pace over a mile away. Not long after that, we spied a lone hunter along the same ridge. We kept going and finally located two good rams feeding up a ridge. We were over two miles in at this point and it was after 11:00 a.m. One of the rams appeared to be in the 180-190 class and that was good enough for me. They were both beautiful and I was very anxious to put on a stalk. We quickly circled ahead of the rams and picked the ridgeline we expected them to be feeding up. During this stalk, I was lucky enough to be the first one to spot a nice four-point mule deer shed antler.

As I was coming around a tree, I happened to spot one of the rams already bedded down facing right toward me. If I took one more step forward, it would have seen me and bolted. There was only 100 yards between us, but as open as it was, it might as well have been half a mile. We slowly and quietly retraced our steps until we were on the other side of the ridge. We decided to try and circle around the basin for a different look.

We bumped out two nice mule deer bucks, but we never saw those two rams again. We were getting hungry at this point, as it was almost 1:00 p.m., so we decided to sit and have a sandwich. We hiked up to a good vantage point and set up the spotting scopes. As it turned out, we couldn't have picked a better spot to have lunch.

I immediately noticed some white rumps almost a mile away. We all quickly put our glasses on them and found it to be a band of seven rams. The first good look I got of them showed one ram that stood out from the rest. It was moving away from us, but its horns came up, back, down, out and up again. All the studying I did

BIGHORN SHEEP
Fourth Award – 200 $\frac{1}{8}$
▼ ▼ ▼ ▼ ▼
DAVID J. NYGARD

in preparation for this hunt now was going to be tested.

We watched them from where we were as we ate. Eventually, they picked a spot to bed down. Once they settled, we moved down the backside of a ridge opposite of them. There were two really good heads that we initially figured would go above 190 B&C. We moved closer yet and set up our scopes to get a really good look at them. Kim and Joe were watching them closely, and I was trying to figure out how in the world I could get across the deep canyon and within bow range. Where they bedded definitely proved that they knew something about survival from predators.

We debated back and forth as to which ram was the oldest, largest, and which would score the best. I found myself always going to the long-horned ram and liking its looks the best. We were blessed enough to get a very long look at these magnificent animals and observe their behavior. I kept asking Joe what he would do. All he ever did was just grin at me. He liked the look of the ram that was more broomed off, but he said they were both great rams.

About 4:30 p.m., the ram I liked the best stood up, walked over to the other large ram and laid its massive horns on the back of the bedded ram. Then it got up and they both were side by side. As if they knew what we were all thinking, they actually hooked horns and twisted our direction. We got a perfect side by side comparison of each ram's bases and overall mass. It was then very evident which ram was the best; the long-horned ram would be the one I would try to take. The whole band then stirred and started feeding along the hillside back toward the direction we first saw them. Grabbing my bow, I said, "Let's go boys."

Joe manned the rifle, and Kim was ready with the video camera. We hustled back down the ridge we had come up, and when we figured we were ahead of the band on the opposite side of the canyon, we literally dropped off several eight-foot and ten-foot ledges on our way to the canyon floor. We scrambled up the side that the sheep were on until we felt that we were about the same level. We then shucked our packs and all non-essential gear and moved very slowly forward, checking every inch of the curving hillside as it came into view. We didn't know if the band had kept the same general direction of travel or if they had simply vanished.

I finally spotted a ram below me in the bottom of a fold in the hillside. I froze and hunkered down and made ready with my arrow. If that single ram hadn't seen me, they were on a trail that would have brought them to within four yards. However, it did see me and the whole band proceeded to come out of the little depression in the hill and bunch up. I had come to full draw and was surprisingly calm and steady. I looked back at Joe and asked what he thought the yardage was and to check with his rangefinder. He indicated that he had left it back with our packs. I felt that the range was somewhere between 45 and 50 yards. When the large ram came out, I held on it and waited for it to get clear of the other rams. The ram stopped, but was not

David J. Nygard, center, took this award-winning bighorn sheep with the help of his close friend and hunting partner, Joe Weingand, right, and Kim Latterell, who had previously hunted in the area. David's ram scores 200-1/8 points.

as clear as I wanted it to be. I didn't feel that I could risk a shot at that distance with the other subordinate ram that close. I chose not to release and I let them walk off around the hill.

That encounter left me shaking and excited. To get that close was such a rush! We quietly discussed our options at that point. Should I continue the next day with the bow and arrow, or switch to a rifle and try to get on them again? Observing the size of the long-horned ram at such a close distance sealed the deal. I would switch to the rifle despite the fact that I had really wanted to harvest this game animal with bow and arrow.

We went back, retrieved our gear, and set out after the band again. It wasn't long before we caught up with them and set up for the shot. They were about 160 yards away across a small canyon, and although they knew we were there, they didn't get nervous for some time. Joe and I belly-crawled up to the sagebrush and made sure we were on the right ram. It wasn't that hard to figure out, but I wanted Joe right there just in case.

All the rams stood like statues for a couple minutes. Unfortunately, the long-horned ram's vitals were somewhat covered by its horns. The ram finally moved, but was with the band and moving off before a clear shot presented itself. It finally got clear of the other sheep, but was quartering away and walking steadily. I had a good rest and fired. At the report, I could hear the bullet strike. The band instantly moved as one and raced down the hill out of view. We were up and running ahead immediately. We came up on a sharp rise and saw below us only six rams running around the hill out of view. We knew that our ram was somewhere else. A few feet more and we located the long-horned ram on a trail below, standing still. I knew it was hit hard, but decided to finish it before it got lower on the mountain and further from the camp. One final shot brought the ram down for good.

Kim and Joe went down ahead of me while I kept watch from above. I followed its trail from the first shot. It was evident that a second shot would not have been needed. As I came up on this great animal, I was in awe. It was and is a perfect specimen and a great representative of its species.

We all celebrated with handshakes, hugs, and smiles. It was about 5:25 p.m. and we had plenty of work ahead of us. We couldn't help ourselves and Kim soon had a tape out and started measuring. In the field, we taped its right horn length at 44-1/2 inches, and its left horn at 41-1/2 inches. The ram's bases were amazingly well over 16 inches! I couldn't have been more pleased.

After spending some more time measuring, we finally got busy with the task at hand. We cleaned the ram up and took several pictures and video footage. It was a great moment for all of us. We didn't have our pack frames with us, so we boned out all the meat and set it out to cool for the night. We would return for it first thing in the morning. I was on such a high that I hauled the head and cape out on my back by putting my arms through the horns and bunching over. Needless to say, the next morning, I was more than a little sore. We did not get back to camp until 10:30 p.m. or so and we hit our beds very tired, but very happy.

The next day, we were up early and noticed an extreme change in the weather. It had clouded up and was starting to rain. I called on my cell phone to the landowner to let him know of our success. He kindly offered to drive my truck in from the locked gate so we didn't have to haul all of our gear and an animal all the way out. We agreed on a spot where he would leave the truck, and then we hustled back to the kill site to retrieve and pack out the meat. We took one of the game carts with us, but this ended up being worthless due to the rain and gumbo mud.

It rained that whole day and night. We had a small river running behind the tent and there was mud everywhere. For those who have never experienced the Breaks country gumbo, it's hard to find an adequate description. We couldn't get my pickup back to camp due to a very slick and steep road that was hard to walk down, let alone drive a truck down. We were effectively stranded. We passed time in camp fleshing the cape, measuring and re-measuring the horns, and mopping water out of the tent that had leaky seams. We were so happy, we didn't mind.

On Wednesday the rain finally stopped in mid-morning, and the sun came out. In order to get the truck down the hill, we had to shovel mud three inches thick to get to dry dirt and make a track for the tires. It was nerve racking, but we finally made it out to the main county road late in the day.

We made it a point on the way out to stop and thank the landowner for all his generosity and help. We stopped at a crossroad, had a celebratory beer, and then Kim went off to the east in search of elk. Joe and I went on into Lewistown to meet with the biologist. The ram was aged at 9-1/2 years old, and a plug was inserted per department regulations. Our hunt was over. I cannot express how thankful I am that I was lucky enough to draw the coveted tag, to have great friends to share in the hunt, and to find and harvest such a magnificent animal. This was definitely a hunt-of-a-lifetime.

TROPHY STATS

▼　▼　▼　▼　▼

Category
　desert sheep

Score
　$179^3/_8$

Location
　Hidalgo County, New Mexico — 2001

Hunter
　James A. Schneider

Length of Horn
　Right: $37^1/_8$　　Left: $37^2/_8$

Circumference of Base
　Right: $15^6/_8$　　Left: $15^6/_8$

Greatest Spread
　$21^3/_8$

DESERT SHEEP
First Award – 179 $^3/_8$

▼ ▼ ▼ ▼ ▼ ▼ ▼ ▼ ▼

JAMES A. SCHNEIDER - HUNTER   MᾹHUNT FOUNDATION - OWNER

Harry Chapin long ago sang:

"It's the going, not the getting there that counts."

The pursuit of my 179-3/8 B&C desert bighorn ram really started with my bowhunt for Stone's sheep in August 1998 in British Columbia. As I entered the airport at Watson Lake, Yukon Territory, in August 1998 after a superb, but stalk-free Stone's sheep hunt with Stan Lancaster in northern British Columbia, I was still reveling in the mountains' magnetic mystery combined with sensational Stone's sheep splendor. As Aldo Leopold wrote:

"Poets sing and hunters scale the mountains primarily for one and the same reason, the thrill to beauty. Critics write and hunters outwit their game for one and the same reason, to reduce that beauty to possession."

Stan was relating his hope for a better Stone's sheep-filled hunt in two years when I was scheduled to return. His intuition was correct, as two years later I ultimately took a fabulous Stone's sheep with Bart Lancaster.

My spirit was still celebrating the hunt when he asked me if I recognized Larry Heathington at the gate. Larry Heathington's reputation for guiding dedicated hunters for magnificent desert bighorn sheep was unparalleled. I had tried to contact him over a number of years at the FNAWS convention, but to no avail.

Stan introduced me to Larry. I instantly advanced my hopeful desert bighorn sheep hunts by a number of years, since the opportunity to hunt with Larry Heathington and learn some of his insight on desert bighorn rams was as irresistible as the Stone's sheep and mountains of northern British Columbia. The following year, one arrow, delivered from 50 yards after clamoring along a narrow ledge high above the broken rocks far below, yielded my first archery-taken desert bighorn ram. It would be entered in Boone and Crockett at 165-6/8. The ram also ranked as the longest horned (37-3/8 inches) desert bighorn ever taken with archery as recognized by Pope and Young Club.

That was Larry's last guided hunt for desert bighorn sheep. He handed the baton to Marvin James. At the 2000 FNAWS convention, I was the silver medal bidder for the Arizona bighorn, Montana bighorn, and British Columbia bighorn auction sheep tags. As I bid (all puns intended) Marvin goodbye, I said "Maybe it is for the best; I will probably draw an Arizona desert bighorn sheep tag with my nine preference points!"

His glance indicated that he was less sanguine and doubted my luck. Luck was with me though. The winner of the New Mexico auction tag decided to sell, and I also drew on my Arizona desert bighorn tag. Instead of one sheep hunt for 2000, I now had three (August

Stone's sheep in B.C., October desert bighorn in New Mexico, and December desert bighorn in Arizona.)

The Stone's sheep hunt was the most demanding, depleting, and exhilarating sheep hunt up to that point in my life. As the last day of the hunt dawned and a 10-hour horseback ride loomed, Bart said, "We still might find a great ram on the way home."

His premonition exceeded mine, although my intuition for the day also included a majestic ram. A close call with my preferred mode of archery led to a view down the barrel of my .300 Winchester Magnum. The scene featured a puff of smoke from a single shot at a ram running straight away at 210 yards followed by the ram's tumbling. The Stone's sheep was certainly a grand slam home run in the bottom of the ninth with one strike to end the game.

As October 2000's crispness greeted each dawn, I found myself with Marvin James and Randy Elmer in the Peloncillo Mountains of New Mexico. With prevalent mountain lions, the desert bighorns resembled pronghorn by staying far from overhangs and cliffs. The bow was idled for the rifle. The video camera rolled and captured the 173-1/8 net B&C desert bighorn ram roll at 250 yards.

Early December's lower slanting sun still seared my face in the Cabeza Prieta Wildlife Area of Arizona, if I did not shield it with my hat. December's temperate days had kept the distinctive red-horned (from rubbing area-specific elephant shrubs) desert bighorn sheep undiscovered. Maybe the end of December (just before the hunting season's end) would bring a chill in the air that would warm the desert bighorn rams' urge to move.

Eventually, we were able to spot a ram at 320 yards. It was now or never. I looked up through the scope. Suddenly the ram stood. I estimated a nine-inch drop at 320 yards. The cross hairs were quieted at the top of the ram's back just behind its front shoulder. The crystal clear silence of the Cabeza Prieta was shattered as I pulled the trigger. A large explosion of dust erupted behind the ram. As the ram instantaneously bolted forward out of view, Marvin said "You shot high."

I said, "I thought I was on it."

Marvin volunteered to make the 45 minute climb to the ram's throne. Marvin's parallel raised arms signaled that a last second deep pass completion into the end zone meant a 2000 wild sheep hat trick — three spectacular rams in 2000, with three desert bighorn rams in 13 months.

When the 2001 FNAWS convention ram awards concluded and the state auction of tags began, my brush with Midas spurred me to bid convincingly for the New Mexico desert bighorn tag, to attempt to take archery's World's Record desert bighorn sheep. As the funds to help continue New Mexico's preservation/propagation of desert bighorn rams in the Peloncillo Mountains were transferred to FNAWS for the New Mexico desert bighorn tag, I hoped that ample rains and nutritious grasses would lead to longer and thicker horns. Also, that mountain lion predator balance/control would erase the rams' imitation of pronghorn.

The fresh air and splendor of the Peloncillo Mountains in mid-October 2001 invigorated both hunter and rutting rams. It ensures that the enthusiasm of searching for a high 170s desert ram must not wane, even when none has been found after searching, looking, and glassing. Finally, near the end of the day, an apparition of two never-before-seen rams emerged just below the top of the mountain. As quickly as they materialized, they laid down for the night. Although they appeared large-

DESERT SHEEP
First Award – 179³/₈
▼ ▼ ▼ ▼ ▼
JAMES A. SCHNEIDER

horned, the limited light and vast distance meant confirmation would need to wait until morning.

As we waited in the dark on October 15, 2001, peering into the mountain peaks, the silence was sumptuously supplanted by the deep thumping within my chest. Were the rams still there? Were they moving to a fateful destination far away beyond our purview? Did mountain lions roust them during the night? Would they move to a place where a close approach was problematic? Would they begin to bash heads and splinter their hardened horns into stubs?

As the gray mountains turned rosy, so did our outlook. The two rams stood and trotted down the mountain and up the other side of the valley. As we traced their progress, we hoped their trek would cease soon. Remarkably they laid down in the shade about 60 yards below a large rock. They both appeared larger than the 173-1/8 B&C desert ram that I had taken in these mountains the year before. The plan entailed me climbing the mountain and stealthily stalking from above until I could see the top of their horns, and then waiting for them to stand in perhaps an hour or two.

The climb proceeded quickly and well, but the glacial downhill sneak had not conjured either monarch. I decided that a closer approach would bust the rams so I backed off. Marvin had joined me in the climb, but headed around the mountain to garner a different view. He emerged farther up the mountain and waved to me. He said the rams had moved to the east around the mountain and that we should try another downward stalk. We began as the brilliant hot sun turned the still air very warm.

Marvin was slightly behind me as he whispered, "Freeze! The two rams are looking toward our position from 60 yards below."

As 10 minutes turned to 20 and felt like 500, Our "statues" felt like they were growing cracks. Suddenly, I heard and Marvin saw the rams slowly move farther around the mountain to our left. He whispered "If we can get to that ledge 10 yards below and to our left, they should be 40 to 50 yards broadside."

As I took my first cautious step, a ram jumped up from below us to the right 30 yards away and sprinted toward the other two rams. A third never-before-seen ram had busted us. How had a third ram crossed a valley and joined these two rams without us seeing it? Had the two rams been looking at the new ram and not toward us?

As we hurried to the ledge, we saw the northeast ends of three southwest-bound running rams go around the mountain and head toward Mexico. Would they stop before reaching Mexico City?

As late morning turned to late afternoon, our glassing had not yielded the new resting

Photograph courtesy of Jame A. Schneider

James A. Schneider took this award-winning desert sheep in Hidalgo County, New Mexico, in 2001. The ram received a First Place Award at the 25th Awards Program in Kansas City and scores 179-3/8 points.

or running place of the rams. Again, just as light diminished to the point the color was gone, the rams were found higher in the impenetrable mountains about a mile away from where we made the stalk.

The next morning would bring the same questions and worries as yesterday morning. In the dark, we traversed the bottom of the new mountain to try to glass from the backside of the mountain where the rams were seen late the afternoon before. One of the three rams was found, but in a place where only a long rifle shot would suffice. The largest of the rams was not seen. We decided to retrace our steps to the side of the mountain where the rams were spotted at the end of the day before.

As we proceeded with the climb, we peeked around a large overhang about 200 yards from the saddle where we intended to sneak. Marvin said, "The ram is looking down the mountain, not toward us. It looks like it is about to head out and not be found again. This is a once-in-a-lifetime ram. If you want it, the rifle is your best choice."

I quickly shot as the ram ambled toward the saddle about 175 yards away. The gigantic-bodied dark chocolate brown desert bighorn ram had completed one role in the wild. Now it would begin a new place of esteem and distinction that reminds us that the wild in nature must be saved for desert bighorn rams and hunters.

The ram's wide deep divot in its left horn magnifies its awesome means to propel its progeny into an unlimited future, if hunters survive to help ensure that New Mexico's desert bighorns flourish.

Imagine what the official score might have been if the deep gouge in its left horn had not occurred. The magnificent ram received the bronze Desert Bighorn Rifle Award at the 2002 Reno Convention of FNAWS.

With an official score of 179-3/8 B&C, 37-1/8-inch and 37-2/8-inch horn lengths, and matched bases of 15-6/8 inches, this ram demonstrates the Boone and Crockett Club's focus on excellence that translates into preserving the wild and wildness for future generations of hunters.

A sincere and long remembered thank you goes to every guide who facilitated our adventure in the wild by pursuing royal rams (especially Stan Lancaster, Bart Lancaster, Larry Heathington, Marvin James, Randy Elmer, and Greg Koons). That thank you, however, would miss the mark unless it was combined with a never forgotten thank you to the fish and game departments of North America (especially Arizona, British Columbia, and New Mexico), the landowners (especially Bill Miller, Jr.), and FNAWS for their passion, insight, effort, protection, patience, and sacrifice to put wild sheep on the mountains.

Photograph by Cliff White

TROPHY STATS

▼ ▼ ▼ ▼ ▼

Category
   Dall's sheep

Score
   177

Location
   Chugach Mountains, Alaska — 1994

Hunter
   William J. Dunbar

Length of Horn
   Right: $40^1/_8$ Left: $39^7/_8$

Circumference of Base
   Right: 15   Left: $15^1/_8$

Greatest Spread
   $23^1/_8$

DALL'S SHEEP
First Award - 177

▼ ▼ ▼ ▼ ▼ ▼ ▼ ▼ ▼

WILLIAM J. DUNBAR

By F. Jeffrey Peterson

Until now, winning the prestigious FNAWS "Gold Rifle" Award was a once in a lifetime opportunity. But, Billy Dunbar's 1994 Dall's sheep hunt changed that rule when he struck gold a second time in Alaska's Chugach Mountains.

Descending a 500-foot slope, we entered a dream world. It's not every day you find yourself walking through the middle of a high hanging valley surrounded by no less than 60 Dall's sheep. It was the most beautiful valley in which I had ever set foot. I had to keep pinching myself to make sure it was all real.

The valley was carpeted with beautiful green grass stretching up slope and fanning out to touch the mouths of five glaciers, each producing a small stream of water. When the streams joined, a deep rocky gorge formed that ran to the end of the hanging valley and then fell 1,500 feet to the river below. Above the glaciers, the gray and brown rocks of mountain peaks reached up to touch an occasional cloud floating in the blue Alaska sky. Fabulous can't describe it. Trying to comprehend the valley and take in all the activity around us were more than the senses could absorb.

Stalking sheep in a wide open valley with only an occasional scrub is not an easy task. We were trying the ultimate stalking deception and it was working. You've heard of "wolves in sheep's clothing?" Well this was a twist on that routine.

From our vantage point at the rim of the hanging valley, we had counted 42 ewes and lambs on a ridge across the gorge. Up the valley, we had spotted three single rams that we nicknamed "Flare," "Kenny," (he reminded us of a stocky guy we played high school football with), and "The Kid." It's hard to score sheep at a range of two miles. While two of the rams were big, they didn't motivate us to enter the valley. After all, it was late afternoon and we had been hiking for two days to reach the rim where we could peek into the hanging valley.

The first four miles of the trek had been easy — up a trail used by hikers to photograph waterfalls in the Chugach. However, the trail soon ended and the going got tough. Fighting alders and rock slides, we earned every mile. We encountered more bear sign here than in any drainage I have experienced. I banged rocks, Bill broke branches, but our singing is what really kept the bears at a distance.

On the second day, the packs were lightened and a cache hung in a tree. Then the route turned straight uphill. Not knowing if there was water on the mountain caused us to carry additional water in case of a dry camp.

Photograph courtesy of Willam J. Dunbar

William J. Dunbar and his hunting partner used hazardous waste clean-up jump suits to make their way across the open hillside without spooking the rams.

Billy made sure we kept ourselves hydrated, and we took plenty of rest breaks. Our 37-year-old bodies seemed to recover faster with several short rests rather than pushing ourselves past the point of recovery. During one of the rest breaks, I asked Billy why so many people applied for these tags. "It's pretty close to Anchorage and people think it's easy," he responded. Easy? Yeah, right!

The top of the mountain seemed elusive, but with persistence it was finally obtained. We then traversed two miles along the mountain and at 4 p.m., the torture racks (backpacks) were thrown on the ground. A small water seep was found nearby. The water purifier could pump faster than the seep flowed; but we were relieved that we weren't in a dry camp. "Should we set up camp or peek at the sheep?" Billy asked.

"We've hiked two solid days to look into this valley, camp can wait," I responded.

When Billy found out he had drawn a tag in the Chugach Range, an expert sheep hunter and former guide chided him, "Why did you get that tag? There hasn't been a book sheep taken from that area for years!"

Billy was a little concerned and scheduled a mid-summer hike into the hunting area with his trusted taxidermist, Joe Romero. The hike allowed Billy to check the route to the mountain and allowed Joe to score from a distance a couple of good rams.

After this first scouting trip, Bill called me with an excited voice. "I saw two or three rams that we think will make the book! You've got to come up and help with the hunt," he exclaimed. That's all it took to get me to book the flight from Boise to Anchorage and to get a daily routine started on the stair stepper.

DALL'S SHEEP
First Award – 177
▼ ▼ ▼ ▼ ▼
WILLIAM J. DUNBAR

From our vantage point on the rim, we had been spotting sheep in the hanging valley for nearly two hours. It was then that I located an additional ram feeding through a patch of willows more than two miles away. "Bill, I've got one you need to look at," I said as I slid the spotting scope his direction.

The scope was cranked to 45x, but still didn't give a lot of detail. Billy looked for a few seconds then he turned the scope to compare the ram in the willows with the three rams spotted earlier. He then turned back and took a long look at this latest ram.

"Jeff, don't take my word on it, but I think we've found the one," Billy said. "It's getting late in the day and I'm tired. However, if that ram beds down, we've got to try for it now."

As Billy was speaking those words, the ram started pawing a bed on a dirt point near one of the glacier streams. Twenty seconds later, the ram was quietly bedded.

A stalking route was picked. It would hopefully bring us to a point on the opposite side of the glacier stream about 150 yards from where the ram had bedded. The last 300 yards would be on the backside of a slope where the ram could not see us. The problem we had was how to move two miles across an open valley through 60 sheep without getting them excited.

"It's time for the secret weapons," Billy said. And with that he pulled out two white jump suits used for hazardous waste clean-up. After donning the suits, Billy handed out the hoods. "I know people who use white suits or coats, but I don't know anyone who uses the hoods. We may be testing new technology," he joked.

So there we were in the middle of the hanging valley dressed like a couple of ewes (our slang pronunciation is "E-We's".) To my amazement, it was working! We had eight ewes and lambs, which were just 400 yards to our right, moving the same direction. As we moved forward, we could see more and more of the hillside to our left. "Whoa, Bill! There's a group of rams, 12 in all."

One was looking at us at 300 yards. The rest were scattered over an area out to 600 yards. I set the scope up and looked at the rams. "There is one here you should look at Bill," I whispered.

Billy took a quick look. "It's nice, probably go 40 maybe 41 inches, but the mass isn't great. Let's find that one ram and then we'll decide."

"It's your tag," I responded while taking one more look at a fabulous Dall's ram.

Ten of 12 rams never gave us more than a glance. One stared from his bed and one stood and moved a few yards away. We kept moving, being careful not to point or reach

William J. Dunbar with his award-winning Dall's sheep. The ram was taken in Alaska's Chugach Mountains in 1994. It scores 177 points and received a First Award at the 25th Awards Program in Kansas City.

with an outstretched arm. We walked slightly hunched over and faces down. "We're just a couple of sheep going to the grocery store," I whispered.

The suits became very hot and we were both perspiring heavily while climbing the final 300 yards to our intended position. We stopped to gain breathing control before crawling over the top. Billy was in the lead. "The ram is gone," Billy whispered back with alarm.

It had been 20 minutes since our last glimpse of the ram, and a lot can go on in 20 minutes. The other sheep, which we could see from our position (mostly ewes and lambs), were not alarmed. "The ram may have left, but let's move slowly to make sure," Billy whispered.

"Don't move," I said. "There's a ram on our side of the stream."

The spotting scope was quickly set up. The ram was 300 yards away feeding through the willows heading in our direction. "What's it look like?" Billy asked.

"You tell me," I responded as I slid sideways to let Bill move to the scope.

"That's it! Good mass!" Billy was excited.

Billy slid back to the rifle and I slid to the scope. The ram moved to 250 yards. Any closer and it might have moved out of view underneath us. "I'm going to take it," Billy whispered.

Through the spotting scope, I saw the hair part in the rib section as the bullet entered. The ram whirled around, but could not leave. "It's dead," I said.

The traditional congratulatory handshake was made and we advanced to the ram. As we approached it, Billy had second thoughts. "It's a small body. I've heard of dwarf rams, they make the horns look larger than they really are."

I stared in disbelief. "It looks like a hog to me!"

Being somewhat fatigued from the hard climbing, we had not brought backpacks on the stalk. After caping and cleaning the ram, we hiked back to camp.

The long days in Alaska are incredible. We climbed to camp at 11 p.m. and tried to get some sleep.

We awoke to the sheep hunter's nightmare — fog so dense you couldn't see 50 yards. "I'm glad we didn't wait to make that stalk today," Billy said with a great deal of relief.

The trip back to the airstrip took two days with packs weighing around 90 to 100 pounds. The Koflack mountaineering boots worked terrific with the heavy loads, especially while sidehilling. Billy's pilot friend, Richard Pulley, met two tired yet happy hunters at the airstrip. He got within ten feet of us and exclaimed, "Whoa! You boys need to bathe!"

After a short flight to a grass landing strip near Eagle, we taxied into Richard's yard. We each enjoyed a welcomed shower and some Alaskan hospitality of homemade chili and sourdough bread. We ate on the porch and admired the horns in the August Alaskan sun.

TROPHY STATS

▼ ▼ ▼ ▼ ▼

Category
Dall's sheep

Score
173 $^6/_8$

Location
Brooks Range, Alaska — 2003

Hunter
Chris E. Kneeland

Length of Horn
Right: 45$^1/_8$ Left: 42$^5/_8$

Circumference of Base
Right: 13$^1/_8$ Left: 13$^2/_8$

Greatest Spread
26

DALL'S SHEEP
Second Award – 173⁶/₈

▼ ▼ ▼ ▼ ▼ ▼ ▼ ▼ ▼

CHRIS E. KNEELAND

When Chris Kneeland left his home one August morning, he was absolutely filled to the brim with anticipation. He was headed to the Brooks Range in Alaska for a Dall's sheep hunt. The thought of those remote, wild mountains was pure heaven for Chris. Dreams of white rams running rampant on the mountains filled his thoughts and dreams.

He arrived on August 6, 2003, for what could have potentially been a 15-day hunt. There he met Mike Vanning, of Gateway Outfitting, who would be his guide for this adventure.

Ten full days later, they awoke for yet another grueling day of chasing rams on the mountain. The weather was awful. Heavy overcast skies and heavy rain was again the order of the day, with a 10 mile-per-hour wind thrown in just to take any feeling of warmth away. Fog complicated things further.

The hunt didn't last long that day. They were out hiking on the gorgeous and barren mountain slopes when they spotted a ram. Chris had the ram of his dreams in his rifle scope at 5:30 a.m. A 310-yard shot with his 7mm reached out and touched his trophy with a definitive and final decision.

Chris had faced adversity and come out shining in the Alaska rain. It was truly a ram of dreams, with horn lengths of 45-1/8 and 42-5/8 inches. Chris Kneeland's hunt didn't just produce a great ram for Chris; it produced the second-largest Dall's ram taken during the entire 25th Awards Period.

Photograph by Cliff White

TROPHY STATS

▼ ▼ ▼ ▼ ▼

Category
   Dall's sheep

Score
   $172^2/_8$

Location
   Chugach Mountains, Alaska — 1991

Hunter
   William J. Dunbar

Length of Horn
   Right: $40^6/_8$ Left: 43

Circumference of Base
   Right: $14^3/_8$ Left: $14^3/_8$

Greatest Spread
   $25^2/_8$

DALL'S SHEEP
Third Award – 172²/₈

▼ ▼ ▼ ▼ ▼ ▼ ▼ ▼ ▼

WILLIAM J. DUNBAR

Story by F. Jeffrey Peterson

The spotting scope had just come into focus and there they were. Billy Dunbar had a 30-power view of the back half of two rams. "Of all the luck!" he thought to himself as they vanished within moments of being spotted. "I spent six hours of hard climbing for that!" Bill muttered to himself. "Where are those other two?"

The sun disappeared as quietly as the sheep had. Billy should have been heading down the mountain two hours earlier. However, the group of rams he had seen only momentarily with his 10x40 binoculars had prompted him to bust his tail to get a better look. "What did this uphill charge get me?" He answered himself, "Another cold lonely night on the mountain."

Billy had not planned to spend the night away from the spike camp, but he was prepared. Years of Alaska weather and the dynamics of hunting had taught him to never venture out without essential gear. For him, that gear included a survival kit, a parka, and Gore-tex pants. It had also taught him that in the last frontier, plans can change in a hurry.

Darkness was upon him as he settled into a rock outcrop to spend the night. He took the parka and pants from the military pack board. They would serve as a sleeping bag — not total comfort, but he would fair alright. This was some of the roughest country in which he had ever hunted Dall's sheep. The dumbest thing he could do was try to get back to spike camp. It would be suicide to panic and try to go down in the dark.

Billy exhaled a deep breath and smiled. It was September and the 1991 Alaska Dall's sheep season had finally started for him and he was a part of it! The season had opened a month earlier for everyone else.

Supper consisted of a granola bar and an apple. Sometimes climbing light has its drawbacks. Alone and in a vast glacial valley, a man can feel quite insignificant and it often inspires deep thoughts. Billy sat in the darkness and wondered if the magnificent ram he had seen earlier in the summer was one of the four that had vanished, or if he had wasted his energy on "pinheads." The hindquarter view through the spotting scope had not answered a thing.

Billy was exhausted, but could not sleep. His thoughts went back to his first sheep hunt in 1975. He remembered taking pictures on the steep slope where his first ram fell. It was a 3/4 curl, smaller than any ram he had taken since, but it was his first. He was thrilled to be in the Dall's sheep club.

He thought of the pictures of that first ram which he had sent to all his friends back in Utah. They were just out of high school and could only dream of the North Country. His mind wandered back to high school and how he had learned to hunt deer, pheasants, and ducks in the Duchesne River drainage of Eastern Utah before his dad moved the family to Alaska. He remembered a few high school classes that had been "cut" to allow extra hours in the field. He thought, too, about a high school teacher (Mr. Aycock) who had managed to disappear from a few classes himself with Billy and his friends. Those were the "no worry" days.

A small breeze kicked up and he thought of the plane. Had he buried the sand bag anchors deep enough? And that landing strip! He had nicknamed it "the blind runway" because on the approach, the entire strip is hidden until you round the glacier. By then, it's too late to change your mind. The valley is too narrow to turn around and if you are too high, you're going to crash. One thing about it, it scares most pilots away from this mountain.

Billy saw the runway as a minor risk. He had paid extra to get a 180 engine in the Super Cub and relied heavily on good equipment. Accused of having ice water in his veins, deep inside Billy knew it was the hours of detailed training Troy Hodges had given him. He could hear Troy's words now: "Lock your mind on the landing you want, Billy Bob, then rely on your equipment and don't flinch when you go for it."

Troy would have been proud of his student on yesterday's landing. The Cub had come around the glacier a little low, but with the extra 180 power, Billy was able to stretch out and "stick" the landing. Billy thought it would be interesting to know his heart rate and blood pressure at such a moment. He has often rehearsed the old adage: "My goal is not to be the best pilot in Alaska, but to be the oldest pilot in Alaska." Sometimes the two go together.

Billy thought forward to the Stone's sheep hunt he had scheduled for the following month. The Stone's and the desert were the rams lacking from his "grand slam" and he wondered what the 23-day hunt would be like.

Billy seldom hunted alone because of the additional risk from unforeseen problems and accidents. However, the rams he had seen on this mountain before had locked him into coming back to this spot. Billy had invited several friends to come along, but for one reason or another, they had conflicts or excuses that caused them to cancel the hunt. Besides, he has been known to stretch a story from time to time, so Bill's tale of finding Big Head Mountain was smiled at and not taken too seriously. But he knew the rugged area had sheep with good genetics. It was worth every effort to be in the area on opening day.

The moon was a welcome sight as it peeked over the rugged snow-covered crags. He gazed at its beauty on such a clear night and felt again the awe of being surrounded by true majesty. Billy's thoughts turned to how those folks who live in great cities no longer experience the mountains at night and lose touch with some of life's greatest treasures. "Regardless of the outcome of the hunt, I'm a richer person for being here" he said to himself.

As the moon ascended, the Northern Lights began to add their illumination to the grand scene. Billy started thinking that if it got any lighter, he could walk back to the spike camp. He could see in some detail the slope he had climbed. As he turned to attempt some sleep, he glanced at the slope and rocks where the rams had disappeared. He could see the rocks in some detail and a few patches of snow on the slope. "What the...? Am I seeing things or did that patch of snow move?" Billy questioned himself.

DALL'S SHEEP
Third Award – 172 2/8

▼ ▼ ▼ ▼ ▼

WILLIAM J. DUNBAR

Confident he was seeing things, Billy reached for his 10x40s just so he could convince himself and go to sleep. As the 10x40s focused, Billy had conflicting thoughts, "Rams don't feed at night, do they?"

At 1,000 yards, Billy could see what he swore were four sheep feeding on the slope. His imagination got the best of him, like a young boy gazing into a cloudy sky looking for shapes — in this case, sheep shapes. He studied the shapes once more and agreed to not look that direction for five minutes to see if the shapes appeared the same. The time went ever so slowly. "I must be going nuts," he muttered to himself. "You are supposed to count sheep to fall asleep, but this is crazy."

Peering back after the allotted time, Billy could only identify two of the shapes. Over the next hour, he studied and restudied the slope, first with the glasses then with the spotting scope. Each optic gathered light differently and it was hard to correlate what he saw. However, what he saw convinced him to take another risk.

He had charted a traverse that could get him to the edge of a deep chute separating him from the objects on the slope. On all fours for the majority of the way, knowing that one bad move and he would be spending several nights on the mountain, Billy navigated to the new vantage point. It had taken nearly two hours to make what he estimated as 100 yards. The white shapes were no where to be seen. Unable to venture any further forward, Billy was content to wait until sunup.

First the stars began to disappear, along with the Northern Lights, and last of all the moon gave way to the pre-dawn. In this pre-dawn state, objects can become confusing to distinguish. Billy scanned the slope for movement, glassing up and down and looking for any off-colored object. His heart suddenly jumped. There were the four rams. They were 500 yards away feeding slowly toward him, but on an angle toward a group of rocks where they had disappeared yesterday. The rocks would conceal them if they traveled another 100 yards in their present direction.

Billy waited for more light. He quickly surveyed the chute in front of him. Chutes in Alaska are no trivial matter; it would take half the day to get down through and onto the far slope. If he was going to get a shot, it would be at the edge of the rocks. The sheep were doing more moving and less feeding now. Billy estimated the distance at 400 to 450 yards.

He decided that he should try to quickly field judge them. With that he lifted his rifle. The rams were moving steadily. The first ram had nearly made it to the rocks, but Billy knew he wasn't the ram he wanted. He could not see the second one clearly as it was being blocked by the third ram, which was heavy, but had a broken horn.

The fourth one was lagging behind. The words of an old Native Alaskan friend who had tutored Billy in the ways of sheep came to his mind, "Billy, a very old ram will surround itself with young rams for additional eyes. These old rams become slow with arthritis and age and you can spot them from a distance as the one who lags behind when moving uphill."

With that thought and a single glance, Billy knew which ram he wanted. The echo of the .300 Mag broke the silence of the dawn. The shot was drowned away by rolling and sliding rock caused by three rams escaping uphill and the fourth sliding and tumbling down. The ram descended into the chute and out of Billy's view, but from its falling motion, he knew it was dead.

Billy looked back over the 100 yards he had covered in the dark. He then looked over the chute. He knew it would take two or three hours of careful climbing to reach the ram. His heart was still pounding, so he sat down and ate breakfast — a granola bar and an apple (it tasted like supper.)

As Billy strapped his parka and pants to the pack board, he began to second-guess the fourth ram. "Was it as good as I thought? I never really scored the ram or got the spotting scope on it. Was the second ram better?" he worried. "Enough! The answer lies in the chute!"

Billy had been working his way downhill for about an hour and a half when he finally saw the body of the ram in the rocks below. Rock masses in Alaska are generally competent to climb on, but the loose stuff will take you down fast. Billy had to fight his excitement and urge to hurry.

At 20 yards, Billy knew that second-guessing was wasted mind power. He examined the head with the care and attention that a jeweler examines a fine diamond. Billy looked at the horns from one angle and then another. This was the biggest ram he had seen in the field! He looked at the head again. This was as beautiful a ram as he had seen on any wall. He counted the growth rings — only eight and one-half. This ram wasn't lagging behind because it was old, it was behind because it was carrying the heaviest horns on the mountain.

The Piper 5656Y flew proud on the trip back to Anchorage. The head was first measured on a pickup tailgate at the airport and then again at home. It ended up being one of the best Dall's sheep taken in 1991. His only regret was not getting a good picture of the ram in the field.

Moments in Measuring...

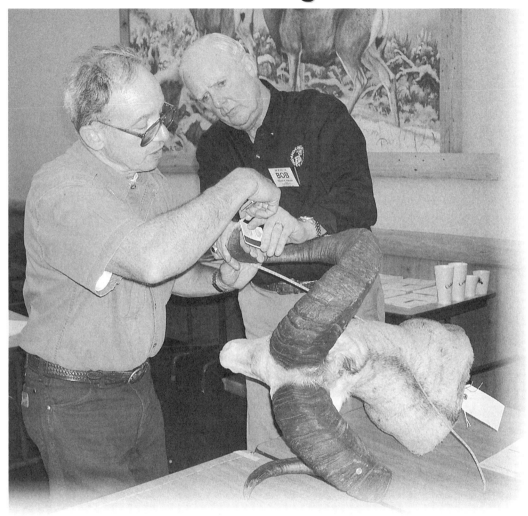

Photograph courtesy of Mark O. Bara

25th Awards Judges Panel team, Mark O. Bara, left, and Bob Hanson, right, measure the length of horn of Ronald G. Selby's Stone's sheep.

Photograph by Cliff White

TROPHY STATS

▼ ▼ ▼ ▼ ▼

Category
　Dall's sheep

Score
　171⁶/₈

Location
　Talkeetna Mountains, Alaska — 2003

Hunter
　Andrew G. Kelso

Length of Horn
　Right: 41⁶/₈　Left: 43²/₈

Circumference of Base
　Right: 14¹/₈　Left: 14¹/₈

Greatest Spread
　24⁶/₈

Photograph by Jack Renea

Andrew G. Kelso accepting his plaque and
medal from Buck Buckner, Chair of the
Big Game Records Committee.

DALL'S SHEEP
Fourth Award – 171 $^6/_8$

▼ ▼ ▼ ▼ ▼ ▼ ▼ ▼ ▼

ANDREW G. KELSO

This hunt really started in 1999, after harvesting my 177-5/8 B&C Washington State California bighorn sheep. After that hunt, I became addicted to sheep and sheep hunting. I looked at a lot of outfitters and finally made my choice: Dan Montgomery's Alaska Trophy Adventures. I booked the first hunt for the 2003 season.

Dan wanted me out in the field before opening day, August 10, so we could do some scouting. So on August 6, I found myself on the doorstep of Dan's cabin.

On the afternoon of the 7th, Dan flew me and my gear out to the Chugach Mountains in his Super Cub floatplane, landing on a lake just below a glacier. By late afternoon, my guide, Mark Schwartz, and I were settled into a perfect camp.

Mountain Marathon 2003

The first morning we hiked down to the glacier and walked nearly to the end, zigzagging between crevasses. It was my first experience on a glacier, but certainly not my last. We only found a couple of small rams and one good-sized goat.

The next day, we took three days worth of food and a tarp to sleep under and hiked over the top, through a mountain pass and set up a fly camp just below the snowfields. From camp we saw eight rams, none of which were legal (legal being either full curl, eight years old, or broomed on both horns).

Opening day arrived with nine rams in sight from camp. One was close to full curl, but I didn't think it was enough to be legal. Even if it was legal, it was not big enough to be an opening day ram. Mark and I hunted the rest of the afternoon in some extremely rough terrain without seeing another sheep. That evening, we set up another fly camp just above the glacier. The weather had been wonderful, but as night fell, the wind kicked up and you could feel a drastic change coming on.

During the next four days we managed to locate several rams as the weather shifted from rain, to wind, to rain. Any ram is a good ram when you're glassing and hiking hard all day, but none of the rams we spotted were legal. We ended up losing a day and a half to the high winds and fog that had socked in, making glassing any distance impossible.

By the morning of the 15th, the weather finally broke in our favor and Dan was able to fly in to move our camp and bring in another hunter, Mark Deibert. With camp moved to a different glacier, and high hopes for seeing a new area, I anxiously awaited the next day's hunt.

The following morning, we spotted almost 20 sheep on the far side of the glacier. As we hiked along our side we got the chance to study all of the rams. We were looking for two par-

Andrew G. Kelso, pictured above, and his guide, Mark Schwartz camped out on several different glaciers during the hunt for Andrew's Dall's sheep.

ticular rams that Dan had seen on previous trips. We eventually spotted a long-horned ram across the glacier. Even from a mile away, it was obvious that it was a legal ram, well past full curl. Since I had been out the longest, it was my choice if I wanted the ram. From what I could see through the spotting scope, this ram was a shooter.

It took a lot of zigzagging to cross the glacier, but we made fairly good time. The stalk was touch and go at times, but we were able to move without being spotted. For the last few hundred yards of the stalk, we were well hidden from view by a thin rock wall. We peeked through a crack in the wall and saw the rams moving out with a purpose, about 800 yards away. The swirling winds had warned them of our presence. We were able to get a very good look at the ram we were after. Dan thought it only had about 12-inch bases and about 39 inches of length. He was certainly a fine-looking ram, very even, and a nice corkscrew shape to its horns, but the ram's horns looked thin.

The hunting was done for the day and it was time to head back to camp. On the way, Dan asked if I could get more time off from work. I told him that I could. We discussed the thin ram, its size, how much time I had to hunt, and what I wanted to do. Dan told me that he knew where there had been two really good rams, but it would mean another move and another day or two of hunting lost. I made my choice and told Dan that I wanted to move.

Mark Deibert was going to stay and hunt the thin ram with another guide, and Mark Schwartz; Dan and I would move camp. Dan said that the rams he had in mind were in Mark

Schwartz's area in the Talkeetna Mountains. Dan told me that Butch Kuflak, a FNAWS board member, was flying in to hunt with me. He also told me that both sheep were very good, mature rams. He said that the bigger

DALL'S SHEEP
Fourth Award – 171 6/8
▼ ▼ ▼ ▼ ▼
ANDREW G. KELSO

ram would go about 42 inches and might make the book. The other ram was wide flaring, about 39 inches in length, and was fairly heavy. This, of course, put me back in good spirits; I again felt optimistic about my chances for a good ram. That evening, Dan flew me back to his cabin. It was good to come back and get cleaned up, and eat some of Loren's (the camp manager) great cooking.

We were delayed flying out the following morning because of the weather, but that afternoon it cleared enough to fly. Dan flew Mark Schwartz out, then me. Mark and I set up camp while Dan went to get Butch. Snow started to fall and the light was fading fast. Mark and I had just about figured out that Dan and Butch were not going to make it back out, when we heard the buzz of Dan's Super Cub coming in.

After another night on the ice, we made our way off the glacier and down the river to a good campsite. Dan went to have a look at the rams while we got camp in order. After his return he broke the news that he now knew the big ram was only around 40 inches and did not think it would go "book."

It was well before dawn the next morning when we struck out, guided by the beams of our headlamps. At about 4:15 a.m., I felt a slight wind slap me in the back of my neck. We completed our planned stalk and confirmed the three rams winded us. They were making their way up into some really nasty stuff at the top of a bowl.

I got my first good look at the two big rams. Both were fine rams. Butch named them T.C. (for tight curl) and Flare. T.C. was a very beautiful ram well over full curl, heavy, and its lamb tips curled out at the end. Flare was just that, flaring and heavy.

Butch had an Oregon bighorn sheep raffle tag in his pocket and his hunt was already scheduled. These plans did not give Butch the time for a second chance at the rams so Dan and Butch headed out to get back in time to catch Butch's commercial flight. Mark and I stayed on the mountain watching the rams. It was not long before they went over the top. We tried to follow them, but near the top of the bowl's knife-edge, the rocks became extremely loose and it was simply too dangerous to continue.

On the 20th, we packed up and headed back up to the glacier. I think this was my lowest point during the trip. I knew my ram was nearby and I did not want to leave without it on my back. When we got back on the glacier near the landing strip it started to snow. We set the tent up and climbed inside. The weather was getting worse and the cloud ceiling was dropping. A call on the satellite phone confirmed that Dan was not going to make it in that night.

The next day was also lost to weather. I was really not in the mood for more tent time, but had no choice. Our only entertainment was listening for boulders falling from the cliffs and onto the glacier; which was a fairly frequent occurrence.

Andrew held out for 19 days in the Talkeetna Mountains of Alaska before he took his award-winning Dall's sheep. His ram scores 171-6/8 points and received a Fourth Award at the 25th Awards Program in Kansas City.

The dawn of the next morning was bright, clear, and beautiful. As luck would have it the rams were back in the bowl. My spirits soared once again at the thought of a second chance at T.C.! We packed up everything, but the tent, and met Dan at the plane as soon as he rolled to a stop. Dan told me to pack down to a flat spot about half a mile below the bowl the sheep were in. As the plane disappeared in the distance, I struck the tent, packed up extra food and gear and headed out. I had everything set up and was napping when Kyle, my new guide, arrived in camp. Later that afternoon Dan and another hunter, Stan, also arrived.

The next morning found us up early and hiking in the dark. This time we took a different approach. We sidehilled past the bowl holding the rams and then headed up, angling toward the next bowl. After some serious elevation gain, we finally made it into the bowl below the mountain crest. After a short break, we started the long climb up to the top through the loose granite.

When we finally made it to the crest, Dan peeked over the top. He spotted the rams directly below about 300 yards away. T.C., Flare, and a smaller ram were all there and feeding, unaware of our presence. When they fed out of sight, we went over the top and set up on a little outcropping. When the rams came back into view, I moved into position to watch T.C. Stan set up and watched Flare.

Dan planned it so I would shoot when I was ready; Stan would then take his shot. The prone position I was in was not the best. I was facing downhill at quite an angle. Kyle held onto my left ankle, so I would not slide down the mountain on my face. Despite the awkward position, I was steady. The big ram was about 250 yards away, but it was a steep downhill shot. Dan reminded me to aim low. I did and when everything felt right, I put pressure on the trigger of my .30-06. In short order, the 150-grain bullet was on its way. The ram whirled and ran behind some rocks before I could finish working the bolt. Dan said "I think you hit it."

I waited for the ram to reappear, but it never did. Just after my shot, Dan went over to Stan and I heard Stan's rifle bark. Stan's ram dropped in sight. His ram was closer and was also near the edge of a cliff. Dan hurried down to to make sure the ram did not fall off the edge. After securing Stan's ram, Dan headed over toward mine. Dan yelled up that my ram was dead. I yelled back "Is it as big as we thought?"

Dan answered, "No. It's bigger...43!"

Dan later told me that he had underestimated my ram because of its absolutely huge body size.

We went to Stan's fine ram first. It actually ended up scoring 162-7/8. We then went on to my ram. It was huge in both body and horn. I paid my respects to the ram and admired it for a while. After several pictures we took care of the rams and then packed both of them back to camp.

The next day we packed up to the plane. Dan took off loaded with the meat, capes and horns. The plan was to meet him on the glacier the following day to be picked up and flown out. That night the weather changed for the worse and the cloud ceiling dropped; Dan was not able to get to us for another 36 hours.

I had been in the field for 19 days. It had been a long, hard hunt, but that is the way I prefer it. I cannot say enough about how well I was treated by Dan, Loren, Mark, Kyle and everyone else at Alaska Trophy Adventures.

Photograph by Cliff White

TROPHY STATS

▼ ▼ ▼ ▼ ▼

Category
  Stone's sheep

Score
  $174^6/_8$

Location
  Muncho Lake, British Columbia — 2000

Hunter
  Donald L. Mann

Length of Horn
  Right: $39^3/_8$ Left: $42^3/_8$

Circumference of Base
  Right: $14^4/_8$ Left: $14^3/_8$

Greatest Spread
  $24^6/_8$

Photograph by Jack Renea

Donald L. Mann accepting his plaque and
medal from Buck Buckner, Chair of the
Big Game Records Committee.

STONE'S SHEEP
First Award – 174⁶/₈

▼ ▼ ▼ ▼ ▼ ▼ ▼ ▼ ▼

Donald L. Mann

"Its color was so magnificent, with distinct gray muzzle markings, blue to black coloring in its hide...the challenges of these mountains, the excitement of our stalk, the moments and feelings of the animal before me... all these thoughts came rushing in."

I'm sure I'm just another sheep hunter bitten by the bug. My first taste of sheep hunting came in the fall of 1999 after a 10-year wait in Colorado for a Rocky Mountain bighorn resident tag. It was a successful, self-guided hunt in the company of

My First Guided Hunt – What an Award It Was

my wife, Barbara, who was a true hunting partner. Once I had bagged the majestic bighorn, I knew I would attempt to complete the grand slam of sheep hunting. I absorbed all I could from both FNAWS and the Grand Slam Club; I joined both of these groups to help in my pursuit of a grand slam.

I started researching Dall's and Stone's sheep hunts in the spring of 2000. A phone call to Dennis Campbell of the Grand Slam Club, a tremendous resource, proved to be a great starting point. I had never been on a guided hunt and, up to now, had never needed a guide to achieve success hunting big game. My goal was a Stone's sheep in Canada by 2002, and then a Dall's sheep by 2004. The final animal, the desert sheep, would not be so easy to pin down. It would be the longest wait.

In the summer, my list of prospective outfitters was narrowed to three by speaking to a number of hunters who provided exciting conversation and excellent referrals. I was excited to learn of a possible fall hunt opening with the new owners of Muncho Lake Outfitters, Art and Crystal Thompson. After a few conversations by radio telephone with Art and Crystal, who

Photograph courtesy of Donald L. Mann

Donald L. Mann, above, and his guide, Willie Edwards, built a snow cave to spend a long, cold night on the mountain.

were already in the field guiding other hunters, my scheduled 2002 Stone's sheep hunt would now happen in 2000.

After several hours in the air to Vancouver, and two more flights on a small, propeller commuter aircraft, I arrived in Ft. Nelson, British Columbia. I was met by Arnold Henhapl, former owner of Muncho Lake Outfitters, who would give me a ride to base camp. We were joined by Arnold's wife, Isa, for the three-hour ride. The trip flew by with great conversation and fantastic scenery.

Once at base camp, Crystal got me settled into comfortable accommodations followed by a great moose roast dinner that afternoon. Art Thompson and I talked about the type of sheep he thought I would be interested in taking. I told him my expectations were to find a dark, traditional ram of respectable size, nothing more. I told him of my willingness to give it my best effort. We discussed the importance of physical and mental preparation.

The following day I met my guide, Willie Edwards. I had heard about Willie the night before from an Arizona hunter who had just returned from a goat hunt with him. This hunter told me that I wouldn't believe it; he had spent the night in a cave with a freezing wind howling outside. He had had a successful hunt, but he said to be prepared. Other hunters I had talked with earlier in the summer while doing my research had also mentioned their high regard for Willie.

Willie and I hit it off right from the start. We took the first day getting the pack string together and organizing our supplies and gear for the next day's hunt. Crystal told me that our area had received about 50 consecutive days of rain and fog. Willie added warnings that some deep stream crossings lay ahead because of that rain. We headed out of base camp at mid-morning. Our campsite was a mere nine-hour horseback ride ahead of us. During the day we stopped occasionally, glassing the mountains and high valleys with our binoculars. The sights were spectacular with splashes of fall color gracing the hillsides. Those brief stops were welcome relief from the saddle. I hadn't spent nearly the amount of time on a horse as Willie had.

I was amazed at the number of goats we were able to spot. Truly this is a Mecca for goat, moose, caribou, and elk, all of which we were easily able to spot throughout the hunt. True to his word, several high and fast stream crossings made for an exciting first day's trek. We finally arrived at the campsite late in the evening.

We spent the next two days glassing the hillsides extensively while scouring maps of the area, which helped us make decisions on how and where to access the mountains we would hunt. Willie decided that as a result of my years of athletic conditioning we would be hunting an area that neither he nor any other guide had hunted in four years. We were going into one of Willie's "hell-holes," as he coined it.

We were up early the next morning with a lunch packed for the day. It included your three basic sandwiches, cookies and four or so candy bars between us. We rode again for several hours, spotting many goats along the way. Once reaching the terminus of our riding destination and tethering our horses, a backpacking expedition was in order. After five hours of climbing, clinging, and clamoring through the shin tangle and rock slides on the steep alpine ridges, we reached a mountain-top. Willie was in excellent condition and possessed a wealth of knowledge. I intently listened to him.

STONE'S SHEEP
First Award – 174⁶/₈
▼ ▼ ▼ ▼ ▼

DONALD L. MANN

We spotted a large regal caribou, for which I possessed a tag, but we agreed that now was not the time. The Stone's sheep would be the priority. I'm sure many hunters encounter this dilemma. We pressed on.

British Columbia scenery is second to none. The views from the tops of these mountains are breathtaking. This is an observation from a person who lives at 9,200 foot elevation with 14,000 foot peaks out his front door.

Willie and I cruised the high tundra for another hour and a half, spotting three ewes en route. Finally, we arrived in the general vicinity that Willie had earmarked. We set up the sheep hunter's best friend, the spotting scope. With a wide grin on his face, Willie said some words I'll never forget, "I've got them, six in the band, and your ram is among them."

We watched them for 30 minutes. Willie isolated a black ram with a gray-striped muzzle for me. Only one other black ram was of interest in this group, but its curl might not have been legal, according to Willie. The rams were about 1,000 yards out.

We started to stalk deliberately across the cliffs high above the rams, which were in a basin. The terrain was intensely demanding. We clung to each handhold on the cliffs while straining under the load of fully-laden backpacks. My rifle made the traverse even more cumbersome and arduous. Despite our care in picking the route above the animals, the smallest ram, acting as a sentinel, spotted us. We froze and were pinned down by its glare. We decided it was best to retreat and Willie said in his Canadian accent, "Looks like a night on the mountain. We'll get that ram tomorrow, eh?"

It was 7:30 p.m. and a six-hour hike from the horses. We had neither sleeping bags nor tent. Willie said we would make a snow cave. I looked at a 12-foot high cornice in front of us. "How many snow caves have you made over the years?" I asked.

Willie answered, "None. This will be my first."

We strategically dug our cave and used shale rock for the floor and for backing. We used one of the survival blankets for a roof. It would be our shelter for a long, cold night. Before we had left base camp, Willie and I discussed the vital necessities of a backpack. We were both short of a few needed items of clothing. I did not have a survival blanket, so Willie lent me one. But as sheep hunting goes, you can't always carry the kitchen sink so you have to deal with the unexpected.

The fourth day of the hunt would be spent in a snow cave. Willie's technique to combat the cold was to walk for 45 minutes in a track outside the cave to warm up. Then he would curl up in the snow cave with part of our remaining blanket until the cold woke him up again, at which time he would get up and walk his circle. Alternating 15 minutes of sleep and 45 minutes of walking was not my idea of rest. I just curled up the best I could and managed little sleep myself. Dreaming of what the next day would bring helped keep my mind off of the cold.

Donald's Stone's sheep scores 174-6/8 points and received a First Award at the 25th Awards Program in Kansas City. The ram was taken on a 2000 hunt near Muncho Lake, British Columbia.

Sunday morning flooded our hillside with a spectacular sunrise. I was up by 6 a.m. Willie had already pinpointed the ram's location. I was stiff and cold. Willie and I talked about the approach and I hung on his every word. Our rams had moved to the east at a slow, methodical pace below us. I now had a first-hand understanding of the exceptional vision Stone's sheep possess. The most feasible plan of attack was to go straight backward across the cliffs we had just traversed the night before. We tried to keep our silhouetted figures off the skyline and away from their view below. We would then be at the top of the mountain where we could descend on the rams in the basin below.

After three hours, we got our break. The rams moved to a small drainage further below, their heads pointing away from our position. A couple more hours put us in the general vicinity where we anticipated they might go. We edged our way carefully to a knoll, where we took up a position about 450 yards out and above the rams. Willie asked me about the distance. I asked for another hundred yards closer in, which was a more comfortable range for me. The wind was picking up from our right.

We began the final stage of our stalk, ever so slowly and silently clinging to the tundra. We perched on another knoll 100 yards closer, which was also the end of our cover. Willie ranged this distance to be about 350 yards. I sighted the ram with the gray-striped nose in my scope. It was standing broadside. Willie helped me steady my thoughts by talking about the placement of the shot with such heavy winds. Up until now, Willie had orchestrated every step like he was reading it from a book. He continued this trend now.

My heart was racing with the adrenaline of the reality of the situation. Heavy winds continued to gust from my right. I steadied my rifle on my backpack and relaxed my breathing. It would not be an easy shot. It seemed as if time stopped. I saw the shot and fired the rifle. Willie said, "It's a hit, the ram is ours!"

I shot one more time at the ram, which was now running. It came to rest about 500 yards away. Willie and I began our short journey to this fine trophy. As we proceeded closer, Willie remarked, "I believe your dark traditional ram is about to be bigger than your dreams!"

With the final 50 feet remaining, Willie commented, "This ram is even bigger than I thought. You've got what I believe is a book ram!"

Once upon this Stone's sheep, with its color so magnificent, with distinct gray muzzle markings, blue to black coloring in his hide, everything came into focus. The challenges of these mountains, the excitement of our stalk, the moments and feelings of the animal before me, all came rushing in. Willie shook my hand and congratulated me. He said rams like this don't come along that often. I was still digesting the trophy before me.

Willie and I took pictures of this fine animal. After caping and quartering the ram, a trip out of the basin and up the mountain was before us. We started out with our heavily-loaded backpacks at 4:30 p.m., after finishing off the last of our food supplies except for a couple of candy bars. We made it across the basin in about two hours, but we had to ascend the mountain again. With time once again running short, we decided to ledge the meat and cape and try to make it to the horses, ride out, and return with empty packs.

We reached the summit at about 7:45 p.m. After traveling the ridges in the dark, it was apparent after several hours that another night on the mountain was our destiny. With clouds obscuring the guiding stars and mountaintops, it was best. Lying on the tundra while wrapped in our survival blankets, we knew our voyage was close to being complete. These thoughts, along with some Northern Lights exploding in the sky, helped us get through another cold breezy night. All the events in this sheep hunt have truly been an adventure with many lessons.

Descending the mountain tired and hungry the next morning was no less difficult than the trip in. On Monday, we arrived back at camp. We enjoyed a meal and some sleep before the final excursion back in to retrieve our trophy. Our supplies were gone quite some time ago. Time passed by so quickly since packing our lunch two and a half days ago! We decided all would be fine until Tuesday. It would give us another full day to ascend the mountains two more times, once from both sides, into the basin and back out.

Our quest ended late Tuesday, at midnight, after negotiating the steep slopes in half walking and sliding fashion for better than 12 hours. Once the ram was placed on the horses, we headed back, riding out at night under the stars. It finally set in what was accomplished: a true trophy hunt and my first guided hunt.

The British Columbia Ministry of Environment, Lands and Parks aged this monarch at 12-1/2 years. A special thanks to my wife Barbara, Art and Crystal Thompson, and guide Willie Edwards for all their support.

Photograph by Cliff White

TROPHY STATS

▼ ▼ ▼ ▼ ▼

Category
Stone's sheep

Score
$174^1/_8$

Location
Marker Lake, Yukon Territory — 2001

Hunter
Ronald G. Selby

Length of Horn
Right: $43^7/_8$ Left: 41

Circumference of Base
Right: $13^7/_8$ Left: 14

Greatest Spread
$23^6/_8$

STONE'S SHEEP
Second Award – 174¹/₈

▼ ▼ ▼ ▼ ▼ ▼ ▼ ▼ ▼

RONALD G. SELBY

This was my first sheep hunt, and I was living a dream. My wife, Laura, wanted me to go on this trip before we started a family. The timing couldn't have been better because the week before I left for the hunt, I found out I was going to be a dad. So many things were happening so fast since booking my hunt through Troy Ginn with Outdoor Consultants. He had encouraged me to go on this Stone's sheep hunt with Teslin Outfitters based on the potential for quality animals. Teslin Outfitters is headquartered in Teslin, Yukon Territory. Stan Stewart was only in his third year as the manager of Teslin Outfitters, but he had been in the sheep hunting business for a long time. After checking with several references I was confident in my choice and was off to my first sheep hunt.

Bush pilot Shane Pasotto flew us across the Cassiar Mountain Range to Marker Lake. The plane shook and bumped, as we were experiencing crosswinds funneling through the mountain passes. Shane smiled at my nervousness and ensured me that this was a smooth flight. I soon forgot about my queasiness as I saw the awesome view of dark bluish-black mountains with patches of green carpet, topped with an occasional snow pack. I looked for animals, but saw none, realizing later that these Stone's sheep blend in really well with their terrain. When we began our descent, Marker Lake appeared to be a small target. However, our pilot glided us safely onto the smooth lake located 4,500 feet above sea level. With base camp located right on the lake, it wasn't long before our guides, wrangler, and cook greeted us with warm coffee and smiles.

James Dick was to be my guide. James was a Tlinglet Indian (pronounced Klinglet) who had been trained by a German sheep guide. He had worked for several sheep outfitters in Northwest Territories, but decided to come back to guide closer to home. James was very knowledgeable about sheep and had a keen eye for spotting them. He was also very amiable and seemed to always smile regardless of how desperate the circumstances.

That evening we ate a good meal prepared by Liver (his real name was Livingston) the camp cook. The mess tent had a gas stove along with many shelves loaded with cooking utensils, pots, pans, condiments, canned goods, etc. In addition to the mess tent, the camp consisted of three other wall tents including two bunk tents and a supply tent. The tent bases were steadied with Balsam logs on which plywood floors rested. The walls were blue tarpaulins braced by balsam wood poles. Each tent had a wood stove with flashing surrounding the pipes to keep from burning the blue tarpaulin walls.

The first day of August (and sheep season) we rode out on our horses with our sack lunches packed and prepared by Liver. We headed northwest of the camp, glassing the peaks and basins of the surrounding mountains as we rode. These were some fine horses and no doubt they were trail hardy. The alpine was thick below timberline, and if it were not for the established game trails, it would have been a tough ride. As we entered a creek bottom of willow tangles, James's horse was spooked by an old moose skull that someone had placed on the trail as a marker. It was not going to be the first time this old horse would be spooked.

We traveled across the creek and into a basin of a mountain ridge. We glassed the basin from below before we entered. As we approached timberline, the marmots whistled from all directions. James said these marmots are also known as "whistlers" and are "good eating." We parked our horses and hiked up to the top of the mountain ridge, glassing as we went.

We found quite a few fresh sheep tracks, but most were from lambs and ewes. We did see one set of ram tracks. James said there was an active salt lick nearby that may have been the reason for all the ewe and lamb tracks. We scouted several basins throughout the day while remaining on the same ridge as we traveled. We glassed distant basins, but unfortunately we only saw one small mountain caribou, a golden eagle, and a porcupine. James wanted to take the porcupine. He said it was some of the best eating a man could experience. He asked me not to tell the other fellows at camp that we passed up the porcupine, because they would be upset with him for not bringing the porcupine back for supper. It is legal for the natives of this area to harvest these critters for food. We traveled back to camp as it was getting dark. Of course, we had to pass by the moose skull, which the horse managed to steer well away from.

The next morning we traveled south of camp. I was astride Feetso, a nimble-hoofed horse that turned out to be a pleasure to ride. We traveled along a creek that emptied from Marker Lake, following some game trails as we went. Several times we hit bogs and had to walk our horses to give them some rest after passing through these low areas.

We finally reached our destination and began glassing the green, grassy basin, which was loaded with springs. We worked our way up to the top of the ridge and glassed a nice draw that led upwards to a peak. As we worked our way toward the peak, we glassed several canyons.

Then the weather changed dramatically. While we were glassing from the peak, the weather changed from warm and sunny to cloudy and cold with sleet; then it changed back to warm and sunny, all within an hour.

I told James we were going to see a ram today, I could just feel it. After several hours of glassing, I looked down into the canyon and saw two animals the size of ants running in the center of the canyon. As I focused my binoculars, I realized that I was looking at my first Stone's rams. James and I studied them intently as one of the rams jumped on top of a large boulder and stood proudly. James figured it to be about 3/4 curl. The second ram decided to join its buddy on top of the boulder, but its companion would have nothing of it as it head-butted the other ram off the rock. James figured it to be only a half-curl. We watched these rams for quite awhile and looked for others, but to no avail. The first ram decided to get off the boulder while the second ram took over the spot and began head-butting the boulder.

Obviously the second ram was venting some frustration after being knocked off the rock earlier by the first ram.

We then traveled around the steep peak and flushed at least a dozen ptarmigan. We saw quite a bit of fresh

STONE'S SHEEP
Second Award – 174 1/8
▼ ▼ ▼ ▼ ▼
RONALD G. SELBY

sign and knew we were about to see more sheep when James spotted a distant animal standing on the edge of a cliff. We took out the spotting scope and determined there were two ewes and a lamb. One ewe looked completely white and stood on the cliff nodding. We watched these sheep awhile and found no others in the vicinity. It was getting late so we eventually gave up and headed back to camp. Today was a good day. We had finally seen some sheep.

Day three found us heading due north of camp. Earl, the other guide, had joined us after his hunter, Bob Friel, had become ill. Earl had us stop and glass every basin we saw, no matter how unremarkable. Earl and Bob had glassed many of these basins six times already. I asked Earl if any rams had ever been taken from these basins in the past. Earl replied "absolutely not" and left it at that. I figured Earl never gave up on a basin regardless of its lack of sheep history or appearance.

Suddenly James spotted what looked to be a good ram on a distant peak over two miles away. The spotting scope revealed two other rams. We crossed a deep draw and followed a creek to the base of the mountain. We glassed the basin and discovered not three, but five rams, one of which was extraordinary. This ram was a lighter-colored ram than the rest, so we called it the "White Ram" even though it was more of a salt and pepper color. The ram's horns seemed as heavy as a bighorn's and they curled down below its jaw and up again to well above the bridge of its nose and the base of its horns.

The wind was not in our favor so we held back and glassed the sheep from a distant butte that was on the same ridgeline. We managed to get pinned down by the sheep as they moved around the narrow ridgeline. We ranged the closest one at about 700 yards. There was nothing but wide-open pasture between us and the ewes, and we could not get any closer. The sheep eventually bedded, with each of the smaller rams settling down strategically as if they were sentries for the White Ram. They could literally view 360 degrees around the small precipice.

The White Ram bedded down at the peak and it began to rain. We had left our horses in such a hurry that we had forgotten our rain gear. Aggravated by our mistake, I suggested that we head back and get a good night's rest. Night was approaching and we had no means to build a fire without spooking the sheep. I would have been willing to camp in the rocks had we kept dry and had the proper equipment, but why risk hypothermia and possible illness when we had another 10 days of hunting. The clouds moved in, allowing us to depart our vantage point unseen by the rams.

After a restless night, we headed back to the north basin looking for the White Ram and its compadres. The other hunter, Bob Friel, came along for there were two other legal rams

Ronald G. Selby took this award-winning Stone's sheep on his first sheep hunt ever. He hunted near Marker Lake in Yukon to find this ram that scores 174-1/8 points.

in the bunch, and we were hoping to get a double. As my guide had spotted the White Ram, it was determined that I would get the first shot.

As we headed up a narrow draw, Bob's horse could not make a steep bank and horse and hunter rolled backwards into the creek. It was a real scare for all of us, but fortunately neither was hurt; we continued on the trail.

As we approached the basin, the sheep were not where they had been the night before. After some glassing, we found that they had moved further south on the backbone ridge between two basins. We could not see the White Ram, but we were certain it was near. We then decided to circle around and try to cut them off. We managed to get to the corner of the far basin undetected and could see four rams, but no White Ram. We hid in some rocks on the edge of a cliff, which left us a 300-yard shot at the nearest of the four rams making their way down the backbone ridge. The second largest ram remained about 600 yards and bedded. As we watched it, I noticed the younger rams making their way towards us. I had read that subordinate rams tend to follow the largest ram, so I positioned myself higher in the rocks while the other three guys remained low and hidden. I could view the open pasture that lay behind us where it seemed the younger sheep were headed.

After glassing for an hour I decided to take a break and eat an apple. As I reached in my daypack and pulled out an apple, the White Ram appeared in front of me in the open pasture not 40 yards away! I dropped the apple and slowly reached for my rifle. Anticipating that the ram would bolt any second, I chambered a round in the barrel as I raised my gun. The vision of this stoic, beautiful ram just standing there broadside will be forever etched in my memory. Its large horns looked out of proportion with the rest of its body. I found the ram in my scope and pulled the trigger, but it didn't go down. It turned and began to run directly away from me. As I fired a second round from my .300, James shouted, "Shoot 'im again, shoot 'im again!"

The ram began to stumble, which allowed me to place a final bullet behind its shoulder. Apparently, my first shot had grazed its right horn and obviously didn't anchor the animal.

We waited before we approached the downed ram, in hopes of Bob getting a shot at the second ram. Unfortunately, the other rams spooked and left the mountain. The White Ram was even more impressive up close. We measured its longest horn at 44 inches, with bases over 14 inches. We then said a prayer and gave thanks for such a truly magnificent animal. After pictures and a lot of backslapping, we packed the ram out to the horses. James's spooky horse would have nothing to do with the ram. She bucked and snorted so we had to pack the ram on my horse.

It began to rain. It was a long walk back to camp, but we managed to get back around midnight after some close calls with "ole spooky." A spooked horse on slippery-sloped mountains in the dark can be a real exercise in patience and sanity.

The following day, the guides caped out the animal, and we ate ribs for dinner. It was a welcomed day of rest. The bush plane returned for my departure, and I wished my new friends well and headed for home.

It was a memorable hunt and I want to thank my wife, Laura, and my son, John Luther, for allowing me to take time away from them to experience a dream. I also want to thank Troy Ginn, James Dick, and Teslin Outfitters for providing the direction, accommodations, and a great hunt.

TABULATIONS OF RECORDED TROPHIES 25TH AWARDS PROGRAM 2001-2003

TABULATIONS OF RECORDED TROPHIES IN THE 25TH AWARDS ENTRY PERIOD

The trophy data shown herein have been taken from score charts in the Records Archives of the Boone and Crockett Club for the 25th Awards Program, 2001-2003. Trophies listed are those that meet minimum score and other stated requirements of trophy entry for the period.

The final scores and rank shown in the book are official, except for trophies shown with an asterisk. An asterisk is assigned to trophies accepted in this Awards Program with entry scores that were subject to verification by the 25th Awards Program Judges Panel. The asterisk can be removed (except in the case of a potential new World's Record) by submitting two additional, independent scorings by official measurers of the Boone and Crockett Club. The Records Committee of the Club will review the three scorings available and determine which, if any, will be accepted in lieu of the Judges' Panel measurement.

When the score has been accepted as final by the Records Committee, the asterisk will be removed in future editions of the all-time records book, Records of North American Big Game, and other publications by the Boone and Crockett Club. In the case of a potential new World's Record, the trophy must come before a Judges' Panel. Only a Judges' Panel can certify a new World's Record and finalize its score. Asterisked trophies are shown at the end of the listings for their category. They are not ranked, as their final score is subject to revision by a Judges' Panel or by the submission of additional scorings, as described above.

Note that "PR" preceding the date of kill indicates "prior to" the year shown for kill.

The scientific and vernacular names, and the sequence of presentation, follows that suggested in the *Revised Checklist of North American Mammals North of Mexico*, 1979 (J. Knox, et al; Texas Tech University, 14 December 1979.)

TROPHY BOUNDARIES

Many of the categories recognized in the Boone and Crockett Club's North American Big Game Awards Program are based upon subspecies differences. In nature, subspecies freely interbreed where their ranges overlap, thus necessitating the setting of geographic boundaries to keep them, as well as hybrids, separate for records-keeping purposes.

Geographic boundaries are described for a number of categories. These include: Alaska brown and grizzly bear; Atlantic and Pacific walrus; American, Roosevelt's, and tule elk; mule, Columbia, and Sitka blacktail deer; whitetail and Coues' deer; moose; and caribou. Pertinent information for several of these boundaries is included in the trophy data listings that follow, but the complete, detailed description for each is to be found in *Measuring and Scoring North American Big Game Trophies*, 2nd Edition, revised 2000, or on the Club's web site at www.booneandcrockettclub.com.

In addition to category specific boundaries, all trophies must be from North America, north of the south border of Mexico, to be eligible. For pelagic trophies such as walrus and polar bear, they must be from Canada, Greenland, and the United States of America side of the International Date Line to be eligible.

Trophy boundaries are set by the Boone and Crockett Club's Records of North American Big Game Committee, working with the latest and best available information from scientific researchers, guides, hunters, and other parties with serious interest in our big game resources. Boundaries are set so that it is highly unlikely specimens of the larger category or hybrids can be taken within boundaries set for the smaller category, thus upsetting the rankings of the smaller category. Trophy boundaries are revised as necessary to maintain this separation of the categories.

BLACK BEAR

Ursus americanus americanus and related subspecies

Score	Greatest Length of Skull Without Lower Jaw	Greatest Width of Skull	Locality	Hunter	Owner	Date Killed	Rank
22 14/16	14 5/16	8 9/16	McCreary, MB	John J. Bathke	John J. Bathke	1998	1
22 10/16	13 14/16	8 12/16	Lincoln Co., WI	Daniel J. Kufahl	Daniel J. Kufahl	2002	2
22 5/16	14 3/16	8 2/16	Hubbard Co., MN	Brian A. Gross	Brian A. Gross	2000	3
22 4/16	13 11/16	8 9/16	Rusk Co., WI	Ben R. Brandstatter	Ben R. Brandstatter	2000	4
22 3/16	13 12/16	8 7/16	Burnett Co., WI	Dustin Luke	Dustin Luke	2003	5
22 2/16	13 15/16	8 3/16	Rusk Co., WI	Dean R. Ecker	Dean R. Ecker	2001	6
22 2/16	14 1/16	8 1/16	St. Croix Co., WI	Gary L. Kurtz	Gary L. Kurtz	2002	6
22	14 2/16	7 14/16	Hertford Co., NC	Joseph C. Lowe	Joseph C. Lowe	1997	8
22	14 4/16	7 12/16	Mille Lacs Co., MN	Michael P. Haberman	Michael P. Haberman	2000	8
22	13 12/16	8 4/16	Polk Co., WI	Roy C. Basham	Roy C. Basham	2000	8
22	13 15/16	8 1/16	Suffolk Co., VA	Donald W. Howard	Donald W. Howard	2000	8
22	13 8/16	8 8/16	Utah Co., UT	Rupert M. Satterthwaite	Rupert M. Satterthwaite	2002	8
22	13 10/16	8 6/16	Polk Co., WI	Dale Ostenson	Dale Ostenson	2002	8
22	13 6/16	8 10/16	Lycoming Co., PA	Steve D. Flook	Steve D. Flook	2002	8
22	13 11/16	8 5/16	Sturgis, SK	Tyler Bazansky	Tyler Bazansky	2003	8
21 14/16	13 10/16	8 4/16	Benton Co., MN	Randy J. Hamers	Randy J. Hamers	1999	16
21 14/16	13 12/16	8 2/16	Mille Lacs Co., MN	Charles D. Huber	Charles D. Huber	2000	16
21 14/16	13 9/16	8 5/16	Crow Wing Co., MN	Ricky J. Carlson	Ricky J. Carlson	2000	16
21 14/16	13 8/16	8 6/16	Monroe Co., PA	Scott H. Mosier	Scott H. Mosier	2001	16
21 14/16	13 8/16	8 6/16	Carswell Lake, SK	Richard P. Smith	Richard P. Smith	2002	16
21 14/16	13 11/16	8 3/16	Echols Co., GA	Everett D. Sirk	Everett D. Sirk	2002	16
21 13/16	14	7 13/16	Aitkin Co., MN	Thomas A. Kubiak	Thomas A. Kubiak	2000	22
21 13/16	13 3/16	8 10/16	Pouce Coupe, BC	Dan R. Therrien	Dan R. Therrien	2000	22
21 13/16	13 11/16	8 2/16	Apache Co., AZ	R. Terrell McCombs	R. Terrell McCombs	2000	22
21 13/16	13 12/16	8 1/16	Ventura Co., CA	Picked Up	Loren C. Nodolf	2000	22
21 13/16	13 11/16	8 2/16	Bedford Co., PA	John W. Colliflower, Sr.	John W. Colliflower, Sr.	2000	22
21 13/16	13 9/16	8 4/16	Rusk Co., WI	Daryl Risler	Daryl Risler	2001	22
21 13/16	13 13/16	8	Lycoming Co., PA	Scott Cummings	Scott Cummings	2001	22
21 13/16	13 9/16	8 4/16	Searchmont, ON	Gregory E. Meredith	Gregory E. Meredith	2002	22
21 13/16	13 1/16	8 12/16	Luzerne Co., PA	Earl J. Cichy, Jr.	Earl J. Cichy, Jr.	2002	22
21 13/16	14	7 13/16	Navajo Co., AZ	Nick C. Williams	Nick C. Williams	2003	22
21 12/16	14 1/16	7 11/16	Hyde Co., NC	Jeffrey D. Gibbs	Jeffrey D. Gibbs	2000	32
21 12/16	13 8/16	8 4/16	Peace River, AB	Ronny F. Register	Ronny F. Register	2001	32

BLACK BEAR

Ursus americanus and related subspecies

Score	Greatest Length of Skull Without Lower Jaw	Greatest Width of Skull	Locality	Hunter	Owner	Date Killed	Rank
21 12/16	13 8/16	8 4/16	Langlade Co., WI	Cary W. Krueger	Cary W. Krueger	2001	32
21 12/16	13 7/16	8 5/16	Sublette Co., WY	Dan W. McCann	Dan W. McCann	2002	32
21 11/16	13 10/16	8 1/16	Carbon Co., UT	Matthew Christy	Matthew Christy	2000	36
21 11/16	13 7/16	8 4/16	Prince of Wales Island, AK	Kelly J. King	Kelly J. King	2001	36
21 11/16	13 14/16	7 13/16	Apache Co., AZ	Ty Ryland	Ty Ryland	2001	36
21 11/16	13 8/16	8 2/16	Prince of Wales Island, AK	Ian K. Chase-Dunn	Ian K. Chase-Dunn	1999	39
21 10/16	13 6/16	8 4/16	Wayne Co., PA	Joseph Simyan, Jr.	Joseph Simyan, Jr.	1999	39
21 10/16	13 9/16	8 1/16	Bradford Co., PA	Stephen E. Watkins	Stephen E. Watkins	2000	39
21 10/16	13 9/16	8 1/16	Peace River, AB	Randy L. Stadler	Randy L. Stadler	2002	39
21 10/16	13 9/16	8 4/16	Sawyer Co., WI	LeRoy McGary	LeRoy McGary	2002	39
21 10/16	13 6/16	8 1/16	Kelwood, MB	John N. Pardun, Sr.	John N. Pardun, Sr.	2003	39
21 9/16	13 9/16	8	Chitek Lake, SK	Steve Grassmid	Steve Grassmid	2000	45
21 9/16	13 5/16	8 4/16	Mantagao Lake, MB	Bruce V. Huewan	Bruce V. Huewan	2001	45
21 9/16	13 7/16	8 2/16	Delta Co., CO	Bryan Livengood	Bryan Livengood	2001	45
21 9/16	13 12/16	7 13/16	Price Co., WI	Troy M. Collins	Troy M. Collins	2001	45
21 9/16	13 4/16	8 5/16	Shawano Co., WI	Dale Van Gheem	Dale Van Gheem	2001	45
21 9/16	13 5/16	8 4/16	Comox Lake, BC	Chantelle R. Bartsch	Chantelle R. Bartsch	2002	45
21 9/16	13 5/16	8 4/16	Prince of Wales Island, AK	Ian K. Chase-Dunn	Ian K. Chase-Dunn	2002	45
21 9/16	13 3/16	8 6/16	Navajo Co., AZ	Lon Hoffman	Lon Hoffman	2002	45
21 9/16	13 5/16	8 4/16	Saddle Hills, AB	David W. Watson	David W. Watson	2003	45
21 8/16	13 4/16	8 4/16	McKean Co., PA	Donald L. Magno	Donald L. Magno	1992	54
21 8/16	13 10/16	7 14/16	Sawyer Co., WI	James M. Slepika, Sr.	James M. Slepika, Sr.	2000	54
21 8/16	13 10/16	7 14/16	Beaufort Co., NC	Danny L. Bowling	Danny L. Bowling	2000	54
21 8/16	13 8/16	8	Duck Mt., MB	Jeffrey A. Lute	Jeffrey A. Lute	2001	54
21 8/16	13 12/16	7 12/16	Lycoming Co., PA	Anthony F. Campana	Anthony F. Campana	2002	54
21 8/16	13 8/16	8	Clam Cove, AK	Thomas J. Stevens	Thomas J. Stevens	2003	54
21 7/16	13 6/16	8 1/16	Bayfield Co., WI	Jane M. Paulson	Jane M. Paulson	2000	60
21 7/16	13 4/16	8 3/16	Burnett Co., WI	Picked Up	Bill Klugow	2001	60
21 7/16	13 6/16	8 1/16	Becker Co., MN	Michael J. Honek	Michael J. Honek	2001	60
21 7/16	13 8/16	7 15/16	Sawyer Co., WI	Daniel A. Solie	Daniel A. Solie	2001	60
21 7/16	13 12/16	7 11/16	Rusk Co., WI	Audrey M. Vandeberg	Audrey M. Vandeberg	2002	60
21 7/16	13 3/16	8 4/16	Sheffield Lake, NL	Jerry L. Beck	Jerry L. Beck	2003	60
21 6/16	13 4/16	8 2/16	Pamlico Co., NC	Randall K. Russell	Randall K. Russell	1999	66

			Locality			Date	Score
21 6/16	13 4/16	8 2/16	Tyrrell Co., NC	Terry L. Sherman	Terry L. Sherman	2000	66
21 6/16	13 3/16	8 3/16	Prince of Wales Island, AK	James F. Baichtal	Picked Up	2001	66
21 6/16	13 6/16	8	Ventura Co., CA	Kevin J. Edwards	Kevin J. Edwards	2001	66
21 6/16	13 10/16	7 12/16	Hyde Co., NC	James P. Pridgen	James P. Pridgen	2001	66
21 6/16	13 10/16	7 12/16	Lac du Bonnet, MB	Jason M. Singbeil	Jason M. Singbeil	2002	66
21 6/16	13 4/16	8 2/16	Catron Co., NM	Ernest R. Gutierrez	Ernest R. Gutierrez	2002	66
21 6/16	13 2/16	8 4/16	Ashland Co., WI	James D. Truttschel	James D. Truttschel	2002	66
21 5/16	13 2/16	8 4/16	Mesa Co., CO	M. Scott Ghan	M. Scott Ghan	2003	66
21 5/16	12 15/16	8 6/16	Portage Co., WI	Craig E. Solinsky	Craig E. Solinsky	1999	75
21 5/16	13 5/16	8	Nechako River, BC	Dean McNolty	Dean McNolty	2000	75
21 5/16	13 5/16	8	Cass Co., MN	Mike Mellema	Mike Mellema	2001	75
21 5/16	13 7/16	7 14/16	Rossburn, MB	William E. Clink	William E. Clink	2001	75
21 5/16	13 8/16	7 13/16	Shawano Co., WI	Diane M. Henry	Diane M. Henry	2002	75
21 5/16	13 13/16	7 8/16	Washburn Co., WI	Armand D. Van Vleet	Armand D. Van Vleet	2002	75
21 4/16	13 8/16	7 13/16	Rossman Lake, MB	John R. Evans	John R. Evans	2003	75
21 4/16	13 10/16	7 10/16	Buckingham Co., VA	Michael D. Nixon	Michael D. Nixon	2003	75
21 4/16	13 5/16	7 15/16	Chippewa Co., WI	Rick A. Sokup	Rick A. Sokup	2000	83
21 4/16	13 6/16	7 14/16	Richards Lake, SK	M.R. James	M.R. James	2001	83
21 4/16	13 6/16	7 14/16	Oscoda Co., MI	Gus Harris	Gus Harris	2001	83
21 4/16	13 2/16	8 2/16	Shasta Co., CA	Sal E. Santoro	Sal E. Santoro	2001	83
21 4/16	13 3/16	8 1/16	Prince of Wales Island, AK	William A. Fedorko	William A. Fedorko	2002	83
21 3/16	13 4/16	8	Kelvington, SK	Mike J. Ryan	Mike J. Ryan	2002	83
21 3/16	13 4/16	8	Price Co., WI	Tim Gehrke	Tim Gehrke	2002	83
21 3/16	13 10/16	7 10/16	King Co., WA	Tyler Seubert	Tyler Seubert	2003	83
21 3/16	13 8/16	7 11/16	Morrison Co., MN	Linda Brummer	Linda Brummer	2000	91
21 3/16	13 2/16	8 1/16	Besnard Lake, SK	Tony Milliken, Sr.	Tony Milliken, Sr.	2001	91
21 3/16	13 5/16	8 2/16	Koochiching Co., MN	Kirby D. Sorensen	Kirby D. Sorensen	2001	91
21 3/16	13 1/16	7 14/16	Bronson Lake, SK	Stanley C. Benson	Stanley C. Benson	2002	91
21 3/16	12 14/16	8 5/16	Prince of Wales Island, AK	William T. Stevens	William T. Stevens	2002	91
21 3/16	13 6/16	7 13/16	Marshall Co., MN	Michael R. Powell	Michael R. Powell	2002	91
21 3/16	13	8 3/16	Oconto Co., WI	Christopher J. Burg	Christopher J. Burg	2002	91
21 3/16	13 3/16	8	Gila Co., AZ	Scott Keetch	Scott Keetch	2003	91
21 3/16	13 1/16	8 2/16	Beatty Brook, NB	Jay S. Conrad	Jay S. Conrad	2003	91
21 3/16	13 3/16	7 15/16	Cass Co., MN	Toni M. Gross	Toni M. Gross	2003	91
21 2/16	13 3/16	7 15/16	Rusk Co., WI	Rainer J. Bidinger	Rainer J. Bidinger	1988	100
21 2/16	13 7/16	7 11/16	Perry Co., AR	Dillard R. Graves	Dillard R. Graves	1996	100
21 2/16	13 3/16	7 15/16	Duck Mt., MB	R. Steve Martin	R. Steve Martin	1996	100
21 2/16	13	8 2/16	Burnett Co., WI	Don S. Karastes	Don S. Karastes	1999	100
21 2/16	13 3/16	7 15/16	Washburn Co., WI	Peter Schomin	Peter Schomin	2000	100
21 2/16	13 4/16	7 14/16	Gila Co., AZ	Fred Peters	Fred Peters	2000	100
21 2/16	13 5/16	7 13/16	Menominee Co., MI	Chris M. Christophersen	Chris M. Christophersen	2001	100

BLACK BEAR

Ursus americanus americanus and related subspecies

Score	Greatest Length of Skull Without Lower Jaw	Greatest Width of Skull	Locality	Hunter	Owner	Date Killed	Rank
21 2/16	13 2/16	8	Langlade Co., WI	Harvey R. Roth	Harvey R. Roth	2001	100
21 2/16	13 3/16	7 15/16	Price Co., WI	James F. Voborsky	James F. Voborsky	2001	100
21 2/16	13 2/16	7 12/16	Craven Co., NC	Thomas J. Denesha	Thomas J. Denesha	2001	100
21 2/16	13 6/16	8	Athabasca River, AB	Walter Krom	Walter Krom	2002	100
21 2/16	13 2/16	7 15/16	Fish Lake, MB	David R. Bryce	David R. Bryce	2002	100
21 2/16	13 3/16	8 3/16	Sullivan Co., NY	Charles W. Hahl	Charles W. Hahl	2002	100
21 2/16	12 15/16	8	Chitek Lake, SK	John H. Vance	John H. Vance	2003	100
21 2/16	13 2/16	8 2/16	Gila Co., AZ	Robert L. Long, Jr.	Robert L. Long, Jr.	2003	100
21 1/16	12 15/16	7 13/16	Edith Lake, BC	Brittany K. Thomas	Brittany K. Thomas	1999	116
21 1/16	13 4/16	7 14/16	Marinette Co., WI	Neal A. Ruechel	Neal A. Ruechel	1999	116
21 1/16	13 3/16	8 1/16	Grey River, NL	Christopher L. Fischer	Christopher L. Fischer	1999	116
21 1/16	13	7 14/16	Prince of Wales Island, AK	Marvin G. DeVore, Sr.	Marvin G. DeVore, Sr.	2000	116
21 1/16	13 3/16	7 11/16	Pacific Co., WA	Greg J. Bryant	Greg J. Bryant	2000	116
21 1/16	13 6/16	8 1/16	Pine Co., MN	William N. Hegge, Jr.	William N. Hegge, Jr.	2000	116
21 1/16	13 1/16	8 1/16	Cass Co., MN	Robert L. Stephan	Robert L. Stephan	2000	116
21 1/16	13	7 9/16	Sawyer Co., WI	William J. Vander Zouwen	William J. Vander Zouwen	2000	116
21 1/16	13 8/16	7 9/16	Pike Co., PA	Timothy M. Biehl	Timothy M. Biehl	2001	116
21 1/16	13 4/16	7 13/16	Itasca Co., MN	John M. Warneke	John M. Warneke	2001	116
21 1/16	13 1/16	8	Prince of Wales Island, AK	Kristy J. King	Kristy J. King	2002	116
21 1/16	12 13/16	8 4/16	Menominee Co., MI	Owen R. Koppelberger	Owen R. Koppelberger	2002	116
21 1/16	13 4/16	7 13/16	Trinity Co., CA	Eric A. Chatham	Eric A. Chatham	2002	116
21 1/16	13 1/16	8	Whitemud Hills, AB	Alfred C. Faber, Jr.	Alfred C. Faber, Jr.	2003	116
21 1/16	12 13/16	8 4/16	Lincoln Co., WI	Timothy J. Grzesiak	Timothy J. Grzesiak	2003	116
21	13 2/16	8 2/16	Lincoln Co., MT	Ian K. Chase-Dunn	Ian K. Chase-Dunn	1994	131
21	12 14/16	7 13/16	Peace River, AB	Mikael Andersson	Mikael Andersson	2000	131
21	13 3/16	7 14/16	Iron Co., WI	Donald B. Morris	Donald B. Morris	2000	131
21	13 2/16	7 10/16	Duck Mt., MB	Wayne R. Schatzman	Wayne R. Schatzman	2000	131
21	13 6/16	8 1/16	Carteret Co., NC	David T. Beveridge	David T. Beveridge	2000	131
21	12 15/16	7 14/16	Thorne Bay, AK	Ian K. Chase-Dunn	Ian K. Chase-Dunn	2001	131
21	13 2/16	7 14/16	Chitek Lake, SK	Todd E. Stahley	Todd E. Stahley	2001	131
21	13 4/16	7 12/16	Frobisher Lake, SK	Robert L. Holder	Robert L. Holder	2001	131
21	12 15/16	8 1/16	Seech Lake, MB	Duane Seiler II	Duane Seiler II	2001	131
21	13 5/16	7 11/16	Polk Co., WI	Michael D. Mader	Michael D. Mader	2001	131

Score	Length	Width	Locality	Hunter	Owner	Date	Rank
21	12 14/16	8 2/16	Mendocino Co., CA	Henry W. Anderson	Henry W. Anderson	2001	131
21	13	8	Mount Martley, BC	Steven A. Krossa	Steven A. Krossa	2001	131
21	13 2/16	7 14/16	Prince of Wales Island, AK	Rudolph O. Wilson, Jr.	Rudolph O. Wilson, Jr.	2002	131
21	13 4/16	7 12/16	Sundown, MB	Mel A. Ortmann	Mel A. Ortmann	2002	131
21	12 13/16	8 3/16	Yavapai Co., AZ	Todd A. Hyslip	Todd A. Hyslip	2002	131
21	13 2/16	7 14/16	Pine Co., MN	Daniel J. Fischer	Daniel J. Fischer	2002	131
21	13	8	Price Co., WI	Thomas P. Stenborg	Thomas P. Stenborg	2002	131
21	13 2/16	7 14/16	Sawyer Co., WI	Robin R. Zillmer	Robin R. Zillmer	2002	131
21	13 5/16	7 11/16	Beaufort Co., NC	Kenneth W. Bateman, Jr.	Kenneth Bateman, Jr.	2002	131
21	12 13/16	8 3/16	Valleyview, AB	Paul J. Kruger	Paul J. Kruger	2003	131
20 15/16	13 3/16	7 12/16	Gogebic Co., MI	Stanley R. Pewoski	Stanley R. Pewoski	1999	151
20 15/16	13	7 15/16	Pamlico Co., NC	Jeremy R. Boyd	Jeremy R. Boyd	2001	151
20 14/16	12 12/16	8 2/16	Mesa Co., CO	Clark R. Milsap	Clark R. Milsap	2000	153
20 14/16	13 1/16	7 13/16	Vilas Co., WI	Ronald J. Latzl	Ronald J. Latzl	2000	153
20 14/16	12 10/16	8 4/16	San Juan Co., UT	Zachary G. May	Zachary G. May	2001	153
20 14/16	13 2/16	7 12/16	Lackawanna Co., PA	Jerry L. Laughman	Jerry L. Laughman	2001	153
20 14/16	12 14/16	8	Kuiu Island, AK	Daniel D. Kreis	Daniel D. Kreis	2002	153
20 14/16	12 12/16	8 2/16	Mora Co., NM	K.L. Ebbens & R. Bassett	Kenneth L. Ebbens	2002	153
20 14/16	12 15/16	7 13/16	Bayfield Co., WI	Albert J. Fremstad	Albert J. Fremstad	2003	153
20 13/16	13	7 13/16	Somerset Co., PA	Richard P. Eans	Richard P. Eans	1996	160
20 13/16	12 13/16	8	Selwyn Lake, SK	Wayne W. Franzen	Wayne W. Franzen	2000	160
20 13/16	12 12/16	8 1/16	Mendocino Co., CA	Michael E. Clasom	Michael E. Clasom	2000	160
20 13/16	13 2/16	7 11/16	Bedford Co., PA	Daniel G. Robinette	Daniel G. Robinette	2000	160
20 13/16	13 2/16	7 11/16	Crow Wing Co., MN	Ricky A. Hines	Ricky A. Hines	2001	160
20 13/16	12 13/16	8	Mesa Co., CO	Rick W. Snellstrom	Rick W. Snellstrom	2001	160
20 13/16	11 9/16	9 4/16	Marquette Co., MI	Picked Up	Todd Crow	2001	160
20 13/16	12 13/16	8	Elk Co., PA	David L. Martino	David L. Martino	2001	160
20 13/16	12 12/16	8 1/16	Prince of Wales Island, AK	Terry Seem	Terry Seem	2002	160
20 13/16	12 11/16	8 2/16	Temagami, ON	Timothy J. Eldridge	Timothy J. Eldridge	2002	160
20 13/16	12 11/16	8 2/16	Koochiching Co., MN	Dennis W. Lagergren	Dennis W. Lagergren	2002	160
20 13/16	13 5/16	7 8/16	Warren Co., PA	Jason Allen	Jason Allen	2002	160
20 13/16	12 13/16	8	Elk Co., PA	David L. Martino	David L. Martino	2002	160
20 12/16	13 9/16	7 3/16	Becker Co., MN	Rex T. Kemmer	Rex T. Kemmer	2001	173
20 12/16	13	7 12/16	Aitkin Co., MN	Jerry R. Clement	Jerry R. Clement	2001	173
20 12/16	12 9/16	8 3/16	Oakburn, MB	Robert L. Behnke	Robert L. Behnke	2001	173
20 12/16	13 2/16	7 10/16	Rusk Co., WI	David E. Fisher	David V. Fisher	2001	173
20 12/16	13 6/16	7 6/16	Bronson Lake, SK	Albert C. England	Albert C. England	2003	173
20 11/16	13 2/16	7 9/16	Huntingdon Co., PA	Derek G. Wright	Derek G. Wright	1996	178
20 11/16	12 12/16	7 15/16	Peter Lake, SK	Henry J. Lohmeier	Henry J. Lohmeier	2000	178
20 11/16	12 13/16	7 14/16	McKean Co., PA	David A. Johnson	David A. Johnson	2000	178
20 11/16	13 1/16	7 10/16	Bear Creek, AB	Daric Isenor	Daric Isenor	2001	178

BLACK BEAR

Ursus americanus americanus and related subspecies

Score	Greatest Length of Skull Without Lower Jaw	Greatest Width of Skull	Locality	Hunter	Owner	Date Killed	Rank
20 11/16	12 12/16	7 15/16	Qu'Appelle River, SK	Rene O. Fortin	Rene O. Fortin	2001	178
20 11/16	13 3/16	7 8/16	Price Co., WI	Barb Boyer	Barb Boyer	2002	178
20 11/16	12 6/16	8 5/16	Hyde Co., NC	Rick Shelton	Rick Shelton	2002	178
20 11/16	12 10/16	8 1/16	Gypsumville, MB	David D. Waldschmidt	David D. Waldschmidt	2003	178
20 11/16	12 14/16	7 13/16	Prince of Wales Island, AK	Wayne P. Fontenelle	Wayne P. Fontenelle	2003	178
20 10/16	13	7 10/16	Bonneville Co., ID	Adrian N. McConeghy	Adrian N. McConeghy	1999	187
20 10/16	12 11/16	7 15/16	Marinette Co., WI	Jan B. Moll	Jan B. Moll	2000	187
20 10/16	13 1/16	7 9/16	Lincoln Co., WI	Wayne S. Schmitz	Wayne S. Schmitz	2000	187
20 10/16	12 10/16	8	Bedford Co., PA	Michael A. Cox	Michael A. Cox	2000	187
20 10/16	12 8/16	8 2/16	Essex Co., NY	Michael P.M. Pond	Michael P.M. Pond	2000	187
20 10/16	12 13/16	7 13/16	Grand Bay, NB	Marino Capulli	Marino Capulli	2001	187
20 10/16	13 2/16	7 8/16	Yavapai Co., AZ	Tony J. Mang	Tony J. Mang	2002	187
20 10/16	12 9/16	8 1/16	Somerset Co., ME	Michael A. Hermstedt	Michael A. Hermstedt	2002	187
20 10/16	13	7 10/16	Prince of Wales Island, AK	Kenneth A. Lyon	Kenneth A. Lyon	2003	187
20 9/16	12 14/16	7 11/16	Clearwater Co., MN	Roger J. Ryant	Roger J. Ryant	2000	196
20 9/16	12 9/16	8	Eden Lake, MB	Becky Johnston	Becky Johnston	2001	196
20 9/16	13 2/16	7 7/16	Ashland Co., WI	Paul T. Bruckner	Paul T. Bruckner	2001	196
20 9/16	13 2/16	7 7/16	Sawyer Co., WI	Robert W. Huck	Robert W. Huck	2002	196
20 9/16	12 8/16	8 1/16	Beaverhead Co., MT	Patrick T. McCarthy	Patrick T. McCarthy	2002	196
20 9/16	12 15/16	7 10/16	Grant Co., NM	Trey A. Whitley	Trey A. Whitley	2003	196
20 8/16	12 11/16	7 13/16	McKean Co., PA	Gayle V. Patterson	Terry L. Patterson	1964	202
20 8/16	12 13/16	7 11/16	Gila Co., AZ	John L. Lundin	John L. Lundin	1999	202
20 8/16	12 10/16	7 14/16	Prince of Wales Island, AK	Steven Arlow	Steven Arlow	2000	202
20 8/16	12 6/16	8 2/16	Grand Co., UT	William N. Fenimore	William N. Fenimore	2000	202
20 8/16	12 8/16	8	Greenwater Lake, SK	Alan J. Stieg	Alan J. Stieg	2001	202
20 8/16	12 8/16	8	Gogebic Co., MI	Michael G. Voelker	Michael G. Voelker	2001	202
20 8/16	12 14/16	7 10/16	Marinette Co., WI	Jeremy J. DeBoth	Jeremy J. DeBoth	2001	202
20 8/16	12 10/16	7 14/16	Ashland Co., WI	Leon L. Klueckman	Leon L. Klueckman	2001	202
20 8/16	12 10/16	7 14/16	Carroll Co., NH	Jeffrey B. Arkebauer	Jeffrey B. Arkebauer	2001	202
20 8/16	13	7 8/16	Mendocino Co., CA	Ben F. Carter III	Ben F. Carter III	2002	202
20 8/16	12 8/16	8	Kuiu Island, AK	Douglas A. Salomon	Douglas A. Salomon	2002	202
20 8/16	13 2/16	7 6/16	Heart Lake, AB	Brent N. Harwood-Lynn	Brent N. Harwood-Lynn	2002	202
20 8/16	12 9/16	7 15/16	Prince of Wales Island, AK	Eric Minneti	Eric Minneti	2002	202

			Locality	Hunter	Owner	Date	Score
20 8/16	12 9/16	7 15/16	Eagle Co., CO	Philip K. Keltner	Philip K. Keltner	2002	202
20 8/16	12 8/16	8	Prince of Wales Island, AK	Greg James	Greg James	2003	202
20 8/16	12 14/16	7 10/16	Meadow Lake, SK	Edward P. Fleetwood, Jr.	Edward P. Fleetwood, Jr.	2003	202
20 7/16	12 12/16	7 11/16	Sublette Co., WY	Picked Up	Louis Roberts	1987	218
20 7/16	12 5/16	8 2/16	Vancouver Island, BC	William H. Hintze	William H. Hintze	1990	218
20 7/16	13	7 7/16	Riding Mt., MB	Dana M. Draper	Dana M. Draper	1997	218
20 7/16	13	7 7/16	Cambria Co., PA	John W. Ostrosky	John W. Ostrosky	1998	218
20 7/16	12 14/16	7 9/16	Taylor River, MB	Ronald Paksi	Ronald Paksi	2000	218
20 7/16	12 12/16	7 11/16	Kern Co., CA	Kevin J. Hunt	Kevin J. Hunt	2000	218
20 7/16	12 12/16	7 11/16	Prince of Wales Island, AK	Kevin G. Camastral	Kevin G. Camastral	2001	218
20 7/16	12 10/16	7 13/16	Hat Lake, BC	Jeff Holland	Jeff Holland	2001	218
20 7/16	12 7/16	8	Egenolf Lake, MB	P. Bruce Easter	P. Bruce Easter	2001	218
20 7/16	13	7 7/16	Mille Lacs Co., MN	Ronald K. Webeck	Ronald K. Webeck	2001	218
20 7/16	12 10/16	7 13/16	Chelan Co., WA	Michelle Bean	Michelle Bean	2001	218
20 7/16	12 13/16	7 10/16	Carbon Co., WY	Seth D. Hamburger	Seth D. Hamburger	2001	218
20 7/16	12 12/16	7 11/16	Armstrong Co., PA	Brian D. Garmong	Brian D. Garmong	2001	218
20 7/16	13 2/16	7 5/16	Indiana Co., PA	Douglas Kostella	Douglas Kostella	2001	218
20 7/16	12 6/16	8 1/16	Montezuma Co., CO	Thelbert J. Pollard, Jr.	Thelbert J. Pollard, Jr.	2002	218
20 7/16	12 10/16	7 13/16	Frank Lake, AB	Douglas K. Evert	Douglas K. Evert	2002	218
20 7/16	13 1/16	7 6/16	Barron Co., WI	Paul Mosentine	Paul Mosentine	2002	218
20 7/16	12 15/16	7 8/16	Grand Co., UT	Robert Butler	Robert Butler	2003	218
20 6/16	12 9/16	7 13/16	Marquette Co., MI	William C. Ochadleus	William C. Ochadleus	1987	236
20 6/16	12 14/16	7 8/16	Greene Co., NY	Scott M. Conlee	Chloe Conlee	1998	236
20 6/16	12 9/16	7 13/16	Apache Co., AZ	J. Michael Goodart	J. Michael Goodart	1999	236
20 6/16	12 12/16	7 10/16	Grays Harbor Co., WA	George C. Atkinson	George C. Atkinson	2000	236
20 6/16	13 5/16	7 1/16	Cass Co., MN	Edward O'Hearn	Edward O'Hearn	2000	236
20 6/16	13 3/16	7 3/16	Washburn Co., WI	James J. Johnson	James J. Johnson	2000	236
20 6/16	13	7 6/16	Moresby Island, BC	William H. Hintze	William H. Hintze	2001	236
20 6/16	12 12/16	7 10/16	Otero Co., NM	Joe A. Salkeld	Joe A. Salkeld	2001	236
20 6/16	12 14/16	7 8/16	Swan River, MB	Chet Hassemer	Chet Hassemer	2001	236
20 6/16	12 15/16	7 7/16	Ashland Co., WI	Kerrie L. Gonnering	Kerrie L. Gonnering	2001	236
20 6/16	12 11/16	7 11/16	Sawyer Co., WI	Ronald D. Fetkenheuer	Ronald D. Fetkenheuer	2001	236
20 6/16	12 12/16	7 12/16	Presque Isle Co., MI	Joette J. Wozniak	Joette J. Wozniak	2001	236
20 6/16	12 10/16	7 7/16	Humboldt Co., CA	Kenneth W. Springer	Kenneth W. Springer	2001	236
20 6/16	12 15/16	7 1/16	Green Lake, SK	Chris Whytock	Chris Whytock	2002	236
20 6/16	13 5/16	7 14/16	Washburn Co., WI	James R. Jenderny	James R. Jenderny	2002	236
20 6/16	12 8/16	7 6/16	Fremont Co., WY	Randy A. Cragoe	Randy A. Cragoe	2002	236
20 6/16	13	7 8/16	Rappahannock Co., VA	Brandon Longmire	Brandon Longmire	2002	236
20 6/16	12 14/16	7 8/16	Graham Co., AZ	John L. Lundin	John L. Lundin	2003	236
20 6/16	12 14/16	7 8/16	Black Bear Island Lake, SK	Steven Bowman	Steven Bowman	2003	236
20 6/16	13 3/16	7 3/16	Jackson Co., OR	Larry W. Anderson III	Larry W. Anderson III	2003	236

BLACK BEAR

Ursus americanus americanus and related subspecies

Score	Greatest Length of Skull Without Lower Jaw	Greatest Width of Skull	Locality	Hunter	Owner	Date Killed	Rank
20 5/16	12 10/16	7 11/16	Susitna River, AK	Abed S. Radwan	Abed S. Radwan	1998	256
20 5/16	12 13/16	7 8/16	Clearfield Co., PA	David E. Sylvis	David E. Sylvis	1998	256
20 5/16	13	7 5/16	Etomami River, SK	Clifford L. Pechota	Clifford L. Pechota	1999	256
20 5/16	12 12/16	7 9/16	Navajo Co., AZ	Dennis Nemeth	Dennis Nemeth	1999	256
20 5/16	12 13/16	7 8/16	Blair Co., PA	David H. Feathers	David H. Feathers	1999	256
20 5/16	12 8/16	7 13/16	Wythe Co., VA	Sharon K. Ball	Sharon K. Ball	1999	256
20 5/16	12 11/16	7 10/16	Mahnomen Co., MN	Scott L. McConkey	Scott L. McConkey	2000	256
20 5/16	12 9/16	7 12/16	Quevillon Lake, QC	Stephane Roberge	Stephane Roberge	2001	256
20 5/16	12 6/16	7 15/16	Iron Mt., LB	James B. Bridge	James B. Bridge	2001	256
20 5/16	12 6/16	7 15/16	Montezuma Co., CO	Buddy Rogers	Buddy Rogers	2001	256
20 5/16	12 5/16	8	Apache Co., AZ	Patti-Lu Mitchell	Patti-Lu Mitchell	2001	256
20 5/16	12 13/16	7 8/16	Kupreanof Island, AK	Timothy J. Sears	Timothy J. Sears	2002	256
20 5/16	12 7/16	7 14/16	Marinette Co., WI	Robert G. Cormier	Robert G. Cormier	2002	256
20 5/16	13 1/16	7 4/16	Oconto Co., WI	Robert Leurquin	Robert Leurquin	2002	256
20 5/16	12 7/16	7 14/16	Washburn Co., WI	Aaron D. Lutze	Aaron D. Lutze	2002	256
20 5/16	12 8/16	7 13/16	White Creek, BC	Steven A. Krossa	Steven A. Krossa	2002	256
20 5/16	12 12/16	7 9/16	Flathead Co., MT	Matthew R.F. Knight	Matthew R.F. Knight	2002	256
20 5/16	13 2/16	7 3/16	Douglas Co., WI	Jerry Volgren	Jerry Volgren	2002	256
20 4/16	12 9/16	7 11/16	Camas Co., ID	Archie E. Malone	Archie E. Malone	1992	274
20 4/16	12 13/16	7 7/16	Douglas Co., WI	Rick Hanson	Rick Hanson	1994	274
20 4/16	12 14/16	8	Dolores Co., CO	Jeremy Gallegos	Jeremy Gallegos	1999	274
20 4/16	12 4/16	7 6/16	Clearfield Co., PA	Randy J. Little	Randy J. Little	1999	274
20 4/16	12 10/16	8	La Pause Lake, QC	Michel Vezina	Michel Vezina	2000	274
20 4/16	12 8/16	7 10/16	Jackson Co., OR	Billy C. Rutherford	Billy C. Rutherford	2000	274
20 4/16	12 8/16	7 12/16	Caniapiscau River, QC	Ivica Hrdjun	Ivica Hrdjun	2000	274
20 4/16	12 12/16	7 12/16	Carswell Lake, SK	Neil Demant	Neil Demant	2001	274
20 4/16	12 11/16	7 8/16	Carswell Lake, SK	Thomas R. Conrardy	Thomas R. Conrardy	2001	274
20 4/16	12 7/16	7 9/16	Coconino Co., AZ	John D. Audsley	John D. Audsley	2001	274
20 4/16	12 10/16	7 13/16	La Plata Co., CO	Randall E. Shepard	Randall E. Shepard	2001	274
20 4/16	12 9/16	7 10/16	Oconto Co., WI	Lawrence J. Woodke	Lawrence J. Woodke	2001	274
20 4/16	12 12/16	7 11/16	Kuiu Island, AK	Nathan L. Andersohn	Nathan L. Andersohn	2002	274
20 4/16	12 13/16	7 8/16	Florence Co., WI	Lee N. Hennes	Lee N. Hennes	2002	274
20 4/16	12 13/16	7 7/16	Desbergeres Lake, QC	John C. Bartsch	John C. Bartsch	2002	274

			Location	Hunter	Owner	Year	Score
20 4/16	12 6/16	7 14/16	Mendocino Co., CA	Tom D. Clark	Tom D. Clark	2002	274
20 4/16	12 8/16	7 12/16	Lane Co., OR	Max Zeller	Max Zeller	2003	274
20 3/16	12 13/16	7 6/16	Wallowa Co., OR	Ron Hebdon	Ron Hebdon	1996	291
20 3/16	13 2/16	7 1/16	Pierce Co., WA	David L. Montgomery	David L. Montgomery	1999	291
20 3/16	12 9/16	7 10/16	Ventura Co., CA	Loren C. Nodolf	Loren C. Nodolf	2000	291
20 3/16	13	7 3/16	Carlton Co., MN	Ted Sherga	Ted Sherga	2000	291
20 3/16	12 10/16	7 9/16	Aroostook Co., ME	Dennis Z. Mock	Dennis Z. Mock	2000	291
20 3/16	12 8/16	7 11/16	Raleigh Co., WV	Dan Willis	Dan Willis	2000	291
20 3/16	12 14/16	7 5/16	Idaho Co., ID	Shayne R. Ellis	Shayne R. Ellis	2001	291
20 3/16	12 11/16	7 8/16	Rio Arriba Co., NM	Clinton Wallace	Clinton Wallace	2001	291
20 3/16	12 12/16	7 7/16	Meadow Lake, SK	Steve C. Parker	Steve C. Parker	2001	291
20 3/16	12 11/16	7 8/16	Douglas Co., WI	John E. Parker	John E. Parker	2001	291
20 3/16	12 10/16	7 9/16	Tuolumne Co., CA	Martin E. McKellips	Martin E. McKellips	2001	291
20 3/16	12 5/16	7 14/16	Huerfano Co., CO	Kevin D. DeWeber	Kevin D. DeWeber	2002	291
20 3/16	12 3/16	8	Mesa Co., CO	Robert Hurst	Robert Hurst	2002	291
20 3/16	12 11/16	7 8/16	Burnett Co., WI	Rick Hanson	Rick Hanson	2002	291
20 3/16	12 13/16	7 6/16	Sweet Grass Co., MT	Paul J. Meyers	Paul J. Meyers	2003	291
20 2/16	12 10/16	7 8/16	Potter Co., PA	Robert B. Snyder	Robert B. Snyder	1997	306
20 2/16	12 10/16	7 8/16	Snow Lake, MB	Charles R. Neuman	Charles R. Neuman	1999	306
20 2/16	12 13/16	7 5/16	Centre Co., PA	Paul M. Martin, Sr.	Paul M. Martin, Sr.	1999	306
20 2/16	12 13/16	7 5/16	Taylor Co., WI	Scott A. Selting	Scott A. Selting	2000	306
20 2/16	12 10/16	7 8/16	Cass Co., MN	Kenny Schlangen	Kenny Schlangen	2001	306
20 2/16	12 14/16	7 4/16	Lincoln Co., WI	Thomas J. Clark	Thomas J. Clark	2001	306
20 2/16	12 11/16	7 5/16	Allegany Co., NY	Mark Kogut	Mark Kogut	2001	306
20 2/16	12 6/16	7 12/16	Turnor Lake, SK	Peter L. Bucklin	Peter L. Bucklin	2002	306
20 2/16	12 5/16	7 13/16	Otter Lake, SK	Doug R. Long	Doug R. Long	2002	306
20 2/16	12 10/16	7 8/16	Washburn Co., WI	Picked Up	Brad Thompson	2002	306
20 2/16	12 7/16	7 11/16	Washington Co., ME	Greg Mendenhall	Greg Mendenhall	2002	306
20 2/16	12 8/16	7 10/16	Vancouver Island, BC	Lorne D. Rinkel	Lorne D. Rinkel	2003	306
20 2/16	12 5/16	7 13/16	Lac La Biche, AB	Harry J. Beckham	Harry J. Beckham	2003	306
20 1/16	12 10/16	7 7/16	Clallam Co., WA	Harry E. Reed	Harry E. Reed	1998	319
20 1/16	12 13/16	7 4/16	Apache Co., AZ	Robert M. Amante	Robert M. Amante	2001	319
20 1/16	12 10/16	7 7/16	Baker Co., OR	Darin A. Weaver	Darin A. Weaver	2001	319
20 1/16	12 4/16	7 13/16	San Juan Co., UT	Zebula H. May	Zebula H. May	2001	319
20 1/16	13 2/16	6 15/16	Lincoln Co., WI	Tony G. Vanden Heuvel	Tony G. Vanden Heuvel	2001	319
20 1/16	12 5/16	7 12/16	Iron Co., MI	Stanley W. Tanner	Stanley W. Tanner	2001	319
20 1/16	12 13/16	7 4/16	Nez Perce Co., ID	Sean M. Wilson	Sean M. Wilson	2002	319
20 1/16	12 12/16	7 5/16	Prince of Wales Island, AK	Alison Chase-Dunn	Alison Chase-Dunn	2002	319
20 1/16	12 6/16	7 11/16	Black Bear Island Lake, SK	Gary L. Mucilli	Gary L. Mucilli	2002	319
20 1/16	12 3/16	7 14/16	Boise Co., ID	Michael C. Lower	Michael C. Lower	2002	319
20 1/16	12 9/16	7 8/16	Christopher Lake, SK	Michael C. Johnson	Michael C. Johnson	2002	319

BLACK BEAR

Ursus americanus americanus and related subspecies

Score	Greatest Length of Skull Without Lower Jaw	Greatest Width of Skull	Locality	Hunter	Owner	Date Killed	Rank
20 1/16	12 8/16	7 9/16	Snohomish Co., WA	Neil Hollo	Neil Hollo	2002	319
20 1/16	12 8/16	7 9/16	Florence Co., WI	Scott E. Weaver	Scott E. Weaver	2002	319
20 1/16	12 6/16	7 11/16	Florence Co., WI	Lee N. Hennes	Lee N. Hennes	2002	319
20 1/16	12 1/16	8	Shikatehawk Stream, NB	Brian J. Glodowski	Brian J. Glodowski	2002	319
20 1/16	12 4/16	7 13/16	Idaho Co., ID	Daniel D. Drover	Daniel D. Drover	2003	319
20 1/16	12 6/16	7 11/16	Berkshire Co., MA	John F. Fitzgerald	John F. Fitzgerald	2003	319
20	12 9/16	7 7/16	Itasca Co., MN	Ronnie L. Snell	Ronnie L. Snell	1993	336
20	12 8/16	7 8/16	Ministikwan Lake, SK	Harold W. Smith	Harold W. Smith	1997	336
20	12 12/16	7 4/16	Marinette Co., WI	Walter Pezall	Walter Pezall	1998	336
20	12 6/16	7 10/16	Fergus Co., MT	Tony Stein	Tony Stein	1999	336
20	12 4/16	7 12/16	High Level, AB	Brian R. Butkiewicz	Brian R. Butkiewicz	2000	336
20	13	7	Jackson Co., WI	Robert B. Nemitz	Robert B. Nemitz	2000	336
20	12 14/16	7 2/16	Clearfield Co., PA	Robert L. Duvuvei	Robert L. Duvuvei	2000	336
20	12 15/16	7 1/16	Magpie River, ON	Jay J. Kaster	Jay J. Kaster	2001	336
20	12 4/16	7 12/16	Umatilla Co., OR	Christopher J. Broderson	Christopher J. Broderson	2001	336
20	12 4/16	7 12/16	Sheridan Co., WY	Jonathon Atkinson	Jonathon Atkinson	2002	336
20	12 4/16	7 12/16	Park Co., MT	Matthew V. Henry	Matthew V. Henry	2002	336
20	12 4/16	7 10/16	Kuiu Island, AK	Dirk D. Dieterich	Dirk D. Dieterich	2002	336
20	12 6/16	7 10/16	San Juan Co., UT	David M. Argyle	David M. Argyle	2002	336
20	12 13/16	7 3/16	Bayfield Co., WI	Daniel C. Keith	Daniel C. Keith	2002	336
20	12 5/16	7 11/16	Klickitat Co., WA	Bryan C. Wilson	Bryan C. Wilson	2002	336
20	12 6/16	7 10/16	Cold Lake, SK	Jeffrey M. Lade	Jeffrey M. Lade	2003	336
22 12/16*	14 4/16	8 8/16	Queen Charlotte Islands, BC	Raymond J. Fournier	Raymond J. Fournier	1992	
22 12/16*	14 5/16	8 7/16	Washburn Co., WI	George Spaulding	George Spaulding	2002	
22 9/16*	13 9/16	9	Huntington Co., PA	Raymond K. Pruss	Raymond K. Pruss	2001	

* Final score subject to revision by additional verifying measurements.

GRIZZLY BEAR
Ursus arctos horribilis

Score	Greatest Length of Skull Without Lower Jaw	Greatest Width of Skull	Locality	Hunter	Owner	Date Killed	Rank
26 $^{14}/_{16}$	16 $^{11}/_{16}$	10 $^{3}/_{16}$	Kala Creek, AK	Eugene C. Williams	Eugene C. Williams	2001	1
26 $^{12}/_{16}$	16 $^{6}/_{16}$	10 $^{6}/_{16}$	Kuskokwim River, AK	Richard E. Jobe	Richard E. Jobe	2001	2
26 $^{10}/_{16}$	16 $^{9}/_{16}$	10 $^{1}/_{16}$	Windy Creek, AK	Kyle R. Moffat	Kyle R. Moffat	2001	3
26 $^{6}/_{16}$	15 $^{14}/_{16}$	10 $^{8}/_{16}$	Nulato Hills, AK	Larry A. Meyer	Larry A. Meyer	2002	4
26 $^{6}/_{16}$	16 $^{3}/_{16}$	10 $^{3}/_{16}$	Kuskokwim River, AK	William G. Farley	William G. Farley	2003	4
26 $^{5}/_{16}$	16 $^{3}/_{16}$	10 $^{2}/_{16}$	Vreeland Creek, AK	Leo P. Caito, Jr.	Leo P. Caito, Jr.	2000	6
26 $^{3}/_{16}$	16 $^{2}/_{16}$	10 $^{1}/_{16}$	Otter Creek, AK	Daniel S. Bolek	Daniel S. Bolek	2001	7
26 $^{1}/_{16}$	16 $^{5}/_{16}$	9 $^{12}/_{16}$	Kokrine Hills, AK	Vernon Spencer	Vernon Spencer	2000	8
26 $^{1}/_{16}$	15 $^{12}/_{16}$	10 $^{5}/_{16}$	Kigluaik Mts., AK	Joseph P. Small	Scott C. Babcock	2001	8
25 $^{10}/_{16}$	16 $^{4}/_{16}$	9 $^{6}/_{16}$	Bonnifield Creek, AK	Picked Up	Jerry D. Lees	2000	10
25 $^{7}/_{16}$	15 $^{9}/_{16}$	9 $^{14}/_{16}$	Elk River, BC	Harry E. Seratt	Harry E. Seratt	2002	11
25 $^{6}/_{16}$	15 $^{12}/_{16}$	9 $^{10}/_{16}$	Anvik River, AK	Tracy Samuelson	Tracy Samuelson	2001	12
25 $^{2}/_{16}$	15 $^{4}/_{16}$	9 $^{14}/_{16}$	Level Mt., BC	George W. Jacobson	George W. Jacobson	2000	13
25 $^{2}/_{16}$	15 $^{8}/_{16}$	9 $^{10}/_{16}$	Mess Creek, BC	Marty Halpern	Marty Halpern	2000	13
25 $^{1}/_{16}$	16	9 $^{1}/_{16}$	Kauk River, AK	Jack B. Robins	Jack B. Robins	2002	15
25	15 $^{8}/_{16}$	9 $^{8}/_{16}$	Golsovia River, AK	Dennis G. Rulewicz	Dennis G. Rulewicz	2002	16
25	15 $^{13}/_{16}$	9 $^{3}/_{16}$	Ungalik River, AK	Aaron I. James	Aaron I. James	2002	16
24 $^{15}/_{16}$	15 $^{15}/_{16}$	9	Pilgrim River, AK	Daniel R. Fiehrer	Daniel R. Fiehrer	1999	18
24 $^{15}/_{16}$	15 $^{10}/_{16}$	9 $^{5}/_{16}$	Mt. Lathrop, AK	Tor Wittussen	Tor Wittussen	2000	18
24 $^{14}/_{16}$	15 $^{10}/_{16}$	9 $^{4}/_{16}$	Salmon Creek, AK	Bradford G. McDavid	Bradford G. McDavid	2003	20
24 $^{14}/_{16}$	15 $^{8}/_{16}$	9 $^{6}/_{16}$	Dean Creek, AK	Mark D. Etchart	Mark D. Etchart	2003	20
24 $^{13}/_{16}$	15 $^{7}/_{16}$	9 $^{6}/_{16}$	Noatak River, AK	Morris A. Link	Morris A. Link	2000	22
24 $^{13}/_{16}$	15 $^{10}/_{16}$	9 $^{3}/_{16}$	Swan Hills, AB	Allan P. Keats	Allan P. Keats	2001	22
24 $^{13}/_{16}$	15 $^{7}/_{16}$	9 $^{6}/_{16}$	Soule Lake, AK	Jeffery Belongia	Jeffery Belongia	2002	22
24 $^{11}/_{16}$	15 $^{5}/_{16}$	9 $^{6}/_{16}$	Virginia Creek, AK	Mike L. Wade	Mike L. Wade	2001	25
24 $^{9}/_{16}$	15 $^{10}/_{16}$	8 $^{15}/_{16}$	Taku River, BC	Kent Deligans	Kent Deligans	2003	26
24 $^{8}/_{16}$	15 $^{5}/_{16}$	9 $^{3}/_{16}$	Koyuk River, AK	Holly E. Oliver II	Holly E. Oliver II	2001	27
24 $^{8}/_{16}$	14 $^{13}/_{16}$	9 $^{11}/_{16}$	Kobuk River, AK	Timothy S. Moermond	Timothy S. Moermond	2001	27
24 $^{6}/_{16}$	15 $^{4}/_{16}$	9 $^{2}/_{16}$	Anvik River, AK	Douglas G. Sansone	Douglas G. Sansone	2000	29
24 $^{5}/_{16}$	15 $^{4}/_{16}$	9 $^{1}/_{16}$	Two Pete Mt., YT	Luke R. Viravec	Luke R. Viravec	2001	30
24 $^{5}/_{16}$	15 $^{7}/_{16}$	8 $^{14}/_{16}$	Big River, AK	L.N. Wisner	L.N. Wisner	2003	30
24 $^{2}/_{16}$	15 $^{8}/_{16}$	8 $^{10}/_{16}$	Caribou Co., ID	Picked Up	Bill E. Lovely	PR1900	32
24 $^{2}/_{16}$	15 $^{7}/_{16}$	8 $^{11}/_{16}$	Little Salcha River, AK	Randy A. Cravener	Randy A. Cravener	2000	32

GRIZZLY BEAR

Ursus arctos horribilis

Score	Greatest Length of Skull Without Lower Jaw	Greatest Width of Skull	Locality	Hunter	Owner	Date Killed	Rank
24 2/16	14 12/16	9 6/16	Squirrel River, AK	Tim D. Hiner	Tim D. Hiner	2001	32
24 2/16	14 15/16	9 3/16	Nabesna River, AK	Joseph Rendeiro	Joseph Rendeiro	2001	32
24 2/16	15 2/16	9	Kantishna River, AK	Thomas C. Brown	Thomas C. Brown	2002	32
24 1/16	15 3/16	8 14/16	Anvik River, AK	Jorge M. Rodriguez	Jorge M. Rodriguez	2001	37
24 1/16	14 12/16	9 5/16	Nass River, BC	Marvin Kwiatkowski	Marvin Kwiatkowski	2001	37
24 1/16	14 15/16	9 2/16	Canyon Creek, AK	Lance M. Cannon	Scott C. Babcock	2002	37
24	14 14/16	9 2/16	Mt. Bendeleben, AK	Chad Farley	Chad Farley	1999	40
24	15 4/16	8 12/16	Quekilok Creek, AK	Mike McDonald	Mike McDonald	2001	40
24	14 12/16	9 4/16	Ungalik River, AK	Theodore D. James III	Theodore D. James III	2002	40
24	15 3/16	8 13/16	Preston Lake, AB	Travis S. Peterson	Travis S. Peterson	2003	40
23 15/16	14 14/16	9 1/16	Gates Creek, BC	Francesco Puricelli	Francesco Puricelli	2000	44
23 14/16	15 8/16	8 6/16	Cascade Inlet, BC	Michaux Nash, Jr.	Michaux Nash, Jr.	2001	45
23 13/16	14 10/16	9 3/16	Melozitna River, AK	Daniel M. Hawkins	Daniel M. Hawkins	2003	46
23 11/16	14 15/16	8 12/16	Kwiktalik Mts., AK	Gregory W. Kasten	Gregory W. Kasten	2002	47
23 11/16	15 1/16	8 10/16	Koyuk River, AK	Brent Hickey	Brent Hickey	2003	47
23 10/16	14 10/16	9	Asikpak River, AK	Paul E. Johnson	Paul E. Johnson	2001	49
23 5/16	14 8/16	8 13/16	Siksikpuk River, AK	Mark E. Ensor	Mark E. Ensor	2001	50
23 4/16	15	8 4/16	Wiminasik Lake, BC	John A. Keats	John A. Keats	2000	51
23 1/16	14 6/16	8 11/16	Fishing Creek, YT	George T. Law	George T. Law	2001	52
23	15	8	Circle Creek, AK	Randall K. Sears	Randall K. Sears	2003	53

ALASKA BROWN BEAR

Ursus arctos middendorffi and certain related subspecies

Minimum Score 26   World's Record 30 12/16

Score	Greatest Length of Skull Without Lower Jaw	Greatest Width of Skull	Locality	Hunter	Owner	Date Killed	Rank
29 3/16	17 9/16	11 10/16	Deadman Bay, AK	Robert M. Ortiz	Robert M. Ortiz	2001	1
29 3/16	18 10/16	10 9/16	Cold Bay, AK	Gene White	Gene White	2001	1
29 3/16	18 11/16	10 8/16	Egegik Bay, AK	Steve Rakes	Steve Rakes	2003	1
28 15/16	17 10/16	11 5/16	Terror Bay, AK	Terry A. Monson	Terry A. Monson	2003	4
28 14/16	17 11/16	11 3/16	Afognak Island, AK	Ricardo E. Longoria	Ricardo E. Longoria	2001	5
28 14/16	17 12/16	11 2/16	Meshik River, AK	Doyle D. Patterson	Doyle D. Patterson	2001	5
28 14/16	18	10 14/16	Pumice Creek, AK	Larry F. O'Brian	Larry F. O'Brian	2001	5
28 13/16	17 15/16	10 14/16	Mt. Veniaminof, AK	Roger L. McCosker	Roger L. McCosker	2001	8
28 11/16	18 1/16	10 10/16	Olga Bay, AK	Melvin F. Hendricks	Melvin F. Hendricks	1996	9
28 11/16	16 14/16	11 13/16	Uganic Bay, AK	Paul G. Mater	Paul G. Mater	2001	9
28 10/16	18	10 10/16	Alaska Pen., AK	John A. Dolan	John A. Dolan	2002	11
28 9/16	17 5/16	11 4/16	Kodiak Island, AK	Richard E. Bennett	Richard E. Bennett	2000	12
28 9/16	17 5/16	11 4/16	Olga Bay, AK	Michael E. Kuglitsch	Michael E. Kuglitsch	2000	12
28 7/16	17 6/16	11 1/16	Pavlof Bay, AK	Gordon L. Dorn	Gordon L. Dorn	2001	14
28 6/16	16 9/16	11 13/16	Black Point, AK	Richard E. Hunnewell	Richard E. Hunnewell	2000	15
28 6/16	17 9/16	10 13/16	Aliulik Pen., AK	Charles W. Stevens	Charles W. Stevens	2001	15
28 6/16	17 12/16	10 10/16	Caribou River, AK	Ronald S. Schmidt	Ronald S. Schmidt	2001	15
28 5/16	17 8/16	10 13/16	Cold Bay, AK	Charles B. Edwards	Charles B. Edwards	1999	18
28 5/16	17 13/16	10 8/16	Port Heiden, AK	Picked Up	Shawn R. Andres	2001	18
28 5/16	17 11/16	10 10/16	Cold Bay, AK	Richard W. Van Valkenburg	Richard W. Van Valkenburg	2002	18
28 5/16	17 4/16	11 11/16	Kodiak Island, AK	Steven Gauvin	Steven Gauvin	1999	18
28 2/16	16 14/16	11 4/16	Lake Rose Tead, AK	Scott K. Parcell	Scott K. Parcell	2000	22
28 2/16	17 1/16	11 1/16	Kodiak Island, AK	Michael P Horstman	Michael P. Horstman	2000	22
28 2/16	17 7/16	10 11/16	Alinchak Bay, AK	Matthew M. Perman	Matthew M. Perman	2001	22
28 2/16	17 8/16	10 10/16	Shotgun Hills, AK	Curt L. Bradford	Curt L. Bradford	1980	22
28 1/16	17	11 1/16	Kenai Pen., AK	Charles Steele	AK Dept. of Fish & Game	2001	26
28 1/16	17 14/16	10 3/16	Cold Bay, AK	Phillip R. Barker	Phillip R. Barker	2002	26
28 1/16	17 1/16	11	Aliulik Pen., AK	Tony Paden	Tony Paden	2002	26
28 1/16	17 11/16	10 6/16	Nelson Lagoon, AK	Ronald G. Skloss	Ronald G. Skloss	2002	26
28 1/16	17 14/16	10 3/16	Cinder River, AK	Ronald V. Hunter	Ronald V. Hunter	2002	26
28 1/16	17 10/16	10 7/16	Big Creek, AK	Nicholas J.H. Borchert	Nicholas J.H. Borchert	2002	26
28	16 15/16	11 1/16	Ugak Bay, AK	Harry V. Fitzpatrick	Harry V. Fitzpatrick	2001	32
28	16 7/16	11 9/16	Port Lions, AK	Thomas E. Gannon	Thomas E. Gannon	2001	32

ALASKA BROWN BEAR

Ursus arctos middendorffi and certain related subspecies

Score	Greatest Length of Skull Without Lower Jaw	Greatest Width of Skull	Locality	Hunter	Owner	Date Killed	Rank
27 14/16	17 7/16	10 7/16	Bruin Bay, AK	Glenn J. Rasmussen	Glenn J. Rasmussen	2002	34
27 14/16	17 1/16	10 13/16	King Salmon, AK	Louis C. Heller	Louis C. Heller	2002	34
27 13/16	17 2/16	10 11/16	Unimak Island, AK	Roger L. Wesley	Roger L. Wesley	2001	36
27 11/16	16 15/16	10 12/16	Orca Bay, AK	James F. Muse	James F. Muse	2000	37
27 11/16	17 3/16	10 8/16	Kejulik River, AK	L. Dean Jones	L. Dean Jones	2002	37
27 10/16	16 9/16	11 1/16	Copper River, AK	Shane W. Woods	Shane W. Woods	2003	39
27 9/16	17 7/16	10 2/16	Kogrukluk River, AK	John S. Newton	John S. Newton	2001	40
27 9/16	17 4/16	10 5/16	Port Moller, AK	Thomas A. Kooistra	Thomas A. Kooistra	2002	40
27 8/16	16 8/16	11	Lower Sturgeon River, AK	James M. Jeppesen, Jr.	James M. Jeppesen, Jr.	2002	42
27 8/16	17 2/16	10 6/16	Port Moller, AK	Keith P. Trader	Keith P. Trader	2002	42
27 7/16	17 2/16	10 5/16	Wide Bay, AK	Jerry D. Lees	Jerry D. Lees	2000	44
27 7/16	17	10 7/16	Pedro Bay, AK	Robert D. Grace	Robert D. Grace	2002	44
27 7/16	16 7/16	11	Barling Bay, AK	Robert Y. Childers	Robert Y. Childers	2003	44
27 5/16	17 3/16	10 2/16	Becharof Lake, AK	Edward N. Cerkowski	Edward N. Cerkowski	2000	47
27 5/16	16 13/16	10 8/16	Tenakee Inlet, AK	Louise E. Henry	Louise E. Henry	2003	47
27 4/16	17 11/16	9 9/16	Cold Bay, AK	Richard L. Smith	Richard L. Smith	2002	49
27 1/16	17 1/16	10	Bear Lake, AK	William J. Dunbar	William J. Dunbar	2000	50
27	16 10/16	10 6/16	Kodiak Island, AK	Roger R. Swanson	Roger R. Swanson	2000	51
26 15/16	17	9 15/16	Chukowan River, AK	Dale J. Francar	Dale J. Francar	1990	52
26 12/16	16 6/16	10 6/16	Ugak Bay, AK	Anthony J. Conte	Anthony J. Conte	2000	53
26 11/16	16 12/16	9 15/16	Sandy River, AK	Thomas C. Merritt	Thomas C. Merritt	1999	54
26 10/16	16 7/16	10 3/16	Bering Glacier, AK	Vol S. Davis, Jr.	Vol S. Davis, Jr.	1984	55
26 9/16	16 4/16	10 5/16	Karluk River, AK	Marc A. Martel	Marc A. Martel	2002	56
26 9/16	16 11/16	9 14/16	Muklung Hills, AK	Byron Lamb	Byron Lamb	2003	56
26 8/16	15 15/16	10 9/16	Ursus Cove, AK	Jerry M. Baker	Jerry M. Baker	2002	58
26 7/16	16 13/16	9 10/16	Stuyahok River, AK	Kevin E. Johnson	Kevin E. Johnson	2000	59
26 5/16	16 5/16	10	Red Lake, AK	Kent Deligans	Kent Deligans	2001	60
26 5/16	16 1/16	10 4/16	Tenakee Inlet, AK	Richard W. Lemon	Richard W. Lemon	2003	60
26 4/16	16 5/16	9 15/16	Kizhuyak Bay, AK	Robert J. Beaulieu	Robert J. Beaulieu	2000	62
26 3/16	16 3/16	10	Muddy Creek, AK	Butch Meilinger	Butch Meilinger	1994	63
26 2/16	16 12/16	9 6/16	Redoubt Creek, AK	Richard R. Bailey	Richard R. Bailey	2001	64
26 2/16	16 4/16	9 14/16	Port Gravina, AK	Mark A. Rufledt	Mark A. Rufledt	2001	64
26 1/16	16 5/16	9 12/16	Alsek River, AK	William H. Hintze	William H. Hintze	1986	66

26 1/16	10	Kodiak Island, AK	Ron C. Heidemann	2002	66
26 1/16	9 12/16	Klehini River, AK	Ronald R Heurich, Jr.	2002	66
26	9 10/16	Bristol Bay, AK	Robert I. Kelly	1999	69
26	9 3/16	Beaver Bay, AK	Ben F. Carter III	2000	69
26	9 14/16	Icy Bay, AK	Dennis Ream	2002	69
28 14/16*	11 1/16	Hinchinbrook Island, AK	Theodore A. Winnen	2001	

* Final score subject to revision by additional verifying measurements.

COUGAR

Felis concolor hippolestes and related subspecies

Minimum Score 14 8/16 — World's Record 16 4/16

Score	Greatest Length of Skull Without Lower Jaw	Greatest Width of Skull	Locality	Hunter	Owner	Date Killed	Rank
16	9 4/16	6 12/16	Archuleta Co., CO	Brian K. Williams	Brian K. Williams	2001	1
15 13/16	9 5/16	6 8/16	Jefferson Co., WA	David Medley	David Medley	2002	2
15 8/16	9	6 8/16	Rio Arriba Co., NM	Max D. Martinez	Max D. Martinez	2001	3
15 8/16	9 3/16	6 5/16	Tamaulipas, MX	Carlos A. Del Valle	Carlos A. Del Valle	2001	3
15 8/16	9 4/16	6 4/16	Elmore Co., ID	Daniel C. Weber	Daniel C. Weber	2002	3
15 8/16	9 4/16	6 4/16	Mora Co., NM	Robert M. Ortiz	Robert M. Ortiz	2002	3
15 7/16	9 3/16	6 4/16	Navajo Co., AZ	Fred Peters	Fred Peters	2000	7
15 7/16	9 3/16	6 7/16	Idaho Co., ID	Daniel R. Helterline	Daniel R. Helterline	2001	7
15 7/16	9	6 4/16	King Co., WA	Roy B. Hisler	Roy B. Hisler	2002	7
15 5/16	9 3/16	6 6/16	Idaho Co., ID	Bruce A. Peletier	Bruce A. Peletier	1999	10
15 5/16	8 15/16	6 2/16	Washoe Co., NV	John D. McCollum, Jr.	John D. McCollum, Jr.	2001	10
15 5/16	9 3/16	6 2/16	Colfax Co., NM	Patrick H. Lyons	Patrick H. Lyons	2001	10
15 5/16	9 1/16	6 4/16	Idaho Co., ID	George R. Naugle	George R. Naugle	2002	10
15 4/16	8 12/16	6 8/16	Revelstoke Lake, BC	Travis M. Schiller	Travis M. Schiller	1999	14
15 4/16	8 14/16	6 6/16	Jumpingpound Creek, AB	Jay J. Fuller	Jay J. Fuller	2000	14
15 4/16	9	6 4/16	Silver Bow Co., MT	Gene White	Gene White	2000	14
15 4/16	9 2/16	6 2/16	Thurston Co., WA	Jonathan A. Adams	Jonathan A. Adams	2003	14
15 3/16	8 15/16	6 4/16	Jefferson Co., WA	Willie Nation	J. Stevens & J. Rankin	1996	18
15 3/16	8 14/16	6 5/16	James River, AB	Donald E. Taylor	Donald E. Taylor	2000	18
15 3/16	8 12/16	6 7/16	Hawkins Creek, BC	Gary R. McMillan	Gary R. McMillan	2000	18
15 3/16	9 1/16	6 2/16	Bullock Creek, BC	John A. Dolan	John A. Dolan	2000	18
15 3/16	8 15/16	6 4/16	Willowbank Mt., BC	Gilles M. Rondeau	Gilles M. Rondeau	2000	18
15 3/16	8 13/16	6 6/16	Flathead Co., MT	Ronald C. Gronitz	Ronald C. Gronitz	2001	18
15 3/16	8 13/16	6 6/16	Taos Co., NM	Albert R. Tuepell	Albert R. Tuepell	2002	18
15 3/16	9	6 3/16	Tsuniah Lake, BC	William C. Boehm	Adam W.J. Boehm	2002	18
15 3/16	8 15/16	6 4/16	Summit Co., UT	Jared L. Brown	Jared L. Brown	2002	18
15 2/16	8 13/16	6 5/16	Navajo Co., AZ	Fred Peters	Fred Peters	2001	27
15 2/16	8 14/16	6 4/16	Missoula Co., MT	Anthony Knuchel	Anthony Knuchel	2002	27
15 2/16	9	6 2/16	Elko Co., NV	Michael A. Algerio	Michael A. Algerio	2002	27
15 2/16	9 1/16	6 1/16	Park Co., CO	Michael F. Kwak	Michael F. Kwak	2002	27
15 2/16	8 14/16	6 4/16	Fraser River, BC	Tom L. Sword	Tom & Mary Sword	2002	27
15 1/16	8 14/16	6 3/16	Missoula Co., MT	Dale A. Rivers	Dale A. Rivers	1994	32
15 1/16	8 11/16	6 6/16	Lamb Creek, BC	W. Justin McCormick	W. Justin McCormick	2000	32

			Locality	Hunter	Owner	Year	Rank
15 1/16	8 12/16	6 5/16	Missoula Co., MT	Gary L. Zabel	Gary L. Zabel	2000	32
15 1/16	8 15/16	6 2/16	Rio Arriba Co., NM	Dean McInnis	Dean McInnis	2001	32
15 1/16	8 14/16	6 3/16	Archuleta Co., CO	Kenneth D. Smith	Kenneth D. Smith	2002	32
15 1/16	8 12/16	6 5/16	Castle River, AB	Flint J. Simpson	Flint J. Simpson	2003	32
15 1/16	8 12/16	6 5/16	Lake Koocanusa, BC	Joseph Kotlarz	Joseph Kotlarz	2003	32
15 1/16	8 12/16	6 5/16	Rio Arriba Co., NM	Michael J. Leonard	Michael J. Leonard	2003	32
15	8 14/16	6 2/16	Wallowa Co., OR	John M. Chung	John M. Chung	1998	40
15	8 13/16	6 3/16	Rio Arriba Co., NM	Bruce E. Young	Bruce E. Young	2000	40
15	8 12/16	6 4/16	Carbon Co., WY	Jody T. Nordin	Jody T. Nordin	2000	40
15	9	6	Custer Co., ID	Jay D. Roche	Jay D. Roche	2001	40
15	8 10/16	6 6/16	Carbon Co., UT	Gary A. Sholund	Gary A. Sholund	2002	40
15	8 15/16	6 1/16	Okanogan Co., WA	Randy L. Anderson	R.L. & M. Anderson	2002	40
15	9	6	Bull River, BC	Joseph A. Borgna	Joseph A. Borgna	2002	40
14 15/16	8 11/16	6 4/16	Wallowa Co., OR	Houston W. Landrus	Houston W. Landrus	1994	47
14 15/16	8 13/16	6 2/16	Caribou Co., ID	Charles Faulkner	Charles Faulkner	2002	47
14 15/16	8 15/16	6	Tooele Co., UT	Robert E. Brown	Robert E. Brown	2002	47
14 14/16	8 12/16	6 2/16	Carbon Co., UT	John Z. Wise	John Z. Wise	2001	50
14 13/16	8 13/16	6	Drywood Creek, AB	Martin B. Gregory	Martin B. Gregory	2000	51
14 13/16	8 12/16	6 1/16	Buckskin Lake, BC	Kenneth R. Sardegna	Kenneth R. Sardegna	2001	51
14 13/16	8 11/16	6 2/16	Deer Lodge Co., MT	Chad M. Klanecky	Chad M. Klanecky	2002	51
14 12/16	8 11/16	6 1/16	Moffat Co., CO	Michael W. Brown	Michael W. Brown	2000	54
14 12/16	8 14/16	5 14/16	Piute Co., UT	Carl L. Biscontini	Carl L. Biscontini	2001	54
14 12/16	8 12/16	6	Lewis Co., ID	Paul R. DuPont, Jr.	Paul R. DuPont, Jr.	2001	54
14 12/16	8 12/16	6	Archuleta Co., CO	Daniel F. Sehr	Daniel F. Sehr	2002	54
14 12/16	8 11/16	6 1/16	Valley Co., ID	Floyd L. Walters, Jr.	Floyd L. Walters, Jr.	2002	54
14 11/16	8 10/16	6 1/16	San Juan Co., NM	Michael J. Leonard	Michael J. Leonard	1990	59
14 11/16	8 9/16	6 2/16	Johnson Co., WY	Bradley R. Vargo	Bradley R. Vargo	2001	59
14 11/16	8 9/16	6 2/16	San Miguel Co., CO	Chris Conley	Chris Conley	2003	59
14 11/16	8 14/16	5 12/16	Moffat Co., CO	David L. Burke	David L. Burke	1995	62
14 10/16	8 8/16	6 2/16	Idaho Co., ID	Ralph F. Lafferty, Jr.	Ralph F. Lafferty, Jr.	2000	62
14 10/16	8 8/16	6 2/16	Spokane Co., WA	Monty L. Pyle	Monty L. Pyle	2001	62
14 10/16	8 11/16	5 15/16	Duchesne Co., UT	Robert C. Chapoose, Jr.	Robert C. Chapoose, Jr.	2001	62
14 10/16	8 9/16	6 1/16	Elko Co., NV	Ben F. Carter III	Ben F. Carter III	2001	62
14 10/16	8 11/16	5 15/16	Juab Co., UT	David B. Nielsen	David B. Nielsen	2002	62
14 10/16	8 10/16	5 15/16	Las Animas Co., CO	Jarrod S. Wiggins	Jarrod S. Wiggins	1999	68
14 9/16	8 9/16	6	Madison Co., MT	Lloyd L. Wilson III	Lloyd L. Wilson III	2001	68
14 9/16	8 9/16	6	Daggett Co., UT	Michael W. Still	Michael W. Still	2001	68
14 9/16	8 9/16	6	Dolores Co., CO	Jason H. Pieper	Jason H. Pieper	2002	68
14 9/16	8 9/16	6	Eureka Co., NV	Anton Gossein	Anton Gossein	2002	68
14 9/16	8 10/16	5 15/16	Elko Co., NV	Robert L. Badger	Robert L. Badger	2003	68
14 8/16	8 6/16	6 2/16	Sublette Co., WY	Louis Roberts	Louis Roberts	1997	74

489

COUGAR

Felis concolor hippolestes and related subspecies

Score	Greatest Length of Skull Without Lower Jaw	Greatest Width of Skull	Locality	Hunter	Owner	Date Killed	Rank
14 8/16	8 5/16	6 3/16	Sanders Co., MT	Butch Meilinger	Butch Meilinger	1998	74
14 8/16	8 8/16	6	Lemhi Co., ID	David S. Erway, Jr.	David S. Erway, Jr.	2000	74
14 8/16	8 8/16	6	Lewis & Clark Co., MT	Delmar E. Hayden	Delmar E. Hayden	2000	74
14 8/16	8 9/16	5 15/16	Elko Co., NV	James A. Boulton	James A. Boulton	2000	74
14 8/16	8 10/16	5 14/16	Larimer Co., CO	Thomas D. Lundgren	Thomas D. Lundgren	2002	74
15 10/16*	9 3/16	6 7/16	Sibbald Flat, AB	Richard J. Howden	Richard J. Howden	2002	
15 9/16*	9 2/16	6 7/16	Heath Creek, AB	Frank Popson	F. & K. Popson	2001	

* Final score subject to revision by additional verifying measurements.

ATLANTIC WALRUS

Odobenus rosmarus rosmarus

The geographical boundary for Atlantic walrus is basically the Arctic and Atlantic coasts south to Massachusetts. More specifically the Atlantic walrus boundary in Canada extends westward to Mould Bay of Prince Patrick Island, to just east of Cape George Richards of Melville Island and to Taloyoak, Nunavut Province (formerly known as Spence Bay, Northwest Territories); and eastward to include trophies taken in Greenland.

Score	Entire Length of Loose Tusk R.	L.	Circumference of Base R.	L.	Circumference at the Third Quarter R.	L.	Locality	Hunter	Owner	Date Killed	Rank
95 6/8	24 4/8	25 1/8	6 6/8	6 4/8	4 3/8	4 3/8	Foxe Basin, NU	Porter Hicks	B&C National Collection	2001	1
95 2/8	22 4/8	22 1/8	7 2/8	7 1/8	4 6/8	4 3/8	Foxe Basin, NU	Ralph F. Merkley	Ralph F. Merkley	2002	2

PACIFIC WALRUS

Odobenus rosmarus divergens

Minimum Score 100

World's Record 147 4/8

The geographical boundary for Pacific walrus is: That portion of the Bering Sea east of the International Dateline; south along coastal Alaska, including the Pribilof Islands and Bristol Bay; extending eastward into Canada to the southwest coasts of Banks and Victoria Islands and the mouth of Bathurst Inlet in Nunavut Province (formerly the northwest portion of Northwest Territories).

Score	Entire Length of Loose Tusk R.	L.	Circumference of Base R.	L.	Circumference at the Third Quarter R.	L.	Locality	Hunter	Owner	Date Killed	Rank
132 4/8	31 5/8	31 6/8	9	9	7 6/8	7 1/8	Goodnews Bay, AK	Picked Up	Jim Riggle	2000	1
115 2/8	32 2/8	31 5/8	6 6/8	6 7/8	5 4/8	5 4/8	St. Lawrence Island, AK	Unknown	P.J. Londo	2001	2
108 6/8	24 6/8	24 5/8	8 3/8	8 6/8	5 6/8	5 7/8	Naknek, AK	Picked Up	Dean Collins	1982	3

492

AMERICAN ELK - TYPICAL ANTLERS

Cervus elaphus nelsoni and certain related subspecies

Minimum Score 360

Score	Length of Main Beam R.	L.	Inside Spread	Circumference at Smallest Place Between First & Second Points R.	L.	Number of Points R.	L.	Locality	Hunter	Owner	Date Killed	Rank
411 3/8	55 5/8	56 5/8	52 3/8	9 6/8	9 5/8	6	7	Rosebud Co., MT	Chuck Adams	Chuck Adams	2000	1
410 5/8	59 2/8	59	41 1/8	8 6/8	8 4/8	7	8	Routt Co., CO	Henry Staats	Cabela's, Inc.	1879	2
407 4/8	52	54 6/8	43	8 6/8	9 1/8	6	6	Carbon Co., WY	Picked Up	Clarence D. Heinrich	1999	3
401 7/8	59 7/8	59 5/8	39 3/8	8 5/8	8 6/8	6	6	White Mtn. Indian Res., AZ	Picked Up	Cabela's, Inc.	1991	4
396 7/8	51 7/8	49 5/8	33 3/8	8 6/8	8 4/8	6	6	Catron Co., NM	Picked Up	Robert J. Seeds	2002	5
396 1/8	56 6/8	56 7/8	39 5/8	8 2/8	8 2/8	7	7	Moffat Co., CO	Ron Moser	Cabela's, Inc.	PR1958	6
394 2/8	52 3/8	52 1/8	49	9 2/8	8 6/8	7	7	Utah Co., UT	Lynn O. Grant	Lynn O. Grant	2003	7
393 6/8	54 7/8	53 5/8	40	9 6/8	9 6/8	6	6	Greenlee Co., AZ	R. Alan Pennington	R. Alan Pennington	1999	8
393 2/8	51 4/8	53	43 6/8	7 6/8	7 4/8	6	6	Sanders Co., MT	Kenneth R. Groh	Kenneth R. Groh	2000	9
392 1/8	58 6/8	59 5/8	53 4/8	7 4/8	7 6/8	6	8	Coconino Co., AZ	Calvin Newmann	Cabela's, Inc.	1993	10
391 6/8	55 6/8	55 7/8	49 6/8	10 4/8	10	6	7	El Paso Co., CO	Fred Long	Cabela's, Inc.	1903	11
391 5/8	63 6/8	62	45 3/8	9 4/8	8 7/8	7	6	Jefferson Co., OR	Unknown	Chuck Hoyt	PR1940	12
391 2/8	57 4/8	59 7/8	47 4/8	8 6/8	8 5/8	6	6	Montana	Doug Dawson	Cabela's, Inc.	1939	13
390 6/8	53 6/8	53 5/8	47 6/8	8 2/8	8 1/8	6	6	Cibola Co., NM	Lee A. Schawe	Lee A. Schawe	2001	14
390 5/8	58	61	44 3/8	9 4/8	9	6	7	Catron Co., NM	Picked Up	Robert J. Seeds	2001	15
389 7/8	64 4/8	64 4/8	42 7/8	8 1/8	8 7/8	6	6	Chelan Co., WA	Unknown	RMEF - Colockum Chapter	1947	16
389 7/8	54 1/8	55 5/8	48 7/8	9 4/8	9 3/8	6	6	Sevier Co., UT	O. Howard Shattuck	O. Howard Shattuck	2002	16
389 3/8	60 3/8	63 4/8	48 3/8	11 5/8	11 5/8	5	5	Modoc Co., CA	Kasey M. Criss	Kasey M. Criss	2003	18
388	55	57 2/8	42	9 5/8	9 4/8	7	7	White Pine Co., NV	Thomas M. Brunson	Thomas M. Brunson	2001	19
385 6/8	53 3/8	59 2/8	40 4/8	8 6/8	9	7	6	Graham Co., AZ	Dwayne E. Heikes	Dwayne E. Heikes	2003	20
385 3/8	51	51 5/8	36 1/8	9 6/8	10 1/8	7	6	Park Co., WY	Don W. Rogers	Don W. Rogers	2001	21
385 3/8	51 7/8	52 1/8	40 7/8	10 7/8	10 2/8	7	7	Garfield Co., UT	Raymond D. Fowler	Raymond D. Fowler	2003	21
385 2/8	57 1/8	57	44	9 4/8	10 3/8	7	6	Park Co., WY	Brian R. Morency	Brian R. Morency	2000	23
384 3/8	56 4/8	53 3/8	36 6/8	11 4/8	12 6/8	6	7	Apache Co., AZ	John A. Cardwell	John A. Cardwell	2001	24
384 3/8	53 4/8	54 5/8	52 5/8	9 3/8	9 2/8	6	6	Beaver Co., UT	Greg D. Myers	Greg D. Myers	2002	24
383 7/8	56 3/8	56 6/8	41 1/8	8 5/8	8 6/8	6	6	Apache Co., AZ	Jerry Wascom	Jerry Wascom	2001	26
383 2/8	57 6/8	58	39 6/8	8 4/8	8 4/8	7	7	Otero Co., NM	Larry Stifflemire	Larry Stifflemire	2001	27
382 5/8	52 5/8	53 2/8	37 1/8	10 4/8	10 5/8	7	7	Dolores Co., CO	Andrea Holley	Andrea Holley	2000	28
382 5/8	53 7/8	53 3/8	44	9 4/8	9 3/8	6	7	Rich Co., UT	Thomas C. Hodges	Thomas C. Hodges	2003	28
382 3/8	53 7/8	56 2/8	41 7/8	9 2/8	8 6/8	6	6	Klickitat Co., WA	Johnny T. Walker	Johnny T. Walker	1965	30
382 2/8	57 6/8	56 3/8	38 4/8	8 7/8	9 2/8	7	7	Apache Co., AZ	Alan D. Hamberlin	Alan D. Hamberlin	2000	31
382 2/8	50 2/8	50 7/8	42 4/8	9 5/8	9 5/8	6	6	Rich Co., UT	Marty Halpern	Marty Halpern	2002	31

AMERICAN ELK - TYPICAL ANTLERS

Cervus elaphus nelsoni and certain related subspecies

Score	Length of Main Beam R.	L.	Inside Spread	Circumference at Smallest Place Between First & Second Points R.	L.	Number of Points R.	L.	Locality	Hunter	Owner	Date Killed	Rank
381 5/8	60 7/8	60 5/8	38 3/8	9 3/8	9 1/8	6	6	White Pine Co., NV	Zane D. Terry	Zane D. Terry	2002	33
381 2/8	61 6/8	61	51 2/8	9 3/8	8	6	6	Coconino Co., AZ	Bernie Smits	Bernie Smits	2001	34
380 7/8	56 2/8	55 2/8	38 3/8	8 5/8	8	7	7	Navajo Co., AZ	Thomas D. Friedkin	Thomas D. Friedkin	2003	35
380 5/8	62 4/8	65 3/8	49	8 5/8	8 4/8	6	8	Custer Co., ID	Mark Williams	Cabela's, Inc.	1976	36
380 4/8	57 2/8	57 7/8	42 6/8	8 7/8	9 5/8	6	6	Grant Co., NM	Ryhan I. Peralta	Ryhan I. Peralta	2001	37
380	53 1/8	54	43 6/8	7 4/8	7 3/8	6	6	Blaine Co., ID	Howard W. Holmes	Howard W. Holmes	2001	38
379 6/8	56 2/8	54	47	11 5/8	9 5/8	6	6	Carbon Co., UT	Paul J. Barton	Paul J. Barton	2002	39
379 5/8	54 5/8	52 3/8	40 1/8	9 2/8	9 5/8	7	6	Gila Co., AZ	Bennie J. Rossetto	Bennie J. Rossetto	2001	40
379 4/8	59 2/8	61	39 6/8	7 5/8	7 5/8	6	6	King Co., WA	M. Sayers & L. Read	Michael L. Sayers	2003	41
378 7/8	59 5/8	57 6/8	47 6/8	9 6/8	8 6/8	7	6	Millard Co., UT	Michael T. Kinney	Michael T. Kinney	2000	42
378 5/8	50 7/8	53 3/8	44 7/8	8 4/8	8 4/8	6	6	White Pine Co., NV	George N. DeLong	George N. DeLong	2001	43
378	52 6/8	51 7/8	42 2/8	8 2/8	8 1/8	7	7	Cache Co., UT	Cory L. Jensen	Cory L. Jensen	2000	44
378	57 3/8	53 7/8	40 4/8	9 2/8	9 4/8	7	7	Teton Co., WY	Jessica L. Hedges	Jessica L. Hedges	2000	44
378	55 3/8	50 7/8	40	9 5/8	9	6	6	Otero Co., NM	Scott M. Spangler	Scott M. Spangler	2001	44
378	50	50 5/8	42 2/8	8 5/8	8 6/8	6	6	Johnson Co., WY	Richard A. Paradis	Richard A. Paradis	2001	44
378	56 2/8	56	46 2/8	8 3/8	8 2/8	6	6	Piute Co., UT	Michael G. Burr	Michael G. Burr	2003	44
377 7/8	52	51 6/8	41 5/8	8 1/8	9	6	6	Millard Co., UT	Reed Mellor	Reed Mellor	2002	49
377 4/8	56 7/8	54 1/8	46 2/8	9 1/8	9 2/8	6	6	Jefferson Co., MT	Paul H. Temple	Gary L. Temple	1927	50
377 3/8	53 6/8	53 6/8	45 7/8	9 1/8	9 2/8	6	6	Lawrence Co., SD	Larry Miller	Larry Miller	1980	51
376 5/8	54 6/8	56 2/8	45 3/8	9 2/8	9 4/8	6	6	Coconino Co., AZ	Brent V. Trumbo	Brent V. Trumbo	1999	52
376 2/8	52 4/8	52 4/8	46 2/8	10 1/8	10	7	7	Juab Co., UT	Andrea McPherson	Andrea McPherson	2003	53
376 1/8	51	51 2/8	42 1/8	9	8 4/8	6	6	Bear Lake Co., ID	Gary J. Christiansen	Gary J. Christiansen	2002	54
375 5/8	55 6/8	57 6/8	41 7/8	9 3/8	9 4/8	6	6	Billings Co., ND	Monte Hoggarth	Monte Hoggarth	2000	55
375 4/8	53 1/8	53 1/8	38 6/8	7 6/8	8 1/8	7	7	Broadwater Co., MT	Joel S. Taylor	Joel S. Taylor	2001	56
375 2/8	54 4/8	54	47 2/8	8 3/8	8	6	6	Multnomah Co., OR	Charles E. Feldhacker	Charles E. Feldhacker	2001	57
375 2/8	55 2/8	55 6/8	49	8 6/8	8 1/8	6	6	Coconino Co., AZ	John H. Noble III	John H. Noble III	2003	57
372 6/8	53	55	43 6/8	8 6/8	8 6/8	6	6	Socorro Co., NM	Douglas H. Sharp	Douglas H. Sharp	2002	59
372 6/8	50 3/8	51 6/8	38 2/8	8	7 4/8	7	7	Natrona Co., WY	Grant E. Pozarnsky	Grant E. Pozarnsky	2002	59
372 1/8	53 2/8	52 5/8	48 5/8	8 7/8	8 2/8	6	6	Catron Co., NM	Robert S. Sanders	Robert S. Sanders	2001	61
371 7/8	52 6/8	50	46 5/8	8 5/8	8 1/8	6	6	Todd Co., SD	Justin B. Boyd	Justin B. Boyd	2001	62
371 2/8	53 4/8	54 2/8	45 2/8	8 5/8	8	6	6	Park Co., WY	Victoria J. Palen	Victoria J. Palen	2001	63
371	54 6/8	53 2/8	36 6/8	9 6/8	9 7/8	6	7	Birch Hills, SK	Gerald H. Hills	Gerald H. Hills	2002	64

Score								Locality			Date	Rank
370 6/8	57 3/8	56 5/8	41 4/8	8 2/8	8 2/8	6	7	Montana	Unknown	Robert E. Clark	1930	65
370 6/8	56	55 6/8	40 2/8	9 3/8	9 2/8	6	6	Park Co., MT	John H. King	John H. King	1960	65
370 4/8	52 6/8	52 5/8	48 4/8	8 3/8	7 7/8	7	6	Catron Co., NM	Barry L. Stafford	Barry L. Stafford	2001	67
370 4/8	52 4/8	55	45 4/8	7 6/8	7 5/8	6	6	Coconino Co., AZ	William J. Mayer	William J. Mayer	2002	67
370 2/8	48 6/8	49 6/8	41 6/8	8 6/8	8 5/8	6	7	Clearwater Co., ID	Gordon F. Larson	Gordon F. Larson	1973	69
370 1/8	51 1/8	52 7/8	43 5/8	8	7 5/8	6	6	Douglas Co., CO	Gregory J. Voeltz	Gregory J. Voeltz	2002	70
370	58 1/8	59 5/8	40	9 3/8	9 3/8	6	6	Iron Co., UT	Dean Davis	Dean Davis	2002	71
369 2/8	57 6/8	55 1/8	38	11 1/8	10 3/8	6	6	Sierra Co., NM	Jerome C. Garcia	Jerome C. Garcia	2001	72
369	51 2/8	50 4/8	55	7	7	6	6	Las Animas Co., CO	Grant C. Adkisson	Grant C. Adkisson	2003	73
368 7/8	50	49 2/8	44 1/8	9 4/8	8 7/8	6	6	Teton Co., WY	William K. Douglas	William K. Douglas	2002	74
368 6/8	52	54 1/8	39 2/8	9 1/8	8 6/8	6	6	Tooele Co., UT	Gary L. Gray	Gary L. Gray	2002	75
368 6/8	48 6/8	45 4/8	37 4/8	8 2/8	8 2/8	6	6	Wasatch Co., UT	Leroy Hampton	Leroy Hampton	2003	75
368 4/8	54 4/8	54 1/8	39	8 5/8	9	6	6	Sheridan Co., WY	Edward R. Kline, Jr.	Edward R. Kline, Jr.	2001	77
367 7/8	54 2/8	54 7/8	42 5/8	8 3/8	7 4/8	7	7	Elko Co., NV	Raylene L. Naveran	Raylene L. Naveran	2002	78
367	53 5/8	55 5/8	45 4/8	8 7/8	8 7/8	6	6	Boulder Co., CO	Keith B. Bergum	Keith B. Bergum	2002	79
367	54 1/8	52	50 6/8	7 2/8	7 3/8	6	6	Sevier Co., UT	Jason T. Slatter	Jason T. Slatter	2003	79
366 1/8	52 1/8	51 2/8	38 1/8	10 5/8	10 2/8	6	6	Beaver Co., UT	Douglas L. Marx	Douglas L. Marx	2001	81
365 4/8	51 1/8	51 2/8	39 6/8	7 4/8	7 7/8	6	6	Uintah Co., UT	Steven F. Thompson	Steven F. Thompson	2001	82
365	58 1/8	53 4/8	45 4/8	9 4/8	9 3/8	6	6	Sweet Grass Co., MT	Dennis D. McDonald	Dennis D. McDonald	2001	83
364 7/8	55 1/8	53 5/8	40 7/8	8 1/8	9 4/8	6	6	Catron Co., NM	Todd M. Hewing	Todd M. Hewing	2001	84
363 2/8	53 7/8	54	46 6/8	9	9	6	6	Catron Co., NM	Lowry W. Hunt III	Lowry W. Hunt III	2003	85
363	56 2/8	54 1/8	43 2/8	8 7/8	8 3/8	6	6	Powder River Co., MT	Mark Kayser	Mark Kayser	2002	86
362 4/8	52 6/8	55 1/8	49 2/8	7 4/8	7 5/8	7	6	Kittitas Co., WA	Frank A. Walker	Douglas W. Walker	1933	87
362 1/8	55 2/8	57 3/8	43 3/8	8 2/8	8 5/8	6	6	Teton Co., ID	Robert Hansen	Robert Hansen	1994	88
362	55 2/8	56 2/8	47 2/8	8 3/8	8 7/8	6	6	Mineral Co., MT	Tony Gullie	Darren J. Page	1982	89
362	54	53 7/8	54 4/8	9 2/8	9 6/8	7	7	Lewis & Clark Co., MT	Jerald Buck	Jerald Buck	2001	89
361 7/8	47 7/8	46 3/8	42 7/8	9 1/8	9 1/8	6	6	Apache Co., AZ	Richard J. Burick	Richard J. Burick	2001	91
361 2/8	52 3/8	52 1/8	41 6/8	9 5/8	9 1/8	7	7	Garfield Co., MT	Bryant A. Shermoe	Bryant A. Shermoe	2001	92
361 1/8	56 3/8	56 7/8	47 3/8	9 1/8	8 4/8	6	6	Sanpete Co., UT	Sharon R. Sterud	Sharon R. Sterud	2002	93
361	52 5/8	53 1/8	37 5/8	9 3/8	9 3/8	6	7	McBride Lake, SK	Donald R. Urzada	Donald R. Urzada	2003	94
360 5/8	49 7/8	48 5/8	33 1/8	8 7/8	9 5/8	6	6	Lincoln Co., NM	Trevor H. Enoch	Trevor H. Enoch	2001	95
360 3/8	51	50 6/8	46 1/8	9 7/8	10 6/8	6	6	Teton Co., WY	Brian B. Frost	Brian B. Frost	2001	96
360 2/8	51 3/8	53 1/8	39 2/8	7 5/8	8	6	6	White Pine Co., NV	Roger B. Whomes	Roger B. Whomes	2002	97
360 1/8	47	47 3/8	36 3/8	8 1/8	8 1/8	6	6	Park Co., WY	William D. Lee	William D. Lee	2003	98
360 1/8	52 5/8	52 6/8	46 5/8	8 1/8	8 6/8	7	8	Hot Springs Co., WY	Joseph A. Skorupski	Joseph A. Skorupski	2001	98
360	56 7/8	57 4/8	38	8 6/8	8 6/8	6	6	Park Co., WY	Samuel Z. Chamberlain	Samuel Z. Chamberlain	2002	100
360	51 5/8	52	38	7 7/8	7 5/8	6	6	Garfield Co., UT	Mitch L. Ellis	Mitch L. Ellis	2003	100
402 4/8*	56 3/8	58 4/8	44 6/8	10 1/8	10 6/8	6	6	Emery Co., UT	Brian J. Gilson	Brian J. Gilson	2003	
399 6/8*	51 3/8	52 2/8	36	9 6/8	9 4/8	7	7	White Pine Co., NV	Troy A. Means	Troy A. Means	2000	
396 7/8*	55 3/8	55 5/8	44 1/8	9 3/8	10 3/8	7	6	Garfield Co., UT	Ryan D. Brindley	Ryan D. Brindley	2003	

* Final score subject to revision by additional verifying measurements.

AMERICAN ELK - NON-TYPICAL ANTLERS

Cervus elaphus nelsoni and certain related subspecies

Minimum Score 385

World's Record 465 2/8

Score	Length of Main Beam R.	L.	Inside Spread	Circumference at Smallest Place Between First & Second Points R.	L.	Number of Points R.	L.	Locality	Hunter	Owner	Date Killed	Rank
444 4/8	54 6/8	52 6/8	52 2/8	9 4/8	9 4/8	9	10	Coconino Co., AZ	Ronald N. Franklin	Ronald N. Franklin	2003	1
442 3/8	53 7/8	49 7/8	44	8 7/8	9 2/8	7	8	Gila Co., AZ	Dan J. Agnew	Dan J. Agnew	2001	2
434 3/8	48 4/8	47	35 3/8	9 2/8	9 1/8	8	9	Colfax Co., NM	Lawrence Sanchez	Ed Sanchez	PR1962	3
430 2/8	56	55 7/8	49 7/8	7 7/8	8 2/8	8	9	Rio Blanco Co., CO	William D. Deweese	Royal Gorge Reg. Mus. & Hist. Cent.	1888	4
429 6/8	49 1/8	49 6/8	40	9 7/8	10 1/8	9	9	Navajo Co., AZ	Clay R. Heuett	Clay R. Heuett	2003	5
421 7/8	55	54	50 1/8	8 1/8	8 4/8	8	9	Kittitas Co., WA	Jeffrey G. Thorpe	Jeffrey G. Thorpe	2003	6
416 5/8	56 5/8	55 4/8	46	8 7/8	9 6/8	7	8	Cibola Co., NM	Jack Mettler	Jack Mettler	2001	7
415 3/8	53 7/8	56 4/8	46 1/8	8 1/8	8 1/8	9	8	Steamboat Springs, CO	O.V. Johnson	Cabela's, Inc.	1952	8
414 6/8	56 1/8	46 2/8	41	9 1/8	9 3/8	7	8	Navajo Co., AZ	James M. Cardwell	James M. Cardwell	2001	9
414	43 6/8	44 7/8	34 5/8	10 2/8	11	9	10	Unknown	Unknown	Daniel F. Habjanetz	1858	10
413 2/8	56	57	45 5/8	8 6/8	8 4/8	7	7	Coconino Co., AZ	Erik W. Swanson	Erik W. Swanson	2001	11
412	53 4/8	53 4/8	44	11 5/8	11 1/8	7	8	Utah Co., UT	Jeffrey L. Didericksen	Jeffrey L. Didericksen	2002	12
411 6/8	52 7/8	50 4/8	49	9 6/8	9 2/8	9	7	Gallatin Co., MT	Unknown	Cabela's, Inc.	1965	13
407 2/8	53 7/8	47 2/8	48 7/8	9 7/8	9 1/8	8	8	Apache Co., AZ	Jay A. Kellett	Jay A. Kellett	2001	14
406 3/8	55 5/8	51 2/8	49 6/8	9 5/8	9 3/8	7	7	Beaver Co., UT	Donald J. Willden	Donald J. Willden	2003	15
405 5/8	53 1/8	50	38 4/8	9 4/8	8 5/8	7	8	Gila Co., AZ	R.J. Smith	R.J. Smith	2003	16
404 6/8	53 2/8	53 6/8	36 7/8	9 6/8	11 3/8	8	8	Juab Co., UT	David L. Naylor	David L. Naylor	2003	17
404 4/8	48	47 5/8	48 6/8	8 2/8	8 3/8	9	8	Flathead Indian Res., MT	Jimmie Walker	Cabela's, Inc.	PR1991	18
403	57 2/8	53 6/8	31 6/8	10 5/8	10 4/8	8	8	Park Co., MT	Casey E. Turner	Casey E. Turner	2003	19
402 3/8	53 3/8	49 6/8	47 5/8	8 3/8	8 5/8	7	8	Idaho	Unknown	Cabela's, Inc.	PR1997	20
401 7/8	54 3/8	52	46 3/8	9	10	7	8	Fergus Co., MT	Raymond J. Koch	Raymond J. Koch	2000	21
400 6/8	55 1/8	55	50 5/8	7 6/8	7 7/8	7	7	Mesa Co., CO	Leland J. Cox	Leland J. Cox	2003	22
400 2/8	52 7/8	52 3/8	42 1/8	8	7 6/8	8	7	Lemhi Co., ID	Bill Kelly	Bill Kelly	1967	23
399 6/8	56 7/8	52	42 5/8	8 4/8	8 4/8	7	6	White Pine Co., NV	Stephanie C. Hull	Stephanie C. Hull	2000	24
399 3/8	59 3/8	60 4/8	43 3/8	9 2/8	10 2/8	7	7	Navajo Co., AZ	Marvin Brawley, Jr.	Pat E. Powell	2003	25
396 4/8	42 5/8	46 4/8	40 6/8	10 7/8	12 2/8	9	7	Tooele Co., UT	Jess Scott	Jess Scott	2003	26
395	54	52 2/8	39 2/8	8 2/8	7 7/8	7	6	Unknown	Unknown	Cabela's, Inc.	PR2001	27
394 4/8	31 6/8	30 3/8	33 2/8	10 4/8	10 2/8	10	12	Greenlee Co., AZ	Picked Up	Jaclyn M. Serfass	2002	28
394 4/8	46	47 2/8	35 1/8	11	10 1/8	9	9	Sandridge, MB	Joel Kayer	Joel Kayer	2003	28
393 6/8	55 2/8	51 6/8	39 5/8	9 3/8	9 1/8	7	7	Yakima Co., WA	Jim Swanson	Cabela's, Inc.	PR1963	30
392 7/8	54 1/8	56 4/8	41	8 5/8	8 4/8	9	8	Morkill River, BC	Picked Up	BC Mineral, Water, Land & Air	2003	31

392 7/8	55	54 1/8	45 3/8	8 7/8	9 1/8	7	7	Bowron River, BC	Greg Loring	Greg Loring	2003	31
392 2/8	54	55 2/8	47 2/8	9	8 1/8	8	8	Granite Co., MT	Robert E. Steffan	Robert E. Steffan	1956	33
392 2/8	55 6/8	56 1/8	39 5/8	10 6/8	10	8	6	Powder River Co., MT	Picked Up	Mark Kayser	1998	33
391 6/8	50 4/8	50 5/8	38 1/8	8 1/8	8 6/8	7	7	Columbia Co., WA	Ryan W. Block	Ryan W. Block	1999	35
391 3/8	54 7/8	55 2/8	42 6/8	10 2/8	10 4/8	7	7	Cibola Co., NM	Charlie Tamez, Jr.	Charlie Tamez, Jr.	1999	36
391 3/8	49	51 2/8	48 5/8	8 5/8	8 6/8	8	6	Gila Co., AZ	James P. Mellody, Jr.	James P. Mellody, Jr.	2001	36
391 1/8	49 4/8	49 5/8	46 3/8	10	10 6/8	8	7	Fergus Co., MT	Matthew D. McWilliams	Matthew D. McWilliams	2001	38
389 7/8	50 4/8	52 5/8	34 2/8	8 6/8	8	9	7	Apache Co., AZ	Mark C. Harlow	Mark C. Harlow	2001	39
389 7/8	50 7/8	49 7/8	43 3/8	8 6/8	8 6/8	7	7	Albany Co., WY	Paul H. Reeder	Paul H. Reeder	2001	39
388 6/8	50 5/8	48 1/8	45	8 6/8	8 1/8	7	7	Shoshone Co., ID	Roger R. Davis	Aly M. Bruner	1978	41
388 4/8	50 2/8	50 5/8	42	9 3/8	9 1/8	7	6	Saguache Co., CO	Anthony J. Heil	Anthony J. Heil	2000	42
387 3/8	52 4/8	54 5/8	30 5/8	7 2/8	7 7/8	7	7	Pierce Co., WA	Wayne C. Milton	Craig S. Milton	2000	43
387 3/8	50	52 1/8	51 2/8	9 4/8	9 5/8	6	7	Garfield Co., UT	David R. Martin	David R. Martin	2003	43
387 2/8	48 6/8	48 3/8	37 3/8	8 5/8	8 5/8	7	7	Catron Co., NM	Robert J. Brooks	Cabela's, Inc.	1992	45
387	46 2/8	44	43	9	8 6/8	8	8	Crook Co., WY	Birch A. Negaard	Birch A. Negaard	2000	46
387	55 6/8	53 4/8	45 1/8	7	7 1/8	7	9	Navajo Co., AZ	Gary W. Crowe	Gary W. Crowe	2003	46
386 6/8	45 5/8	45 7/8	47 3/8	7	7	8	11	Unknown	Unknown	Donald F. Belker	PR1981	48
386 1/8	56	54 1/8	39	10 2/8	10 3/8	7	6	Lincoln Co., NV	Jason House	Jason House	2001	49
385 6/8	47 2/8	50	37	7 3/8	8 2/8	8	8	Socorro Co., NM	Kim C. Haberland	Kim C. Haberland	2002	50
444 4/8*	56 5/8	54 2/8	40	9 1/8	11 4/8	8	13	Arm Lake, AB	John Almberg	John Almberg	1999	
434 1/8*	53 5/8	54 3/8	51	10 4/8	10 4/8	7	10	British Columbia	Picked Up	Neal Hutchinson	PR1993	
424 6/8*	56 2/8	51 7/8	52 6/8	10 2/8	10 2/8	7	6	Lincoln Co., NV	Cindy S. Marques	Cindy S. Marques	2002	
423 4/8*	58	55 1/8	38 4/8	8 5/8	9 1/8	8	7	Yavapai Co., AZ	Lynn E. Munoz	Lynn E. Munoz	1998	
422 4/8*	55	56 1/8	39 4/8	11 7/8	10 7/8	7	8	Battle River, AB	Brent A. Kuntz	Brent A. Kuntz	2002	

* Final score subject to revision by additional verifying measurements.

ROOSEVELT'S ELK

Cervus elaphus roosevelti

Minimum Score 275

New World's Record 404 6/8

Roosevelt's elk includes trophies from: west of Interstate Highway I-5 in Oregon and Washington; Del Norte, Humboldt, and Trinity Counties, California, as well as that portion of Siskiyou County west of I-5 in Northern California; Afognak and Raspberry Islands of Alaska; and Vancouver Island, British Columbia.

Score	Length of Main Beam R.	L.	Inside Spread	Circumference at Smallest Place Between First & Second Points R.	L.	Number of Points R.	L.	Locality	Hunter	Owner	Date Killed	Rank
404 6/8	54 1/8	57 5/8	40 6/8	8 2/8	9 4/8	9	8	Benton Co., OR	Jason S. Ballard	Jason S. Ballard	2002	1
374 3/8	50	47	42	9 2/8	8 5/8	8	8	Bonanza Lake, BC	Ronald K. Bridge	Ronald K. Bridge	2002	2
357 7/8	54 6/8	56 1/8	42 7/8	8 6/8	8 5/8	7	6	Siskiyou Co., CA	Angela M. Cheula	Angela M. Cheula	2000	3
356 2/8	48 5/8	50 7/8	38 1/8	9 2/8	9 6/8	8	7	Campbell River, BC	James L.M. Amos	James L.M. Amos	1998	4
356	48 3/8	49 3/8	44 3/8	9 7/8	10 7/8	6	7	Douglas Co., OR	Thomas B. Swanton	Thomas B. Swanton	1953	5
355 4/8	50	52 1/8	42 1/8	9 7/8	10	6	8	Vancouver Island, BC	Picked Up	Bruce Williamson	1955	6
353 5/8	43 1/8	47 5/8	38 2/8	8 4/8	8 2/8	8	6	Coos Co., OR	Ken Wilson	Ken Wilson	1957	7
353 1/8	53 2/8	53 4/8	40 7/8	7 7/8	7 6/8	7	7	Benton Co., OR	William Pitcher	William Pitcher	2003	8
349 3/8	48 2/8	46 2/8	40 3/8	9 3/8	9 3/8	7	7	Bonanza River, BC	Ted Brookman	Ted Brookman	2001	9
345 6/8	54 1/8	54 3/8	35 2/8	8 7/8	9 4/8	7	7	Pacific Co., WA	Norman W. Scott	Raymond W. Scott	1971	10
341 4/8	40 7/8	40 6/8	45	10 6/8	9 2/8	7	7	Grays Harbor Co., WA	Unknown	Jack Adams, Jr.	1997	11
340 4/8	47	48 2/8	36 7/8	9 2/8	9 2/8	7	7	Perry River, BC	Joseph S. Brannen	Joseph S. Brannen	2002	12
340 2/8	49 1/8	43 6/8	33 7/8	11 5/8	10	8	7	Benton Co., OR	Thomas R. Sherman	Thomas R. Sherman	2002	13
336	46 3/8	46 3/8	39 6/8	7 2/8	7 2/8	8	7	Humboldt Co., CA	Jeremy W. Flick	Jeremy W. Flick	2001	14
335 1/8	47 2/8	49 4/8	46 3/8	9 4/8	9 1/8	7	8	Wahkiakum Co., WA	J.W. Robinson & W. Robinson	Jim W. Robinson	1966	15
329	44 2/8	49	38 3/8	7 7/8	8	8	7	Clatsop Co., OR	David G. Bigsby	David G. Bigsby	1962	16
325 7/8	48 4/8	48 2/8	33 5/8	7 5/8	8 1/8	6	8	Humboldt Co., CA	Kevin Atkinson	Kevin Atkinson	2001	17
322 2/8	50	50 4/8	38 6/8	8	7 7/8	6	6	Benton Co., OR	Samuel R. Gray	Samuel R. Gray	2000	18
320 6/8	50	48 7/8	41	7 2/8	7 1/8	7	7	Humboldt Co., CA	Brian J. Noel	Brian J. Noel	2003	19
319 5/8	49 5/8	50 6/8	48	7 6/8	8 3/8	8	9	Curry Co., OR	Jamie L. White	Jamie L. White	1978	20
319 1/8	46 4/8	48	32	7 7/8	7 4/8	7	8	Humboldt Co., CA	Claire C. Hawkins	Claire C. Hawkins	2003	21
318 4/8	51 2/8	48 6/8	38 1/8	9 1/8	9 2/8	8	8	Conuma River, BC	Jason C. Hird	Jason C. Hird	2000	22
318 4/8	49 1/8	48	33 2/8	8 3/8	8 1/8	8	7	Coos Co., OR	Todd Freitag	Todd Freitag	2003	22
316 3/8	48	47 2/8	35	9 7/8	10 4/8	6	7	Del Norte Co., CA	Gary Towers	Gary Towers	2002	24
316 1/8	48 6/8	48 3/8	32 5/8	8	8 1/8	7	6	Humboldt Co., CA	Tod O. Droege	Tod O. Droege	2003	25
313 2/8	47 6/8	48 6/8	31 2/8	8	7 7/8	7	7	Humboldt Co., CA	William Blunt	William Blunt	2002	26
313 1/8	43 5/8	44 1/8	50 1/8	9 1/8	9 1/8	6	7	Yamhill Co., OR	Britt R. Madison	Britt R. Madison	2002	27
312 6/8	41 7/8	43 4/8	33 5/8	9 2/8	8 1/8	9	8	Humboldt Co., CA	Glenn W. Bjorklund	Glenn W. Bjorklund	2002	28
308 3/8	46 4/8	45 7/8	35 3/8	9 5/8	9 6/8	7	8	Clatsop Co., OR	Brian D. Bonnell	Brian D. Bonnell	2000	29

Score								Locality	Hunter	Owner	Date	Rank
308 3/8	49 2/8	44 2/8	41 4/8	7 6/8	7 4/8	6	6	Benton Co., OR	Mark Goracke	Mark Goracke	2002	29
305 7/8	44 7/8	46	38 7/8	9 2/8	9 2/8	7	6	Del Norte Co., CA	Steven Gauvin	Steven Gauvin	2003	31
303	46 6/8	44 3/8	35 3/8	7 5/8	7 4/8	7	7	Humboldt Co., CA	Walter M. Gibson	Walter M. Gibson	2002	32
301 7/8	48 3/8	48	34 5/8	8 2/8	7 6/8	6	7	Benton Co., OR	James R. Rice	James R. Rice	2003	33
301 6/8	39 5/8	40	33 2/8	8 2/8	8 5/8	7	8	Benton Co., OR	Scott Staten	Scott Staten	2000	34
301 5/8	44 5/8	45 5/8	37 7/8	8 1/8	7 6/8	6	6	Columbia Co., OR	Bud Holmes	Bud Holmes	1949	35
301 5/8	44 3/8	48 2/8	37 2/8	9 2/8	9 6/8	6	7	Grays Harbor Co., WA	T. Franklin Stinchfield, Jr.	T. Franklin Stinchfield, Jr.	2001	35
301 4/8	48 2/8	49 3/8	35 7/8	8 5/8	8 6/8	6	7	Jefferson Co., WA	Jeff D. Halsey	Jeff D. Halsey	2001	37
301 1/8	47 4/8	45	35 5/8	9	9 2/8	6	6	Siskiyou Co., WA	Joseph B. Rightmier	Joseph B. Rightmier	2001	38
298	47	47 7/8	34 5/8	7 4/8	7 2/8	6	6	Columbia Co., OR	Richard D. Banzer	Joseph D. Banzer	1959	39
296 6/8	44 2/8	43 7/8	38 5/8	9 1/8	9 1/8	6	6	Coos Co., OR	Ryan K. Gardner	Ryan K. Gardner	2001	40
296 3/8	44 6/8	44 2/8	35 7/8	8 3/8	8 4/8	7	7	Douglas Co., OR	Matthew R. Fullerton	Matthew R. Fullerton	2000	41
295 6/8	43 7/8	45 1/8	34 7/8	8 1/8	8	7	7	Coos Co., OR	Wesley A. Plummer	Wesley A. Plummer	2001	42
294 4/8	46 4/8	48 2/8	34 7/8	9 1/8	8 4/8	6	8	Washington Co., OR	Chris Zurbrugg	Chris Zurbrugg	1996	43
293 3/8	43 6/8	44 1/8	43 7/8	8 4/8	8 5/8	6	6	Coos Co., OR	Ken Wilson	Ken Wilson	2001	44
292 7/8	44 1/8	47 4/8	36 4/8	8 4/8	8 4/8	6	7	Siskiyou Co., CA	Gearen L. Nugent	Gearen L. Nugent	2001	45
291 7/8	39 6/8	38	34 3/8	9 3/8	9 5/8	8	6	Wahkiakum Co., WA	Brian S. Boudreau	Brian S. Boudreau	2002	46
291 3/8	43 5/8	43 7/8	37 3/8	9 1/8	8 7/8	6	7	Washington Co., OR	Matthew D. Schmidlin	Matthew D. Schmidlin	2001	47
290 5/8	42	41 4/8	37 3/8	9 4/8	8 4/8	8	8	Columbia Co., OR	Joseph D. Banzer	Joseph D. Banzer	2000	48
290	43 7/8	44 3/8	39 6/8	8 2/8	7 7/8	6	6	Jefferson Co., WA	Elmer Loose	Elmer Loose	2000	49
281 6/8	44 4/8	45 4/8	34 7/8	8 5/8	7 7/8	6	6	Clatsop Co., OR	Larry W. Atkins	Larry W. Atkins	1996	50
278 5/8	45 3/8	45 2/8	44 1/8	9 5/8	9 5/8	5	6	Jefferson Co., OR	Lewis Dickman	Harry H. Dickman	1957	51
276 1/8	40 1/8	43 3/8	41 5/8	10 4/8	9 4/8	5	5	Clallam Co., WA	Scott Williams	Scott Williams	2003	52
369 *	50 5/8	48 2/8	40 4/8	7 4/8	7 2/8	8	7	Coos Co., OR	George J. Yost	Rudy A. Yost	1936	
367 1/8*	49 5/8	49	39 4/8	8	7 6/8	7	8	Humboldt Co., CA	John J. Aboud	John J. Aboud	2003	
364 *	53 7/8	54 6/8	41 2/8	9	9	9	7	Adams River, BC	Michael R. Finnell	Michael R. Finnell	2000	

* Final score subject to revision by additional verifying measurements.

TULE ELK

Cervus elaphus nannodes

Minimum Score 270

World's Record 365

Tule elk are from selected areas in California. For a complete description of the boundary, check the Official Measurer's manual, *Measuring and Scoring North American Big Game Trophies*, or visit the Club's web site at www.booneandcrockettclub.com.

Score	Length of Main Beam R.	L.	Inside Spread	Circumference at Smallest Place Between First & Second Points R.	L.	Number of Points R.	L.	Locality	Hunter	Owner	Date Killed	Rank
309 7/8	40 1/8	41 2/8	40 7/8	7 5/8	7 4/8	7	6	Monterey Co., CA	Chuck Adams	Chuck Adams	1990	1
292	40 1/8	36 5/8	43 2/8	8 2/8	7 1/8	6	8	San Luis Obispo Co., CA	Lee M. Wahlund	Lee M. Wahlund	2003	2
289 2/8	42 5/8	43 7/8	43 6/8	7 5/8	7 3/8	8	6	Solano Co., CA	Dino W. Markette	Dino W. Markette	1990	3
287	38 6/8	39 2/8	38	7 4/8	7 5/8	7	8	San Luis Obispo Co., CA	Edward R. Frey	Kathleen A. Frey	2001	4
284 6/8	44 6/8	47 3/8	40 3/8	6 6/8	7 5/8	7	7	Solano Co., CA	Ted F. Volken	Ted F. Volken	1999	5
279 4/8	37 1/8	38 7/8	44 3/8	7 7/8	7 1/8	8	8	Monterey Co., CA	Picked Up	Matthew R. Goodson	1999	6
272 5/8	38 6/8	39 1/8	36 2/8	8	7 6/8	6	7	San Luis Obispo Co., CA	George W. Windolph	George W. Windolph	2003	7
342 6/8*	47 1/8	46 2/8	41 7/8	8 5/8	8 6/8	9	7	Solano Co., CA	Picked Up	Richard A. Cox	1996	
304 4/8*	41 4/8	43 4/8	45 3/8	7 7/8	8	8	8	Solano Co., CA	Patrick J. Gilligan	Patrick J. Gilligan	2003	
299 5/8*	40 6/8	46 4/8	44 2/8	7 3/8	8 4/8	10	8	Solano Co., CA	Patrick J. Gilligan	Patrick J. Gilligan	1991	

* Final score subject to revision by additional verifying measurements.

MULE DEER - TYPICAL ANTLERS

Odocoileus hemionus hemionus and certain related subspecies

Minimum Score 180   World's Record 226 4/8

Score	Length of Main Beam R.	Length of Main Beam L.	Inside Spread	Circumference at Smallest Place Between Burr & First Point R.	Circumference at Smallest Place Between Burr & First Point L.	Number of Points R.	Number of Points L.	Locality	Hunter	Owner	Date Killed	Rank
207 5/8	27	25 3/8	31	5 1/8	5 2/8	6	6	Sonora, MX	Unknown	James E. Arias	1978	1
206 1/8	24 5/8	24 5/8	25 2/8	5	5 1/8	5	5	Summit Co., CO	Robb R. Rishor	Robb R. Rishor	2002	2
204 5/8	25 5/8	26 1/8	24 6/8	4 7/8	4 7/8	6	5	Routt Co., CO	Paul Brenner	Craig Hoyer	1960	3
204 5/8	26 7/8	28 1/8	29 3/8	6 1/8	6 2/8	5	5	Adams Co., ID	Alvin Yantis	Alvin Yantis	1967	3
204 4/8	27 6/8	26 6/8	28	4 5/8	4 5/8	6	5	Carbon Co., UT	Harold Wimmer	Tony Allred	1933	5
203 4/8	28 6/8	28 1/8	29 4/8	5	5 1/8	6	5	Utah Co., UT	Carl B. Webb	Carl B. Webb	2000	6
203 2/8	26 5/8	26 5/8	22	5 2/8	5 2/8	5	6	McLeese Lake, BC	Dean Barlow	Dean Barlow	1980	7
202 3/8	23 7/8	25 2/8	24 5/8	5 3/8	5 6/8	5	5	Whitebear Lake, SK	Robert E. Code	Robert E. Code	2000	8
201 4/8	27 4/8	24 6/8	25 1/8	5 4/8	5 4/8	5	6	Dolores Co., CO	James H. Becher	Jerry Schwaderer	1963	9
201 4/8	29 3/8	29 3/8	26 6/8	4 6/8	5	6	5	Washington Co., UT	Clyde Cannon	Troy T. Truman	1979	9
201 4/8	29 2/8	28 5/8	28	5 6/8	5 4/8	9	6	Franklin Co., ID	Forrest Christensen	Forrest Christensen	2000	9
201 3/8	27 5/8	27	25 5/8	5 4/8	5 4/8	5	5	Idaho	Scott Rehn	D.J. Hollinger & B. Howard	1968	12
201 2/8	26	26	24 2/8	5 4/8	5 2/8	7	6	Lincoln Co., WY	Gavin S. Lovell	Gavin S. Lovell	2003	13
201	28 1/8	26	26 2/8	5 4/8	5 4/8	5	5	Las Animas Co., CO	Jerry D. Dye	Jerry D. Dye	2001	14
200 6/8	25 2/8	23 7/8	25 3/8	5 3/8	5 3/8	5	5	Montrose Co., CO	Dennis Carr	Dennis Carr	1963	15
200 5/8	25 3/8	26 7/8	22 5/8	5 3/8	5 4/8	5	6	Shoshone Co., ID	Jerry Madsen	Cabela's, Inc.	1989	16
200 4/8	26 3/8	27	27 2/8	5 5/8	5 6/8	6	6	Baker Co., OR	Oliver D. Markle	Gene Markle	1924	17
200 3/8	28 2/8	28 2/8	25 4/8	5 2/8	5 2/8	6	5	Modoc Co., CA	F.M. Huglin	Frank M. Huglin	1948	18
200 3/8	27	27 3/8	23 3/8	4 6/8	4 6/8	5	5	Ouray Co., CO	Ernest L. Veo	Ernest L. Veo	1961	18
200	26 1/8	27 4/8	29	4 6/8	4 6/8	4	4	Fremont Co., CO	W.E. Canterbury	Jerry E. Canterbury	1951	20
199 7/8	26	26 3/8	22 5/8	5 1/8	5 3/8	6	5	Pelletier Lake, SK	Tyson N. Faucher	Tyson N. Faucher	2003	21
199 4/8	25	24 7/8	22 1/8	6 2/8	6 4/8	7	6	Logan Co., KS	Stacy C. Hoeme	Stacy C. Hoeme	2001	22
199 4/8	26 2/8	26	27 7/8	5 4/8	5 2/8	5	5	Yuma Co., CO	Kerry G. Weed	Kerry G. Weed	2003	22
199 3/8	27 2/8	25 1/8	25 7/8	6 4/8	6 2/8	7	6	Mt. Blackstrap, SK	Gordon Kyler	Gordon Kyler	2001	24
199 1/8	27 6/8	28 1/8	26 4/8	5 5/8	5 6/8	6	5	Adams Co., ID	Wallace E. Averett	Larry G. Averett	1976	25
199 1/8	24 3/8	24 7/8	23 5/8	4 4/8	4 4/8	5	5	Elmore Co., ID	Teresa R. Crone	Teresa R. Crone	2000	25
199	25 5/8	25 4/8	23 1/8	5 4/8	5 2/8	5	7	Pondera Co., MT	Jim Luoma	Jim Luoma	2000	27
198 7/8	28 7/8	28 3/8	26 2/8	4 5/8	4 6/8	6	5	S. Saskatchewan River, SK	Barry D. Miller	Barry D. Miller	2000	28
198 5/8	25 3/8	24 2/8	25 3/8	5	5	6	5	Rio Arriba Co., NM	Picked Up	Robert J. Seeds	2002	29
198 4/8	27 5/8	26 2/8	27 2/8	6	5 6/8	5	6	Rio Arriba Co., NM	Lambert Callado	Lambert Callado	2003	30
198 1/8	25 5/8	25	26 1/8	5	5 2/8	5	5	Caribou Co., ID	Arlo T. Hopkins	Arlo T. Hopkins	1962	31
198 1/8	26 4/8	27 1/8	21	4 5/8	4 6/8	6	5	Swift Current, SK	Bryce Stan	Bryce Stan	2003	31
198	28 5/8	27 7/8	30 6/8	5	5	6	5	Adams Co., ID	Allen Solterbeck	Ryan B. Hatfield	1975	33

MULE DEER - TYPICAL ANTLERS

Odocoileus hemionus hemionus and certain related subspecies

Score	Length of Main Beam R.	L.	Inside Spread	Circumference at Smallest Place Between Burr & First Point R.	L.	Number of Points R.	L.	Locality	Hunter	Owner	Date Killed	Rank
198	24 2/8	23 7/8	26 2/8	6 1/8	6	5	5	Colorado	Unknown	D.J. Hollinger & B. Howard	PR1980	33
197 7/8	27 6/8	26 3/8	25 3/8	5 4/8	5 5/8	5	5	Rio Arriba Co., NM	Aric DeJesus	Aric DeJesus	2000	35
197 4/8	24 4/8	25 5/8	22 2/8	6	6 1/8	6	8	Routt Co., CO	John E. Simmons	John E. Simmons	1977	36
197 4/8	24 1/8	24 4/8	26 1/8	5 2/8	5 2/8	5	5	Lincoln Co., WY	Douglas L. Stephens	Douglas L. Stephens	2001	36
197 2/8	26 1/8	26 6/8	26	4 6/8	4 7/8	5	5	Shoshone Co., ID	Roger R. Davis	Aly M. Bruner	1987	38
197 1/8	27 4/8	28 4/8	25	4 7/8	4 6/8	5	6	Diefenbaker Lake, SK	Alvin Onofriechuck	Alvin Onofriechuck	2001	39
197	27 4/8	27 5/8	22 6/8	5 2/8	5 2/8	5	5	Rio Arriba Co., NM	Unknown	Robert M. Ortiz	1999	40
196 6/8	25 3/8	27 1/8	21 2/8	5 1/8	5	5	6	Montrose Co., CA	Howard S. Thrift	H.S. & B. Thrift	1962	41
196 4/8	25 3/8	25 3/8	21 2/8	4 4/8	4 3/8	5	5	Park Co., WY	Thomas E. Ault	Thomas E. Ault	1991	42
196 3/8	23 7/8	24 4/8	23 5/8	4 5/8	4 4/8	5	5	Hermosillo, MX	Glenn Bailey	Glenn Bailey	2001	43
196 3/8	25 1/8	26 5/8	23 3/8	5 1/8	5 3/8	5	5	Gunnison Co., CO	James A. Manuel	James A. Manuel	2002	43
196 3/8	27 1/8	27 7/8	27 3/8	5 6/8	5 3/8	5	5	Sonora, MX	Christopher T. Moser	Christopher T. Moser	2003	43
196 3/8	25	27 5/8	28 1/8	6 4/8	6	5	5	Gunnison Co., CO	Leland J. Cox	Leland J. Cox	2003	43
196	25	24 7/8	21 6/8	4 6/8	4 6/8	5	6	Rio Arriba Co., NM	Picked Up	Steven C. Erquhart	1988	47
196	25	24 7/8	27	5 2/8	5	5	5	Adams Co., ID	Jim Hostetler	Jim Hostetler	2001	47
195 7/8	25 4/8	25	22 5/8	4 7/8	4 7/8	5	6	Sioux Co., NE	Clarence Dout	Heath L. Serres	1949	49
195 7/8	25 3/8	23 5/8	20 3/8	5 5/8	5 6/8	6	5	Walla Walla Co., WA	Unknown	Rick H. Russo	1961	49
195 7/8	23 3/8	23 5/8	30 3/8	5 2/8	5 2/8	6	6	Sonora, MX	John L. Mussell	John L. Mussell	2002	49
195 6/8	26 4/8	27 2/8	23	5 1/8	6	6	6	Rio Arriba Co., NM	Herman A. Bennett	Herman A. Bennett	1968	52
195 6/8	26 6/8	23 3/8	21 4/8	5 6/8	5 7/8	5	6	Rio Arriba Co., NM	Cevero Caramillo	Cevero Caramillo	2001	52
195 5/8	25 2/8	26 1/8	26 2/8	4 7/8	5	5	5	Garfield Co., CO	Jack A. Fitzgerald	Jack A. Fitzgerald	1967	54
195 3/8	27 3/8	26 6/8	25 7/8	5	5	7	8	Coconino Co., AZ	Bradford Eden	D.J. Hollinger & B. Howard	1949	55
195 2/8	26 4/8	27 1/8	23 2/8	5 3/8	5 2/8	6	6	Notukeu Creek, SK	Ron Boskill	Ron D. Button	2000	56
195 2/8	25 4/8	26 1/8	27 5/8	5 1/8	5 2/8	5	6	Gunnison Co., CO	Randy Clark	Randy Clark	2002	56
195 1/8	24	24 7/8	30	5	5 2/8	5	5	Sonora, MX	Grant A. Medlin	Grant A. Medlin	2002	58
195	28 1/8	27 5/8	25 4/8	5 1/8	5 1/8	6	5	Lincoln Co., WY	Randy S. Mixon	Randy S. Mixon	2001	59
195	27 5/8	27 4/8	24 5/8	5 7/8	6	5	6	Sonora, MX	Steven R. Huntley	Steven R. Huntley	2002	59
194 7/8	25 1/8	24 3/8	22 7/8	5 5/8	5 5/8	5	5	Sublette Co., WY	Gil Winters	Gil Winters	1998	61
194 7/8	25 1/8	28 1/8	23 7/8	5 1/8	5 1/8	5	5	Tooele Co., UT	Wade L. Hanks	Wade L. Hanks	2002	61
194 3/8	24 6/8	26	21 3/8	5	5	5	5	Grant Co., OR	Joey Wood	Joey Wood	1985	63
194 3/8	25	25 3/8	23 3/8	4 6/8	4 6/8	5	5	San Juan Co., UT	Roy T. Hume	Roy T. Hume	2001	63
194 3/8	27 2/8	27 3/8	25 3/8	4 5/8	4 5/8	6	6	Unknown	Unknown	Cabela's, Inc.	PR2003	63
194 1/8	27 1/8	25 5/8	22 7/8	5 2/8	5 1/8	4	4	Rio Arriba Co., NM	Picked Up	Robert J. Seeds	1994	66

Score	Main Beam R	Main Beam L	Inside Spread	Circ. R	Circ. L	Pts. R	Pts. L	Locality	Hunter	Owner	Date	Rank
193 7/8	26 6/8	27 2/8	28 3/8	5 1/8	5 3/8	5	7	Madison Co., MT	Edgar Allard	R.G. Stroup	1948	67
193 6/8	25 5/8	23 2/8	25 2/8	5	5 1/8	5	6	Unknown	Unknown	Paul Sides	PR1960	68
193 6/8	28 1/8	27 5/8	23 4/8	4 6/8	4 6/8	4	4	British Columbia	Picked Up	Cabela's, Inc.	PR2001	68
193 6/8	24 4/8	25 4/8	21 6/8	4 5/8	4 4/8	5	5	Franklin Co., ID	Nicholas Q. Shumway	Nicholas Q. Shumway	2001	68
193 5/8	28 7/8	25 3/8	32 1/8	5 5/8	5 5/8	6	6	Adams Co., CO	Phillip E. Hupp	Phillip E. Hupp	2001	71
193 4/8	23 4/8	23 5/8	18 4/8	4 4/8	4 3/8	5	5	Utah Co., UT	Seth A. Poulson	Seth A. Poulson	2001	72
193 2/8	23 7/8	25 5/8	21 6/8	5 1/8	5	5	5	Lincoln Co., WY	Michael J. Garrett	Michael J. Garrett	2001	73
193 2/8	26 5/8	26 4/8	21	4 7/8	5	6	6	Bear Lake Co., ID	Brad J. Michel	Brad J. Michel	2002	73
193 1/8	24 3/8	24 3/8	22 2/8	5 4/8	5 4/8	6	5	Fraser River, BC	Kent Lawlor	Kent Lawlor	2000	75
193 1/8	27 2/8	27 1/8	23	5	4 7/8	6	6	Rio Arriba Co., NM	Picked Up	Lambert Callado	2001	75
193	25	25 6/8	22 2/8	4 6/8	5	5	7	Carbon Co., WY	Jeff Pfau	Jeff Pfau	1985	77
193	24 2/8	24 4/8	25 3/8	4 6/8	4 6/8	5	5	Uintah Co., UT	Unknown	D.R. & J. Harrow	PR1986	77
192 7/8	25 5/8	26 6/8	21 6/8	5	4 7/8	5	7	Cartier Creek, AB	Wayne Price	Wayne Price	1971	79
192 5/8	25 3/8	25	24 6/8	4 5/8	4 6/8	6	5	Lincoln Co., WY	James M. Snowden	James M. Snowden	2000	80
192 4/8	28 1/8	26 6/8	27 6/8	4 7/8	4 7/8	4	5	Mesa Co., CO	Lacy J. Harber	Lacy J. Harber	1963	81
192 4/8	24 1/8	24	23 7/8	4 4/8	4 5/8	6	5	Summit Co., UT	Boyd J. Pendleton	Boyd J. Pendleton	2000	81
192 4/8	24 3/8	24 2/8	19 6/8	4 6/8	4 6/8	6	5	Slope Co., ND	Jennifer A. Belland	Jennifer A. Belland	2000	81
192 4/8	26 3/8	25 4/8	21 3/8	5 6/8	5 5/8	6	6	Grizzly Creek, BC	Deller Watson	Deller Watson	2000	81
192 3/8	26 6/8	27	28 5/8	4 6/8	4 7/8	7	5	Klamath Co., OR	Douglas S. Golden	Douglas S. Golden	1955	85
192 3/8	25 6/8	25 7/8	27 6/8	4 4/8	4 4/8	5	5	Unknown	Unknown	Cabela's, Inc.	PR2001	85
192 3/8	23 6/8	23 6/8	21 7/8	5 2/8	5 2/8	5	5	Wilkie, SK	Melvin B. Gillis	Melvin B. Gillis	2001	85
192 3/8	28 1/8	27 7/8	25 1/8	4 7/8	4 5/8	5	5	Rio Arriba Co., NM	Eudane Vicenti	Eudane Vicenti	2002	85
192 3/8	26 4/8	26 5/8	25	4 7/8	5 1/8	6	6	Routt Co., CO	James S. Farleigh	James S. Farleigh	2003	85
192 2/8	27 3/8	27 5/8	28 3/8	5	5	10	5	Valley Co., ID	Bruce Myers	Bruce Myers	1976	90
192 2/8	26 2/8	27 4/8	27 6/8	5 5/8	5 3/8	5	5	Sonora, MX	Picked Up	Kirk Kelso	2003	90
191 7/8	24 2/8	24 4/8	21 5/8	5 1/8	5 1/8	5	5	Unknown	Unknown	Jeffrey W. Robinson	1970	92
191 7/8	25 6/8	25 6/8	21 7/8	4 1/8	4 2/8	5	5	Utah	Unknown	D.R. & J. Harrow	PR1976	92
191 7/8	27 3/8	26 3/8	24 5/8	5 1/8	5 2/8	5	5	Great Sand Hills, SK	Richey Lane	Richey Lane	1983	92
191 7/8	26 4/8	26 1/8	22 4/8	5 2/8	5	7	8	Duchesne Co., UT	Brandon K. Rowley	Brandon K. Rowley	2000	92
191 6/8	26 4/8	27 3/8	27 3/8	5 1/8	5	6	6	Dolores Co., CO	Jim Becher	Jerry Schwaderer	1961	96
191 6/8	26 7/8	26 3/8	21 3/8	4 6/8	4 6/8	6	6	Unknown	Unknown	Thomas J. Lovrin	PR1970	96
191 6/8	24 5/8	24 5/8	22 7/8	4 7/8	5	5	7	Tooele Co., UT	Cody L. Warren	Cody L. Warren	2000	96
191 5/8	25 1/8	25	24 4/8	5 3/8	5 3/8	6	5	Larimer Co., CO	N. Duane Wygant	N. Duane Wygant	1966	99
191 5/8	26 6/8	26 7/8	20 6/8	5 7/8	5 5/8	5	5	Mesa Co., CO	Thomas W. White	Thomas W. White	1972	99
191 5/8	26 6/8	25 7/8	24 1/8	5 6/8	5 4/8	7	7	Unknown	Unknown	Gary P. Farley	PR1993	99
191 4/8	25 2/8	26 2/8	21 3/8	5 4/8	5 6/8	5	5	Mesa Co., CO	Arlie Manship	Arlie Manship	1957	102
191 4/8	25	25 6/8	20 7/8	5 3/8	5 2/8	5	7	Power Co., ID	Stephen E. Wegner	Stephen E. Wegner	1965	102
191 3/8	27 6/8	27 6/8	25 6/8	5 4/8	5 4/8	5	5	Rio Arriba Co., NM	Edward R. Frey	Kathleen A. Frey	2000	104
191 2/8	24 4/8	25 2/8	24 3/8	4 6/8	4 6/8	5	6	Carbon Co., WY	Kermit D. Russell	Patrick McKee	2000	105
191 2/8	24 7/8	24 7/8	27 6/8	4 7/8	5 1/8	5	5	Gooding Co., ID	Donald W. Larson	Donald W. Larson	2000	105
191 1/8	24 1/8	24 7/8	19 7/8	5 4/8	4 5/8	6	6	Lincoln Co., WY	Unknown	DeWayne A. Williams	1967	107
191 1/8	25 3/8	23	23	5 1/8	4 1/8	5	5	Lincoln Co., WY	Darin D. Kerr	Darin D. Kerr	2001	107

MULE DEER - TYPICAL ANTLERS

Odocoileus hemionus hemionus and certain related subspecies

Score	Length of Main Beam R.	L.	Inside Spread	Circumference at Smallest Place Between Burr & First Point R.	L.	Number of Points R.	L.	Locality	Hunter	Owner	Date Killed	Rank
191 2/8	22 1/8	23 2/8	23	4 6/8	4 6/8	5	5	Larimer Co., CO	Albert Valles, Jr.	Albert Valles, Jr.	2001	107
191 2/8	26 2/8	27 3/8	21 6/8	5 4/8	5 2/8	5	6	Malheur Co., OR	Tom Markle	Tom Markle	2002	107
191 2/8	25 3/8	24 3/8	25	4 2/8	4 1/8	5	5	Washoe Co., NV	Daniel A. Grayson	Daniel A. Grayson	2002	107
191 2/8	26 3/8	25 7/8	22 4/8	5 2/8	5 2/8	6	5	Mesa Co., CO	Mark Blair	Mark Blair	2003	107
191 1/8	25 5/8	24 1/8	22 2/8	4 6/8	4 6/8	6	5	Wallowa Co., OR	William Bruck	Robert P. Romine, Sr.	1976	113
191 1/8	26 4/8	26 7/8	24 7/8	4 7/8	4 7/8	5	5	Eagle Co., CO	Ralph L. Nygren	Ralph L. Nygren	1978	113
191 1/8	24	23 2/8	22	4 7/8	4 7/8	6	5	Washington Co., ID	Mike Meyer	Mike Meyer	1980	113
191 1/8	24 3/8	23 2/8	23 1/8	4 7/8	4 7/8	8	6	Sublette Co., WY	Gil Winters	Gil Winters	2001	113
191 1/8	25 4/8	26 1/8	27 5/8	5	5	5	4	Sonora, MX	Gerald P. McBride	Gerald P. McBride	2003	113
191	27 3/8	25 1/8	24 6/8	4 3/8	4 4/8	5	5	Montrose Co., CO	Johnny A. Grimes	Johnny A. Grimes	1999	118
191	26 6/8	26 6/8	24 4/8	5 1/8	5	6	6	Eagle Co., CO	Stephen V. Vallone	Stephen V. Vallone	2000	118
191	26	25 1/8	25 1/8	5	5 1/8	5	6	Rio Arriba Co., NM	Russell J. Jackson	Russell J. Jackson	2002	118
190 7/8	24	24 7/8	26	5 2/8	5 2/8	5	5	Dolores Co., CO	Unknown	Henry A. Anderson	1945	121
190 7/8	27 7/8	27 6/8	25 1/8	5 1/8	5 1/8	4	5	Sonora, MX	Stan A. Hanes	Stan A. Hanes	2001	121
190 7/8	26	25 7/8	20 5/8	5	4 7/8	4	4	Lincoln Co., NV	Dan Goff	Dan Goff	2001	121
190 6/8	24 5/8	24 7/8	19 4/8	4 7/8	4 7/8	5	5	Garfield Co., UT	Arthur L. Holt	Tom E. Reese	1950	124
190 6/8	24 4/8	26 2/8	24 4/8	4 7/8	4 6/8	5	5	Dolores Co., CO	Jess Guynes	Jess Guynes	1974	124
190 6/8	27 2/8	28 6/8	23 4/8	4 5/8	4 5/8	5	5	Klickitat Co., WA	Gary R. Hess	Gary R. Hess	2000	124
190 6/8	28 2/8	26 4/8	22 7/8	5 2/8	5 1/8	6	6	Carbon Co., WY	Archie P. Kirsch	Archie P. Kirsch	2002	124
190 6/8	25 2/8	24 1/8	24	5 3/8	5 3/8	7	6	Rio Arriba Co., NM	Terry R. Chapman	Terry R. Chapman	2002	124
190 5/8	25 4/8	27	25 4/8	5 7/8	5 2/8	8	5	Elmore Co., ID	Robert Bentley	Robert Bentley	1970	129
190 5/8	25 4/8	25 3/8	23 7/8	4 5/8	4 6/8	5	5	Twin Falls Co., ID	William L. McCall, Sr.	William L. McCall, Sr.	1995	129
190 5/8	22 7/8	23 3/8	22 7/8	4 7/8	4 7/8	5	5	Flathead Co., MT	Richard D. Clark	Richard D. Clark	2000	129
190 4/8	28 5/8	26 6/8	29 4/8	5 2/8	5 6/8	5	6	Okanogan Co., WA	John A. Propp	John A. Propp	1973	132
190 3/8	26 3/8	27 4/8	22 7/8	4 5/8	4 6/8	5	5	Kane Co., UT	Craig I. Haskell	Craig I. Haskell	1997	133
190 3/8	24 6/8	26 3/8	25 7/8	4 5/8	4 7/8	5	5	Rio Arriba Co., NM	Picked Up	Jicarilla Game & Fish	2002	133
190 2/8	24 2/8	25	19 2/8	4 7/8	4 7/8	6	6	Lincoln Co., WY	Picked Up	Marvin Fralich	2000	135
190 2/8	27 4/8	28 5/8	26	4 4/8	4 5/8	4	4	Malheur Co., OR	Alan E. Hebert	Alan E. Hebert	2000	135
190 2/8	27 1/8	26 5/8	29 6/8	5 3/8	5 4/8	5	6	French Creek, SK	Rod Roberts	Rod Roberts	2001	135
190 2/8	25 3/8	24 2/8	22 6/8	4 7/8	4 7/8	5	5	Rio Arriba Co., NM	Allan R. Cypert	Allan R. Cypert	2002	135
190 1/8	27 1/8	26 2/8	28 5/8	5	5 1/8	5	5	Unknown	Unknown	Timothy C. Sweeney	PR1992	139
190 1/8	23 3/8	23 4/8	22 5/8	5 1/8	5	5	5	Lincoln Co., WY	Kenneth E. Brown	Kenneth E. Brown	2001	139
190 1/8	27 2/8	27 4/8	22	5 6/8	5 4/8	7	6	Ten Mile Lake, BC	Denis Hocevar	Denis Hocevar	2001	139

Score	Length R	Length L	Inside Spread	Circ. R	Circ. L	Points	Points	Locality	Hunter	Owner	Date	Rank
190	24	24 3/8	23 2/8	4 1/8	4 3/8	5	5	Stillwater Co., MT	Saschia Herman	S. Davies & G. Davies IV	PR1953	142
190	24	24 2/8	21 2/8	4 7/8	5	5	5	Fir Mt., SK	Randy J. Fehr	Randy J. Fehr	2000	142
189 5/8	27 2/8	27 5/8	27 4/8	4 7/8	4 6/8	5	5	Archuleta Co., CO	Kyle R. Bramwell	Kyle R. Bramwell	2000	144
189 5/8	24 7/8	25 2/8	22 5/8	5 4/8	4 5/8	7	5	Nye Co., NV	Picked Up	Tory Cantrell	2000	144
189 5/8	26 4/8	23 5/8	27 7/8	4 3/8	5 4/8	5	6	Eureka Co., NV	Taylor A. Lund	Taylor A. Lund	2002	144
189 4/8	24 6/8	24 5/8	24 6/8	4 5/8	4 3/8	6	6	Montrose Co., CO	Robert W. Miller	Robert W. Miller	1950	147
189 3/8	25 1/8	23 1/8	22 3/8	4 3/8	4 4/8	6	6	Baker Co., OR	Mark Melgard	Mark Melgard	1949	148
189	23 6/8	29	22 5/8	5 6/8	4 5/8	6	6	Sublette Co., WY	Louis Roberts	Louis Roberts	1987	149
189	28 1/8	26	26 2/8	4 6/8	5 7/8	9	5	Cache Creek, BC	Glen Okino	Glen Okino	1992	149
188 6/8	26	25 7/8	26 6/8	4 3/8	4 6/8	5	6	Delta Co., CO	James A. McCormick	James A. McCormick	1982	151
188 6/8	26	26 4/8	21 2/8	4 4/8	4 1/8	6	5	Moffat Co., CO	Gary E. Farley	Gary E. Farley	1999	151
188 6/8	26 6/8	24 6/8	23 4/8	5	4 4/8	5	6	Gregory Co., SD	Phillip L. Johnson	Phillip L. Johnson	2001	151
188 3/8	24 6/8	27 2/8	22	4 6/8	5	6	5	Madison Co., MT	Jack F. Beals	Jack F. Beals	1951	154
188 3/8	26 2/8	24 3/8	25 2/8	6	4 7/8	5	5	Sonora, MX	Fred E. Borton	Fred E. Borton	2002	154
188 1/8	28	25 3/8	21 2/8	6	5 3/8	6	6	Lincoln Co., NV	Darren Hansen	Darren Hansen	1986	156
188 1/8	23 4/8	24 4/8	26	4 6/8	5 6/8	5	5	Gooding Co., ID	Ernie N. Menchaca	Ernie N. Menchaca	2000	156
188	23 3/8	22	22 6/8	5	5	5	5	Owyhee Co., ID	Brandon Boone	Brandon Boone	2001	158
187 7/8	25 2/8	26 6/8	24 1/8	5	4 7/8	5	5	Cache Co., UT	Bliss W. Law	Bliss W. Law	1964	159
187 7/8	24	25	19 7/8	4 7/8	4 7/8	5	6	Lincoln Co., WY	Stefan K. White	Stefan K. White	2000	159
187 7/8	26 7/8	25 2/8	22 1/8	4 7/8	4 7/8	6	5	Rio Arriba Co., NM	Gene Thompson	Gene Thompson	2001	159
187 6/8	25 4/8	24 7/8	22	5 1/8	5 1/8	5	5	Missoula Co., MT	Jeffrey Hahn	Jeffrey Hahn	1984	162
187 5/8	21 7/8	23 3/8	20 7/8	4 4/8	4 4/8	5	5	Boulder Co., CO	Wendy M. Hahn	Wendy M. Hahn	2002	163
187 4/8	25	26 4/8	26 7/8	4 3/8	4 3/8	5	5	Baca Co., CO	Steven F. Voges	Steven F. Voges	2000	164
187 3/8	23 5/8	25 7/8	21	4 6/8	4 5/8	6	5	Wallowa Co., OR	Arvey D. Nelson	Arvey D. Nelson	2000	165
187 1/8	26 4/8	26 2/8	22 5/8	5 3/8	5 1/8	5	6	Morrow Co., OR	Walter P. Inskeep	Walter P. Inskeep	1962	166
187 1/8	27 1/8	23 3/8	20 1/8	5 4/8	5 2/8	4	4	Sublette Co., WY	Jim Tardif	Jim Tardif	2001	166
187	23 4/8	26 2/8	21 2/8	5 4/8	4 7/8	6	5	Blaine Co., ID	B.R. Hanks & D.L. Smith	Brent R. Hanks	1998	168
187	23 6/8	27	25 6/8	4 7/8	5 1/8	7	5	Gunnison Co., CO	Ray W. Dinsmore, Jr.	Ray W. Dinsmore, Jr.	2001	168
187	26 7/8	25	24 4/8	4 7/8	5 1/8	5	5	Cochise Co., AZ	Bradley D. Grap	Bradley D. Grap	2003	168
186 6/8	25 3/8	26 3/8	27 7/8	5 1/8	4 6/8	5	5	Dolores Co., CO	Francis Becher	Jerry Schwaderer	1954	171
186 6/8	25	26 3/8	22 7/8	4 5/8	5 2/8	5	5	Morrow Co., OR	Stefanie A. Skultety	Stefanie A. Skultety	2001	171
186 4/8	26 6/8	22	27 2/8	5 2/8	5 1/8	5	5	Eagle Co., CO	Douglas L. Kailey	Douglas L. Kailey	1978	173
186 1/8	24 4/8	23 3/8	20 5/8	5 1/8	5 4/8	5	5	Fremont Co., CO	Grant C. Adkisson	Grant C. Adkisson	1968	174
186	25 6/8	25 3/8	21 6/8	5 6/8	4 5/8	7	5	Dolores Co., CO	James H. Becher	Jerry Schwaderer	1959	175
186	24 7/8	23 7/8	21 4/8	4 5/8	5	5	5	Bonneville Co., ID	Ken Schiess	Ken Schiess	1980	175
185 7/8	26	25	17 3/8	5 2/8	4 3/8	5	5	Merritt, BC	Ben Young	John Young	1971	177
185 7/8	23 7/8	23 1/8	22	4 5/8	4 6/8	5	5	Red Deer River, AB	Keith Balfourd	Keith Balfourd	1993	177
185 6/8	25 1/8	25 3/8	26 4/8	4 5/8	4 7/8	6	5	Mesa Co., CO	J. Harold Whatley, Jr.	J. Harold Whatley, Jr.	1978	179
185 6/8	26 3/8	26 7/8	22	5	4 4/8	7	5	Andrews Co., TX	Roger D. Hooten	Roger D. Hooten	2002	179
185 5/8	26 6/8	26 3/8	26 3/8	4 4/8	5 3/8	6	6	Sonora, MX	Richard N. Kimball	Richard N. Kimball	1999	181
185 5/8	22	23 3/8	25 1/8	5 1/8	4 7/8	6	6	La Plata Co., CO	Robert D. Cleveland	Robert D. Cleveland	1999	181
185 5/8	26 2/8	25 3/8	25 4/8	4 7/8		5	6	Teton Co., MT	Kurt D. Rued	Kurt D. Rued	2001	181

MULE DEER - TYPICAL ANTLERS

Odocoileus hemionus hemionus and certain related subspecies

Score	Length of Main Beam R.	L.	Inside Spread	Circumference at Smallest Place Between Burr & First Point R.	L.	Number of Points R.	L.	Locality	Hunter	Owner	Date Killed	Rank
185 4/8	24 2/8	24 5/8	18 1/8	5 1/8	5	6	7	Delta Co., CO	H. Robert Bruce	H. Robert Bruce	1966	184
185 4/8	26 2/8	24 6/8	26	4 4/8	4 4/8	6	6	Teton Co., ID	Virgil Beard	Virgil Beard	1992	184
185 4/8	23 1/8	24 4/8	23	5 2/8	5 1/8	5	5	Lincoln Co., WY	William H. Koenig	William H. Koenig	2000	184
185 4/8	27 1/8	26 3/8	29 3/8	5 1/8	5 1/8	8	7	Washakie Co., WY	Marvin W. Matthiesen	Marvin W. Matthiesen	2000	184
185 4/8	24 7/8	25 2/8	21 4/8	5 1/8	5	5	6	Grand Co., CO	Timothy A. Holinka	Timothy A. Holinka	2001	184
185 4/8	24 6/8	24 4/8	24 2/8	6 3/8	6 2/8	7	5	Peace River, AB	Brad W. McPhee	Brad W. McPhee	2003	184
185 3/8	25 7/8	26	20 2/8	5 6/8	5 6/8	6	6	Alberta	George Papineau	Chad Lewis	PR1987	190
185 3/8	28 3/8	27 4/8	21 3/8	4 5/8	4 7/8	4	5	Eagle Co., CO	Steven C. Croell	Steven C. Croell	1988	190
185 2/8	26 6/8	26 4/8	24 2/8	4 5/8	4 6/8	5	5	La Plata Co., CO	David R. Buffalow	David R. Buffalow	1984	192
185 2/8	22 7/8	23 4/8	21 2/8	5 1/8	5 1/8	4	5	Mesa Co., CO	Douglas A. Hobbick	Douglas A. Hobbick	1989	192
185 2/8	24	24 6/8	25 1/8	4 5/8	4 5/8	5	5	S. Saskatchewan River, SK	Roger A. Arseneault	Roger A. Arseneault	2002	192
185 1/8	27 3/8	27 5/8	28 4/8	5 4/8	5 3/8	5	5	Malheur Co., OR	Mark L. Joyce	Mark L. Joyce	2000	195
185 1/8	25 4/8	25	19 2/8	5 2/8	5 3/8	5	4	Ferry Co., WA	Mike J. Cartwright	Mike J. Cartwright	2001	195
185 1/8	22	21 7/8	21 7/8	5 4/8	5 5/8	6	6	Gooding Co., ID	Dallas E. Smith	Dallas E. Smith	2001	195
185	23	23	21 4/8	5 2/8	5 1/8	5	5	Eagle Co., CO	Fred M. Upchurch	Fred M. Upchurch	1979	198
185	25 2/8	25 2/8	22 2/8	5 2/8	5 7/8	5	6	Lincoln Co., WY	Terence C. Luttrell	Terence C. Luttrell	1999	198
184 6/8	25 2/8	26 6/8	26 6/8	4 7/8	4 7/8	5	5	La Plata Co., CO	Jim Benavidez	Jim Benavidez	1987	200
184 6/8	23 4/8	23 2/8	22 2/8	5	4 7/8	6	6	Garfield Co., CO	John W. Colliflower	John W. Colliflower	2000	200
184 6/8	25 6/8	25 6/8	23 2/8	4 4/8	4 4/8	5	5	Custer Co., NE	Alan Estergard	Alan Estergard	2000	200
184 6/8	26 5/8	25 1/8	27 2/8	5 1/8	4 7/8	6	8	Oneida Co., ID	Jason L. Evans	Jason L. Evans	2002	200
184 5/8	26 3/8	26 1/8	21 6/8	5 2/8	4 6/8	8	8	Carbon Co., WY	Todd T. Loomis	Todd T. Loomis	2000	204
184 5/8	24	24 7/8	23	5 4/8	5 6/8	6	5	Unknown	Unknown	Mark J. Tobin	PR2002	204
184 4/8	26	22 3/8	22 6/8	4 5/8	4 4/8	4	4	Pike Lake, SK	Mark P. Belchamber	Mark P. Belchamber	2002	206
184 4/8	22 5/8	24 3/8	22 2/8	4 4/8	4 4/8	5	5	Rio Arriba Co., NM	Picked Up	Jaymes Panzy	2002	206
184 3/8	22	22 4/8	18 7/8	5 1/8	5 1/8	5	5	Eagle Co., CO	Murl E. Seeley	Murl E. Seeley	2002	208
184 2/8	26 6/8	27	23 7/8	5 2/8	5 1/8	7	6	Larimer Co., CO	George A. Zimmerman	Mike G. Fergus, Jr.	1937	209
184 2/8	27 4/8	27 1/8	30 4/8	4 4/8	4 5/8	6	7	Valley Co., ID	Don R. Freeman	Matt J. Perry	1965	209
184	25 5/8	24 7/8	21 2/8	4 6/8	4 5/8	5	5	Nye Co., NV	Jim Biondo	Jim Biondo	2002	211
183 7/8	24 7/8	26	22 2/8	5	4 7/8	5	6	Deschutes Co., OR	Keith D. Franklin	Keith D. Franklin	2002	212
183 6/8	24	24	20 4/8	4 4/8	4 4/8	5	5	Fremont Co., CO	Justin G. Adkisson	Justin G. Adkisson	1996	213
183 5/8	24 3/8	23 7/8	26	4 6/8	4 3/8	7	6	Garfield Co., CO	Robert H. Peters	Robert H. Peters	1983	214
183 5/8	21 3/8	23	18 7/8	5 1/8	5	5	5	Treasure Co., MT	Clinton D. Sowden	Clinton D. Sowden	2000	214
183 5/8	24 1/8	23 7/8	24 3/8	4 2/8	4 2/8	5	5	Boise Co., ID	Jerry W. Simmons	Jerry W. Simmons	2002	214

Score							Locality	Owner	Hunter	Date	Rank
183 4/8	25 1/8	24 6/8	25	4 7/8	4 7/8	6 5	Garfield Co., CO	David G. Arcand	David G. Arcand	2002	217
183 4/8	24	24	20	5	4 7/8	5 5	Lincoln Co., WY	Craig C. Coolahan	Craig C. Coolahan	2003	217
183 1/8	25 6/8	25 5/8	24 1/8	4 3/8	4 1/8	5 4	Delta Co., CO	Eric J. Marcoe	Eric J. Marcoe	2002	219
183	24 6/8	24 2/8	21 2/8	5 1/8	5	5 5	San Miguel Co., CO	Frayne Whiteskunk	Frayne Whiteskunk	1999	220
182 7/8	24 5/8	24 1/8	23 2/8	5 1/8	5	6 6	Sonora, MX	Dean Collins	Dean Collins	2001	221
182 6/8	25 1/8	24 1/8	24 4/8	5	5	5 5	Chaffee Co., CO	Colin J. Canterbury	Colin J. Canterbury	2003	222
182 4/8	23 2/8	23	21	5 3/8	5 1/8	5 5	Golden Valley Co., ND	Chris J. Meek	Chris J. Meek	2001	223
182 4/8	25 6/8	25 6/8	23 7/8	5 2/8	5 4/8	5 5	Lake Diefenbaker, SK	Garry J. Landstad	Garry J. Landstad	2003	223
182 3/8	25 6/8	24	20 5/8	5	5	5 6	Baker Co., OR	James A. Curtiss	James A. Curtiss	1991	225
182	26 6/8	25 3/8	23 3/8	5 6/8	5 4/8	5 5	Klickitat Co., WA	Kenneth D. Tilley	Kenneth D. Tilley	2001	226
182	24 5/8	25 4/8	25 4/8	5 1/8	5 4/8	6 5	Natrona Co., WY	Brent Stalkup	Brent Stalkup	2003	226
181 7/8	24 1/8	22 5/8	26 3/8	4 6/8	5 5/8	5 6	Lake Co., MT	Picked Up	USFWS National Bison Range	1988	228
181 6/8	24	24 1/8	24 1/8	4 5/8	4 5/8	6 5	Gunnison Co., CO	Gary T. White	Gary T. White	1997	229
181 6/8	24 5/8	26 4/8	21 6/8	4 6/8	4 7/8	4 6	Sublette Co., WY	Wayne A. Schmidt	Wayne A. Schmidt	2000	229
181 5/8	21 1/8	23 4/8	16 1/8	5 2/8	5 2/8	7 7	Pitkin Co., CO	Gary A. Johnston	Gary A. Johnston	1986	231
181 5/8	25 3/8	23 4/8	23 2/8	4 4/8	4 6/8	5 5	Milk River, AB	Karey A. Seward	Karey A. Seward	2001	231
181 4/8	24 3/8	24 4/8	21 6/8	4 6/8	5	5 6	Lincoln Co., ID	Andrew M. Callistini	Andrew M. Callistini	2001	233
181 3/8	24	24 2/8	22 6/8	5 7/8	5 1/8	5 7	Owyhee Co., ID	Lucas M. Johnson	Lucas M. Johnson	1996	234
181 3/8	24 6/8	23 4/8	17 4/8	4 6/8	4 6/8	5 8	Moffat Co., CO	Matthew E. Wagner	Matthew E. Wagner	2000	234
181 2/8	23 7/8	24	25 6/8	5 2/8	5 2/8	5 5	Gunnison Co., CO	John S. Pedretti	John S. Pedretti	1997	236
181 1/8	23 6/8	23 6/8	18 1/8	4 5/8	4 5/8	5 6	Rio Blanco Co., CO	Ryan S. Holmlund	Ryan S. Holmlund	2000	237
181 1/8	25	23 7/8	24 1/8	4 4/8	4 4/8	5 5	Lincoln Co., WY	Jared D. Gray	Jared D. Gray	2001	237
181	22 5/8	22 3/8	22 5/8	4 7/8	5	6 7	Crook Co., OR	Teresa L. Davis	Teresa L. Davis	2001	239
180 7/8	25	25 2/8	21 1/8	4 6/8	5	6 6	Carbon Co., WY	Jon P. McDowell	Jon P. McDowell	1982	240
180 7/8	21 5/8	22 5/8	23 4/8	5	4 7/8	6 5	Lincoln Co., NV	Phillip DeShazo	Phillip DeShazo	2001	240
180 7/8	22 6/8	24 1/8	22 3/8	5 1/8	5 1/8	4 4	Nechako River, BC	Terry Raymond, Jr.	Terry Raymond, Jr.	2001	240
180 7/8	24 4/8	26 1/8	25 4/8	5 3/8	5 1/8	7 7	Grant Co., OR	Charles Tompkins	Charles Tompkins	2002	240
180 7/8	21 7/8	22 4/8	22 4/8	5	5	5 6	Montezuma Co., CO	Picked Up	Chris Hansen	2002	240
180 6/8	24 1/8	24 6/8	26 3/8	5 1/8	5 4/8	6 6	Montana	Unknown	Lavern Reil	PR1945	245
180 6/8	25 2/8	27 5/8	19 2/8	5 4/8	5 6/8	6 5	Klamath Co., OR	Glen E. Beeman	Glen E. Beeman	1964	245
180 6/8	23 1/8	24	19 6/8	4 6/8	4 6/8	5 5	Routt Co., WY	Arthur F. Richter, Jr.	Arthur F. Richter, Jr.	2001	245
180 6/8	24 3/8	24 7/8	26 5/8	5 2/8	5 5/8	9 5	Peace River, AB	Ralph J. Demicco	Ralph J. Demicco	2002	245
180 5/8	27 4/8	27 3/8	28	5 1/8	5 2/8	5 6	Shasta Co., CA	Michael D. Vaiana	Michael D. Vaiana	2003	249
180 4/8	24 1/8	24 5/8	23 3/8	4 5/8	4 7/8	5 5	Las Animas Co., CO	Picked Up	Grant C. Adkisson	2001	250
180 4/8	24	24	21 5/8	5	4 7/8	6 5	Grand Co., CO	Morris G. Kimmell	Morris G. Kimmell	2001	251
180 3/8	27 1/8	27	22	5 7/8	5 6/8	5 5	Teton Co., MT	Orville Alfson	Randy Lindgren	1987	252
180 2/8	24 6/8	25 1/8	19 6/8	4 6/8	4 6/8	5 8	Rio Arriba Co., NM	Russell C. Vigil	Russell C. Vigil	2001	252
180 2/8	26 2/8	23 7/8	22 7/8	5	4 3/8	5 5	Elbert Co., CO	Jon A. Fuerst	Jon A. Fuerst	1997	254
180 1/8	22 7/8	22 5/8	24 1/8	4 3/8	5	4 4	Moffat Co., CO	Bobby R. Klein	Bobby R. Klein	2000	254
180 1/8	25 2/8	24 7/8	25 2/8	4 5/8	4 6/8	5 5	Eagle Co., CO	John M. Grobecker	John M. Grobecker	2001	254
180 1/8	24 7/8	25 1/8	19 7/8	4 6/8	4 3/8	4 5	Agnellice Lake, SK	Blaine P. Miller	Blaine P. Miller	2001	254
180 1/8	25 7/8	25 2/8	24 4/8	4 4/8	4 3/8	5 7	Montrose Co., CO	Kenneth W. Felderhoff	Kenneth W. Felderhoff	2002	254

MULE DEER - TYPICAL ANTLERS

Odocoileus hemionus hemionus and certain related subspecies

Score	Length of Main Beam R.	L.	Inside Spread	Circumference at Smallest Place Between Burr & First Point R.	L.	Number of Points R.	L.	Locality	Hunter	Owner	Date Killed	Rank
180 1/8	23 5/8	25 3/8	26 4/8	4 5/8	4 3/8	6	5	Pitkin Co., CO	Shane D. Fossett	Shane D. Fossett	2002	254
180	24 6/8	24 3/8	24 3/8	4 1/8	4 3/8	6	6	Garfield Co., CO	John S. Bouchard	John S. Bouchard	1962	260
180	23 2/8	23 7/8	22	5 1/8	4 7/8	5	6	Ferry Co., WA	Henry E. Goff	Henry E. Goff	1978	260
180	29 2/8	27 6/8	31 2/8	4 5/8	5	5	5	Duchesne Co., UT	Virgil L. Jensen	Virgil L. Jensen	1991	260
180	25 5/8	25 5/8	25 2/8	4 4/8	4 4/8	5	5	Sonora, MX	Glenn Bailey	Glenn Bailey	2002	260
205 7/8*	25 2/8	25 3/8	25 4/8	6 1/8	5 3/8	5	5	Luck Lake, SK	Douglas Erickson	Douglas Erickson	2001	
205*	26	25 7/8	26 3/8	5 6/8	5 4/8	5	5	Sonora, MX	Russell G. Brice	Russell G. Brice	2003	

* Final score subject to revision by additional verifying measurements.

MULE DEER - NON-TYPICAL ANTLERS

Odocoileus hemionus hemionus and certain related subspecies

Minimum Score 215

World's Record 355 2/8

Score	Length of Main Beam R.	L.	Inside Spread	Circumference at Smallest Place Between Burr & First Point R.	L.	Number of Points R.	L.	Locality	Hunter	Owner	Date Killed	Rank
307 6/8	23 7/8	22 1/8	21 5/8	4 4/8	4 5/8	23	16	Idaho	Unknown	D.J. Hollinger & B. Howard	PR1935	1
291 6/8	21 5/8	22 7/8	17 5/8	8 7/8	5 3/8	66	5	Linn Co., OR	Unknown	D.J. Hollinger & B. Howard	1992	2
287 5/8	29	28 6/8	29 5/8	4 7/8	4 7/8	15	16	Montezuma Co., CO	Travis Shippy	Cabela's, Inc.	1985	3
281 6/8	27 2/8	27 4/8	22	5 3/8	5 3/8	14	13	Black Hills, SD	William Olsen	Cabela's, Inc.	1944	4
274 7/8	23 7/8	26 2/8	27	6 4/8	6 2/8	23	11	Morgan Co., CO	Kenneth W. Plank	Cabela's, Inc.	1987	5
274 6/8	24 5/8	22 6/8	22 4/8	5 3/8	5 1/8	14	18	Washington	Unknown	Cabela's, Inc.	PR2003	6
274 2/8	25 7/8	25 6/8	25 3/8	6	5 5/8	15	12	Shackleton, SK	Glen A. Miller	Glen A. Miller	2003	7
273 4/8	25 4/8	24 2/8	22 2/8	5 7/8	5 2/8	20	19	Deschutes Co., OR	Picked Up	OR Dept. of Fish & Wildlife	1956	8
273	24 2/8	22 7/8	35 2/8	5 1/8	5	15	16	Cassia Co., ID	Donald Porter	Ron J. Hulse	1964	9
271 4/8	26	26 6/8	26 7/8	5 6/8	5 5/8	22	18	Colorado	Unknown	Cabela's, Inc.	PR1985	10
271 2/8	22 7/8	24 4/8	23 6/8	5 3/8	5	16	14	British Columbia	G.L. Popp	Cabela's, Inc.	PR1960	11
269 4/8	27 7/8	26 4/8	20 3/8	5 5/8	5 5/8	13	13	Unknown	Unknown	Ron Hall	PR1987	12
269	25 4/8	26 5/8	17 4/8	5 4/8	5 4/8	13	14	Weston Co., WY	Lavonne M. Bucey-Bredehoeft	Lavonne M. Bucey-Bredehoeft	1961	13
267 5/8	28 1/8	28 2/8	29 2/8	6	6 2/8	16	12	Wallowa Co., OR	Mark Thompson	Dale Potter	1924	14
266 2/8	25 1/8	26	20 5/8	5 4/8	5 4/8	12	12	Williams Lake, BC	Robert R. Letts	D.J. Hollinger & B. Howard	1984	15
264 4/8	28 5/8	26 5/8	29 5/8	5 1/8	4 7/8	16	12	Colorado	Unknown	Cabela's, Inc.	PR1950	16
263 2/8	29 1/8	29 1/8	28 2/8	4 7/8	5	9	13	Rio Arriba Co., NM	Picked Up	Robert J. Seeds	1988	17
262 3/8	27 7/8	25 5/8	24 5/8	5 2/8	5 1/8	9	12	Cassia Co., ID	Ron Woodall	D.J. Hollinger & B. Howard	1984	18
262 2/8	22 5/8	28 2/8	24 1/8	4 3/8	4 5/8	8	9	Adams Co., ID	Carolyn Menichetti	Raymond R. Cross	1959	19
261 6/8	23 6/8	25 4/8	21 4/8	5 4/8	5 3/8	14	16	Montezuma Co., CO	Travis Shippy	Cabela's, Inc.	1986	20
261 3/8	25 2/8	26 5/8	19 4/8	4 6/8	4 6/8	10	10	111 Mile House, BC	Picked Up	D.J. Hollinger & B. Howard	1998	21
259 7/8	19 3/8	31 1/8	25 6/8	5 3/8	5 2/8	15	19	Coconino Co., AZ	Picked Up	Alvin C. West	1967	22
259 5/8	25 1/8	25 4/8	20 7/8	5 2/8	5 2/8	10	11	Sublette Co., WY	H. Duane Hermon	H. Duane Hermon	1973	23
257 4/8	25	26 6/8	25 2/8	5 3/8	5 5/8	12	10	Colorado	Ed Hiler	Aly M. Bruner	1957	24
257	23 1/8	23 2/8	23 2/8	5 5/8	5 4/8	15	13	Lincoln Co., ID	Zach Shetler	Cabela's, Inc.	2001	25
252 7/8	21 7/8	22 6/8	26 6/8	5 4/8	5 5/8	15	11	S. Saskatchewan River, SK	Glenn A. Vestre	Glenn A. Vestre	2001	26
251 2/8	26 4/8	27 1/8	24 1/8	6 4/8	6 1/8	10	15	Grant Co., OR	Edward Kock	Daniel E. Williams	1930	27
250 3/8	27 2/8	27 7/8	24 4/8	4 4/8	4 4/8	12	9	Grant Co., OR	Manford Pate	D.J. Hollinger & B. Howard	1946	28
248 6/8	27 1/8	26 5/8	16 3/8	6	6	8	19	Idaho	Unknown	D.J. Hollinger & B. Howard	1962	29
248 6/8	22 2/8	25 6/8	23 3/8	5 4/8	6	10	8	Adams Co., CO	Picked Up	US Fish & Wildlife Service	1989	29
248 4/8	22 6/8	26 3/8	26 6/8	5 4/8	5	9	6	Lincoln Co., NV	Alan B. Shepherd	Alan B. Shepherd	2001	31
248 3/8	28	26 4/8	25 2/8	6 2/8	6 2/8	12	12	Okanogan Co., WA	William L. Tedford	Steve Nordness	1940	32

MULE DEER - NON-TYPICAL ANTLERS

Odocoileus hemionus hemionus and certain related subspecies

Score	Length of Main Beam R.	L.	Inside Spread	Circumference at Smallest Place Between Burr & First Point R.	L.	Number of Points R.	L.	Locality	Hunter	Owner	Date Killed	Rank
247 7/8	27 4/8	28	28 5/8	4 4/8	4 4/8	11	11	Grant Co., OR	Manford Pate	D.J. Hollinger & B. Howard	1946	33
247 1/8	24 2/8	23 5/8	24 2/8	5 2/8	5 1/8	11	13	Campbell Co., WY	Ron Fresuik	D.J. Hollinger & B. Howard	1979	34
246 1/8	26 7/8	27 4/8	27 4/8	5 7/8	5 6/8	8	9	Twin Falls Co., ID	Jed Seamons	Jed Seamons	2000	35
246	29 6/8	31 1/8	23 4/8	6 7/8	6 6/8	9	11	Unknown	Unknown	D.J. Hollinger & B. Howard	PR1993	36
244 5/8	23 7/8	24 2/8	20 5/8	5 3/8	5 1/8	8	9	Cibola Co., NM	Picked Up	Picked Up	1989	37
244 3/8	26 2/8	25 7/8	24 4/8	5 3/8	5 4/8	13	10	Lemhi Co., ID	Picked Up	Cabela's, Inc.	PR1958	38
244 2/8	24	24 6/8	20 6/8	6	6 1/8	16	16	British Columbia	Unknown	Douglas V. Grant	1958	39
242 7/8	24	25 6/8	22 7/8	5 1/8	5 6/8	18	13	Elko Co., NV	Edgar Meek	D.J. Hollinger & B. Howard	1971	40
242 5/8	27 6/8	28 2/8	27 3/8	4 6/8	4 6/8	13	9	Camas Co., ID	Jeff M. Ashmead	Jeff M. Ashmead	1981	41
242 4/8	23 2/8	26 2/8	21 6/8	5 5/8	5 2/8	14	6	Sanders Co., MT	Ernest Butte	Roy Butte	1929	42
242 4/8	26 4/8	26 7/8	24 7/8	5 3/8	5 1/8	10	10	Moffat Co., CO	Robert K. Kissling	Robert K. Kissling	2000	42
241 4/8	25 7/8	22 3/8	25 3/8	4 7/8	5	13	18	Park Co., MT	James H. Batzloff	James H. Batzloff	1959	44
241 3/8	25 2/8	25 2/8	22 4/8	5 3/8	5 4/8	12	11	Unknown	Unknown	Aly M. Bruner	PR1989	45
241	27	25 4/8	27 4/8	5 6/8	5 6/8	10	8	Colorado	Unknown	Cabela's, Inc.	PR2001	46
241	24 5/8	25 7/8	23 4/8	5 1/8	5 5/8	12	11	Moffat Co., CO	Gary W. Christensen	Gary W. Christensen	2003	46
240 6/8	23	23 5/8	20 2/8	4 6/8	4 5/8	13	12	Norton Co., KS	Bill Bussen	Cabela's, Inc.	1996	48
240 4/8	23 6/8	26 6/8	19	5 6/8	5 6/8	10	13	Montrose Co., CO	Albin C. Wood	Albin C. Wood	1961	49
240 3/8	25 1/8	25 4/8	24 1/8	6 3/8	6	10	12	Unknown	Unknown	Terry L. Amos	PR2000	50
240 1/8	28 1/8	28 4/8	25 5/8	7 1/8	5 3/8	13	8	Caribou Co., ID	Roy M. McIntosh	Roy M. McIntosh	1967	51
239 7/8	26 6/8	24 5/8	21 4/8	5 5/8	5 7/8	11	10	Caribou Co., ID	Jack E. Detmer	Jack E. Detmer	1964	52
239 1/8	24 4/8	24	23 6/8	4 4/8	4 4/8	10	9	San Miguel Co., CO	Vodne O. Chapoose	Vodne O. Chapoose	2002	53
238	26 3/8	26	26 4/8	5	5 1/8	12	10	Mesa Co., CO	James D. Greer	James D. Greer	1969	54
236 6/8	25 2/8	25 7/8	24 2/8	5	4 5/8	14	12	Opuntia Lake, SK	Tom D. Jiricka	Tom D. Jiricka	2003	55
236 5/8	25 6/8	26 5/8	22 2/8	5 5/8	5 6/8	12	11	Lincoln Co., NV	Ronald N. Anderson	Ronald N. Anderson	2001	56
236	28 1/8	29 1/8	23 6/8	4 7/8	4 6/8	5	7	Summit Co., CO	Ray Alt	Ray Alt	1987	57
235 7/8	22 6/8	22	25 2/8	5 2/8	5 3/8	12	10	Nevada Co., CA	Unknown	Charles L. Leavell	1920	58
235 5/8	23 6/8	25 5/8	25 7/8	5 4/8	5 3/8	11	8	Kane Co., UT	Rance Rollins	Rance Rollins	1965	59
235	25 4/8	25 5/8	22 4/8	4 6/8	4 7/8	10	10	Garnier Lakes, AB	Arthur Gallagher	Richard C. Nelson	1936	60
235	27 1/8	29 2/8	27 4/8	5 2/8	5 3/8	8	11	Eagle Co., CO	Charles D. Elam	Charles D. Elam	2002	60
234 6/8	28	29 2/8	32 3/8	5 2/8	5 2/8	6	7	Modoc Co., CA	Unknown	D.J. Hollinger & B. Howard	1950	62
234 1/8	24 5/8	24 1/8	22 4/8	5 4/8	5 4/8	9	11	Salmon Arm, BC	Jeffrey M. Snow	Jeffrey M. Snow	2002	62
234	24 5/8	24 4/8	22	5 2/8	5	9	9	Lincoln Co., NV	Jason G. Carter	Jason G. Carter	2003	64

Score						Points		Locality	Hunter	Owner	Date	Rank
233 4/8	29 2/8	28	5	5	23 6/8	8	10	Blaine Co., ID	Art Richards	Kyle J. Kimball	1984	65
233 3/8	25	26 1/8	6 2/8	6 3/8	21 7/8	11	9	S. Saskatchewan River, AB	Kelvin J. Clary	Kelvin J. Clary	2003	66
233 2/8	25 6/8	25 6/8	6 2/8	6	24 4/8	11	12	San Juan Co., UT	Leon P. Rush, Jr.	Leon P. Rush, Jr.	2001	67
232 4/8	25	24 2/8	5 4/8	5 1/8	20 3/8	10	10	Adams Co., ID	Allen Solterbeck	Ryan B. Hatfield	1973	68
232 3/8	26 1/8	26	5 4/8	5 3/8	23 5/8	12	12	Eagle Co., CO	Unknown	D.J. Hollinger & B. Howard	PR1960	69
232 2/8	24 3/8	25 1/8	5	5	22 1/8	10	9	Elmore Co., ID	David R. Heck	David R. Heck	2002	70
232	24 6/8	26	6	5 7/8	21 3/8	10	10	Garfield Co., CO	Vern Williams	D.J. Hollinger & B. Howard	1961	71
232	26	25 2/8	4 7/8	5	23 1/8	8	8	Rio Arriba Co., NM	Picked Up	Robert J. Seeds	1998	71
231 7/8	26	25 3/8	6 2/8	5 7/8	25	10	10	Lake Co., OR	Marion J. Rossiter	Marion J. Rossiter	1961	73
231 6/8	25 1/8	24 7/8	5 2/8	5 2/8	23 2/8	8	7	Yuma Co., AZ	Gregg W. Stults	Gregg W. Stults	2000	74
231 4/8	26 5/8	24 7/8	5 5/8	5 5/8	23 2/8	10	10	Yuma Co., CO	I. Dwayne Bullock	I. Dwayne Bullock	1986	75
231 2/8	23 4/8	22 4/8	5 1/8	4 7/8	30 2/8	9	5	Bannock Co., ID	Kevin D. Linford	Kevin D. Linford	1982	76
231 1/8	24 4/8	25 6/8	5 1/8	5 3/8	22	12	11	Stevens Co., WA	David Kilmartin	David Kilmartin	1985	77
231	24 1/8	21 5/8	5 4/8	5 2/8	16 4/8	9	6	Coconino Co., AZ	Robert E. Anderson	Robert E. Anderson	1988	78
231	27 7/8	28 1/8	5	5 1/8	19 6/8	11	9	S. Saskatchewan River, SK	Sheldon C. McNabb	Sheldon C. McNabb	2001	78
230 5/8	22 1/8	23 2/8	5 4/8	5 3/8	24 3/8	8	7	Salmon Arm, BC	Jack W. Stewart	Jack W. Stewart	2000	80
230 1/8	27	26 7/8	4 5/8	4 5/8	21 4/8	13	8	Delta Co., CO	Frank W. Penland	Frank W. Penland	1978	81
230 1/8	26	24 5/8	5 3/8	5 5/8	27 4/8	10	8	Mohave Co., AZ	Shane Memmott	Shane Memmott	2002	81
230	25 7/8	25 5/8	5 4/8	5 4/8	22 7/8	7	8	Boise Co., ID	Leland R. Nevill	Leland R. Nevill	1986	83
230	24 5/8	23 4/8	6 2/8	6 2/8	20 1/8	10	8	Pitkin Co., CO	Joseph J. Stroh	Joseph J. Stroh	2002	83
229 7/8	26 2/8	25 7/8	5 1/8	5	29 6/8	8	10	Ferry Co., WA	Gus Krug	Michael R. Damery	1958	85
229 3/8	25 7/8	26 3/8	4 7/8	4 7/8	19 3/8	13	13	Cascade Co., MT	Thomas W. Hood	Thomas W. Hood	1974	86
228	25 4/8	26	5 2/8	5 2/8	16 2/8	7	9	Rio Arriba Co., NM	Picked Up	NM Dept. of Game & Fish	2000	87
227 5/8	20 1/8	23 1/8	5 1/8	5	25 6/8	10	7	Toole Co., MT	Kenneth Thompson	Kenneth Thompson	1957	88
227 4/8	22 7/8	23 3/8	8 6/8	8 4/8	21 7/8	9	10	San Juan Co., NM	Martin Mareno	D.J. Hollinger & B. Howard	1957	89
227 3/8	23 6/8	23 6/8	4 7/8	4 7/8	17 1/8	14	16	Fremont Co., WY	James P. Lovely	James P. Lovely	1946	90
227 2/8	26 2/8	26 6/8	5 3/8	5 4/8	21 2/8	11	12	Adams Co., ID	Hank Widener	Dan Schledewitz	1963	91
226 7/8	24	27 4/8	5 5/8	5	32 2/8	11	8	Mesa Co., CO	Picked Up	D.J. Hollinger & B. Howard	1997	92
226 6/8	24 5/8	25	5 4/8	5	20 3/8	11	9	Delburne, AB	Calvin A. Watts	Calvin A. Watts	2000	93
226 3/8	25 4/8	25 4/8	5 7/8	5 5/8	23 5/8	9	12	Coconino Co., AZ	Richard D. Nelson	Richard D. Nelson	2001	94
226 1/8	24 4/8	27 5/8	5 3/8	5 2/8	22	9	8	Nekeenet Indian Res., SK	John C. Pavlakis	John C. Pavlakis	2001	95
226	25 1/8	25 4/8	4 4/8	4 4/8	26 3/8	9	8	Mesa Co., CO	James R. Story	James R. Story	2000	96
225 6/8	26 6/8	25	5 4/8	5	24 6/8	9	9	Elko Co., NV	Picked Up	D.R. Aschenbach & D. Pearson	1999	97
225 3/8	24 5/8	21 1/8	4 5/8	4 7/8	19 1/8	10	10	Pelletier Lake, SK	Darcy L. Faucher	Darcy L. Faucher	2003	98
225 2/8	29 6/8	28 2/8	5	5 1/8	26 2/8	7	9	Lemhi Co., ID	Arthur Scott	J. & L.S. Massey	1953	99
225 2/8	22	22 2/8	5 1/8	5 4/8	20 2/8	11	11	Coconino Co., AZ	Ed Pfeifer	Ed Pfeifer	1968	99
225	25 1/8	25	5	5	25	11	11	Payette Co., ID	Howard L. Alexander	Howard D. Alexander	1955	101
224 6/8	28 5/8	28 6/8	5 2/8	5	27 1/8	9	9	Montrose Co., CO	Herbert L. Swalley	Tim Alberti	1961	102
224 1/8	28 4/8	28 4/8	4 6/8	4 6/8	28 6/8	7	8	Nez Perce Co., ID	Jack O'Connor	University of Idaho	1960	103
224	26 2/8	25 6/8	5 2/8	5 1/8	36 5/8	8	10	Caribou Co., ID	Parley Hopkins	Arlo T. Hopkins	1935	104
223 7/8	27 5/8	26 4/8	5 3/8	5 2/8	20	12	13	Crook Co., OR	Clarence L. Fitzwater	W. Dean Fitzwater	PR1933	105

MULE DEER - NON-TYPICAL ANTLERS

Odocoileus hemionus hemionus and certain related subspecies

Score	Length of Main Beam R.	L.	Inside Spread	Circumference at Smallest Place Between Burr & First Point R.	L.	Number of Points R.	L.	Locality	Hunter	Owner	Date Killed	Rank
223 7/8	26 1/8	26 1/8	24 3/8	4 6/8	4 4/8	7	9	Campbell Co., WY	Richard A. Stone	Richard A. Stone	2000	105
223	22 4/8	23	25 7/8	5 1/8	5 5/8	8	11	Sanders Co., MT	Picked Up	USFWS National Bison Range	1986	107
223	27	27 5/8	26 4/8	6	5 5/8	9	10	Klickitat Co., WA	Joseph M. Hirko	Joseph M. Hirko	1986	107
222 6/8	25 6/8	24 2/8	24	5 6/8	5 2/8	12	9	Dixon Lake, BC	Phil D'Entremont	Phil D'Entremont	2000	109
222 4/8	26 1/8	25	25 1/8	5 6/8	5 5/8	9	7	Beechy, SK	Cecil S. Bryson	Cecil S. Bryson	2003	110
222 3/8	26 3/8	26 4/8	27 3/8	5	5 3/8	8	8	Idaho	Picked Up	Patrick J. Gilligan	1980	111
222 1/8	24 2/8	26 4/8	22 4/8	5 1/8	5 1/8	11	10	Garfield Co., CO	Wayne Anderson	D.J. Hollinger & B. Howard	1956	112
222 1/8	26 3/8	27 1/8	21	5 4/8	5 2/8	12	14	Eagle Co., CO	W. King Stubbs	W. King Stubbs	2001	112
221 3/8	22 7/8	26 4/8	18 5/8	6	6 2/8	10	10	Sheridan Co., WY	Michael A. Barrett	Michael A. Barrett	2003	114
220 7/8	23 6/8	23	19 6/8	4 6/8	4 6/8	8	8	Jeff Davis Co., TX	John Z. Means	John Z. Means	2002	115
220 6/8	24 1/8	24	22 5/8	5	4 7/8	10	8	Colorado	William P. Betts	Coby Betts	1944	116
220 5/8	24 6/8	25 7/8	23 1/8	5	5 1/8	9	8	Cheyenne Co., KS	David J. Asleson	David J. Asleson	2001	117
220 4/8	25 6/8	23 6/8	20	5 5/8	5 5/8	10	10	Twin Falls Co., ID	Ivan Molyneux	William C. Pulsipher	1948	118
220 2/8	27	26 4/8	22	5 5/8	5 4/8	8	10	S. Saskatchewan River, SK	Jim Clary	Jim Clary	2001	119
219 2/8	23 4/8	25 4/8	23 3/8	4 7/8	4 7/8	7	7	Sanpete Co., UT	William W. Goodridge	William W. Goodridge	1950	120
219 1/8	25	26 5/8	25 4/8	6	6 3/8	12	10	Mohave Co., AZ	Frank Zuern, Sr.	Frank Zuern, Sr.	1994	121
218 1/8	23 6/8	24 3/8	24	6 2/8	6 2/8	8	8	Sonora, MX	Picked Up	Billy Havens	2001	122
217 6/8	27 3/8	26	22 7/8	5	4 7/8	9	8	Rio Arriba Co., NM	Alfred W. Vigil	Alfred W. Vigil	2003	123
216 6/8	25 1/8	27	26 6/8	4 6/8	4 6/8	8	9	Morgan Co., UT	Unknown	L. Dwight Israelsen	1965	124
216 5/8	26 2/8	27 4/8	27	5	4 6/8	8	9	Sheridan Co., WY	Zach Peters	Zach Peters	2001	125
216 2/8	25	25 4/8	21 4/8	5 7/8	5 4/8	10	7	Arapahoe Co., CO	Jim Bashor	Jim Bashor	2001	126
216 2/8	27 1/8	27 3/8	19	5 1/8	5 4/8	8	8	Blackwater River, BC	Greg Petersen	Greg Petersen	2002	126
216 1/8	24 5/8	25	23	5 2/8	5 1/8	10	7	Carbon Co., WY	Robert E. Bergquist	Robert E. Bergquist	2003	128
215 7/8	24 7/8	24 3/8	20 3/8	4 3/8	4 3/8	12	8	Deschutes Co., OR	Ben Myers	Ben Myers	1974	129
215 3/8	24 5/8	24 4/8	21 5/8	5 1/8	5 3/8	9	6	Great Sand Hills, SK	Hamid Zanidean	Hamid Zanidean	1998	130
215	27 6/8	26 7/8	24 6/8	4 7/8	4 7/8	6	9	Deschutes Co., OR	Glen D. Clark	Glen D. Clark	1980	131
215	27	28	21 1/8	5 1/8	5 1/8	7	10	Coconino Co., AZ	Danny F. Monnett	Danny F. Monnett	2001	131
248 4/8*	27 6/8	24 5/8	22 5/8	6	5	13	13	Rio Arriba Co., NM	Aaron Q. Howell	Aaron Q. Howell	2001	

* Final score subject to revision by additional verifying measurements.

COLUMBIA BLACKTAIL - TYPICAL ANTLERS

Odocoileus hemionus columbianus

Minimum Score 125

World's Record 182 2/8

Score	Length of Main Beam R	L	Inside Spread	Circumference at Smallest Place Between Burr & First Point R	L	Number of Points R	L	Locality	Hunter	Owner	Date Killed	Rank
172 5/8	23 6/8	23 1/8	21	4 7/8	4 6/8	6	5	Washington Co., OR	Fred Wolford	Gary A. French	1919	1
170 1/8	26	24 5/8	17 2/8	4 4/8	4 4/8	5	6	Trinity Co., CA	Eric Helms	Eric Helms	2000	2
166 2/8	25 5/8	25 3/8	21 6/8	4 2/8	4 1/8	5	5	Polk Co., OR	Earl Starks	Earl Starks	1959	3
164 6/8	23 4/8	23 6/8	17 4/8	5 1/8	5 2/8	5	5	Clackamas Co., OR	Howard D. Bunnell	Howard D. Bunnell	2003	4
163 5/8	21 6/8	22 1/8	20 3/8	4 3/8	4 3/8	4	5	Lake Co., CA	Bill L. Conn	Bill L. Conn	1976	5
162 7/8	23 2/8	23 4/8	19 4/8	4 7/8	4 7/8	5	5	Josephine Co., OR	John E. Webb, Jr.	John E. Webb, Jr.	1973	6
162 6/8	22 4/8	22 4/8	20 2/8	5 2/8	5 2/8	5	5	Jackson Co., OR	Ken Wilson	Ken Wilson	1979	7
160 4/8	23	22 7/8	17 6/8	4 3/8	4 4/8	5	5	Siskiyou Co., CA	Tommy McCaw	John A. Crawford	1934	8
160 1/8	22 5/8	22 1/8	15 7/8	4 7/8	4 7/8	5	5	Chilliwack Lake, BC	Mike Tenbos	Mike Tenbos	2000	9
158 6/8	21 3/8	20 7/8	17 6/8	4 4/8	4 4/8	5	5	Josephine Co., OR	Glen R. Wooldridge	Glen R. Wooldridge	PR1950	10
154	23 4/8	24 3/8	23 2/8	4 2/8	4 2/8	8	7	Mendocino Co., CA	Ernest McKee	Ralph McKee, Jr.	1957	11
153 7/8	22 4/8	22 2/8	22 3/8	4 6/8	4 5/8	5	5	Jackson Co., OR	Mike J. Prohoroff	Mike J. Prohoroff	2000	12
153 5/8	23 2/8	22 4/8	21 7/8	3 6/8	3 6/8	6	5	Jackson Co., OR	Ken Wilson	Ken Wilson	2000	13
153	19 7/8	19 7/8	15 6/8	4 7/8	4 7/8	5	5	Douglas Co., OR	James W. Martin, Jr.	James W. Martin, Jr.	2001	14
151 4/8	23 7/8	23 3/8	22 6/8	4 4/8	4 5/8	5	5	Mendocino Co., CA	Ely O. Sanderson	Ely O. Sanderson	2000	15
151 3/8	20 7/8	20 3/8	14 1/8	4 4/8	4 4/8	5	5	Clackamas Co., OR	David Wolford	David Wolford	1999	16
151 3/8	24 3/8	24 6/8	20 4/8	4 2/8	4 2/8	4	4	Trinity Co., CA	Leonard C. Waterman	Leonard C. Waterman	2003	16
151 2/8	22	22 3/8	17 6/8	4 1/8	4 1/8	5	5	Clallam Co., WA	Joe Pavel	Patrick M. Lockhart	1962	18
150 6/8	21 3/8	21	18 1/8	5	4 7/8	5	6	Humboldt Co., CA	Jason R. McCanless	Jason R. McCanless	2001	19
150 6/8	22 6/8	23 6/8	21 4/8	4 6/8	4 6/8	5	5	Trinity Co., CA	Cameron L. Brown	Cameron L. Brown	2002	19
150	21 5/8	22	17	5 6/8	5 5/8	6	6	Mendocino Co., CA	Mark A. Pennacchio	Mark A. Pennacchio	2002	21
149 7/8	22 4/8	23 4/8	19 7/8	4 3/8	4 3/8	6	6	Lewis Co., WA	Elvon A. Self	Elvon A. Self	1966	22
149 6/8	22 3/8	22 3/8	19	4 4/8	5	5	5	Mendocino Co., CA	Redhawk R. Pallesen	Redhawk R. Pallesen	1996	23
149 5/8	20 2/8	20	16 1/8	4 7/8	5	5	5	Trinity Co., CA	Craig Brown	Craig Brown	2002	24
149 4/8	23 7/8	22 6/8	15 3/8	5 1/8	5	5	6	Lewis Co., WA	Scotty Mullins	James Stafford	1977	25
148 3/8	18 6/8	18 6/8	15 3/8	5 2/8	5 4/8	6	5	Snohomish Co., WA	C.T. Hasler	C.T. Hasler	1955	26
147 1/8	20 3/8	20 5/8	21 6/8	3 4/8	3 3/8	5	5	Humboldt Co., CA	Jimmy Lennon	Kenneth W. Springer	1930	27
147 1/8	22 1/8	22 1/8	16 4/8	4 2/8	4 2/8	5	7	Trinity Co., CA	Picked Up	Bruce D. Ringsmith	1961	27
147 1/8	21 7/8	21 6/8	18 7/8	4 3/8	4 3/8	6	5	Santa Clara Co., CA	Domenic V. Genco	Domenic V. Genco	2003	27
146 5/8	23 6/8	23 2/8	18 7/8	5 3/8	5 4/8	7	6	Pierce Co., WA	Roy E. Erickson	Dwayne R. Erickson	1942	30
146 2/8	24 2/8	24	17	5 2/8	5 4/8	6	7	Clallam Co., WA	Earl Stone	Patrick M. Lockhart	1946	31
145 7/8	22 4/8	22	18 7/8	4 4/8	4 5/8	5	5	Glenn Co., CA	George W. Wiget	Kathleen W. Dunn	1939	32
145 4/8	22	21 4/8	16 6/8	5 6/8	6 3/8	6	6	Lewis Co., WA	Adolph M. Borden	Glenn M. Borden	1939	33

COLUMBIA BLACKTAIL - TYPICAL ANTLERS

Odocoileus hemionus columbianus

Score	Length of Main Beam R.	L.	Inside Spread	Circumference at Smallest Place Between Burr & First Point R.	L.	Number of Points R.	L.	Locality	Hunter	Owner	Date Killed	Rank
145 3/8	21 2/8	22 4/8	19 6/8	4 4/8	4 4/8	6	6	Clallam Co., WA	Ernest Hanewell	Patrick M. Lockhart	1964	34
145 1/8	19 7/8	20 1/8	20 1/8	4 4/8	4 4/8	5	5	Jefferson Co., WA	Bryan L. Bukovnik	Bryan L. Bukovnik	2001	35
145	20 5/8	20 1/8	17 1/8	5	4 4/8	7	5	Tehama Co., CA	Douglas R. Jost	Douglas R. Jost	2002	36
144 7/8	21 6/8	21 5/8	19 5/8	5 6/8	5 7/8	4	3	Grays Harbor Co., WA	Ken Frank	Mitch Myers	1935	37
144 6/8	22 4/8	22 7/8	16 5/8	4 4/8	4 4/8	5	5	Benton Co., OR	Martin C. Goracke	Thomas Goracke	PR1950	38
144 6/8	22 4/8	22	16 4/8	4 2/8	4 4/8	5	5	Linn Co., OR	Angeline Fischer	Angeline Fischer	1968	38
144 6/8	23 1/8	22 2/8	19 7/8	4 7/8	4 5/8	5	5	Humboldt Co., CA	Kevin R. Hunt	Kevin R. Hunt	2002	38
144 5/8	21	21 1/8	17 7/8	4 2/8	4 3/8	5	5	Lewis Co., WA	LeRoy F. Benge	LeRoy F. Benge	1974	41
144 1/8	20 2/8	19 2/8	17 7/8	4 6/8	4 6/8	5	5	Humboldt Co., CA	Richard L. Barsanti	Richard L. Barsanti	2000	42
144 1/8	22	21 4/8	16 3/8	4 2/8	4 1/8	5	5	Lane Co., OR	John W. Wheeler	John W. Wheeler	2001	42
144	21 6/8	23 2/8	19 2/8	4	3 7/8	5	5	Jackson Co., OR	Robert D. Davidson	Robert D. Davidson	2000	44
143 6/8	21 4/8	21 7/8	15 6/8	4 6/8	5	5	5	Linn Co., OR	Michael D. Owen	Michael D. Owen	1973	45
143 4/8	21 7/8	21 7/8	18 2/8	4 1/8	4 3/8	4	5	Clackamas Co., OR	Richard L. Schwichtenberg	Richard L. Schwichtenberg	2002	46
143 2/8	22 4/8	22 6/8	17 2/8	4 1/8	4 2/8	7	5	Polk Co., OR	S. Mike Jacobsen	S. Mike Jacobsen	2000	47
143 1/8	21	21 5/8	17 1/8	4 2/8	4 4/8	5	5	Coos Co., OR	Ken Wilson	Ken Wilson	1980	48
142 5/8	20 1/8	20 4/8	15 5/8	4	4	5	5	Alameda Co., CA	Dino W. Markette	Dino W. Markette	1999	49
142	23 6/8	23 2/8	20	5 4/8	5 3/8	8	6	Lewis Co., WA	Calvin Harris	Pete Harris	1963	50
140 7/8	22 7/8	22 6/8	17 3/8	4 3/8	4 3/8	4	4	Clallam Co., WA	Irving C. Hansen	Kurt C. Hansen	PR1950	51
140 7/8	21 1/8	19 4/8	16 3/8	4 2/8	4 5/8	5	5	Tehama Co., CA	Donald J. Giottonini, Jr.	Donald J. Giottonini, Jr.	2002	51
140 6/8	23 5/8	23 6/8	20	5	5	5	5	Clallam Co., WA	Darrell J. Johnson	Darrell J. Johnson	2003	53
140 4/8	20 2/8	22 2/8	18 4/8	4 4/8	4 4/8	5	4	Mendocino Co., CA	Bill L. Conn	Bill L. Conn	1977	54
140 4/8	21 1/8	21 2/8	19 4/8	4 1/8	4 1/8	5	5	Mendocino Co., CA	Ronald L. Christensen	Ronald L. Christensen	2002	54
140 3/8	23 1/8	22 6/8	19 2/8	4 4/8	4 2/8	6	5	Jackson Co., OR	Dusty S. McGrorty	Dusty S. McGrorty	2000	56
139 5/8	19 1/8	19 4/8	16 1/8	4 4/8	4 4/8	5	5	Yolo Co., CA	Paul S. Matsumura	Paul S. Matsumura	2001	57
139 2/8	22 4/8	22 2/8	16	4	4	5	5	Tehama Co., CA	Paul J. Carlisle, Jr.	Paul J. Carlisle, Jr.	2000	58
139 1/8	23 2/8	23 3/8	20 3/8	5 3/8	4 5/8	5	4	Santa Clara Co., CA	Jack G. James	William R. James	1945	59
139	19 2/8	20 5/8	17 6/8	4 4/8	4 4/8	5	5	Mendocino Co., CA	Emilio Flores	Emilio Flores	2001	60
139	20	20 3/8	17 4/8	3 7/8	4 2/8	4	5	Trinity Co., CA	Summer L. Brown	Summer L. Brown	2003	60
138 6/8	20 3/8	19 7/8	16 7/8	4 6/8	4 5/8	5	6	Clackamas Co., OR	Timothy P. Brown	Timothy P. Brown	2001	62
138 4/8	22 6/8	23 1/8	20 6/8	4 2/8	4 4/8	4	4	Tehama Co., CA	Dean A. Chambers	Dean A. Chambers	2002	63
138 3/8	19	21 1/8	18 1/8	4 7/8	4 7/8	4	5	Mendocino Co., CA	Gus J. Kerry	Gus J. Kerry	2002	64
138 2/8	21 7/8	21 2/8	15 2/8	3 5/8	3 7/8	4	5	Coos Co., OR	Lynn A. Schrag	Lynn A. Schrag	1996	65
138 1/8	21 2/8	21	16 3/8	4 2/8	4 1/8	5	5	Polk Co., OR	Douglas G. Ellis	Douglas G. Ellis	2000	66

Score								Locality	Hunter	Owner	Date	Rank
138 1/8	19 7/8	19 7/8	19 1/8	3 6/8	4	5	5	Siskiyou Co., CA	Gary G. Pitt	Gary G. Pitt	2001	66
138 1/8	22 1/8	21 6/8	16 6/8	4	4	4	5	Humboldt Co., CA	Donald C. Miller	Donald C. Miller	2002	66
138	20 4/8	20 2/8	14	4 1/8	4 1/8	5	5	Marion Co., OR	Lawrence Sowa	Tim Sowa	1960	69
137 4/8	21 5/8	19 4/8	15 7/8	4 5/8	4 5/8	5	6	Marion Co., OR	John D. Lulay	John D. Lulay	2001	70
137 3/8	20 5/8	20 7/8	15 7/8	4 7/8	4 5/8	5	5	Coos Co., OR	Eli P. Mast	Glenn E. Sickels	1876	71
137 3/8	20 6/8	20 7/8	16 5/8	4 3/8	4 1/8	5	5	Clackamas Co., OR	Timothy P. Brown	Timothy P. Brown	2000	71
137 2/8	20 4/8	20 4/8	18 2/8	3 7/8	3 6/8	5	5	Mendocino Co., CA	Norman Brown, Jr.	Norman Brown, Jr.	2000	73
137 2/8	20	21 2/8	19 3/8	4 2/8	4 4/8	6	5	Mendocino Co., CA	Cliff E. Jacobson	Cliff E. Jacobson	2001	73
137 2/8	21 3/8	21 1/8	15 2/8	4 1/8	4 4/8	5	5	Lane Co., OR	Glen E. Butler	Glen E. Butler	2001	73
137 1/8	19 4/8	20 1/8	16 5/8	4 5/8	4 6/8	4	5	King Co., WA	John A. Grosvenor	John A. Grosvenor	1983	76
137 1/8	20 7/8	20 7/8	14 1/8	3 5/8	3 6/8	5	4	Lewis Co., WA	Bill C. Boehm	Bill C. Boehm	1997	76
137 1/8	20 5/8	20 3/8	15 7/8	4 3/8	4 2/8	5	5	Lane Co., OR	Noah C. Hoiland	Noah C. Hoiland	2000	78
136 7/8	23 1/8	22 7/8	20 2/8	4 4/8	4 7/8	3	4	Linn Co., OR	Mike Martell	Mike Martell	1985	79
136 6/8	20 6/8	20 6/8	17 2/8	4 2/8	4 1/8	5	5	Jackson Co., OR	Scott L. Ruppel	Scott L. Ruppel	2002	79
136 3/8	21 7/8	21 7/8	18 1/8	4 2/8	4 2/8	3	3	Clallam Co., WA	Bill Wilder	V. Birkland & M. Lewis	1953	81
136 3/8	21 4/8	22 3/8	19 1/8	4 2/8	4 2/8	5	5	Chehalis River, BC	A. Larry Kahl	A. Larry Kahl	2001	81
136 2/8	21 4/8	21 3/8	21 5/8	4 4/8	4 4/8	5	6	Santa Clara Co., CA	Glenn D. Brem	Glenn D. Brem	1941	83
136 1/8	18 5/8	18 5/8	14 5/8	5 1/8	4 6/8	6	6	Humboldt Co., CA	Brian E. Hornberger	Brian E. Hornberger	2003	84
135 7/8	21 2/8	21	22 3/8	4 4/8	4 4/8	6	6	Trinity Co., CA	Gregory C. Koehler	Gregory C. Koehler	2000	85
135 7/8	21 3/8	21 4/8	20 3/8	4 2/8	4 3/8	5	5	San Mateo Co., CA	Robert Caughey	Robert Caughey	2002	85
135 7/8	20 2/8	21	14 5/8	4 4/8	4 4/8	5	5	Skamania Co., WA	Kevin J. Lueders	Kevin J. Lueders	2002	85
135 7/8	19 3/8	19 7/8	19 1/8	4 6/8	4 2/8	5	5	Mendocino Co., CA	Joseph B. Ricard	Joseph B. Ricard	2003	85
135 4/8	22 7/8	22 3/8	17 2/8	4 2/8	3 4/8	5	4	Pierce Co., WA	Joseph G. Williams	Joseph G. Williams	1954	89
135 4/8	21 3/8	20 7/8	19 4/8	4 6/8	4 3/8	5	5	Glenn Co., CA	Charles W. Abbott	Charles W. Abbott	2000	89
135 4/8	20 3/8	19 2/8	16 2/8	4 1/8	4 1/8	6	5	Skamania Co., WA	Joseph J. Boggioni	Joseph J. Boggioni	2000	89
135 4/8	20 5/8	20 3/8	18 6/8	4 2/8	4 2/8	5	5	Mendocino Co., CA	Richard A. Rajeski	Richard A. Rajeski	2002	89
135 3/8	19 7/8	20	13 7/8	4 6/8	4 6/8	5	5	Sonoma Co., CA	William M. Somma	William M.Somma	2002	93
135 2/8	21	20 6/8	17 2/8	5 1/8	5 1/8	4	4	Linn Co., OR	Dennis R. Middleton	Dennis R. Middleton	2000	94
135 2/8	19 4/8	20 1/8	15 6/8	4 1/8	4 4/8	5	5	Humboldt Co., CA	Scott S. Eskra	Scott S. Eskra	2002	94
135 1/8	19 5/8	19 4/8	15 5/8	4 2/8	4 1/8	5	5	Lewis Co., WA	William A. Logan	William A. Logan	1975	96
135 1/8	22 1/8	21 4/8	22 4/8	4 1/8	4 2/8	5	5	Sonoma Co., CA	Michael R. Williams	Michael R. Williams	2002	96
135 1/8	20 6/8	21 6/8	19 1/8	4	3 7/8	5	5	Mendocino Co., CA	Thomas W. Atterbury	Thomas W. Atterbury	2002	96
135 1/8	22 1/8	21 3/8	20 1/8	6	5 6/8	4	4	Santa Clara Co., CA	Phillip A. Corral	Phillip A. Corral	2003	96
135	19 3/8	19 3/8	16 2/8	4 1/8	4 1/8	5	5	Trinity Co., CA	Kevin D. Clair	Kevin D. Clair	2001	100
135	21 7/8	22 3/8	17	3 7/8	3 5/8	6	5	Lane Co., OR	Walt Metcalfe	Walt Metcalfe	2002	100
134 1/8	21	20 6/8	18 5/8	4 3/8	4 6/8	5	5	Clackamas Co., OR	Scott J. Fuge	Scott J. Fuge	2001	102
134	21 2/8	20 5/8	16 6/8	4 2/8	4	5	5	Humboldt Co., CA	Harold Fisher	Harold Fisher	1982	103
133 7/8	20 6/8	19 6/8	14 5/8	5 1/8	5	5	5	Clackamas Co., OR	Lawrence Sowa	Tim Sowa	1955	104
133 7/8	21 2/8	20 7/8	20 7/8	5	4 6/8	6	6	Glenn Co., CA	Al J. Santos	Al J. Santos	2002	104
133 5/8	21 6/8	21 3/8	16 7/8	3 7/8	3 6/8	5	5	Mendocino Co., CA	Fred E. Borton	Fred E. Borton	1998	106
133 3/8	22	21 5/8	20 4/8	4 3/8	4 3/8	5	5	Santa Clara Co., CA	Joel G. Sakamoto	Joel G. Sakamoto	2001	107
133	20 1/8	19 7/8	15	3 6/8	3 6/8	4	5	Humboldt Co., CA	Robert L. Currier	Robert L. Currier	1983	108

COLUMBIA BLACKTAIL - TYPICAL ANTLERS

Odocoileus hemionus columbianus

Score	Length of Main Beam R.	L.	Inside Spread	Circumference at Smallest Place Between Burr & First Point R.	L.	Number of Points R.	L.	Locality	Hunter	Owner	Date Killed	Rank
133	18 3/8	18 6/8	19	4 3/8	4 4/8	5	5	Napa Co., CA	Robert C. Covey	Robert C. Covey	2001	108
132	21 7/8	21 7/8	16 6/8	4 7/8	4 4/8	5	5	Lewis Co., WA	Marion Bays	Brian Dickason	1937	110
131 7/8	20 5/8	20 4/8	18 1/8	4 7/8	4 7/8	4	4	Douglas Co., OR	Lynn A. Schrag	Lynn A. Schrag	1989	111
131 5/8	22 1/8	22	23 4/8	4	4 2/8	3	5	Napa Co., CA	Henry Samuels	Tim H. Mathison	1928	112
131 1/8	19 7/8	19 7/8	15 7/8	4	4	5	5	Mendocino Co., CA	Brent W. Seehafer	Brent W. Seehafer	2000	113
131	21 6/8	20	17 4/8	4 1/8	4 1/8	5	5	Mendocino Co., CA	Robert W. Logan	Robert W. Logan	2001	114
130 7/8	20 2/8	19 7/8	12 7/8	4 1/8	4 2/8	5	5	Pierce Co., WA	Dean E. Voelker	Dean E. Voelker	1976	115
130 6/8	22 6/8	22 5/8	18 6/8	4 5/8	4 4/8	5	7	Trinity Co., CA	Donald A. Dunn	Donald A. Dunn	2002	116
130 5/8	19 4/8	20	15 3/8	4 3/8	4 2/8	5	5	Lewis Co., WA	Robert L. Shannon, Jr.	Robert L. Shannon, Jr.	1989	117
130 5/8	20 4/8	21	15 7/8	4 3/8	4 1/8	5	5	Coos Co., OR	Lynn A. Schrag	Lynn A. Schrag	1992	117
130 5/8	21 5/8	21	16 3/8	4 2/8	4 4/8	5	5	Mason Co., WA	Pete Kruger, Sr.	Pete Kruger, Sr.	2001	117
130 1/8	22 4/8	22 7/8	17	4	3 7/8	6	8	Lane Co., OR	Calvin A. Speckman	Calvin A. Speckman	2002	120
130	20 3/8	20 1/8	14 4/8	4 1/8	3 6/8	5	5	Siskiyou Co., CA	Craig Wyosnick	Craig Wyosnick	1990	121
129 7/8	21 6/8	21 3/8	19 7/8	4 5/8	4 5/8	5	5	Trinity Co., CA	Robert L. Currier	Robert L. Currier	2000	122
129 4/8	19 1/8	21	17 6/8	3 5/8	3 6/8	5	5	Humboldt Co., CA	Richard J. Banko, Jr.	Richard J. Banko, Jr.	2003	123
129 3/8	19 6/8	19 6/8	17 3/8	4 6/8	4 6/8	5	5	Trinity Co., CA	Roxane R. Kelso	Roxane R. Kelso	2002	124
129	20 1/8	20 5/8	15 4/8	4 1/8	4 1/8	5	5	Yamhill Co., OR	Rick Grout	Rick Grout	2001	125
129	22 5/8	19	17 6/8	4 2/8	4 3/8	5	5	Humboldt Co., CA	Nick Albert	Nick Albert	2002	125
127 7/8	19 5/8	20 2/8	15 3/8	4 6/8	4 5/8	5	5	Trinity Co., CA	Robert P. Agnew	Robert P. Agnew	1997	127
127 2/8	20 1/8	20 1/8	14 6/8	4 4/8	4 5/8	7	6	Humboldt Co., CA	Kent Ingalls	Kent Ingalls	2002	128
127 1/8	20 5/8	21	16 5/8	4 4/8	4 4/8	5	5	Island Co., WA	Danny D. Waite	Danny D. Waite	2002	129
126 6/8	22 7/8	22 5/8	18 6/8	3 7/8	4	3	4	Lewis Co., WA	Scott D. Falk	Scott D. Falk	1977	130
126 2/8	19 3/8	19 7/8	19 6/8	4 2/8	4 3/8	6	5	Napa Co., CA	Thomas G. Van Scyoc	Thomas G. Van Scyoc	2000	131
125 7/8	20 2/8	19 2/8	15 1/8	4 1/8	4 1/8	5	5	Cowlitz Co., WA	Reuben C. Grendahl	Reuben C. Grendahl	1994	132
125 6/8	20 2/8	20 1/8	19 2/8	4 3/8	4 3/8	4	4	San Mateo Co., CA	Picked Up	Daniel R. Caughey III	2001	133
125 4/8	19 5/8	19 7/8	14 2/8	4 2/8	4 1/8	5	5	Lane Co., OR	Cameron R. Hanes	Cameron R. Hanes	2000	134
125 3/8	19	19 5/8	18 7/8	4 3/8	4 6/8	4	4	Tehama Co., CA	Monte D. Matheson	Monte D. Matheson	2001	135
125	21 5/8	21 3/8	18 6/8	4 4/8	4 4/8	4	5	Pierce Co., WA	Terry McDonald	Terry McDonald	1970	136

COLUMBIA BLACKTAIL - NON-TYPICAL ANTLERS

Minimum Score 155

Odocoileus hemionus columbianus

New World's Record 208 1/8

Score	Length of Main Beam R.	L.	Inside Spread	Circumference at Smallest Place Between Burr & First Point R.	L.	Number of Points R.	L.	Locality	Hunter	Owner	Date Killed	Rank
208 1/8	21 7/8	20 4/8	17 5/8	4 2/8	4 3/8	9	9	Polk Co., OR	Frank S. Foldi	Steve D. Crossley	1962	1
197 4/8	23 7/8	22 6/8	19 1/8	4 1/8	4 1/8	11	11	Trinity Co., CA	Newt Boren	Richard Shepard	1955	2
188 6/8	23 4/8	19 7/8	17 4/8	4 3/8	5 1/8	7	9	Shasta Co., CA	Brad E. Wittner	Brad E. Wittner	1981	3
187	21 5/8	22 6/8	18 4/8	4 2/8	4 2/8	9	8	Douglas Co., OR	Alva J. Flock	Alva J. Flock	1967	4
178 4/8	24 1/8	23	22 1/8	5 2/8	5	6	12	Mendocino Co., CA	Russel F. Roach	Russel F. Roach	2002	5
177 4/8	22 7/8	23 5/8	17 2/8	4 6/8	4 7/8	6	6	Washington Co., OR	John Susee	Randal P. Olsen	1954	6
176 5/8	20 4/8	20 3/8	13 4/8	4 7/8	4 6/8	8	10	Trinity Co., CA	Harland C. Moore, Sr.	James A. Swortzel	1947	7
176 5/8	21 4/8	22	16 5/8	4 2/8	4 3/8	8	8	Clackamas Co., OR	Ronald G. Searls	Ronald G. Searls	1970	7
173 7/8	20 6/8	21 3/8	18 6/8	5 2/8	5 1/8	6	8	Clark Co., WA	James D. Gipe	James D. Gipe	1976	9
167 1/8	22 7/8	21 1/8	20 1/8	4 1/8	4 2/8	8	8	Jackson Co., OR	Richard Falls	Richard Falls	1971	10
167	22 4/8	22 3/8	16 2/8	4 4/8	4 4/8	7	7	Tehama Co., CA	Mark S. Swarsbrook	Mark S. Swarsbrook	1996	11
165	24	24 6/8	24 6/8	5 3/8	5 1/8	8	6	Clatsop Co., OR	Gerald E. Ryan	Gerald E. Ryan	1972	12
162	20 2/8	22 6/8	14	6 2/8	4 7/8	11	6	Benton Co., OR	David L. Barker	David L. Barker	1992	13
160 3/8	22 1/8	22 5/8	22 7/8	4 3/8	4 3/8	8	7	Linn Co., OR	Brian J. Cook	Brian J. Cook	2000	14
158	25 6/8	24 7/8	18 6/8	4 4/8	4 7/8	6	9	Siskiyou Co., CA	William H. Smith	William H. Smith	1966	15
155 6/8	20 5/8	21	16 6/8	5 2/8	5 2/8	6	8	San Mateo Co., CA	Robert Caughey	Robert Caughey	2002	16
201 3/8*	23 6/8	25 7/8	26 3/8	5 1/8	5 1/8	12	11	Jackson Co., OR	Merle Brainard	Vern Dollar	1936	

* Final score subject to revision by additional verifying measurements.

SITKA BLACKTAIL - TYPICAL ANTLERS

Odocoileus hemionus sitkensis

Minimum Score 100

World's Record 133

Sitka blacktail deer includes trophies from coastal Alaska and the Queen Charlotte Islands of British Columbia.

Score	Length of Main Beam R	L	Inside Spread	Circumference at Smallest Place Between Burr & First Point R	L	Number of Points R	L	Locality	Hunter	Owner	Date Killed	Rank
120 6/8	18 7/8	18 2/8	15 4/8	3 6/8	4	6	5	Kizhuyak Bay, AK	Walter W. Woodward	Walter W. Woodward	2001	1
116 7/8	16 6/8	16 7/8	13 3/8	4 1/8	3 7/8	5	5	Prince of Wales Island, AK	James W. Bauers	James W. Bauers	2003	2
114 4/8	17 4/8	17	14 6/8	3 5/8	3 6/8	5	5	Kodiak Island, AK	Danny J. Lee	Danny J. Lee	2001	3
113 6/8	18	16 7/8	14 2/8	4	4 1/8	5	5	Kasaan Bay, AK	Charles Escoffon	Charles Escoffon	1994	4
112 4/8	16	15 7/8	15 6/8	3 4/8	3 5/8	5	5	Cumshewa Inlet, BC	Harold Larsen	Harold Larsen	1970	5
111 7/8	14 4/8	15 4/8	14 1/8	3 5/8	3 5/8	5	5	Prince of Wales Island, AK	Dick D. Hamlin	Dick D. Hamlin	1965	6
110 1/8	16 6/8	16 1/8	14 1/8	3 5/8	3 4/8	5	5	Prince of Wales Island, AK	Jared Azure	Jared Azure	2002	7
110 1/8	17 2/8	16 4/8	13 7/8	4	3 7/8	5	5	Kosciusko Island, AK	Bob Ameen	Bob Ameen	2003	7
109 6/8	17 5/8	17 4/8	15 4/8	4	4	5	4	Kodiak Island, AK	Lonnie L. Ritchey	Lonnie L. Ritchey	2001	9
109 3/8	16 7/8	16 6/8	13 6/8	3 4/8	3 5/8	6	5	Prince of Wales Island, AK	Dick D. Hamlin	Dick D. Hamlin	PR1960	10
108 4/8	16 4/8	15 6/8	15	3 6/8	3 5/8	5	5	Kodiak Island, AK	Chuck Adams	Chuck Adams	1986	11
108 2/8	17 3/8	17 2/8	15 2/8	3 7/8	3 7/8	5	5	Kodiak Island, AK	Warren D. Winger	Warren D. Winger	1989	12
108 1/8	14 5/8	15	13 5/8	4 2/8	4	5	5	Spiridon Bay, AK	John T. Schloeder	John T. Schloeder	2001	13
107 5/8	17 3/8	18	14 3/8	3 5/8	3 4/8	5	4	Larsen Bay, AK	Dave Melton	Dave Melton	2002	14
107 3/8	17	17 3/8	17 1/8	3 6/8	3 6/8	5	5	Prince of Wales Island, AK	Picked Up	Scott E. McDonald	1995	15
107	17 3/8	17 1/8	14 2/8	4	4	5	5	Kodiak Island, AK	Jeff Wells	Jeff Wells	2001	16
105 6/8	16 6/8	16 4/8	16 4/8	3 5/8	3 6/8	5	4	Sitkoh Lake, AK	David J. Oen	David J. Oen	2002	17
105 2/8	17 2/8	16 6/8	14 2/8	4 2/8	4 1/8	6	6	Prince of Wales Island, AK	Dee-O Whitehead	Dee-O Whitehead	1990	18
105	17 5/8	17 2/8	15 4/8	4 1/8	4 1/8	6	6	Larsen Bay, AK	John T. Schloeder	John T. Schloeder	2002	19
104 7/8	17 3/8	15 7/8	15 7/8	3 7/8	4 2/8	5	6	Prince of Wales Island, AK	Dale L. Hayes	Dale L. Hayes	1991	20
104 4/8	15 6/8	15 7/8	14 6/8	3 4/8	3 5/8	5	5	Prince of Wales Island, AK	Danny Hoggard	Danny Hoggard	2003	21
104 1/8	16 1/8	16 4/8	13 7/8	3 4/8	3 5/8	5	5	Kasaan Bay, AK	Charles Escoffon	Charles Escoffon	1985	22
103 3/8	17 1/8	17 2/8	14 7/8	3 5/8	3 4/8	5	5	Revillagigedo Island, AK	Jeff Gilmon	Jeff Gilmon	1998	23
102 2/8	16 4/8	15 7/8	14 4/8	3 5/8	3 4/8	5	5	Uganik Bay, AK	Justin T. Dubay	Justin T. Dubay	2001	24
102 2/8	15 3/8	16	15	4 2/8	4 2/8	4	4	Little Creek, AK	William F. Kneer, Jr.	William F. Kneer, Jr.	2003	24
101 4/8	16 6/8	17	14 2/8	3 5/8	3 5/8	5	5	Kasaan Bay, AK	Charles Escoffon	Charles Escoffon	1983	26
101 1/8	15 2/8	15 3/8	14 3/8	3 3/8	3 3/8	5	5	Zachar Bay, AK	Rebecca M. Branson	Rebecca M. Branson	2000	27
121 2/8*	17 4/8	18 2/8	16 2/8	3 6/8	3 7/8	5	5	Prince of Wales Island, AK	Picked Up	Jack A. Adams	1989	
115 5/8*	18 1/8	18 3/8	14 3/8	3 6/8	3 6/8	5	5	Larsen Bay, AK	Stephen J. Dambacher	Stephen J. Dambacher	2001	

* Final score subject to revision by additional verifying measurements.

SITKA BLACKTAIL - NON-TYPICAL ANTLERS

Odocoileus hemionus sitkensis

Minimum Score 118

New World's Record 134

Sitka blacktail deer includes trophies from coastal Alaska and the Queen Charlotte Islands of British Columbia.

Score	Length of Main Beam R.	L.	Inside Spread	Circumference at Smallest Place Between Burr & First Point R.	L.	Number of Points R.	L.	Locality	Hunter	Owner	Date Killed	Rank
134	19 6/8	20 3/8	16 3/8	4 5/8	4 4/8	5	6	Control Lake, AK	William B. Steele, Jr.	William B. Steele, Jr.	1987	1
126 7/8	17	17 5/8	13 7/8	4 2/8	4 4/8	6	8	Prince of Wales Island, AK	Dan L. Hayes	B&C National Collection	1984	2
126 4/8*	18 7/8	20 3/8	17	4 3/8	4 2/8	6	5	Little Coal Bay, AK	Charles Escoffon	Charles Escoffon	1985	
120 1/8*	18 1/8	17 5/8	13 7/8	3 6/8	4 2/8	5	6	Revillagigedo Island, AK	Dick D. Hamlin	Dick D. Hamlin	PR1970	

* Final score subject to revision by additional verifying measurements.

WHITETAIL DEER - TYPICAL ANTLERS

Odocoileus virginianus virginianus and certain related subspecies

Score	Length of Main Beam R.	L.	Inside Spread	Circumference at Smallest Place Between Burr & First Point R.	L.	Number of Points R.	L.	Locality	Hunter	Owner	Date Killed	Rank
203 3/8	25 7/8	27 2/8	19 3/8	5 7/8	5 5/8	6	6	Sturgeon River, SK	Hubert Collins	Hubert Collins	2003	1
199 2/8	27 2/8	27 1/8	21 3/8	5 7/8	5 7/8	6	7	Kansas	Picked Up	KS Dept. of Wildlife & Parks	1999	2
198 6/8	26 6/8	26 6/8	21 5/8	4 1/8	4 1/8	6	5	Lewis Co., MO	Daryl L. Blum	Daryl L. Blum	2002	3
196 6/8	29 6/8	29	21	5 2/8	5 6/8	6	8	Kane Co., IL	Ray Schremp	Ray Schremp	2000	4
194	28 4/8	28 6/8	22 2/8	5	5	6	6	Kent Co., MD	Kevin C. Miller	Kevin C. Miller	2002	5
193 3/8	27 7/8	29	25 4/8	5 3/8	5 5/8	7	5	Franklin Co., MA	Kajetan R. Sovinski	Kajetan R. Sovinski	2002	6
192 7/8	28 2/8	28 5/8	22	5 2/8	5 2/8	7	7	Mercer Co., IL	Jerry W. Whitmire	Cabela's, Inc.	2000	7
192 2/8	29 1/8	27 7/8	21 4/8	5 7/8	5 4/8	6	5	Souris River, MB	T.K. Patterson & D. Dickson	T.K. Patterson & D. Dickson	2002	8
191 5/8	31 1/8	29 4/8	21	5 2/8	4 6/8	8	8	Scioto Co., OH	Lowell E. Kinney	Lowell E. Kinney	2000	9
191 2/8	29	28 6/8	23 6/8	4 7/8	4 7/8	5	5	Monroe Co., MI	Michael A. Kelly	MI Whitetail Hall of Fame Mus.	1997	10
191	27 6/8	28 3/8	19	5	5 3/8	5	5	Cass Co., MO	John D. Meyer	John D. Meyer	2001	11
190 7/8	26 6/8	26	20 4/8	4 4/8	4 3/8	6	5	Wayne Co., IA	Douglas M. Eldridge	Douglas M. Eldridge	2000	12
190 6/8	26 5/8	27	17 6/8	5 1/8	5	7	7	Whiteshell Prov. Park, MB	Darrin Murash	Cabela's, Inc.	1999	13
190 5/8	27 6/8	29 2/8	20 1/8	4 6/8	5	5	5	Ogle Co., IL	Geoff Lester	Geoff Lester	2000	14
190 5/8	26 3/8	26 5/8	18 5/8	4 5/8	4 6/8	8	7	Hillsdale Co., MI	Gregory D. McCuiston	Gregory D. McCuiston	2001	14
190	26	24 6/8	21 1/8	6 2/8	6 4/8	6	9	Turtleford, SK	Dick Rooney	D.J. Hollinger & B. Howard	1989	16
189 5/8	26 4/8	26 1/8	18 3/8	4 7/8	4 6/8	7	5	Geary Co., KS	Ron Wolford	Cabela's, Inc.	2002	17
189 1/8	30 2/8	30 1/8	18 7/8	5 2/8	5 2/8	5	5	Washtenaw Co., MI	Mark C. Ritchie	MI Whitetail Hall of Fame Mus.	1984	18
188 6/8	27 4/8	27 4/8	25	5 1/8	4 7/8	5	6	Stafford Co., KS	Robin L. Austin	Robin L. Austin	2002	19
188 4/8	30 3/8	30 6/8	21 3/8	5 3/8	5 1/8	8	7	Macon Co., MO	Eugene J. Bausch	Eugene J. Bausch	2001	20
188 4/8	23	23 4/8	18 6/8	5	4 7/8	7	7	Sandy Lake, MB	Darren L. Yanchycki	Darren L. Yanchycki	2001	20
188 4/8	27 4/8	27 3/8	18 3/8	5	5 1/8	5	6	Fulton Co., OH	Scott E. May	Scott E. May	2002	20
188	28 4/8	27 2/8	17 1/8	5 2/8	5 2/8	7	6	Williams Co., OH	Brad A. McNalley	Brad A. McNalley	2000	23
188	27 6/8	25 6/8	20 7/8	4 6/8	4 4/8	5	5	Schuyler Co., IL	Donald L. Smith	Donald L. Smith	2001	24
187 7/8	27 5/8	26 7/8	23 3/8	5 2/8	5	6	6	Whitesand Lake, SK	Stan Eskovich	Stan Eskovich	2002	24
187 7/8	27 2/8	28 1/8	22 2/8	4 5/8	4 6/8	7	7	Franklin Co., MO	Mickey R. Montee	Mickey R. Montee	2001	26
187 5/8	26 7/8	26 4/8	19 7/8	5 3/8	5 4/8	6	7	Pine Creek, MB	C. Anne Reddon	C. Anne Reddon	2001	27
187 3/8	24 7/8	24 7/8	18 4/8	5 7/8	5 5/8	6	6	Unknown	Unknown	MI Whitetail Hall of Fame Mus.	1962	28
187	24 6/8	24 7/8	19	4 7/8	4 7/8	6	6	Swift Co., MN	George A. Piotter	George A. Piotter	2002	28

Score								Locality	Hunter	Owner	Date	Rank
186 7/8	30 4/8	29 2/8	20 7/8	4 7/8	4 7/8	7	7	Greene Co., OH	Dale A. Heathcook	Dale A. Heathcook	2001	30
186 6/8	27 7/8	28 5/8	19 6/8	4 5/8	4 3/8	6	5	Bullitt Co., KY	Troy Gentry	Troy Gentry	2002	31
186 2/8	25 6/8	26 6/8	18	5 4/8	5 4/8	7	5	Adams Co., OH	Larry D. Napier	Larry D. Napier	2001	32
186 1/8	24 7/8	26 2/8	19 1/8	4 7/8	5	6	8	Columbia Co., KS	Jared T. MacNees	Jared T. MacNees	2000	33
186 1/8	29 2/8	28 2/8	20 3/8	4 6/8	4 5/8	7	7	Franklin Co., KS	Stephen P. Edwards	Stephen P. Edwards	2001	33
185 2/8	26 4/8	24 3/8	17 2/8	4 5/8	4 6/8	6	7	Adair Co., MO	Ronald Lene	Bobby D. Lene	1976	35
185	28	27 3/8	26 5/8	5 2/8	5 4/8	10	11	Lyon Co., KS	Ronald L. Sleisher	Ronald L. Sleisher	2001	36
184 5/8	26 7/8	26 5/8	23 1/8	5 2/8	5 2/8	6	5	Birch Lake, SK	Michael G. Taylor	Michael G. Taylor	2000	37
184 5/8	27	27	19 1/8	5 1/8	5 1/8	7	6	Champaign Co., OH	Eric Coleman	Eric Coleman	2000	37
184 5/8	25 7/8	26 6/8	19 5/8	4 5/8	5 1/8	6	5	Walworth Co., WI	Scot Zajdel	Scot Zajdel	2002	37
184 5/8	23 3/8	22 5/8	20 7/8	4 6/8	4 6/8	6	6	Jasper Co., MO	Picked Up	Andy S. Johnson	2002	37
184 2/8	27	27 4/8	20 6/8	4 6/8	4 6/8	5	5	Shelby Co., TN	Picked Up	Sammy Beesinger	2001	41
184 1/8	28 3/8	27 5/8	20 3/8	4 5/8	4 5/8	6	7	Wapello Co., IA	Ryan W. Scott	Ryan W. Scott	2000	42
184 1/8	24 6/8	25 1/8	20 7/8	5 6/8	5 6/8	5	5	Allamakee Co., IA	Steve Heim	Steve Heim	2002	42
183 7/8	26 5/8	26 5/8	18 5/8	3 7/8	3 7/8	6	6	Adams Co., IA	Gregory L. Andrews	Gregory L. Andrews	2000	44
183 7/8	26	26 2/8	18 3/8	4 2/8	4 2/8	5	5	Angelina Co., TX	Jeffery T. Capps	Jeffery T. Capps	2000	44
183 7/8	24 2/8	24	20 6/8	4 6/8	5	9	7	Naramata Creek, BC	Al J. Thibodeau	Al J. Thibodeau	2002	44
183 7/8	27 2/8	27 4/8	20 5/8	5 3/8	5 4/8	6	5	Scott Co., IA	Marlon J. Vander Heiden	Marlon J. Vander Heiden	2003	44
183 6/8	26 7/8	26 4/8	21 2/8	5 7/8	5 5/8	5	6	Winona Co., MN	Picked Up	Kevin J. Nelsen	1967	48
183 6/8	27 6/8	27 5/8	19	5 1/8	5 1/8	5	5	Soundng Lake, AB	David W. Higman	David W. Higman	2001	48
183 6/8	26 5/8	26 6/8	20 6/8	6	6	5	7	Bureau Co., IL	Rebecca Ratay	Rebecca Ratay	2002	48
183 5/8	30	29 3/8	24 5/8	5 1/8	4 7/8	5	5	Clark Co., IN	Donald B. Minnich	Donald B. Minnich	1999	51
183 5/8	28 2/8	28 6/8	21 5/8	4 4/8	4 5/8	7	7	Qu'Appelle River, SK	Anthony Roberts	Anthony Roberts	2000	51
183 5/8	27 6/8	27 1/8	20 3/8	5 7/8	5 6/8	5	5	Guthrie Co., IA	Charles S. Callaway	Charles S. Callaway	2001	51
183 5/8	28 4/8	28 2/8	18 1/8	4 6/8	5	5	5	Clay Co., IL	Scott Fritschle	Scott Fritschle	2002	51
183 3/8	28	27 3/8	19 1/8	4 6/8	4 5/8	6	6	Pulaski Co., KY	Billy M. Haynes	Billy M. Haynes	2000	55
183 3/8	27 4/8	27 2/8	17	5 2/8	5 2/8	5	6	Wayne Co., OH	Lloyd K. Eshler	Lloyd K. Eshler	2000	55
183 3/8	28	27 2/8	19 7/8	5 4/8	5 4/8	7	7	Anderson Co., KS	Brian K. Hanes	Brian K. Hanes	2001	55
183 1/8	26 2/8	26 5/8	20 3/8	5 4/8	5 4/8	6	6	Chisago Co., MN	Timothy L. Ryan	Timothy L. Ryan	2000	58
182 7/8	29 6/8	27 6/8	18 3/8	5 3/8	5 3/8	6	5	Sedgwick Co., CO	Glenn W. Vinton	Glenn W. Vinton	2000	59
182 5/8	30	30 1/8	19 2/8	5 1/8	4 5/8	5	7	Cross Co., AR	B. Jason Franklin	B. Jason Franklin	1995	60
182 5/8	27 2/8	27 2/8	19 3/8	5	5	6	6	Monroe Co., IA	Les A. Bateman	Les A. Bateman	2001	60
182 3/8	28 3/8	27 7/8	23 5/8	5 1/8	5 3/8	4	5	Viking, AB	Charles D. Dobbs	Charles D. Dobbs	2001	62
182 3/8	29 4/8	30 4/8	27 1/8	5 3/8	5 5/8	7	7	McPherson Co., NE	Leonard Bergantzel	Leonard Bergantzel	1999	63
182 2/8	26 2/8	26 5/8	17 7/8	5	5	5	5	Polk Co., MN	Benjamin D. Faldet	Benjamin D. Faldet	2000	63
182 2/8	29 6/8	27 6/8	18 3/8	5 1/8	5 1/8	6	6	Hancock Co., IL	Jeffrey L. Akers	Jeffrey L. Akers	2000	65
182 1/8	30 1/8	30	19 2/8	4 5/8	4 5/8	5	5	Muskingum Co., OH	Charles E. Goldsmith	Charles E. Goldsmith	2001	65
182 1/8	27 2/8	28 6/8	20 1/8	5 5/8	5 7/8	8	7	Richland Co., OH	Bruce L. King	Bruce L. King	2000	67
182 1/8	27 4/8	28 5/8	20 3/8	5 1/8	5 1/8	6	6	Jackson Co., MI	Brian T. Kessman	Brian T. Kessman	2002	67
182	29 1/8	27 4/8	19 5/8	4 7/8	4 6/8	5	5	Unknown	Bernie Benson	Kenneth W. Springer	1976	69
182	24 1/8	23 6/8	22 3/8	5 4/8	5 5/8	6	6	Henderson Co., IL	Jeffrey A. Bloise	Jeffrey A. Bloise	2000	69

WHITETAIL DEER - TYPICAL ANTLERS

Odocoileus virginianus virginianus and certain related subspecies

Score	Length of Main Beam R.	L.	Inside Spread	Circumference at Smallest Place Between Burr & First Point R.	L.	Number of Points R.	L.	Locality	Hunter	Owner	Date Killed	Rank
182	27 7/8	28 1/8	23 7/8	4 5/8	5 1/8	7	7	Hancock Co., OH	Larry G. Rader	Larry G. Rader	2000	69
182	27 1/8	27 1/8	25	5	5	5	6	Peoria Co., IL	Thomas Missen	Thomas Missen	2001	69
181 7/8	26 5/8	26 5/8	20 4/8	5 2/8	5 2/8	7	7	Washington Co., MN	Daniel F. Gallagher	Daniel F. Gallagher	2001	73
181 5/8	25 4/8	25 2/8	16 6/8	5 5/8	5 4/8	6	6	Sawyer Co., WI	Picked Up	Teresa Kleutsch	1996	74
181 5/8	26 7/8	27 7/8	22 3/8	5 2/8	5 1/8	5	5	Berrien Co., MI	Steven E. Coleman	Steven E. Coleman	2000	74
181 5/8	24	26 5/8	19	5 4/8	5 2/8	6	8	Edgar Co., IL	Christopher L. Newhart	Christopher L. Newhart	2001	74
181 4/8	27 5/8	28 4/8	20 1/8	5 4/8	4 7/8	9	9	Cole Co., MO	Douglas S. Middleton	Douglas S. Middleton	2000	77
181 4/8	25 6/8	25 4/8	20	5 4/8	5 4/8	5	6	Valley Lake, AB	Terry O. Hobbs	Terry O. Hobbs	2000	77
181 4/8	26 1/8	26 6/8	18	5 3/8	5 3/8	6	7	Vernon Co., WI	Timothy T. Nordengren	Timothy T. Nordengren	2001	77
181 4/8	26 3/8	26 3/8	20 3/8	4 4/8	4 4/8	7	5	Bureau Co., IL	William J. Calbow, Jr.	William J. Calbow, Jr.	2002	77
181 3/8	27	27 4/8	17 6/8	6 4/8	6 6/8	5	7	Lawrence Co., IL	Charles Morehead	Charles Morehead	2002	81
181 2/8	26 5/8	26 3/8	23 2/8	6 1/8	6 3/8	5	5	Morrison Co., MN	Scott A. Shonka	Scott A. Shonka	2000	82
181 1/8	30 1/8	29 1/8	22 3/8	5 1/8	5 3/8	8	6	Waushara Co., WI	Kenneth G. Wilson	Kenneth G. Wilson	2001	83
181	29 3/8	29 1/8	18	5 6/8	5 4/8	5	5	Rutland Co., VT	Picked Up	Gary E. Merrill	1971	84
181	26 4/8	27 6/8	20 2/8	4 7/8	5	7	7	Saskatchewan	Unknown	Tom Eustace	1999	84
180 7/8	27 1/8	26	18 1/8	6 4/8	6 1/8	7	5	Monona Co., IA	Picked Up	David E. Fender	1991	86
180 7/8	27 6/8	25 4/8	18 7/8	4 5/8	4 4/8	6	7	Audubon Co., IA	Michael M. Miller	Keith E. Brock	1996	86
180 6/8	27 4/8	27	20	4 4/8	4 4/8	5	5	Iosco Co., MI	Zack T. Shellenbarger	Zack T. Shellenbarger	2000	88
180 5/8	27 3/8	27 4/8	17 5/8	4 3/8	4 4/8	5	5	Wabasha Co., MN	Bradley S. Kreofsky	Bradley S. Kreofsky	2000	89
180 5/8	24 5/8	23 4/8	19 1/8	5 1/8	5 1/8	6	6	Saline Co., MO	Alvin Croka	Alvin Croka	2001	89
180 4/8	26 5/8	26 3/8	18 6/8	5 4/8	5 3/8	5	5	Dawson Co., NE	Jerry Lauby	Jerry Lauby	1983	91
180 4/8	28 6/8	26 5/8	21 3/8	4 7/8	5 3/8	7	9	Pottawatomie Co., KS	Picked Up	Cabela's, Inc.	2001	91
180 4/8	27 1/8	26 6/8	20 1/8	5 4/8	5 1/8	6	5	Rock Island Co., IL	Douglas J. Hood	Douglas J. Hood	2002	91
180 3/8	26 5/8	26 4/8	16 3/8	5 4/8	5 4/8	7	6	Minnesota	Unknown	Isaak Walton League	PR1901	94
180 3/8	28 3/8	28 2/8	22 5/8	5	4 7/8	5	5	Dodge Co., WI	Herman Pautsch	Brian E. Neitzel	1965	94
180 3/8	32 6/8	32 4/8	22 3/8	5 2/8	5 3/8	4	4	Hillsdale Co., MI	Victor L. Bulliner	Victor L. Bulliner	2001	94
180 3/8	25 7/8	24 5/8	17 1/8	4 6/8	4 6/8	8	7	Mountain Lake, SK	James Sinclair	James Sinclair	2002	94
180 3/8	27 6/8	28 1/8	19 7/8	5 1/8	5 3/8	7	6	Allamakee Co., IA	Joseph Lieb	Joseph Lieb	2002	94
180 2/8	27	26 6/8	20 2/8	5 4/8	5 3/8	5	5	Clinton Co., MI	John L. Benedict	John L. Benedict	2002	99
180 2/8	25 5/8	25 7/8	17 4/8	5	4 5/8	7	7	Rock Island Co., IL	Andrew K. Crippen	Andrew K. Crippen	2002	99
180 1/8	28 7/8	28 5/8	20 2/8	4 5/8	4 5/8	6	5	Ohio Co., KY	Anthony Goff	Anthony Goff	2000	101
180 1/8	25	25 3/8	23 4/8	4 6/8	4 5/8	7	6	Clark Co., IN	Matthew D. Miller	Matthew D. Miller	2000	101
180	26 5/8	26 5/8	18 2/8	4 7/8	5 1/8	6	6	Winona Co., MN	James R. Walkes	James R. Walkes	2001	103

Score	L. Main Beam R	L. Main Beam L	Inside Spread	Circ. R	Circ. L	Pts. R	Pts. L	Locality	Hunter	Owner	Date	Rank
179 7/8	26 7/8	26 6/8	21 3/8	4 3/8	4 6/8	6	7	Beltrami Co., MN	Richard L. Dickinson	Richard L. Dickinson	2001	104
179 6/8	28 4/8	28	21	4 7/8	4 6/8	5	5	Porter Co., IN	Herbert R. Smith	Herbert R. Smith	2001	105
179 6/8	26 4/8	26 4/8	22 1/8	5 5/8	5 6/8	6	6	Cutarm Creek, SK	Rick Schuster	Rick Schuster	2001	105
179 6/8	24 5/8	24 4/8	20 4/8	5	5	6	6	Red Deer River, SK	Robert Abbott	Robert Abbott	2001	105
179 6/8	26 5/8	28 2/8	22 1/8	5 1/8	5 1/8	6	8	Lawrence Co., IL	Donald E. Stangle	Donald E. Stangle	2001	105
179 5/8	26 3/8	25 6/8	19 3/8	5 4/8	5 1/8	6	6	Pike Co., IL	Dale B. Karns	Dale B. Karns	2002	109
179 4/8	26 5/8	25 3/8	22	4 5/8	5 2/8	8	6	Barber Co., KS	Picked Up	Bill J. Timms	1999	110
179 2/8	27 5/8	26 1/8	20 2/8	4 5/8	4 5/8	8	8	Kalamazoo Co., MI	Steve J. Williams	Steve J. Williams	2000	111
179 2/8	25 1/8	25	19 4/8	5 4/8	5 5/8	7	7	St. Landry Parish, LA	Shannon R. Deville	Shannon R. Deville	2001	111
179 1/8	27	27 2/8	19 3/8	5 4/8	5 5/8	6	7	Bremer Co., IA	Blaine A. Davis	Blaine A. Davis	2000	113
179 1/8	25 7/8	25 6/8	17 4/8	5 6/8	5 6/8	9	7	N. Saskatchewan River, SK	Miles A. Johnson	Miles A. Johnson	2003	113
179	26	26 6/8	16	6 1/8	6 2/8	6	6	Dauphin Lake, MB	Maurice Theoret	Maurice Theoret	2001	115
178 5/8	25 5/8	25 5/8	22 1/8	5 2/8	5 1/8	5	5	Franklin Co., NE	Robert L. Lennemann	Robert L. Lennemann	2000	116
178 5/8	25	24 7/8	17 1/8	5 5/8	5 5/8	6	6	Noble Co., IN	William M. Hart, Jr.	William M. Hart, Jr.	2001	116
178 4/8	28 2/8	29	21 4/8	5 1/8	5 1/8	6	5	Jo Daviess Co., IL	Jack R. Herman	Jack R. Herman	2001	118
178 4/8	25 2/8	25 2/8	19 1/8	4 4/8	4 6/8	6	8	Buffalo Co., WI	Edward P. Brannen	Edward P. Brannen	2001	118
178 3/8	25 2/8	23 2/8	19 1/8	4 1/8	4 2/8	7	6	Phillips Co., KS	Harold Dusin	Robert C. Dusin	1973	120
178 3/8	24 3/8	24 2/8	25 3/8	5 4/8	5 3/8	5	6	Fillmore Co., NE	Jan Rischling	Jan Rischling	2000	120
178 3/8	25 2/8	25 3/8	19 5/8	4 3/8	4 4/8	6	6	Crawford Co., IA	Clark A. Corbin	Clark A. Corbin	2000	120
178 3/8	27 3/8	27 4/8	18 6/8	5 1/8	5 1/8	7	7	Perry Co., KY	Henry Sizemore	Henry Sizemore	2001	120
178 3/8	27 2/8	26 4/8	21 3/8	4 6/8	4 6/8	5	5	Morgan Co., IL	Allen Gerberding	Allen Gerberding	2002	120
178 1/8	25 1/8	25 1/8	18 1/8	4 5/8	4 6/8	6	6	Kleberg Co., TX	Eugene Werlin, Jr.	Eugene Werlin, Jr.	2002	120
178 1/8	26 7/8	25	18 6/8	6 1/8	6 3/8	5	5	Union Co., IL	K. Kent Treece	K. Kent Treece	1997	126
178	25	25	22 1/8	4 3/8	4 4/8	5	6	Greene Co., VA	Clyde E. Eppard, Sr.	Clyde E. Eppard, Sr.	2000	126
177 7/8	26 7/8	26 6/8	25 3/8	5 3/8	5 3/8	6	6	Cass Co., MN	Robert C. Palmer, Jr.	Robert C. Palmer, Jr.	1997	128
177 7/8	25 5/8	25 5/8	19 6/8	5 5/8	5 5/8	5	6	Johnson Co., IL	Jordan R. Lewis	Jordan R. Lewis	2000	128
177 5/8	28 1/8	28 2/8	21 6/8	5 2/8	5 2/8	5	6	Chariton Co., MO	G. Duane Gunn	G. Duane Gunn	2001	130
177 5/8	28 1/8	25 4/8	22 5/8	5 1/8	5	5	5	Houston Co., MN	Oscar W. Bernsdorf	Roger Bernsdorf	1959	131
177 5/8	26 3/8	28 1/8	23 5/8	4 7/8	5 1/8	6	5	Morgan Co., IL	Clint A. Rhea	Clint A. Rhea	2002	133
177 5/8	25 5/8	25 5/8	15 6/8	4 7/8	5	5	5	Roger Mills Co., OK	Dusty W. Davis	Dusty W. Davis	2000	133
177 4/8	25 7/8	25 7/8	21 5/8	4 3/8	4 3/8	6	6	Frio Co., TX	Guy S. Perkins	Guy S. Perkins	2001	133
177 4/8	23	24 3/8	18 6/8	5 7/8	6	6	7	Fulton Co., IL	Justin Hillman	Justin Hillman	2002	133
177 4/8	28 1/8	28 1/8	21 1/8	5 5/8	5 4/8	4	4	Pierce Co., WI	Robert H. Zich	Robert H. Zich	2002	133
177 4/8	28 3/8	28	20 3/8	4 6/8	5 4/8	8	7	Warren Co., IL	Matthew J. Lovdahl	Matthew J. Lovdahl	2002	138
177 3/8	27 6/8	26 6/8	25	5 2/8	4 6/8	6	5	Simpson Co., KY	Mickel J. Norris	Mickel J. Norris	1992	138
177 3/8	28 6/8	27 2/8	20 5/8	5 1/8	5 2/8	6	6	Pike Co., IL	Chad S. Lankford	Chad S. Lankford	2001	138
177 2/8	28 3/8	29 5/8	20	5 2/8	5	7	5	Meeting Lake, SK	Carl C. Sankey	Carl C. Sankey	2001	141
177 2/8	26	25 2/8	23 7/8	4 6/8	5 3/8	5	4	Madison Co., IL	Joseph S. Cannon	Joseph S. Cannon	1998	141
177 2/8	25 2/8	28 2/8	18 5/8	4 5/8	5 4/8	6	6	Lee Co., IL	Picked Up	Paul A. Harmon	2002	143
177 2/8	28 7/8	28 7/8	18 7/8	5 4/8	5 4/8	6	5	Pendleton Co., KY	John C. Bowers	John C. Bowers	2000	143
177 2/8	30	29 4/8	20 6/8	5	5 1/8	5	6	Monroe Co., WI	Mark A. Schmitz	Mark A. Schmitz	2000	143

WHITETAIL DEER - TYPICAL ANTLERS

Odocoileus virginianus virginianus and certain related subspecies

Score	Length of Main Beam R.	L.	Inside Spread	Circumference at Smallest Place Between Burr & First Point R.	L.	Number of Points R.	L.	Locality	Hunter	Owner	Date Killed	Rank
177 2/8	28 7/8	29 2/8	22 6/8	5 1/8	5 1/8	5	4	Page Co., IA	Darrel L. Vogel	Darrel L. Vogel	2000	143
177 2/8	25 4/8	24 6/8	21 6/8	4 6/8	4 7/8	5	5	Grundy Co., IL	Brandon Smith	Brandon Smith	2001	143
177 2/8	25 4/8	25 7/8	18 6/8	5 6/8	5 7/8	5	5	Stockholm, SK	Justin Banga	Justin Banga	2001	143
177 2/8	25	25 1/8	20 4/8	5 5/8	5 4/8	6	5	Allamakee Co., IA	Mark E. Walleser	Mark E. Walleser	2002	143
177 1/8	26 6/8	26 6/8	25 1/8	5 3/8	5 3/8	8	7	Golden City Lake, ON	Beverly E. Bennett	Beverly E. Bennett	2001	149
177 1/8	25 5/8	25 7/8	23 5/8	4 7/8	4 7/8	6	6	Clay Co., IA	Jeff D. Tiefenthaler	Jeff D. Tiefenthaler	2001	149
177	27 7/8	28 1/8	26 2/8	4 5/8	4 7/8	8	8	Lake Co., OH	Thomas A. Lasko	Thomas A. Lasko	2000	151
177	25 4/8	25 1/8	18	4 3/8	4 3/8	6	6	Union Co., IA	Michael A. Herrick	Michael A. Herrick	2000	151
177	28 3/8	26 6/8	17 6/8	4 7/8	4 6/8	5	5	Casey Co., KY	Jeff Bastin	Jeff Bastin	2001	151
176 7/8	27 3/8	25 6/8	20 1/8	6 5/8	6 7/8	4	4	Harrison Co., IA	Jay D. Jensen	Jay D. Jensen	2000	154
176 6/8	28 1/8	28 6/8	24 6/8	5 1/8	5 1/8	5	4	Saskatchewan	Jim McCrea	D.J. Hollinger & B. Howard	1992	155
176 6/8	25 4/8	24 7/8	20 4/8	5 7/8	6 1/8	5	5	Athabasca, AB	Nikki G. Wescott Haley	Nikki G. Wescott Haley	2000	155
176 6/8	26 1/8	25 1/8	19 6/8	4 4/8	4 4/8	6	7	Jasper Co., IL	Marty A. Draves	Marty A. Draves	2001	155
176 6/8	26 5/8	28	18 4/8	4 5/8	4 4/8	8	6	Washtenaw Co., MI	Walter J. Kempher	Walter J. Kempher	2002	155
176 5/8	23	22 6/8	20 1/8	4 7/8	5	6	6	Saunders Co., NE	John I. Kunert	John I. Kunert	2000	159
176 5/8	25 2/8	25 2/8	18 3/8	4 1/8	4 2/8	6	6	Linn Co., MO	Joel Head	Joel Head	2000	159
176 5/8	23 1/8	22 7/8	17 1/8	4 5/8	4 5/8	6	8	Buffalo Co., WI	Michael A. Ward	Michael A. Ward	2001	159
176 5/8	25 1/8	25	15 4/8	5 5/8	5 4/8	5	5	Carrot River, SK	Larry K. Trout	Larry K. Trout	2001	159
176 4/8	26	26 4/8	23 1/8	4 2/8	4 1/8	6	7	Todd Co., SD	Richard B. Carlson	Richard B. Carlson	2000	163
176 4/8	27 2/8	28	20 6/8	5 7/8	5 7/8	6	8	Kingman Co., KS	Jonathon C. Henning	Jonathon C. Henning	2002	163
176 3/8	24 3/8	23 3/8	17 3/8	5 2/8	5 2/8	6	5	Pope Co., MN	Richard M. Thompson	Richard M. Thompson	1976	165
176 3/8	25 2/8	26 2/8	17 7/8	4 7/8	5	6	5	Van Buren Co., IA	Bruce C. Spiller	Bruce C. Spiller	2000	165
176 3/8	25 7/8	25 5/8	18 1/8	4 5/8	4 3/8	7	9	Lanigan, SK	Derek Fisher	Derek Fisher	2000	165
176 3/8	25 4/8	26 1/8	17 4/8	5 6/8	5 6/8	6	6	S. Saskatchewan River, SK	Cory M. Schommer	Cory M. Schommer	2000	165
176 2/8	24	23 6/8	15 6/8	5	5 2/8	5	5	Jefferson Co., AR	Arthur Hubbard	Charles Burnett	1953	169
176 1/8	25 4/8	24 4/8	21 5/8	4 6/8	5 1/8	6	6	Solberg Lake, SK	Dale W. Brinkman	Dale W. Brinkman	2001	170
176 1/8	27	27 4/8	21 2/8	5	5 1/8	8	8	Jefferson Co., IA	Dale E. Manor	Dale E. Manor	2001	170
176 1/8	27	27 2/8	19 7/8	4 7/8	4 5/8	6	6	Hillsborough Co., NH	Phillip J. Marrotte	Phillip J. Marrotte	2002	170
176	25 5/8	25 5/8	17 6/8	4 2/8	4 1/8	6	7	Monroe Co., MO	David J. Godat	David J. Godat	2001	173
176	27 6/8	27 2/8	26 4/8	5	5	4	5	Penobscot Co., ME	David R. Morrison	David R. Morrison	2001	173
175 7/8	28 1/8	28 2/8	21 3/8	3 7/8	3 7/8	5	6	Iowa Co., IA	Chris Adams	Chris Adams	2000	175
175 7/8	28 6/8	29 4/8	18 5/8	4 2/8	4 3/8	6	6	Switzerland Co., IN	Dale A. Dixon, Jr.	Dale A. Dixon, Jr.	2000	175
175 7/8	24 5/8	23 1/8	18 7/8	5 1/8	5	6	6	Nez Perce Co., ID	Rusty P. Kirtley	Rusty P. Kirtley	2000	175

Score	Main Beam R	Main Beam L	Inside Spread	Circ. R	Circ. L	Pts R	Pts L	Locality	By	Owner	Date	Rank
175 6/8	29 2/8	28 6/8	21 3/8	4 6/8	5 1/8	6	5	Brown Co., OH	Robert W. Young	Robert W. Young	1991	178
175 6/8	24 1/8	24 2/8	21 1/8	5 7/8	5 7/8	6	7	Logan Co., CO	Thomas P. Grainger	Thomas P. Grainger	2000	178
175 6/8	25 2/8	25 3/8	18 3/8	5 2/8	5 3/8	6	8	Hart Co., KY	Patrick Devore	Patrick Devore	2000	178
175 6/8	27	27 4/8	19 4/8	5 2/8	5 2/8	5	5	Wayne Co., IN	Brent E. Ferguson	Brent E. Ferguson	2000	178
175 6/8	25 5/8	24 6/8	19	4 7/8	4 7/8	5	5	Allen Co., KS	Gary L. Cleaver	Gary L. Cleaver	2002	178
175 5/8	28 4/8	27 7/8	18 2/8	5 2/8	5 1/8	5	6	Sullivan Co., NH	Robert Lucas, Jr.	Robert Lucas, Jr.	2002	183
175 4/8	26 6/8	26 1/8	17 7/8	5 1/8	5 6/8	6	5	Grant Co., WI	Picked Up	Andrew J. Nelson	2000	184
175 3/8	27	27	18 6/8	6 2/8	5 1/8	8	7	Richland Co., WI	Vince L. Fairchild	Vince L. Fairchild	2000	185
175 3/8	26 4/8	26 6/8	22 1/8	5 2/8	5	5	6	Jefferson Co., ID	Daniel R. Merrill	Daniel R. Merrill	2001	185
175 2/8	26 7/8	27 2/8	21	4 7/8	4 5/8	5	6	Jersey Co., IL	Jacob J. Laramee	Jacob J. Laramee	1998	187
175 2/8	26	28 3/8	21 3/8	5	5 3/8	7	5	Logan Co., OH	Larry E. Pooler	Larry E. Pooler	2000	187
175 2/8	28 7/8	27 6/8	19 1/8	4 5/8	5	8	7	Pike Co., IL	Lewis W. Henry, Jr.	Lewis W. Henry, Jr.	2000	187
175 2/8	28 6/8	28 5/8	19	5 6/8	5 3/8	6	4	Neshoba Co., MS	Charlie G. Wilson II	Charlie G. Wilson II	2001	187
175 2/8	28	28 3/8	20 3/8	5 5/8	4 7/8	9	8	Lake Co., IN	Matthew A. Kelnhofer	Matthew A. Kelnhofer	2002	187
175 2/8	24 6/8	24 2/8	16	5	5 1/8	7	6	Lucas Co., IN	Larry L. Davis	Larry L. Davis	2002	187
175 1/8	26 6/8	26 6/8	19 5/8	4 1/8	5 3/8	6	5	Lac St. Anne, AB	Shane A. Thue	Shane A. Thue	1981	193
175	24	24	18 6/8	5 2/8	5 3/8	6	6	Ohio Co., IN	Rick T. Henry	Rick T. Henry	1998	194
175	28 1/8	28 2/8	21 4/8	5 1/8	5	6	5	Lake Co., IL	Picked Up	Nancy L. Egbert	2000	194
175	27	26 6/8	18 3/8	4 3/8	5 6/8	5	6	Cooper Co., MO	Bradley M. Baker	Bradley M. Baker	2000	194
175	26 2/8	25 3/8	19	5 2/8	4 4/8	7	6	Lac La Biche, AB	Tony J. Mitchell	Tony J. Mitchell	2000	194
175	26 6/8	26 7/8	21 3/8	5 3/8	5 4/8	6	6	Torch River, SK	Leo L. Arcand	Leo L. Arcand	2001	194
175	26 2/8	25 7/8	20 2/8	5 2/8	4 7/8	5	5	Knox Co., IL	Joel P. Catlin	Joel P. Catlin	2001	194
175	24 4/8	24 2/8	21 2/8	4 6/8	4 5/8	6	6	Leavenworth Co., KS	Dennis L. Yarnell	Dennis L. Yarnell	2001	194
175	22 7/8	23 5/8	18 6/8	5	5	5	5	Sheridan Co., KS	Les S. Brown	Les S. Brown	2002	194
174 7/8	27 6/8	28 1/8	23 4/8	5 7/8	5 3/8	6	6	Ottawa Co., OH	John L. Biggert, Sr.	John L. Biggert, Sr.	1976	194
174 7/8	25	25 2/8	18 7/8	4 3/8	4 7/8	7	5	Decatur Co., IA	Mike Boswell	Mike Boswell	1999	203
174 7/8	27 6/8	27 3/8	20 2/8	5 5/8	4 7/8	6	4	St. Louis Co., MN	Randy Fredlund	Randy Fredlund	2000	203
174 7/8	23	24 1/8	17 7/8	4 6/8	4 4/8	6	6	Pipestone River, SK	Brent M. Urschel	Brent M. Urschel	2000	203
174 7/8	25 4/8	26 6/8	18 1/8	4 4/8	4 5/8	6	5	Goodsoil, SK	Richard C. Moulton	Richard C. Moulton	2000	203
174 7/8	25 7/8	25 2/8	17 4/8	4 7/8	5	5	6	Elbow River, AB	James W. Taylor	James W. Taylor	2001	203
174 7/8	28 6/8	27 5/8	21 3/8	5 3/8	5 3/8	7	6	Clayton Co., IA	Scott D. Geater	Scott D. Geater	2001	203
174 7/8	24 1/8	24 1/8	18 1/8	5	4 7/8	7	7	Barron Co., WI	Wayne Phillips	Wayne Phillips	2001	203
174 7/8	24 3/8	25 4/8	20 7/8	4 7/8	4 7/8	5	6	Decatur Co., IA	Thomas G. Krikke	Thomas G. Krikke	2001	203
174 7/8	28 1/8	27 5/8	23 5/8	4 4/8	4 4/8	7	7	Door Co., WI	Keith N. Bink	Keith N. Bink	2001	203
174 6/8	25 7/8	27 1/8	24 4/8	4 5/8	4 6/8	6	5	Winnebago Co., IL	Charles P. Lanzendorf	Brian S. Anderson	1998	212
174 6/8	27 1/8	25	19 2/8	4 7/8	4 6/8	5	6	Vermilion Co., IL	Chris W. Magrini	Chris W. Magrini	2000	212
174 6/8	25	26 4/8	19 6/8	4 6/8	4 4/8	6	6	Oneida Co., WI	Michael J. Krueger	Michael J. Krueger	2000	212
174 6/8	26 4/8	23 5/8	15 4/8	4 4/8	4 3/8	5	6	Jefferson Co., WI	Ronald Jongetjez	Ronald Jongetjez	2000	212
174 6/8	23 3/8	27 6/8	18 6/8	4 3/8	4 3/8	7	6	Avoyelles Parish, LA	Allen J. Gaspard	Allen J. Gaspard	2003	212
174 5/8	25 5/8	24 7/8	19 3/8	5 4/8	5 4/8	5	6	Webb Co., TX	Alan W. Saralecos	Alan W. Saralecos	2000	217
174 5/8	26 2/8	25 4/8	21 5/8	5 2/8	6 1/8	5	6	Lyman Co., SD	Leeman E. Moore, Jr.	Leeman E. Moore, Jr.	2002	217

WHITETAIL DEER - TYPICAL ANTLERS

Odocoileus virginianus virginianus and certain related subspecies

Score	Length of Main Beam R.	L.	Inside Spread	Circumference at Smallest Place Between Burr & First Point R.	L.	Number of Points R.	L.	Locality	Hunter	Owner	Date Killed	Rank
174 5/8	25 4/8	24 6/8	16 7/8	4 5/8	4 6/8	5	6	Maverick Co., TX	Frank A. Wojtek	Frank A. Wojtek	2002	217
174 4/8	26 5/8	25 1/8	20 6/8	4 7/8	4 6/8	6	6	Polk Co., MN	Steven R. Cornell	Steven R. Cornell	2000	220
174 4/8	26 1/8	25 4/8	18 6/8	4 6/8	4 6/8	5	5	Gull Lake, AB	Robert Meredith	Robert Meredith	2001	220
174 4/8	28	27 2/8	20 5/8	5	4 7/8	6	6	Jackson Co., IA	Randy P. Steines	Randy P. Steines	2002	220
174 3/8	28 6/8	27 2/8	20 5/8	5 1/8	5	5	5	Otter Tail Co., MN	Picked Up	Frank Virchow	1999	223
174 3/8	26	25 1/8	20 2/8	5 2/8	5 6/8	5	7	Fulton Co., IL	Robert V. Stevenson, Jr.	Robert V. Stevenson, Jr.	1999	223
174 3/8	24 1/8	24 4/8	16 1/8	4 4/8	4 5/8	7	6	Mineral Co., MT	Dan Woodson	Dan Woodson	2000	223
174 3/8	27	27 2/8	20 1/8	5 6/8	5 3/8	8	9	Jackson Co., MO	Mark A. Trowbridge	Mark A. Trowbridge	2000	223
174 3/8	26	26	20 1/8	4 4/8	4 6/8	6	7	Genesee Co., NY	Jeffrey A. Mullin	Jeffrey A. Mullin	2002	223
174 2/8	26 3/8	26 3/8	22 2/8	4 4/8	4 3/8	5	5	Richland Co., WI	Mitch Shewchuk	Mitch Shewchuk	2000	228
174 2/8	25 4/8	27 3/8	18 6/8	4 6/8	4 7/8	7	8	Saline Co., KS	Robert L. Darrow	Cabela's, Inc.	2000	228
174 2/8	25 2/8	24 5/8	20 4/8	4 4/8	4 4/8	6	6	Brown Co., IL	David A. Bowen	David A. Bowen	2001	228
174 2/8	26	26 1/8	19 7/8	6	5 7/8	5	7	Hudson Bay, SK	Norman Belchamber	Norman Belchamber	2001	228
174 2/8	24 4/8	26	19 5/8	5 6/8	7 2/8	7	8	Fish Lake, AB	Aldo B. Zanon	Aldo B. Zanon	2002	228
174 2/8	28 3/8	28	25 6/8	6 3/8	6 3/8	4	4	Knox Co., IL	Bradley M. Nelson	Bradley M. Nelson	2002	228
174 1/8	26 5/8	26 3/8	21 5/8	5 3/8	5 4/8	5	5	Allamakee Co., IA	Picked Up	IA Dept. of Natl. Resc.	1998	234
174 1/8	25	25 3/8	21 1/8	4 6/8	5	9	9	Starke Co., IN	Charles W. Via	Charles W. Via	2000	234
174 1/8	26	25 6/8	22 7/8	5 1/8	5	6	8	Summit Co., OH	Robert E. Faber	Robert E. Faber	2000	234
174 1/8	26 3/8	25	19 5/8	5	5	5	6	Franklin Co., IN	Clarence G. Hupfer	Clarence G. Hupfer	2001	234
174 1/8	28 4/8	29	21	5 2/8	5 2/8	7	5	Clark Co., IL	Barry Howe	Barry Howe	2002	234
174 1/8	26 2/8	25 2/8	17 2/8	6 1/8	6 3/8	8	7	Cass Co., IL	Christopher C. Gosset	Christopher C. Gosset	2002	234
174 1/8	24 6/8	25 4/8	20 1/8	4 4/8	4 3/8	6	7	Blaine Lake, SK	James Skarpinsky	James Skarpinsky	2002	234
174 1/8	26 4/8	27 1/8	19	4 7/8	4 7/8	7	6	Hocking Co., OH	David C. Jones	David C. Jones	2002	234
174	25 6/8	26	19 6/8	4 3/8	4 3/8	5	5	Desha Co., AR	David Wren	Maurice Abowitz	1962	242
174	25 5/8	24 6/8	17 2/8	4 1/8	4 1/8	5	6	Christian Co., KY	Christopher Cundiff	Christopher Cundiff	1985	242
174	27 2/8	27 3/8	20 5/8	4 4/8	4 4/8	5	4	Otter Tail Co., MN	John D. Thorson	John D. Thorson	2000	242
174	25 4/8	25 4/8	20 2/8	4 4/8	4 3/8	5	6	Saginaw Co., MI	Orrin R. Nothelfer	Orrin R. Nothelfer	2000	242
174	25 5/8	25 6/8	22 5/8	5 4/8	5 4/8	6	8	Van Buren Co., MI	Mark A. Meulendyk	Mark A. Meulendyk	2002	242
174	21 6/8	21	18 6/8	4 5/8	4 4/8	7	8	Tuscarawas Co., OH	Wes S. McMillan	Wes S. McMillan	2003	242
173 7/8	25 7/8	25	19 1/8	4 6/8	4 6/8	5	5	Wadena Co., MN	Picked Up	Kelly C. Marshall	1987	248
173 7/8	27 3/8	27 2/8	19	4 5/8	4 5/8	5	6	Meigs Co., OH	Roger L. Hoffman	Roger L. Hoffman	1993	248
173 7/8	25 4/8	25 5/8	18 7/8	4 7/8	5 1/8	5	5	Appanoose Co., IA	Joel V. Ash	Joel V. Ash	2001	248
173 7/8	28 7/8	28 3/8	17 3/8	4 5/8	4 7/8	6	7	Pittsylvania Co., VA	Picked Up	David Baker	2001	248

Score	Length of Main Beam R	Length of Main Beam L	Inside Spread	Circumference R	Circumference L	Points R	Points L	Locality	By Whom Killed	Owner	Date	Rank
173 7/8	26 1/8	26 4/8	16 4/8	5 3/8	5 3/8	6	5	Pike Co., MO	Marty Niffen	Marty Niffen	2001	248
173 7/8	26	27 4/8	17 2/8	5 5/8	5 6/8	6	7	Franklin Co., OH	Casey M. Murphy, Jr.	Casey M. Murphy, Jr.	2002	248
173 6/8	25 5/8	26	21	5 6/8	5 6/8	5	5	Menominee Co., WI	Picked Up	Ray T. Charles	1994	254
173 6/8	24 1/8	26 6/8	25 3/8	5 5/8	5 5/8	9	7	Ribstone Creek, AB	Morgan J. Williams	Morgan J. Williams	2000	254
173 6/8	26	25 4/8	20	5	5	5	5	Montgomery Co., IN	Andrew A. Horning	Andrew A. Horning	2001	254
173 6/8	25 6/8	25 6/8	21 4/8	5 2/8	5	6	5	Comanche Co., KS	Kenneth W. Williams	Kenneth W. Williams	2001	254
173 6/8	27 5/8	26 7/8	21 4/8	5 2/8	5 2/8	5	5	Adams Co., OH	Stacey E. Blevins	Stacey E. Blevins	2002	254
173 6/8	30 5/8	29 5/8	20 5/8	5 3/8	5 4/8	6	5	Erie Co., OH	James W. Zimmerman	James W. Zimmerman	2002	254
173 6/8	25	26	18 4/8	3 7/8	3 7/8	5	5	Stokes Co., NC	Buddie Adkins	Buddie Adkins	2002	254
173 5/8	26 5/8	26 3/8	20 1/8	5 6/8	5 4/8	8	8	Sedgwick Co., KS	Mary A. Fuller	Mary A. Fuller	2002	254
173 5/8	25 7/8	25	19 2/8	5 6/8	5 7/8	6	6	Adams Co., IL	Mike L. Melton	Mike L. Melton	2000	262
173 5/8	25 5/8	25 5/8	19 7/8	4 3/8	4 2/8	5	5	Jo Daviess Co., IL	William B. Bland	William B. Bland	2001	262
173 5/8	26 2/8	26 7/8	21 5/8	5	5	6	6	Hubbard Co., MN	Justin Sandmeyer	Justin Sandmeyer	2001	262
173 4/8	26 6/8	25 6/8	22	6 1/8	6 2/8	5	5	Decatur Co., IA	Picked Up	Bill J. Timms	1999	265
173 4/8	24	25 2/8	18 4/8	4 6/8	4 6/8	6	6	Clinton Co., IA	Picked Up	Steve Scharf	1999	265
173 4/8	26 4/8	27 3/8	18 4/8	5 5/8	5 5/8	7	6	Meadow Lake, SK	David A. Holmes	David A. Holmes	2000	265
173 4/8	26 2/8	26 3/8	20 5/8	4 7/8	4 5/8	5	6	Torch River, SK	Picked Up	Kurt Rempel	2000	265
173 4/8	25 1/8	24 3/8	18 6/8	5 3/8	5 4/8	5	5	Adams Co., IL	Wayne A Brinkley	Wayne A Brinkley	2000	265
173 4/8	25 4/8	25 4/8	19 4/8	4 7/8	4 6/8	7	7	Trempealeau Co., WI	Ross P. Lambert	Ross P. Lambert	2001	265
173 4/8	26	26 5/8	20 6/8	4 4/8	4 2/8	6	6	Greene Co., IL	Ryan M. Swearingin	Ryan M. Swearingin	2001	265
173 3/8	25 6/8	25 7/8	19 2/8	4 7/8	5	8	7	St. Louis Co., MN	Picked Up	William E. Clink	1960	272
173 3/8	26 3/8	26 7/8	20 7/8	6 2/8	6 2/8	5	5	Clay Co., IN	Rex A. Treadway	Rex A. Treadway	2001	272
173 3/8	26 4/8	26 4/8	18 3/8	5 5/8	5 7/8	6	6	Schuyler Co., IL	Ken J. Shaw	Ken J. Shaw	2002	272
173 2/8	28 3/8	27 3/8	21 2/8	5 3/8	5 2/8	5	5	Pike Co., OH	Kathleen E. Kellough	Kathleen E. Kellough	1999	275
173 2/8	24 3/8	24 4/8	24 4/8	5 2/8	5 2/8	6	8	Henderson Co., IL	David L. Alberts	David L. Alberts	2000	275
173 2/8	26 3/8	25 1/8	20 1/8	5	5 1/8	6	6	Harrison Co., IA	Troy Rath	Troy Rath	2001	275
173 2/8	26 2/8	26 2/8	19 3/8	4 5/8	4 5/8	7	6	Hyde Co., SD	Dillon K. Baloun	Dillon K. Baloun	2001	275
173 2/8	24 5/8	25	18 2/8	4 7/8	4 6/8	6	6	Beaver Co., PA	Robert E. Davenport	Robert E. Davenport	2002	275
173 2/8	27 1/8	26 7/8	21 6/8	5 3/8	5	4	4	Adams Co., OH	Doug N. Ruehl	Doug N. Ruehl	2002	275
173 1/8	25 6/8	25 6/8	17 6/8	5 2/8	5 3/8	7	7	Union Co., AR	James O. Cox	Arkansas County Seed	1973	281
173 1/8	27 3/8	27	22 1/8	4 7/8	5	5	6	Williamson Co., IL	Jay Johns	Jay Johns	1997	281
173 1/8	27 3/8	26 7/8	19 7/8	5 5/8	5 3/8	5	5	Unknown	Unknown	Terry L. Amos	1998	281
173 1/8	22 4/8	22 4/8	16 1/8	4 5/8	4 6/8	7	9	Custer Co., NE	Mitch W. Hickey	Mitch W. Hickey	1999	281
173 1/8	26 6/8	26 6/8	18 1/8	5 1/8	5 1/8	5	5	Jackson Co., WI	David R. Stalheim	David R. Stalheim	1999	281
173 1/8	26 4/8	26	17 7/8	5 3/8	4 5/8	5	5	Saline Co., MO	Jesse H. Little	Jesse H. Little	2000	281
173 1/8	27 6/8	28 2/8	20	5 6/8	6	5	6	Coles Co., IL	Ron Osborne	Ron Osborne	2000	281
173 1/8	26 5/8	25 6/8	20	5 2/8	5 4/8	7	7	Becker Co., MN	Cliff C. Wessels	Cliff C. Wessels	2000	281
173 1/8	26 7/8	26 3/8	20 3/8	4 6/8	4 5/8	5	5	Clayton Co., IA	Alan E. Troester	Alan E. Troester	2000	281
173 1/8	28	28 5/8	23	4 4/8	4 6/8	6	5	Porter Co., IN	Joseph J. Marlow	Joseph J. Marlow	2001	281
173	27 3/8	27	21 3/8	4 5/8	4 3/8	5	7	Jim Hogg Co., TX	Eliverto Cantu	Eddie M. Garza	1985	291
173	24	25 7/8	18 4/8	4 5/8	4 6/8	5	5	Crawford Co., IA	Picked Up	IA Dept. of Natl. Resc.	1994	291

WHITETAIL DEER - TYPICAL ANTLERS

Odocoileus virginianus virginianus and certain related subspecies

Score	Length of Main Beam R.	L.	Inside Spread	Circumference at Smallest Place Between Burr & First Point R.	L.	Number of Points R.	L.	Locality	Hunter	Owner	Date Killed	Rank
173	26 3/8	25 1/8	19 3/8	4 4/8	4 6/8	8	6	Jo Daviess Co., IL	Jim Bielema	Jim Bielema	2000	291
173	24 4/8	24 7/8	18 3/8	4 5/8	4 5/8	7	7	Douglas Co., WI	Raymond J. Dolsen	Raymond J. Dolsen	2000	291
173	26	25 7/8	21 6/8	4 7/8	4 5/8	6	6	McHenry Co., IL	Chase M. Ziller	Chase M. Ziller	2001	291
173	27 7/8	27 3/8	19 6/8	4 6/8	4 4/8	5	7	Webb Co., TX	Betty C. Robison	Betty C. Robison	2002	291
173	27 5/8	26 4/8	24 6/8	4 4/8	4 6/8	4	4	Botetourt Co., VA	James E. Broughman, Jr.	James E. Broughman, Jr.	2002	291
172 7/8	25 5/8	26 5/8	21 5/8	4 6/8	4 7/8	6	5	Minnehaha Co., SD	Daniel D. Anderson	Daniel D. Anderson	2001	298
172 7/8	28 2/8	27 7/8	21 3/8	5 5/8	5 4/8	5	5	Scott Co., IL	Josh L. Roach	Josh L. Roach	2001	298
172 7/8	28 1/8	27 4/8	20 7/8	5 7/8	5 4/8	6	5	Kent Co., MI	Matthew Sikma	Matthew Sikma	2002	298
172 6/8	25 6/8	24 6/8	18	4 6/8	4 6/8	5	5	Mercer Co., PA	Michael D. Heckathorn	Michael D. Heckathorn	2000	301
172 6/8	29 3/8	27 7/8	18 6/8	4 6/8	5	5	6	Elk Co., KS	Michael E. Benge	Michael E. Benge	2000	301
172 6/8	26 3/8	26 4/8	20	4 2/8	4 2/8	5	5	Anne Arundel Co., MD	Gus Andujar	Gus Andujar	2000	301
172 6/8	25 6/8	26	17	5 1/8	5 1/8	5	5	N. Battleford, SK	Chris G. Gilmer	Chris G. Gilmer	2001	301
172 6/8	22 1/8	22 2/8	15 5/8	4 5/8	4 7/8	9	8	Jefferson Co., IL	Picked Up	Randy Banes	2002	301
172 5/8	27 1/8	27 7/8	22 5/8	5	4 7/8	6	5	Long Island Lake, AB	David G. McGraw	David G. McGraw	2000	306
172 5/8	26 1/8	26 3/8	17 7/8	4 3/8	4 3/8	6	5	Stafford Co., KS	David Carlton	David Carlton	2000	306
172 5/8	26 6/8	28 5/8	19 1/8	5 1/8	5 2/8	5	5	Porcupine Plain, SK	Ron Daunheimer	Ron Daunheimer	2001	306
172 5/8	26 2/8	25 6/8	19 3/8	4 3/8	4 4/8	5	6	Grant Co., WI	Pete W. Glassmaker	Pete W. Glassmaker	2001	306
172 5/8	28 7/8	28 5/8	19 3/8	5	4 7/8	5	5	Stafford Co., KS	Trenton L. Teager	Trenton L. Teager	2003	306
172 4/8	25 4/8	25 2/8	17	4 5/8	4 6/8	6	6	Stevens Co., WA	Don Ledbeter	Don Ledbeter	1990	311
172 4/8	24 4/8	24 7/8	23 6/8	4 5/8	4 5/8	5	5	Keokuk Co., IA	Michael D. Wells	Michael D. Wells	2000	311
172 4/8	23 5/8	24 3/8	19 6/8	5 1/8	5 1/8	5	5	Marion Co., IA	Richard P. Johnson	Richard P. Johnson	2000	311
172 4/8	26	27 6/8	21	5	5 1/8	5	5	Harrison Co., MO	Bill Cook	Bill Cook	2001	311
172 4/8	26 6/8	26 4/8	21 6/8	5 7/8	5 7/8	5	5	Mozart, SK	Wesley M. Spuzak	Wesley M. Spuzak	2001	311
172 4/8	25 4/8	25 6/8	18 6/8	4 7/8	5	5	5	Anselmo, AB	Robert J. Wegner	Robert J. Wegner	2001	311
172 4/8	21 4/8	23 4/8	25	4 7/8	5	6	6	Polk Co., AR	Lonnie Cecil	Lonnie Cecil	2002	311
172 3/8	26	24 6/8	24 5/8	5 4/8	5 5/8	5	5	Walworth Co., WI	Daniel Miller	Daniel Miller	2000	318
172 3/8	23 4/8	23 3/8	18 5/8	5 2/8	5 2/8	6	5	Washington Co., KY	Gordon S. Adam	Gordon S. Adam	2000	318
172 3/8	25 6/8	26 3/8	17	6 3/8	6 2/8	7	9	Morgan Co., GA	Jeff L. Banks	Jeff L. Banks	2001	318
172 3/8	25 6/8	25 7/8	16 2/8	5	5	6	7	Grundy Co., MO	Wayne A. Moore, Jr.	Wayne A. Moore, Jr.	2001	318
172 3/8	26 4/8	26 6/8	17 1/8	5	5 2/8	6	6	Credit River, ON	Eugene Bulizo	Eugene Bulizo	2001	318
172 3/8	26 4/8	26 1/8	17 3/8	4 5/8	4 5/8	5	5	Fayette Co., IN	Lisa A. Tarvin	Lisa A. Tarvin	2001	318
172 3/8	25 6/8	27 6/8	20 3/8	4 7/8	4 7/8	4	4	Crawford Co., IL	W. Dave Johnson	W. Dave Johnson	2002	318
172 2/8	25 7/8	26	18	4 7/8	5	5	5	Berrien Co., MI	Mike C. Payne	Mike C. Payne	2000	325

Score	Length of Main Beam R	Length of Main Beam L	Inside Spread	Circumference R	Circumference L	Pts. R	Pts. L	Locality	Hunter	Owner	Date	Rank
172 2/8	23 3/8	22 6/8	17	5 3/8	5 3/8	6	6	Bartholomew Co., IN	Dustin G. Prewitt	Dustin G. Prewitt	2001	325
172 2/8	26	26 6/8	19 2/8	5 1/8	5 2/8	5	6	Martin Co., KY	Julius Jude	Julius Jude	2001	325
172 2/8	25 6/8	25 2/8	25 2/8	4 4/8	4 4/8	5	5	Perkins Co., NE	G. Michael Martin	G. Michael Martin	2001	325
172 2/8	20 2/8	20 2/8	18 4/8	4 7/8	4 7/8	5	5	Tamaulipas, MX	William W. Gouldin	William W. Gouldin	2002	325
172 1/8	26 7/8	25 3/8	16	4 1/8	4	5	6	Price Co., NE	Picked Up	Greg K. Young	1981	330
172 1/8	25 1/8	25 5/8	19 1/8	4 4/8	4 3/8	6	5	Rock Island Co., IL	Ron Baum	Keith Hogan	1985	330
172 1/8	24 5/8	24 4/8	18 5/8	4 4/8	4 5/8	5	5	Buffalo Co., WI	David G. Lyga	David G. Lyga	2000	330
172 1/8	25 6/8	25 4/8	22 3/8	5 2/8	5 4/8	5	5	Van Buren Co., IA	Picked Up	Bob McWilliams	2001	330
172	26 1/8	25 6/8	19	6 1/8	6	5	5	Jackson Co., MI	Justin D. Wright	Justin D. Wright	1998	334
172	25 3/8	24 6/8	17 4/8	4 5/8	4 5/8	7	6	Pike Co., MO	Randall E. Pilliard	Randall E. Pilliard	2000	334
172	25 7/8	26	18 4/8	5	5	5	5	Govan, SK	James J. King	James J. King	2000	334
172	26 3/8	28 1/8	27 4/8	4 7/8	5 1/8	6	7	Crawford Co., OH	William E. Crall	William E. Crall	2000	334
172	26 5/8	28 3/8	17 7/8	4 6/8	4 7/8	6	7	Pettis Co., MO	James R. Ellison	James R. Ellison	2001	334
172	27 1/8	26	24 2/8	5 1/8	5 1/8	5	5	Jennings Co., IN	Guy Euler	Guy Euler	2001	334
172	27 2/8	26 6/8	20 7/8	4 7/8	4 6/8	9	9	St. Clair Co., IL	James R. Smith	James R. Smith	2001	334
172	25 4/8	25 1/8	20 4/8	4 2/8	4 2/8	5	5	Shelby Co., KY	Frank L. Walker	Frank L. Walker	2002	334
172	26 2/8	26 2/8	16	5 4/8	5 3/8	5	5	Yazoo Co., MS	Barry S. Barnes	Barry S. Barnes	2003	334
171 7/8	26 6/8	26 6/8	21 4/8	5 5/8	5 5/8	6	7	Jackson Co., KY	Jessie Mahaffey	Tony Mahaffey	1979	343
171 7/8	26 2/8	26 4/8	20 1/8	4 5/8	4 5/8	5	5	Jackson Co., IA	Harvey Sieler	Steve Scharf	PR1985	343
171 7/8	27 7/8	26 6/8	22 7/8	4 3/8	4 5/8	5	5	Putnam Co., IL	Robert D. Koeppel	Robert D. Koeppel	1985	343
171 7/8	25 3/8	25 1/8	20 5/8	4 6/8	4 5/8	6	5	Meigs Co., OH	Raymond G. Golden	Raymond G. Golden	1997	343
171 7/8	27 7/8	27 4/8	21 1/8	4	4 1/8	5	5	Larue Co., KY	Gary Polly	Gary Polly	2001	343
171 7/8	27 3/8	27 4/8	22 3/8	4 6/8	4 5/8	7	6	Caldwell Co., MO	Robert T. Lobb	Robert T. Lobb	2001	343
171 7/8	26 1/8	28 3/8	21 3/8	5 3/8	5 2/8	8	5	Wayne Co., IL	Donald E. Riley	Donald E. Riley	2002	343
171 7/8	26 1/8	26 1/8	16 7/8	4 6/8	4 6/8	6	6	W. Feliciana Parish, LA	James A. Jackson	James A. Jackson	2003	343
171 6/8	27	27	16 2/8	4 3/8	4 3/8	5	5	Linn Co., IA	Picked Up	IA Dept. of Natl. Resc.	1996	351
171 6/8	25 6/8	26 3/8	21 6/8	4 2/8	4 2/8	5	5	Unknown	Unknown	Bill J. Timms	PR1999	351
171 6/8	26 3/8	24 7/8	17 2/8	4 7/8	4 7/8	5	5	Greene Co., IN	Barry A. Stoner	Barry A. Stoner	1999	351
171 6/8	24 2/8	24 2/8	19 4/8	4 2/8	4 2/8	5	5	Throckmorton Co., TX	D. David Teague	D. David Teague	2000	351
171 6/8	27 1/8	27 3/8	18 7/8	5 4/8	5 4/8	6	6	Kenton Co., KY	Mike White	Mike White	2000	351
171 6/8	25 7/8	24 7/8	20 1/8	5 6/8	6 3/8	6	10	Adams Co., OH	Larry D. Napier	Larry D. Napier	2000	351
171 6/8	28 2/8	27 1/8	21 1/8	5	5	8	8	Monroe Co., OH	Terry L. Bartrug	Terry L. Bartrug	2000	351
171 6/8	28 4/8	29 3/8	21 6/8	4 4/8	4 4/8	4	4	Linn Co., IA	Gerald R. Peters	Gerald R. Peters	2001	351
171 6/8	27 1/8	27 1/8	21 4/8	5	5	5	5	Waukesha Co., WI	Ryan Bischop	Ryan Bischop	2002	351
171 6/8	28 2/8	26 5/8	20	4 4/8	4 4/8	8	7	McPherson Co., KS	Ronald R. Myers	Ronald R. Myers	2002	351
171 6/8	26 5/8	23 6/8	20 2/8	4 4/8	4 4/8	6	7	Jumping Deer Creek, SK	Keegan Benko	Keegan Benko	2002	351
171 6/8	25 2/8	28	17 5/8	4 6/8	5	6	6	Scott Co., IA	Ray Garvin	Greg Garvin	2002	351
171 5/8	27 5/8	27 5/8	19 3/8	4 2/8	4 2/8	6	6	Todd Co., MN	Harlan D. Hinzmann	Harlan D. Hinzmann	1978	363
171 5/8	26 3/8	27 3/8	19 1/8	4 3/8	4 3/8	5	5	Sherburne Co., MN	Jeffrey C. Cox	Jeffrey C. Cox	2000	363
171 5/8	25	25 4/8	18 5/8	4 5/8	4 5/8	7	6	Larue Co., KY	Robert L. Bachuss	Robert L. Bachuss	2000	363
171 5/8	23 4/8	24	24 4/8	4 4/8	4 5/8	5	5	Putnam Co., IN	Sharon K. Lepper	Sharon K. Lepper	2000	363

WHITETAIL DEER - TYPICAL ANTLERS

Odocoileus virginianus virginianus and certain related subspecies

Score	Length of Main Beam R.	L.	Inside Spread	Circumference at Smallest Place Between Burr & First Point R.	L.	Number of Points R.	L.	Locality	Hunter	Owner	Date Killed	Rank
171 5/8	26 7/8	26 3/8	21 7/8	5 1/8	5	5	5	Allamakee Co., IA	John E. Wood	John E. Wood	2000	363
171 5/8	27	26 6/8	18 4/8	4 5/8	4 5/8	6	7	Vermilion Co., IL	Jeff Dodd	Jeff Dodd	2001	363
171 5/8	24 7/8	24 7/8	20 4/8	5 3/8	5 3/8	7	7	Todd Co., KY	Roger Cherry	Roger Cherry	2001	363
171 5/8	25 6/8	26 2/8	21 5/8	4 6/8	4 7/8	5	5	Dewitt Co., IL	William A. Steward	William A. Steward	2001	363
171 5/8	26 5/8	24 4/8	21 4/8	4 5/8	4 4/8	7	7	Webb Co., TX	Xavier Villasenor, Jr.	Xavier Villasenor, Jr.	2001	363
171 5/8	25 6/8	25 6/8	19 7/8	4 6/8	4 4/8	6	6	Vinton Co., OH	Brian Huff	Brian Huff	2002	363
171 5/8	26 3/8	25 4/8	21 7/8	4 6/8	4 6/8	8	6	Adams Co., OH	Mark A. Garman	Mark A. Garman	2002	363
171 5/8	28 4/8	28 2/8	18 7/8	5	5 1/8	8	5	Washington Co., OH	Kenneth G. Kidder	Kenneth G. Kidder	2002	363
171 4/8	25 2/8	26 2/8	25 4/8	4 4/8	4 6/8	6	6	Thickwood Hills, SK	Brian C. Sankey	Brian C. Sankey	1996	375
171 4/8	25 2/8	24 7/8	22	4 5/8	4 5/8	5	5	Webb Co., TX	Willie H. Esse, Jr.	Willie H. Esse, Jr.	2000	375
171 4/8	27 4/8	27 2/8	19	4 7/8	4 5/8	7	5	St. Croix Co., WI	Picked Up	Mike Kessler	2000	375
171 4/8	24 4/8	25 4/8	18 2/8	4	4 1/8	5	5	Jackson Co., IA	Picked Up	Alan Andreson	2001	375
171 4/8	26 3/8	27 3/8	20	5 2/8	5 3/8	8	6	Wabigoon Lake, ON	James H. Trapp	James H. Trapp	2001	375
171 4/8	26 1/8	25 5/8	18 6/8	4 1/8	4 1/8	8	7	Cumberland Co., NC	Lucas J. Hinerman	Lucas J. Hinerman	2001	375
171 4/8	27 2/8	26 6/8	19	5	5	9	7	Pike Co., OH	Terry L. Waits	Terry L. Waits	2001	375
171 4/8	26	25 4/8	18 3/8	5 1/8	5 5/8	6	7	Morgan Co., IN	David L. Wolford	David L. Wolford	2002	375
171 4/8	25	25 4/8	21	4 2/8	4 2/8	5	5	Red River Co., TX	Clint L. Jackson	Clint L. Jackson	2002	375
171 4/8	24 6/8	24 7/8	17	4 4/8	4 4/8	7	7	White Co., AR	Dennis Needham	Dennis Needham	2002	375
171 4/8	25 6/8	25 1/8	23 4/8	4 5/8	4 7/8	8	6	Jefferson Co., OH	Frank J. Rozic	Frank J. Rozic	2002	375
171 3/8	27 2/8	27 2/8	22 5/8	5 1/8	5 1/8	6	6	Parke Co., IN	Ronald A. Keys	Ronald A. Keys	1997	386
171 3/8	26 2/8	26 4/8	20	4 3/8	4 4/8	6	6	Adair Co., MO	Karen White	Karen White	2000	386
171 3/8	25 7/8	27 2/8	19 3/8	4 3/8	4 4/8	5	5	Dearborn Co., IN	Nick T. Lobenstein	Nick T. Lobenstein	2001	386
171 3/8	27 3/8	27	20 1/8	5	5	5	5	Sangamon Co., IL	James V. Holdenried	James V. Holdenried	2001	386
171 3/8	25 3/8	25 5/8	17 5/8	5 1/8	5	5	6	Twin Lakes, AB	Shaun P.W. Proulx	Shaun P.W. Proulx	2002	386
171 3/8	26 2/8	26	18 1/8	4 7/8	5	5	5	St. Francois Co., MO	Edward A. Peterson	Edward A. Peterson	2002	386
171 3/8	27 2/8	27 2/8	18 1/8	4 5/8	4 4/8	6	7	Appanoose Co., IA	Kris A. Shondel	Kris A. Shondel	2002	386
171 3/8	27 2/8	27 1/8	24 1/8	5 1/8	5 2/8	5	8	Randolph Co., IL	James E. Mraz	James E. Mraz	2003	386
171 2/8	27 1/8	27 6/8	20 6/8	5	5 1/8	6	6	Rainy Lake, ON	John N. Nelson	John N. Nelson	2000	394
171 2/8	24 7/8	27	19 6/8	4 2/8	4 4/8	6	6	Warren Co., MO	Billy DeCoster	Billy DeCoster	2000	394
171 2/8	27 2/8	26 5/8	22 1/8	5 5/8	5 2/8	6	7	Warren Co., IA	David G.J. Milby	David G.J. Milby	2000	394
171 2/8	27 1/8	28 7/8	22	5 1/8	5 5/8	7	7	Madison Co., OH	Bartly D. Howerton	Bartly D. Howerton	2000	394
171 2/8	25 4/8	25 4/8	16 6/8	4 3/8	4 3/8	6	6	Onondaga Co., NY	Kenneth L. Lamb	Kenneth L. Lamb	2000	394
171 2/8	25	26 4/8	18 2/8	5 6/8	5 7/8	6	6	Meigs Co., TN	James E. Rose	James E. Rose	2000	394

171 2/8	24 7/8	25 2/8	21 5/8	5 6/8	5 4/8	6	6	Lee Co., IA	Jim D. Wages	Doyle M. Jarrell	2001	394
171 2/8	23 2/8	25 2/8	24 4/8	4 7/8	4 6/8	6	7	Scott Co., IA	Jeffrey R. Coonts	Jeffrey R. Coonts	2002	394
171 2/8	28 2/8	28 4/8	21	5 1/8	5 3/8	6	5	Jefferson Co., WI	Daniel J. Marks	Daniel J. Marks	2002	394
171 2/8	23 6/8	25 1/8	21 4/8	5 5/8	5 6/8	6	5	Bulyea, SK	Fred Hansen	Fred Hansen	2002	394
171 1/8	26	25 7/8	19 2/8	4 7/8	4 7/8	6	5	Nuevo Leon, MX	Jose L. Flores	Jose L. Flores	1986	404
171 1/8	26 6/8	28	21 3/8	4 5/8	4 5/8	5	5	Menominee Co., WI	Robert L. Boyd	Robert L. Boyd	2000	404
171 1/8	24 6/8	25 1/8	18 7/8	5	5 1/8	5	5	Shawano Co., WI	Leo M. McDonald	Leo M. McDonald	2000	404
171 1/8	25 2/8	24 7/8	19 1/8	4 3/8	4 3/8	6	5	Polk Co., WI	Jack G. Fleming	Jack G. Fleming	2000	404
171 1/8	25 7/8	27	18 4/8	5 4/8	5 5/8	5	5	Lamar Co., AL	Richard L. Moore	Richard L. Moore	2001	404
171 1/8	28 1/8	28 1/8	23 3/8	4 6/8	4 5/8	5	6	Fayette Co., IA	Gerald D. Miller	Gerald D. Miller	2001	404
171 1/8	30 5/8	28 3/8	20 4/8	4 6/8	4 6/8	8	5	Kenton Co., KY	Mike White	Mike White	2001	404
171 1/8	26	26 1/8	21 7/8	5 3/8	5 1/8	5	7	Kenton Co., KY	Jim Bezold	Jim Bezold	2002	404
171	25 6/8	26 6/8	23 7/8	5 2/8	5 4/8	5	6	Clark Co., KS	Cullen R. Spitzer	Cullen R. Spitzer	2002	413
171	25	25	16 6/8	4 5/8	4 4/8	6	8	Clinton Co., IA	Thomas J. Straka	Thomas J. Straka	1994	413
171	25 2/8	25 3/8	17 2/8	5	5 2/8	8	6	Bulyea, SK	Tracy K. Hubick	Tracy K. Hubick	2000	413
171	27 1/8	27	19 2/8	4 5/8	4 5/8	6	7	Maverick Co., TX	William A. Jordan III	William A. Jordan III	2001	413
171	26 4/8	26 4/8	20	4 6/8	4 6/8	7	6	Albemarle, VA	Eddie W. Snow	Eddie W. Snow	2001	413
171	29 2/8	29 5/8	19 6/8	4 4/8	4 4/8	5	5	Casey Co., KY	Larry Haggard	Larry Haggard	2002	413
171	25 1/8	25 1/8	18 4/8	5 7/8	6 3/8	5	5	Queenie Creek, AB	Barton F. Toporowski	Barton F. Toporowski	2002	413
171	24 6/8	25 1/8	21	4 1/8	4 1/8	5	7	Lake of the Rivers, SK	Bryan Bogdon	Bryan Bogdon	2003	413
170 7/8	27 4/8	26 4/8	22 5/8	5	5	5	8	Boyle Co., KY	Wilburn Turner	Wilburn Turner	2000	420
170 7/8	23 4/8	21 6/8	16 3/8	5 2/8	5 3/8	6	6	Timeu Creek, AB	Tom A. Wong	Tom A. Wong	2000	420
170 7/8	24 5/8	24 4/8	22	5 1/8	5	7	5	Qu'Appelle River, SK	Mel Tuck	Mel Tuck	2000	420
170 7/8	25 5/8	25	18 6/8	5 6/8	5 5/8	6	7	Porcupine Plain, SK	Edward H. Marinelli	Edward H. Marinelli	2000	420
170 7/8	26 5/8	26 3/8	21	4 6/8	4 6/8	5	4	Perry Co., OH	Ron D. Nash	Ron D. Nash	2001	420
170 7/8	26 5/8	27 4/8	22 3/8	6 3/8	6 5/8	5	7	Lewis Co., KY	Phillip R. Hall	Phillip R. Hall	2001	420
170 7/8	25 7/8	25 4/8	20 6/8	5	5 2/8	6	5	Pierce Co., WI	Donald G. Frandrup	Donald G. Frandrup	2002	420
170 7/8	23 7/8	25 6/8	19 2/8	4 7/8	5 4/8	5	6	Spink Co., SD	William D. Mitchell	William D. Mitchell	2002	420
170 7/8	26 6/8	26 3/8	18 3/8	5 2/8	5	6	6	Oakland Co., MI	Rick L. Holderbaum	Rick L. Holderbaum	2002	420
170 6/8	28 6/8	28 4/8	27 1/8	4 7/8	4 7/8	6	5	Shoshone Co., ID	Clarence Hagerman	Robert D. Myers	1947	429
170 6/8	26 4/8	25 2/8	21 4/8	4 4/8	4 3/8	5	6	Natchitoches Parish, LA	Randy K. Ward	Randy K. Ward	1993	429
170 6/8	25 5/8	25 4/8	18 6/8	4 3/8	4 3/8	5	5	Monona Co., IA	Unknown	George Waters	PR2000	429
170 6/8	29 4/8	29 7/8	27 2/8	4 5/8	4 7/8	5	5	Hart Co., KY	Darryl L. Shelby	Darryl L. Shelby	2000	429
170 6/8	24 4/8	23 4/8	18	4 7/8	4 7/8	5	5	Torch River, SK	William H. Worley, Jr.	William H. Worley, Jr.	2000	429
170 6/8	26 1/8	26	18 2/8	4 7/8	4 4/8	6	5	Moore Co., NC	Jason A. Cole	Jason A. Cole	2000	429
170 6/8	26	28	20 6/8	4 6/8	4 5/8	5	6	Greene Co., IN	Jesse D. Yeryar	Jesse D. Yeryar	2001	429
170 6/8	26 5/8	25 3/8	20 2/8	5	5	6	5	Labette Co., KS	Stefan S. Smith	Stefan S. Smith	2001	429
170 6/8	26 5/8	27 2/8	18 4/8	4 5/8	4 4/8	5	6	Franklin Co., MO	Daryl J. Klekamp	Daryl J. Klekamp	2002	429
170 5/8	26 1/8	25 4/8	16 7/8	5	4 7/8	6	6	Lawrence Co., IL	Tim Golden	Tim Golden	2000	438
170 5/8	22 7/8	26 1/8	18 2/8	4 6/8	4 6/8	6	9	Meadow Lake, SK	John W. Stoothoff, Jr.	John W. Stoothoff, Jr.	2000	438
170 5/8	26 2/8	21 2/8	21 2/8	4 4/8	4 4/8	8	7	Pike Co., OH	Jesse H. Brubacher	Jesse H. Brubacher	2000	438

Score	Length of Main Beam R.	L.	Inside Spread	Circumference at Smallest Place Between Burr & First Point R.	L.	Number of Points R.	L.	Locality	Hunter	Owner	Date Killed	Rank
170 5/8	25 7/8	25 2/8	17 4/8	5 1/8	5 1/8	7	9	Decatur Co., KS	H. Robert Foster	H. Robert Foster	2000	438
170 5/8	27 3/8	27 7/8	18 1/8	5 2/8	5	5	5	Fond du Lac Co., WI	Victor J. Ketchpaw	Victor J. Ketchpaw	2000	438
170 5/8	25 2/8	25	20 7/8	5 2/8	5 3/8	6	5	S. Saskatchewan River, SK	Jack Clary	Jack Clary	2001	438
170 5/8	26 1/8	26 4/8	19 5/8	4 5/8	4 3/8	7	6	Mason Co., IL	Randall E. Ballard	Randall E. Ballard	2001	438
170 5/8	25 6/8	26 1/8	19 1/8	5 3/8	5 4/8	5	5	Union Co., KY	Craig Nally	Craig Nally	2002	438
170 4/8	25 3/8	25 4/8	18 5/8	5 6/8	5 6/8	7	5	Warren Co., IA	George H. Eckstrom II	George H. Eckstrom II	2000	446
170 4/8	23 2/8	23 5/8	19	5	5 1/8	5	5	Etonami River, SK	William K. Batty	William K. Batty	2001	446
170 4/8	26 5/8	26 4/8	19 4/8	5 7/8	5 6/8	5	6	Posey Co., IN	Steve Reed, Jr.	Steve Reed, Jr.	2001	446
170 4/8	26 5/8	26 2/8	21 1/8	5 3/8	5 6/8	6	5	Oneida Co., NY	Tjaart A. Kruger	Tjaart A. Kruger	2002	446
170 4/8	27 6/8	28 7/8	19 4/8	5	5	7	6	Licking Co., OH	Mark E. McCoy	Mark E. McCoy	2002	446
170 4/8	23 1/8	21 5/8	18 4/8	4 6/8	4 6/8	6	6	Mercer Co., MO	Jason T. Goforth	Jason T. Goforth	2002	446
170 4/8	26 5/8	27 6/8	19 1/8	5	5	6	6	Vermilion Co., IL	Ryan D. Sparling	Ryan D. Sparling	2002	446
170 4/8	25 5/8	25 6/8	17	4 3/8	4 4/8	5	5	Ottawa Co., OH	Donald S. Loucks	Donald S. Loucks	2002	446
170 3/8	28 1/8	26 4/8	18 5/8	5 5/8	5 5/8	5	5	Jackson Co., IA	Unknown	Steven Morehead	1983	454
170 3/8	26 1/8	25 5/8	21 3/8	5 2/8	5 2/8	5	5	Whiteside Co., IL	Mark Trent	David Billman	1998	454
170 3/8	24 2/8	24 1/8	21 2/8	4 6/8	4 6/8	5	6	Scott Co., MN	Joe Shotliff	Joe Shotliff	2000	454
170 3/8	27 7/8	26 4/8	17 5/8	4 6/8	4 6/8	5	5	Penobscot Co., ME	Lawrence L. Lord	Lawrence L. Lord	2000	454
170 3/8	25 3/8	24 6/8	18 7/8	5 3/8	5 2/8	6	7	Quill Lake, SK	Eddy Korolchuk	Eddy Korolchuk	2000	454
170 3/8	25 2/8	25 6/8	18 1/8	4 4/8	4 3/8	6	6	Dimmit Co., TX	Robert E. Zaiglin	Robert E. Zaiglin	2001	454
170 3/8	26 2/8	25 3/8	17 7/8	5	5 1/8	5	6	Idaho	Unknown	Larry Haines	PR2002	454
170 3/8	25 7/8	25 4/8	22 3/8	4 6/8	4 7/8	6	5	Concordia Parish, LA	Ronnie L. Wilkinson	Ronnie L. Wilkinson	2002	454
170 2/8	27 7/8	27 4/8	25 6/8	5 1/8	4 7/8	5	5	Jackson Co., IA	Picked Up	Nathan Kilburg	1997	462
170 2/8	25 6/8	25	17 2/8	4 6/8	4 6/8	5	5	Washington Co., MO	William M. Hazer	William M. Hazer	1998	462
170 2/8	29 6/8	27 3/8	17 3/8	5 5/8	6 2/8	8	6	Bedford Co., VA	Picked Up	Michael T. Ingram	2000	462
170 2/8	28 2/8	29 4/8	23 7/8	5 6/8	5 6/8	5	5	Clythe Creek, ON	Bill T. Henshall	Bill T. Henshall	2000	462
170 2/8	27 6/8	28 5/8	20 6/8	4 4/8	4 3/8	6	4	Crane Lake, SK	Jeff M. Slabik	Jeff M. Slabik	2000	462
170 2/8	21 2/8	21 2/8	15	4 4/8	4 3/8	7	8	Maverick Co., TX	Steve E. Holloway	Steve E. Holloway	2001	462
170 2/8	25 5/8	25 3/8	20 1/8	4 6/8	4 7/8	7	6	Monroe Co., IA	Vince L. Feehan	Vince L. Feehan	2001	462
170 2/8	28 1/8	29 2/8	20 4/8	5 6/8	5 4/8	9	7	Clinton Co., IA	Kiner Giddings	Kiner Giddings	2001	462
170 2/8	23 4/8	23 7/8	17 2/8	4 6/8	4 7/8	6	6	Lake Co., IL	Jeffrey B. Keller	Jeffrey B. Keller	2002	462
170 1/8	28 4/8	27	15 1/8	4 3/8	4 3/8	5	5	Jasper Co., GA	Glenn Owens	James E. Owens	1967	471
170 1/8	28 3/8	28 3/8	21 5/8	4 6/8	5	6	6	White Co., AR	Ernest W. Stephenson	Ernest W. Stephenson	1971	471
170 1/8	25 7/8	26 4/8	16 7/8	4 2/8	4 2/8	6	7	Lake of the Woods Co., MN	Kevin L. Olson	Kevin L. Olson	2000	471

Score								Locality	Owner	Hunter	Date	Rank
170 1/8	25 4/8	26	19 7/8	4 6/8	5	5	6	Buffalo Co., WI	Dan Folkedahl	Dan Folkedahl	2000	471
170 1/8	25 4/8	25 3/8	21 2/8	5 6/8	6	7	6	Little Quill Lake, SK	Bennie Buttram	Bennie Buttram	2000	471
170 1/8	29	29 1/8	19 4/8	5	4 7/8	8	6	Allamakee Co., IA	Gary W. Anfinson	Gary W. Anfinson	2000	471
170 1/8	25	25 6/8	22 1/8	4 2/8	4 2/8	7	7	La Salle Co., TX	Weldon L. Nichols	Weldon L. Nichols	2001	471
170 1/8	26 7/8	26 3/8	22 3/8	5 2/8	5 1/8	5	5	Iron Co., WI	Randy D. Szukalski	Randy D. Szukalski	2001	471
170 1/8	26 3/8	26 7/8	19 3/8	4 6/8	4 7/8	6	9	Tomahawk Creek, AB	Jim W. Robertson	Jim W. Robertson	2001	471
170 1/8	23 7/8	23 6/8	17 5/8	4 5/8	4 7/8	5	6	Unknown	Unknown	Richard D. Finkle	PR2002	471
170 1/8	25 6/8	26 2/8	20 1/8	5	4 7/8	6	5	Fairfield Co., OH	Kirk H. Smith	Kirk H. Smith	2002	471
170 1/8	27 6/8	27 6/8	19 1/8	4 5/8	4 4/8	4	4	Geary Co., KS	Picked Up	Carlos Navarro	2002	471
170 1/8	26 6/8	26 2/8	20 1/8	5	4 7/8	5	6	Boone Co., IA	Paul K. Adix	Paul K. Adix	2002	471
170	24 7/8	26 5/8	21 6/8	4 3/8	4 4/8	5	5	Oneida Co., WI	Felix Holewinski, Sr.	Ray T. Charles	1928	484
170	28 2/8	27 4/8	19 2/8	5	5 2/8	5	5	Clayton Co., IA	Kenneth D. Gossman	Darlene Gossman	1955	484
170	27	26 1/8	23 4/8	5 2/8	5 4/8	5	5	Davis Co., IA	Picked Up	IA Dept. of Natl. Resc.	1991	484
170	27	26 2/8	18 2/8	5	4 4/8	6	5	Tazewell Co., IL	Picked Up	Melissa A. Chirello	2000	484
170	27 2/8	25 7/8	22	4 7/8	4 6/8	5	5	Fowler Lake, SK	Stuart J. Bishop	Stuart J. Bishop	2000	484
170	26 3/8	25 7/8	15 4/8	4 7/8	5	5	5	Crawford Co., WI	Joel B. Oppriecht	Joel B. Oppriecht	2000	484
170	26 2/8	26 1/8	18 6/8	4 6/8	4 6/8	7	7	Otsego Co., MI	Robert M. Cannon	Robert M. Cannon	2000	484
170	26 6/8	27 6/8	21 6/8	4 6/8	4 7/8	5	5	Oxford Co., ME	Kenneth A. Zerbst	Kenneth A. Zerbst	2000	484
170	26 6/8	27	20 6/8	5	4 7/8	5	6	Edgar Co., IL	K. David Neal	K. David Neal	2001	484
170	26	24 5/8	20	5	5	5	6	Logan Co., OH	Randy D. Longshore	Randy D. Longshore	2001	484
170	29	27 1/8	21 4/8	4 7/8	4 7/8	5	5	Erie Co., OH	John A. Smith	John A. Smith	2001	484
170	28 1/8	27 5/8	20 5/8	5 3/8	5 3/8	7	6	Unknown	Unknown	Rory J. Petersen	PR2002	484
170	25 4/8	25 3/8	24 4/8	5 1/8	5 3/8	8	7	Buffalo Co., WI	Gilbert A. Arnoldy	Gilbert A. Arnoldy	2002	484
169 6/8	24 3/8	24 4/8	18 1/8	5 4/8	5 2/8	8	8	Saskatchewan River, SK	Trevor Folden	Trevor Folden	2000	497
169 6/8	27 3/8	27 6/8	24 4/8	4 4/8	4 4/8	4	4	Ashland Co., OH	Eric M. Dininger	Eric M. Dininger	2003	497
169 5/8	27 4/8	25 7/8	21	5	5	8	8	Saskatchewan	Jeff Hesketh	Jeff Hesketh	2000	499
169 5/8	25 3/8	25 6/8	17 3/8	4 6/8	4 6/8	6	6	Union Co., IA	John J. Wright	John J. Wright	2002	499
169 4/8	26 1/8	26 1/8	21 6/8	5 3/8	5 2/8	6	5	Webster Co., NE	Matthew Cederburg	Matthew Cederburg	1999	501
169 4/8	27 6/8	27 4/8	22 2/8	4 5/8	4 6/8	5	6	Cook Co., IL	Richard P. Bielik, Sr.	Richard P. Bielik, Sr.	1999	501
169 4/8	23 2/8	23 1/8	17 4/8	5 3/8	5 2/8	7	6	Spencer Co., KY	Keith King	Keith King	2001	501
169 3/8	26 1/8	25 7/8	17 3/8	5 4/8	5 4/8	6	6	Peonan Point, MB	Robert J. Sztorc	Robert J. Sztorc	1998	504
169 3/8	25 7/8	26 2/8	18 7/8	4 2/8	4 5/8	5	6	Pike Co., KY	Jody Scott	Jody Scott	2000	504
169 3/8	23 4/8	23 4/8	19 7/8	5 5/8	5 6/8	6	7	Marshall Co., IA	Matthew J. DeSchamp	Matthew J. DeSchamp	2000	504
169 3/8	26 7/8	24 6/8	23 3/8	5 3/8	5 3/8	5	5	Houston Co., MN	Brook F. Parent	Brook F. Parent	2002	504
169 3/8	28 2/8	27 3/8	20 4/8	5 4/8	5 4/8	7	7	Edmonson Co., KY	Danny E. Vincent	Danny E. Vincent	2002	504
169 2/8	23 7/8	24 6/8	18 6/8	4 6/8	4 6/8	7	7	Shelby Co., IL	Scott Reed	Scott Reed	2001	504
169 2/8	27 1/8	26 6/8	19	4 6/8	4 4/8	9	9	Hopkins Co., KY	William W. Poe	William W. Poe	2002	509
169 2/8	26 4/8	26 7/8	19 6/8	5 2/8	5 2/8	5	5	Harlan Co., NE	Darrell S. Jones	Darrell S. Jones	2002	509
169 2/8	23 4/8	23 4/8	15 6/8	5	5 2/8	7	6	Price Co., WI	Bob E. Karau	Bob E. Karau	2002	509
169 1/8	25 7/8	25 6/8	18 3/8	5 1/8	5 1/8	5	5	Leoville, SK	John B. Triplett	John B. Triplett	2002	513
168 7/8	25 1/8	25 2/8	18	5 2/8	5 2/8	5	6	Chaplin Lake, SK	Angie D. Schlamp	Angie D. Schlamp	2001	514

WHITETAIL DEER - TYPICAL ANTLERS

Odocoileus virginianus virginianus and certain related subspecies

Score	Length of Main Beam R.	L.	Inside Spread	Circumference at Smallest Place Between Burr & First Point R.	L.	Number of Points R.	L.	Locality	Hunter	Owner	Date Killed	Rank
168 7/8	25 7/8	26	21 3/8	5 6/8	5 6/8	5	6	Greene Co., IL	David R. Flatt	David R. Flatt	2001	514
168 7/8	25 6/8	26 3/8	17 1/8	5 1/8	5 1/8	6	5	Ross Co., OH	Leslie H. Merritt	Leslie H. Merritt	2002	514
168 6/8	26 4/8	26 3/8	17	4 3/8	4 5/8	6	7	Todd Co., MN	Gretchen K. Kircher	G.K. & R. Kircher	2000	517
168 5/8	20 3/8	19 6/8	19	7	6 7/8	6	8	Lyon Co., KY	Derek West	Derek West	2000	518
168 5/8	22 7/8	25 7/8	22 6/8	4 7/8	5 2/8	6	6	Pope Co., IL	Gary A. Roepke	Gary A. Roepke	2000	518
168 5/8	25 2/8	23	22 6/8	5 1/8	5 1/8	7	6	Morrison Co., MN	Jody Tomala	Jody Tomala	2001	518
168 5/8	24 6/8	25 6/8	17 5/8	4 6/8	5	6	7	Polk Co., IA	Picked Up	Casey L. Goodhue	2002	518
168 5/8	26 6/8	25 5/8	20 3/8	4 1/8	4 3/8	5	7	Vigo Co., IN	Jason L. Pearman	Jason L. Pearman	2002	518
168 4/8	25 6/8	25 2/8	17 2/8	4 7/8	4 7/8	6	6	Pulaski Co., KY	Kevin Hewitt	Kevin Hewitt	2000	523
168 4/8	23 2/8	23 1/8	22 4/8	5 6/8	5 6/8	6	6	Meadow Lake, SK	Jeffrey A. Arthur	Jeffrey A. Arthur	2003	523
168 3/8	28 6/8	28 2/8	19 6/8	5 1/8	5 2/8	4	5	Lewis Co., KY	Frank B. Smith	Harold Smith	1958	525
168 3/8	25 2/8	25 4/8	17 5/8	4 3/8	4 1/8	5	5	Adams Co., IN	James M. Everett, Jr.	James M. Everett, Jr.	1989	525
168 3/8	26 2/8	26 4/8	22 2/8	5 2/8	5 4/8	6	4	Marion Co., IA	Randy G. Manuel, Sr.	Randy G. Manuel, Sr.	1999	525
168 3/8	26 3/8	25 1/8	19 5/8	4 3/8	4 6/8	5	6	Coal Co., OK	Bryan K. Arms	Bryan K. Arms	2002	525
168 3/8	24 6/8	25	18 4/8	4 5/8	4 7/8	8	9	Lake Co., MN	Jeremy A. Buck	Jeremy A. Buck	2002	525
168 2/8	27 5/8	27 2/8	18 4/8	4 1/8	4 1/8	7	8	Sussex Co., DE	Edward L. Howell, Jr.	Edward L. Howell, Jr.	2000	530
168 2/8	25	25	20 6/8	4 2/8	4 4/8	6	6	Scott Co., KY	Jennifer M. Jacobs	Jennifer M. Jacobs	2000	530
168 2/8	27 4/8		22	5 7/8	5 7/8	5	6	Macon Co., IL	Scott Hartman	Scott Hartman	2001	530
168 2/8	28 3/8	27 7/8	18 2/8	5 4/8	5 4/8	6	8	Jefferson Co., NY	Charles C. Bourquin, Jr.	Charles C. Bourquin, Jr.	2002	530
168 1/8	27 2/8	27 7/8	19 5/8	5	5 2/8	5	5	Hocking Co., OH	Michael W. Masten	Michael W. Masten	1995	534
168 1/8	27 2/8	27 2/8	19 6/8	4 3/8	4 3/8	6	6	Crawford Co., WI	Matthew Malcolm	Matthew Malcolm	1999	534
168 1/8	25 4/8	25	19 7/8	5 2/8	5 2/8	7	7	Calling Lake, AB	David A. Schmidt	David A. Schmidt	2000	534
168 1/8	26 2/8	26 2/8	21 7/8	4 4/8	4 5/8	6	5	Sounding Lake, AB	Edmund L. James	Edmund L. James	2001	534
168 1/8	22 4/8	23	16 1/8	4 4/8	4 5/8	5	5	Trempealeau Co., WI	Thomas A. Clopper	Thomas A. Clopper	2001	534
168 1/8	26 2/8	25	19 1/8	5	5	5	6	Muskingum Co., OH	Chad Fracker	Chad Fracker	2001	534
168 1/8	26 1/8	25 5/8	19 1/8	5	5	6	5	Outagamie Co., WI	Thomas J. Bessette	Thomas J. Bessette	2002	534
168 1/8	24 6/8	25	17 3/8	5 3/8	5 4/8	7	8	Arm River, SK	Ronald N. Riche	Ronald N. Riche	2002	534
168 1/8	23 4/8	22 6/8	19 6/8	4 3/8	4 5/8	5	6	Wynyard, SK	Dennis M. Karakochuk	Dennis M. Karakochuk	2002	534
168	26 1/8	29	18 2/8	5	4 5/8	6	7	Perry Co., KY	Ernie McIntosh	Ernie McIntosh	2000	543
168	20 2/8	22 6/8	17 1/8	5	4 7/8	5	6	Warren Co., KY	Natasha M. Esterley	Natasha M. Esterley	2002	543
167 7/8	26 4/8	26 3/8	19	5 1/8	4 7/8	5	7	Norquay, SK	Patrick H. McKenzie	Patrick H. McKenzie	1981	545
167 7/8	27 7/8	28	20 7/8	4 7/8	4 7/8	7	7	Macoupin Co., IL	Vic G. Christian	Vic G. Christian	2002	545
167 7/8	24 7/8	24 6/8	15 7/8	4 6/8	5	7	5	Outagamie Co., WI	James L. Bleck	James L. Bleck	2002	545

Score	Main Beam R	Main Beam L	Inside Spread	Circ. R	Circ. L	Points R	Points L	Locality	Hunter	Owner	Date Killed	Rank
167 6/8	26	24 6/8	18 5/8	4 6/8	4 7/8	6	6	Lancaster Co., NE	Michael R. Cook	Michael R. Cook	1987	548
167 6/8	26 3/8	26 6/8	17 4/8	5 2/8	5	4	5	Waupaca Co., WI	Robert L. Felkner	Robert L. Felkner	2000	548
167 6/8	24 1/8	25 1/8	20 4/8	5 3/8	5 2/8	5	5	Jackson Co., IA	Dan Oberfoell	Dan Oberfoell	2001	548
167 6/8	28 1/8	27 1/8	18 4/8	4 4/8	4 5/8	5	5	Albemarle Co., VA	James F. Shifflett	James F. Shifflett	2001	548
167 5/8	26 2/8	26 2/8	22 2/8	4 7/8	4 6/8	5	6	Polk Co., WI	Raynold Norling	Jeff C. Norling	1947	552
167 5/8	24 3/8	24 2/8	17 3/8	4 7/8	5 1/8	5	6	Dunn Co., ND	Kyle R. Stefan	Kyle R. Stefan	2001	552
167 5/8	25 4/8	24 7/8	18 2/8	5 1/8	5 2/8	4	7	Oconto Co., WI	Scott E. Samp	Scott E. Samp	2001	552
167 4/8	26 4/8	27 2/8	20 6/8	5	4 5/8	5	3	Oregon	Cayetano Houk	Cayetano Houk	1975	555
167 4/8	28	27 1/8	19	5	4 7/8	6	5	Coshocton Co., OH	John Mucu	John Mucu	2000	555
167 4/8	23	24 5/8	21 3/8	4 5/8	4 7/8	6	6	Coahuila, MX	Thomas W. Powell	Thomas W. Powell	2000	555
167 4/8	24 5/8	24 4/8	20 1/8	5 1/8	5 1/8	6	8	Donley Co., TX	Dan E. McBride	Dan E. McBride	2000	555
167 4/8	25 4/8	24 6/8	17	5 3/8	5	6	9	Cloud Co., KS	Dana M. Alderson	Dana M. Alderson	2002	555
167 3/8	26 4/8	24 4/8	20 5/8	5 4/8	5 5/8	6	7	Reno Co., KS	J. LaVon Bontrager	J. LaVon Bontrager	2000	560
167 3/8	25 1/8	24 6/8	18	4 2/8	4 3/8	6	6	Crawford Co., GA	Grant Allen	Grant Allen	2000	560
167 3/8	26 1/8	25 6/8	19 5/8	4 4/8	4 4/8	5	5	Buffalo Co., WI	Rocky H. Cornelius	Rocky H. Cornelius	2000	560
167 3/8	27 2/8	27 1/8	21 3/8	5	4 7/8	8	7	Waukesha Co., WI	Picked Up	Scott A. Davis	2001	560
167 3/8	25 7/8	25 2/8	20 2/8	5 6/8	5 3/8	6	7	Portage Co., WI	Al Hotterstine	Al Hotterstine	2003	560
167 2/8	25 4/8	24 2/8	19 3/8	5	5 2/8	5	6	Otsego Co., MI	Andrew F. Lustyik	Andrew F. Lustyik	1979	565
167 2/8	24 7/8	24 7/8	19 4/8	4 7/8	5 2/8	5	5	Fall River Co., SD	Donald L. Massa	Donald L. Massa	2000	565
167 1/8	22 3/8	23 3/8	18 5/8	6 2/8	6 1/8	5	5	Fulton Co., IL	Wesley R. Carithers	Wesley R. Carithers	2001	567
167 1/8	24 6/8	23 4/8	20 4/8	4 5/8	4 7/8	6	6	Hutchinson Co., SD	Bryan Maas	Bryan Maas	2001	567
167 1/8	27	27	20 7/8	5	5	4	4	Franklin Co., ME	Guy W. Haines	Guy W. Haines	2002	567
167	27 4/8	26 1/8	20 1/8	4 7/8	4 7/8	5	5	Jackson Co., IL	Theresa L. Davis	Theresa L. Davis	2002	567
167	27 2/8	28 1/8	24 6/8	4 5/8	4 5/8	5	6	Montgomery Co., MS	Darrel J. Wilson	Darrel J. Wilson	2002	567
167	23 5/8	24 5/8	18 4/8	5 5/8	5 4/8	5	5	Iroquois Co., IL	Vance A. Schmid	Vance A. Schmid	1977	567
167	26	24	18 4/8	4 6/8	5 2/8	6	6	Buffalo Co., WI	Edward J. Schlosser	Edward J. Schlosser	1998	572
167	27 2/8	27	16	5 7/8	4 6/8	5	5	Saline Co., NE	Randy J. Adams	Randy J. Adams	1999	572
167	26 6/8	24 1/8	17 1/8	4 4/8	6 4/8	7	7	Calloway Co., KY	Barry B. Canerdy	Barry B. Canerdy	2000	572
167	24 1/8	25 4/8	18 4/8	5 1/8	4 4/8	5	6	Loon Lake, SK	Robert J. Breheney	Robert J. Breheney	2001	572
167	25 5/8	26 2/8	18 2/8	4 3/8	5 1/8	6	5	Eau Claire Co., WI	Brett D. Grill	Brett D. Grill	2001	572
167	25 4/8	26 1/8	22 1/8	5	4 3/8	6	6	Armstrong Co., TX	Lawrence W. Cieslewicz	Lawrence W. Cieslewicz	2001	572
167	27 5/8	25 2/8	16 5/8	4 7/8	4 6/8	7	6	Grayson Co., KY	Jonathan Van Meter	Jonathan Van Meter	2002	572
166 7/8	25 7/8	26 3/8	16 4/8	5 5/8	5 1/8	6	6	Big River, SK	Bret D. Hamm	Bret D. Hamm	2000	580
166 7/8	26 6/8	24 4/8	16 6/8	5 3/8	6	7	7	Adams Co., IL	Beatrice J. Walmsley	Beatrice J. Walmsley	2003	580
166 6/8	26	25 2/8	20	6	5 2/8	6	7	Page Co., IA	Ray F. Stark	Ray F. Stark	2000	580
166 6/8	23 6/8	24 3/8	17 2/8	6	6 1/8	6	5	Calhoun Co., IL	Mel Eltora	Mel Eltora	2000	582
166 6/8	24 3/8	26 1/8	19	3 7/8	3 7/8	5	5	Jefferson Co., IA	Terry J. Hammes	Terry J. Hammes	2000	582
166 6/8	25 1/8	24 4/8	18 7/8	6	6	6	6	Forest Co., WI	Robert A. Karl	Robert A. Karl	2001	582
166 6/8	25 1/8	26 7/8	16	4 4/8	4 6/8	8	5	Price Co., WI	Judith L. Mindock	Judith L. Mindock	2001	582
166 6/8	26	24 7/8	19 2/8	4 1/8	4 1/8	6	6	Pittsburg Co., OK	Dale Atwood	Dale Atwood	2001	582
166 6/8	24 4/8		16 5/8	5 3/8	5 3/8	6	6	Rogers Co., OK	Jesse L. Newton	Jesse L. Newton	2001	582

WHITETAIL DEER - TYPICAL ANTLERS

Odocoileus virginianus virginianus and certain related subspecies

Score	Length of Main Beam R.	L.	Inside Spread	Circumference at Smallest Place Between Burr & First Point R.	L.	Number of Points R.	L.	Locality	Hunter	Owner	Date Killed	Rank
166 6/8	27 2/8	27 2/8	22	4 7/8	4 5/8	6	6	Jim Hogg Co., TX	Mark D. Cooper	Mark D. Cooper	2002	582
166 6/8	28	27 5/8	21 2/8	4 6/8	4 5/8	5	6	Warren Co., IL	Randy L. Hartz	Randy L. Hartz	2002	582
166 5/8	26 6/8	25 5/8	19 2/8	4 4/8	4 5/8	6	5	St. Francis Co., AR	Arden Johnson	Hunter Johnson	1973	591
166 5/8	28 1/8	28 1/8	20 1/8	4 7/8	4 7/8	5	5	Marshall Co., MS	Michael W. Janes	Michael W. Janes	2000	591
166 5/8	27 6/8	27 7/8	22 3/8	4 6/8	4 5/8	6	6	Oldham Co., KY	David Fenley	David Fenley	2002	591
166 5/8	26 1/8	26 4/8	23 3/8	4 6/8	5	6	7	Clinton Co., IL	Brett Thomas	Brett Thomas	2002	591
166 5/8	24 7/8	25 5/8	23 2/8	4 5/8	4 6/8	7	6	Jo Daviess Co., IL	Gaylord A. McKee	Gaylord A. McKee	2002	591
166 4/8	27 2/8	26 1/8	20 4/8	4 6/8	4 4/8	5	5	Portage Co., OH	Daniel S. Behm	Daniel S. Behm	2000	596
166 4/8	26 2/8	24 3/8	19	4 6/8	4 6/8	5	5	Door Co., WI	Sharon F. Gulley	Sharon F. Gulley	2000	596
166 4/8	25	25	19 2/8	4 3/8	4 3/8	6	6	Waushara Co., WI	Donald J. Weinmann	Donald J. Weinmann	2002	596
166 3/8	26 4/8	27 3/8	20 7/8	4 2/8	4 2/8	5	6	Hart Co., KY	Cheryl Wilson	Cheryl Wilson	2001	599
166 2/8	25 2/8	25 7/8	21	4 7/8	4 5/8	5	5	Bell Co., KY	Timothy D. Elliott	Timothy D. Elliott	2000	600
166 1/8	25	24	19 2/8	4 4/8	4 4/8	6	5	N. Saskatchewan River, SK	John P. McMillan	John P. McMillan	2000	601
166 1/8	24	24	18 3/8	4 7/8	4 6/8	5	5	Chisago Co., MN	Jerry A. Smith	Jerry A. Smith	2000	601
166 1/8	24 4/8	24 4/8	17 3/8	4 6/8	4 6/8	6	6	Paulding Co., OH	Timothy G. Copsey	Timothy G. Copsey	2000	601
166 1/8	24 4/8	24 5/8	19	4 3/8	4 2/8	7	6	Duval Co., TX	Gary M. Burch	Gary M. Burch	2000	601
166 1/8	26 1/8	26 7/8	19 1/8	4	4 1/8	5	5	Buffalo Co., WI	Philip L. Raikowski	Philip L. Raikowski	2001	601
166 1/8	25 5/8	26 3/8	19 4/8	5 3/8	5 4/8	6	6	Jo Daviess Co., IL	Jon R. Bourquin	Jon R. Bourquin	2001	601
166	26 4/8	26	17 4/8	5 4/8	5 3/8	7	7	Pike Co., GA	William M. Eppinger	Wanda E. Morris	1970	607
166	26 1/8	26 2/8	15 4/8	4 3/8	4 3/8	5	6	Isle Lake, AB	Gary H. Appleton	Gary H. Appleton	2000	607
166	25 6/8	26 3/8	17 5/8	5	4 7/8	6	8	Beltrami Co., MN	Kenneth A. Hovland	Kenneth A. Hovland	2000	607
166	22 6/8	22 4/8	19	5 2/8	4 6/8	5	5	Howard Co., IA	Boyd Bollman	Boyd Bollman	2002	607
165 7/8	27 5/8	28 1/8	21 1/8	5 4/8	5 5/8	4	5	Green Co., WI	Thomas R. Krause	Thomas R. Krause	2000	611
165 7/8	25 4/8	24 6/8	23 2/8	4 7/8	4 6/8	6	5	Logan Co., NE	Steve S. Lippitt	Steve S. Lippitt	2001	611
165 7/8	24 4/8	23 5/8	19 1/8	4 7/8	4 5/8	5	5	Hunterdon Co., NJ	David L. Tampier	David L. Tampier	2002	611
165 6/8	25	26 2/8	17 7/8	4 2/8	4 2/8	6	5	Juneau Co., WI	Kevin R. Dawson	Kevin R. Dawson	1996	614
165 6/8	24 6/8	25 4/8	20 4/8	5 2/8	5 2/8	5	5	Appanoose Co., IA	Melvin T. Digman	Melvin T. Digman	2000	614
165 6/8	25 6/8	25	21 1/8	5 6/8	5 6/8	6	6	Chippewa Co., WI	Rodney C. Lazarz	Rodney C. Lazarz	2000	614
165 6/8	26	25 7/8	20	4 7/8	4 7/8	5	7	Vermillion Co., IN	Michael A. Still	Michael A. Still	2000	614
165 6/8	25 2/8	26 3/8	18 5/8	5 2/8	5 1/8	6	7	Marion Co., KS	Casey R. Cooper	Casey R. Cooper	2002	614
165 6/8	24 4/8	23 4/8	18 7/8	5 2/8	5 2/8	6	6	Hamilton Co., IL	Bruce E. Thompson	Bruce E. Thompson	2002	614
165 5/8	28 4/8	28 1/8	23 5/8	4	4 1/8	4	4	Madison Co., GA	Jimmy Osborne	Jimmy Osborne	1968	620
165 5/8	24 3/8	23 3/8	23 2/8	5 6/8	5 6/8	6	5	Clayton Co., IA	Michael L. Hertges	Michael L. Hertges	2000	620

Score	L. Main Beam R	L. Main Beam L	Inside Spread	Circ. R	Circ. L	Pts. R	Pts. L	Owner	Hunter	Locality	Date	Rank
165 5/8	26 2/8	26 3/8	18 1/8	4 6/8	4 5/8	5	5	Ramon E. Kohnert	Ramon E. Kohnert	Trempealeau Co., WI	2000	620
165 5/8	28 2/8	29 2/8	22 4/8	5 6/8	5 6/8	4	6	Kenneth D. Toms	Kenneth D. Toms	Adams Co., IA	2000	620
165 5/8	25	23 4/8	17 7/8	5	5 2/8	5	5	Alan D. White	Alan D. White	Yuma Co., CO	2002	620
165 5/8	24 7/8	24 3/8	23 1/8	5 2/8	5 3/8	5	5	Jace Cagle	Jace Cagle	Lyon Co., KY	2002	620
165 4/8	25 1/8	24 1/8	22 4/8	5	5	5	6	Ronald A. Williamson	Ronald A. Williamson	Trempealeau Co., WI	1999	626
165 4/8	24 4/8	23 7/8	19 3/8	4 3/8	4 3/8	8	5	Raymond Nechetsky, Sr.	Raymond Nechetsky, Sr.	Lehigh Co., PA	2000	626
165 4/8	28	27 7/8	18 4/8	5 5/8	5 5/8	7	6	David M. Uhls	David M. Uhls	Johnson Co., IL	2001	626
165 4/8	25 7/8	25 7/8	20	5 3/8	5 1/8	5	5	Benjamin J. Self	Benjamin J. Self	Vermilion Co., IL	2001	626
165 3/8	25 2/8	27 4/8	21 1/8	5 2/8	5 3/8	5	5	Jackie W. Vest	Jackie W. Vest	Giles Co., VA	2000	630
165 3/8	29 1/8	26 3/8	21 3/8	4 7/8	4 7/8	5	6	Charles L. Coffin	Charles L. Coffin	Grafton Co., NH	2000	630
165 3/8	25 1/8	25 1/8	19 7/8	4 5/8	4 4/8	5	5	Jeffrey Johnston	Jeffrey Johnston	Poundmaker Creek, SK	2000	630
165 3/8	23 4/8	23 4/8	20 1/8	5	5 2/8	5	5	Erik C. Ahart	Erik C. Ahart	Uvalde Co., TX	2002	630
165 3/8	25 1/8	25 2/8	18 7/8	5 4/8	5 2/8	7	5	Gary R. Steffan	Picked Up	Woodbury Co., IA	2002	630
165 2/8	26 2/8	26 2/8	19 4/8	5 1/8	4 7/8	5	5	Kenny Brown	Kenny Brown	Christian Co., KY	2000	635
165 2/8	25 5/8	25 5/8	22 4/8	4 7/8	4 5/8	5	6	Jerry M. Williams	Jerry M. Williams	Ray Co., MO	2001	635
165 2/8	27 2/8	25 7/8	21 1/8	4 5/8	4 6/8	6	6	Corbin E. Turpin	Corbin E. Turpin	Sumner Co., KS	2002	635
165 2/8	26	27 1/8	18 2/8	5	5	7	7	Joseph E. Wagner	Joseph E. Wagner	Calumet Co., WI	2002	635
165 2/8	25 4/8	26 4/8	18 5/8	5 3/8	5 1/8	6	5	Paul R. Sankey	Paul R. Sankey	Door Co., WI	2002	635
165 1/8	25 1/8	25 2/8	17 5/8	5	5	7	6	Ricky Strickland	Ricky Strickland	Tallapoosa Co., AL	1981	640
165 1/8	26	25 7/8	21 1/8	4 6/8	4 7/8	7	7	Tim A. Dockendorf	Tim A. Dockendorf	Gregory Co., SD	2000	640
165 1/8	22 1/8	23 6/8	19 1/8	6	6	6	6	Brian M. Fosse	Brian M. Fosse	Sanders Co., NE	2000	640
165 1/8	27 4/8	23 6/8	22 3/8	4 3/8	4 6/8	5	4	Henry Sevcenko	Henry Sevcenko	Duck Mt., MB	2000	640
165 1/8	24 6/8	26 7/8	18 3/8	5	4 6/8	5	4	Greig A. Sims	Greig A. Sims	Reno Co., KS	2001	640
165	24 7/8	24 3/8	17	5 1/8	5	5	5	Karl O. Hamilton	Karl O. Hamilton	Jefferson Co., WV	2000	645
165	24 3/8	24 7/8	19 5/8	4 1/8	3 6/8	6	6	Daniel P. Ginn	Daniel P. Ginn	Dearborn Co., IN	2002	645
165	25	26 3/8	18 1/8	4 5/8	4 6/8	8	8	Ronald D. Searcy	Ronald D. Searcy	Livingston Co., MO	2002	645
165	27 1/8	26 4/8	22	4 7/8	4 7/8	7	5	Russel Macknak	Russel Macknak	Cupar, SK	2002	645
164 7/8	25 6/8	24 3/8	17 1/8	4 1/8	5	8	7	Larry W. Brown	Larry W. Brown	Rappahannock Co., VA	2001	649
164 7/8	25 1/8	24 6/8	19 1/8	4 5/8	4 1/8	5	5	Robert G. Spencer	Robert G. Spencer	Kiowa Co., KS	2002	649
164 6/8	25	24 1/8	18 1/8	4 4/8	4 5/8	6	5	Michael G. Adams	Michael G. Adams	Stony Plain Indian Res., AB	1998	651
164 6/8	26 7/8	26 2/8	18 5/8	4 7/8	4 7/8	6	6	Todd A. Wills	Todd A. Wills	Brown Co., IL	2000	651
164 6/8	24 7/8	25 6/8	19 5/8	5 4/8	5 7/8	7	7	C.L. Dutch Workman	C.L. Dutch Workman	Wicomico Co., MD	2000	651
164 6/8	23 5/8	22 4/8	20 2/8	5 2/8	5 2/8	5	5	Jerry R. Dobbs	Jerry R. Dobbs	Lake Co., IL	2001	651
164 6/8	24	24	19 7/8	4 7/8	4 7/8	5	5	J. David Monaghan	J. David Monaghan	Mason Co., TX	2001	651
164 6/8	27 1/8	27 4/8	19 6/8	5 1/8	5 3/8	6	6	John H. Doherty	John H. Doherty	New Castle Co., DE	2001	651
164 6/8	25	24 7/8	17 4/8	5	5 3/8	8	6	Walter Talandis, Jr.	Walter Talandis, Jr.	Hardin Co., IL	2001	651
164 6/8	24 4/8	24 3/8	21 3/8	5 1/8	5 1/8	6	5	Floyd C. Lowry	Floyd C. Lowry	Usherville, SK	2001	651
164 5/8	23 3/8	23	14 7/8	5 4/8	5 4/8	5	5	Forrest Johnson	Art Siermala	St. Louis Co., MN	PR1950	659
164 5/8	27 6/8	25 7/8	21 3/8	5 1/8	5 1/8	6	5	Doug S. Nitek	Doug S. Nitek	Rusk Co., WI	2000	659
164 5/8	25 2/8	25 5/8	19 4/8	5	5	7	7	Tim L. Touchton	Tim L. Touchton	Berrien Co., GA	2000	659
164 5/8	26 5/8	26	18 6/8	5 5/8	5	6	6	Mark V. Mauro	Mark V. Mauro	Pierce Lake, SK	2001	659

WHITETAIL DEER - TYPICAL ANTLERS

Odocoileus virginianus virginianus and certain related subspecies

Score	Length of Main Beam R.	L.	Inside Spread	Circumference at Smallest Place Between Burr & First Point R.	L.	Number of Points R.	L.	Locality	Hunter	Owner	Date Killed	Rank
164 5/8	25	25	16 7/8	4 2/8	4 2/8	6	6	Kanawaha, WV	William S. Aldridge	William S. Aldridge	2001	659
164 4/8	27 7/8	27 4/8	22	4 3/8	4 3/8	7	7	St. Louis Co., MN	David Willeck	Dan Willeck	1984	664
164 3/8	25 5/8	24 5/8	18 1/8	4 6/8	4 5/8	5	5	Scott Co., AR	Lindsay C. Rudd	Lindsay C. Rudd	2001	665
164 3/8	27 1/8	26 4/8	18 1/8	5 2/8	5 2/8	5	5	Lee Co., VA	Dewayne L. Saylor	Dewayne L. Saylor	2001	665
164 2/8	25 1/8	26 4/8	18	5 1/8	4 6/8	5	5	Butler Co., KS	George A. Cheney	George A. Cheney	2002	667
164 1/8	26 6/8	26 6/8	20 5/8	4	4	5	5	Jackson Co., WI	Carl Randall	Jeannine Lamb	1948	668
164 1/8	24 2/8	25 4/8	19 5/8	4 6/8	4 6/8	5	5	Beltrami Co., MN	Jerry D. Hamilton	Jerry D. Hamilton	2000	668
164 1/8	27 4/8	27 3/8	19 2/8	4 4/8	4 4/8	6	5	Adair Co., KY	Shane Stonecypher	Shane Stonecypher	2001	668
164 1/8	25 4/8	25 5/8	18 7/8	4 6/8	5	5	5	Outagamie Co., WI	Craig C. Koch	Craig C. Koch	2001	668
164 1/8	22 7/8	23 6/8	15 3/8	4 4/8	4 2/8	5	5	Outagamie Co., WI	Matthew R. Heimann	Matthew R. Heimann	2002	668
164 1/8	23 2/8	24 2/8	17 5/8	5 3/8	5 6/8	7	7	White Fox, SK	David L. Main	David L. Main	2002	668
164 1/8	23 1/8	24 5/8	20 3/8	5 6/8	5 6/8	5	5	Macoupin Co., IL	Brian Genetti	Brian Genetti	2002	668
164 1/8	26 7/8	24 4/8	20 7/8	5 1/8	5	6	5	Clay Co., GA	William L. Leaptrot	William L. Leaptrot	2002	668
164 1/8	27 2/8	28 1/8	19 5/8	4 5/8	4 4/8	6	6	Union Co., OH	Todd Tomlin	Todd Tomlin	2002	668
164 1/8	23 6/8	24 2/8	20 3/8	4 1/8	4 2/8	7	7	Warren Co., IA	Larry D. Hill	Larry D. Hill	2002	668
164	25 6/8	26 2/8	18 6/8	5 1/8	5 1/8	5	6	Green Co., WI	James Newman	James Newman	1994	678
164	25	22 7/8	22 4/8	4 7/8	4 7/8	6	5	Kleberg Co., TX	Johnnie R. Walters	Johnnie R. Walters	2000	678
164	24 2/8	23 5/8	16	4 2/8	4 2/8	5	5	Rice Co., MN	Thad A. Sunsdahl	Thad A. Sunsdahl	2000	678
164	26	27 4/8	23	5 4/8	5 5/8	6	5	Benton Co., IA	Brett Pollock	Brett Pollock	2000	678
164	28 6/8	28 2/8	18 4/8	4 6/8	4 7/8	4	4	Madison Co., IA	Raymond Dawson	Raymond Dawson	2001	678
164	27	27 4/8	17 4/8	5 3/8	5 2/8	8	6	Clermont Co., OH	David L. Shouse, Jr.	David L. Shouse, Jr.	2001	678
163 7/8	25 7/8	26 5/8	19 4/8	5 5/8	5 5/8	6	6	Wayne Co., KY	James J. Worley	James J. Worley	2000	684
163 7/8	23 4/8	23	20 1/8	5	5	5	6	Swan River, SK	Milo J. Conklin	Milo J. Conklin	2000	684
163 7/8	24 4/8	24 6/8	19 3/8	4 4/8	4 6/8	5	5	Yankton Co., SD	Jeff A. Sayler	Jeff A. Sayler	2000	684
163 7/8	25 2/8	24 4/8	16 2/8	4 7/8	4 7/8	6	5	Taylor Co., KY	Douglas M. Graham	Douglas M. Graham	2001	684
163 7/8	26 5/8	26 3/8	17 1/8	6 1/8	5 4/8	5	6	Barber Co., KS	Richard M. Young	Richard M. Young	2001	684
163 7/8	25 5/8	24 7/8	16 3/8	4 7/8	4 6/8	5	5	Lewis Co., KY	Michael Graf	Michael Graf	2002	684
163 7/8	26 4/8	26 7/8	23 5/8	5	5 4/8	5	5	Jackson Co., IA	Larry J. Curtis	Larry J. Curtis	2002	684
163 7/8	24	24 2/8	18 1/8	4 3/8	4 6/8	6	6	Sheboygan Co., WI	Larry A. Rach	Larry A. Rach	2002	684
163 7/8	25 6/8	25	18 3/8	5 1/8	5	5	5	Ashland Co., OH	Matt A. Schumaker	Matt A. Schumaker	2003	684
163 7/8	24 5/8	24 2/8	19 6/8	4 7/8	4 7/8	6	6	Butler Co., KY	Dennis E. McElhannon	Dennis E. McElhannon	2003	684
163 6/8	25	25 2/8	19 1/8	5	5 2/8	4	5	Shelby Co., IL	Travis E. Monroe	Travis E. Monroe	1998	694
163 6/8	25 6/8	25 3/8	18 3/8	4 7/8	4 6/8	6	5	Pelicanpouch Lake, ON	Lane Benoit	Lane Benoit	2002	694

Score	L.	R.	Spread	Circ.	Circ.	R	L	Locality	Hunter	Owner	Date	Rank
163 5/8	24 6/8	26 5/8	21 1/8	4 2/8	4 2/8	7	5	Franklin Co., IN	Glenn E. Willis, Jr.	Glenn E. Willis, Jr.	1999	696
163 5/8	25 4/8	25 1/8	19 1/8	4 4/8	4 7/8	5	5	Adams Co., WI	Bruce Sonnenberg	Bruce Sonnenberg	2000	696
163 5/8	23 4/8	24 2/8	21 1/8	4 4/8	4 4/8	5	5	Wilkinson Co., MS	Lynwood Williams III	Lynwood Williams III	2000	696
163 5/8	26 5/8	26 1/8	23 7/8	4 5/8	4 4/8	6	7	Grayson Co., TX	Mark A. Wade	Mark A. Wade	2000	696
163 5/8	26 1/8	25 5/8	18 5/8	4 5/8	4 5/8	5	5	Cook Co., GA	Andrew L. Jaramillo	Andrew L. Jaramillo	2001	696
163 5/8	24 4/8	24 6/8	20	4 3/8	4 2/8	8	7	Bourbon Co., KS	Kevin R. Kraatz	Kevin R. Kraatz	2001	696
163 5/8	30 1/8	27 6/8	23 7/8	5 2/8	5 3/8	5	5	Madison Co., IL	Dustin Bauer	Dustin Bauer	2002	696
163 5/8	22 5/8	24	19 1/8	5 1/8	5	5	5	Clark Co., WI	Bradley A. Fagan	Bradley A. Fagan	2002	696
163 4/8	26 5/8	26 3/8	19 2/8	5	5	5	7	Washington Co., RI	James M. Manni	James M. Manni	2002	705
163 4/8	26	26	21 2/8	4 3/8	4 3/8	5	5	Pike Co., GA	Ronnie G. Newman	Kevin C. Newman	1977	705
163 4/8	26 7/8	26 7/8	19 6/8	5 1/8	5 1/8	7	9	Lake Co., MN	Edward M. Plemel	Edward M. Plemel	2001	705
163 3/8	27	26 7/8	21 3/8	4 5/8	4 5/8	4	6	Forest Co., PA	Brady Mortimer	Brady Mortimer	2002	708
163 3/8	23 6/8	23 1/8	18 2/8	4 4/8	4 5/8	6	7	Onondaga Co., NY	Anthony A. Denison	Anthony A. Denison	2000	708
163 3/8	25 3/8	27 2/8	21	5 1/8	5	6	4	Harvey Co., KS	Tim S. Ross	Tim S. Ross	2001	708
163 3/8	23 4/8	25 4/8	19 3/8	5 3/8	5 3/8	5	6	Jefferson Co., IA	Bryan D. Manor	Bryan D. Manor	2001	708
163 3/8	26 1/8	26 1/8	18 5/8	4 4/8	4 4/8	5	5	Highland Co., OH	John H. McClure	John H. McClure	2001	708
163 3/8	25 6/8	26 7/8	16 6/8	4 7/8	4 4/8	8	6	Bedford Co., VA	Steve A. Williams	Steve A. Williams	2002	708
163 2/8	26 3/8	25 6/8	22 7/8	4 2/8	4 2/8	6	5	Dane Co., WI	Adam Smith	Adam Smith	2002	714
163 2/8	22 4/8	22 3/8	13 4/8	4 2/8	4 2/8	7	7	Walker Co., TX	Ryan M. Lampson	Ryan M. Lampson	2000	714
163 1/8	27 5/8	28 3/8	24	5 3/8	5 1/8	4	4	Linn Co., IA	Trent L. Packingham	Trent L. Packingham	2001	716
163 1/8	20 1/8	21	15 3/8	4 2/8	4 2/8	6	7	Madison Co., MT	Paul S. Bowles	Paul S. Bowles	2000	716
163 1/8	26 1/8	25 1/8	17 1/8	4 6/8	4 5/8	5	6	Kingman Co., KS	Cody B. Purviance	Cody B. Purviance	2000	716
163 1/8	26 2/8	25 5/8	19 5/8	4 7/8	4 6/8	5	5	Bucks Co., PA	Craig D. Kirkman	Craig D. Kirkman	2001	716
163 1/8	25 4/8	26 4/8	19 5/8	5 1/8	5 1/8	5	5	Jessamine Co., KY	Rocky D. Johnson	Rocky D. Johnson	2001	716
163	27 4/8	26 4/8	18 1/8	5	5 1/8	5	5	Waupaca Co., WI	Lee R. Platta	Lee R. Platta	2002	721
163	26 6/8	25 6/8	20 3/8	4 6/8	4 5/8	7	6	Rushing River, ON	Michael J. Eugair	Michael J. Eugair	2000	721
163	24 5/8	25 4/8	20	4 4/8	4 4/8	5	5	McLean Co., KY	Patrick Guynn	Patrick Guynn	2000	721
163	23 5/8	23 5/8	16 2/8	3 7/8	4	6	6	Terrell Co., GA	Gary W. Freeman	Gary W. Freeman	2000	721
163	25 5/8	24 3/8	19 1/8	5 2/8	5 2/8	8	7	Morgan Co., IN	James R. Pritchard	James R. Pritchard	2000	721
163	25 1/8	24 7/8	22 3/8	4 3/8	5 1/8	6	6	Burnett Co., WI	Richard M. Shutt, Jr.	Picked Up	2001	721
163	25	25 3/8	18 4/8	4 4/8	4 4/8	5	5	Chenango Co., NY	James A. Robinson	James A. Robinson	2002	721
162 7/8	29 3/8	30 2/8	25	5 1/8	5 2/8	3	3	Clark Co., KS	Brian King	Brian King	2002	728
162 7/8	25 1/8	25 2/8	18 7/8	4 4/8	4 4/8	5	5	Kewaunee Co., WI	Michael J. Witpalck	Michael J. Witpalck	1994	728
162 7/8	26 2/8	28 1/8	20 7/8	5 2/8	5 2/8	6	6	Ashley Co., AR	Picked Up	AR Game & Fish Comm.	1995	728
162 7/8	25 3/8	26 1/8	17 1/8	5 1/8	5 1/8	5	7	Aitkin Co., MN	Marty Johnson	Marty Johnson	1999	728
162 7/8	24	24 4/8	15 6/8	4 3/8	4 4/8	6	6	Halifax Co., VA	David M. King	David M. King	1999	728
162 7/8	24 3/8	23 5/8	17 6/8	4 1/8	4 3/8	7	6	Crow Wing Co., MN	Jake Oravetz	Jake Oravetz	2000	728
162 7/8	24 3/8	26 5/8	24 3/8	4 7/8	4 5/8	4	4	Schuyler Co., IL	Michael Glasby	Michael Glasby	2000	728
162 6/8	26 6/8	26 3/8	18 6/8	4 5/8	5	7	6	Jasper Co., IA	Ronald W. Brown	Ronald W. Brown	2001	735
162 6/8	25 7/8	29 7/8	24 5/8	4 4/8	4 4/8	5	8	Dodge Co., WI	Duane A. McClyman	Duane A. McClyman	2000	735
162 6/8	23 7/8	22 4/8	16	4 3/8	4 4/8	6	6	Greene Co., IL	Larry A. Marks	Larry A. Marks	2001	735

WHITETAIL DEER - TYPICAL ANTLERS

Odocoileus virginianus virginianus and certain related subspecies

Score	Length of Main Beam R.	L.	Inside Spread	Circumference at Smallest Place Between Burr & First Point R.	L.	Number of Points R.	L.	Locality	Hunter	Owner	Date Killed	Rank
162 6/8	26 2/8	25 4/8	23 3/8	4 4/8	4 5/8	6	5	Chippewa Co., WI	Marlene E. Olson	Marlene E. Olson	2001	735
162 6/8	25	26 5/8	21	5	5 2/8	5	5	Geauga Co., OH	Alan C. Snyder	Alan C. Snyder	2002	735
162 5/8	26 6/8	26 6/8	19 1/8	5	5 2/8	6	6	Beltrami Co., MN	Wallace Lamon	Wallace Lamon	1970	739
162 5/8	28	26 7/8	18 6/8	4 2/8	4 2/8	7	8	Cuyahoga Co., OH	Jeffery C. Perry	Jeffery C. Perry	2000	739
162 5/8	24 1/8	24 7/8	16 7/8	4	4 1/8	7	5	Indiana Co., PA	Joseph E. Hess	Joseph E. Hess	2000	739
162 5/8	25 6/8	25	20 5/8	5	5	6	6	Marwayne, AB	Michael D. Wade	Michael D. Wade	2000	739
162 5/8	23 2/8	23 4/8	17 2/8	4 2/8	4 2/8	6	7	Atascosa Co., TX	James N. Meissner	James N. Meissner	2000	739
162 5/8	24 4/8	24	19 3/8	5 4/8	5 4/8	8	5	Macoupin Co., IL	Curtis A. Reznicek	Curtis A. Reznicek	2001	739
162 5/8	26 2/8	24 6/8	20 5/8	4 5/8	4 3/8	6	7	McLean Co., IL	Picked Up	Steve McGarvey	2002	739
162 5/8	27 5/8	26 6/8	19 5/8	4 6/8	4 6/8	4	4	Jackson Parish, LA	Joey L. Neatherland	Joey L. Neatherland	2002	739
162 4/8	26 1/8	25 3/8	19 3/8	5	4 7/8	5	8	Oakland Co., MI	Keith W. Headley	Keith W. Headley	2000	747
162 4/8	24	25	16 4/8	4 2/8	4 2/8	5	5	La Porte Co., IN	Gary Leslie	Gary Leslie	2001	747
162 4/8	26 5/8	26 6/8	22 5/8	5 6/8	6 1/8	5	8	Ohio Co., KY	Bruce M. Mitchell	Bruce M. Mitchell	2002	747
162 4/8	25	23 5/8	18 6/8	4 3/8	4 3/8	5	5	Montgomery Co., IA	David C. Morgan	David C. Morgan	2002	747
162 4/8	23 4/8	23 4/8	16 9/8	4 6/8	4 5/8	6	6	Wallace Co., KS	Kyle L. Sexson	Kyle L. Sexson	2002	747
162 3/8	25 3/8	26	22 3/8	5 6/8	5 6/8	6	5	Johnson Co., IN	Ricky Hall, Sr.	Ricky Hall, Sr.	2002	752
162 3/8	26 6/8	26 4/8	22 3/8	4 1/8	4 4/8	6	7	Chautauqua Co., NY	Joseph E. Kaluza	Joseph E. Kaluza	2002	752
162 2/8	25 3/8	25 4/8	16	4 2/8	4 5/8	5	7	Worth Co., GA	J.L. Pritchard	Marcus E. Evans	1963	754
162 2/8	25 4/8	27 5/8	16 6/8	4 2/8	4 2/8	7	9	Ogema Bay, ON	Daniel C. Johnson	Daniel C. Johnson	2000	754
162 2/8	26 5/8	25 5/8	20 6/8	4 4/8	4 2/8	5	5	Nodaway Co., MO	Jeremy L. Richardson	Jeremy L. Richardson	2000	754
162 2/8	27	27	19 2/8	5	4 6/8	5	5	Yates Co., NY	Robert A. Bradley	Robert A. Bradley	2000	754
162 2/8	27 2/8	26 1/8	19 4/8	5 2/8	5 1/8	5	5	Highland Co., OH	Travis Ison	Travis Ison	2000	754
162 2/8	24 4/8	25 3/8	16 6/8	4 7/8	4 7/8	5	5	Ashland Co., WI	Mark K. Hultman	Mark K. Hultman	2001	754
162 2/8	24 1/8	28 1/8	19 4/8	4 4/8	4 4/8	6	6	Waupaca Co., WI	Duane E. Koeller	Duane E. Koeller	2001	754
162 2/8	27 6/8	24 5/8	20 6/8	4 2/8	4 4/8	6	6	Caldwell Co., KY	Wayne Boatright	Wayne Boatright	2002	754
162 2/8	24 7/8	25 7/8	17 1/8	4 6/8	4 6/8	6	6	Tuscola Co., MI	Paul S. King	Paul S. King	2002	754
162 2/8	27 2/8	25 6/8	19 4/8	5 2/8	4 6/8	7	6	Buffalo Pound Lake, SK	Mario T. Sinotte	Mario T. Sinotte	2003	754
162 1/8	24 6/8	24 3/8	20 1/8	5 4/8	5 4/8	5	7	Du Page Co., IL	Richard S. Pawelczyk	Richard S. Pawelczyk	2002	764
162 1/8	25 7/8	25 2/8	20 3/8	4 6/8	4 4/8	5	6	Boyd Co., NE	Jim D. Alford	Jim D. Alford	2002	764
162	25 4/8	22 7/8	18 2/8	4 5/8	4 5/8	4	4	Fairfield Co., CT	Stephen M. Ruttkamp	Stephen M. Ruttkamp	1989	766
162	23 5/8	27 7/8	19 4/8	4 4/8	4 3/8	5	5	Lincoln Co., MT	Jerry D. Ambrose	Jerry D. Ambrose	2001	766
161 7/8	27 5/8	27 7/8	16 5/8	4 1/8	4 2/8	6	6	Belmont Co., OH	Sampson Michael III	Sampson Michael III	2000	768
161 7/8	23 7/8	23 2/8	16 2/8	5 6/8	5 7/8	7	6	Hudson Bay, SK	Scott Griswold	Scott Griswold	2001	768

Score							Locality	Hunter	Owner	Date	Rank
161 7/8	25 5/8	29 1/8	21 3/8	4 4/8	4 4/8	6	6	Jackson Co., WI	Lawrence S. Graf	Lawrence S. Graf	2002	768
161 6/8	26 3/8	25	19 5/8	5	4 6/8	5	5	Orleans Co., NY	Duane H. Phillips	Duane H. Phillips	2001	771
161 6/8	24 4/8	24 6/8	21	5 3/8	5 5/8	7	5	Gibson Co., IN	Mark A. Hasenour	Mark A. Hasenour	2002	771
161 5/8	23 4/8	24 1/8	21 1/8	4 3/8	4 3/8	6	6	Garrard Co., KY	Timothy L. Poynter	Timothy L. Poynter	2000	773
161 5/8	26	23 2/8	21 1/8	4 5/8	5	5	5	Sioux Co., IA	Myron Van Ginkel	Myron Van Ginkel	2000	773
161 5/8	25 1/8	24 2/8	18 1/8	5 3/8	5 2/8	7	5	Oconto Co., WI	Michael E. O'Connell	Michael E. O'Connell	2000	773
161 5/8	23 4/8	24 4/8	23 1/8	5	5	6	6	Adair Co., MO	Timothy J. Schepers	Timothy J. Schepers	2001	773
161 5/8	25 3/8	24 4/8	20 4/8	5 1/8	5	5	5	Chase Co., KS	Michael J. Cudlipp	Michael J. Cudlipp	2001	773
161 5/8	23 5/8	24 1/8	19 2/8	4 3/8	4 4/8	7	5	Butler Co., OH	Gregory W. Davis	Gregory W. Davis	2001	773
161 5/8	23 5/8	23 1/8	20 1/8	4 3/8	4 4/8	5	5	Jackson Co., OH	David C. Haynes	David C. Haynes	2002	773
161 5/8	24 1/8	23 5/8	22 1/8	4 7/8	5 1/8	5	5	Noble Co., IN	Richard A. Green	Richard A. Green	2002	773
161 5/8	26 6/8	26 4/8	22 3/8	5 4/8	5 1/8	4	4	Coffey Co., KS	Doug Witteman	Doug Witteman	2002	773
161 4/8	24 7/8	25 5/8	18	4 6/8	4 5/8	5	5	Merrimack Co., NH	Harry Heath	Harry Heath	1949	782
161 4/8	27 4/8	28 3/8	20 1/8	4 3/8	4 3/8	5	5	Green Co., WI	Robert Taylor	Ann M. Brown	1974	782
161 4/8	27 7/8	27 1/8	23 4/8	4 6/8	4 5/8	6	6	Aroostook Co., ME	Picked Up	William Patton, Sr.	2000	782
161 4/8	25	24 4/8	17 2/8	4 3/8	4 6/8	5	5	Athens Co., OH	Michael V. Schaffer	Michael V. Schaffer	2000	782
161 4/8	27	27	20 4/8	5 2/8	5 2/8	4	4	Sampson Co., NC	C. Brady Freeman	C. Brady Freeman	2000	782
161 4/8	27	26	19 4/8	5 1/8	5 3/8	5	5	Warren Co., NY	Paul J. Tubbs	Paul J. Tubbs	2001	782
161 4/8	25 4/8	24 5/8	20 1/8	5 4/8	5 4/8	5	9	Franklin Co., OH	Christopher E. Brungarth	Christopher E. Brungarth	2001	782
161 4/8	25 1/8	25 1/8	16 7/8	4 6/8	4 5/8	6	6	Dallas Co., IA	David H. Andrews	David H. Andrews	2001	782
161 4/8	23	23 3/8	16 6/8	4 2/8	4 3/8	5	5	Rockcastle Co., KY	Joseph D. Durham	Joseph D. Durham	2002	782
161 4/8	23 7/8	24 3/8	17 6/8	5	5	7	6	Shawano Co., WI	Brian R. Hagel	Brian R. Hagel	2002	782
161 3/8	27 5/8	26 6/8	20 5/8	5 5/8	5 5/8	6	5	Norman Co., MN	Kevin C. Bitker	Kevin C. Bitker	1978	792
161 3/8	27 6/8	27 4/8	17 6/8	5 4/8	5 2/8	6	6	Definace, OH	Gerald A. Snyder, Jr.	Gerald A. Snyder, Jr.	1998	792
161 3/8	24 5/8	24 7/8	20 7/8	5 3/8	5 1/8	6	5	Otoe Co., NE	Keith G. Merkel	Keith G. Merkel	2000	792
161 3/8	23 1/8	23 1/8	18 5/8	4 6/8	5	5	5	Wright Co., MN	Victor L. Peterson	Victor L. Peterson	2002	792
161 2/8	25 1/8	24 4/8	19 6/8	4 2/8	4 2/8	5	5	Charles Co., MD	Jeremy L. Pugh	Jeremy L. Pugh	2000	796
161 2/8	24 1/8	23 3/8	17 6/8	5 2/8	5 1/8	6	6	Cherry Co., NE	Chris A. Benson	Chris A. Benson	2001	796
161 1/8	25 3/8	25 4/8	18 7/8	4 7/8	4 4/8	5	5	Douglas Co., WI	John Wohlwend	John Wohlwend	1998	798
161 1/8	24 1/8	24 1/8	18 7/8	4 2/8	4 2/8	5	5	Barren Co., KY	James G. Haynes	James G. Haynes	2000	798
161 1/8	24 2/8	25 1/8	17 3/8	5	5	5	6	Floyd Co., IN	Earl D. Whitworth III	Earl D. Whitworth III	2001	798
161 1/8	26 1/8	25 5/8	18 5/8	4 7/8	4 7/8	5	5	Natchidoches Parish, LA	Coy Birdwell	Coy Birdwell	2001	798
161 1/8	24 2/8	25	18 2/8	4 7/8	4 5/8	5	7	Northampton Co., PA	Asher G. Abel	Asher G. Abel	2002	798
161 1/8	25 1/8	25 3/8	17 1/8	5 2/8	5	5	6	Steuben Co., NY	Gary D. Wilson	Gary D. Wilson	2002	798
161 1/8	26 4/8	26 3/8	18 7/8	4 4/8	4 3/8	5	5	Cattaraugus Co., NY	Gregg P. Kaczmarczyk	Gregg P. Kaczmarczyk	2002	798
161 1/8	25	25 3/8	19	5 2/8	5 2/8	6	5	Granite Co., MT	Thomas L. Jacobson	Thomas L. Jacobson	2002	798
161 1/8	26 5/8	26 6/8	18 7/8	4 4/8	4 4/8	5	6	Val Verde Co., TX	Robert D. Jones III	Robert D. Jones III	2002	798
161	25 5/8	25 3/8	21	4 2/8	4 2/8	5	5	Pushmataha Co., OK	Hez F. Ray	Claude E. Hicks, Jr.	1895	807
161	25 7/8	25 6/8	17 4/8	5	5	5	5	St. Louis Co., MN	Steven T. Nelson	Steven T. Nelson	1998	807
161	23 5/8	23 4/8	17	4 4/8	4 3/8	6	5	Washington Co., IL	John V. Rickhoff	John V. Rickhoff	1999	807
161	24 3/8	25 1/8	20	4 6/8	4 6/8	5	5	Fayette Co., IL	Scott L. Hunt	Scott L. Hunt	2000	807

WHITETAIL DEER - TYPICAL ANTLERS

Odocoileus virginianus virginianus and certain related subspecies

Score	Length of Main Beam R.	L.	Inside Spread	Circumference at Smallest Place Between Burr & First Point R.	L.	Number of Points R.	L.	Locality	Hunter	Owner	Date Killed	Rank
161	26 2/8	27 3/8	20 7/8	4 4/8	4 6/8	6	6	Mitchell Co., GA	Jerome J. Tallent	Jerome J. Tallent	2000	807
161	25 4/8	26 1/8	15 4/8	4 7/8	4 7/8	6	6	Dunn Co., WI	Joseph G. Treiber	Joseph G. Treiber	2000	807
161	25 6/8	25 2/8	17 6/8	4 3/8	4 3/8	6	6	Preston Co., WV	Ronald B. Kopanko	Ronald B. Kopanko	2000	807
161	25 4/8	23 3/8	17 2/8	4 6/8	4 6/8	5	5	Missaukee Co., MI	Jeffrey S. Orr	Jeffrey S. Orr	2001	807
161	24 4/8	25 4/8	17 2/8	4 7/8	4 6/8	6	6	Caroline Co., MD	Laura L. Kreis	Laura L. Kreis	2001	807
161	27 1/8	27 6/8	23 2/8	4 6/8	4 7/8	5	5	Henderson Co., KY	Picked Up	John M. Beckham	2002	807
161	24 3/8	22 7/8	17 7/8	5 2/8	5 2/8	7	6	Pope Co., IL	Jerry F. Thomas	Jerry F. Thomas	2002	807
161	23 7/8	24	18	4 6/8	5	5	5	Gentry Co., MO	Jay C. Cook	Jay C. Cook	2002	807
160 7/8	24 7/8	24 5/8	15 6/8	4 7/8	5	5	5	Bonner Co., ID	Richard C. Speaks	Richard C. Speaks	2002	807
160 7/8	23 6/8	23 7/8	20 4/8	4 4/8	4 5/8	5	8	Fremont Co., WY	Ben L. Wilkes	Ben L. Wilkes	1999	820
160 7/8	27 2/8	27	19 6/8	4 6/8	4 6/8	5	5	Oxford Co., ME	Stephen A. Marston	Stephen A. Marston	2000	820
160 7/8	25	24 2/8	20 2/8	4 6/8	4 5/8	5	6	Amisk Creek, AB	Brian S. Setree	Brian S. Setree	2000	820
160 7/8	23 7/8	25 2/8	21 7/8	4 3/8	4 5/8	5	5	Graves Co., KY	Stephen C. Lyell	Stephen C. Lyell	2000	820
160 7/8	26 2/8	25 5/8	17 5/8	5	5 2/8	5	5	Marathon Co., WI	Frank Hojnacki	Frank Hojnacki	2000	820
160 7/8	25	25 1/8	17 7/8	4 2/8	4 3/8	5	5	Colquitt Co., GA	W. Neal Hager	W. Neal Hager	2000	820
160 7/8	25 6/8	25 5/8	17 3/8	5 4/8	5 4/8	5	7	Hall Co., GA	Bonnie L. Harrison	Bonnie L. Harrison	2001	820
160 7/8	24 2/8	23 7/8	18 2/8	5	5 1/8	5	7	Adair Co., MO	Bruce May	Bruce May	2001	820
160 6/8	25 3/8	24 4/8	16 4/8	4 4/8	4 3/8	7	7	Grundy Co., IA	Jeff D. Billerbeck	Jeff D. Billerbeck	1996	828
160 6/8	25 5/8	25 5/8	21 1/8	4 6/8	4 5/8	7	6	Avoyelles Parish, LA	Tammy J. Lemoine	Tammy J. Lemoine	2000	828
160 6/8	23 5/8	23 6/8	16 7/8	5 4/8	5 4/8	5	6	Adams Co., WI	Todd W. Hajos	Todd W. Hajos	2000	828
160 6/8	24 5/8	25 7/8	22 7/8	4 2/8	4 3/8	6	5	Madison Co., IA	Gale R. Plynesser	Gale R. Plynesser	2000	828
160 6/8	23 7/8	23 7/8	17 7/8	4 6/8	4 5/8	5	6	Jefferson Co., NE	Larry Stafford	Larry Stafford	2001	828
160 6/8	25 4/8	25 2/8	19 6/8	5	4 6/8	4	5	Sussex Co., DE	Harry H. Isaacs III	Harry H. Isaacs III	2001	828
160 6/8	26 5/8	26 6/8	21 6/8	5	5	6	8	Forsyth Co., NC	Ronald W. James	Ronald W. James	2001	828
160 6/8	26 7/8	27 4/8	21 2/8	5	5 2/8	6	6	Sumner Co., KS	David W. Troutman	David W. Troutman	2001	828
160 6/8	25 2/8	26 1/8	20	4 6/8	4 4/8	5	5	Miami Co., OH	Craig A. Peters	Craig A. Peters	2002	828
160 5/8	27 1/8	28 3/8	21 6/8	4 6/8	5	6	7	Hubbard Co., MN	Jerry Potratz	James C. Treat	1974	837
160 5/8	22 4/8	23	21 3/8	6	6 4/8	4	5	Logan River, AB	Walter L. Goas III	Walter L. Goas III	2000	837
160 5/8	26 1/8	26	23 3/8	4 6/8	4 4/8	5	5	Iowa Co., IA	Rodney L. Exline	Rodney L. Exline	2000	837
160 5/8	26 7/8	27	16 2/8	5	4 7/8	7	6	Warren Co., IN	Tim Wadkins	Tim Wadkins	2001	837
160 5/8	26	25	20	4 6/8	4 6/8	5	6	Caldwell Co., KY	Jimmy D. Fuller	Jimmy D. Fuller	2002	837
160 5/8	25 1/8	25 2/8	20	5 1/8	4 7/8	5	6	Menard Co., IL	George E. Hypke	George E. Hypke	2002	837
160 5/8	25	24 3/8	18	5 7/8	5 6/8	7	7	Meadow Lake, SK	Frank Campano	Frank Campano	2002	837

844
844
844
847
847
847
847
852
852
852
852
852
852
852
852
852
852
852
862
862
862
862
862
862
862
862
862
862
862
873
873
873

Score								Locality	Owner	Hunter	Year	Rank
160 4/8	25 5/8	26 5/8	16 7/8	5 5/8	5 5/8	9	8	Nelson Co., VA	William W. Cross	William W. Cross	2001	844
160 4/8	24 2/8	24 2/8	18 3/8	4 6/8	5	7	6	Vernon Co., WI	Misty L. Coates	Misty L. Coates	2002	844
160 4/8	28	28 1/8	23 2/8	4 7/8	4 5/8	4	4	Hartford Co., CT	William J. White	William J. White	2002	844
160 3/8	25 2/8	24 7/8	20 4/8	5 5/8	5 3/8	6	5	Wilkinson Co., MS	Danny W. Frazier	Danny W. Frazier	2000	847
160 3/8	25	25 5/8	21 7/8	5 1/8	5	5	5	Geauga Co., OH	Andrew F. Ule	Andrew F. Ule	2001	847
160 3/8	25 4/8	25	21 4/8	4 7/8	4 7/8	8	7	LaCrosse, WI	Greg D. Kastenschmidt	Greg D. Kastenschmidt	2001	847
160 3/8	28 1/8	27 4/8	23 5/8	4 4/8	4 3/8	5	6	Clinton Co., IL	Kyle Varel	Kyle Varel	2002	847
160 3/8	25 3/8	25 3/8	20 3/8	4 6/8	4 7/8	5	5	Grant Co., WI	Ronald H. Martin	Ronald H. Martin	2002	847
160 2/8	24 1/8	24 2/8	16 3/8	5 3/8	5 3/8	7	9	Orangeburg Co., SC	Jason M. Doremus	Jason M. Doremus	2000	852
160 2/8	24 2/8	23 4/8	15 6/8	4 3/8	4 3/8	5	5	Loudoun Co., VA	Richard C. Vance	Richard C. Vance	2000	852
160 2/8	25 4/8	25 2/8	16	4 3/8	5	5	5	Logan Co., ND	Denise R. Groce	Denise R. Groce	2000	852
160 2/8	26 5/8	27 3/8	24 4/8	4 6/8	4 6/8	5	5	Pepin Co., WI	Michael J. Anderson	Michael J. Anderson	2000	852
160 2/8	24 2/8	24 6/8	22 2/8	5	5 4/8	5	5	Ogle Co., IL	Philip H. Nye, Jr.	Philip H. Nye, Jr.	2000	852
160 2/8	23 4/8	23 4/8	22	5 1/8	5 2/8	5	6	Washington Co., PA	Robert L. Dhans	Robert L. Dhans	2000	852
160 2/8	25 6/8	25 2/8	19 4/8	4 5/8	4 5/8	5	5	Franklin Co., IN	James C. Wilson	James C. Wilson	2000	852
160 2/8	24 5/8	22 7/8	19	4 5/8	4 5/8	6	6	Whitley Co., KY	Chris Tompkins	Chris Tompkins	2001	852
160 2/8	27 4/8	25 7/8	20 4/8	5 2/8	5 2/8	6	6	Ashtabula Co., OH	John J. Spinda III	John J. Spinda III	2002	852
160 2/8	25 4/8	25 4/8	20 1/8	5 2/8	5 6/8	6	7	Jackson Co., IA	Dennis L. Petersen	Dennis L. Petersen	2002	852
160 1/8	22 1/8	22 5/8	17 2/8	5 1/8	5 3/8	5	7	Chisago Co., MN	Steven F. Zupon	Steven F. Zupon	2000	862
160 1/8	23 1/8	23 2/8	16 3/8	4 2/8	4 2/8	5	5	Hinds Co., MS	Roger A. Hudson	Roger A. Hudson	2000	862
160 1/8	25 6/8	25 5/8	17 2/8	4 4/8	4 4/8	6	5	Keya Paha Co., NE	Robert W. Schmidt	Robert W. Schmidt	2000	862
160 1/8	25 5/8	24 4/8	20 7/8	5 3/8	5 2/8	5	6	Jo Daviess Co., IL	Scott L. Havens	Scott L. Havens	2000	862
160 1/8	27 3/8	27 3/8	18 7/8	5 7/8	5 6/8	7	6	Metcalfe Co., KY	Mark Shirley	Mark Shirley	2000	862
160 1/8	25 5/8	26 2/8	16 5/8	4 4/8	4 4/8	7	6	Franklin Co., VA	James D. Baker	James D. Baker	2000	862
160 1/8	24 6/8	24 1/8	17 7/8	5	5 1/8	5	5	Claiborne Parish, LA	Kenneth B. Harrison	Kenneth B. Harrison	2000	862
160 1/8	24 7/8	25 6/8	18 5/8	4 5/8	4 6/8	5	5	Clark Co., MO	Thomas F. Casey	Thomas F. Casey	2001	862
160 1/8	26 6/8	26 6/8	17 7/8	4 7/8	5	4	4	Sawyer Co., WI	Christopher M. Schloesser	Christopher M. Schloesser	2001	862
160 1/8	25 4/8	24 6/8	16 5/8	4 4/8	4 6/8	5	5	Noble Co., OH	David Hodges II	David Hodges II	2002	862
160 1/8	25	24 6/8	21 7/8	4 6/8	4 6/8	5	7	Allamakee Co., IA	Adrian V. McGeough	Adrian V. McGeough	2002	862
160	23 1/8	23 1/8	17 4/8	4 7/8	5	5	7	Clark Co., WI	Mark R. Lamers	Mark R. Lamers	2000	873
160	24 3/8	25 2/8	18 4/8	5 1/8	5	6	5	Loudoun Co., VA	Stephen Marshall	Stephen Marshall	2001	873
160	28	27 4/8	20 6/8	5 5/8	5 4/8	7	6	Cumberland Co., KY	Chris Bunch	Chris Bunch	2002	873
204 2/8*	30 2/8	29 6/8	20 4/8	4 5/8	4 5/8	6	5	Pendleton Co., KY	Robert W. Smith	Robert W. Smith	2000	873

* Final score subject to revision by additional verifying measurements.

WHITETAIL DEER - NON-TYPICAL ANTLERS

Minimum Score 185   *Odocoileus virginianus virginianus* and certain related subspecies   World's Record 333 7/8

Score	Length of Main Beam R.	L.	Inside Spread	Circumference at Smallest Place Between Burr & First Point R.	L.	Number of Points R.	L.	Locality	Hunter	Owner	Date Killed	Rank
307 5/8	26 3/8	23 5/8	22	8	6 4/8	21	17	Monroe Co., IA	Tony W. Lovstuen	Bass Pro Shops	2003	1
304 3/8	27 3/8	27 2/8	23 1/8	5 1/8	5 7/8	17	20	Fulton Co., IL	Jerry D. Bryant	Jerry D. Bryant	2001	2
260 1/8	24 1/8	24 1/8	23 4/8	5 5/8	5 5/8	18	17	Garrard Co., KY	Benjamin J. Brogle	Bass Pro Shops	2002	3
259 2/8	24 4/8	23 3/8	21 7/8	5 3/8	5 6/8	12	14	Souris River, MB	Howard G. Pauls	Bass Pro Shops	2000	4
254 2/8	29 1/8	27 7/8	21 3/8	6 1/8	6 2/8	16	15	Caroline, AB	Mike Chrustawka	Cabela's, Inc.	1991	5
250 4/8	29 6/8	29 7/8	20 5/8	5 5/8	5 7/8	13	9	Alexander Co., IL	Andrew French III	Andrew French III	2000	6
245 6/8	24 1/8	24 3/8	18 7/8	5 5/8	5 6/8	13	13	Souris River, MB	Richard D. Pauls	Richard D. Pauls	2000	7
244 3/8	22 1/8	23 1/8	17 4/8	5 4/8	4 7/8	25	24	Sumner Co., TN	David K. Wachtel III	David K. Wachtel III	2000	8
244 1/8	25 6/8	25	20	4 7/8	5 6/8	10	15	Kenton, MB	Frank Smart	Cabela's, Inc.	1949	9
242	24 6/8	27 2/8	22 5/8	6 6/8	6 1/8	14	12	McDonough Co., IL	Picked Up	Danny L. Powell	2002	10
241 7/8	28	27 2/8	21 2/8	6 3/8	6 4/8	10	9	Henry Co., IL	Andy S. Carlson	Andy S. Carlson	2002	11
241 6/8	25 7/8	26 1/8	19 3/8	5 6/8	5 3/8	11	10	Des Moines Co., IA	Picked Up	IA Dept. of Natl. Resc.	1999	12
241 3/8	23 5/8	23 2/8	20 7/8	6 5/8	6 7/8	13	8	Putnam Co., IL	Michael D. Ublish	Michael D. Ublish	2001	13
240 4/8	27 7/8	26 4/8	20 7/8	5	5 1/8	13	15	Allamakee Co., IA	David Gordon	David Gordon	2000	14
240 2/8	28 4/8	30 5/8	22 4/8	6 1/8	6 1/8	15	12	Warren Co., IA	Rick L. Dye	Rick L. Dye	2000	15
239 3/8	27 7/8	26 6/8	20 2/8	7 1/8	6 2/8	21	12	White Co., IL	Reed T. Rountree	Reed T. Rountree	2002	16
237 6/8	26 3/8	26 4/8	25	5 5/8	6	9	13	Des Moines Co., IA	Harlan Swehla	Harlan Swehla	2002	17
237 1/8	28 3/8	28 1/8	17 1/8	6 1/8	6	13	11	Wayne Co., KY	Jessie D. Fulton	Cabela's, Inc.	2000	18
234 4/8	27 1/8	26 3/8	24 2/8	5 7/8	5 7/8	14	11	Knox Co., IL	James R. Hensley, Jr.	James R. Hensley, Jr.	2000	19
234 4/8	24	23 4/8	17 4/8	5 6/8	4 6/8	9	9	Peterson, SK	Murray A. Pulvermacher	Murray A. Pulvermacher	2002	19
233 5/8	27 4/8	28 1/8	19 3/8	4 7/8	5	11	17	Chippewa Co., WI	Russell W. Jones	Russell W. Jones	2000	21
233 4/8	21 1/8	26	18 5/8	5 4/8	4	14	10	Saskatchewan	Unknown	Cabela's, Inc.	1962	22
232 7/8	21 2/8	20 3/8	15 6/8	4	4	18	19	Haywood Co., TN	Justin K. Samples	Justin K. Samples	2001	23
232 3/8	28	27 1/8	17	5 4/8	5 5/8	10	11	Glass Lake, SK	Karpo S. Stokalko	Karpo S. Stokalko	2001	24
232	17 4/8	16 6/8	18 3/8	4 4/8	4 4/8	26	22	Monroe Co., AR	Picked Up	Kirk Brann	2000	25
231 5/8	27 3/8	26 6/8	18 4/8	6 1/8	6 2/8	10	11	Porter Co., IN	Robert J. Johannsen	Robert J. Johannsen	2002	26
231 2/8	30	30 4/8	22 5/8	5	5	9	11	Nebraska	Unknown	Cabela's, Inc.	PR1993	27
230 6/8	22 3/8	23 3/8	19 7/8	5 7/8	5 4/8	13	10	Peoria Co., IL	Picked Up	David T. Lockhart	2000	28
230 5/8	24 7/8	24 6/8	17 4/8	5 2/8	5	14	11	Okfuskee Co., OK	Joe A. Green	Johnny J. Green	1971	29
230 2/8	24 4/8	25 1/8	15 5/8	5 7/8	5 6/8	17	20	Lawrence Co., PA	Michael D. Ambrosia	Michael D. Ambrosia	2001	30
229 5/8	31 7/8	26	23 7/8	5	5	12	13	Scioto Co., OH	Ron Vastine	Ron Vastine	2002	31
228 6/8	27 7/8	28 5/8	22 2/8	5 6/8	6 2/8	9	10	Unknown	Unknown	Steven Miller	PR1972	32
228 6/8	27 1/8	29 1/8	21 7/8	6	5 6/8	11	7	Frenchman Butte, SK	Dan Fedirko	Cabela's, Inc.	1998	32

Score								Locality	Hunter	Owner	Date	Rank
228 6/8	28 3/8	26 4/8	17 1/8	5 1/8	5	9	14	Perry Co., IN	Richard L. Hubert	Richard L. Hubert	2002	32
228 3/8	24 5/8	26 5/8	15 4/8	6 5/8	5 6/8	13	10	Randolph Co., IL	Aaron L. Eggemeyer	Aaron L. Eggemeyer	2001	35
228 2/8	28 3/8	28 2/8	19 1/8	6 4/8	6 3/8	7	8	Dubuque Co., IA	Arthur D. Wille	Arthur D. Wille	2000	36
228 2/8	24 5/8	26 1/8	20 4/8	6 4/8	6 4/8	15	12	Weld Co., CO	Ronald E. Kammerzell	Ronald E. Kammerzell	2001	36
228	27 3/8	26 4/8	21 3/8	6 1/8	5 7/8	11	14	Manitoba	Unknown	Gale Sup	PR1998	38
227 6/8	24 5/8	25 3/8	18 6/8	4 6/8	4 5/8	13	13	Sumner Co., KS	Matthew L. Dalton	Matthew L. Dalton	2001	39
227 5/8	23 6/8	24 4/8	15 2/8	5 3/8	5 2/8	10	10	Pike Co., IL	Gavin Risley	Gavin Risley	2002	40
227 4/8	22 6/8	23 6/8	24	4 7/8	4 7/8	17	12	Fannin Co., TX	Joe P. Moore, Jr.	Joe P. Moore, Jr.	2001	41
227 3/8	27 2/8	26 5/8	17 1/8	5 4/8	5 5/8	7	10	Madison Co., IA	Jerry L. Wells	Jerry L. Wells	2001	42
226 6/8	24 4/8	22 3/8	19 7/8	5 2/8	5 4/8	13	12	Polk Co., IA	Picked Up	IA Dept. of Natl. Resc.	1998	43
226 6/8	27 3/8	27 2/8	21 2/8	6 2/8	6 1/8	10	9	Piatt Co., IL	Mark Wimpy	Mark Wimpy	2000	43
226 1/8	25 1/8	22 3/8	14 6/8	4 6/8	6	8	15	Iowa Co., WI	Robert Odey	Robert Odey	2002	45
226	28 1/8	27	20 4/8	4 7/8	5 2/8	17	17	Morgan Co., MO	Art Sousley	Cabela's, Inc.	1962	46
225 7/8	22 5/8	19 4/8	17 4/8	5 2/8	4 7/8	13	13	Grayson Co., TX	Jeffery L. Duncan	Jeffery L. Duncan	2001	47
225 7/8	24 5/8	24 3/8	18	5 2/8	5 2/8	10	8	Linn Co., KS	Douglas L. Below	Douglas L. Below	2001	47
225 3/8	26	26 2/8	19 2/8	5 4/8	5 5/8	12	13	Chitek Lake, SK	Wade L. Higgins	Wade L. Higgins	2003	49
224 5/8	26 6/8	27 1/8	14 2/8	5 1/8	5 3/8	17	15	Hart Co., KY	Picked Up	S. Colvin & J. Coe	2003	50
224 4/8	27 7/8	27 7/8	26 3/8	5 4/8	6	8	12	Marshall Co., IL	Frank A. McKean	Frank A. McKean	2000	51
224 3/8	30 5/8	30 1/8	21 2/8	4 7/8	4 5/8	11	8	Chisago Co., MN	Nathan Stimson	Nathan Stimson	2001	52
224 1/8	19 7/8	21 7/8	18 3/8	6 4/8	6	13	10	Rose Prairie, BC	Rob White	Rob White	2000	53
224	27 6/8	27 4/8	23 5/8	6 4/8	6 3/8	10	8	Will Co., IL	Picked Up	Rita O. Luedtke	2002	54
223 2/8	29 6/8	32 4/8	22 1/8	6 5/8	5 7/8	7	13	Fulton Co., IL	Lyle Mason	Lyle Mason	2000	55
223 1/8	28 6/8	23 6/8	18	5 6/8	5 7/8	13	13	Wilson Co., KS	John Bowser	Cabela's, Inc.	2002	56
223	24 5/8	22 6/8	14 3/8	6 6/8	6 5/8	14	17	Callaway Co., MO	Herman D. Stiefferman, Jr.	Herman D. Stiefferman, Jr.	2000	57
222 4/8	25 3/8	29 3/8	20 6/8	4 7/8	4 7/8	12	9	Richland Co., IL	Lloyd E. Lemke	Lloyd E. Lemke	2000	58
222 4/8	26	26 1/8	18 5/8	6 3/8	5 5/8	11	11	Clinton Co., OH	Jonathan K. Hale	Jonathan K. Hale	2001	58
222 3/8	28 1/8	29 3/8	19 7/8	5 4/8	5 7/8	9	12	Van Buren Co., IA	Le Roy G. Everhart	Grundy Co. Cons. Center	1969	60
222 3/8	26 2/8	25 3/8	23 5/8	5 4/8	5 4/8	11	12	Hancock Co., IL	James E. Bowdish	James E. Bowdish	2000	60
222 3/8	29 1/8	27 7/8	16 4/8	6 4/8	7	13	9	Wilson Co., KS	Kent Marr	Kent Marr	2003	60
222 1/8	22 2/8	24 2/8	14 3/8	4 2/8	4 4/8	11	13	Ellis Co., TX	David Krajca	David Krajca	2001	63
221 4/8	26 2/8	24 2/8	22	5	5 2/8	11	16	Comanche Co., OK	Ted M. Evans	Ted M. Evans	2001	64
221 2/8	25 6/8	26 7/8	20 1/8	5	5	10	9	Jersey Co., IL	Ross A. Eggebrecht	Ross A. Eggebrecht	2002	65
220 6/8	27 4/8	22 6/8	18	5 4/8	6 4/8	9	15	Crawford Co., IA	Picked Up	Raymond H. Schulte	2000	66
220 5/8	25 3/8	24 7/8	23 1/8	5 7/8	5 7/8	8	12	Berrien Co., MI	Robert C. Sexton	Robert C. Sexton	2002	67
220 1/8	27	26 7/8	22 1/8	6 6/8	6	13	10	Ashland Co., OH	Jeffrey J. Spreng	Jeffrey J. Spreng	2002	68
220	26 3/8	26 2/8	18 7/8	4 4/8	4 5/8	16	13	Scott Co., AR	Daniel Boyd	Daniel Boyd	2001	69
220	29 1/8	29 4/8	20 4/8	5	5	8	7	Fayette Co., WV	Jess E. Kelly	Jess E. Kelly	2002	69
219 6/8	24 6/8	26	21 2/8	5 3/8	5 5/8	12	11	Cass Co., MI	Bruce C. Heslet II	Bruce C. Heslet II	2000	71
219 5/8	28 4/8	24 2/8	20	5 2/8	4 7/8	9	11	Meeting Lake, SK	Earl Braun	Earl Braun	2002	72
219 3/8	26 2/8	26 5/8	18 4/8	5 3/8	5 2/8	10	10	Schuyler Co., IL	James R. Lehman	James R. Lehman	2000	73
219 1/8	24 6/8	24 6/8	17 4/8	4 5/8	4 6/8	10	9	S. Saskatchewan River, SK	Picked Up	Thad W. Karwandy	2000	74

Score	Length of Main Beam R.	L.	Inside Spread	Circumference at Smallest Place Between Burr & First Point R.	L.	Number of Points R.	L.	Locality	Hunter	Owner	Date Killed	Rank
219 1/8	26 6/8	26 3/8	19 1/8	5 3/8	5 3/8	13	12	Porter Co., IN	John S. Biggs, Jr.	John S. Biggs, Jr.	2000	74
218 1/8	27 2/8	27 1/8	15	5 7/8	5 7/8	13	8	Iron Co., MI	Carl Mattson	Mary J. Wellman	1945	76
217 7/8	25 6/8	25 1/8	16 4/8	5 7/8	5 5/8	13	7	Jefferson Co., IL	Steve Gum	Steve Gum	2002	77
217 5/8	25 4/8	26 1/8	19 3/8	5 5/8	5 3/8	16	14	Butler Co., KS	Trent A. Busenitz	Trent A. Busenitz	2002	78
217 3/8	28 1/8	25 2/8	21 2/8	5 7/8	6 4/8	11	8	Douglas Co., WI	Unknown	Ross A. Manthey	1939	79
217 2/8	19	24 4/8	16 5/8	7 4/8	6 2/8	16	10	Benewah Co., ID	Daniel Dodd	Cabela's, Inc.	1996	80
216 7/8	25 4/8	27 1/8	22 3/8	5 5/8	5 4/8	12	7	Wayne Co., IL	Kenneth L. Tucker	Kenneth L. Tucker	2000	81
216 2/8	26 6/8	26 3/8	20	4 6/8	5 5/8	8	11	Lyon Co., KS	Rodney D. Watson	Rodney D. Watson	2000	82
216 1/8	26	26 6/8	22 2/8	6 3/8	6 3/8	9	10	Grundy Co., IL	Steven E. Claypool	Steven E. Claypool	2001	83
216	24 6/8	22 1/8	16 2/8	4	4 4/8	13	12	Kiowa Co., KS	Ray L. Magby	Ray L. Magby	2001	84
215 7/8	27 7/8	26	24 1/8	6 1/8	6 2/8	10	10	Taney Co., MO	Roy S. Smith	Ronald L. Smith	1986	85
215 7/8	28	25 1/8	21 2/8	5 5/8	5 6/8	9	11	Trego Co., KS	Stephen G. Chaffee	Stephen G. Chaffee	2000	85
215 6/8	25 1/8	25 3/8	21	4 4/8	5 4/8	12	10	Idaho	Leroy Shaffer	D.J. Hollinger & B. Howard	1968	87
215 4/8	25	24 6/8	20 3/8	4 7/8	5 1/8	10	11	Drayton Valley, AB	Mitch B. Reimer	Mitch B. Reimer	2002	88
215 2/8	23 2/8	23 1/8	17 7/8	7 1/8	7 2/8	12	12	Henderson Co., KY	Gary E. Boucherie	Gary E. Boucherie	1991	89
215 2/8	25 6/8	25 1/8	16 6/8	5 6/8	5 5/8	11	14	La Crosse Co., WI	Mark R. Thorn	Mark R. Thorn	2000	89
215 1/8	24 4/8	26 2/8	19 3/8	6 7/8	7 2/8	13	11	Racine Co., WI	Mike T. Thelen	Mike T. Thelen	2001	91
215	28 1/8	27 5/8	19 5/8	6 7/8	7 2/8	8	10	Todd Co., MN	Picked Up	Tom Kendall	2000	92
214 7/8	27 6/8	27	20 1/8	6 7/8	7	7	11	Concordia Parish, LA	W.E. Beazley	Mike Harper	1938	93
214 6/8	27 1/8	25 4/8	16 4/8	5	4 7/8	11	11	Audrain Co., MO	John D. Burgher	Cabela's, Inc.	2002	94
214 4/8	26 7/8	26 6/8	26 6/8	5 6/8	5 6/8	11	15	Payne Co., OK	Chad Hane	Chad Hane	2003	95
214 3/8	27 4/8	25 3/8	23	5 4/8	6	10	9	McDonough Co., IL	Neil A. Twidwell	Neil A. Twidwell	2002	96
214 3/8	26 1/8	23 7/8	14 6/8	5 7/8	6 2/8	8	14	Wicomico Co., MD	Michael D. Lawhorn	Michael D. Lawhorn	2002	96
214 3/8	27 3/8	26 4/8	23 2/8	5 5/8	5	10	9	Macoupin Co., IL	Clifford Bressler	Clifford Bressler	2002	96
214 2/8	23 3/8	22 3/8	15 6/8	4 4/8	4 2/8	12	16	Pickett Co., TN	Ronnie D. Perry, Jr.	Ronnie D. Perry, Jr.	2001	99
214 2/8	27 2/8	27 2/8	20	4 5/8	4 5/8	6	10	Little Fishing Lake, SK	Larry R. Kobsar	Larry R. Kobsar	2003	99
214 1/8	25 5/8	27	15 4/8	4 4/8	4 4/8	10	9	Michigan	Unknown	MI Whitetail Hall of Fame Mus.	1934	101
214 1/8	28	28 3/8	21 4/8	6 1/8	6 2/8	7	9	Van Buren Co., IA	Douglas W. Farrell	Douglas W. Farrell	2001	101
214	24 3/8	20 5/8	19 7/8	6	7 3/8	9	12	Scott Co., IL	James K. Garrett	James K. Garrett	1994	103
213 7/8	29 1/8	29 2/8	19 3/8	5 3/8	5 5/8	8	9	Bonner Co., ID	Fred B. Post	Michael R. Damery	1978	104
213 7/8	24 5/8	25 2/8	18 5/8	5 7/8	5 6/8	10	8	S. Saskatchewan River, SK	Keith A. Graves	Keith A. Graves	2000	104
213 2/8	24	24 4/8	16 4/8	5 5/8	5 3/8	11	8	Washington Co., KS	Lance D. Black	Lance D. Black	2002	106

Score	Main Beam R	Main Beam L	Inside Spread	Burr R	Burr L	Points R	Points L	Locality	Hunter	Owner	Date	Rank
213 1/8	28 4/8	27 3/8	21 2/8	6 3/8	6	8	9	Buffalo Co., WI	Picked Up	Byron H. Hoch	2000	107
213 1/8	24 5/8	24 6/8	20 7/8	5 3/8	5 3/8	10	10	Leech Lake, AB	Greg J. Gilbertson	Greg J. Gilbertson	2001	107
212 7/8	25 2/8	25 6/8	17 4/8	5 3/8	5 5/8	10	10	Carroll Co., MO	John L. Crose	John L. Crose	2002	109
212 5/8	27 2/8	25	20 3/8	5	4 4/8	12	8	Licking Co., OH	J. Chris Lepley	J. Chris Lepley	2001	110
212 4/8	25 4/8	25 4/8	21	6 1/8	6 3/8	10	11	Randolph Co., IL	Mark E. Houba	Mark E. Houba	2000	111
212 3/8	22 7/8	25 2/8	22 2/8	6 2/8	6 1/8	17	14	Brown Co., IL	Martin L. Brobst	Martin L. Brobst	2000	112
212 1/8	28 5/8	27	18 5/8	5 6/8	6 2/8	11	1	Koochiching Co., MN	Tom Sutch	Tom Sutch	2000	113
212	25 7/8	26 4/8	22 6/8	6 2/8	6	11	11	Kankakee Co., IL	Thomas Miller	Thomas Miller	2002	114
211 6/8	26 4/8	27 1/8	23 5/8	6 4/8	6 2/8	10	9	Clark Co., KS	Cullen R. Spitzer	Cullen R. Spitzer	2001	115
211 4/8	22 4/8	24 6/8	18 6/8	5 5/8	5 4/8	10	11	Saskatchewan	Vernon Nokinsky	D.J. Hollinger & B. Howard	1976	116
211 3/8	27 6/8	29 2/8	20 5/8	5 7/8	6	10	9	Chase Co., KS	Picked Up	Tom Crump	1998	117
211 3/8	27 1/8	27 3/8	18 1/8	6 4/8	6 4/8	7	10	Fayette Co., IL	Greg A. Raterman	Greg A. Raterman	2000	117
211 3/8	26 2/8	27 6/8	19 2/8	4 6/8	5 1/8	9	8	Perry Co., IL	Richard W. Murphy	Richard W. Murphy	2002	117
211 2/8	26 2/8	25	18 4/8	5 7/8	5 4/8	7	9	Breathitt Co., KY	Michael D. Johnson	Michael D. Johnson	2000	120
210 7/8	27 4/8	27 5/8	20 6/8	5 4/8	5 7/8	10	12	Wayne Co., IA	Jack J. Pershy	Jack J. Pershy	2001	121
210 6/8	25 4/8	24 2/8	17 4/8	6	5 7/8	11	13	Unknown	Unknown	Charles J. Kramer	2001	122
210 5/8	23 7/8	23 7/8	19 3/8	5 4/8	5 2/8	13	14	Wapello Co., IA	Picked Up	IA Dept. of Natl. Resc.	1996	123
210 5/8	21 1/8	21 1/8	18 2/8	5 6/8	6	9	11	Dawson Creek, BC	Kenn F. Chysyk	Nick Trenke	1999	123
210 5/8	25 4/8	25 5/8	21 6/8	6 2/8	6 4/8	8	12	Fork River, MB	Jimmy D. Blaine	Jimmy D. Blaine	2000	123
210 5/8	25 2/8	22 5/8	20 4/8	5 3/8	5 1/8	10	10	Qu'Appelle Valley, SK	Bryce Burns	Bryce Burns	2000	123
210 4/8	25	25 2/8	20 4/8	5 5/8	5	11	9	Mason Co., IL	Jesse Stinauer	Jesse Stinauer	2002	127
210 3/8	27 7/8	26 7/8	19 2/8	6 4/8	6 4/8	9	8	Linn Co., KS	Randall W. Hinde	Randall W. Hinde	2001	128
210	23 1/8	23 5/8	17 3/8	5 4/8	5 4/8	12	10	Wright Co., MN	Picked Up	John R. Thole	1998	129
209 5/8	27 3/8	28	21 3/8	5 1/8	5	8	10	Van Buren Co., IA	Allen C. Funk	Allen C. Funk	2000	130
209 5/8	24 3/8	22 5/8	16 4/8	5 7/8	5 7/8	10	14	Jasper Co., IL	Chris Rush	Chris Rush	2002	130
209 4/8	26 3/8	25 4/8	17 7/8	5 1/8	5	10	12	Manitou Lake, SK	Dustin Elchyson	Dustin Elchyson	2001	132
209 3/8	24 5/8	24 3/8	19 6/8	6 4/8	6 5/8	8	6	Macon Co., MO	Bryan Dickbernd	Bryan Dickbernd	2002	133
209 2/8	26 3/8	27 1/8	18 7/8	5 7/8	5 5/8	7	12	Crawford Co., KS	Jason C. Ball	Jason C. Ball	2000	134
209 1/8	28	24 4/8	17 1/8	5 7/8	6	10	11	Butler Co., OH	Ronald N. Fields	Ronald N. Fields	2001	135
209	23 3/8	22 4/8	17 3/8	5 6/8	6 2/8	9	14	Highland Co., OH	Eddie Hunter, Sr.	Eddie Hunter, Sr.	2000	136
208 5/8	27	26 1/8	24 2/8	6 5/8	6 2/8	7	7	Red River, MB	Unknown	Jeffrey Gustafson	1977	137
208 4/8	25 4/8	25 6/8	19 1/8	5 6/8	5 5/8	13	10	Mille Lacs Co., MN	Picked Up	Louis J. Los	2002	138
208 3/8	26 2/8	28 6/8	19 3/8	4 4/8	4 4/8	10	6	Okanogan Co., WA	Kenneth Anderson	Thomas S. Anderson	1959	139
208 2/8	25 6/8	24	21 1/8	4 6/8	4 6/8	8	11	Guthrie Co., IA	Jay Miller	Jay Miller	2002	140
208 1/8	23 5/8	24 2/8	21	5 3/8	6 2/8	10	11	Monroe Co., AR	Picked Up	Donald Barkley	2000	141
208	27 5/8	27 5/8	21 3/8	5 5/8	5 4/8	9	11	Pinehurst Lake, AB	Steve Onciul	Steve Onciul	2001	142
207 7/8	25 2/8	23 3/8	17 6/8	6 1/8	6	12	11	Fort Sill, OK	R.B. Robertson	Jessie L. Salisbury	1968	143
207 4/8	27 7/8	27 7/8	17 3/8	5 4/8	5 4/8	12	8	Winona Co., MN	Picked Up	Ray T. Charles	2001	144
207 3/8	18 5/8	12 1/8	17 1/8	4 1/8	4	15	14	Madison Co., MS	Kenneth L. Reece	Kenneth L. Reece	2001	145
207 1/8	27 3/8	27 1/8	20 2/8	4 7/8	4 6/8	8	9	Waseca Co., MN	Scott Schaible	Scott Schaible	1998	146
207 1/8	27	26 3/8	19 1/8	5 1/8	4 7/8	10	9	Montgomery Co., IN	Michael R. Davis	Michael R. Davis	2000	146

WHITETAIL DEER - NON-TYPICAL ANTLERS

Odocoileus virginianus virginianus and certain related subspecies

Score	Length of Main Beam R.	L.	Inside Spread	Circumference at Smallest Place Between Burr & First Point R.	L.	Number of Points R.	L.	Locality	Hunter	Owner	Date Killed	Rank
207 1/8	24 4/8	23 3/8	16 1/8	6	5 7/8	12	12	Linn Co., KS	Charles E. Jasper	Charles E. Jasper	2000	146
206 7/8	26	26	17 4/8	5 1/8	5 1/8	8	8	St. Louis, SK	Kelvin Tate	D.J. Hollinger & B. Howard	1987	149
206 7/8	27 1/8	27 7/8	19 5/8	5 2/8	5 2/8	10	10	Jo Daviess Co., IL	Picked Up	Doug D. Jones	1998	149
206 7/8	26 7/8	26 5/8	18 6/8	5 1/8	5 1/8	7	13	Crawford Co., WI	Thomas Oppriecht	Thomas Oppriecht	2001	149
206 7/8	24 6/8	22 5/8	15 5/8	5 4/8	5 3/8	9	12	Adair Co., MO	Mearl Janes	Scott Janes	2002	149
206 6/8	23 7/8	27	23 1/8	5 6/8	5 4/8	12	11	Vermilion Co., IL	Ronald Weddle	Ronald Weddle	2001	153
206 5/8	24 4/8	24 4/8	14 6/8	7 1/8	6	13	11	Penobscot Co., ME	Jay L. McLellan	Jay L. McLellan	2001	154
206 4/8	24 6/8	23 7/8	18 1/8	5 3/8	5 3/8	9	13	Chippewa Co., WI	Richard C. Bennesch	Richard C. Bennesch	2000	155
206 3/8	26 6/8	26 5/8	21 6/8	5 7/8	5 4/8	9	8	St. Louis Co., MN	Picked Up	Paul Coughlin	2002	156
206 2/8	26 6/8	27 5/8	23 3/8	5 1/8	5 4/8	10	12	Henry Co., IL	Jon R. Wolf	Jon R. Wolf	2000	157
206 2/8	24 6/8	25 5/8	24 1/8	5 1/8	6 2/8	8	13	Jefferson Co., KS	Michael J. Navrat, Jr.	Michael J. Navrat, Jr.	2001	157
206 2/8	26 7/8	27 6/8	20 6/8	5 6/8	5 5/8	10	9	Gull Lake, AB	Jack K. Mulder	Jack K. Mulder	2001	157
206 2/8	26 2/8	26 5/8	19	5	5	9	13	Pike Co., IN	William J. Goeppner	William J. Goeppner	2003	157
206	25 3/8	25 4/8	18 5/8	5	5 4/8	13	13	Lincoln Co., MO	Robert J. Leacock	Robert J. Leacock	2002	161
205 7/8	25 5/8	25 5/8	20 6/8	4 6/8	5 2/8	9	16	Franklin Co., MO	Alfred Osborn	Jack E. Osborn	1957	162
205 7/8	27 3/8	26 2/8	18 1/8	5 6/8	5 7/8	10	10	Todd Co., MN	Ben Sadlovsky	Matthew K. Sadlovsky	1973	162
205 7/8	26 6/8	25 1/8	19 7/8	5 3/8	5 2/8	10	11	Lawrence Co., AL	Ronald R. Laymon	Ronald R. Laymon	2000	162
205 6/8	26 2/8	25 7/8	16 6/8	5 3/8	5 3/8	9	11	Trimble Co., KY	Billy A. Riddell, Jr.	Billy A. Riddell, Jr.	2001	165
205 5/8	29 1/8	27 7/8	21 4/8	5 3/8	5 1/8	11	8	Doniphan Co., KS	Fran E. Wiederholt	Fran E. Wiederholt	1996	166
205 4/8	23 5/8	22	18 2/8	5 7/8	5 6/8	10	12	Adams Co., OH	Mike Theuil	Bruce Bruening	2002	167
205 4/8	28 6/8	28 4/8	22 1/8	4 5/8	4 6/8	9	7	Geauga Co., OH	R. Chris Harris	R. Chris Harris	2002	167
205 3/8	28 4/8	28	20 2/8	4 7/8	5	7	8	Allamakee Co., IA	Picked Up	Frank Miller	1993	169
205 3/8	26 3/8	23 2/8	23 1/8	4 7/8	4 6/8	14	9	Henderson Co., KY	Stephen L. Arend	Stephen L. Arend	2000	169
205 2/8	25 6/8	25 1/8	19 7/8	6 2/8	6 2/8	8	8	Morgan Co., IL	Shawn R. Keegan	Shawn R. Keegan	2000	171
205 1/8	25 7/8	25 7/8	25 3/8	4 6/8	4 6/8	8	9	Moose Mountain Creek, SK	Darrell Arndt	Darrell Arndt	1999	172
205	24 2/8	25 6/8	15 6/8	4 6/8	4 5/8	10	8	Grady Co., OK	Rickie L. Jenkins	Rickie L. Jenkins	2001	173
205	27 2/8	26 5/8	17 6/8	5 1/8	5 1/8	8	9	Warren Co., IL	Brad Wike	Brad Wike	2002	173
204 7/8	23 3/8	23 1/8	22 7/8	4 7/8	4 5/8	10	11	Minnesota	Steve Scholl	Steve Scholl	1941	175
204 7/8	23 3/8	24 6/8	20 2/8	5 3/8	5 1/8	12	10	Ogle Co., IL	Troy W. O'Brien	Troy W. O'Brien	2001	175
204 6/8	25	26 5/8	19 1/8	5 4/8	5 4/8	9	9	Harris Co., GA	Lauren C. Atwell	Lauren C. Atwell	2002	177
204 6/8	27 4/8	22 6/8	19 4/8	5 6/8	7 4/8	6	12	Warren Co., OH	Rex A. Gill	Rex A. Gill	2002	177
204 5/8	26	27 2/8	17 4/8	5 4/8	5 6/8	11	10	Richland Co., MT	Harold R. Moran	Harold R. Moran	1956	179
204 5/8	27 1/8	25 7/8	21 6/8	5 4/8	5 7/8	6	11	Spruce Grove, AB	Darryl Legge	Darryl Legge	1999	179

Score	L	R	Inside	Circ. L	Circ. R	Pts L	Pts R	Location	Owner	Hunter	Year	Rank
204 4/8	21 4/8	22 1/8	22 6/8	5 1/8	5 3/8	9	8	Dogpound Creek, AB	Patrick F. Kinch	Patrick F. Kinch	2002	181
204 3/8	27 2/8	28	20 1/8	4 4/8	4 4/8	7	9	Dimmit Co., TX	Knox Miller	Clayton R. Johnson	1938	182
204 3/8	23 1/8	25	17 2/8	6 1/8	5 2/8	9	6	Lincoln Co., NE	Clyde L. Albers	Clyde L. Albers	2000	182
204 3/8	24 3/8	25	19 6/8	4 1/8	4 1/8	10	10	Assiniboine River, SK	Karen R. Seginak	Karen R. Seginak	2000	182
204 3/8	26 2/8	26 2/8	17 2/8	5 2/8	4 5/8	12	7	Otter Tail Co., MN	John L. Sabbin	John L. Sabbin	2001	182
204 3/8	27 5/8	28 1/8	25 4/8	5 3/8	5 4/8	6	8	Allen Co., IN	Charles E. Dennis	Charles E. Dennis	2002	182
204 2/8	28 3/8	28 1/8	18 4/8	4 7/8	5	11	11	Grant Co., WI	Michael M. White	Michael M. White	2001	187
204 1/8	26	25 4/8	19 7/8	4 5/8	4 5/8	9	11	Jefferson Co., OH	Ronald J. Ault	Ronald J. Ault	2002	188
204	24 3/8	23 2/8	19 2/8	4 4/8	4	13	8	Hardin Co., KY	Picked Up	Dennis J. Haberkorn	1990	189
204	24 6/8	24 6/8	13 1/8	4 4/8	4 5/8	15	13	Saskatchewan	Picked Up	Steve Scharf	PR2001	189
204	29	28 7/8	20 7/8	5 7/8	6 3/8	10	9	McHenry Co., IL	Rick Lagerhausen	Rick Lagerhausen	2002	189
203 7/8	25	25 6/8	20 5/8	5 4/8	5 3/8	14	9	Carver Co., MN	Peter Kamann	Eugene L. Kamann	1900	192
203 7/8	25 2/8	25 5/8	24 1/8	6 7/8	6 5/8	7	10	Greene Co., IN	Robert J. Cornwell	Robert J. Cornwell	2000	192
203 5/8	26 6/8	26 4/8	20 4/8	6 4/8	6 1/8	9	10	Spokane Co., WA	Jeff Whitman	Jeff Whitman	1992	194
203 4/8	28 4/8	29	22 3/8	4 7/8	5 1/8	6	7	Greene Co., IL	Greg L. Griswold	Greg L. Griswold	2001	195
203 3/8	22 3/8	21 2/8	18 2/8	4 4/8	4 3/8	10	13	Cumberland Co., NJ	Darrell T. Capps	Darrell T. Capps	2000	196
203 3/8	22 3/8	24 1/8	17 5/8	4 3/8	4 4/8	11	10	Monroe Co., WI	Darrell G. Schultz	Darrell G. Schultz	2001	196
203 3/8	22 4/8	23 3/8	20 6/8	4 4/8	4 4/8	10	9	Candle Lake, SK	Joseph R. Conard	Joseph R. Conard	2001	196
203 2/8	26 2/8	25 1/8	24 4/8	4 7/8	5	6	6	Logan Co., CO	Wade D. Shults	Wade D. Shults	2000	199
203 2/8	22 2/8	21 3/8	15 4/8	4 7/8	4 7/8	9	10	Pike Co., IL	J. Brett Evans	J. Brett Evans	2001	199
203 2/8	25 7/8	27 2/8	19	6 1/8	5 6/8	8	8	Iroquois Co., IL	Michael A. Lucht	Michael A. Lucht	2002	199
203 1/8	24 5/8	26 1/8	24	5 2/8	5 5/8	10	7	Bureau Co., IL	Jack E. Davis	Jack E. Davis	2001	202
203	26 3/8	26 5/8	16 2/8	5 2/8	5 1/8	6	11	Cooper Co., MO	Tim Folmer	Tim Folmer	2000	203
203	29 1/8	27 6/8	22 2/8	6	6	10	12	Lake of the Prairies, SK	Eldon Conrad	Eldon Conrad	2000	203
202 7/8	27 6/8	27 6/8	20 6/8	5 2/8	5 1/8	8	7	Cutarm River, SK	Charles Bassingthwaite	Charles Bassingthwaite	2001	205
202 6/8	27 2/8	27 6/8	22	5 5/8	5 5/8	7	6	McHenry Co., IL	Jim Kunde	Jim Kunde	2001	206
202 6/8	25	24 7/8	19	5 2/8	4 7/8	12	7	Sullivan Co., IN	Tate R. Graves	Tate R. Graves	2002	206
202 5/8	29	28 2/8	20 5/8	4 7/8	4 7/8	7	8	Weld Co., CO	Picked Up	Matt Yocam	1999	208
202 5/8	24 3/8	24 5/8	16 4/8	5 2/8	6	7	13	Johnson Co., IL	Timothy J. Boyle	Timothy J. Boyle	2001	208
202 5/8	26	26 4/8	22 3/8	5 4/8	5 4/8	9	10	Spiritwood, SK	Donald J. Chamberlain	Donald J. Chamberlain	2001	208
202 4/8	28 5/8	27 4/8	17 6/8	5 1/8	5 1/8	11	9	Muskingum Co., OH	Gil W. Gard II	Gil W. Gard II	2002	208
202 4/8	26 5/8	27 1/8	20 6/8	6	6 1/8	8	8	Fond du Lac Co., WI	Warren Miller	Warren Miller	2000	212
202 4/8	23 3/8	24 2/8	19 5/8	5 6/8	5 3/8	10	8	Pontotoc Co., MS	William H. Westmoreland	William H. Westmoreland	2001	212
202 3/8	27 2/8	27 5/8	22 4/8	5	5 2/8	11	15	Keweenaw Co., MI	Bernard J. Jackovich	Bernard J. Jackovich	2000	214
202 2/8	25 5/8	25 3/8	17	6	6 3/8	13	9	Pike Co., IL	Picked Up	George R. Metcalf	1996	215
202 2/8	22 5/8	22 2/8	13 6/8	5 7/8	5 5/8	9	8	Crow Wing Co., MN	Michael L. Daly	Michael L. Daly	2000	215
202 2/8	25 4/8	25	18 6/8	5 3/8	5 2/8	8	6	Audrain Co., MO	Barbara L. Blackmore	Barbara L. Blackmore	2001	215
202 2/8	25	25 5/8	19 5/8	5	5 1/8	11	9	Mitchell Co., GA	Tommy S. Burford	Tommy S. Burford	2001	215
202 1/8	25 5/8	28	25	5 3/8	5 2/8	9	10	Wood Co., OH	Wynn A. Brinker	Wynn A. Brinker	2001	219
202	29 3/8	25 7/8	17 7/8	4 2/8	4 3/8	11	9	Falls Co., TX	Rudy Garcia	Rudy Garcia	2000	220
201 7/8	27	26 5/8	21	4 4/8	4 4/8	12	8	Michigan	Unknown	Steve Crossley	1945	221

WHITETAIL DEER – NON-TYPICAL ANTLERS

Odocoileus virginianus virginianus and certain related subspecies

Score	Length of Main Beam R.	Length of Main Beam L.	Inside Spread	Circumference at Smallest Place Between Burr & First Point R.	Circumference at Smallest Place Between Burr & First Point L.	Number of Points R.	Number of Points L.	Locality	Hunter	Owner	Date Killed	Rank
201 7/8	28 2/8	28 4/8	24	5 1/8	5 2/8	10	9	New London Co., CT	Henry M. Konow, Jr.	Henry M. Konow, Jr.	2000	221
201 6/8	25 1/8	25	19 4/8	5 2/8	5 4/8	7	8	Minnesota	Unknown	Larry D. Bollier	1969	223
201 5/8	26 3/8	25 7/8	16 2/8	5 7/8	5 7/8	9	13	Tama Co., IA	Rod L. Waschkat	Rod L. Waschkat	2001	224
201 4/8	25 7/8	25	23 4/8	5 2/8	5 4/8	9	14	Jefferson Co., PA	James D. Rowles	James D. Rowles	2000	225
201 4/8	26 7/8	28	20 2/8	5 6/8	5 6/8	13	11	Jackson Co., IL	Mark D. Ralph	Mark D. Ralph	2000	225
201 4/8	23 1/8	23 2/8	20 2/8	4 7/8	5	13	13	Monroe Co., AR	Jerry Griggs	Jerry Griggs	2002	225
201 4/8	27 7/8	27 1/8	18	5 5/8	5 4/8	9	10	Dauphin Co., PA	Darron A. Erdman	Darron A. Erdman	2002	225
201 3/8	24 6/8	26 5/8	18 1/8	4 6/8	4 5/8	12	10	Dickinson Co., MI	Ludvic Riihimaki	Mary J. Wellman	1948	229
201 3/8	25 4/8	25 6/8	18 4/8	6 2/8	6 4/8	9	9	De Kalb Co., MO	Charles F. Christensen	Charles F. Christensen	1998	229
201 3/8	24 5/8	26 5/8	18 6/8	4 1/8	4 2/8	9	10	Le Flore Co., OK	William M. Russell	William M. Russell	2001	229
201 3/8	25 1/8	29 3/8	21	5 4/8	5 7/8	13	10	Licking Co., OH	Ty L. Yoho	Ty L. Yoho	2002	229
201 3/8	26 7/8	26 2/8	22 6/8	5 1/8	5	9	12	Washington Co., MS	Shelby R. Barrett, Jr.	Shelby R. Barrett, Jr.	2002	229
201 2/8	25 7/8	25 7/8	18 6/8	5 1/8	5	8	11	Jefferson Co., IL	Dwight N. Pfeiffer	Dwight N. Pfeiffer	1999	234
201 1/8	27 5/8	25 5/8	21 5/8	5 2/8	5 2/8	7	9	Coffey Co., KS	Lance W. Jacob	Cabela's, Inc.	2000	235
201	24 2/8	24	16 5/8	6	5 6/8	12	9	Republic Co., KS	Bucky D. Barber	Bucky D. Barber	2000	236
201	27	26 2/8	20 4/8	5 7/8	5 5/8	9	12	Pottawatomie Co., KS	M. Evan Porterfield	M. Evan Porterfield	2002	236
200 7/8	28	29 7/8	19	5	4 7/8	11	9	Cochrane, AB	Terry L. Raymond	Terry L. Raymond	2001	238
200 6/8	28	28 1/8	22	5 6/8	5 5/8	15	12	Clay Co., MN	Unknown	Richard L. Meyer	1975	239
200 6/8	25 2/8	25 7/8	22 3/8	6	6 1/8	7	10	Oktibbeha Co., MS	Pamela Reid-Rhoades	Will Sanders	1993	239
200 6/8	28	26 2/8	19 3/8	6	6	9	9	Sarpy Co., NE	Mark A. Dillon	Mark A. Dillon	2001	239
200 6/8	23 6/8	23 6/8	16 3/8	4 6/8	4 4/8	11	9	Uvalde Co., TX	James R. Schroeder	James R. Schroeder	2003	239
200 5/8	25 5/8	26 2/8	17 1/8	5	5	14	8	Adams Co., IL	Edward B. Tucker	Edward B. Tucker	1999	243
200 5/8	22 1/8	23 5/8	16 1/8	5 3/8	5 1/8	16	10	Lewis Co., MO	Bennett E. Nation	Bennett E. Nation	2000	243
200 5/8	29 6/8	29 7/8	19 6/8	5 5/8	5 4/8	9	10	Clinton Co., OH	Robert C. Sargent	Robert C. Sargent	2002	243
200 5/8	22 3/8	27 4/8	22 3/8	5 7/8	6	10	6	Barber Co., KS	Rick Behrends	Rick Behrends	2003	243
200 4/8	27 4/8	28	21 1/8	5 4/8	5 5/8	9	9	Sawyer Co., WI	Gary A. Haus	Gary A. Haus	2000	247
200 4/8	25 6/8	23 5/8	17 7/8	4 4/8	4 5/8	7	9	Allamakee Co., IL	Bruce L. Schuttemeier	Bruce L. Schuttemeier	2000	247
200 4/8	26	28	16	5 1/8	5 5/8	13	11	Menominee Co., WI	Michael G. Firgens	Michael G. Firgens	2001	247
200 4/8	27 6/8	27 3/8	20 4/8	5	5 3/8	8	7	Webb Co., TX	James Robison	James Robison	2003	247
200 3/8	24 4/8	24 2/8	20 7/8	5 6/8	5 6/8	10	11	Lancaster Co., NE	Tyler Fountain	Tyler Fountain	2000	251
200 3/8	24 7/8	25 7/8	19 3/8	5 6/8	5 4/8	7	7	Washington Co., NE	Elton O. Jones	Elton O. Jones	2002	251
200 3/8	23 6/8	22 1/8	18 5/8	5 2/8	7 6/8	8	9	Sauk Co., WI	Rob Horton	Rob Horton	2003	251
200 2/8	26 6/8	26 7/8	21 6/8	4 5/8	4 5/8	8	7	Greenup Co., KY	Eric E. Sparks	Eric E. Sparks	2000	254

Final Score	Main Beam R	Main Beam L	Inside Spread	Circ. R	Circ. L	Pts R	Pts L	Locality	Owner	By Whom Taken	Date	Rank
200 2/8	25 6/8	26 4/8	22 5/8	5 2/8	5 2/8	6	8	Athabasca, AB	John M. Gibbs	John M. Gibbs	2000	254
200 2/8	26 1/8	26 3/8	18 1/8	5 4/8	5 5/8	7	10	Isanti Co., MN	Michael W. Shattuck	Michael W. Shattuck	2001	254
200 2/8	29 2/8	29 1/8	23 7/8	5 3/8	5 7/8	8	9	Marion Co., KY	Chris Lyvers	Chris Lyvers	2002	254
200 1/8	27 1/8	27 2/8	23 2/8	6 3/8	6	11	9	Marion Co., OH	Brent E. Dorfe	Brent E. Dorfe	1999	258
200 1/8	28 3/8	28 6/8	18 7/8	4 5/8	4 5/8	8	8	Colquitt Co., GA	Jacky R. Stanfill	Jacky R. Stanfill	2002	258
200 1/8	24 3/8	24 3/8	19 5/8	5 4/8	5 3/8	8	11	Marion Co., IA	Boyd L. Mathes	Boyd L. Mathes	2002	258
200	25 3/8	26	19	4 7/8	4 6/8	8	10	Clay Co., IA	Picked Up	IA Dept. of Natl. Resc.	1987	261
200	24 4/8	25 2/8	18 2/8	5 1/8	4 7/8	11	7	James River, AB	Picked Up	Chad Lenz	1999	261
200	22 7/8	21 6/8	18 4/8	4 7/8	5	10	12	Buffalo Co., WI	John E. Blanchar	John E. Blanchar	2000	261
200	26 4/8	27	23 4/8	5 6/8	5 5/8	10	10	Clayton Co., IA	Michael A. Hinzman	Michael A. Hinzman	2000	261
200	30 2/8	28 6/8	19 5/8	5 4/8	5 4/8	8	8	Breckenridge, KY	James Bowles	James Bowles	2000	261
200	27 1/8	27 7/8	22 5/8	5 7/8	5 7/8	9	10	Lake Co., IN	John E. Quinlan	John E. Quinlan	2002	261
199 7/8	24 5/8	24	16 6/8	5 4/8	5 2/8	8	12	Vernon Co., WI	D. & K.D. McClurg	D. & K.D. McClurg	2001	267
199 6/8	26 7/8	27 5/8	24	5 2/8	5	10	11	Red River Parish, LA	Jason I. Dupree	Jason I. Dupree	2001	268
199 6/8	27 3/8	27 5/8	18 6/8	6	5 6/8	8	10	Licking Co., OH	Terry L. Garee	Terry L. Garee	2002	268
199 5/8	30	30 6/8	23	5 1/8	4 7/8	6	10	Jasper Co., GA	Hugh Barber	Donald A. Barber	1959	270
199 5/8	27 3/8	26 4/8	21	5 6/8	5 5/8	11	9	Douglas Co., MT	Timothy J. Hoel	Timothy J. Hoel	1999	270
199 4/8	25 3/8	25 4/8	21 2/8	5	5 1/8	9	7	Columbia Co., WI	Cameron L. Gramse	Cameron L. Gramse	2001	272
199 4/8	27 2/8	28 2/8	19 3/8	6 1/8	6	6	10	Seneca Co., OH	Gerald D. Terry	Gerald D. Terry	2002	272
199 3/8	20 6/8	22 2/8	15	6	6 6/8	13	9	Talbot Co., MD	William H. Shields	William H. Shields	2001	274
199 2/8	23 4/8	22 3/8	15 5/8	4 4/8	4 6/8	14	13	Johnson Co., KY	Gary L. Music	Gary L. Music	2001	275
199 2/8	26	26 4/8	19 5/8	6 2/8	6	7	9	Nodaway Co., MO	Sandra K. Gillenwater	Sandra K. Gillenwater	2002	275
199 1/8	25 1/8	25 7/8	17 5/8	4 6/8	5 3/8	11	7	Lucas Co., IA	J.J. Keller & J.R. Keller	J.J. Keller & J.R. Keller	2000	277
199 1/8	26 6/8	26 6/8	19 2/8	5 2/8	5 2/8	11	10	Richland Co., IL	Picked Up	Roy A. Albertson	2001	277
198 7/8	26 2/8	27 2/8	19 4/8	5 3/8	5 2/8	9	7	Randolph Co., IL	Mark Houba	Mark Houba	2002	279
198 7/8	26 7/8	27 2/8	18 6/8	6 7/8	6	11	14	Knox Co., OH	James T. Hlay	James T. Hlay	2002	279
198 6/8	23 3/8	23 1/8	17 3/8	4	4	11	12	Cherokee Co., TX	Randall L. Chandler	Randall L. Chandler	1994	281
198 6/8	26	24	16 7/8	5 1/8	5	9	12	Story Co., IA	Jarod J. Pederson	Jarod J. Pederson	1999	281
198 6/8	25	22 2/8	14 6/8	4 6/8	4 6/8	11	12	Greenwater Lake, SK	Picked Up	Don Kjelshus	2000	281
198 6/8	28 3/8	28 3/8	15 1/8	5 3/8	5 3/8	9	7	Madison Co., IL	Eric W. Barach	Eric W. Barach	2001	281
198 5/8	26 6/8	27	17 2/8	4 5/8	4 5/8	8	8	Jackson Co., IA	James M. Ruggeberg	James M. Ruggeberg	1997	285
198 4/8	29	29 4/8	23 4/8	5 1/8	5	9	5	Missisquoi, QC	Mario L. Quintin	Mario L. Quintin	1990	286
198 4/8	26 1/8	25 3/8	19 6/8	6	5 6/8	8	7	Pottawattamie Co., IA	Picked Up	IA Dept. of Natl. Resc.	2000	286
198 4/8	25 1/8	22 5/8	19 1/8	5 7/8	5 7/8	10	5	Smoky River, AB	Jim Boland	Jim Boland	2000	286
198 4/8	21 5/8	23	17 5/8	4 3/8	4 4/8	7	9	Rapides Parish, LA	William A. Jordan, Jr.	William A. Jordan, Jr.	2001	286
198 4/8	28 2/8	27 4/8	19 4/8	6 4/8	6 7/8	11	10	Issaquena Co., MS	John T. Campbell	John T. Campbell	2001	286
198 2/8	25 5/8	24 7/8	16 6/8	5 3/8	5 2/8	11	10	Marinette Co., WI	Stephen R. Couveau	Stephen R. Couveau	2001	291
198 2/8	22 5/8	21 7/8	16 6/8	4 5/8	4 5/8	9	9	Dogpound Creek, AK	Steve K. Thompson	Steve K. Thompson	2001	291
198 2/8	27	28 1/8	19 1/8	4 6/8	4 3/8	9	9	Lewis Co., KY	Phillip R. Hall	Phillip R. Hall	2002	291
198 2/8	27 3/8	28 3/8	23 3/8	5 3/8	5 3/8	8	8	Fairfield Co., OH	Rodney A. McManus	Rodney A. McManus	2002	291
198 1/8	27 5/8	26 5/8	21	6	6 1/8	7	9	Jefferson Co., WI	Charles E. Emery	Charles E. Emery	2001	295

WHITETAIL DEER - NON-TYPICAL ANTLERS

Odocoileus virginianus virginianus and certain related subspecies

Score	Length of Main Beam R.	Length of Main Beam L.	Inside Spread	Circumference at Smallest Place Between Burr & First Point R.	Circumference at Smallest Place Between Burr & First Point L.	Number of Points R.	Number of Points L.	Locality	Hunter	Owner	Date Killed	Rank
198	27 5/8	26 7/8	22 4/8	5	4 7/8	7	9	Holt Co., NE	Randy D. Sell	Randy D. Sell	2000	296
198	26 5/8	26 5/8	19 4/8	5 3/8	5 1/8	12	8	Meigs Co., OH	Jack Satterfield, Jr.	Jack Satterfield, Jr.	2000	296
198	25 5/8	27 5/8	18 7/8	4 7/8	4 6/8	8	9	Jackson Co., IA	Jesse H. Smith	Jesse H. Smith	2001	296
198	27 1/8	25 5/8	17 3/8	5 5/8	6 3/8	10	7	Jefferson Co., IA	Jesse Rebling	Jesse Rebling	2001	296
197 7/8	24 1/8	23 2/8	17 6/8	4 5/8	4 6/8	6	7	Willacy Co., TX	Clifton L. Smith	Garcia Estate	2000	300
197 7/8	28 7/8	27	21 2/8	5 2/8	4 5/8	8	6	Hardin Co., KY	Ellis E. Givens	Ellis E. Givens	2001	300
197 7/8	25 3/8	25 3/8	22	4 1/8	4 5/8	1	8	Richland Co., OH	James C. Carpenter	James C. Carpenter	2001	300
197 6/8	24 5/8	22 6/8	18	4 5/8	4 5/8	21	16	Barber Co., KS	Barte G. Miller	Barte G. Miller	2002	303
197 5/8	26 5/8	23 1/8	22 4/8	4 7/8	4 6/8	9	11	Appanoose Co., IA	Bill R. Clark	Bill R. Clark	2001	304
197 4/8	25 1/8	23 7/8	17 3/8	5 5/8	5 6/8	8	11	Iowa Co., WI	Roger S. Venden	Roger S. Venden	2002	305
197 4/8	23 3/8	26 1/8	17 1/8	5 7/8	5 5/8	12	11	Harrison Co., MO	William M. White	William M. White	2002	305
197 4/8	26 1/8	26 2/8	21 3/8	4 2/8	4 3/8	11	9	Aroostook Co., ME	Robert W. Cameron, Jr.	Robert W. Cameron, Jr.	2002	305
197 3/8	22 1/8	21	17 5/8	4 4/8	4 4/8	16	14	Mifflin Co., PA	Garry L. Forgy	Garry L. Forgy	2000	308
197 3/8	28 5/8	27 6/8	21 6/8	6 4/8	5 2/8	16	14	Suffolk Co., NY	John E. Hansen	John E. Hansen	2001	308
197 3/8	24 5/8	24 2/8	21 1/8	6 3/8	6 4/8	10	9	Black Hawk Co., IA	Michael R. Lichty	Michael R. Lichty	2002	308
197 2/8	25 5/8	26 7/8	19	5 2/8	5 1/8	14	9	Washington Co., MN	Albert J. Cotton	Margie Barnett	1930	311
197 2/8	23 5/8	23 7/8	23 1/8	5	5	14	9	Vilas Co., WI	Unknown	Ross A. Manthey	1943	311
197 2/8	28 6/8	28 2/8	22 4/8	5 3/8	5 3/8	9	14	Noxbee Co., MS	Edward A. Halfacre	Edward A. Halfacre	1998	311
197 2/8	27 6/8	29 4/8	19 7/8	5 2/8	5 2/8	9	8	Fayette Co., IL	Todd L. Hodson	Todd L. Hodson	2000	311
197 2/8	23 1/8	22 7/8	20 3/8	5 5/8	5 3/8	10	10	Van Buren Co., MI	John Pierson	John Pierson	2000	311
197 2/8	25	23 7/8	19 5/8	5 6/8	5 6/8	7	8	Fulton Co., IL	Nicholas P. McElroy	Nicholas P. McElroy	2000	311
197 1/8	26	25 5/8	24 1/8	5	5 5/8	8	9	Caddo Co., OK	Jerid C. Avery	Jerid C. Avery	2000	317
197	26 4/8	26 4/8	21	4 3/8	5	8	9	La Salle Co., IL	Ken Sparks, Jr.	Ken Sparks, Jr.	2002	318
196 7/8	24 6/8	24 5/8	16	5 3/8	4 5/8	13	14	Allegheny Co., PA	Charles E. Main	Charles E. Main	2000	319
196 7/8	23 6/8	23	22 4/8	5	5 3/8	12	11	Hart Co., KY	John L. Seymour	John L. Seymour	2000	319
196 6/8	25 7/8	26	21 2/8	4 4/8	4 5/8	10	8	Lewis Co., MO	Kenneth W. Brocksmith	Kenneth W. Brocksmith	2000	321
196 6/8	21 2/8	20 6/8	18 2/8	5 2/8	4 3/8	10	11	Butler Co., IA	Edwin T. Blanchard	Edwin T. Blanchard	2000	321
196 6/8	27 2/8	26 2/8	21 2/8	5 1/8	5	10	9	Pike Co., IL	Larry D. Grant	Larry D. Grant	2001	321
196 6/8	25 5/8	24 5/8	15	5 3/8	5 1/8	9	8	Dakota Co., NE	David J. Miller	David J. Miller	2002	321
196 6/8	24 3/8	23 2/8	16 3/8	6 3/8	6 3/8	13	11	Jackson Co., IA	Wayne M. Harvey	Wayne M. Harvey	2002	321
196 5/8	27 7/8	27 5/8	20 6/8	6 3/8	6 3/8	9	9	Nottawasaga River, ON	James P. Baird	James P. Baird	2000	326
196 5/8	29 2/8	28 5/8	19 1/8	6 2/8	5 6/8	7	9	Winnipeg River, MB	Mark S. Ilijanic	Mark S. Ilijanic	2000	326
196 5/8	26 7/8	26 5/8	20 2/8	5	4 7/8	9	9	Kayosuar Creek, SK	Kelly Schuster	Kelly Schuster	2000	326

Score								Locality	Owner	Hunter	Year	Rank
196 5/8	23 1/8	23 2/8	19 3/8	4 7/8	4 5/8	9	11	Rabbit Lake, SK	Jim Clary	Jim Clary	2000	326
196 5/8	27	27 2/8	19 4/8	7	7	9	10	Bates Co., MO	Joseph E. Favre	Joseph E. Favre	2002	326
196 4/8	26 4/8	25 6/8	17 1/8	5 4/8	5 3/8	8	10	Page Co., IA	Michael L. Hughes	Michael L. Hughes	1999	331
196 4/8	24 4/8	24 2/8	18 6/8	6	6 2/8	8	10	Crystal Lakes, SK	Andrew Gazdewich	Andrew Gazdewich	2001	331
196 4/8	24 1/8	25 1/8	19 6/8	5 1/8	5	12	10	Wayne Co., NY	Jonathan S. Countryman	Jonathan S. Countryman	2001	331
196 3/8	26	25 7/8	21	4 7/8	5	8	10	Baldwin Co., AL	Kyle Ferguson	Carl Raley	1962	334
196 3/8	26 3/8	26 6/8	20 7/8	4 4/8	4 3/8	7	9	Spokane Co., WA	Eric Friesen	Eric Friesen	1986	334
196 3/8	25 6/8	25 3/8	20 3/8	5 6/8	5 6/8	11	11	Clayton Co., IA	David D. Sadewasser	David D. Sadewasser	2000	334
196 3/8	24 4/8	23 7/8	22 3/8	5 5/8	5 6/8	10	8	Franklin Co., KY	Gene C. Brown	Gene C. Brown	2001	334
196 3/8	24 5/8	20 7/8	14 3/8	6 4/8	7 3/8	7	12	St. Mary's Co., MD	Terry L. Starr	Terry L. Starr	2001	334
196 2/8	25 4/8	25	24	5 2/8	6 3/8	5	14	Henderson Co., KY	Nathan A. Peak	Nathan A. Peak	2000	339
196 2/8	25	25 7/8	18 3/8	4 7/8	5 2/8	12	8	Putnam Co., IN	Todd G. Barnes	Todd G. Barnes	2000	339
196 2/8	23 4/8	24 3/8	16 4/8	6 1/8	5 6/8	7	9	Pierce Co., WI	Mark P. Dolan	Mark P. Dolan	2001	339
196 1/8	25 2/8	24 4/8	17 3/8	5 7/8	5 2/8	8	7	Lyon Co., KS	A. Scott Ritchie	A. Scott Ritchie	2000	342
196 1/8	26 1/8	25 7/8	13 6/8	6 1/8	5 7/8	7	9	Whitley Co., KY	Douglas Angel	Douglas Angel	2001	342
196 1/8	21 6/8	19 5/8	21	4 5/8	4 5/8	20	13	Montgomery Co., NC	Roger D. Hunt	Roger D. Hunt	2001	342
196 1/8	25 2/8	25	19 3/8	5 6/8	5 5/8	8	8	Wabasha Co., MN	Angela Reinhardt	Angela Reinhardt	2002	342
196 1/8	23 5/8	23 6/8	18 4/8	4 3/8	4 2/8	13	9	Lincoln Co., OK	Joshua A. Shade	Joshua A. Shade	2002	342
196	24 6/8	26 2/8	20 4/8	5 3/8	5 4/8	9	12	Mercer Co., MO	James W. Berryman	James W. Berryman	2001	347
196	24 4/8	25 6/8	19 7/8	4 7/8	5 4/8	9	7	Franklin Co., IN	John D. Burkhart	John D. Burkhart	2002	347
195 7/8	26	27	20 4/8	5 2/8	5 2/8	10	8	Florence Co., WI	Barbara R. Bowman	E.J. Nichols	PR1940	349
195 7/8	25 2/8	27 6/8	20 6/8	4 6/8	5	11	7	Marshall Co., MN	Vernon Blazejewski	Picked Up	1997	349
195 7/8	23 3/8	23 6/8	15 6/8	6 5/8	6 6/8	12	15	Thorhild, AB	Beau Lyons	Picked Up	2000	349
195 7/8	26 7/8	27 5/8	18 3/8	5	4 7/8	11	11	Blueberry River, BC	Ernie Kuehne	Ernie Kuehne	2000	349
195 7/8	26 4/8	27	19 2/8	4 7/8	4 7/8	9	6	Webb Co., TX	Jimmie L. Speake	Jimmie L. Speake	2000	349
195 7/8	24 7/8	24	18 2/8	4 4/8	4 4/8	11	10	Kleberg Co., TX	Allyn Archer	Allyn Archer	2002	349
195 7/8	25 3/8	27	20	6 2/8	6 3/8	7	9	Peoria Co., IL	Stanley E. Goard	Stanley E. Goard	2002	349
195 6/8	21	19 6/8	15	4 5/8	4 6/8	8	12	Park Co., MT	Larry R. Faust	Larry R. Faust	2001	356
195 6/8	25 5/8	25 7/8	20 7/8	5 1/8	5 1/8	10	9	Little Moose Lake, SK	Carl Grundman	Carl Grundman	2001	356
195 6/8	25	24 2/8	14	5 2/8	5 1/8	9	10	Madison Co., IL	James M. Hoefert	James M. Hoefert	2001	356
195 6/8	24 2/8	25 2/8	20 7/8	5 5/8	5 4/8	8	9	Johnston Co., OK	Rhonda L. Upchurch	Rhonda L. Upchurch	2002	356
195 5/8	24 3/8	24	18 3/8	4 2/8	4	7	7	Madison Co., MS	Damon C. Saik	Damon C. Saik	2001	360
195 5/8	29 2/8	28 3/8	22 4/8	5 5/8	5 3/8	8	6	Pike Co., MO	Zachary E. Sutter	Zachary E. Sutter	2002	360
195 4/8	24 2/8	23 7/8	19 7/8	5 4/8	5 2/8	9	10	Angus Brook, NS	John Breslin, Jr.	John Breslin, Jr.	1995	362
195 4/8	22 3/8	22 4/8	17 6/8	4 7/8	4 6/8	12	10	Comanche Co., OK	Jerry L. Timmons	Jerry L. Timmons	2000	362
195 4/8	24 4/8	25 3/8	16 6/8	6 3/8	6 1/8	8	9	Boone Co., IA	Joe R. Busch	Joe R. Busch	2001	362
195 4/8	24 2/8	24 1/8	18 4/8	4 6/8	4 6/8	10	9	Door Co., WI	Robert F. Meingast	Robert F. Meingast	2002	362
195 4/8	24 5/8	24 4/8	20 4/8	5 1/8	5 2/8	11	10	Livingston Co., MO	Wayne D. Cunningham	Wayne D. Cunningham	2002	362
195 3/8	25 5/8	26 1/8	19 3/8	5 1/8	5 2/8	7	9	Hopkins Co., KY	Brad Nelson	Picked Up	2000	367
195 3/8	26 1/8	24 2/8	18	5 1/8	5 1/8	7	11	Outagamie Co., WI	Michael S. Schernick	Michael S. Schernick	2000	367
195 3/8	23	24 7/8	20 7/8	6 6/8	6 6/8	10	9	Stephens Co., OK	David J. Vassella	David J. Vassella	2001	367

Odocoileus virginianus virginianus and certain related subspecies

Score	Length of Main Beam R.	L.	Inside Spread	Circumference at Smallest Place Between Burr & First Point R.	L.	Number of Points R.	L.	Locality	Hunter	Owner	Date Killed	Rank
195 3/8	24 5/8	25 2/8	18 3/8	5 2/8	5 1/8	14	6	Vermilion River, MB	Greg O'Hare	Greg O'Hare	2001	367
195 3/8	28 7/8	26 1/8	20 5/8	6 3/8	6 3/8	7	6	Marion Co., OH	Douglas S. Campbell	Douglas S. Campbell	2002	367
195 2/8	31 6/8	31	21 5/8	4 7/8	5	10	9	Brooks Co., GA	Donald K. Duren	Latrelle D. Burkholder	1970	372
195 2/8	28 3/8	28 6/8	20 5/8	6	5 6/8	9	6	Jefferson Co., IL	William C. Bell	William C. Bell	2000	372
195 2/8	23 3/8	23 5/8	21 2/8	5	5	8	8	Dimmit Co., TX	Guinn D. Crousen	Guinn D. Crousen	2001	372
195 2/8	24 6/8	23	20 4/8	5 3/8	5 4/8	8	11	Tunica Co., MS	Leland N. Dye, Jr.	Leland N. Dye, Jr.	2001	372
195 1/8	20 5/8	23 3/8	14 2/8	6 3/8	5 7/8	11	13	Dukes Co., MA	Picked Up	Daniel C. Feeney	1999	376
195 1/8	24 3/8	23 1/8	17	5 4/8	5 3/8	7	9	Sylvan Lake, AB	Les Diehl	Les Diehl	1999	376
195 1/8	23 6/8	23 2/8	16 6/8	5 1/8	5 1/8	10	8	Woods Co., OK	Stephen C. Elias	Stephen C. Elias	2000	376
195 1/8	26 2/8	26 3/8	23	5 1/8	5	10	8	Maury Co., TN	Chris Hagan	Chris Hagan	2002	376
195 1/8	26 7/8	26	24	4 5/8	4 5/8	7	8	Washington Co., IL	Leo M. Suchomski	Leo M. Suchomski	2002	376
195	24 4/8	24 4/8	23 6/8	3 7/8	3 7/8	7	8	St. Francis Co., AR	John H. Parker	John H. Parker	1996	381
195	22 6/8	26 6/8	19 6/8	5 3/8	5 7/8	10	8	Shawnee Co., KS	Mark E. Conaway	Mark E. Conaway	1999	381
195	26	25 4/8	19 3/8	4 5/8	4 5/8	9	7	Shell River, MB	Wayne Todoschuk	Wayne Todoschuk	2000	381
195	22 6/8	21 7/8	20	5 4/8	5 4/8	12	14	Carter Co., OK	William A. Crosby	William A. Crosby	2000	381
195	26 6/8	26 6/8	19 3/8	5 5/8	5 5/8	8	7	Delaware Co., IA	Joseph D. Hoeger	Joseph D. Hoeger	2000	381
195	26 4/8	26 1/8	15 2/8	5 5/8	5 6/8	7	7	Dubuque Co., IA	Adam W. Anglin	Adam W. Anglin	2001	381
194 6/8	27 6/8	27 2/8	19 5/8	5	5 3/8	8	7	Iowa Co., WI	Mark A. Klosterman	Mark A. Klosterman	2000	387
194 5/8	27 6/8	28 3/8	20 1/8	5 6/8	5 5/8	7	10	Walworth Co., WI	Michael R. Senft	Michael R. Senft	2000	388
194 5/8	26 1/8	24 1/8	20 2/8	5	5	12	8	Pottawatomie Co., KS	Gary W. Schafer	Gary W. Schafer	2002	388
194 4/8	25 3/8	25	17 3/8	4 7/8	5 2/8	11	7	Stafford Co., KS	Jarred E. Hitz	Jarred E. Hitz	2002	390
194 1/8	29 1/8	30 1/8	19	5 2/8	5 2/8	9	10	Licking Co., OH	Roger J. Holbrook	Roger J. Holbrook	2000	391
194 1/8	25 7/8	24 7/8	20 5/8	5	5	9	7	Du Page, IL	Picked Up	Christopher T. Vasey	2000	391
194 1/8	23 4/8	24 4/8	20 2/8	5 6/8	5 1/8	7	10	Dubuque Co., IA	Kyle S. Koltes	Kyle S. Koltes	2002	391
193 6/8	22 6/8	24 1/8	16 3/8	5	8 2/8	5	14	Butler Co., KS	Lucas Mott	Lucas Mott	2001	394
193 5/8	27 7/8	24 5/8	19 5/8	5 2/8	5	9	7	Meadow Lake, SK	Keith A. Field	Keith A. Field	2000	395
193 5/8	24 4/8	24 5/8	18	5 7/8	6 1/8	6	10	Mercer Co., IL	David F. Flickinger	David F. Flickinger	2000	395
193 4/8	26	26 6/8	17 6/8	5 5/8	5 7/8	9	10	Dane Co., WI	Aaron G. Tachon	Aaron G. Tachon	2000	397
193 2/8	24 6/8	24 3/8	19 5/8	5	5	11	10	Fergus Co., MT	Michael C. Smith	Michael C. Smith	1969	398
193 1/8	24 7/8	24 7/8	22 1/8	5	4 7/8	7	7	Marion Co., MO	David E. Moss	David E. Moss	2001	399
193	24 1/8	22 7/8	20	6 5/8	7 2/8	6	7	Outagamie Co., WI	James C. Snortum	James C. Snortum	2001	400
193	25 5/8	25 2/8	22	5	4 6/8	7	8	Strafford Co., NH	Joseph A. Jacques	Joseph A. Jacques	2002	400
192 7/8	26	26 5/8	18 2/8	6 2/8	5 7/8	7	8	Morrison Co., MN	Brent M. Beimert	Brent M. Beimert	2001	402

Score	R. Main Beam	L. Main Beam	Inside Spread	R. Circ.	L. Circ.	R. Points	L. Points	Locality	Owner	Hunter	Year	Rank
192 7/8	27 4/8	27 4/8	22 1/8	5 7/8	5 4/8	9	9	Edwards Co., IL	Ronald D. Pritchett	Ronald D. Pritchett	2001	402
192 5/8	24 2/8	23 5/8	15 1/8	4 6/8	4 6/8	10	12	Johnson Co., MO	M. Scott Stehwien	M. Scott Stehwien	2002	404
192 5/8	21 6/8	21 4/8	17	4 4/8	4 5/8	12	10	Dubuque Co., IA	Greg Wille	Greg Wille	2002	404
192 4/8	27 6/8	26 3/8	19 7/8	5 4/8	6	7	9	Garfield Co., NE	Jerry B. Horwart	Jerry B. Horwart	2000	406
192 4/8	25 4/8	26 1/8	19 1/8	4 6/8	4 7/8	7	7	Buffalo Co., WI	Dale G. Hoch	Dale G. Hoch	2000	406
192 3/8	22 5/8	22 3/8	20 5/8	4 7/8	5 1/8	8	8	Clark Co., MO	Larry D. Foust	Larry D. Foust	2000	408
192 3/8	28 6/8	27 6/8	19 5/8	5 2/8	5	8	10	Knox Co., KY	Barry F. Yancosek	Barry F. Yancosek	2001	408
192 1/8	26 2/8	27	23	5 2/8	5 2/8	7	7	Kansas	Picked Up	Dusty Van Dorn	1970	410
192 1/8	25 7/8	26 7/8	20	4 4/8	4 3/8	9	8	Fayette Co., OH	Scott A. Boyer	Scott A. Boyer	2000	410
191 5/8	24 7/8	24 6/8	17 6/8	5	4 6/8	9	9	Allamakee Co., IA	Michael J. Manning	Michael J. Manning	2000	412
191 5/8	25 7/8	26 3/8	19 7/8	4 5/8	4 7/8	8	10	Cass Co., IN	Jay Stidham	Jay Stidham	2002	412
191 5/8	25 4/8	26	19 3/8	5 1/8	5 1/8	6	6	Todd Co., MN	MN Dept. of Natl. Resources	Picked Up	1994	414
191 4/8	26 7/8	27 1/8	23 4/8	6 2/8	6 2/8	7	6	Kingman Co., KS	Collins F. Kellogg, Sr.	Collins F. Kellogg, Sr.	2001	414
191 4/8	25 3/8	24 7/8	21 7/8	4 6/8	5	6	9	Red Willow Co., NE	Cody L. Ervin	Bud Max	PR1994	416
191 3/8	27	27 2/8	22 2/8	5 4/8	5 4/8	12	9	Crawford Co., WI	Mary Osterhaus	Mary Osterhaus	2001	416
191 3/8	22 6/8	23 4/8	18 2/8	5 3/8	5 3/8	7	6	Calhoun Co., IL	Eric D. Friedel	Eric D. Friedel	2002	416
191 2/8	24 6/8	24 2/8	17 3/8	4 6/8	4 3/8	11	10	Boone Co., IA	Paul Whitmore	Paul Whitmore	1980	419
191 2/8	24	24 2/8	20 1/8	5 2/8	4 7/8	13	8	Breckinridge Co., KY	Eddie Dutschke	Eddie Dutschke	2002	419
191 2/8	26 2/8	24	17	5 1/8	5 1/8	9	8	Meigs Co., OH	Kenneth A. Turley	Kenneth A. Turley	2002	419
191 2/8	26 5/8	28 1/8	25 7/8	5 2/8	5 2/8	9	9	Monmouth Co., NJ	William A. Brown	William A. Brown	2002	419
191 1/8	25 7/8	27 1/8	20 3/8	5 5/8	5 6/8	8	6	Vanderburgh Co., IN	Rodney J. Schutz	Rodney J. Schutz	2000	423
191	27 4/8	27 4/8	21	4 6/8	4 5/8	8	9	Warren Co., IN	Roger A. Parient, Jr.	Roger A. Parient, Jr.	2000	424
191	23 4/8	22 4/8	16 2/8	5	4 7/8	8	9	Holt Co., NE	Bruce E. Coburn	Bruce E. Coburn	2001	424
191	23 3/8	23 5/8	18	4 6/8	4 6/8	15	11	Tulsa Co., OK	Kelly G. Wendlandt	Kelly G. Wendlandt	2002	424
190 7/8	25 7/8	26 2/8	18 3/8	5 7/8	5 5/8	8	10	Parke Co., IN	Burk Collings	Burk Collings	2000	427
190 7/8	23 6/8	24 2/8	18	4 7/8	4 7/8	15	8	McDonald Co., MO	Clinton W. Helm	Clinton W. Helm	2002	427
190 6/8	24 2/8	21 7/8	15 5/8	5 2/8	5 2/8	12	11	Stony Plain, AB	Audrey F. Martin	Audrey F. Martin	2000	429
190 5/8	19 5/8	24 6/8	19 4/8	4 6/8	4 7/8	6	6	Jackson Co., IL	Heath R. Rushing	Heath R. Rushing	2001	430
190 5/8	26 5/8	27 1/8	22 1/8	4 7/8	4 6/8	7	7	Des Moines Co., IA	David F. Hackett	David F. Hackett	2002	430
190 5/8	28	27 3/8	21 3/8	5 3/8	5 3/8	9	9	Doniphan Co., KS	David P. Harrison	David P. Harrison	2002	430
190 4/8	26 2/8	22	14 2/8	5 1/8	5 2/8	18	13	Carter Co., OK	Walt Spradling	Walt Spradling	2001	433
190 3/8	19 2/8	23 5/8	18 1/8	4 6/8	4 5/8	11	11	Foster Co., ND	Brad A. Schulz	Brad A. Schulz	2001	434
190 3/8	22 1/8	21 2/8	17 2/8	5 1/8	5 1/8	7	9	Macon Co., IL	Matt E. Westbay	Matt E. Westbay	2002	434
190 1/8	21 5/8	25 5/8	20 6/8	4 7/8	5	8	10	Ranfurly, AB	Kevin C. Bertin	Kevin C. Bertin	1996	436
190 1/8	27 2/8	25 3/8	20 3/8	5 5/8	6 2/8	13	12	Fayette Co., IA	Timothy R. Cummings	Timothy R. Cummings	2002	436
190	25 4/8	24 5/8	14 3/8	6	6	8	9	Crittenden Co., AR	Warren H. Barry, Jr.	Warren H. Barry, Jr.	2000	438
190	24 6/8	21 3/8	17 4/8	4 4/8	4 3/8	10	9	Glendon, AB	Philip Kozak III	Philip Kozak III	2001	438
189 7/8	21 7/8	29 2/8	21 1/8	4 7/8	4 7/8	9	9	Warren Co., KY	James R. Devore	James R. Devore	2002	440
189 6/8	29 2/8	25 4/8	20 3/8	5 7/8	5 7/8	9	8	Woodford Co., IL	Gunnar R. Darnall	Gunnar R. Darnall	2001	441
189 6/8	25 4/8	23 7/8	15	4 5/8	4 5/8	7	8	Macon Co., MO	Greg P. Bruno	Greg P. Bruno	2001	441
189 5/8	24 7/8	23 7/8	17	6 3/8	6 5/8	7	9	Jackson Co., WI	Kevin L. Tegels	Kevin L. Tegels	2002	443

WHITETAIL DEER - NON-TYPICAL ANTLERS

Odocoileus virginianus virginianus and certain related subspecies

Score	Length of Main Beam R	L	Inside Spread	Circumference at Smallest Place Between Burr & First Point R	L	Number of Points R	L	Locality	Hunter	Owner	Date Killed	Rank
189 4/8	24 6/8	25 5/8	18 3/8	5 5/8	6 1/8	8	11	McDonough Co., IL	Les Twidwell	Les Twidwell	2001	444
189 3/8	24 6/8	25 3/8	19 4/8	5 3/8	5	8	7	Marion Co., KY	Picked Up	Dan Thompson	2000	445
189 3/8	20 6/8	21 1/8	15 1/8	4 5/8	4 2/8	17	6	Montague Co., TX	Chris R. Burns	Chris R. Burns	2001	445
189 2/8	24	24	16 5/8	4 2/8	4 3/8	8	8	Grant Co., KY	Gary W. Humphrey	Gary W. Humphrey	2002	447
189	27 7/8	28 2/8	22	5 5/8	5 6/8	8	8	Ogle Co., IL	Russell A. Young	Russell A. Young	2000	448
188 7/8	25 3/8	25 1/8	17 2/8	5 3/8	5 1/8	8	9	Elkhart Co., IN	Kenny H. Cowles	Kenny H. Cowles	2000	449
188 5/8	23 2/8	24 1/8	16 1/8	4 7/8	5	8	11	Todd Co., MN	H. & G. Tschida	Harold Tschida	1965	450
188 4/8	23 7/8	24 4/8	19 6/8	5	5 1/8	9	9	Fairfield Co., OH	Ronald A. Waits	Ronald A. Waits	2001	451
188 4/8	23 6/8	22 2/8	16	5 1/8	5 7/8	10	10	Pontotoc Co., MS	William T. Roberts	William T. Roberts	2001	451
188 3/8	22 6/8	23 5/8	15 6/8	5 5/8	5 1/8	11	9	Muhlenburg, KY	Kelly B. Richey	Kelly B. Richey	2000	453
188 3/8	23 1/8	23 2/8	17	4 6/8	4 7/8	7	11	Comanche Co., OK	John P. Sklaney, Jr.	John P. Sklaney, Jr.	2000	453
188 3/8	23 4/8	21 6/8	17 2/8	4 3/8	5	8	10	Sawyer Co., WI	James H. Tiffany	James H. Tiffany	2000	453
188 3/8	22 7/8	23 5/8	19	4 7/8	4 6/8	7	7	Benson Co., ND	Gerald J. Jaeger	Gerald J. Jaeger	2001	453
188 3/8	22 2/8	23 7/8	19	7 2/8	5 7/8	8	5	Ripley Co., IN	Dwayne E. Roth	Dwayne E. Roth	2002	453
188 2/8	23	22 3/8	15 1/8	4 3/8	4 2/8	8	8	Webb Co., TX	Ronnie D. Wolter	Ronnie D. Wolter	2000	458
188 2/8	23 1/8	21 5/8	17 4/8	6 2/8	6 7/8	9	8	Morgan Co., IL	Timothy P. Mason	Timothy P. Mason	2001	458
188 2/8	22 4/8	24	17 2/8	5 4/8	5 6/8	7	8	Hancock Co., IL	Larry E. Clark	Larry E. Clark	2002	458
188 1/8	26 3/8	26 6/8	17 7/8	5 2/8	5 2/8	8	10	King & Queen Co., VA	Gerald R. Collier, Jr.	Gerald R. Collier, Jr.	1997	461
188 1/8	23 6/8	23 3/8	16 5/8	4 6/8	4 4/8	12	10	St. Louis Co., MN	Leslie J. Soular	Leslie J. Soular	1999	461
188 1/8	23 1/8	23	23 4/8	5 4/8	5 4/8	8	7	La Salle Co., IL	James E. Giese	James E. Giese	2002	461
187 7/8	23 6/8	25 7/8	19 1/8	5 2/8	5 1/8	9	10	Washington Co., IN	R. Jeread Abner	R. Jeread Abner	2000	464
187 7/8	24 2/8	23 2/8	17 5/8	5	5 2/8	7	9	La Porte Co., IN	Daniel Hildreth	Daniel Hildreth	2000	464
187 7/8	22 2/8	23	16 2/8	4 7/8	4 4/8	12	11	Carbon Co., WY	John C. Heinrich, Jr.	John C. Heinrich, Jr.	2001	464
187 7/8	27	25 6/8	19 7/8	5	5 1/8	9	7	Warren Co., MO	Richard Buxton	Richard Buxton	2001	464
187 7/8	24 2/8	23 6/8	17 4/8	4 7/8	4 7/8	10	11	Cowley Co., KS	Hal S. Atkinson, Jr.	Hal S. Atkinson, Jr.	2001	464
187 6/8	23	24 2/8	18 1/8	5 6/8	5 6/8	8	9	Holmes Co., MS	Laurence H. Walker	Frank A. Eakin	1950	469
187 6/8	26	27	21 3/8	7 3/8	6 7/8	8	5	Peoria Co., IL	Stanley D. Hayes	Stanley D. Hayes	2000	469
187 6/8	24	25 4/8	22 6/8	5 6/8	5 2/8	8	6	Clayton Co., IA	Virgil High	Virgil High	2002	469
187 5/8	29 1/8	29 6/8	16 1/8	4 3/8	4 5/8	6	12	Grayson Co., KY	James E. Crick	James E. Crick	2000	472
187 4/8	23 5/8	23 2/8	27 5/8	6 3/8	5 2/8	14	6	Angus Brook, NS	Jim M. O'Keefe	Jim M. O'Keefe	2002	473
187 3/8	26	26 3/8	17 1/8	5	4 4/8	6	7	Custer Co., NE	Jerry D. Snitker	Jerry D. Snitker	1963	474
187 3/8	23 3/8	24 7/8	21 6/8	5 1/8	5 1/8	9	9	McKenzie Co., ND	James V. McKenzie	Kenneth H. McKenzie	1969	474
187 3/8	28	28 2/8	20 3/8	5 6/8	5 5/8	6	10	Adams Co., IL	Douglas J. Schutte	Douglas J. Schutte	1996	474

Score								Locality	Hunter	Owner	Date	Rank
187 3/8	24 6/8	25 5/8	21	5 1/8	4 5/8	8	10	Montgomery Co., IN	Gary W. Harrison	Gary W. Harrison	2000	474
187 3/8	26 3/8	24 5/8	15 4/8	5 2/8	5	7	10	Linn Co., IA	Charles E. Ganoe	Charles E. Ganoe	2000	474
187 3/8	22 3/8	22 4/8	15 5/8	5 3/8	5 1/8	9	12	Pawnee Co., NE	Scott W. Stehlik	Scott W. Stehlik	2002	474
187 3/8	29 1/8	26 2/8	23 1/8	4 6/8	4 6/8	8	6	Berkshire Co., MA	Peter J.M. Kiendzior	Peter J.M. Kiendzior	2002	474
187 2/8	24 4/8	24 6/8	17 3/8	5	5	8	8	Monroe Co., NY	William J. Lerkins	William J. Lerkins	2000	481
187 1/8	24 6/8	25 4/8	17 6/8	5 6/8	5 3/8	8	6	Pike Co., IL	Joseph Rizzo	Joseph Rizzo	2001	482
187 1/8	25 1/8	25 1/8	20 1/8	5 2/8	5	8	8	Kosciusko Co., IN	Edward E. Miller, Jr.	Edward E. Miller, Jr.	2001	482
187 1/8	23 2/8	21 6/8	15 5/8	4 4/8	4 4/8	11	11	Somervell Co., TX	Edwin E. Smith	Edwin E. Smith	2002	482
187 1/8	20 6/8	22 6/8	17 5/8	5	4 7/8	9	9	Koochiching Co., MN	Bill Hanson	Bill Hanson	2002	482
187	26 3/8	26 7/8	17 6/8	5 3/8	5 3/8	9	9	Jackson Co., WI	Jamie E. Peterson	Jamie E. Peterson	2000	486
186 7/8	26 1/8	27	19	5 4/8	5 3/8	10	7	Pawnee Co., KS	Gary J. Dechant	Gary J. Dechant	2000	487
186 6/8	25 2/8	26 6/8	18	6	6 1/8	11	13	Carter Co., KY	Alva R. King	Alva R. King	2000	488
186 6/8	24 7/8	23 7/8	23 4/8	4 3/8	4 2/8	8	10	Windham Co., CT	Theodore G. Decyk	Theodore G. Decyk	2002	488
186 5/8	26 5/8	28	22	4 4/8	4 5/8	7	7	Pike Co., OH	Randall S. Martin	Randall S. Martin	2002	488
186 4/8	19 3/8	22 4/8	18 4/8	5 1/8	5 2/8	12	10	Dillberry Lake, AB	William M. Ruttan	William M. Ruttan	2002	491
186 4/8	25 7/8	25 7/8	19 5/8	6 1/8	6 3/8	7	9	Livingston Co., KY	Justin Layne	Justin Layne	2002	491
186 4/8	26	25 5/8	15 6/8	7 5/8	6 5/8	8	8	Harvey Co., KS	Phil Yutzy	Picked Up	2002	491
186 3/8	27 2/8	26 3/8	20 7/8	5 4/8	5 6/8	5	11	Clinton Co., OH	Bryan S. Coffey	Bryan S. Coffey	2002	494
186 3/8	26 2/8	25 5/8	20 1/8	5	5	8	8	Rice Co., KS	Kevin Emmerich	Kevin Emmerich	2002	494
186 2/8	25 2/8	24 2/8	18 3/8	5	4 7/8	10	6	Shawano Co., WI	Nathan Morris	Nathan Morris	2000	496
186 2/8	24 2/8	25 3/8	19 2/8	5 2/8	5 1/8	8	11	Burt Co., NE	Leroy G. Townsend	Leroy G. Townsend	2001	496
186 1/8	25 6/8	24 6/8	18 7/8	4 6/8	4 6/8	11	9	Warren Co., KY	Stephen M. Young	Stephen M. Young	2000	498
186 1/8	24 6/8	25 2/8	18 6/8	5	5 3/8	7	7	Stratton, ON	Joseph K. Sharp	Joseph K. Sharp	2001	498
186	22	21 2/8	21 2/8	4 6/8	5 1/8	9	10	Logan Co., CO	Bucky D. Barber	Bucky D. Barber	2000	500
186	26 4/8	25 5/8	18 4/8	4 4/8	4 4/8	9	11	Bath Co., VA	Michael B. Renzi	Michael B. Renzi	2002	500
186	27 4/8	27 4/8	19 4/8	5 2/8	5 2/8	6	5	Wayne Co., MI	Kevin H. Olson	Kevin H. Olson	2002	500
185 7/8	26 7/8	26 2/8	18 6/8	5 2/8	5 2/8	6	6	Cook Co., IL	Timothy L. Harkness	Timothy L. Harkness	2000	503
185 7/8	21 1/8	22 7/8	16 7/8	5 6/8	5 7/8	8	10	Jones Co., GA	Victor Montford	Victor Montford	2002	503
185 6/8	30 3/8	26 2/8	21 3/8	4 5/8	4 6/8	6	7	Grayson Co., KY	Kermit W. Ayer	Kermit W. Ayer	2000	505
185 6/8	23 6/8	23 6/8	18	5 1/8	5 4/8	9	10	Sharp Co., KS	Witt Stephens, Jr.	Witt Stephens, Jr.	2001	505
185 6/8	23 6/8	19 6/8	18 4/8	5 4/8	5 2/8	8	8	Newton Lake, AB	John J. McKeown	John J. McKeown	2001	505
185 5/8	27	27 2/8	17 4/8	4 5/8	4 5/8	6	9	Stevens Co., WA	Robert E. Dudding	Robert E. Dudding	1991	508
185 4/8	26 5/8	26 4/8	17 1/8	3 7/8	4	10	9	Rowan Co., KY	Keith Dotson	Keith Dotson	2001	509
185 3/8	23 6/8	22 5/8	15	5 2/8	5 2/8	9	8	Billings Co., ND	Ray Brunsvold	Verna Brunsvold	1967	510
185 3/8	24 4/8	25 3/8	21 2/8	5 2/8	5 4/8	8	9	Oldman Lake, AB	Allen T. Carstairs	Allen T. Carstairs	2000	510
185 3/8	26 7/8	23	15 6/8	7 2/8	8	8	10	McPherson Co., KS	Harvey D. Hagen	Harvey D. Hagen	2000	510
185 2/8	21 5/8	21 2/8	19 2/8	4 2/8	4 5/8	8	5	Palo Pinto Co., TX	Michael L. Baze	Michael L. Baze	2001	513
185 2/8	25	24 2/8	21 1/8	4 4/8	4 5/8	5	9	Charron Lake, AB	Glenn Duigou	Glenn Duigou	2001	513
185 2/8	26 6/8	26 6/8	18 2/8	4 6/8	5 5/8	7	9	Bedford Co., VA	Randy G. Patterson	Picked Up	2002	513
185 2/8	25 6/8	25 5/8	18 1/8	5 4/8	5 4/8	9	9	Allen Co., KY	Dewayne Cheek	Dewayne Cheek	2002	513
185 1/8	26 1/8	26 4/8	17 3/8	4 6/8	4 6/8	8	9	St. Francois Co., MO	Timothy R. Williams	Timothy R. Williams	1996	517

WHITETAIL DEER - NON-TYPICAL ANTLERS

Odocoileus virginianus virginianus and certain related subspecies

Score	Length of Main Beam R.	L.	Inside Spread	Circumference at Smallest Place Between Burr & First Point R.	L.	Number of Points R.	L.	Locality	Hunter	Owner	Date Killed	Rank
185 1/8	24 5/8	24 1/8	17 3/8	4 4/8	4 5/8	6	8	Phillips Co., MT	Kipp Sjostrom	Kipp Sjostrom	2000	517
185 1/8	22 5/8	22 3/8	18 7/8	4 5/8	4 4/8	8	8	Kent Co., MD	Ralph Fleegle	Ralph Fleegle	2001	517
185	22 4/8	22 1/8	25	5 2/8	5	11	8	Long Lake, AB	Bryan D. Hill	Bryan D. Hill	2000	520
185	24 6/8	23 1/8	16	5 3/8	5 3/8	6	13	Webster Co., NE	Leonard D. Delka	Leonard D. Delka	2000	520
185	25 1/8	25 5/8	17 1/8	4 7/8	4 7/8	9	12	Christian Co., KY	John Blakeley	John Blakeley	2001	520
185	24 3/8	23 2/8	20 1/8	4 4/8	4 4/8	7	10	Lincoln Co., WI	Ryan K. Stebnitz	Ryan K. Stebnitz	2001	520
185	25 3/8	24 6/8	22 6/8	4 6/8	4 7/8	6	7	Winneshiek Co., IA	Craig M. Eggert	Craig M. Eggert	2001	520
185	24 5/8	25	22 1/8	5 5/8	5 6/8	8	7	Marion Co., IN	Jason S. Losee	Jason S. Losee	2001	520
185	20 6/8	19 5/8	14 5/8	5	5 2/8	9	11	Dubuque Co., IA	Tyler J. Vorwald	Tyler J. Vorwald	2002	520
185	23 3/8	24 1/8	17 4/8	6	5 7/8	7	8	Warrick Co., IN	James S. Drake	James S. Drake	2002	520
251 2/8*	27 2/8	27 5/8	22 1/8	6 3/8	6 5/8	10	13	Lorain Co., OH	Kirk W. Gott	Kirk W. Gott	2000	520

* Final score subject to revision by additional verifying measurements.

COUES' WHITETAIL DEER - TYPICAL ANTLERS

Minimum Score 100

World's Record 144 1/8

Odocoileus virginianus couesi

Score	Length of Main Beam R.	L.	Inside Spread	Circumference at Smallest Place Between Burr & First Point R.	L.	Number of Points R.	L.	Locality	Hunter	Owner	Date Killed	Rank
128 3/8	20 1/8	20 3/8	16 7/8	4 1/8	4 1/8	5	5	Sonora, MX	Picked Up	Kirk Kelso	2002	1
127 4/8	19 5/8	20 3/8	12 6/8	3 6/8	4	6	5	Sonora, MX	Picked Up	Kirk Kelso	PR2003	2
125	19 6/8	19 5/8	15 4/8	4 1/8	4 3/8	7	6	Graham Co., AZ	Bradley Johns	Bradley Johns	2000	3
124 7/8	20 6/8	20 5/8	14 3/8	4 3/8	4 3/8	5	4	Santa Cruz Co., AZ	Kirk Kelso	Kirk Kelso	2001	4
123 6/8	19 7/8	19 6/8	14 4/8	3 7/8	3 7/8	5	4	Sonora, MX	William J. Mills	William J. Mills	2002	5
123 3/8	20 2/8	20 5/8	16 1/8	4	4	4	4	Pima Co., AZ	Picked Up	Brian A. Rimsza	2002	6
121 3/8	21	20	15 3/8	4 2/8	4 3/8	4	4	Sonora, MX	Picked Up	Kirk Kelso	2003	7
121	20 6/8	20 7/8	16	4	3 7/8	4	4	Sonora, MX	Picked Up	Kirk Kelso	2003	8
120	18 5/8	17 7/8	14 2/8	4 2/8	4 1/8	4	4	Sonora, MX	Picked Up	Kirk Kelso	2000	9
116 6/8	19 2/8	17 7/8	14 2/8	4 2/8	3 7/8	4	4	Sonora, MX	Len H. Guldman	Len H. Guldman	2003	10
115 6/8	20	19 5/8	16	4	3 7/8	4	6	Sonora, MX	Richard G. Bailey	Richard G. Bailey	2003	11
115 4/8	21 3/8	22 4/8	18	4	4	4	3	Sonora, MX	Picked Up	Kirk Kelso	2003	12
114	18 5/8	18 3/8	13	3 5/8	3 4/8	4	5	Pima Co., AZ	Jeffrey K. Volk	Michael E. Duperret	2001	13
113 7/8	18 1/8	17 7/8	12 1/8	4 2/8	4 2/8	6	5	Sonora, MX	Craig T. Boddington	Craig T. Boddington	2000	14
113 5/8	19	19	14 7/8	3 5/8	3 6/8	4	4	Socorro Co., NM	Gerad Montoya	Gerad Montoya	1999	15
113 2/8	19 5/8	19 3/8	14 6/8	3 7/8	3 7/8	4	4	Sonora, MX	Brian K. Murray	Brian K. Murray	2001	16
113 2/8	17 4/8	17 5/8	12 2/8	3 7/8	3 6/8	5	5	Sonora, MX	Betsy S. Grainger	Betsy S. Grainger	2001	16
113	18 2/8	18 3/8	11 4/8	4 3/8	4 3/8	4	5	Pima Co., AZ	Frank C. Benvenuto	Frank C. Benvenuto	1967	18
112 5/8	17 7/8	18 2/8	10 3/8	4 1/8	4 1/8	4	5	Sonora, MX	Michael C. Cupell	Michael C. Cupell	2000	19
112 4/8	17 2/8	16 7/8	13 6/8	4 1/8	4 1/8	4	5	Sonora, MX	Kirk Kelso	Kirk Kelso	2001	20
112 3/8	17 3/8	16 3/8	12 3/8	3 4/8	3 6/8	5	5	Sonora, MX	Michael M. Golightly	Michael M. Golightly	2001	21
112 1/8	18 6/8	19	13 6/8	3 6/8	3 6/8	4	5	Sonora, MX	Kerry L. Mailloux	Kerry L. Mailloux	1996	22
112	19 1/8	19 3/8	16 5/8	4 1/8	4	5	6	Grant Co., NM	Charles Arendt	Bud Arendt	1924	23
111 6/8	19 2/8	19 6/8	11 4/8	3 7/8	3 7/8	4	5	Sonora, MX	Lynn H. Stinson	Lynn H. Stinson	2000	24
111 1/8	18 5/8	18 4/8	14 2/8	4	4	5	4	Sonora, MX	David J. Lechel	David J. Lechel	2001	25
110 6/8	17	17	12 6/8	3 3/8	3 3/8	5	5	Santa Cruz Co., AZ	Andrew M. Lopez	Andrew M. Lopez	2000	26
110 6/8	17 2/8	17 2/8	13 4/8	4	4 1/8	4	4	Sonora, MX	Travis J. Adams	Travis J. Adams	2001	26
110 6/8	16	15 6/8	11	3 4/8	3 5/8	5	6	Sonora, MX	Joe McDowell	Joe McDowell	2003	26
110 5/8	19 5/8	19 2/8	16 1/8	3 7/8	4	4	4	Pinal Co., AZ	Chuck Adams	Chuck Adams	1989	29
110 4/8	17 2/8	17 2/8	13 6/8	3 5/8	3 6/8	4	4	Sonora, MX	Lynn H. Stinson	Lynn H. Stinson	2001	30
110 3/8	18 4/8	18 7/8	13 5/8	3 3/8	3 4/8	4	4	Santa Cruz Co., AZ	Benjamin H. Richardson	Benjamin H. Richardson	2000	31
110 2/8	15	16 7/8	13 6/8	4	4	5	5	Pima Co., AZ	Kurt J. Kreutz	Kurt J. Kreutz	2000	32
110 1/8	16 6/8	18 4/8	13 5/8	4	4	5	5	Sonora, MX	Picked Up	Kirk Kelso	2003	33

COUES' WHITETAIL DEER - TYPICAL ANTLERS

Odocoileus virginianus couesi

Score	Length of Main Beam R.	L.	Inside Spread	Circumference at Smallest Place Between Burr & First Point R.	L.	Number of Points R.	L.	Locality	Hunter	Owner	Date Killed	Rank
108 5/8	17 5/8	18 4/8	13 7/8	3 5/8	3 5/8	4	4	Sonora, MX	Michael D. Moore	Michael D. Moore	2002	34
108 4/8	17 4/8	16 3/8	13 4/8	4 1/8	4	4	4	Sonora, MX	Picked Up	Kirk Kelso	1999	35
108 3/8	19 1/8	19 1/8	15 3/8	3 7/8	3 7/8	4	4	Sonora, MX	Mark D. Nuessle	Mark D. Nuessle	2003	36
107 4/8	16 2/8	15 6/8	14 6/8	3 4/8	3 3/8	5	5	Sonora, MX	Peter W. Spear	Peter W. Spear	2000	37
106 4/8	16 2/8	16 5/8	12	3 7/8	3 7/8	4	5	Chihuahua, MX	Richard M. Young	Richard M. Young	2001	38
106 3/8	16 1/8	15 4/8	13 1/8	3 7/8	3 6/8	5	5	Sonora, MX	Michael J. Hoppis	Michael J. Hoppis	2002	39
105 5/8	17 4/8	17 4/8	16 1/8	4 1/8	4 2/8	4	5	Pima Co., AZ	Frank C. Benvenuto	Frank C. Benvenuto	1971	40
105 5/8	16 4/8	16 4/8	14 7/8	4	4 2/8	5	5	Gila Co., AZ	Jack R. Cook	Jack R. Cook	1993	40
105 1/8	18 4/8	18 4/8	14 1/8	3 4/8	3 4/8	4	5	Sonora, MX	Jerry D. Dye	Jerry D. Dye	2003	42
104 5/8	17 2/8	17 5/8	12 3/8	3 6/8	3 6/8	4	4	Chihuahua, MX	Louie I. Venturacci	Louie I. Venturacci	2000	43
104 5/8	17	17 3/8	11 3/8	3 7/8	3 6/8	4	4	Sonora, MX	Brent W. Bunger	Brent W. Bunger	2003	43
104 3/8	18	17 4/8	13 1/8	3 5/8	3 5/8	4	4	Sonora, MX	Kirk Kelso	Kirk Kelso	2002	45
104	17 3/8	17 2/8	16 4/8	3 6/8	4	4	4	Sonora, MX	Jon R. Reardon	Jon R. Reardon	2002	46
103 3/8	18 3/8	17 7/8	12 7/8	3 6/8	3 5/8	4	4	Sonora, MX	Scott S. Snyder	Scott S. Snyder	2001	47
103 2/8	17 4/8	17 7/8	15 6/8	3 4/8	3 5/8	5	4	Pima Co., AZ	Kirk Kelso	Kirk Kelso	1997	48
102 7/8	17 7/8	17 7/8	13 7/8	3 6/8	3 6/8	4	4	Pima Co., AZ	Kirk Kelso	Kirk Kelso	1994	49
102 1/8	16 4/8	17 3/8	14 1/8	4 4/8	4 4/8	5	5	Sonora, MX	Kirk Kelso	Kirk Kelso	2002	50
101 7/8	17 2/8	16 5/8	14 5/8	4 1/8	4 2/8	4	5	Pima Co., AZ	Kirk Kelso	Kirk Kelso	1992	51
101 7/8	16 6/8	17	12 3/8	3 6/8	3 4/8	4	5	Sonora, MX	Kirk Kelso	Kirk Kelso	2000	51
101 5/8	16 6/8	17	15 3/8	3 5/8	3 4/8	5	6	Sonora, MX	Kirk Kelso	Kirk Kelso	2002	53
101 4/8	19 1/8	17 4/8	13	4 2/8	4	4	4	Gila Co., AZ	Jack R. Cook	Jack R. Cook	1994	54
100 5/8	17 6/8	17 1/8	16 1/8	3 2/8	3 1/8	4	4	Sonora, MX	George F. Daum	George F. Daum	2000	55
100 5/8	17	17 4/8	15 3/8	3 7/8	4	3	4	Sonora, MX	Gary L. Barneson	Gary L. Barneson	2001	55
100 4/8	19	17 7/8	16	3 4/8	3 4/8	5	5	Chihuahua, MX	T.R. White	T.R. White	2002	57
100 3/8	17 6/8	17 7/8	12 3/8	3 5/8	3 4/8	4	4	Sonora, MX	Kirk Kelso	Kirk Kelso	1998	58
100 1/8	17 2/8	18	13 7/8	4	4	4	4	Pima Co., AZ	Frank C. Benvenuto	Frank C. Benvenuto	1959	59
132 7/8*	20 5/8	20 7/8	15 3/8	4	4	5	6	Santa Cruz Co., AZ	Sergio Orozco	Sergio Orozco	2001	

* Final score subject to revision by additional verifying measurements.

COUES' WHITETAIL DEER - NON-TYPICAL ANTLERS

Minimum Score 105

Odocoileus virginianus couesi

New World's Record 196 2/8

Score	Length of Main Beam R.	L.	Inside Spread	Circumference at Smallest Place Between Burr & First Point R.	L.	Number of Points R.	L.	Locality	Hunter	Owner	Date Killed	Rank
196 2/8	20 4/8	19 3/8	12 3/8	4 6/8	4 6/8	11	15	Graham Co., AZ	Native American	D.J. Hollinger & B. Howard	PR1971	1
141	21 6/8	22	15 3/8	4 6/8	4 5/8	5	6	Sonora, MX	Picked Up	Jorge Camou	2001	2
138 5/8	16 6/8	16 6/8	11 5/8	4 3/8	4 3/8	9	6	Sonora, MX	Glenn Hall	Glenn Hall	2000	3
133 4/8	19 4/8	19 5/8	15 3/8	3 2/8	3 3/8	5	7	Sonora, MX	Picked Up	Kirk Kelso	2002	4
129 7/8	20 6/8	20 5/8	17 3/8	4	4	5	7	Apache Co., AZ	Picked Up	Donald H. McBride	1999	5
127 7/8	20 2/8	20 2/8	15 4/8	4 1/8	4	5	8	Grant Co., NM	Unknown	Mike W. Leonard	PR1960	6
126 2/8	17	16 3/8	15 6/8	4 2/8	5	6	8	Graham Co., AZ	Steve T. Letcher	Steve T. Letcher	2001	7
124 2/8	17 1/8	17	15 5/8	5 5/8	5 2/8	8	7	Gila Co., AZ	Denny L. Hunsaker	Denny L. Hunsaker	1997	8
123 1/8	16 6/8	18 5/8	14 3/8	4	4	7	6	Pima Co., AZ	Doug Field	Doug Field	2001	9
122 4/8	19 1/8	18	15 2/8	4	3 7/8	7	7	Sonora, MX	Michael L. Braegelmann	Michael L. Braegelmann	2002	10
121 5/8	17 2/8	16 1/8	15 2/8	4 2/8	4 3/8	8	7	Graham Co., AZ	Stuart Hancock	Stuart Hancock	2001	11
121 1/8	19	19 2/8	13	3 3/8	3 3/8	7	8	Sonora, MX	Michael L. Braegelmann	Michael L. Braegelmann	2000	12
120	17 2/8	17 4/8	13 7/8	3 5/8	3 5/8	6	5	Sonora, MX	William A. Keebler	William A. Keebler	2001	13
117 4/8	17 4/8	18 5/8	15 4/8	4 3/8	4 3/8	6	6	Chihuahua, MX	William G. Farley	William G. Farley	2002	14
116 1/8	20 3/8	19 3/8	12 7/8	3 3/8	3 5/8	8	5	Pima Co., AZ	Thomas Bowman	Thomas Bowman	2002	15
154 1/8*	15 6/8	15 6/8	15 6/8	4 1/8	4 2/8	7	7	Sonora, MX	Picked Up	Jorge Camou	2001	
152 *	20 2/8	20	17 4/8	4 4/8	4 4/8	8	8	Graham Co., AZ	Picked Up	Mike Sullivan	1971	

* Final score subject to revision by additional verifying measurements.

CANADA MOOSE

Alces alces americana and *Alces alces andersoni*

Minimum Score 185

World's Record 242

Canada moose includes trophies from Newfoundland and Canada (except for Yukon Territory and Northwest Territories), Maine, Minnesota, New Hampshire, North Dakota, and Vermont.

Score	Greatest Spread	Length of Palm R.	L.	Width of Palm R.	L.	Circumference of Beam at Smallest Place R.	L.	Number of Normal Points R.	L.	Locality	Hunter	Owner	Date Killed	Rank
240 6/8	63 4/8	48 7/8	47 2/8	18	19 4/8	7 7/8	8	16	16	Kinaskan Lake, BC	Doug E. Frank	Doug E. Frank	2002	1
220 3/8	61 3/8	43 7/8	43 4/8	14 4/8	17 3/8	7 4/8	8 1/8	16	14	Hancock Co., ME	James T. Robertson	James T. Robertson	2002	2
217 5/8	64 3/8	44 3/8	42 7/8	16 3/8	15 4/8	7 6/8	7 2/8	11	16	Buffalo River, AB	Abe Teichroeb	Abe Teichroeb	2001	3
213	61 4/8	40 1/8	41	14	13 2/8	8 3/8	8 3/8	14	14	Thunder Bay, ON	Claude R. Vincent	Claude R. Vincent	2001	4
211 4/8	60 2/8	39 6/8	40 6/8	18 5/8	14 5/8	7 5/8	7 2/8	14	16	Ptarmigan Lake, BC	Jack W. Ahart, Sr.	Jack W. Ahart, Sr.	2002	5
210 7/8	60 1/8	40 2/8	44 2/8	15 7/8	14 6/8	7 6/8	7 3/8	15	13	Clova, QC	R. Theriault & J.P. Lavoie	R. Theriault & J.P. Lavoie	2002	6
210 6/8	61	43 3/8	43	14 6/8	14 6/8	7 2/8	7 1/8	10	11	Toad River, BC	Jerry D. Bechard	Jerry D. Bechard	2001	7
209 5/8	58 1/8	42 3/8	43 6/8	14 5/8	14 4/8	7 7/8	8	11	11	Dover River, AB	Allan M. Fenerty	Allan M. Fenerty	2001	8
209 4/8	57	41 2/8	40 4/8	14 6/8	13 6/8	7	7 1/8	15	16	Hayes Peak, BC	Richard Kling	Richard Kling	2000	9
208	62	40 6/8	43	12 3/8	12	6 2/8	6 2/8	14	15	Thorhild, AB	Ross F. Lyons	Ross F. Lyons	2001	10
207	53 4/8	41	40 4/8	15 4/8	16 4/8	6 6/8	6 7/8	14	16	Tabor Lake, BC	Carolynn Quamme	Carolynn Quamme	2000	11
206	61 2/8	42	38 5/8	13 2/8	16 1/8	8 5/8	8 4/8	13	12	Oxford Co., ME	Gerard L. Roy	Gerard L. Roy	2000	12
205 2/8	60	41	42 4/8	13 3/8	13 4/8	7 2/8	7 3/8	11	12	Charlie Lake, BC	Thomas C. Bieberle	Thomas C. Bieberle	2001	13
204 7/8	59 1/8	42	42 4/8	14 5/8	14 4/8	6 7/8	6 7/8	10	12	Thorpe Creek, BC	Gary W. Cunningham	Gary W. Cunningham	2001	14
204 6/8	64	38 3/8	38 6/8	14 2/8	14	8 2/8	8	12	12	Aroostook Co., ME	Michael G. Mele	Michael G. Mele	2003	15
203 7/8	58 1/8	37 2/8	39 1/8	13 6/8	14	8	7 7/8	15	14	Glundebery Creek, BC	Ronald K. Pettit	Ronald K. Pettit	2003	16
203 6/8	63 2/8	41	40 5/8	13	12 5/8	7 1/8	7	10	11	Muskwa River, BC	Martin W. Lowe	Martin W. Lowe	2001	17
203 4/8	56 4/8	42	41 6/8	16 1/8	14	7 6/8	8	13	10	Otter Lake, BC	Melissa J. Lawrence	Melissa J. Lawrence	2001	18
203 2/8	54	40 2/8	41 1/8	15 4/8	15 4/8	8 2/8	7 7/8	12	11	Halfway River, BC	Dan P. Adams	Dan P. Adams	2002	19
202 6/8	58 2/8	41 2/8	38 4/8	15	16 7/8	8	7 6/8	11	13	Tommy Lakes, BC	David G. Clary	David G. Clary	2001	20
202 2/8	53	44 5/8	46 3/8	11 6/8	12 4/8	7 2/8	7 2/8	11	15	Mitch Lake, AB	John Maryanski	John Maryanski	2001	21
202 2/8	54 2/8	40 1/8	44 7/8	12	12 3/8	7 7/8	8	14	14	Milo Lake, BC	Lisa K. Allen	Lisa K. Allen	2001	21
202	54 4/8	39 7/8	41 1/8	16	15 1/8	7 2/8	7 2/8	12	12	Dease Lake, BC	Dan Franzen	Dan Franzen	2003	23
201 4/8	55	40 5/8	43 6/8	12 4/8	14	7 1/8	7 3/8	13	15	Coos Co., NH	Ricky A. Matulaitis	Ricky A. Matulaitis	1997	24
201 3/8	52 1/8	43 6/8	44 3/8	13 2/8	15 6/8	7 5/8	7 6/8	10	10	Peace River, AB	Kenneth R. Gray	Kenneth R. Gray	2001	25
201 1/8	60 5/8	38	40	13 1/8	14 1/8	7 3/8	7 1/8	13	12	Porcupine Forest, SK	Ted Yuzek	Robert Yuzek	1967	26
201	54 2/8	38 1/8	36 3/8	17 3/8	17 2/8	7 6/8	8	13	15	Aroostook Co., ME	Mark P. Olson	Mark P. Olson	2000	27
201	60 6/8	38 4/8	43	12 6/8	15 6/8	6 7/8	7 1/8	12	12	Wolverine River, AB	Arlan C. Castner	Arlan C. Castner	2000	27
200 6/8	55 6/8	39 4/8	38 7/8	13 2/8	13 7/8	7 3/8	7 4/8	13	14	Cassiar Mts., BC	Gale B. Miller	Gale B. Miller	2000	29
200 6/8	61 4/8	37 5/8	37 4/8	12 7/8	14 3/8	7 2/8	7 7/8	12	14	Franklin Co., ME	Adam Tibbetts	Adam Tibbetts	2002	29

Score										Locality	Owner	Hunter	Date	Rank
200 3/8	53 1/8	38 4/8	38 6/8	13 7/8	13 4/8	7 5/8	7 5/8	16	14	Buffalo River, AB	Alan M. Jesse	Alan M. Jesse	2001	31
196 5/8	57 6/8	38 7/8	37 3/8	13 3/8	13 3/8	7 2/8	7 2/8	13	16	Bear Creek, BC	L. Scot Jenkins	L. Scot Jenkins	1997	32
195 6/8	56 3/8	41 6/8	40 7/8	13 3/8	14 5/8	7 4/8	7 3/8	10	10	Sawn Lake, AB	Dean V. Manz	Dean V. Manz	2003	33
194 4/8	61 6/8	35 7/8	38 3/8	11 7/8	11 3/8	7 6/8	7 5/8	14	14	Tutsingale Mt., BC	Keith Frederiksen	Keith Frederiksen	2001	34
192 6/8	55	37 6/8	36 4/8	14 6/8	14 6/8	6 7/8	7	15	14	McGraw Brook, NB	David A. McCrea	David A. McCrea	2000	35
185 5/8	47 7/8	40 4/8	39 6/8	13 4/8	13 2/8	7 3/8	7 5/8	16	15	Scoop Lake, BC	Donnie Moffat	Donnie Moffat	2001	36
185 5/8	58 5/8	40 6/8	36 4/8	16 2/8	18 2/8	7 4/8	7 2/8	10	12	Penobscot Co., ME	James B. Crowley	James B. Crowley	2001	36
183 3/8	57 3/8	43 4/8	42 3/8	12	10 6/8	8	7 3/8	10	11	Aroostook Co., ME	George A. Pickel	George A. Pickel	1999	38
181 1/8	63 5/8	40 4/8	41 6/8	15	13 1/8	7 1/8	7 3/8	7	10	Windsor Co., VT	Eli Holmquist	Picked Up	2001	39
181 1/8	57 3/8	44 4/8	38 2/8	12 5/8	12 5/8	6 4/8	6 5/8	13	13	Dease Lake, BC	Andres Garza-Tijerina	Andres Garza-Tijerina	2001	39
177 7/8	58 1/8	45	42 3/8	16	12 5/8	6 7/8	6 7/8	15	8	Jennings River, BC	Dean L. Rehbein	Dean L. Rehbein	2003	41
175 5/8	67 1/8	39	36	10 5/8	10 7/8	7 5/8	8	11	12	Smuts Lake, ON	Ronald S. Regan	Ronald S. Regan	1981	42
174 4/8	58	37 3/8	41 1/8	13 2/8	13 2/8	7 5/8	7 1/8	12	13	Porcupine Mts., MB	Sidney G. Humphries	Sidney G. Humphries	2001	43
174 4/8	62 2/8	40 3/8	42	9 4/8	12 4/8	6 6/8	6 6/8	11	11	Gnat Creek, BC	Jody J. Marcks	Jody J. Marcks	2003	43
197	51 2/8	41 3/8	40 5/8	14 6/8	12 4/8	7 5/8	7 4/8	7	9	Level Mt. Range, BC	Thomas R. Conrardy	Thomas R. Conrardy	2000	45
165 5/8	61 5/8	42 6/8	36 6/8	14 6/8	13 1/8	7 5/8	7 5/8	13	10	Piscataquis Co., ME	Dieter Tiarks	Dieter Tiarks	2002	45
163 3/8	52 7/8	41 2/8	41 2/8	13 1/8	13 1/8	7 2/8	7 2/8	9	10	Aroostook Co., ME	Marcie M. Shoulders	Marcie M. Shoulders	2002	47
163 3/8	51 3/8	42 1/8	41 2/8	14 2/8	15 2/8	7 2/8	7 5/8	10	10	Ft. McMurray, AB	Bruce A. Friedel	Bruce A. Friedel	2001	48
162 2/8	57	40 3/8	41 2/8	14 4/8	14 4/8	7 6/8	7 5/8	12	10	Somerset Co., ME	Jared Mitchell	Jared Mitchell	2001	48
157	46 6/8	37 5/8	38 7/8	13 6/8	14 5/8	7 2/8	7 3/8	13	11	French Creek, BC	Wes Peters	Wes Peters	1999	50
156 5/8	59 4/8	44	44	11 6/8	11 6/8	7 6/8	7 6/8	6	7	Nipigon Bay, ON	David L. Keith	David L. Keith	2002	51
152 2/8	51 2/8	36	37 3/8	13 2/8	12 7/8	7 3/8	7 2/8	12	12	Deadwood Lake, BC	J. George Williams	J. George Williams	2003	52
152 2/8	63	43	38 4/8	13 3/8	13 5/8	8 1/8	8 6/8	12	14	Wapiti River, AB	Kevin D. Wojciechowski	Kevin D. Wojciechowski	2001	53
194 2/8	35 1/8	32	12 6/8	13 4/8	7 4/8	7 3/8	14	14	13	Penobscot Co., ME	Kati J. Deane	Kati J. Deane	2001	53
193 6/8	37 4/8	37 2/8	11 2/8	10 2/8	6 4/8	6 4/8	13	13		Ghost Lake, AB	Norman P. Charchun	Norman P. Charchun	2000	55
193 2/8	38 6/8	38 5/8	12 5/8	12 6/8	7 4/8	7 4/8	10	11		Thoradson Creek, AB	Derwin W. Doll	Derwin W. Doll	2001	56
193 1/8	36 6/8	37 4/8	12 6/8	12 4/8	7 1/8	7	14	12		Halfway Creek, BC	John G. Williams	John G. Williams	2003	57
192 7/8	38 2/8	40 2/8	12 6/8	13 7/8	6 5/8	6 5/8	13	10		Cry Lake, BC	Troy D. Larson	Troy D. Larson	2003	58
191 6/8	38 1/8	36 2/8	13 6/8	12 3/8	7 7/8	7 7/8	14	16		Franklin Co., ME	Delmont L. Ward	Delmont L. Ward	2002	59
191 5/8	39 2/8	39 6/8	13 1/8	13 1/8	7 7/8	7 7/8	10	11		Oxford Co., ME	D.A. Sasse & J.R. Sheets	D.A. Sasse & J.R. Sheets	2001	60
191 5/8	38	40 2/8	13 2/8	12 2/8	6 6/8	6 4/8	9	13		Rancheria River, BC	Remo Pizzagalli	Remo Pizzagalli	2002	61
191	36 4/8	36 6/8	12	12 1/8	6 4/8	6 3/8	13	12		Mt. Meehaus, BC	Edward A. Petersen	Edward A. Petersen	2001	61
190 7/8	38 6/8	35 4/8	12	11	6 4/8	6 4/8	17	13		Mt. Farnsworth, BC	Ronald L. Smits	Ronald L. Smits	2001	63
190 4/8	42	40 1/8	12 3/8	10 6/8	7 2/8	7 3/8	10	12		Toad River, BC	Bob C. Strahan	Bob C. Strahan	2001	64
189 5/8	36 1/8	39 2/8	11 1/8	11 4/8	7 4/8	7 2/8	14	12		Aroostook Co., ME	Lavern C. Holden	Lavern C. Holden	2000	65
189 5/8	36	37 4/8	13	14 4/8	7 5/8	7 4/8	12	13		Line Lake, BC	Frank A. Villa	Frank A. Villa	2001	66
189 3/8	39 3/8	39	9 5/8	10 6/8	7 5/8	7 5/8	9	11		Kawdy Plateau, BC	Thomas P. Powers	Thomas P. Powers	2003	66
188 7/8	39 5/8	39 4/8	10 7/8	14 6/8	7 6/8	7 7/8	10	12		Stuart Lake, BC	Allyn T. Kerr	Allyn T. Kerr	2003	68
188 6/8	40 4/8	40 1/8	9	9 2/8	7 6/8	7 6/8	14	12		Ames Creek, BC	Jessica Novak	Jessica Novak	2001	69
188 1/8	33 3/8	35 4/8	13 6/8	14 3/8	7 3/8	7 2/8	11	12		Aroostook Co., ME	Leonide G. Daigle	Leonide G. Daigle	2001	70
186 6/8	41 7/8	38	10 1/8	11 1/8	7	7 2/8	13	9		Pelican Mt., AB	Steve P. Rosychuk	Steve P. Rosychuk	2000	71

CANADA MOOSE

Alces alces americana and *Alces alces andersoni*

Score	Greatest Spread	Length of Palm R.	L.	Width of Palm R.	L.	Circumference of Beam at Smallest Place R.	L.	Number of Normal Points R.	L.	Locality	Hunter	Owner	Date Killed	Rank
185 5/8	62 7/8	37	37	10 6/8	12	7 1/8	7 3/8	8	9	Essex Co., VT	Cassandra E. Hamwey	Cassandra E. Hamwey	2003	72
184 4/8	60	37 6/8	40 3/8	13 6/8	12 4/8	7	7 1/8	11	7	Coos Co., NH	Brent D. Bouchard	Brent D. Bouchard	2001	73
181 1/8	47 7/8	39 3/8	40 4/8	11 3/8	15	7 5/8	7 3/8	12	12	Tahoots Creek, BC	Ronald D. Zelewski	Ronald D. Zelewski	2001	74
176 7/8	55 2/8	38 6/8	37 3/8	15 1/8	15	6 7/8	7	7	11	Cody Creek, BC	Charles W. Mace	Charles W. Mace	2001	75
176 6/8	45 4/8	38 4/8	34 3/8	15 4/8	14	8 6/8	8 7/8	14	14	Inzana Lake, BC	R. Carson Hyndman	R. Carson Hyndman	2002	75
176 6/8	55 2/8	37 2/8	35 2/8	13 5/8	14 2/8	7 4/8	7 3/8	10	10	Murray River, BC	Loren Alm	Loren Alm	2003	75
173 7/8	55 7/8	41 2/8	37	12 2/8	15	7 4/8	7 5/8	9	14	Lake Co., MN	Robert C. Nielsen	Robert C. Nielsen	2002	78
172 7/8	54 6/8	36 4/8	36 1/8	13	11 3/8	7 7/8	7 6/8	11	11	Liard River, BC	Gary J. Swoboda	Gary J. Swoboda	1998	79
172 7/8	57	38 3/8	37 5/8	14 4/8	11 4/8	7 5/8	7 4/8	15	10	French Range, BC	Fred J. Hansen	Fred J. Hansen	2002	79
167 7/8	59 5/8	36 4/8	40 3/8	12 3/8	11	7 1/8	7 2/8	11	9	Coos Co., NH	Picked Up	Lionel Dalton	2000	81
186	52 4/8	36 4/8	37	12	11 7/8	7 4/8	7 3/8	11	11	Oxford Co., ME	Steven L. Pelletier	Steven L. Pelletier	2001	82
157 7/8	50 5/8	38 5/8	38 4/8	13 4/8	13 6/8	7 6/8	7 5/8	8	8	Tuya River, BC	Bradley R. Jackle	Bradley R. Jackle	2003	83
155 5/8	65 5/8	36 3/8	38 2/8	11 4/8	9 5/8	6	6 1/8	8	9	Wainwright, AB	Aldo B. Zanon	Aldo B. Zanon	2001	84
152 2/8	50 2/8	37 3/8	41 2/8	12 4/8	12 5/8	6 5/8	6 7/8	11	15	Fish Lake, BC	Fabrizio Weber	Fabrizio Weber	2000	85
152 2/8	54 2/8	38 4/8	37	11 6/8	11 4/8	7	7	10	13	Hyland Lake, BC	Ron Morton	Ron Morton	2002	85
152 2/8	59	36 7/8	40 5/8	12	14 1/8	7 2/8	7 2/8	7	10	Parton River, BC	Richard E. Day	Richard E. Day	2002	85
228 5/8*	68 5/8	44 1/8	44 2/8	16 7/8	16 1/8	7 6/8	8 2/8	12	12	Parton River, BC	Randy E. Miller	Randy E. Miller	2001	
219 3/8*	59 5/8	48 2/8	44 6/8	15 4/8	14 3/8	8	7 6/8	15	13	Kahntah River, BC	Michael Green	Michael Green	2001	

* Final score subject to revision by additional verifying measurements.

ALASKA-YUKON MOOSE

Alces alces gigas

Minimum Score 210   World's Record 261 5/8

Alaska-Yukon moose includes trophies from Alaska, Yukon Territory, and Northwest Territories.

Score	Greatest Spread	Length of Palm R.	L.	Width of Palm R.	L.	Circumference of Beam at Smallest Place R.	L.	Number of Normal Points R.	L.	Locality	Hunter	Owner	Date Killed	Rank
247 7/8	80 3/8	45 6/8	46 2/8	21 2/8	18 5/8	83 3/8	9 3/8	11	11	Rapid Creek, AK	Mark S. Rose	Mark S. Rose	2003	1
238	70 4/8	49 2/8	46 4/8	15	15 4/8	82 3/8	83 3/8	14	16	Kenai Pen., AK	Richard K. Mayer	Richard K. Mayer	2002	2
238	65 4/8	51 7/8	51	17 3/8	20 3/8	8	7 7/8	10	12	Dennison Creek, AK	Lynda S. Donahoe	Michael L. Cronk	2003	2
237 6/8	75 2/8	47 1/8	43 1/8	24 6/8	19 2/8	9	8 7/8	12	13	Timberline Lake, AK	Dan K. Presley	Dan K. Presley	2002	4
237 6/8	67	50 6/8	49 5/8	14 3/8	13 1/8	8 5/8	8 6/8	14	14	Kenai Pen., AK	Robert M. Stacy	Robert M. Stacy	2003	4
237 5/8	68 7/8	46 6/8	44 6/8	17 6/8	22 4/8	7 7/8	8 1/8	14	20	Birch Lakes, AK	Kassem Meiss	Kassem Meiss	2002	6
236	68 6/8	48 6/8	54 2/8	13 4/8	17 4/8	7 7/8	7 7/8	14	14	Cook Inlet, AK	Robert L. Godwin	Robert L. Godwin	2000	7
235 1/8	67 3/8	47 2/8	46 3/8	15 5/8	15 6/8	8 4/8	7 7/8	15	16	Kantishna River, AK	James L. Munsell	James L. Munsell	2000	8
234 6/8	67 4/8	47 1/8	47 3/8	18 1/8	18	7 4/8	7 4/8	11	15	Mackenzie Mts., NT	Thomas M. Roles	Thomas M. Roles	2002	9
234 1/8	65 3/8	51 1/8	51 7/8	15	14 7/8	7 3/8	7 5/8	11	13	Alaska	Unknown	Ronald F. Lax	1972	10
233 7/8	68 3/8	53 4/8	50 4/8	15 4/8	15 5/8	8 4/8	7 6/8	9	12	Kuskokwim River, AK	Brian G. Mangold	Brian G. Mangold	2001	11
232 5/8	68 1/8	51 1/8	49 1/8	13 3/8	14	7 7/8	7 6/8	12	12	Lachbuna Lake, AK	Lavern W. Kind	Lavern W. Kind	2002	12
232 4/8	69 4/8	44 5/8	46 2/8	16 7/8	16 7/8	8 2/8	8	14	12	Tuck Creek, AK	Thomas J. O'Neill	Thomas J. O'Neill	2001	13
231 7/8	68 5/8	42	46 7/8	17 4/8	17 7/8	7 1/8	7 2/8	15	16	Allen River, AK	Gordon L. Stewart	Gordon L. Stewart	2003	14
230 2/8	73 6/8	44 5/8	45 6/8	16 6/8	17 6/8	6 7/8	7	10	12	Branch River, AK	Don W. Noah	Don W. Noah	1977	15
230 2/8	66 2/8	46	48 2/8	19 4/8	16	9 2/8	9	11	13	Lakina River, AK	Robert E. Farone	Robert E. Farone	2002	15
230	65 2/8	43 3/8	46 4/8	18 1/8	16 4/8	7 4/8	7 4/8	18	15	Ogilvie River, YT	Dean L. Benner	Dean L. Benner	2002	17
229 4/8	69 6/8	46 1/8	47	16 4/8	16 4/8	7 6/8	7 7/8	10	11	Bear Creek, AK	J. Arden Meyer	J. Arden Meyer	1999	18
229 2/8	69 2/8	45 2/8	47 1/8	13 1/8	14 2/8	8 2/8	8 1/8	15	15	Pilot Mt., AK	Todd L. Johnson	Todd L. Johnson	2002	19
229 1/8	70 1/8	45 5/8	47 2/8	15	14 7/8	8	8 3/8	11	11	Coleen River, AK	Rick J. Schikora	Rick J. Schikora	2002	20
229	70 2/8	44 4/8	42 6/8	15 2/8	15 2/8	8 3/8	8 4/8	13	14	Old Womens Mountain, AK	Ralph L. Ivanoff	Ralph L. Ivanoff	2003	21
228 7/8	70 3/8	46 3/8	46 4/8	15	14 4/8	7 7/8	7 3/8	12	11	Tazimina River, AK	Samuel P. Albanese, Jr.	Samuel P. Albanese, Jr.	2001	22
228 4/8	57 4/8	48 6/8	50	18 1/8	16 2/8	8 4/8	8 5/8	12	13	Emerald Lake, YT	J. George Williams	J. George Williams	1979	23
228 4/8	63 4/8	49 4/8	48 4/8	14	14 6/8	7	7 1/8	13	14	Fuller Mt., AK	Richard S. Edelen	Richard S. Edelen	2002	23
228 3/8	73 7/8	43 7/8	44 4/8	12	15 4/8	7 3/8	7 4/8	14	16	Nushagak River, AK	William C. Thorp	William C. Thorp	2003	25
228 2/8	69 4/8	44 4/8	43 1/8	17 4/8	17 1/8	7 7/8	7 5/8	12	12	Kateel River, AK	Thomas O. Sandsmark	Thomas O. Sandsmark	2002	26
228 1/8	64 7/8	44 7/8	47	17 7/8	20 6/8	7 3/8	7 3/8	12	13	Tay River, YT	William L. Cox	William L. Cox	2001	27
227 6/8	61 6/8	45 7/8	46 3/8	15 3/8	15 7/8	8 6/8	8 6/8	13	15	Koyukuk River, AK	Ted R. Ramirez	Ted R. Ramirez	2001	28
227 4/8	68 6/8	42 4/8	45 4/8	14 2/8	16 6/8	7 5/8	7 6/8	15	16	Squirrel River, AK	James E. Wolfe	James E. Wolfe	2000	29
227 4/8	69 6/8	47 4/8	44 4/8	13 6/8	14	8 1/8	8 2/8	13	13	Canyon Creek, AK	Jeremy S. Davis	Jeremy S. Davis	2002	29

ALASKA-YUKON MOOSE

Alces alces gigas

Score	Greatest Spread	Length of Palm R.	Length of Palm L.	Width of Palm R.	Width of Palm L.	Circumference of Beam at Smallest Place R.	Circumference of Beam at Smallest Place L.	Number of Normal Points R.	Number of Normal Points L.	Locality	Hunter	Owner	Date Killed	Rank
226 4/8	67 6/8	44	46 5/8	14 5/8	16 2/8	7 7/8	7 6/8	13	13	Nisling River, YT	Harmon D. Maxson	Harmon D. Maxson	1994	31
226 3/8	74 5/8	41 5/8	43 2/8	17 1/8	16 2/8	8	8 1/8	10	10	Tikchik Mt., AK	Norman D. Abell	Norman D. Abell	2003	32
226	65	49	49 4/8	15 1/8	17 3/8	8 4/8	8 3/8	9	10	Cantwell, AK	Monson Nicklie, Jr.	Monson Nicklie, Jr.	2001	33
225 7/8	66 7/8	46 1/8	47	14 2/8	15 3/8	7 1/8	7 1/8	12	12	White Mts., AK	Vince A. Osborne	Vince A. Osborne	2002	34
225 5/8	69 3/8	45 6/8	46 5/8	15 1/8	17 3/8	7 7/8	7 6/8	10	12	Koyukuk River, AK	Paul B. Cochran	Paul B. Cochran	2003	35
225 3/8	68 1/8	45 6/8	43 6/8	15 6/8	13 6/8	8 2/8	8 1/8	13	12	Teklanika River, AK	Roger D. Speer	Roger D. Speer	2000	36
225 3/8	70 1/8	45 3/8	45 2/8	15 4/8	14 4/8	7 7/8	8	11	11	Selawik Hills, AK	Daniel A. Marks	Daniel A. Marks	2001	36
225	68	46 2/8	46	15 5/8	15	7 6/8	7 4/8	11	10	Squirrel River, AK	David F. Witmer	David F. Witmer	2000	38
224 5/8	63 5/8	49 6/8	48 5/8	13 5/8	13 4/8	8 3/8	8 5/8	10	11	Mountain River, NT	Jerome N. Ida	Jerome N. Ida.	2001	39
224 5/8	68 3/8	45	45 5/8	16 2/8	19 2/8	7 7/8	8 1/8	9	13	Aishihik Lake, YT	C. Don Steepleton	C. Don Steepleton	2002	39
224 4/8	57	45 7/8	46 5/8	19 4/8	20	8	7 7/8	11	15	Caribou Hills, AK	Dan K. Presley	Dan K. Presley	2001	41
224 4/8	67 2/8	48 3/8	49 5/8	13 1/8	12 2/8	8	8	10	12	Nowitna River, AK	Jeffrey H. Bushke	Jeffrey H. Bushke	2003	41
224 2/8	70 4/8	46 6/8	48 1/8	13 6/8	16	7 4/8	7 3/8	9	12	Alaska Pen., AK	Gary J. Pals	Gary J. Pals	2001	43
223 3/8	61 3/8	47 2/8	45 2/8	13 4/8	14 2/8	7 2/8	7 2/8	15	15	Lucky Lake, YT	Chad M. Pung	Chad M. Pung	2003	44
222 4/8	68 6/8	43 2/8	42 2/8	14 3/8	14 6/8	7 2/8	7 2/8	13	13	Chilchitna River, AK	M. Blake Patton	M. Blake Patton	2000	45
222 4/8	71 2/8	43	41 2/8	15 6/8	15 3/8	7 4/8	7 4/8	12	14	Selawik River, AK	Bruce A. Miklautsch	Bruce A. Miklautsch	2002	45
222	68 6/8	45 5/8	42 5/8	16 7/8	16 2/8	7 7/8	7 6/8	10	10	Koktuli River, AK	David B. Reed	David B. Reed	2001	47
221 3/8	54 7/8	48	46 6/8	16 6/8	15 2/8	8 4/8	8 2/8	14	13	Hart Lake, YT	M. Robert Delaney	M. Robert Delaney	2001	48
221 2/8	65 2/8	44 4/8	43 4/8	15 3/8	15 7/8	7 1/8	7 2/8	12	12	Mosquito Mt., AK	Randall L. Jansma	Randall L. Jansma	2000	49
220 5/8	69 1/8	39 4/8	42 6/8	14 6/8	15	7 4/8	7 4/8	14	17	Nowitna River, AK	Bernard G. Lusk	Bernard G. Lusk	2002	50
220 5/8	67 1/8	45 5/8	42 7/8	14 3/8	16 6/8	7	7	13	16	Kougarok River, AK	J. Marshall Jones, Jr.	J. Marshall Jones, Jr.	2002	50
220 4/8	68 2/8	44	40 5/8	17 6/8	16 2/8	7 2/8	7 2/8	12	15	Selawik River, AK	Dolan Baker	Dolan Baker	2002	52
220	65 2/8	43 4/8	46 3/8	13 5/8	15 1/8	7 2/8	7 4/8	13	15	Utopia Creek, AK	Robert A. Shotts	Robert A. Shotts	2002	53
220	63 2/8	44	43 2/8	15 6/8	16 2/8	7 3/8	7 4/8	13	14	Kanuti River, AK	Joseph P. Kitko	Joseph P. Kitko	2003	53
219 7/8	66 3/8	40 6/8	46	18	16	8	8 6/8	12	14	Judd Lake, AK	Douglas R. Danforth	Douglas R. Danforth	1963	55
219 5/8	62 7/8	44	41 2/8	16 7/8	17 1/8	7 2/8	7 4/8	15	13	Tanana River, AK	Morris W. Nagl	Morris W. Nagl	1973	56
218 4/8	66 4/8	49 3/8	43 2/8	15 1/8	14 6/8	8 1/8	8	11	10	Koyukuk River, AK	Jack L. Brickner	Jack L. Brickner	2002	57
217 6/8	67 6/8	41 6/8	40	17	16 4/8	8 4/8	8 4/8	11	14	Selawik River, AK	Stephen R. Haufsk	Stephen R. Haufsk	1998	58
217 6/8	68 2/8	43 1/8	43 1/8	14 6/8	14 4/8	7 2/8	7 1/8	11	10	Titna River, AK	Will R. Coleman	Will R. Coleman	2003	58
217 4/8	63 4/8	39 6/8	42 3/8	19 2/8	16 4/8	7 7/8	7 6/8	16	13	Mackenzie Mts., NT	Bruce K. Ostenson	Bruce K. Ostenson	2003	60
217 2/8	66	44 3/8	45 2/8	15 3/8	15 3/8	7 7/8	7 7/8	8	12	Askin Lake, YT	Joe L. Perry	Joe L. Perry	2000	61
217 2/8	71	46 2/8	43 4/8	13 1/8	12 5/8	7 5/8	7 4/8	10	10	Babel River, AK	J.D. Andrews	J.D. Andrews	2003	61
216 7/8	71 3/8	47 2/8	44	15	15 2/8	8 2/8	9 6/8	6	7	Fog Creek, AK	Gary A. Rose	Gary A. Rose	2003	63

216 1/8	66 7/8	44	41 4/8	14 3/8	13 6/8	7 5/8	7 3/8	12	12	Swift River, AK	Michael D. Bishop	Michael D. Bishop	2000	64
215 2/8	59 6/8	42 4/8	45 7/8	14 1/8	17 3/8	7 1/8	7 2/8	14	14	Koyukuk River, AK	Jack L. Brickner	Jack L. Brickner	2000	65
214 7/8	66 1/8	45 3/8	43 1/8	16 4/8	15 4/8	7 7/8	7 6/8	8	15	Upper Kandik River, AK	Gerald L. Beall	Gerald L. Beall	2002	66
214 6/8	67 6/8	40 4/8	38 2/8	17 5/8	15 3/8	8	7 7/8	12	16	Lost Lake, AK	Charlie Pearce	Charlie Pearce	2001	67
214 6/8	68 2/8	43 2/8	43 2/8	14 7/8	15 7/8	7 6/8	7 5/8	8	8	Half Moon Lake, AK	Curtis C. Hood	Curtis C. Hood	2001	67
213 7/8	70 1/8	42 6/8	44 4/8	18 3/8	18 2/8	9 5/8	9 3/8	6	9	Farewell Lake, AK	Daniel A. Niedert	Daniel A. Niedert	2001	69
213 2/8	63	44 1/8	42 5/8	14	13 1/8	7 3/8	7 3/8	13	12	Lachbuna Lake, AK	Kenneth D. Sisneros	Kenneth D. Sisneros	2000	70
212 6/8	70	37 7/8	37 1/8	15 3/8	15 4/8	6 7/8	6 7/8	12	12	McKinley Creek, AK	Mark Graham	Mark Graham	1999	71
212 6/8	64 6/8	42 4/8	41 2/8	13 6/8	15 1/8	7	7	12	12	Tay River, AK	George F. Wegner	George F. Wegner	1999	71
212 6/8	61 4/8	41 4/8	45 3/8	18 5/8	16 3/8	7 7/8	7 6/8	10	15	Nowitna River, AK	Johnnie R. Walters	Johnnie R. Walters	2000	71
212 5/8	73 3/8	41 3/8	42 2/8	12 4/8	14	7 6/8	7 6/8	8	9	Billy Lake, AK	George E. Lindsey, Jr.	George E. Lindsey, Jr.	2001	74
211 7/8	62 3/8	45 2/8	39 4/8	15 1/8	15 4/8	7 4/8	7 1/8	13	13	Dulbi River, AK	Michael J. Godfrey	Michael J. Godfrey	2002	75
211 5/8	62 1/8	40	41 1/8	18 5/8	16	7 6/8	7 7/8	11	11	Twitya River, NT	Gary Nehring	Gary Nehring	2002	76
211 4/8	61 2/8	41 6/8	44 1/8	13 6/8	13 6/8	7 5/8	7 5/8	12	13	Dillingham, AK	Shean M. Hardesty	Shean M. Hardesty	2001	77
211 4/8	72 2/8	42	41	12 4/8	12 4/8	8 5/8	8 6/8	11	13	Fisher Creek, YT	Dale C. Rettinghouse	Dale C. Rettinghouse	2002	77
211 3/8	58 3/8	44 7/8	42 4/8	19 7/8	17 1/8	6 7/8	7	10	10	No Name Creek, AK	Timothy H. Shawl	Timothy H. Shawl	2000	79
211	60	43	43	14 4/8	13 6/8	7 6/8	7 7/8	14	11	Marys Mt., AK	Dallas C. Anderson	Dallas C. Anderson	2000	80
210 1/8	62 5/8	41	39	21	15 6/8	7	7	14	12	Pilot Point, AK	Kathleen S. Lischkge	Kathleen S. Lischkge	1999	81
240 6/8*	72 4/8	44 6/8	46 5/8	19 4/8	16 4/8	7 7/8	8 2/8	17	15	Ogilvie River, YT	John L. Croft	John L. Croft	2002	
240 6/8*	70 6/8	48 2/8	48 7/8	18 6/8	19 4/8	8	8 3/8	10	10	Becharof Lake, AK	Chad A. Reel	Chad A. Reel	2002	

* Final score subject to revision by additional verifying measurements.

WYOMING MOOSE

Alces alces shirasi

Wyoming moose includes trophies taken in Colorado, Idaho, Montana, Utah, Washington, and Wyoming.

Score	Greatest Spread	Length of Palm R.	L.	Width of Palm R.	L.	Circumference of Beam at Smallest Place R.	L.	Number of Normal Points R.	L.	Locality	Hunter	Owner	Date Killed	Rank
193	51	40 4/8	42 2/8	14 1/8	11 7/8	7	6 5/8	12	14	Bingham Co., ID	Richard K. Smith	Richard K. Smith	2000	1
187 3/8	50 3/8	42 4/8	42 7/8	12 7/8	12 4/8	6 5/8	6 4/8	13	7	Bonneville Co., ID	Robin R. Pearson	Robin R. Pearson	2000	2
181	52 4/8	35 4/8	35 6/8	11 3/8	11 6/8	6 3/8	6 5/8	11	12	Jackson Co., CO	Dennis Pahlisch	Dennis Pahlisch	2001	3
178 3/8	42 5/8	37 1/8	36	12 6/8	13 1/8	7 1/8	7 3/8	12	13	Sublette Co., WY	Christopher W. Doak	Christopher W. Doak	2002	4
176 4/8	51 6/8	36 4/8	38 1/8	11 6/8	12 4/8	7 2/8	7 1/8	9	8	Morgan Co., UT	Larry R. Brower	Larry R. Brower	2003	5
175 7/8	50 7/8	34	35	13 3/8	12 6/8	6 7/8	6 6/8	11	9	Uinta Co., WY	Kurt P. Argyle	Kurt P. Argyle	2000	6
175 5/8	45 5/8	41 1/8	40 2/8	12 6/8	9 4/8	6 2/8	6 4/8	10	9	Caribou Co., ID	Robert V. Kimball	Robert V. Kimball	1987	7
174 7/8	48 5/8	38 6/8	34 4/8	9 5/8	10 4/8	7	7 2/8	12	13	Sublette Co., WY	Christopher S. Dauphin	Christopher S. Dauphin	2001	8
173 2/8	50 4/8	35 4/8	34	11 3/8	9 3/8	7	7	12	11	Lincoln Co., WY	David W. Whitesell	David W. Whitesell	2000	9
173 1/8	45 1/8	38 1/8	38	10	13 4/8	7	7 2/8	10	9	Larimer Co., CO	Picked Up	Dustin H. Bailey	2003	10
172 1/8	51 5/8	35	37 1/8	11 2/8	10 7/8	6 3/8	6 6/8	8	11	Summit Co., UT	David R. Gualazzi	David R. Gualazzi	2002	11
171 6/8	56 4/8	33 1/8	35 7/8	9 2/8	10	7 2/8	7 3/8	8	9	Grand Co., CO	Kenneth S. Gates	Kenneth S. Gates	2001	12
171 2/8	56	32 1/8	31 4/8	11 2/8	12 2/8	6 3/8	6 5/8	9	9	Teton Co., WY	Scott N. Carter	Scott N. Carter	2001	13
171 2/8	48 2/8	36 7/8	33 5/8	13 5/8	13 5/8	6 5/8	6 2/8	13	8	Larimer Co., CO	Billy Havens	Billy Havens	2002	13
169 3/8	53 1/8	34 6/8	30 4/8	9 4/8	11 7/8	7 1/8	7 1/8	11	13	Freemont, ID	W.H. Mitchell & R.F. Henry	W.H. Mitchell & R.F. Henry	2001	15
169	47 4/8	31 4/8	33 2/8	11 7/8	12 4/8	6 3/8	6 3/8	11	11	Madison Co., ID	Ronald K. Farris	Ronald K. Farris	2000	16
169	50 6/8	30 4/8	31 2/8	11 5/8	9 5/8	7	7 1/8	13	12	Jackson Co., CO	George Whisenhunt	George Whisenhunt	2001	16
168 4/8	50 4/8	31 3/8	31 5/8	11 5/8	12 6/8	6	6	10	11	Wyoming	Unknown	Bill H. McCabe	1958	18
168 3/8	47 3/8	35 5/8	35 4/8	10 4/8	10 5/8	6 4/8	6 4/8	8	9	Fremont Co., CO	Alfred C. Deshaw	Alfred C. Deshaw	2000	19
167 2/8	48	33	33	9 4/8	12 6/8	7 1/8	7 1/8	10	10	Sheridan Co., WY	Bill E. Hitt	Bill E. Hitt	2001	20
167 2/8	49 2/8	36 4/8	33 6/8	8 6/8	11 1/8	6 4/8	6 4/8	12	10	Sheridan Co., WY	Mark B. Steffen	Mark B. Steffen	2003	20
166 6/8	45 4/8	34 3/8	35 1/8	9 3/8	9 2/8	6 1/8	6	11	11	Sublette Co., WY	Dianne Boroff	Dianne Boroff	1997	22
166 3/8	49 3/8	35 4/8	36	11 2/8	10	6 1/8	6	9	7	Boundary Co., ID	Ronald R. Frederickson	Ronald R. Frederickson	2001	23
165 7/8	50 3/8	34 2/8	30 4/8	11 3/8	11 5/8	6 7/8	6 7/8	13	9	Morgan Co., UT	Alfred E. Cornelison	Alfred E. Cornelison	2003	24
165 5/8	47 3/8	36	32	10 6/8	12 1/8	7 3/8	7 4/8	9	10	Carbon Co., WY	Tana E. Sullivan	Tana E. Sullivan	2000	25
165 2/8	44 6/8	31 4/8	31 4/8	12 4/8	13 2/8	6 2/8	6 2/8	10	11	Granite Co., MT	Larry E. Clark	Larry E. Clark	2001	26
164 7/8	52 1/8	31 6/8	33	11 4/8	11 3/8	6 3/8	6 3/8	7	7	Shoshone Co., ID	John L. Amistoso	John L. Amistoso	2001	27
164 5/8	44 1/8	33 3/8	32 2/8	9 5/8	11 3/8	6 3/8	6 3/8	12	14	Caribou Co., ID	Wendel E. Hetzler	Wendel E. Hetzler	2002	28
164	47 2/8	32 3/8	37 2/8	11	11 6/8	6	6 1/8	9	10	Teton Co., ID	Picked Up	Ken V. Beard	2001	29
163 7/8	50 1/8	34	33	9 4/8	11 2/8	6 3/8	6 3/8	8	12	Summit Co., UT	Wade Wilde	Wade Wilde	2001	30
163 1/8	51 1/8	34 6/8	31	10 1/8	10 1/8	5 7/8	5 7/8	9	11	Bear Lake Co., ID	Toni R. Walo	Toni R. Walo	2000	31

Score										Locality	Owner	Hunter	Year	Rank
162 3/8	46 7/8	35 6/8	36 6/8	8 6/8	9 4/8	6 2/8	6 3/8	7	9	Bonner Co., ID	Chris Culbertson	Chris Culbertson	2001	32
162 3/8	46 5/8	35 1/8	34	11 3/8	9 2/8	6 5/8	6 5/8	8	8	Idaho Co., ID	Gerhardt L. Phillips III	Gerhardt L. Phillips III	2003	32
161 7/8	47 1/8	32 6/8	31 4/8	9 7/8	13 2/8	6	6	10	8	Carbon Co., MT	Stephen Tylinski	Stephen Tylinski	2001	34
161 7/8	51 1/8	33 6/8	31 2/8	11 5/8	9 6/8	5 7/8	6	9	9	Bonner Co., ID	Troy L. Black	Troy L. Black	2001	34
161 5/8	48 5/8	30 6/8	32	9 4/8	10 1/8	6 2/8	6 2/8	11	10	Cache Co., UT	Richard E. Reeder	Richard E. Reeder	2001	36
161 3/8	51 7/8	30 4/8	31 2/8	10 4/8	10 3/8	5 7/8	5 7/8	8	10	Teton Co., WY	Dean Collins	Dean Collins	2000	37
161 2/8	50 6/8	32	33 6/8	8 6/8	9 3/8	6 4/8	6 4/8	8	11	Sheridan Co., WY	Danny R. Hart	Danny R. Hart	1996	38
161 2/8	56	31 1/8	25 4/8	12 4/8	12	6 5/8	6 5/8	10	9	Teton Co., WY	Jerrie L. Eaton	Jerrie L. Eaton	2000	38
161 2/8	50	29 4/8	32 7/8	10 2/8	11 2/8	7	6 7/8	9	9	Pend Oreille Co., WA	Eric B. Walker	Eric B. Walker	2001	38
161 1/8	43 1/8	35 4/8	30 6/8	13 4/8	11 6/8	5 4/8	5 5/8	11	11	Teton Co., WY	Patrick J. Baumann	Patrick J. Baumann	2001	41
160 6/8	47 2/8	30 2/8	30	10 2/8	9 4/8	7 3/8	7 2/8	10	10	Jackson Co., CO	Bill Dalley	Bill Dalley	2001	42
160 6/8	38 6/8	35 2/8	36 4/8	11 6/8	9 7/8	5 7/8	6 1/8	12	10	Summit Co., UT	Catherine D. Mower	Catherine D. Mower	2002	42
160 6/8	50	32 3/8	31 5/8	9 4/8	9	5 7/8	5 6/8	9	9	Flathead Co., MT	Shawn P. Price	Shawn P. Price	2003	42
160 4/8	45 6/8	35	37 2/8	9 2/8	10 3/8	6 1/8	6 1/8	7	9	Clark Co., ID	David L. Denny	David L. Denny	2002	45
159 6/8	43 6/8	33 4/8	33 3/8	10	13 4/8	6 5/8	6 5/8	5	10	Bonneville Co., ID	Eric P. Horman	Eric P. Horman	2001	46
159 4/8	48 4/8	33 4/8	36 3/8	15	11 2/8	5 6/8	5 6/8	5	5	Boundary Co., ID	Marcus Byler	Marcus Byler	1999	47
159 3/8	49 5/8	33 3/8	29 4/8	10 4/8	9 6/8	6 6/8	6 5/8	9	9	Teton Co., WY	Warren J. Hatton	Warren J. Hatton	2000	48
159 3/8	44 3/8	31 1/8	30 4/8	11	11 4/8	6	6 3/8	11	10	Teton Co., WY	Scott L. Ray	Scott L. Ray	2001	48
159 2/8	53 6/8	33 7/8	33 2/8	9	7 4/8	6	6	6	7	Pend Oreille Co., WA	Eric F. Rebitzer	Eric F. Rebitzer	2000	50
159 1/8	45 1/8	32	34 7/8	11 2/8	9 4/8	6 5/8	6 4/8	12	9	Bonneville Co., ID	Brian G. Edgerton	Brian G. Edgerton	2000	51
159	44 6/8	28 2/8	28 2/8	11	12 1/8	5 7/8	5 7/8	12	12	Caribou Co., ID	Kenneth W. Logue	Kenneth W. Logue	2002	52
158 7/8	49 1/8	32 3/8	31 3/8	10 4/8	10 2/8	6 3/8	6 2/8	7	9	Madison Co., MT	Paul A. Pernak	Paul A. Pernak	2001	53
158 6/8	51	32	32 5/8	11 1/8	12 4/8	6 2/8	6 2/8	6	7	Idaho Co., ID	Loren R. Alley	Loren R. Alley	2003	54
158 3/8	46 7/8	31 6/8	35 4/8	8 5/8	11 7/8	6 3/8	6 5/8	9	10	Fremont Co., ID	Rance B. Dye	Rance B. Dye	1998	55
158 2/8	44	34 4/8	32	11 1/8	13 4/8	6	6 3/8	8	11	Idaho Co., ID	Ray Brown	Ray Brown	2001	56
158 2/8	46	34 2/8	32 4/8	9 6/8	9	6 6/8	6 5/8	8	8	Albany Co., WY	J. Darroll Bennett	J. Darroll Bennett	2002	56
158	47	30 7/8	33 6/8	9	9 4/8	5 5/8	5 5/8	10	10	Boundary Co., ID	John P. Thomas	John P. Thomas	2000	58
158	48 4/8	33 6/8	32 4/8	9	9	6 2/8	6 2/8	7	7	Sublette Co., WY	Maureen Montgomery	Maureen Montgomery	2001	58
157 6/8	51 2/8	28 7/8	31 6/8	10 1/8	9 4/8	5 7/8	5 7/8	8	12	Carbon Co., MT	Mark Theroux	Mark Theroux	2001	60
157 3/8	44 3/8	31 4/8	33 5/8	10 6/8	12 3/8	6 2/8	6 3/8	8	13	Carbon Co., WY	Chad D. Blake	Chad D. Blake	2002	61
157 2/8	43 6/8	30 3/8	30 2/8	10 4/8	11 4/8	6 4/8	6 4/8	12	10	Teton Co., WY	Thomas L. Buller	Thomas L. Buller	2000	62
157 2/8	49 6/8	32 6/8	30 5/8	7 6/8	8 3/8	6 3/8	6 3/8	10	9	Jackson Co., CO	James E. Schmid	James E. Schmid	2001	62
157 1/8	46 7/8	30 4/8	36 3/8	9 3/8	12 1/8	6 2/8	6 2/8	9	11	Teton Co., WY	Gary J. Amrine	Gary J. Amrine	2000	64
157 1/8	53 1/8	29 3/8	34 4/8	9 5/8	13 2/8	6	6 1/8	7	12	Flathead Co., MT	Larry A. Fenster	Larry A. Fenster	2000	64
156 6/8	44 6/8	35 4/8	32 6/8	9	10	6 2/8	6 4/8	8	10	Sublette Co., WY	Dianna L. Trapp	Dianna L. Trapp	2001	66
156 5/8	41 7/8	32	31 7/8	11 1/8	10 2/8	6 5/8	6 2/8	11	9	Power Co., ID	Wesley T. Port	Wesley T. Port	1999	67
156 5/8	53 1/8	27 1/8	26 2/8	11 4/8	11 3/8	6 2/8	6 1/8	8	9	Jackson Co., CO	Frank S. Noska IV	Frank S. Noska IV	2002	67
156 4/8	42 6/8	30 1/8	28 5/8	11 1/8	11	6 4/8	6 2/8	11	11	Beaverhead Co., MT	Dan Alzheimer	Dan Alzheimer	2001	69
156 2/8	47 2/8	31 2/8	31 4/8	8 4/8	9 6/8	5 6/8	5 6/8	9	9	Beaverhead Co., MT	Lori J. Ginn	Lori J. Ginn	2002	70
156	42 4/8	32	30	10 6/8	11 1/8	6	6 4/8	10	10	Teton Co., WY	Thomas Covert	Thomas Covert	2001	71
155 5/8	42 1/8	30 4/8	30 5/8	10 5/8	12	6 6/8	6 5/8	10	9	Beaverhead Co., MT	Larry G. Marshall	Larry G. Marshall	1999	72

WYOMING MOOSE

Alces alces shirasi

Score	Greatest Spread	Length of Palm R.	L.	Width of Palm R.	L.	Circumference of Beam at Smallest Place R.	L.	Number of Normal Points R.	L.	Locality	Hunter	Owner	Date Killed	Rank
1555 4/8	46 2/8	28 3/8	30 7/8	10 3/8	10	6 2/8	6 3/8	10	10	Madison Co., ID	Richard W. Woodfin	Richard W. Woodfin	1998	73
1555 4/8	47 6/8	31 4/8	31 2/8	8 7/8	8 4/8	6 1/8	6 1/8	8	8	Teton Co., WY	J. George Williams	J. George Williams	2001	73
1555 4/8	49 2/8	29 1/8	31 1/8	9 3/8	8 7/8	5 2/8	5 1/8	10	10	Caribou Co., ID	Bruce Dodson	Bruce Dodson	2002	73
1552 2/8	40 4/8	33 1/8	29 2/8	11 7/8	13 2/8	7 2/8	7 3/8	11	9	Cache Co., UT	William F. Kneer, Jr.	William F. Kneer, Jr.	2003	76
1551 1/8	51 5/8	29 4/8	30	8 3/8	9 7/8	5 7/8	6	10	8	Spokane Co., WA	Mike R. Coyle	Mike R. Coyle	2001	77
1555	48 2/8	31 4/8	29 5/8	10 6/8	10 6/8	6 3/8	6	8	7	Teton Co., WY	Leonard J. Kosirog	Leonard J. Kosirog	2001	78
1546 6/8	45 6/8	30 4/8	29 2/8	9 3/8	9 2/8	6	6	10	8	Sublette Co., WY	Leisa Roberts	Leisa Roberts	2001	79
1544 4/8	46 6/8	30 4/8	35 2/8	9 4/8	8 7/8	6 4/8	6 5/8	9	10	Weber Co., UT	Kent Larsen	Kent Larsen	2003	80
1534 6/8	45 6/8	28	29 2/8	10	10 3/8	6	6	10	9	Cassia Co., ID	Picked Up	Gene B. Pitchford	2001	81
1532 2/8	41 2/8	29 1/8	30 5/8	10 3/8	10 5/8	6	5 7/8	11	10	Bonneville Co., ID	Cathie Owen	Cathie Owen	2000	82
1517 7/8	39 3/8	34 1/8	27 6/8	10 6/8	11 6/8	6 6/8	6 6/8	13	11	Teton Co., ID	Willard O. Olson	Willard O. Olson	1987	83
1515 5/8	44 1/8	28 4/8	29 2/8	11 1/8	9 7/8	6 3/8	6 4/8	11	13	Sheridan Co., WY	Bruce T. Berger	Bruce T. Berger	2002	84
151	43 6/8	32 1/8	27 7/8	11 4/8	10 5/8	6 1/8	6 1/8	11	11	Morgan Co., UT	Kevin Parry	Kevin Parry	2003	85
1507 1/8	50 3/8	30	30	7 4/8	10	6 2/8	5 6/8	7	9	Pend Oreille Co., WA	Michael L. Albaugh	Michael L. Albaugh	2000	86
1506 6/8	47 4/8	27 2/8	26 6/8	11	11 6/8	5 7/8	5 7/8	8	8	Mineral Co., MT	Brian Palmer	Brian Palmer	2002	87
1502 6/8	47	30 2/8	30	7 7/8	7 7/8	5 6/8	5 7/8	8	8	Lincoln Co., WY	Allan E. Kaas	Allan E. Kaas	2001	88
1501 1/8	44 1/8	30 2/8	29 3/8	9 7/8	11 2/8	5 7/8	5 6/8	8	8	Teton Co., WY	Heidi Anderson	Sage & Kylie Anderson	2003	89
1492 2/8	47 2/8	30 2/8	28 6/8	8 4/8	9 3/8	5 6/8	6	9	8	Beaverhead Co., MT	Robert K. Des Jardins	Robert K. Des Jardins	2001	90
1487 5/8	45 1/8	31 4/8	27	10	10 2/8	5 7/8	6	8	9	Larimer Co., CO	Wesley J. Lowrie	Wesley J. Lowrie	2001	91
1486 6/8	43 4/8	31 1/8	29 2/8	9	9 2/8	6	5 7/8	9	9	Missoula Co., MT	Va Yee Leng K. Moua	Va Yee Leng K. Moua	2000	92
1486 6/8	41 4/8	30	27 1/8	11 7/8	10 7/8	5 5/8	5 5/8	12	10	Caribou Co., ID	Louis C. Uhl	Louis C. Uhl	2002	92
1484 4/8	41 6/8	32 6/8	30	10 2/8	10	6 3/8	6 3/8	9	8	Flathead Co., MT	Waylon W. Wolvert	Waylon W. Wolvert	2002	94
1483 5/8	41 3/8	29	29 6/8	9 4/8	10	6	6 2/8	9	9	Lincoln Co., MT	James F. Myers	James F. Myers	2002	95
1477 1/8	39 7/8	29 5/8	29 4/8	10 6/8	10 6/8	5 6/8	5 7/8	8	12	Jackson Co., CO	Lawrence M. Kochevar	Lawrence M. Kochevar	2000	96
1476 6/8	49	30	26 4/8	7 7/8	9 5/8	6 1/8	6	9	10	Caribou Co., ID	Blaine G. Atkinson	Blaine G. Atkinson	2002	97
1474 1/8	50 6/8	28 4/8	29 5/8	8 5/8	10 5/8	6 2/8	6 3/8	6	5	Madison Co., MT	Steve A. Hallgren	Steve A. Hallgren	2001	98
1471 4/8	46 7/8	30 4/8	34	6 3/8	10 4/8	6 2/8	6 4/8	7	10	Bonneville Co., ID	Todd C. Sorenson	Todd C. Sorenson	1998	99
1467 5/8	39 1/8	29 5/8	26 4/8	10 2/8	10 1/8	6 2/8	6 2/8	11	11	Bonneville Co., ID	Lisa M. Pascadlo	Lisa M. Pascadlo	2001	100
1462 4/8	43 2/8	27 7/8	25 6/8	9 7/8	8 5/8	6 2/8	6 1/8	12	11	Caribou Co., ID	Thomas E. Myers	Thomas E. Myers	2002	101
146	46 2/8	28 6/8	31	9 3/8	9 6/8	5 6/8	5 7/8	6	7	Daggett Co., UT	Paul T. Alexander	Paul T. Alexander	2002	102
1451 1/8	42 7/8	27	26 4/8	9 2/8	11	6 3/8	6 4/8	9	9	Teton Co., WY	Ellen J. Strube	Ellen J. Strube	1973	103
1451 1/8	45 7/8	25 1/8	24	8 4/8	9	6 1/8	6 2/8	11	11	Weber Co., UT	Scott M. Bond	Scott M. Bond	2001	103

Score										Locality	Hunter	Owner	Date Killed	Rank
145	39 4/8	32 7/8	29 1/8	11 6/8	11 2/8	6 4/8	6 3/8	6	10	Flathead Co., MT	Ron Holton	Ron Holton	1993	105
147 4/8	46 3/8	26 2/8	27 1/8	9 7/8	9 6/8	6 2/8	6 3/8	7	8	Pend Oreille Co., WA	John T. Handy	John T. Handy	2002	106
144 6/8	46	26 6/8	25 2/8	8 7/8	10 4/8	6 2/8	6 2/8	9	9	Pend Oreille Co., WA	Shawn K. MacFarlane	Shawn K. MacFarlane	2001	107
144 6/8	46 2/8	28 7/8	25 6/8	10 4/8	9	6 4/8	6 6/8	9	8	Teton Co., WY	Benjamin D. Smith	Benjamin D. Smith	2003	107
144 5/8	40 7/8	29 5/8	30 1/8	8 5/8	9 2/8	5 5/8	5 6/8	8	9	Pend Oreille Co., WA	Douglas D. Kikendall	Douglas D. Kikendall	2002	109
144	43 6/8	26 3/8	27 5/8	8 5/8	9 6/8	6 1/8	6 1/8	9	9	Jefferson Co., ID	Val Hymas	Val Hymas	1999	110
143 5/8	52 3/8	27 1/8	23 7/8	9 7/8	8 4/8	5 3/8	5 2/8	11	8	Sublette Co., WY	David A. Brown	David A. Brown	1983	111
141 7/8	46 5/8	28 6/8	29 4/8	7 5/8	8 2/8	7 2/8	7 2/8	7	4	Jackson Co., CO	Mark D. Thomson	Mark D. Thomson	2001	112
141 3/8	44 7/8	29	28 5/8	6 6/8	7	6	5 7/8	7	8	Utah Co., UT	Don M. Hunter	Don M. Hunter	2003	113
141 1/8	38 3/8	28 2/8	28 3/8	9 4/8	8 1/8	6	6	11	9	Lincoln Co., WY	Stacy J. Willoughby	Stacy J. Willoughby	2003	114
141	48 2/8	26	32 1/8	7 4/8	9	6 2/8	5 7/8	7	7	Flathead Co., MT	Jon W. Cole	Jon W. Cole	1999	115
140 5/8	38 5/8	28 3/8	27 6/8	8 4/8	10 6/8	5 6/8	5 6/8	9	9	Jackson Co., CO	Michael J. O'Brien	Michael J. O'Brien	2000	116
140 2/8	41 6/8	24 1/8	25 4/8	10 6/8	9 7/8	6 2/8	6 3/8	9	10	Fremont Co., ID	John L. Lyon	John L. Lyon	2001	117
183 7/8*	49 7/8	36 4/8	36 4/8	13 3/8	14 4/8	7 1/8	7 3/8	12	10	Johnson Co., WY	Scott A. Wodahl	Scott A. Wodahl	2002	
180 4/8*	54 4/8	35 1/8	34 5/8	11 4/8	10 2/8	6 1/8	6 1/8	12	12	Duchesne Co., UT	Jon H. Phillips	Jon H. Phillips	2003	

* Final score subject to revision by additional verifying measurements.

MOUNTAIN CARIBOU

Rangifer tarandus caribou

Minimum Score 360 — World's Record 453

Mountain caribou includes trophies from Alberta, British Columbia, southern Yukon Territory, and the Mackenzie Mountains of Northwest Territories.

Score	Length of Main Beam R.	L.	Inside Spread	Circumference at Smallest Place Between Brow and Bez Points R.	L.	Length of Brow Points R.	L.	Width of Brow Points R.	L.	Number of Points R.	L.	Locality	Hunter	Owner	Date Killed	Rank
440 7/8	57 2/8	55 3/8	42 6/8	6 4/8	6	20 2/8	18 1/8	11 2/8	9	16	16	Nisling River, YT	Larry D. Merillat	Larry D. Merillat	2003	1
416 7/8	50 3/8	49 5/8	45 2/8	6 6/8	5 5/8	17 1/8	16 2/8	10	5	18	21	Arctic Red River, NT	Garth W. Peterson	Garth W. Peterson	2002	2
413 6/8	47 2/8	46	39 1/8	6 6/8	7	16 3/8	17 4/8	9 6/8	7 2/8	18	15	Divide Lake, NT	Chuck Adams	Chuck Adams	1995	3
410 6/8	54 5/8	55 6/8	43 1/8	6 1/8	5 6/8	20 3/8	20	11 5/8	6 7/8	12	11	Prospector Mt., YT	Allen Gunson	Allen Gunson	1998	4
406 5/8	47 6/8	49 6/8	30 1/8	7 5/8	6 6/8	17 1/8	17 1/8	8 4/8	8 2/8	13	20	Ruby Range, NT	Bill Strange	Bill Strange	1986	5
404 3/8	43	43 4/8	33 4/8	8 2/8	8 2/8	19 1/8	11 3/8	12 6/8	3 3/8	20	17	Kawdy Mt., BC	Mark Drake	Mark Drake	2002	6
404 3/8	52 5/8	52 6/8	36 7/8	7 7/8	7 6/8	18 2/8	16	12 2/8	2 6/8	19	19	Nisling River, YT	Richard R. Anspaugh	Richard R. Anspaugh	2003	6
404	48 1/8	48 7/8	32 3/8	7 7/8	8 5/8	15	14 5/8	11 5/8	6 5/8	19	20	French Range, BC	Mike Harvella	Mike Harvella	2000	8
404	48	48 1/8	33 6/8	6 3/8	6 4/8	17 2/8	14 7/8	7	7 3/8	16	17	Mountain River, NT	Carles A. Webb	Carles A. Webb	2003	8
402 7/8	46 1/8	47 7/8	28 4/8	7 1/8	6 5/8	18 4/8	15 2/8	14 4/8	1/8	20	14	Tootsee River, BC	David Unruh	David Unruh	2000	10
401 3/8	54 3/8	52 4/8	45 4/8	6 6/8	6 4/8	5 7/8	21 4/8	1/8	17 3/8	12	14	Cassiar Mts., BC	Tim D. Caldwell	Tim D. Caldwell	2001	11
400	43 2/8	41 1/8	33 4/8	6 2/8	6 6/8	15 2/8	19 2/8	4 2/8	14 4/8	19	22	Pine Lake, YT	William Watson	William Watson	2001	12
398 7/8	52 2/8	53 2/8	31 1/8	6 1/8	5 5/8	18 3/8	19 7/8	6 2/8	8	16	16	Telegraph Creek, BC	James J. Kass	James J. Kass	2002	13
397 1/8	45 2/8	47 2/8	37 7/8	6 2/8	5 6/8	15 6/8	15	8 5/8	7 1/8	20	18	Little Cottonwood Lake, BC	William J. Kuehn	William J. Kuehn	2001	14
396 4/8	47 3/8	46 2/8	38 2/8	6 6/8	6 7/8	17 3/8	17 1/8	11	5 2/8	12	13	Mackenzie Mts., NT	Kirk M. Cavanaugh	Kirk M. Cavanaugh	2001	15
396 3/8	49 4/8	48 7/8	40 1/8	6 1/8	5 7/8	20 1/8	18 7/8	15 6/8	3	19	14	Pelly Mts., YT	Ken Taylor	Ken Taylor	2002	16
394 2/8	51 2/8	54 5/8	39 3/8	6 6/8	6 6/8	14 6/8	18 6/8	2 7/8	11 4/8	14	18	Niven Creek, BC	Jamie Gunn	Jamie Gunn	2002	17
393 7/8	54	51 6/8	49 3/8	7 4/8	6 5/8	18 2/8	5 6/8	13 3/8	1/8	16	13	Pelly Mts., YT	Thomas J. Grogan	Thomas J. Grogan	2000	18
393 6/8	42 3/8	46	41 6/8	6 6/8	6 7/8	17 4/8	3 2/8	12 1/8	1/8	19	13	Blanchet Lake, BC	Rick E. Abbott	Rick E. Abbott	2000	19
390	51 2/8	47	30 4/8	6	6 1/8	18 5/8	19 5/8	7 7/8	11 3/8	13	15	Mountain River, NT	Gary Nehring	Gary Nehring	2002	20
389 4/8	46 1/8	44 1/8	32 1/8	6 6/8	7	17 1/8	15 1/8	11 3/8	3 4/8	19	16	Caribou Creek, BC	William O. Anderson	William O. Anderson	2001	21
384 5/8	51 4/8	54 6/8	37	4 5/8	5	16 5/8	16 6/8	6 6/8	7 6/8	16	14	Johiah Lake, BC	Robert W. Elka	Robert W. Elka	2000	22
381 6/8	47 3/8	46 4/8	38 5/8	5 7/8	5 7/8	14 6/8	11 2/8	10 4/8	1/8	21	16	Spatzizi Plateau, BC	Brad Villnow	Rebecca Villnow	2000	23
380	47 6/8	47 6/8	42 5/8	6 4/8	6 6/8	17 4/8	3 7/8	10 1/8	1/8	17	13	Kitchener Lake, BC	Ryan Huntsman	Ryan Huntsman	2001	24
380	45 2/8	45 5/8	34 3/8	6 5/8	6 6/8	15 6/8	14 1/8	6 2/8	4 6/8	14	14	Mackenzie Mts., NT	D. Belton Noseworthy	D. Belton Noseworthy	2002	24
379 4/8	46 3/8	47	31 7/8	5 7/8	6 2/8	6 4/8	16 4/8	1/8	10 4/8	15	18	Todd Creek, BC	Geofrey S. Moss	Geofrey S. Moss	2003	26
378 3/8	40 7/8	39 3/8	38 7/8	7 1/8	7 2/8	19 6/8	4 1/8	14 4/8	5/8	17	17	Kawdy Plateau, BC	Shawn Powers	Shawn Powers	2003	27
377 2/8	48 1/8	46 2/8	36 2/8	6 6/8	6 6/8	16 3/8	15 3/8	2 7/8	7 7/8	15	15	Mount Logan, YT	Michael D. Moore	Michael D. Moore	2001	28
377	45 1/8	48 5/8	34	7 6/8	6 7/8	14 1/8	14 6/8	4 5/8	4 2/8	14	14	Twitya River, NT	Thomas L. Pregler	Thomas L. Pregler	2001	29

Score											Locality	Hunter	Owner	Date	Rank
376 1/8	49 7/8	49 2/8	40 7/8	6 4/8	18 1/8	11 2/8	14	1/8	17	9	Cassiar Mts., BC	Billy H. Boyd	Billy H. Boyd	2001	30
373 5/8	46 2/8	45	32 4/8	6	5 4/8	16 7/8	1/8	12 1/8	16	18	Divide Lake, NT	Raymond P. Cartonia	Raymond P. Cartonia	2001	31
372 4/8	52	50 7/8	41 6/8	5 7/8	16 1/8	12 7/8	12 2/8	4 4/8	17	15	Johiah Lake, BC	Robert A. Elka	Robert A. Elka	2000	32
365 2/8	44 6/8	45 2/8	40 4/8	6 2/8	13 7/8	2	6 6/8	1/8	16	15	Kawdy Plateau, BC	Bradley R. Jackle	Bradley R. Jackle	1998	33
441*	49 3/8	48 3/8	48 2/8	6 2/8	19 5/8	19 7/8	17 2/8	11 6/8	16	12	Gana River, NT	Allen A. Meyer	Allen A. Meyer	2001	
438 1/8*	51 5/8	52 7/8	37 5/8	7 5/8	17 5/8	17 5/8	4 1/8	12 1/8	18	20	Mackenzie Mts., NT	Mark J. Sheridan	Mark J. Sheridan	2002	
419 6/8*	48 5/8*	48 6/8*	37 5/8	6 4/8	18 3/8	10 6/8	10 3/8	1/8	17	15	Calata Lake, BC	Terry A. Street	Terry A. Street	2002	

* Final score subject to revision by additional verifying measurements.

WOODLAND CARIBOU

Rangifer tarandus caribou

Woodland caribou includes trophies from Nova Scotia, New Brunswick, and Newfoundland.

Score	Length of Main Beam R.	L.	Inside Spread	Circumference at Smallest Place Between Brow and Bez Points R.	L.	Length of Brow Points R.	L.	Width of Brow Points R.	L.	Number of Points R.	L.	Locality	Hunter	Owner	Date Killed	Rank
329 2/8	40 3/8	40 2/8	40 7/8	5	5	16 5/8	17 6/8	13 3/8	11 1/8	10	13	Parsons Pond, NL	Donald L. Strickler	Donald L. Strickler	2000	1
327 3/8	33 5/8	36 3/8	32 3/8	6	5 4/8	13 7/8	17 7/8	12 2/8	13 6/8	19	18	Caribou Lake, NL	Robert Sparks	Robert Sparks	2002	2
324 7/8	39 6/8	38 7/8	38 5/8	6 2/8	6 2/8	16 2/8	16 4/8	11 6/8	15 4/8	13	17	Gander River, NL	Robert P. Meyers, Jr.	Robert P. Meyers, Jr.	2002	3
324 3/8	39 6/8	40 3/8	33 3/8	5 4/8	5 3/8	18 4/8	17 2/8	13 1/8	13 3/8	18	13	Belle Isle, NL	Aaron D. Coomer	Aaron D. Coomer	2002	4
323 6/8	39 6/8	41 3/8	31 2/8	5 7/8	5 4/8	14 5/8	17	12 4/8	1/8	15	13	West River, NL	Thomas L. Nederveld	Thomas L. Nederveld	2002	5
320 6/8	45	39 6/8	36 3/8	5 6/8	6 3/8	5 4/8	15 4/8	1/8	12 6/8	11	15	Owl Pond, NL	Michael J. Kennedy	Michael J. Kennedy	2000	6
316 4/8	37 4/8	36 3/8	34 4/8	5 2/8	4 7/8	16 5/8	20 7/8	13 4/8	7 4/8	12	12	Middle Ridge, NL	Kenneth J. Miller	Kenneth J. Miller	2002	7
313 4/8	35 4/8	35 4/8	30 4/8	5 2/8	5	16 7/8	19 5/8	11 5/8	7 1/8	14	12	Cat Arm River, NL	Michael P. Jones	Michael P. Jones	1999	8
313 3/8	37 4/8	34 7/8	30 7/8	5 1/8	5 1/8	17 7/8	15 4/8	9	7 1/8	23	13	Hinds Lake, NL	William D. Graham	William D. Graham	2002	9
312 1/8	38 6/8	35 6/8	28 7/8	5 3/8	5	15 5/8	14 2/8	11 1/8	12 2/8	19	20	Sandy Lake, NL	Cecil S. Reaser, Jr.	Cecil S. Reaser, Jr.	1998	10
310 2/8	37 4/8	35 5/8	38	5 7/8	5 4/8	12 3/8	13 5/8	8 5/8	9 1/8	14	16	Third Pond, NL	Keith C. Halstead	Keith C. Halstead	2002	11
308 1/8	39	38 2/8	25 7/8	5 1/8	4 7/8	16 1/8	13 7/8	14 6/8	9	19	16	Northern Pen., NL	George M. Jerry	George M. Jerry	1999	12
307 5/8	37	38 3/8	29 1/8	5 3/8	5 4/8	13 5/8	17	2 4/8	13 5/8	12	19	West River, NL	Timothy S. Nederveld	Timothy S. Nederveld	2002	13
306 6/8	39 5/8	42 7/8	34 6/8	5 4/8	5 6/8	13 6/8	16 4/8	9 1/8	14 5/8	10	14	White Hills, NL	Donald Z. Detwiler	Donald Z. Detwiler	2000	14
304 6/8	39 4/8	35 4/8	34 5/8	5 6/8	5 4/8	15 5/8	14 3/8	11 4/8	10 1/8	15	13	Deer Lake, NL	John F. Babler	John F. Babler	2002	15
302	38 4/8	36 2/8	29 7/8	5 4/8	5 2/8	16 2/8	16 3/8	15	13 6/8	15	16	River of Ponds, NL	Harold L. Nyce	Harold L. Nyce	1998	16
300 3/8	37 5/8	38	25 5/8	6	5 7/8	14 1/8	18 6/8	1 5/8	13 2/8	13	11	Deer Lake, NL	William L. Cochran	William L. Cochran	2001	17
299 2/8	35 7/8	36 6/8	28 2/8	5 5/8	5 7/8	12 7/8	14 1/8	10	11 4/8	17	14	SW Gander River, NL	Anthony C. Crowell	Anthony C. Crowell	2002	18
298 4/8	35 6/8	37 2/8	28 7/8	4 4/8	4 6/8	13 4/8	15 5/8	7 4/8	11 2/8	12	11	Western Brook Pond, NL	Norbert D. Bremer	Norbert D. Bremer	2003	19
294 1/8	38 5/8	40 7/8	26 2/8	6	5 4/8	14 2/8	12 2/8	10 3/8	4 6/8	15	14	Buchans Plateau, NL	Donald Clifford	Brian J. Emerson	1975	20
292 6/8	38 5/8	39 1/8	23 4/8	4 6/8	5	15 5/8	16 7/8	12	10 6/8	11	14	Cormack Lake, NL	Dale J. Francar	Dale J. Francar	1996	21
291 6/8	41 6/8	40 1/8	42 2/8	5 3/8	5 1/8	13 3/8	15 2/8	6 7/8	9	10	10	Goose Lake, NL	Robert E. Wrenn	Robert E. Wrenn	2000	22
288 6/8	41 2/8	39 6/8	35 2/8	4 5/8	4 5/8	11 1/8	15 6/8	9 1/8	11 2/8	11	13	Cloud River, NL	David D. Landig	David D. Landig	2001	23
286 3/8	38 4/8	35 4/8	32 1/8	5 3/8	6	13	13 2/8	10 4/8	9 4/8	14	13	Island Pond, NL	Carlton E. Dixon, Jr.	Carlton E. Dixon, Jr.	2000	24
285 1/8	37	36 2/8	27 5/8	5 2/8	4 7/8	11	12 3/8	7 6/8	11 5/8	16	18	Sam's Pond, NL	Raymond L. Todd, Sr.	Raymond L. Todd, Sr.	2002	25
284 7/8	39 3/8	36 4/8	33 4/8	5 1/8	5 3/8	16	14 7/8	12 6/8	10 2/8	15	12	Baie Verte Pen., NL	Daniel C. Pyzik	Daniel C. Pyzik	2001	26
284 2/8	32	29 7/8	30 3/8	5 1/8	5 1/8	12 2/8	16 4/8	10 5/8	5 3/8	10	14	Hinds Lake, NL	Stephen L. Cartwright	Stephen L. Cartwright	2002	26
283 7/8	35 4/8	36 2/8	25 7/8	5 4/8	5 5/8	16 4/8	16 2/8	12	11	13	16	Deer Lake, NL	John R. Mathews	John R. Mathews	2000	28
282 1/8	38	37 5/8	31 4/8	4 7/8	4 5/8	12 3/8	15 3/8	1/8	12	10	16	Northern Pen., NL	Gregory R. Green	Gregory R. Green	2000	29

Score												Locality	By whom killed	Owner	Date killed	Rank
281 2/8	35 4/8	36 5/8	30 7/8	4 7/8		11 1/8	11	9 7/8	7 1/8	17	17	Daniel's Harbor, NL	Terry D. Braden	Terry D. Braden	1998	30
278 4/8	34 1/8	35 5/8	29 1/8	4 6/8	5	13 1/8	11 5/8	10 5/8	10	17	13	Grand Falls, NL	Gene M. Ptaszkiewicz	Gene M. Ptaszkiewicz	2002	31
276	32 2/8	34 7/8	25	5 1/8	5 1/8	14 2/8	14 2/8	12 1/8	5 3/8	14	12	Sams Pond, NL	Jake Weise	Jake Weise	2000	32
274	35 2/8	37 7/8	29 6/8	5	5 1/8	15 7/8	12 6/8	14 3/8	4 6/8	14	12	River Pond, NL	David M. Hippeli	David M. Hippeli	1998	33
267	31 6/8	32 6/8	34 3/8	5 3/8	5 1/8	11 5/8	12 1/8	8 6/8	10 6/8	17	13	Ten Mile Lake, NL	Jerome A. Mastel	Jerome A. Mastel	2003	34
266	30 4/8	31 4/8	28 6/8	5 7/8	5 2/8	12 7/8	10 4/8	10 4/8	10 3/8	14	15	Middle Ridge, NL	Robert G. Callender	Robert G. Callender	2002	35
265 5/8	34 1/8	38 5/8	32	4 5/8	5	15	14 4/8	12 1/8	11 4/8	12	16	Island Pond, NL	Carlton E. Dixon, Sr.	Carlton E. Dixon, Sr.	2000	36
333 6/8*	40 1/8	38 6/8	31 3/8	6 1/8	6 7/8	16	16	16 6/8	9 1/8	20	22	Caribou Lake, NL	Jason P. Keber	Jason P. Keber	2000	
332 6/8*	40 6/8	40 5/8	38	5 2/8	5 4/8	16 6/8	15 2/8	13	2 6/8	17	15	Great Harbour Deep, NL	Rolland G. Bohm	Rolland G. Bohm	2000	

* Final score subject to revision by additional verifying measurements.

BARREN GROUND CARIBOU

Rangifer tarandus granti

Barren ground caribou includes trophies from Alaska and northern Yukon Territory.

Score	Length of Main Beam R	L	Inside Spread	Circumference at Smallest Place Between Brow and Bez Points R	L	Length of Brow Points R	L	Width of Brow Points R	L	Number of Points R	L	Locality	Hunter	Owner	Date Killed	Rank
426 6/8	55 3/8	54 2/8	34 1/8	7	8 4/8	18	19 3/8	6 4/8	9 2/8	19	16	Shagak Bay, AK	James A. McIntosh	James A. McIntosh	2002	1
424 6/8	48	46 5/8	34 5/8	5 6/8	5 5/8	24	1 5/8	1	19 2/8	13	30	Shotgun Hills, AK	Clinton E. Hanson, Jr.	Clinton E. Hanson, Jr.	2003	2
418 3/8	50 4/8	51 1/8	37 7/8	5 7/8	5 1/8	20	17 4/8	15 1/8	8 1/8	20	18	Agenuk Mt., AK	James L. Johnson	James L. Johnson	2000	3
413 4/8	53 4/8	52 4/8	41 6/8	5 7/8	5 2/8	17 5/8	20 1/8	14 2/8	11	18	20	Grayling Creek, AK	Jack W. McElmurry	Jack W. McElmurry	2002	4
413 1/8	50 1/8	49 6/8	37 5/8	6 3/8	7	18 4/8	18 7/8	9 7/8	14 6/8	15	18	Kuskokwim River, AK	Dewey F. Gibson	Dewey F. Gibson	1996	5
412 5/8	47 3/8	45 5/8	33 6/8	8 4/8	9	17 4/8	18 4/8	4 4/8	11 5/8	16	15	Nishlik Lake, AK	Randy L. Jansma	Randy L. Jansma	2003	6
409 5/8	53 2/8	52 3/8	43	6 2/8	6 4/8	19 2/8	16 2/8	13 1/8	5 6/8	15	14	Iliamna Lake, AK	William R. Deiley	William R. Deiley	1984	7
409	47 6/8	48 1/8	36 2/8	5 5/8	6 2/8	18 5/8	17	14 4/8	8 1/8	17	16	Funny River, AK	Kam P. St. John	Kam P. St. John	2002	8
407 6/8	43	43 7/8	29 4/8	7 3/8	6 5/8	17 7/8	17 7/8	9 6/8	15 4/8	22	25	Fern Lake, AK	Ralph B. Feriani	Ralph B. Feriani	1976	9
407 4/8	51 7/8	50 4/8	35 2/8	6 7/8	6 5/8	1 1/8	20 4/8	1/8	16	16	18	Adak Island, AK	Delbert R. Oney	Delbert R. Oney	2003	10
406 6/8	47 3/8	47 3/8	30	5 7/8	6 3/8	19	22 1/8	4 4/8	16 1/8	15	21	Hart River, YT	Daniel J. Galles	Daniel J. Galles	2002	11
406 2/8	54 1/8	50 6/8	43	5 5/8	6	19 6/8	20 3/8	8 2/8	12 3/8	13	16	Alaska Range, AK	Chuck A. Oeleis	Chuck A. Oeleis	2000	12
405 1/8	54 4/8	54	36 5/8	6 4/8	6 5/8	19	15 2/8	9 6/8	13 4/8	13	16	Swan Lake, AK	Tanya N. Dickinson	Tanya N. Dickinson	2003	13
404 3/8	46 7/8	45 6/8	37 3/8	6 3/8	6	14	15	2 5/8	9 1/8	20	24	Brooks Range, AK	Dale E. Helmbrecht	Dale E. Helmbrecht	2003	14
401 3/8	54 4/8	52 7/8	47 6/8	6 2/8	5 7/8	17 7/8	18 4/8	5 2/8	8 6/8	14	14	Swan Lake, AK	Loren B. Hollers	Loren B. Hollers	2001	15
400 7/8	56 5/8	56 3/8	39	6 3/8	6 4/8	14 4/8	15 4/8	6 3/8	8 6/8	13	14	Snake River, YT	William W. Goodridge	William W. Goodridge	2001	16
400 5/8	49 7/8	49 6/8	36 1/8	8 3/8	8 5/8	15 6/8	15 6/8	10 7/8	9 5/8	17	21	Nishlik Lake, AK	Rollie J. Smith	Rollie J. Smith	2001	17
398 2/8	50 2/8	47 7/8	36 4/8	6 2/8	6 2/8		16 4/8	12		19	25	Kanektuk River, AK	Jeffrey Singley	Jeffrey Singley	2003	18
395 7/8	59 3/8	60 3/8	46 6/8	4 7/8	5	18	6 5/8	12 1/8	1/8	16	14	Kenai Pen., AK	David C. Campbell, Jr.	David C. Campbell, Jr.	1970	19
395 4/8	47 6/8	44 3/8	34 5/8	6 7/8	6 3/8	17 3/8	20 5/8	11 3/8	13 4/8	15	17	Mulchatna River, AK	Harry W. Hagelund	Harry W. Hagelund	2002	20
394 7/8	48	47	41 2/8	6 6/8	6 2/8	18 7/8	11 4/8	13 7/8	1/8	23	14	Kuskokwim River, AK	Mark A. Haglund	Mark A. Haglund	2001	21
394 4/8	50	50 1/8	38 1/8	5 2/8	6 6/8	20 1/8	18 5/8	6 4/8	10 7/8	13	16	Adak Island, AK	Jon L. Schleiger	Jon L. Schleiger	1991	22
393 7/8	55 7/8	53 5/8	41 5/8	5 2/8	5 4/8	16 7/8	18 3/8	11 3/8	12 1/8	14	16	Blackstone River, YT	Michael D. Bright	Michael D. Bright	2001	23
392 3/8	54 3/8	54 3/8	50 2/8	6 4/8	6 7/8	18 1/8		11		19	11	Denali Hwy., AK	Billie J. Durham	Virginia K. Vinson	1959	24
392 1/8	52 1/8	50	38 2/8	5 2/8	6	17 4/8	15 5/8	13 1/8	9 5/8	18	17	Grayling Creek, AK	Carl H. Spaeth	Carl H. Spaeth	2002	25
390 7/8	53 7/8	55 6/8	42 3/8	5 4/8	5 2/8	12 6/8	20 4/8	3 4/8	11 6/8	15	19	Alaska Pen., AK	John V. Vargo, Jr.	John V. Vargo, Jr.	1995	26
390 1/8	48 4/8	50 7/8	32 5/8	6 4/8	6 2/8	14 2/8	15 1/8	11 5/8	9 2/8	17	21	Killbuck Mts., AK	Chris J. Coody	Chris J. Coody	2001	27
390 1/8	53 7/8	54 4/8	37 6/8	7 3/8	7 3/8	3 2/8	18 6/8	1/8	9 4/8	13	17	Adak Island, AK	David B. Garrigus	David B. Garrigus	2003	27
388 2/8	51 1/8	52 1/8	48 5/8	5 7/8	6 3/8	2 6/8	17 3/8	6/8	11 6/8	13	14	Pegati Lake, AK	Jeff S. Mitchell	Jeff S. Mitchell	2003	29
387 3/8	49 7/8	51 4/8	36 3/8	5 7/8	6 1/8	16 1/8	19 6/8	10 7/8	8 4/8	16	19	Swan Lake, AK	Tony M. Sikora	Tony M. Sikora	2001	30

Score												Locality	Hunter	Owner	Date	Rank
387 1/8	57	54	38 6/8	6 2/8	6	16 7/8	8 2/8	12 3/8	1/8	20	13	Tikchik Lakes, AK	Bryan L. McGregor	Bryan L. McGregor	2002	31
386 7/8	54 5/8	53 3/8	36	8 7/8	8	16 3/8	19 6/8	6 6/8	9 6/8	15	15	Adak Island, AK	Frank A. Bertolli	Frank A. Bertolli	2002	32
385 6/8	48 3/8	44 3/8	33 2/8	5 3/8	5 5/8	17 6/8	17 5/8	9 3/8	9 4/8	19	16	King Salmon, AK	David R. Lautner	David R. Lautner	1983	33
384 6/8	51 2/8	50 2/8	46 1/8	5 3/8	5 2/8	5 5/8	17 5/8	1/8	10 4/8	11	15	Ilianna Lake, AK	Leonard F. Sauer	Leonard F. Sauer	1996	34
379 6/8	43 7/8	47 7/8	40 6/8	6 6/8	6 4/8		15 1/8		6 7/8	15	13	Ugashik River, AK	Guy C. Powell	Guy C. Powell	1967	35
378 7/8	48 5/8	49 1/8	42 3/8	6 6/8	5 5/8	1 1/8	19 3/8	1/8	15 5/8	13	19	Cairn Mt., AK	Howie J. Pentony	Howie J. Pentony	1997	36
378 3/8	47 7/8	47 1/8	41 3/8	5 6/8	6	4 2/8	18 5/8	1/8	15	13	21	Unimak Island, AK	William F. Nye	William F. Nye	2001	37
377 3/8	55 1/8	52 7/8	35 3/8	4 7/8	4 7/8	17 2/8	15 3/8	14 2/8	7 1/8	13	16	Tulugak Lake, AK	Jeff Snow	Jeff Snow	2001	38
375 6/8	52 1/8	53 7/8	39 6/8	5 6/8	5 6/8	14 1/8	17 2/8	2	9 7/8	16	20	Nishlik Lake, AK	Elise M. Giezentanner	Elise M. Giezentanner	2002	39
375 5/8	52 6/8	54 1/8	40 5/8	7	6 6/8	17 7/8	17 1/8	10 2/8	14 2/8	18	16	Aniak Lake, AK	Robert G. Childress	Robert G. Childress	2001	40
375 4/8	39 7/8	43 3/8	28 1/8	9 6/8	6 2/8	18 6/8	17 5/8	4 6/8	11	20	18	Stony River, AK	Laurie Porter	Laurie Porter	1980	41
431 3/8*	50 4/8	48	42 2/8	8 5/8	8 1/8	17 3/8	10 4/8			22	18	Chulitna River, AK	Harry E. Buzby III	Harry E. Buzby III	2001	
426 6/8*	54 3/8	51 4/8	43 6/8	8 5/8	7	17 4/8	7 6/8	10 1/8	1/8	14	14	Twin Lakes, AK	Paul A. Lautner	Paul A. Lautner	2002	
418 4/8*	48 2/8	49 1/8	24 3/8	7 4/8	7 6/8	15 5/8	23 2/8	1/8	19 1/8	16	22	Kenai Mts., AK	Jack C. Standiford	Jack C. Standiford	2001	

* Final score subject to revision by additional verifying measurements.

CENTRAL CANADA BARREN GROUND CARIBOU

Minimum Score 345　　　　*Rangifer tarandus groenlandicus*　　　　World's Record 433 4/8

Central Canada barren ground caribou occur on Baffin Island and the the mainland of Northwest Territories, with geographic boundaries of the Mackenzie River to the west; the north edge of the continent to the north (excluding any islands except Baffin Island); Hudson Bay to the east; and the southern boundary of Northwest Territories to the south. The boundary also includes the northwest corner of Manitoba north of the south limit of township 87 and west of the Little Churchill River, Churchill River, and Hudson Bay.

Score	Length of Main Beam R.	L.	Inside Spread	Circumference at Smallest Place Between Brow and Bez Points R.	L.	Length of Brow Points R.	L.	Width of Brow Points R.	L.	Number of Points R.	L.	Locality	Hunter	Owner	Date Killed	Rank
404	51 3/8	54 2/8	42 7/8	5 2/8	5 3/8	18 3/8	21 4/8	1/8	15 3/8	12	16	Courageous Lake, NT	Gordon A Welke	Doris Welke	2001	1
402 6/8	49 7/8	49 4/8	46 7/8	4 6/8	4 7/8	16 6/8	19 2/8	13 6/8	14 5/8	23	17	MacKay Lake, NT	Gordon Carpenter	Gordon Carpenter	2001	2
400 3/8	53 6/8	57	40 6/8	5 7/8	5 4/8	21	19 1/8	19 1/8	6 7/8	18	17	Little Marten Lake, NT	Joel C. Garner	Joel C. Garner	2001	3
399 6/8	50 3/8	54 7/8	42 5/8	5 3/8	4 5/8	17 2/8	16 7/8	13	11	32	17	Nicholson Lake, MB	Francis N. George	Francis N. George	2001	4
397 2/8	55 5/8	51 5/8	30 1/8	4 4/8	4 4/8	17 6/8	17	15 1/8	14	20	21	Humpy Lake, NT	Tracy A. Peterson	Tracy A. Peterson	2000	5
394 5/8	54 5/8	53 7/8	37 5/8	5	4 7/8	21 7/8	17 1/8	15	9	16	12	Schmok Lake, MB	Dennis A. Branfield	Dennis A. Branfield	2001	6
394 4/8	45 6/8	46 2/8	33 6/8	5 5/8	5 3/8	15	17 4/8	1/8	15 7/8	20	25	Courageous Lake, NT	Thomas E. Kriz	Thomas E. Kriz	2000	7
391 7/8	45 4/8	48 2/8	27	6	5 7/8	20 2/8	22 5/8	6 2/8	20 6/8	13	18	Rendezvous Lake, NT	Diana L. Ross	Diana L. Ross	2003	8
390	53 5/8	54 7/8	35 2/8	7 4/8	5 5/8	17 4/8	20 1/8	14 1/8	14	13	17	Little Marten Lake, NT	Adolfo R. Gutierrez	Adolfo R. Gutierrez	2002	9
386 6/8	45 6/8	43 6/8	28 1/8	5 2/8	5 2/8	16	17 1/8	13 1/8	14 3/8	22	19	Jolly Lake, NT	James J. Hudson	James J. Hudson	2001	10
383 7/8	47	45 7/8	41 1/8	5 2/8	5 6/8	14 5/8	18 2/8	8 4/8	14 5/8	12	21	Nejanilini Lake, MB	Michael A. Dahlheimer	Michael A. Dahlheimer	2003	11
382 5/8	49 4/8	48 2/8	31 1/8	4 6/8	5	2 6/8	18 6/8	1/8	14 3/8	24	37	Little Marten Lake, NT	Jerrold L. Nye	Jerrold L. Nye	2001	12
382 4/8	47 3/8	49 7/8	34 3/8	5	6 4/8	19 7/8	13	17 1/8	1/8	29	17	MacKay Lake, NT	Ron Kerr	Ron Kerr	2001	13
380 5/8	52 6/8	50 6/8	44 1/8	6	5 7/8	6 6/8	17 5/8	1/8	14 4/8	12	16	Courageous Lake, NT	Bernie L. Zimmerman	Bernie L. Zimmerman	2002	14
380 4/8	51 3/8	49 5/8	33 2/8	5 5/8	5	11 4/8	17 3/8	5	15 1/8	13	19	Rendezvous Lake, NT	Brent W. Ross	Brent W. Ross	2003	15
376 3/8	50 7/8	51 5/8	42 5/8	5	5	17 4/8	16 4/8	7 7/8	10 5/8	17	16	Courageous Lake, NT	Gary Nehring	Gary Nehring	2001	16
374 2/8	50 2/8	49	35 2/8	4 3/8	5 4/8	17 2/8	14 4/8	14 5/8	7 1/8	22	19	Little Marten Lake, NT	Houston Smith	Houston Smith	1999	17
374 1/8	54 5/8	53 2/8	37 3/8	6 2/8	5 2/8	1 3/8	19 4/8	1/8	17 2/8	14	19	Warburton Bay, NT	J. Aaron Dillabough	J. Aaron Dillabough	2001	18
373 6/8	51 3/8	51 5/8	38 5/8	4 4/8	4 4/8	15 1/8	16	10 1/8	7 1/8	11	14	Aylmer Lake, NT	James Holzberger	James Holzberger	2003	19
373 2/8	45 2/8	47 4/8	23 4/8	4 5/8	5 5/8	20 4/8	20 3/8	6 2/8	16 7/8	14	17	Rendezvous Lake, NT	George R. Breiwa II	George R. Breiwa II	2000	20
373	44 2/8	44 4/8	31 5/8	5 2/8	4 7/8	17 4/8	19 5/8	12 4/8	14	16	19	Granet Lake, NT	Joe Hocevar	Joe Hocevar	2002	21
372 7/8	49 1/8	48 5/8	32 3/8	6 2/8	5 5/8	11 4/8	11 1/8	7	4 5/8	18	17	Rendezvous Lake, NT	Charles H. Rohrer	Charles H. Rohrer	2001	22
372 5/8	48 2/8	47 2/8	28 1/8	5	5	11 4/8	17 7/8		14 3/8	16	24	Little Forehead Lake, NT	Thomas P. Grainger	Thomas P. Grainger	2003	23
371 2/8	53 6/8	54 1/8	37 3/8	5 2/8	5 2/8	17 6/8	16	8 4/8	12 3/8	13	13	MacKay Lake, NT	Bob J. Williams	Bob J. Williams	2001	24
369 7/8	48 5/8	48 2/8	32 1/8	4 7/8	4 7/8	16 3/8	6 7/8	13 7/8	1/8	30	24	Whitewolf Lake, NT	Aaron Levine	Aaron Levine	2001	25
369 7/8	56 1/8	54 1/8	37 4/8	4 5/8	4 2/8	19 3/8	19 6/8	14 1/8	8 1/8	14	15	Schmok Lake, MB	Thomas W. Petry	Thomas W. Petry	2001	25

Score												Location	Hunter	Owner	Year	Rank
369 3/8	54 4/8	53 2/8	46 1/8	4 7/8	5	14 4/8	15 1/8	1 2/8	9 5/8	14	15	Humpy Lake, NT	Scott S. Snyder	Scott S. Snyder	2000	27
369 1/8	48 3/8	48 3/8	29	5 6/8	5 6/8	14 1/8	15 2/8	12 2/8	11 6/8	26	24	Rendez-vous Lake, NT	Sherwood Mack	Sherwood Mack	2002	28
368 4/8	48 4/8	51	31 2/8	5	4 7/8	16 4/8	17 2/8	5 2/8	13 6/8	14	16	MacKay Lake, NT	Kevin R. Williams	Kevin R. Williams	2001	29
364 3/8	51 4/8	50 5/8	32 4/8	6	5	18 7/8	17 2/8	14 7/8	6 1/8	14	15	Humpy Lake, NT	Robert M. Anderson	Robert M. Anderson	2001	30
361 6/8	45 1/8	47 4/8	26 6/8	5 6/8	5 7/8	14 4/8	18 1/8	11 1/8	10 4/8	23	22	MacKay Lake, NT	Donald C. Norheim	Donald C. Norheim	2001	31
360 7/8	48 4/8	49 2/8	30 1/8	5 5/8	5 3/8	6	13 7/8	1/8	7 4/8	14	15	Humpy Lake, NT	John J. D'Alessandro	John J. D'Alessandro	2002	32
358 6/8	49 1/8	49 3/8	37 1/8	5 4/8	5 4/8	14 2/8	15 6/8	7 3/8	10 4/8	14	17	Little Marten Lake, NT	Chuck Adams	Chuck Adams	2000	33
358 4/8	53	52 3/8	38	4	4 1/8	13 6/8	16 5/8	1/8	13 2/8	13	19	MacKay Lake, NT	Joe L. Perry	Joe L. Perry	1999	34
358	51 4/8	51 2/8	44 1/8	4 7/8	5 1/8	20 6/8	16 4/8	16 1/8	2 4/8	19	12	MacKay Lake, NT	William Janega	William Janega	2001	35
358	44 3/8	43 1/8	24 3/8	5 2/8	5 3/8	13 1/8	17 6/8	4	14	16	26	Rendez-vous Lake, NT	Metod Novak	Metod Novak	2002	35
356 5/8	49 5/8	51 4/8	35 6/8	5 2/8	4 6/8	16 4/8	17	14 1/8	11 4/8	15	15	Snare River, NT	Randy J. Henrichs	Randy J. Henrichs	2002	37
355	52 7/8	52 2/8	39 5/8	4 6/8	5	1 6/8	18 4/8	1/8	16	13	24	Humpy Lake, NT	Lanny Rominger	Lanny Rominger	2000	38
352 7/8	46 1/8	48	29 2/8	5	5	15 7/8	15 5/8	8 7/8	12 2/8	22	22	Courageous Lake, NT	William H. Moyer	William H. Moyer	2003	39
352 3/8	54 6/8	54 3/8	39 2/8	5 5/8	6 5/8	18 2/8	13 1/8			14	9	MacKay Lake, NT	Chad A. Dillabough	Chad A. Dillabough	2002	40
351	52 5/8	52 7/8	33	5 5/8	6	2 3/8	16 1/8	1/8	12 1/8	12	13	Rendez-vous Lake, NT	David A. Ross	David A. Ross	2003	41
350	51 4/8	55 7/8	35 4/8	5 3/8	5	17 1/8	2 2/8	8 4/8	1/8	17	13	Farnie Lake, MB	Thomas G. Kestly	Thomas G. Kestly	2001	42
345 1/8	55 2/8	55 3/8	39	4 6/8	4 5/8	14 4/8	6 2/8	7 6/8	1/8	17	14	Schmok Lake, MB	Thomas W. Petry	Thomas W. Petry	2001	43
400 6/8*	46 7/8	49 4/8	34 3/8	5	5 7/8	13 5/8	14 6/8	9 1/8	10 7/8	18	20	Blevins Lake, MB	Ron Shykitka	Ron Shykitka	2001	

* Final score subject to revision by additional verifying measurements.

QUEBEC-LABRADOR CARIBOU

Rangifer tarandus

Quebec-Labrador caribou includes trophies from Quebec and Labrador.

Score	Length of Main Beam R.	L.	Inside Spread	Circumference at Smallest Place Between Brow and Bez Points R.	L.	Length of Brow Points R.	L.	Width of Brow Points R.	L.	Number of Points R.	L.	Locality	Hunter	Owner	Date Killed	Rank
423 6/8	50 2/8	49 1/8	52 5/8	5 7/8	6 1/8	15 4/8	21 4/8	7 4/8	16 2/8	26	24	Helluva Lake, QC	Jeff C. Wright	Jeff C. Wright	2001	1
402 6/8	56 5/8	53 4/8	45 5/8	5 1/8	4 7/8	18 4/8	17 1/8	13 3/8	15 5/8	22	21	Mollet Lake, QC	James C. Johnson	James C. Johnson	2001	2
397 3/8	53	51 6/8	45 2/8	5 4/8	5 2/8	16	11 3/8	13	4	21	20	Fel Lake, QC	Roscoe Blaisdell	Roscoe Blaisdell	2001	3
394 3/8	47 2/8	47 1/8	43	4 6/8	4 5/8	19 2/8	20 1/8	16 2/8	11 4/8	30	25	Caniapiscau River, QC	Jerilyn K. Zwolinski	Jerilyn K. Zwolinski	2001	4
392 7/8	49 4/8	48 6/8	46 4/8	5	5 3/8	17	17 1/8	8 6/8	12 2/8	21	25	Mollet Lake, QC	Stephen M. Van Poucke	Stephen M. Van Poucke	2001	5
392 3/8	53 6/8	55 1/8	43 4/8	6 1/8	5 6/8	18	15	13 2/8	1/8	22	16	Maki Lake, QC	Sharon M. Pack	Sharon M. Pack	2001	6
392 3/8	54 4/8	54 4/8	44 2/8	5 5/8	5 5/8	3 4/8	18 2/8	1/8	12 6/8	15	13	Caniapiscau Lake, QC	Matthew Christy	Matthew Christy	2001	6
392 2/8	51 6/8	51 2/8	43 5/8	5 1/8	5 2/8	16 4/8	17	11 5/8	11 4/8	19	16	False River, QC	Serge Danis	Serge Danis	1998	8
391 1/8	53 3/8	53 4/8	37 4/8	5 4/8	5 4/8	18 5/8	4 3/8	12	1/8	18	17	Mollet Lake, QC	William K. Herndon	William K. Herndon	2001	9
390 2/8	46 1/8	45 3/8	41 1/8	4 6/8	4 5/8	23	20 6/8	15 1/8	17 2/8	21	23	Musset Lake, QC	Gerald C. Gilbert	Gerald C. Gilbert	2000	10
387 1/8	54 2/8	53 7/8	51 4/8	6 1/8	5 7/8	18	17 4/8	7 7/8	6 6/8	15	14	Mollet Lake, QC	William M. Wheless III	William M. Wheless III	2002	11
387	51 2/8	50 3/8	40 6/8	5 1/8	5	14 6/8	20 2/8	10 4/8	15 3/8	20	19	Minto Lake, QC	Duane Armitage	Duane Armitage	2002	12
386 2/8	50 2/8	51 6/8	49 7/8	5 6/8	6 2/8	16 4/8	19	1/8	13 6/8	14	15	Massie Lake, QC	W.T. Garry Drummond	W.T. Garry Drummond	2001	13
386	57 4/8	56 6/8	40 4/8	4 7/8	4 7/8	1 1/8	18 4/8	12 1/8	13 3/8	15	20	Horse Lake, NL	Ronald J. Bartels	Ronald J. Bartels	2001	14
385 2/8	48	49 6/8	45 3/8	4 6/8	4 7/8	20 1/8	18 6/8	9 6/8	13 4/8	21	21	Minto Lake, QC	Randy Spedoske	Randy Spedoske	2001	15
385 1/8	42 3/8	45 5/8	42 3/8	5 1/8	5 5/8	16 1/8	17 7/8	9 1/8	9 1/8	13	27	May Lake, QC	Michael A. Pilchard	Michael A. Pilchard	2001	16
384 2/8	54 4/8	55 5/8	47 7/8	4 6/8	4 6/8	18 3/8	18	9 7/8	11 4/8	18	15	Minto Lake, QC	Sandra K. Thorn	Sandra K. Thorn	2001	17
384 1/8	48 1/8	48 2/8	44 3/8	4 4/8	4 4/8	17 5/8	20 4/8	4	12 5/8	17	20	Mollet Lake, QC	William H. Taylor	William H. Taylor	2001	18
383 5/8	47 6/8	45 4/8	41 6/8	5 1/8	5 1/8	17 3/8	19 3/8	1/8	13	21	20	Nastapoka River, QC	Robert W. DeVlieger II	Robert W. DeVlieger II	2002	19
383	48	50 1/8	43 6/8	5 3/8	5 1/8	14 3/8	5 4/8	10 3/8	1/8	25	23	Attikamagen Lake, NL	Barbara L. Cole	Barbara L. Cole	2001	20
382 3/8	47 6/8	49 1/8	42 6/8	4 4/8	4 4/8	21 7/8	2	6 1/8	14 2/8	24	21	Lake Chabanel, QC	Ronald D. Britton	Ronald D. Britton	2003	21
380 5/8	48 1/8	51 1/8	41 4/8	4 4/8	4 4/8	12 5/8	16 3/8	15	15	21	24	Torngat Mts., NL	Robert G. Best	Robert G. Best	2001	22
378 3/8	47 5/8	48 3/8	35 3/8	5 6/8	5 4/8	18	20	15	15	20	18	Amiskunipts Lakes, QC	Richard R. Hess	Richard R. Hess	2001	23
378 2/8	52 5/8	52 5/8	62 3/8	5	4 6/8	15 1/8	4 1/8	8 2/8	1/8	13	15	Bobby Lake, QC	Stan L. Saxion	Stan L. Saxion	2002	24
377 6/8	50 1/8	50	37	5	5 1/8	4 1/8	17 6/8	1/8	15 4/8	17	22	Clear Water Lake, QC	Greg A. Abbas	Greg A. Abbas	2001	25
377 4/8	47	50 6/8	38 1/8	4 4/8	4 5/8	14 7/8	19	6	11	13	14	Kakiattualuk Lake, QC	Ronald C. Rockwell	Ronald C. Rockwell	2001	26
377 1/8	43 2/8	44	47 7/8	5 6/8	5 6/8	14 4/8	14 1/8	6 1/8	10 1/8	20	18	Moyer Lake, QC	Ricky L. Gleeson	Ricky L. Gleeson	2002	27
376 4/8	52 6/8	53 2/8	36	4 7/8	5	16 2/8	16 6/8	14 2/8	10 4/8	18	20	Fremin Lake, QC	Floyd E. Osterhoudt	Floyd E. Osterhoudt	2001	28
376 1/8	47 6/8	48	41 3/8	5 2/8	5	16 3/8	17 3/8	12 1/8	11 5/8	17	17	Mollet Lake, QC	Bob Taylor	Bob Taylor	2002	29

Score												Locality	Owner	Hunter	Date Killed	Rank
376	47 5/8	46 4/8	40	5	4 5/8	20	18	14	14 4/8	17	21	Dornon Lake, QC	David A. Ogilvie	David A. Ogilvie	2001	30
375 7/8	44 6/8	46 4/8	29 5/8	4 4/8	4 4/8	15 7/8	20 4/8	11 7/8	11	17	21	Eaton Canyon, QC	Brian J. Gorbutt	Brian J. Gorbutt	2000	31
374 3/8	48 7/8	48 3/8	45 1/8	5 1/8	5	18 1/8	16 1/8	13 3/8	7 7/8	20	16	Little Whale River, QC	Kent Deligans	Kent Deligans	2002	32
373	46 5/8	48 6/8	35 2/8	5 6/8	5 5/8	13 2/8	10 5/8	8 5/8	6	23	21	George River, QC	Bret R. Cary	Bret R. Cary	2001	33
372 7/8	55 5/8	55 5/8	43 5/8	6 1/8	6 1/8	17 3/8	13 4/8	11 7/8	1 4/8	11	13	Minto Lake, QC	Bernard R. Hammond	Bernard R. Hammond	2001	34
372 6/8	45 7/8	46	34 4/8	5 4/8	5 5/8	18 7/8	15 3/8	10 2/8	7	18	13	Aigneau River, QC	L. Steven Ritchey	L. Steven Ritchey	1996	35
371 3/8	50 5/8	52 1/8	48 6/8	4 7/8	4 7/8		20 3/8		16	11	15	Menihec Lake, NL	David C. Stark	David C. Stark	2000	36
370 7/8	50 3/8	53	42 5/8	4 2/8	4 3/8	21 2/8	19 1/8	15 7/8	2 4/8	15	13	Minto Lake, QC	Larry Ahrndt	Larry Ahrndt	2001	37
370 4/8	44 7/8	49 3/8	48 5/8	5 5/8	5 5/8	18 3/8	3 3/8	14 2/8	1/8	18	15	Faribault Lake, QC	Carl E. Cardinal	Carl E. Cardinal	2002	38
370 2/8	51 6/8	51 4/8	44 7/8	5 3/8	5 3/8	13 1/8	16 6/8	6 7/8	12 3/8	17	15	Minto Lake, QC	Carl H. Spaeth	Carl H. Spaeth	1999	39
368 6/8	51 4/8	51 3/8	43 1/8	4 6/8	4 5/8	17 4/8	4	11 2/8	1/8	18	16	La Cosa Lake, NL	Gerald W. Patterson	Gerald W. Patterson	2000	40
367 6/8	48 1/8	49 7/8	46 5/8	4 7/8	5	18 7/8	18 2/8	7 1/8	12 1/8	21	21	Lake Tasiataq, QC	Henry E. Targowski	Henry E. Targowski	2001	41
366 2/8	46 6/8	46	44	5 3/8	5 3/8	17 4/8	14 6/8	11 5/8	1/8	17	13	Simon Lake, QC	John G. Sykes	John G. Sykes	2001	42
366	49 6/8	49 7/8	47 4/8	4 4/8	4 5/8	19 5/8	18 7/8	13	12	15	15	Lake Boismenu, QC	Roger M. Sisco	Roger M. Sisco	2003	43
365 2/8	48 4/8	52	44 7/8	5 1/8	5 3/8	18 4/8	9	17	1/8	16	15	Minto Lake, QC	Anthony Tambasco	Anthony Tambasco	2001	44
405 2/8*	47 4/8	45 5/8	39 7/8	6	5 2/8	17 6/8	15 6/8	11 6/8	13 1/8	12	17	Bull Lake, QC	David A. Parish	David A. Parish	2002	
399 3/8*	46 7/8	46 1/8	44 1/8	5 4/8	5 6/8	20 2/8	21 5/8	7 6/8	19 7/8	20	28	Andrea Lake, NL	Jack D. Stroud	Jack D. Stroud	2001	

* Final score subject to revision by additional verifying measurements.

Minimum Score 80 — New World's Record 95

Score	Length of Horn R.	L.	Circumference of Base R.	L.	Circumference at Third Quarter R.	L.	Inside Spread	Tip to Tip Spread	Length of Prong R.	L.	Locality	Hunter	Owner	Date Killed	Rank
95	19 3/8	18 5/8	7 2/8	7	3 1/8	3	11 7/8	11 5/8	6 7/8	7	Coconino Co., AZ	Dylan M. Woods	Dylan M. Woods	2000	1
95	17 2/8	17 2/8	7 2/8	7 2/8	3 7/8	4	10 1/8	4 3/8	7	6 1/8	Mohave Co., AZ	David Meyer	David Meyer	2002	1
90 4/8	15 7/8	15 5/8	7 6/8	7 5/8	2 7/8	2 7/8	13 7/8	10 5/8	6 6/8	7	Pershing Co., NV	Mark R. Forsmark	Mark R. Forsmark	2001	3
90 4/8	16	17 4/8	7 3/8	7 2/8	2 5/8	3	7 2/8	4	7 7/8	7 3/8	Lincoln Co., NM	Dale Hislop	Dale Hislop	2003	3
90 2/8	15 6/8	15 7/8	7 6/8	7 4/8	3 1/8	3	11 2/8	10	6 2/8	6	Albany Co., WY	Gary W. Spiegelberg	Gary W. Spiegelberg	2001	5
90 2/8	17 2/8	17 1/8	6 3/8	6 2/8	2 5/8	2 5/8	13 5/8	10 2/8	8 5/8	8 5/8	Grant Co., NM	Lanny S. Rominger	Lanny S. Rominger	2002	5
90	16 4/8	16 4/8	7 2/8	7 4/8	2 3/8	2 4/8	11 5/8	11 5/8	7 2/8	7 4/8	Natrona Co., WY	Frank C. Kalasinsky	Frank C. Kalasinsky	2003	7
89 6/8	17 3/8	17 1/8	6 7/8	6 6/8	2 7/8	2 7/8	9 5/8	3 5/8	6 5/8	6 3/8	Harney Co., OR	Debbie E. Cronin	Debbie E. Cronin	2001	8
89 6/8	16 6/8	15 7/8	7 3/8	7 2/8	3 4/8	3 4/8	12 7/8	7 1/8	6	6	Coconino Co., AZ	Dennis J. Waitman	Dennis J. Waitman	2003	8
89 6/8	16 3/8	16 4/8	7 6/8	7 5/8	3	3 1/8	9 4/8	7 6/8	6 3/8	6	Washakie Co., WY	David A. Diede	David A. Diede	2003	8
89 4/8	17 7/8	18 1/8	7 3/8	7	3	2 7/8	10	6 2/8	6	5 6/8	Catron Co., NM	Raymond R. Mong	Raymond R. Mong	1999	11
89 2/8	18	18	7 2/8	7 1/8	2 7/8	2 6/8	9 1/8	3 4/8	5 3/8	5 2/8	Unknown	L.M. Edwards	Doug Millar	PR1950	12
89 2/8	16 3/8	16 2/8	8	7 7/8	3 1/8	3	11 5/8	6 7/8	6	6	Johnson Co., WY	Harlan L. Legried	Harlan L. Legried	2003	12
89	16 4/8	16 6/8	6 7/8	7	3 2/8	3 1/8	11 3/8	7 3/8	7 3/8	6 4/8	Socorro Co., NM	David Meyer	David Meyer	2001	14
89	16	16 1/8	7 5/8	7 5/8	2 5/8	2 5/8	10 5/8	5 4/8	6 3/8	6 4/8	Humboldt Co., NV	Chris R. Winkel	Chris R. Winkel	2002	14
89	17 4/8	17 2/8	7 5/8	7 7/8	2 7/8	2 7/8	8 7/8	4 4/8	6 1/8	5 6/8	Washoe Co., NV	Patrick G. Nicholls	Patrick G. Nicholls	2002	14
88 4/8	16 2/8	16 4/8	7	6 7/8	2 7/8	2 7/8	9 1/8	8 1/8	5 5/8	5 6/8	Manyberries, AB	Fred J. Streleoff	Fred J. Streleoff	2003	17
88 2/8	17 1/8	17 1/8	6 6/8	6 5/8	3	3	13 5/8	13	5 6/8	6 4/8	Pershing Co., NV	Bryan L. Foote	Bryan L. Foote	2001	18
88 2/8	17 1/8	16 7/8	6 5/8	6 5/8	3	3	9 6/8	3 6/8	6	6	Lincoln Co., NM	John Timmons	John Timmons	2003	18
88	16 4/8	17 2/8	7 3/8	7 3/8	2 7/8	2 7/8	14	12 7/8	5 1/8	5 6/8	Coconino Co., AZ	Bill Drake	Bill Drake	2001	20
88	16 3/8	16 2/8	7	6 5/8	2 7/8	2 6/8	12 3/8	8 2/8	7 5/8	6 6/8	Catron Co., NM	Patrick J. Gilligan	Patrick J. Gilligan	2002	20
87 6/8	16 5/8	16 5/8	6 6/8	6 6/8	3	3	10	5 1/8	6 7/8	6 2/8	Pershing Co., NV	Joseph R. Ellington	Joseph R. Ellington	2000	22
87 6/8	17 7/8	18 1/8	6 4/8	6 3/8	3	3	12 2/8	7 2/8	5 6/8	5 4/8	Coconino Co., AZ	A.J. Renkema	A.J. Renkema	2002	22
87 4/8	15 4/8	16	7 2/8	7 3/8	2 7/8	3	8	3	6 3/8	6	Sage Creek, AB	Drew Ramsay	Drew Ramsay	2001	24
87 2/8	16 4/8	16 4/8	7	7	3	3	13 4/8	9 2/8	6 1/8	6	Socorro Co., NM	Kirk E. Winward	Kirk E. Winward	1999	25
87 2/8	16 7/8	16 7/8	6 5/8	6 5/8	3 1/8	3	11 1/8	4 4/8	5 5/8	5 6/8	Fremont Co., WY	Ben L. Wilkes	Ben L. Wilkes	2002	25
87 2/8	15 6/8	15 6/8	7 1/8	7 2/8	3	3 1/8	11 6/8	8 6/8	5 7/8	7 1/8	Navajo Co., AZ	Shatarra DeSpain	Shatarra DeSpain	2003	25
87	16 3/8	16 4/8	7	7	3 2/8	3 2/8	9 3/8	4 5/8	7	5 5/8	Duchesne Co., UT	Joseph Machac	Joseph Machac	2001	28
87	18 3/8	18 1/8	6 6/8	6 7/8	2 5/8	2 5/8	10 5/8	5 1/8	5 3/8	5 4/8	Gilliam Co., OR	Jeff C. Wilkins	Jeff C. Wilkins	2002	28
86 6/8	15 1/8	15	7	7	2 5/8	2 5/8	12	10 2/8	6 2/8	6 4/8	Carbon Co., WY	Dale B. Jones	Dale B. Jones	2002	30
86 6/8	16 4/8	16 4/8	6 6/8	6 7/8	2 6/8	2 7/8	10 6/8	10 7/8	6 4/8	6 3/8	Carbon Co., WY	Gary A. Spina	Gary A. Spina	2002	30
86 4/8	17 2/8	17 2/8	7	6 7/8	2 5/8	2 5/8	18 5/8	16 7/8	6 1/8	6	Judith Basin Co., MT	Michael D. Hannula	Michael D. Hannula	2001	32
86 4/8	16	15 7/8	7 1/8	7 1/8	2 7/8	2 6/8	11 3/8	8	5 5/8	6 4/8	Humboldt Co., NV	James M. Hill	James M. Hill	2003	32

Score											Locality	Hunter	Owner	Date Killed	Rank
86 4/8	16 3/8	16 4/8	7 1/8	7	2 4/8	2 5/8	14 1/8	9 7/8	6	6 1/8	Carbon Co., WY	Garland E. Sawyers	Garland E. Sawyers	2003	32
86 4/8	14 5/8	14 2/8	6 7/8	7	3 3/8	3 1/8	12 2/8	9 2/8	5 2/8	5 2/8	Fremont Co., WY	Bill Chapman	Bill Chapman	2003	32
86 2/8	16	15 7/8	6 7/8	6 7/8	3	3 2/8	10	6 2/8	6 1/8	6 2/8	Moffat Co., WY	Len H. Guldman	Len H. Guldman	2001	36
86 2/8	14 2/8	14 1/8	7 6/8	7 6/8	3 1/8	3	10 1/8	8 1/8	5 4/8	5 4/8	Sweetwater Co., WY	Jon W. Parker	Jon W. Parker	2003	36
86	18 2/8	17 7/8	6 3/8	6 3/8	2 5/8	2 5/8	9 3/8	4 7/8	4 6/8	5 5/8	Mineral Co., NV	Roger L. Fawcett	Roger L. Fawcett	2002	38
86	15 6/8	15 6/8	7	7	2 5/8	2 6/8	9 5/8	4 7/8	6 4/8	6 4/8	Carbon Co., WY	J. Mike Clegg	J. Mike Clegg	2002	38
85 6/8	16 5/8	16 7/8	6 6/8	6 5/8	2 5/8	2 6/8	13	9 1/8	6 4/8	6 6/8	Goshen Co., WY	Billy G. Lee	Billy G. Lee	2000	40
85 6/8	15 3/8	15 7/8	6 6/8	6 5/8	2 5/8	2 6/8	8 7/8	5 6/8	7	7	Natrona Co., WY	Alex R. Bilek	Alex R. Bilek	2001	40
85 4/8	15 6/8	16 1/8	6 6/8	6 6/8	2 7/8	3	9 2/8	7 1/8	5 6/8	6 1/8	Carbon Co., WY	Lenard E. Brashier	Lenard E. Brashier	2000	42
85 4/8	17 2/8	17	7 2/8	7 2/8	2 5/8	2 5/8	8 4/8	2 4/8	4 5/8	4 5/8	Natrona Co., WY	Scotty J. Tuttle	Scotty J. Tuttle	2000	42
85 4/8	17	17 6/8	6 6/8	6 6/8	2 3/8	2 5/8	11 4/8	5 6/8	5 4/8	5 6/8	Yavapai Co., AZ	David Meyer	David Meyer	2001	42
85 4/8	18 1/8	16 5/8	6 6/8	6 5/8	3	3	15 7/8	12 7/8	5 7/8	5 1/8	Colfax Co., NM	Ed Hengel, Jr.	Ed Hengel, Jr.	2002	42
85 4/8	16 7/8	16 5/8	6 6/8	6 6/8	3	3 3/8	10 6/8	8	6	5 7/8	Duchesne Co., UT	John P. Grimmett	John P. Grimmett	2002	42
85 2/8	15 2/8	15 1/8	6 6/8	6 6/8	3 3/8	3 3/8	10 6/8	7 7/8	6 2/8	6 7/8	Harney Co., OR	Matthew J. Foster	Matthew J. Foster	2000	47
85 2/8	15 3/8	15 6/8	7	7 1/8	2 7/8	3 1/8	10 3/8	5	5 2/8	5	Harney Co., OR	Anthony J. Gardner	Anthony J. Gardner	2001	47
85 2/8	16 6/8	16 6/8	7 2/8	7 1/8	2 4/8	2 4/8	10 6/8	7 7/8	5 3/8	5 2/8	Hudspeth Co., TX	William G. Kyle	William G. Kyle	2002	47
85 2/8	16 5/8	16 6/8	6 7/8	6 7/8	3 2/8	3 4/8	10	9 1/8	4 4/8	4 4/8	Carbon Co., WY	Donald E. Perrien	Donald E. Perrien	2002	47
85 2/8	15 4/8	15 4/8	6 3/8	6 3/8	3 4/8	3 4/8	11 1/8	10 3/8	5 6/8	5 6/8	Carbon Co., WY	John V. Sjogren	John V. Sjogren	2002	47
85 2/8	16 4/8	16 6/8	6 6/8	6 5/8	2 3/8	2 5/8	10	5 5/8	6 5/8	6 5/8	Jackson Co., CO	Karl E. Wondrak	Karl E. Wondrak	2003	47
85 2/8	15 4/8	15 2/8	7	6 7/8	2 6/8	2 6/8	10	8	6 2/8	6 3/8	Coconino Co., AZ	Levi M. Wilson	Levi M. Wilson	2003	47
85 2/8	17	16 6/8	6 5/8	6 5/8	3 1/8	3 2/8	15 5/8	10 3/8	4 6/8	5 3/8	Cypress Lake, SK	Bradley R. Jackle	Bradley R. Jackle	2003	47
85	17	17 1/8	6 2/8	6 3/8	2 4/8	2 5/8	11 1/8	5 2/8	6 4/8	6 7/8	Nye Co., NV	Jared R. Pekuri	Jared R. Pekuri	2000	55
85	16 6/8	16 6/8	6 5/8	6 5/8	2 5/8	2 4/8	10 2/8	4 2/8	6 5/8	6	Baker Co., OR	Russell H. Elms	Russell H. Elms	2001	55
85	16	15 7/8	6 6/8	7	3	3	8 6/8	5 5/8	5 6/8	7	Emery Co., UT	Len H. Guldman	Len H. Guldman	2001	55
85	16	16 2/8	6 7/8	6 4/8	2 5/8	2 7/8	6 3/8	2 6/8	6 4/8	6	Carbon Co., WY	Larry S. Hicks	Larry S. Hicks	2001	55
85	15	14 4/8	7 3/8	7 4/8	3 1/8	3	13 7/8	12	6	6 3/8	Washoe Co., NV	Kawika Fisher	Kawika Fisher	2002	55
85	17 2/8	16 4/8	6 7/8	6 7/8	2 3/8	2 2/8	9 2/8	2 5/8	6 1/8	6	Washoe Co., NV	Jelindo A. Tiberti II	Jelindo A. Tiberti II	2003	55
84 6/8	16	15 6/8	6 6/8	6 6/8	2 5/8	2 5/8	10 6/8	4 6/8	5 2/8	5 4/8	Mora Co., NM	Mark W. Streissguth	Mark W. Streissguth	2000	61
84 6/8	17	17	6	5 7/8	3 1/8	3	11 4/8	9	4 2/8	4 3/8	Colorado	Picked Up	Lance M. Gatlin	PR2001	61
84 6/8	15 5/8	15 5/8	6 5/8	6 5/8	2 7/8	3 1/8	9 6/8	5 6/8	6 4/8	6 3/8	Harney Co., OR	Jim C. Femrite	Jim C. Femrite	2001	61
84 6/8	16 3/8	16 3/8	6 5/8	6 5/8	2 6/8	2 6/8	11 7/8	8 7/8	6	6	Mohave Co., AZ	Steve E. Johns	Steve E. Johns	2001	61
84 6/8	15 6/8	15 7/8	6 6/8	6 6/8	2 7/8	3 1/8	12 3/8	9 7/8	6 1/8	6 1/8	Washakie Co., WY	Mark I. Walker	Mark I. Walker	2001	61
84 6/8	15	14 7/8	7	7 1/8	3	3	10 3/8	9 6/8	6 1/8	6 1/8	Natrona Co., WY	Landon S. Blakeley	Landon S. Blakeley	2001	61
84 6/8	16 4/8	16 3/8	7	7	2 6/8	3	10 4/8	6 3/8	5 4/8	5 2/8	Sweetwater Co., WY	Roy G. Gamblin	Roy G. Gamblin	2002	61
84 6/8	16 6/8	16 5/8	6 6/8	6 4/8	3 2/8	3 2/8	10 3/8	4 4/8	5 2/8	5 4/8	Socorro Co., NM	Gilbert T. Adams III	Gilbert T. Adams III	2002	61
84 6/8	15	15	7	7	3	3	10 5/8	7	6 1/8	6	Sheridan Co., NE	Tim L. Bernard	Tim L. Bernard	2002	61
84 6/8	16 6/8	16 6/8	6 5/8	6 5/8	3	2 2/8	5 5/8	2 2/8	5 1/8	5 3/8	Lincoln Co., WY	Brad D. Lewis	Brad D. Lewis	2002	61
84 6/8	16 5/8	16 4/8	6 2/8	6 2/8	2 5/8	2 5/8	11 3/8	9 7/8	5 3/8	5 1/8	Socorro Co., NM	Angie D. Hall	Angie D. Hall	2003	61
84 4/8	15 7/8	15 6/8	6 3/8	6 3/8	3 3/8	3 3/8	12	11 3/8	6 5/8	6 2/8	Socorro Co., NM	David W. Ogilvie, Jr.	David W. Ogilvie, Jr.	1993	72
84 4/8	15 2/8	15 2/8	7 1/8	7 1/8	2 6/8	2 6/8	13 2/8	6 6/8	5 7/8	5 7/8	Fremont Co., WY	Greg E. Fuechsel	Greg E. Fuechsel	2000	72
84 4/8	15 2/8	15	6 7/8	6 7/8	3 3/8	3 3/8	5 5/8	2 4/8	6 2/8	6 2/8	Emery Co., UT	Len H. Guldman	Len H. Guldman	2002	72

PRONGHORN

Antilocapra americana americana and related subspecies

Score	Length of Horn R.	L.	Circumference of Base R.	L.	Circumference at Third Quarter R.	L.	Inside Spread	Tip to Tip Spread	Length of Prong R.	L.	Locality	Hunter	Owner	Date Killed	Rank
84 4/8	16 5/8	16 3/8	7 1/8	7	2 5/8	2 7/8	9 6/8	4 4/8	5 5/8	5 4/8	Brooks, AB	Shaun E. Steidel	Shaun E. Steidel	2002	72
84 4/8	16 4/8	17 2/8	5 7/8	6	3 6/8	3 5/8	10 1/8	7 6/8	6 1/8	5 7/8	Socorro Co., NM	Michael L Braegelmann	Michael L Braegelmann	2002	72
84 4/8	16 2/8	16 4/8	6 2/8	6 2/8	2 6/8	2 6/8	9 1/8	3 7/8	6 5/8	6 6/8	Lincoln Co., NM	Charles W. Wolcott	Charles W. Wolcott	2002	72
84 4/8	16 2/8	16 4/8	6 6/8	6 5/8	2 5/8	2 5/8	12 5/8	6 7/8	6 5/8	6 6/8	Consul, SK	Greg D. Illerbrun	Greg D. Illerbrun	2002	72
84 4/8	17 2/8	17 3/8	6 5/8	6 5/8	2 7/8	2 6/8	16 3/8	9 6/8	5 3/8	5 1/8	Colfax Co., NM	Robert D. Jones	Robert D. Jones	2003	72
84 4/8	16 6/8	16 6/8	6 3/8	6 3/8	3	3	9	5 5/8	5	5 2/8	Apache Co., AZ	Mel L. Risch	Mel L. Risch	2003	72
84 2/8	17	17	6 2/8	6 2/8	2 5/8	2 5/8	10 3/8	5 7/8	6 1/8	6 1/8	Catron Co., NM	Richard Jaramillo	Richard Jaramillo	1999	81
84 2/8	16 1/8	16	6 6/8	6 7/8	2 5/8	2 5/8	8 7/8	4 2/8	6 2/8	6 3/8	Harney Co., OR	Marvin K. Champ	Marvin K. Champ	1999	81
84 2/8	16 2/8	16 2/8	6 5/8	6 6/8	2 7/8	2 6/8	11 6/8	7 5/8	5 7/8	5 6/8	Sweetwater Co., WY	Joseph L. Koback	Joseph L. Koback	2000	81
84 2/8	16 3/8	15 2/8	7 3/8	7 1/8	3 1/8	2 6/8	12 5/8	10 2/8	5 3/8	5 5/8	Carbon Co., WY	Kip T. Williams	Kip T. Williams	2000	81
84 2/8	16 2/8	16 1/8	6 7/8	6 7/8	2 5/8	2 5/8	9 6/8	5 6/8	5 7/8	6 2/8	Carbon Co., WY	Kim Cooper	Kim Cooper	2001	81
84 2/8	16 2/8	15 5/8	6 4/8	6 3/8	2 6/8	2 6/8	12 6/8	9 1/8	6 1/8	6 1/8	Lincoln Co., NM	Lee Frudden	Lee Frudden	2002	81
84 2/8	16 4/8	16 2/8	6 1/8	6 2/8	3	3 2/8	11 4/8	7	6 1/8	5 5/8	Custer Co., CO	Picked Up	Kevin Travincek	2003	81
84 2/8	14 4/8	14 6/8	7 2/8	7 1/8	2 5/8	2 6/8	9 1/8	3 6/8	6 5/8	6 4/8	Logan Co., CO	Richard L. Smith	Richard L. Smith	2003	81
84	15 5/8	15 4/8	7	7	3	3	11 1/8	6 5/8	6 1/8	6 2/8	Sweetwater Co., WY	Jerry D. Johnson	Jerry D. Johnson	1999	89
84	16 1/8	16 4/8	7	6 7/8	2 4/8	2 3/8	13 2/8	8 6/8	6 7/8	6 3/8	Harney Co., OR	Scott D. Isaak	Scott D. Isaak	2001	89
84	15	15	7	7	3 3/8	3 2/8	10 1/8	6 6/8	5	5	Yavapai Co., AZ	Kevin A. Teston	Kevin A. Teston	2001	89
84	15 2/8	15 2/8	7	7	2 6/8	2 5/8	9	4 2/8	6	6	Eureka Co., NV	Brian J. Fagg	Brian J. Fagg	2002	89
84	16 3/8	17 3/8	6 7/8	6 6/8	2 6/8	3	7 1/8	1	5 5/8	5 5/8	Natrona Co., WY	Craig R. Pierce	Craig R. Pierce	2003	89
83 6/8	15 5/8	15 4/8	7	7	3 1/8	3 1/8	10 1/8	6 1/8	5 4/8	5 4/8	Carbon Co., WY	Larry S. Hicks	Larry S. Hicks	2000	94
83 6/8	17 5/8	17 6/8	6 3/8	6 3/8	2 5/8	2 5/8	9 2/8	5 2/8	5 3/8	5 2/8	Catron Co., NM	R. Steve Bass	R. Steve Bass	2001	94
83 6/8	15 6/8	15 6/8	6 7/8	6 7/8	3 2/8	3 2/8	10 4/8	8 3/8	5	4 7/8	Socorro Co., NM	Todd A. Romsa	Todd A. Romsa	2001	94
83 6/8	17 1/8	17 3/8	5 7/8	5 7/8	2 4/8	2 5/8	12 1/8	10 1/8	5 6/8	5 7/8	Catron Co., NM	Seth R. Edgar	Seth R. Edgar	2001	94
83 6/8	17	17 1/8	6 4/8	6 4/8	2 6/8	3	9 6/8	5 4/8	5 4/8	5	Humboldt Co., NV	Victor Marcuerquiaga	Victor Marcuerquiaga	2002	94
83 6/8	15 2/8	15 2/8	6 4/8	6 4/8	3 2/8	3 2/8	8 1/8	5 2/8	5 6/8	5 5/8	Coconino Co., AZ	Mark D. Roggenbuck	Mark D. Roggenbuck	2002	94
83 6/8	18 7/8	18 6/8	6 2/8	6 1/8	2 5/8	2 4/8	16 2/8	14	5 6/8	4 5/8	Grant Co., NM	H. Hudson DeCray	H. Hudson DeCray	2002	94
83 6/8	16	15 5/8	7	7	3 2/8	2 7/8	13	11 2/8	4 7/8	4 7/8	Washakie Co., WY	Ronald D. Nelson	Ronald D. Nelson	2002	94
83 6/8	15 6/8	15 6/8	6 3/8	6 3/8	3	3 5/8	11	9 5/8	6	5 2/8	Uintah Co., UT	Timothy K. Krause	Timothy K. Krause	2003	94
83 4/8	15 4/8	15 5/8	7 3/8	7 1/8	3	3	11 4/8	8 5/8	5 2/8	5 1/8	Mora Co., NM	Pate Stewart	Pate Stewart	2000	103
83 4/8	14 7/8	14 6/8	7	6 7/8	2 6/8	2 6/8	14 3/8	12 1/8	6 6/8	6 2/8	Fremont Co., WY	Patrick D. Austin	Patrick D. Austin	2000	103
83 4/8	15 6/8	15 6/8	6 3/8	6 3/8	3 1/8	3	13 7/8	11 5/8	5 4/8	5 3/8	Coconino Co., AZ	Kyle L. Wells	Kyle L. Wells	2000	103
83 4/8	15 3/8	15 1/8	7 2/8	7 2/8	2 7/8	2 6/8	13 3/8	11 5/8	6	5 4/8	Moffat Co., CO	Bernard F. Kochevar, Jr.	Bernard F. Kochevar, Jr.	2000	103
83 4/8	15	17	7 4/8	7 1/8	2 3/8	2 6/8	11	8 6/8	6 1/8	6	Harney Co., OR	Randy Hopp	Randy Hopp	2001	103

											Location	Hunter	Owner	Date	Score
83 4/8	15 3/8	15 5/8	7 3/8	7	2 4/8	2 6/8	14 3/8	12 3/8	5 6/8	6	Lincoln Co., WY	LaDee N. Allred	LaDee N. Allred	2001	103
83 4/8	14 4/8	14 3/8	6 7/8	6 7/8	3 4/8	3 4/8	10 6/8	8 7/8	5 7/8	6	Socorro Co., NM	John C. Perkins	John C. Perkins	2001	103
83 4/8	15 5/8	15 5/8	7	6 7/8	2 7/8	2 7/8	7 4/8	5 2/8	5 2/8	5 7/8	Jackson Co., CO	Robert B. Firth, Jr.	Robert B. Firth, Jr.	2001	103
83 4/8	15 4/8	15	6 2/8	6 2/8	3 6/8	3 1/8	9 2/8	3 6/8	6 1/8	5 6/8	Hudspeth Co., TX	James N. Gallagher, Jr.	James N. Gallagher, Jr.	2002	103
83 4/8	15 1/8	15	7	7	2 6/8	2 6/8	7 2/8	5 3/8	6 2/8	5 7/8	Sweetwater Co., WY	Aaron R. Carlson	Aaron R. Carlson	2002	103
83 4/8	15 6/8	16	7	6 7/8	2 5/8	2 6/8	15 1/8	11 6/8	4 6/8	4 7/8	Eureka Co., NV	Robert Loveridge	Robert Loveridge	2003	103
83 4/8	15 3/8	15 5/8	7	6 6/8	2 6/8	2 7/8	10 7/8	7 2/8	6 3/8	5 5/8	Uintah Co., UT	J. Todd Hogan	J. Todd Hogan	2003	103
83 4/8	16	15 5/8	6 5/8	6 6/8	3	3	14 5/8	10 2/8	5 4/8	5 5/8	Coconino Co., AZ	Jeffrey L. May	Jeffrey L. May	2003	103
83 2/8	15 6/8	15 5/8	6 6/8	6 6/8	2 7/8	3	13 3/8	14	5 4/8	5 4/8	Socorro Co., NM	Wade A. Boggs	Wade A. Boggs	2000	116
83 2/8	15 1/8	16 1/8	7 4/8	7 2/8	2 7/8	3	10	4 2/8	5 4/8	6	Hudspeth Co., TX	Bonnie Cross	Bonnie Cross	2000	116
83 2/8	15 6/8	15 5/8	7 4/8	7 4/8	2 6/8	2 4/8	12 1/8	8	4 6/8	4 6/8	Colfax Co., NM	Robert D. Jones	Robert D. Jones	2001	116
83 2/8	16 6/8	16 6/8	6 7/8	6 6/8	3 3/8	2 3/8	11 6/8	7 2/8	5 5/8	5 4/8	Harney Co., OR	Kenneth J. Zander, Jr.	Kenneth J. Zander, Jr.	2001	116
83 2/8	16 3/8	16 3/8	6 7/8	6 5/8	2 5/8	2 5/8	12	7 6/8	6 2/8	5 6/8	Coconino Co., AZ	Charles H. Lewis	Charles H. Lewis	2001	116
83 2/8	15 1/8	15	7 3/8	7 3/8	2 5/8	2 5/8	8 4/8	3 2/8	4 4/8	4 4/8	Carbon Co., WY	Charles P. Ruzicska	Charles P. Ruzicska	2001	116
83 2/8	17 6/8	18 1/8	5 4/8	5 7/8	2 5/8	2 6/8	12 5/8	7 5/8	6	6 3/8	Red Deer River, AB	Ron Peshke	Ron Peshke	2001	116
83 2/8	15 7/8	15 6/8	7 1/8	6 7/8	2 4/8	2 4/8	9 4/8	3 2/8	6 3/8	6	Natrona Co., WY	Justin A. Fernandez	Justin A. Fernandez	2001	116
83 2/8	16 7/8	16 1/8	5 7/8	6	2 3/8	2 4/8	11 6/8	7 1/8	6 2/8	6 6/8	Mineral Co., NV	George C. Mathias, Jr.	George C. Mathias, Jr.	2002	116
83 2/8	15 4/8	15 6/8	6 4/8	6 6/8	2 6/8	2 6/8	9 4/8	3 4/8	5 5/8	5 3/8	Yavapai Co., AZ	John E. Pappas	John E. Pappas	2002	116
83 2/8	15 4/8	15 5/8	6 1/8	6	3 4/8	3 4/8	10 1/8	7	5 4/8	6	Socorro Co., NM	Thomas J. Murphy	Thomas J. Murphy	2002	116
83 2/8	16 3/8	16 1/8	6 4/8	6 4/8	2 4/8	2 4/8	12 1/8	8	5 3/8	5 3/8	Albany Co., WY	Steven R. Maynard	Steven R. Maynard	2003	116
83 2/8	17	16 4/8	6 2/8	6 2/8	2 6/8	2 5/8	12 5/8	8 1/8	5 7/8	5 4/8	Lincoln Co., NM	Bob Nicholas	Bob Nicholas	2003	116
83 2/8	15 6/8	15 7/8	6 4/8	6 4/8	2 3/8	2 5/8	12 2/8	8	6 3/8	6 3/8	Rosebud Co., MT	Todd D. Friez	Todd D. Friez	2003	116
83	16	15 4/8	6 6/8	6 6/8	2 6/8	2 6/8	8	5 3/8	5 7/8	5 7/8	Cascade Co., MT	Henry G. Sivumaki	Henry G. Sivumaki	1998	130
83	14 7/8	15	6 5/8	6 5/8	3	3	9 5/8	7 3/8	6 1/8	6 3/8	Socorro Co., NM	R. Steve Bass	R. Steve Bass	2000	130
83	16 4/8	16 5/8	6 6/8	6 6/8	2 5/8	2 5/8	8 7/8	4 2/8	4 6/8	5	Humboldt Co., NV	David A. Hargrove	David A. Hargrove	2000	130
83	17 1/8	16 7/8	6 4/8	6 3/8	2 6/8	2 6/8	9	3 7/8	5 4/8	4 6/8	Rich Co., UT	Charles A. Lantry	Charles A. Lantry	2000	130
83	16 4/8	16 5/8	6 5/8	6 4/8	2 5/8	2 5/8	13 5/8	9 5/8	5 3/8	5 1/8	Socorro Co., NM	Michaux Nash, Jr.	Michaux Nash, Jr.	2000	130
83	15 6/8	15 7/8	6 4/8	6 1/8	2 5/8	2 5/8	9 2/8	5 2/8	6 3/8	6 2/8	Humboldt Co., NV	Jevon W. Ziegler	Jevon W. Ziegler	2001	130
83	15	15 2/8	7 3/8	7 3/8	3	3	11 3/8	8 2/8	4 5/8	4 5/8	Carbon Co., WY	Dorin D. Blodgett	Dorin D. Blodgett	2001	130
83	16 2/8	16 4/8	6 4/8	6 3/8	2 2/8	2 2/8	10 5/8	5 2/8	6 3/8	7 2/8	Harney Co., OR	Mark W. Scott	Mark W. Scott	2002	130
83	16 1/8	16 3/8	6 6/8	6 4/8	2 5/8	2 7/8	13	7 3/8	5 6/8	6	Emery Co., UT	Susan Tuttle	Susan Tuttle	2002	130
83	15 7/8	16 1/8	6 3/8	6 3/8	2 6/8	2 6/8	11 4/8	5 6/8	5 6/8	6 1/8	Coconino Co., AZ	Ken Goodman	Ken Goodman	2002	130
83	15 4/8	15 4/8	6 1/8	6	2 4/8	2 4/8	10 6/8	5 4/8	7 2/8	7	Hudspeth Co., TX	Ernie Davis	Ernie Davis	2002	130
83	14 6/8	14 7/8	6 6/8	6 5/8	2 5/8	2 5/8	11 3/8	7 7/8	6 3/8	6 3/8	Carbon Co., WY	William L. Larson	William L. Larson	2003	130
82 6/8	15 7/8	15 7/8	6 4/8	6 4/8	2 6/8	2 6/8	11 2/8	5 6/8	5 1/8	5 3/8	Carbon Co., UT	Bonnie M. Powell	Bonnie M. Powell	1999	142
82 6/8	16	16 1/8	6 1/8	6 1/8	2 6/8	2 6/8	10 4/8	6 2/8	5 5/8	5 7/8	Fremont Co., WY	Ken Wilkinson	Ken Wilkinson	2001	142
82 6/8	16 1/8	16 3/8	6 4/8	6 3/8	2 7/8	2 7/8	8 2/8	2 2/8	5 3/8	5 2/8	Quay Co., NM	Joshua M. Panger	Joshua M. Panger	2001	142
82 6/8	16 6/8	16 4/8	6 3/8	6 2/8	2 7/8	2 7/8	9 1/8	7 2/8	4 6/8	5 3/8	Eureka Co., NV	Mike B. Holt	Mike B. Holt	2002	142
82 6/8	15 4/8	15 5/8	6 6/8	6 6/8	2 5/8	2 5/8	12 4/8	9 5/8	6 2/8	6 4/8	Powder River Co., MT	William P. Stuver	William P. Stuver	2003	142
82 4/8	14 6/8	14 3/8	7	7	3 3/8	3 4/8	8	4 4/8	4 4/8	5 2/8	Coconino Co., AZ	Isaac W. Wilson	Isaac W. Wilson	2003	142
82 4/8	16 1/8	16 5/8	7 1/8	6 7/8	2 4/8	2 5/8	9 7/8	5 7/8	5 6/8	5 7/8	Hartley Co., TX	Marvin Willis	Mark Willis	1968	148

PRONGHORN

Antilocapra americana americana and related subspecies

Score	Length of Horn R.	L.	Circumference of Base R.	L.	Circumference at Third Quarter R.	L.	Inside Spread	Tip to Tip Spread	Length of Prong R.	L.	Locality	Hunter	Owner	Date Killed	Rank
82 4/8	14 7/8	14 5/8	6 3/8	6 3/8	3 3/8	3 3/8	10 5/8	8 1/8	6 3/8	6 3/8	Chouteau Co., MT	Jack Willson	Jack Willson	1986	148
82 4/8	16 1/8	16 2/8	7	6 5/8	2 6/8	2 3/8	10 3/8	5 4/8	6 3/8	5 5/8	Carbon Co., WY	John Strand	John Strand	1997	148
82 4/8	15 1/8	15	7 4/8	7 3/8	2 7/8	2 7/8	11 2/8	9 2/8	6 3/8	5 1/8	Musselshell Co., MT	Matt M. Marvel	Matt M. Marvel	1999	148
82 4/8	16 6/8	16 3/8	6 2/8	6 2/8	2 3/8	2 4/8	11 3/8	7 4/8	6 4/8	6 1/8	Humboldt Co., NV	M. Todd McLean	M. Todd McLean	2000	148
82 4/8	16	16 1/8	6 3/8	6 3/8	2 6/8	2 6/8	11 5/8	8 6/8	5 4/8	5 5/8	Harney Co., OR	Travis E. Ingram	Travis E. Ingram	2000	148
82 4/8	14 7/8	15	6 6/8	6 6/8	3	3	9 6/8	7 5/8	6	6	Carbon Co., WY	James E. Schmid	James E. Schmid	2000	148
82 4/8	17	16 7/8	6 3/8	6 4/8	2 6/8	2 6/8	10 6/8	9 2/8	4 6/8	4 7/8	Navajo Co., AZ	Byron L. Eiler	Byron L. Eiler	2000	148
82 4/8	17	17	6 7/8	6 4/8	3	3	11 4/8	6 7/8	4 4/8	4 4/8	Catron Co., NM	Scott M. Kohrs	Scott M. Kohrs	2000	148
82 4/8	15 7/8	15 7/8	6 6/8	6 6/8	2 4/8	2 5/8	8	1 3/8	5 3/8	5 3/8	Humboldt Co., NV	John H. Parker	John H. Parker	2001	148
82 4/8	14 4/8	14 4/8	6 6/8	6 6/8	3 4/8	3 5/8	14 1/8	12 4/8	5 3/8	5 2/8	Luna Co., NM	Hanspeter Giger	Hanspeter Giger	2001	148
82 4/8	15 7/8	15 7/8	6 7/8	6 7/8	3	3	16 3/8	12 3/8	5 5/8	4 5/8	Colfax Co., NM	Robert D. Jones	Robert D. Jones	2002	148
82 4/8	15 3/8	15 4/8	6 4/8	6 4/8	2 5/8	2 6/8	9	5 1/8	5 7/8	5 6/8	Sweetwater Co., WY	Paul H. Comino	Paul H. Comino	2002	148
82 4/8	15 2/8	15 2/8	6 5/8	6 4/8	3 3/8	3 2/8	9 4/8	6 5/8	5 2/8	5	Owyhee Co., ID	Donald E. Perrien	Donald E. Perrien	2002	148
82 4/8	15 7/8	16 4/8	6 3/8	6 2/8	2 5/8	2 6/8	14 2/8	11 4/8	5 5/8	5 4/8	Otero Co., NM	George C. Billings	George C. Billings	2003	148
82 4/8	14 5/8	14 6/8	7 3/8	7 2/8	2 7/8	2 6/8	11 4/8	9	5 2/8	5 2/8	Natrona Co., WY	Cory L. Wolff	Cory L. Wolff	2003	148
82 4/8	17	17	6 1/8	6 1/8	2 6/8	2 6/8	13 2/8	7 1/8	5 3/8	5 2/8	Powder River Co., MT	Floyd Michell	Floyd Michell	2003	148
82 2/8	15 3/8	15 3/8	7 2/8	7 2/8	2 6/8	2 6/8	15 5/8	11 7/8	5 2/8	5 6/8	Natrona Co., WY	Charles K. Williams	Charles K. Williams	1992	165
82 2/8	16 4/8	16 4/8	6	5 5/8	2 6/8	3	14 2/8	12 4/8	6 1/8	5 5/8	Coconino Co., AZ	Keith Martin	Keith Martin	2000	165
82 2/8	15 3/8	15 2/8	6 5/8	6 6/8	2 5/8	2 6/8	14 7/8	12 3/8	5 7/8	4 5/8	Hudspeth Co., TX	Timothy L. Orton	Timothy L. Orton	2000	165
82 2/8	15 3/8	15 3/8	6 2/8	6 2/8	2 6/8	2 6/8	8 3/8	3 3/8	5 7/8	5 3/8	Rosebud Co., MT	Eugene F. Himmel	Eugene F. Himmel	2000	165
82 2/8	16	16	7	7	2 3/8	2 4/8	9 7/8	7	6	6 1/8	Fremont Co., WY	Jeffery K. Harrow	Jeffery K. Harrow	2001	165
82 2/8	16 2/8	15 7/8	7 2/8	7 2/8	2 5/8	2 3/8	12 2/8	10	5 5/8	5 6/8	Sweetwater Co., WY	Kevin Burns	Kevin Burns	2001	165
82 2/8	15 7/8	15 1/8	6 4/8	6 4/8	2 2/8	2 2/8	9	4 2/8	6 6/8	6 6/8	Albany Co., WY	Janan B. Jones	Janan B. Jones	2001	165
82 2/8	14 7/8	14 5/8	7 2/8	7 1/8	2 6/8	2 6/8	11 3/8	8 2/8	5 7/8	6 1/8	Campbell Co., WY	Derek E. Emter	Orin Edwards	2001	165
82 2/8	14 7/8	15	6 1/8	6 1/8	3 4/8	3 2/8	10 2/8	7 6/8	5	5	Taos Co., NM	Donald E. Perrien	Donald E. Perrien	2002	165
82 2/8	15 4/8	15 3/8	6 4/8	6 4/8	2 4/8	2 4/8	11 2/8	6 5/8	6 5/8	6 4/8	Union Co., OR	David J. Barlet	David J. Barlet	2002	165
82 2/8	16	16 2/8	7	6 6/8	2 5/8	2 6/8	14 1/8	9 4/8	6 4/8	5 5/8	Coconino Co., AZ	Robert M. Young	Robert M. Young	2002	165
82 2/8	15	14 7/8	6 3/8	6 3/8	2 7/8	2 7/8	9 6/8	8 2/8	5 7/8	5 7/8	Santa Fe Co., NM	Johnny L. Montoya	Johnny L. Montoya	2002	165
82 2/8	17	16 7/8	6 4/8	6 6/8	2 7/8	2 7/8	10 4/8	5 6/8	4 2/8	5 2/8	Hudspeth Co., TX	Gerald P. McBride	Gerald P. McBride	2002	165
82 2/8	16 2/8	16 2/8	6 1/8	6 1/8	2 4/8	2 6/8	8 3/8	4 2/8	6 1/8	6	Wibaux Co., MT	Gary A. Nunberg	Gary A. Nunberg	2002	165
82 2/8	15 7/8	16 3/8	6 1/8	6 2/8	2 6/8	2 6/8	9 3/8	3 4/8	6 1/8	6 2/8	Laramie Co., WY	Blake C. Prather	Blake C. Prather	2002	165
82 2/8	14 1/8	14	7 1/8	7 1/8	2 2/8	2 2/8	13 7/8	12	6 2/8	6 1/8	Humboldt Co., NV	Valerie J. Moser	Valerie J. Moser	2003	165
82 2/8	17	16 5/8	6 4/8	6 4/8	2 4/8	2 4/8	8 4/8	4 6/8	5 3/8	5 1/8	Carbon Co., WY	Larry S. Hicks	Larry S. Hicks	2003	165

Score										Locality	Hunter	Owner	Date	Rank
82 2/8	15 3/8	15 3/8	6 3/8	6 2/8	3 2/8	3	10 4/8	7 3/8	5 5/8	Socorro Co., NM	Timothy K. Krause	Timothy K. Krause	2003	165
82 2/8	16 3/8	16 3/8	6 4/8	6 3/8	2 5/8	2 6/8	10 4/8	4	5 3/8	Yavapai Co., AZ	Rick J. Levine	Rick J. Levine	2003	165
82 2/8	15 5/8	15 3/8	6 2/8	6 2/8	2 6/8	2 5/8	8 7/8	5 2/8	6	Golden Valley Co., ND	Sean M. Finneman	Sean M. Finneman	2003	165
82	15 5/8	15 7/8	6 4/8	6 6/8	2 6/8	2 6/8	8 4/8	3 4/8	5 5/8	Catron Co., NM	John P. Grimmett	John P. Grimmett	1987	185
82	17 1/8	16 5/8	7 5/8	6 6/8	2 1/8	2 6/8	13 6/8	11 4/8	5 3/8	Washoe Co., NV	Andy H. Riddell	Andy H. Riddell	1992	185
82	16 5/8	16 5/8	6 3/8	6 2/8	2 6/8	2 6/8	7 6/8	4	4 6/8	Lincoln Co., NM	Earl K. Wahl, Jr.	Earl K. Wahl, Jr.	1992	185
82	16 7/8	16	6 4/8	6 5/8	3 1/8	3 1/8	11 1/8	6 3/8	5 4/8	Coconino Co., AZ	John P. Grimmett	John P. Grimmett	1993	185
82	16 6/8	16 5/8	6 4/8	6 5/8	2 6/8	2 6/8	12 2/8	8 4/8	5	Washoe Co., NV	Anthony V. Guillen, Jr.	Anthony V. Guillen, Jr.	2000	185
82	14 7/8	15	7	7	3	3	12 3/8	8 6/8	5	Rio Grande Co., CO	Andrew L. Farish	Andrew L. Farish	2000	185
82	16 1/8	16 1/8	6 6/8	6 5/8	2 5/8	2 5/8	8 2/8	2 4/8	5 3/8	Platte Co., WY	Michael Perkowski	Michael Perkowski	2000	185
82	15 4/8	15 5/8	6 4/8	6 4/8	2 4/8	2 4/8	13	8 5/8	5 1/8	Liberty Co., MT	Joel H. Fenger	Joel H. Fenger	2000	185
82	15 4/8	15 4/8	6 2/8	6 2/8	2 7/8	2 7/8	12 5/8	8 2/8	6	Washoe Co., NV	Thomas W. Caron	Thomas W. Caron	2001	185
82	15	16 1/8	7	7	2 6/8	2 6/8	13	9 4/8	6	Natrona Co., WY	Tom L. Swartz	Tom L. Swartz	2002	185
82	15 2/8	15 2/8	6 3/8	6 3/8	3	2 5/8	8	7 4/8	5 4/8	Albany Co., WY	Curt Apel	Curt Apel	2002	185
82	15 2/8	15 4/8	6 5/8	6 6/8	2 7/8	2 5/8	15 4/8	12 4/8	5 6/8	Larimer Co., CO	Paul W. Hansen	Paul W. Hansen	2002	185
82	14 6/8	14 5/8	6 6/8	6 6/8	2 7/8	3	10 3/8	6 7/8	5 1/8	Washakie Co., WY	Lew W. Raderschadt	Lew W. Raderschadt	2002	185
82	14 6/8	14 6/8	6 2/8	6 1/8	3 3/8	2 7/8	11 4/8	7 4/8	6 2/8	Socorro Co., NM	Brent V. Trumbo	Brent V. Trumbo	2002	185
82	15 4/8	15 1/8	7	6 7/8	2 3/8	2 5/8	12 2/8	9 3/8	5 6/8	Fremont Co., WY	John L. O'Brien	John L. O'Brien	2002	185
82	16 1/8	15 5/8	6 4/8	6 2/8	2 5/8	2 5/8	11	6	5 4/8	Lincoln Co., NM	Robert J. Smalley	Robert J. Smalley	2003	185
82	15 6/8	15 5/8	6 2/8	6 4/8	3 3/8	3	10 2/8	10 2/8	5 4/8	Socorro Co., NM	Robert B. Williams	Robert B. Williams	2003	185
82	15 3/8	15 3/8	6 4/8	6 4/8	2 4/8	2 4/8	9 5/8	6 4/8	5	Carbon Co., WY	Scott R. Strand	Scott R. Strand	2003	185
81 6/8	16 6/8	16 7/8	6 6/8	6	3	2 7/8	14 6/8	11 3/8	5 6/8	Colfax Co., NM	Rodney Hatzman	Rodney Hatzman	2000	203
81 6/8	15 7/8	16 1/8	6 1/8	6 1/8	2 7/8	2 6/8	10	5 5/8	4	Bare Creek, AB	Steven C. Mummery	Steven C. Mummery	2000	203
81 6/8	14 1/8	15 6/8	6 1/8	6 5/8	2 6/8	2 5/8	11 7/8	9 4/8	5 7/8	Yavapai Co., AZ	Mark T. Michaelis	Mark T. Michaelis	2002	203
81 6/8	15 4/8	14 7/8	6 5/8	6 4/8	2 5/8	2 5/8	10 1/8	6 4/8	6 5/8	Washakie Co., WY	Dawn E. Nelson	Dawn E. Nelson	2002	203
81 6/8	15 2/8	15 6/8	6 3/8	6 3/8	3	3	11 7/8	7	5 3/8	Weston Co., WY	Brett D. Stull	Brett D. Stull	2003	203
81 4/8	16 6/8	16 4/8	6 1/8	5 7/8	2 7/8	2 7/8	10 5/8	5 1/8	5 4/8	Custer Co., MT	Matthew L. Nichols	Matthew L. Nichols	2003	209
81 4/8	16 3/8	14 2/8	6 4/8	6 6/8	3 2/8	3 2/8	9 1/8	4 5/8	4 4/8	Natrona Co., WY	David P. Moore	David P. Moore	1970	209
81 4/8	14 3/8	14 2/8	7	7	2 6/8	2 7/8	12 1/8	10 4/8	5 4/8	Sweetwater Co., WY	Robert B. Strasburg	Robert B. Strasburg	2000	209
81 4/8	15 4/8	15 1/8	6 5/8	6 5/8	2 3/8	2 3/8	10 2/8	6 2/8	6 3/8	Campbell Co., WY	David E. Harwood	David E. Harwood	2000	209
81 4/8	15 5/8	15 2/8	6 7/8	6 7/8	2 7/8	2 7/8	9 3/8	5 6/8	4 6/8	Carbon Co., WY	Robert D. Elmore	Robert D. Elmore	2001	209
81 4/8	15 2/8	15 1/8	6 6/8	6 5/8	2 5/8	2 5/8	15 2/8	12	5 2/8	Washakie Co., WY	Curtis J. Kelstrom	Curtis J. Kelstrom	2001	209
81 4/8	15 1/8	15 1/8	6 2/8	6 1/8	2 5/8	2 5/8	12 2/8	8	5 2/8	Colfax Co., NM	Ryan R. Marchand	Ryan R. Marchand	2002	209
81 4/8	16 3/8	15 6/8	6 4/8	6 4/8	2 4/8	2 6/8	8	9 3/8	6 6/8	Johnson Co., WY	Lance Lockwood	Lance Lockwood	2002	209
81 2/8	14 3/8	14 3/8	7 2/8	7 2/8	2 7/8	2 6/8	9 3/8	9 3/8	5 3/8	Sweetwater Co., WY	William D. Angle	William D. Angle	2003	217
81 2/8	16 5/8	16 2/8	6 5/8	6 4/8	2 5/8	2 5/8	9 3/8	6 5/8	5 3/8	Albany Co., WY	Andrew Nordin	Andrew Nordin	2000	217
81 2/8	16	15 4/8	6 6/8	6 1/8	2 5/8	2 5/8	11 3/8	7 4/8	5 1/8	Moffat Co., CO	Frank S. Noska IV	Frank S. Noska IV	2001	217
81 2/8	16 3/8	16 3/8	6 5/8	6 5/8	2 3/8	2 5/8	11 4/8	10 7/8	6 5/8	Elko Co., NV	Michael A. Brown	Michael A. Brown	2001	217
81 2/8	15 7/8	15 3/8	6 1/8	6 2/8	2 4/8	2 6/8	10 7/8	6 3/8	5	Humboldt Co., NV	Nick G. Deffterios	Nick G. Deffterios	2001	217
81 2/8	17 4/8	17 1/8	6 1/8	6 1/8	2 6/8	2 4/8	12	11 6/8	4 1/8	White Pine Co., NV	James C. Maple	James C. Maple	2002	217
81 2/8	15 3/8	15 2/8	6 3/8	6 2/8	2 5/8	2 5/8	7 7/8	3 3/8	6 4/8	Fremont Co., WY	Hyland B. Erickson	Hyland B. Erickson	2002	217

PRONGHORN

Antilocapra americana americana and related subspecies

Score	Length of Horn R.	L.	Circumference of Base R.	L.	Circumference at Third Quarter R.	L.	Inside Spread	Tip to Tip Spread	Length of Prong R.	L.	Locality	Hunter	Owner	Date Killed	Rank
81	15	14 2/8	6 6/8	6 5/8	2 1/8	2 2/8	21 2/8	20 4/8	5	5 4/8	Sublette Co., WY	Louis Roberts	Louis Roberts	1983	223
81	15 7/8	16 3/8	6 6/8	6 4/8	2 3/8	2 5/8	13 2/8	9 6/8	6	5 5/8	Yavapai Co., AZ	Monte A. Arrowsmith	Monte A. Arrowsmith	2000	223
81	16	16	6 4/8	6 4/8	2 4/8	2 4/8	12	7	5 3/8	5	Uintah Co., UT	Buckley Blackburn	Buckley Blackburn	2001	223
81	15 6/8	15 6/8	6 2/8	6 2/8	2 6/8	2 7/8	9 5/8	5 6/8	5 1/8	5 4/8	Yavapai Co., AZ	Mark A. Kessler	Mark A. Kessler	2001	223
81	15 6/8	15 6/8	6 2/8	6 1/8	2 5/8	2 5/8	9 5/8	5 1/8	6	6	Garfield Co., MT	Kurt D. Rued	Kurt D. Rued	2001	223
81	17 5/8	17 5/8	6 4/8	6 3/8	2 5/8	2 5/8	10 6/8	4 4/8	4 2/8	4 2/8	McCone Co., MT	Daniel J. Hibl	Daniel J. Hibl	2001	223
81	16 4/8	16 2/8	6 3/8	6 2/8	2 3/8	2 4/8	8	3 7/8	7	6 5/8	Woodpile Creek, SK	Robert A. Simpson	Robert A. Simpson	2002	223
81	16 1/8	16 2/8	6	5 7/8	3 2/8	3 2/8	8 7/8	5 3/8	5 1/8	5 1/8	Socorro Co., NM	John J. Lazzeroni	John J. Lazzeroni	2002	223
81	15 4/8	15 1/8	6 1/8	5 7/8	3 3/8	3 3/8	9 7/8	6 4/8	5 3/8	5 3/8	Socorro Co., NM	Elizabeth Andrews-Glass	Elizabeth Andrews-Glass	2002	223
81	16 2/8	16 2/8	6 2/8	6 2/8	2 6/8	2 6/8	13 7/8	9 4/8	4 4/8	4 7/8	Coconino Co., AZ	William A. Keebler	William A. Keebler	2003	223
81	16	16 1/8	6 3/8	6 4/8	2 3/8	2 4/8	9 1/8	6 1/8	6	5 6/8	Platte Co., WY	Joseph A. DiPasqua	Joseph A. DiPasqua	2003	223
81	15 4/8	16 1/8	6 2/8	6 2/8	2 4/8	2 5/8	13 4/8	8 4/8	5 7/8	5 3/8	Richland Co., MT	David S. Moore	David S. Moore	2003	223
80 6/8	15 1/8	15 5/8	7 1/8	7 1/8	2 4/8	2 5/8	13 3/8	10 7/8	5 3/8	5 4/8	Johnson Co., WY	D.L. Reyman	D.L. Reyman	1958	235
80 6/8	17 3/8	17 4/8	6 2/8	6 4/8	2 5/8	2 6/8	13 6/8	10 5/8	4 2/8	4 3/8	Mora Co., NM	Picked Up	Gerald R. Gold	1983	235
80 6/8	16 1/8	15 5/8	6 2/8	6 3/8	2 5/8	2 5/8	9 4/8	5 5/8	6 1/8	6 2/8	Lake Co., OR	Craig D. Jordan	Craig D. Jordan	2000	235
80 6/8	14 1/8	14 2/8	6 4/8	6 4/8	3 5/8	3 6/8	7 2/8	4 4/8	4 5/8	4 6/8	Socorro Co., NM	Gilbert T. Adams III	Gilbert T. Adams III	2000	235
80 6/8	14	14 3/8	7 3/8	7 2/8	2 7/8	2 7/8	11 1/8	8 2/8	5	5 1/8	Garfield Co., MT	William B. Hartman	William B. Hartman	2000	235
80 6/8	15 3/8	15 2/8	6 6/8	6 6/8	2 5/8	2 7/8	9 2/8	4 1/8	5 1/8	5 2/8	Albany Co., WY	Rick E. Bickford	Rick E. Bickford	2002	235
80 6/8	15 1/8	14 7/8	5 7/8	6	2 5/8	2 5/8	10 3/8	6 4/8	6 2/8	6 2/8	Hudspeth Co., TX	Susan C. Reneau	Susan C. Reneau	2002	235
80 6/8	15 4/8	14 6/8	6 5/8	6 5/8	3 5/8	3 2/8	15 2/8	11 6/8	5	4 4/8	Torrance Co., NM	Rosemary Bazile	Rosemary Bazile	2003	235
80 4/8	15 1/8	15 2/8	7 3/8	7 3/8	2 6/8	2 7/8	10	5 7/8	5	5 4/8	Fremont Co., WY	David W. Campbell	David W. Campbell	1998	243
80 4/8	15 5/8	15 5/8	6 2/8	6 1/8	3	2 7/8	8 1/8	3	4 4/8	4 7/8	Hidalgo Co., NM	Mark A. Jackson	Mark A. Jackson	2001	243
80 4/8	15 4/8	15 4/8	6 3/8	6 4/8	2 4/8	2 5/8	9 3/8	4 4/8	5 3/8	5 3/8	Blaine Co., MT	Donald E. Shaferly, Jr.	Donald E. Shaferly, Jr.	2001	243
80 4/8	15 4/8	15	6 2/8	6	2 5/8	2 4/8	10	7 1/8	5 7/8	5 6/8	Carbon Co., WY	Brian T. McCulloch	Brian T. McCulloch	2002	243
80 4/8	15	15 1/8	6 3/8	6 3/8	2 5/8	2 6/8	9 3/8	7 3/8	5 7/8	5 7/8	Carbon Co., WY	Peter J. Spehar	Peter J. Spehar	2002	243
80 4/8	14 1/8	14 2/8	6 7/8	6 7/8	2 7/8	2 7/8	13 4/8	10 3/8	5 3/8	5 3/8	Ingebrigt Lake, SK	Jack Clary	Jack Clary	2003	243
80 4/8	14 6/8	15 2/8	6 6/8	6 5/8	2 7/8	3 2/8	14 5/8	11 6/8	5 4/8	5 7/8	Cypress Hills, SK	Howard Jackle	Howard Jackle	2003	243
80 2/8	15 3/8	15 2/8	6 5/8	6 4/8	2 4/8	2 4/8	11 4/8	10 7/8	6 5/8	5 4/8	Sweetwater Co., WY	Dale A. Blum	Dale A. Blum	1992	250
80 2/8	14 6/8	14 5/8	6 5/8	6 5/8	3 2/8	3 1/8	8 6/8	8 3/8	5 3/8	5	Hudspeth Co., TX	Alex W. Kibler	Alex W. Kibler	2000	250
80 2/8	16 2/8	16 1/8	6 2/8	6 6/8	2 7/8	2 7/8	10	5 2/8	5 1/8	5 2/8	Moffat Co., CO	Kenneth W. Springer	Kenneth W. Springer	2001	250
80 2/8	15 4/8	16	6 4/8	6 3/8	2 6/8	3 2/8	12	10 2/8	5 1/8	5 4/8	Harney Co., OR	Daryl G. Whitmore	Daryl G. Whitmore	2001	250
80 2/8	15 2/8	15 4/8	6 4/8	6 4/8	2 3/8	2 5/8	5 2/8	2 4/8	5 7/8	5 5/8	Fremont Co., WY	Howard M. Johnson	Howard M. Johnson	2001	250
80 2/8	16 4/8	14 3/8	6 4/8	6 4/8	2 6/8	2 5/8	5	12 1/8	6	6	Wildhorse, AB	John G. McKay	John G. McKay	2001	250

											Locality	Hunter	Owner	Date	Rank
80 2/8	17 1/8	17 1/8	7 1/8	7	2 6/8	2 6/8	10 2/8	9 1/8	3 3/8	3 3/8	Harney Co., OR	Dennis E. Lambert	Dennis E. Lambert	2002	250
80 2/8	15 2/8	15 4/8	7	7	2 7/8	3 1/8	7 3/8	1 5/8	5 1/8	4 7/8	Torrance Co., NM	Kelly K. Beckstrom	Kelly K. Beckstrom	2002	250
80 2/8	15 7/8	16	6 1/8	6 3/8	2 6/8	2 4/8	8 5/8	5 1/8	5 5/8	6 5/8	Campbell Co., WY	George N. Spitzer	George N. Spitzer	2002	250
80 2/8	15 4/8	15 6/8	6 4/8	6 5/8	2 4/8	2 5/8	9 2/8	4	5 3/8	5 1/8	Sweetwater Co., WY	Jason L. Kirk	Jason L. Kirk	2002	250
80 2/8	15 7/8	15 7/8	6 6/8	6 6/8	2 3/8	2 3/8	10 5/8	5 7/8	5 4/8	4 7/8	Washoe Co., NV	Blake A. Bender	Blake A. Bender	2003	250
80	15 7/8	16 6/8	6 3/8	6 2/8	3	3	12 2/8	7 2/8	4 7/8	4 7/8	Yavapai Co., AZ	Kurt R. Shepherd	Kurt R. Shepherd	1985	261
80	15 1/8	14 5/8	6 6/8	6 6/8	2	2	12 1/8	11	7 2/8	7	Oregon	Unknown	Woodland Taxidermy	2000	261
80	14 4/8	14 2/8	6 1/8	6 2/8	3 1/8	3	12	10 6/8	6 1/8	6 2/8	Converse Co., WY	William L. Pickett	William L. Pickett	2000	261
80	16	15 5/8	5 7/8	5 7/8	2 6/8	2 6/8	12 2/8	6 2/8	5 7/8	6 1/8	Luna Co., NM	Becky Verrips	Becky Verrips	2000	261
80	15 6/8	15 5/8	6 2/8	6 1/8	2 4/8	2 4/8	10 3/8	6 4/8	5 7/8	5 5/8	Sierra Co., NM	Lacy J. Harber	Lacy J. Harber	2001	261
80	15 1/8	15 4/8	6 7/8	6 7/8	2 1/8	2 3/8	8 5/8	5 3/8	5 7/8	5 6/8	Lincoln Co., WY	Jeffrey L. Davison	Jeffrey L. Davison	2001	261
80	14 3/8	14 3/8	6 5/8	6 6/8	2 6/8	3	9 2/8	4 3/8	5 2/8	5 1/8	Emery Co., UT	Benny L. Allred	Benny L. Allred	2001	261
80	16	16 2/8	6 2/8	6 2/8	2 3/8	2 4/8	9 3/8	5	4 5/8	4 4/8	Yavapai Co., AZ	Donald H. Johnson	Donald H. Johnson	2001	261
80	14	14 1/8	6 2/8	6 1/8	2 3/8	2 5/8	7 6/8	2 3/8	7 4/8	7 4/8	Moffat Co., CO	Jared J. Hemmert	Jared J. Hemmert	2001	261
80	15	15 3/8	6 4/8	6 4/8	2 5/8	2 5/8	7 7/8	3 3/8	5 6/8	5 6/8	Humboldt Co., NV	Carl B. Walton	Carl B. Walton	2002	261
80	15 1/8	15 1/8	6 3/8	6 1/8	3 1/8	3 1/8	9	4 7/8	4 6/8	4 6/8	Emery Co., UT	Monte E. Tucker	Monte E. Tucker	2003	261
80	14 2/8	14 7/8	6 5/8	6 4/8	2 7/8	3 1/8	13 3/8	10 3/8	4 6/8	4 6/8	Carbon Co., WY	John C. Vanko	John C. Vanko	2003	261
80	16	16 1/8	6 6/8	6 4/8	2 5/8	2 5/8	14	9 4/8	4 6/8	4 5/8	Brown Co., NE	Brad Gambill	Brad Gambill	2003	261
80	16	16	6 4/8	6 4/8	3 7/8	3 5/8	10 5/8	4 7/8	5 5/8	4 5/8	Sweetwater Co., WY	Nicole Peterson	Nicole Peterson	2003	261
90 6/8*	17 4/8	17 3/8	7 1/8	7	4 3/8	3 7/8	10 2/8	6 6/8	5 1/8	4 6/8	Catron Co., NM	Kirk E. Winward	Kirk E. Winward	2003	261

* Final score subject to revision by additional verifying measurements.

BISON

Bison bison bison and *Bison bison athabascae*

Minimum Score 115

World's Record 136 4/8

Trophies are acceptable only from states and provinces that recognize bison as a wild and free-ranging game animal and for which a hunting license and/or big game tag is required for hunting.

Score	Length of Horn R.	Length of Horn L.	Circumference of Base R.	Circumference of Base L.	Circumference at Third Quarter R.	Circumference at Third Quarter L.	Greatest Spread	Tip to Tip Spread	Locality	Hunter	Owner	Date Killed	Rank
131 6/8	21 5/8	21 4/8	16	15 1/8	5 4/8	5 4/8	19 5/8	30	Coconino Co., AZ	Duane R. Richardson	Duane R. Richardson	2002	1
128 6/8	19	19	14 7/8	15	7 4/8	7 5/8	29 4/8	21 4/8	Garfield Co., UT	Steven R. Farr	Steven R. Farr	2000	2
128 2/8	23	23	14 5/8	14 5/8	4 4/8	4 4/8	33 4/8	24 3/8	Sikanni Chief River, BC	George E. Salazar	George E. Salazar	2001	3
128 2/8	20 2/8	20 6/8	15 3/8	15 3/8	5 7/8	6	33 6/8	29 6/8	Custer Co., SD	William D. Gentner	William D. Gentner	2002	3
128	19 2/8	19 6/8	16 2/8	16 2/8	5 6/8	6	31 1/8	26	Cub Mt., YT	Richard Ward	Richard Ward	2001	5
126 6/8	19 7/8	20 1/8	14 2/8	14	7	7	31 7/8	26 6/8	Custer Co., SD	Thomas P. Powers	Thomas P. Powers	2002	6
125 2/8	19 5/8	19 5/8	15 2/8	15	6 5/8	5 7/8	29 6/8	21 6/8	Custer Co., SD	Adam Ziolkowski	Adam Ziolkowski	2001	7
124 6/8	20 1/8	20 2/8	14 2/8	14 2/8	6 5/8	6 4/8	33 6/8	28 4/8	Custer Co., SD	William J. Smith	William J. Smith	2000	8
124 2/8	18 1/8	18 1/8	15 6/8	15 1/8	6 4/8	7 5/8	28 1/8	22 2/8	Teton Co., WY	Terry Mathes	Terry Mathes	1998	9
123 6/8	19	19	14 1/8	14 1/8	7 1/8	7 1/8	26 6/8	16 3/8	Garfield Co., UT	Gregory N. Brian	Gregory N. Brian	2002	10
123 4/8	18 4/8	18 7/8	15 5/8	14 7/8	5 1/8	4 4/8	32 1/8	26 4/8	Custer Co., SD	Lonnie R. Henriksen	Lonnie R. Henriksen	2001	11
122 2/8	18 7/8	19	15	15	6 4/8	5 4/8	29 1/8	22	Custer Co., SD	Kent Deligans	Kent Deligans	2001	12
122	19	19	15 4/8	15 6/8	5 6/8	6 2/8	31 4/8	24 5/8	Custer Co., SD	Charles A. LeKites	Charles A. LeKites	2001	13
121 4/8	14 4/8	14 4/8	18 2/8	17 6/8	5 7/8	6	30 3/8	25 4/8	Custer Co., SD	Gary W. Derrick	Gary W. Derrick	2001	14
120 4/8	17 6/8	17 3/8	14 4/8	14 4/8	6 6/8	6 7/8	30 4/8	24 6/8	Custer Co., SD	Morgan D. Silvers	Morgan D. Silvers	2002	15
120 2/8	16 3/8	17 1/8	13 4/8	13 2/8	7 7/8	8	32 4/8	29 3/8	Teton Co., WY	Herbert C. Hazen	Herbert C. Hazen	2000	16
120 2/8	17 5/8	17 5/8	14 1/8	14 1/8	5 4/8	6	31 6/8	27 1/8	Teton Co., WY	Jim P. Collins, Jr.	Jim P. Collins, Jr.	2001	16
120 2/8	18 3/8	18 2/8	14	13 7/8	6 4/8	6 7/8	29 7/8	24 5/8	Custer Co., SD	Gary E. Janssen	Gary E. Janssen	2002	16
120	17 1/8	17	14 1/8	14 1/8	6	6 7/8	30	24 4/8	Teton Co., WY	Brandon Egbert	Brandon Egbert	2001	19
120	19 3/8	19 2/8	14 4/8	14 5/8	5 1/8	5	27 4/8	18 4/8	Garfield Co., UT	David Dastrup	David Dastrup	2002	19
119 4/8	19 1/8	19 1/8	13 6/8	13 6/8	6	5 7/8	27 5/8	19 3/8	Garfield Co., UT	Darin D. Kerr	Darin D. Kerr	2000	21
119 4/8	18 6/8	18 6/8	14 3/8	14	6 5/8	7 5/8	31	24 4/8	Custer Co., SD	Charles F. Harris	Charles F. Harris	2001	21
119 2/8	18 1/8	19 7/8	14 3/8	14 3/8	5 4/8	6 5/8	28 2/8	20 2/8	Custer Co., SD	Robert G. Kinna	Robert G. Kinna	2000	23
119	18 4/8	18 6/8	13 7/8	14 1/8	6	6	30 3/8	24 1/8	Teton Co., WY	Kathryn H. Rommel	Kathryn H. Rommel	2000	24
119	18 5/8	17 6/8	13 5/8	13 4/8	6 2/8	6 6/8	28 2/8	18 2/8	Teton Co., WY	Slaton J. Reynoldson	Slaton J. Reynoldson	2002	24
118 4/8	17 7/8	18 1/8	13 6/8	14 2/8	6 4/8	6 5/8	30 6/8	24 4/8	Custer Co., SD	Max G. Bauer, Jr.	Max G. Bauer, Jr.	2001	26
118	18 4/8	18 1/8	14 3/8	14 3/8	5 5/8	5 7/8	30	24 6/8	Coconino Co., AZ	Chuck Adams	Chuck Adams	2000	27
117 4/8	19	18 6/8	14 4/8	14 2/8	5 2/8	5 1/8	26 7/8	19 1/8	Delta Junction, AK	Kenneth L. Carlson	Kenneth L. Carlson	2001	28
117 4/8	18 6/8	18 6/8	14 3/8	14 3/8	5 3/8	5 2/8	27 6/8	20	Coconino Co., AZ	Chuck Adams	Chuck Adams	2002	28
117 2/8	17	16 5/8	14 7/8	14 4/8	5 7/8	6 3/8	28	22 4/8	Davis Co., UT	Jacob B. Mecham	Jacob B. Mecham	2000	30

116 2/8	16 4/8	16 4/8	14 2/8	14 1/8	5 7/8	6 6/8	27 3/8	23 5/8	Garfield Co., UT	Jelindo A. Tiberti II	Jelindo A. Tiberti II	2002	31
115 4/8	19	18 6/8	13 6/8	13 5/8	5	4 6/8	27 3/8	21 2/8	Garfield Co., UT	Thomas M. Sorensen	Thomas M. Sorensen	2001	32
115 2/8	18 6/8	18 6/8	13 4/8	14 2/8	6 1/8	6 1/8	29	22	Kenney Lake, AK	Gloria M. Lannen	Gloria M. Lannen	1999	33
115 2/8	16 3/8	17 1/8	13 4/8	13 7/8	6 4/8	6 6/8	28 2/8	23 7/8	Teton Co., WY	Barry Remington	Barry Remington	2000	33
115 2/8	15 4/8	15 4/8	15 6/8	15 7/8	6	5 2/8	26 1/8	21 1/8	Davis Co., UT	Douglas S. Christensen	Douglas S. Christensen	2002	33
132 *	21 3/8	21 2/8	15 3/8	15 1/8	7	6 7/8	32 4/8	21 3/8	Copper River, AK	Timothy L. Hastings	Timothy L. Hastings	2002	

* Final score subject to revision by additional verifying measurements.

ROCKY MOUNTAIN GOAT

Oreamnos americanus americanus and related subspecies

Score	Length of Horn R.	L.	Circumference of Base R.	L.	Circumference at Third Quarter R.	L.	Greatest Spread	Tip to Tip Spread	Locality	Hunter	Owner	Date Killed	Rank
54 6/8	11 4/8	11 4/8	5 6/8	5 6/8	2	2	6 1/8	6 1/8	Vixen Inlet, AK	Ross M. Groben	Ross M. Groben	2001	1
54	10 3/8	10 2/8	6 1/8	6	2 1/8	2 1/8	7 6/8	7	Stikine River, BC	Shawn K. MacFarlane	Shawn K. MacFarlane	2003	2
53 6/8	10 2/8	10 2/8	6 1/8	6 1/8	2 1/8	2 1/8	7 6/8	7 3/8	Del Creek, BC	Dora L. Hetzel	Dora L. Hetzel	2003	3
53 4/8	10 4/8	10 6/8	6	6	2	2	7 4/8	7 1/8	Elko Co., NV	R. Dean Conley	R. Dean Conley	2002	4
53 2/8	10 4/8	10 4/8	5 7/8	5 7/8	2 1/8	2	6 2/8	5 1/8	Cleveland Pen., AK	Robert M. Ortiz	Robert M. Ortiz	2001	5
53	10 5/8	10 7/8	5 6/8	5 6/8	1 7/8	1 7/8	7 2/8	6 7/8	Shoemaker Creek, BC	Klauss Wolff	Klauss Wolff	2002	6
53	11	10 4/8	5 6/8	5 6/8	2	2	8 3/8	7 6/8	Skeena River, BC	Randy Kucharyshen	Randy Kucharyshen	2003	6
52 4/8	10 5/8	10 6/8	5 6/8	5 6/8	2	2	6 2/8	5 4/8	Cleveland Pen., AK	Robert M. Ortiz	Robert M. Ortiz	2001	8
52 4/8	10 5/8	10 6/8	5 7/8	5 7/8	1 7/8	1 7/8	7 6/8	7 2/8	Tahltan Highland, BC	Peter A. Walker	Peter A. Walker	2001	8
52 4/8	10 5/8	10 4/8	5 4/8	5 5/8	2	2	6 6/8	5 5/8	Boca De Quadra, AK	Jason C. Wrinkle	Jason C. Wrinkle	2001	8
52 2/8	10 2/8	10 4/8	5 7/8	6 1/8	1 7/8	2	8 7/8	8 4/8	Sheslay River, BC	R. Terrell McCombs	R. Terrell McCombs	2002	11
52 2/8	9 4/8	9 4/8	6 2/8	6 2/8	2	2	8 1/8	7 6/8	Piute Co., UT	Cloys D. Seegmiller	Cloys D. Seegmiller	2002	11
52 2/8	9 7/8	9 7/8	5 7/8	5 7/8	2	2	8 6/8	8 3/8	Morice Lake, BC	Rebecca M. Werner	Rebecca M. Werner	2003	11
52 2/8	9 6/8	9 4/8	6 4/8	6 4/8	1 7/8	1 6/8	6 4/8	5 5/8	Adams Co., ID	Rusty P. Kirtley	Rusty P. Kirtley	2003	11
52	10 3/8	10 3/8	5 7/8	5 7/8	1 7/8	1 7/8	8 7/8	8 1/8	Atlin Lake, BC	Frank J. Provencal	Frank J. Provencal	2002	15
52	10 1/8	10 1/8	6	6	2	1 7/8	8 4/8	7 5/8	Atlin Lake, BC	Frank W. Provencal	Frank W. Provencal	2002	15
52	10 3/8	10 3/8	5 6/8	5 6/8	1 7/8	1 7/8	6 4/8	5	Beaver Co., UT	Patrick J. Gilligan	Patrick J. Gilligan	2003	15
51 6/8	10 3/8	10 3/8	5 7/8	5 7/8	2	2	7 3/8	6 2/8	Little Tahltan River, BC	Leon E. Procknow	Leon E. Procknow	2000	18
51 6/8	10 7/8	10 7/8	5 5/8	5 5/8	1 7/8	1 7/8	8 3/8	7 7/8	Flint Creek, BC	Doug H. Cundy	Doug H. Cundy	2001	18
51 6/8	9 6/8	9 6/8	6	6	1 7/8	1 7/8	7 1/8	6 3/8	Telegraph Creek, BC	John C. Marsh	John C. Marsh	2001	18
51 6/8	10 2/8	10 2/8	6	6	2	2	7 5/8	6 7/8	Beaver Co., UT	Troy Christensen	Troy Christensen	2001	18
51 6/8	9 6/8	10	6	6	2	2	7 4/8	6 7/8	Pine Tree Lake, BC	Eric Torgerson	Eric Torgerson	2001	18
51 6/8	10	10 3/8	5 6/8	5 7/8	1 7/8	1 7/8	6 3/8	6 1/8	Kittitas Co., WA	Mark D. Larson	Mark D. Larson	2002	18
51 4/8	10	10 2/8	5 7/8	6	2	2	7 7/8	7 3/8	Sinawa Eddy Mt., BC	Jeffrey A. Sackett	Jeffrey A. Sackett	2002	24
51 2/8	10	10 1/8	6	6	1 7/8	1 7/8	6 6/8	6 2/8	Baker Co., OR	Kenneth R. Mellow	Kenneth R. Mellow	2000	25
51 2/8	10 4/8	10 6/8	5 4/8	5 4/8	2	2	8 1/8	8	Bob Quinn Lake, BC	Larry G. Snyder	Larry G. Snyder	2000	25
51 2/8	9 3/8	9 3/8	6	6	1 7/8	1 7/8	6 4/8	5 7/8	Okanogan Co., WA	Carey D. Mott	Carey D. Mott	2000	25
51	10 3/8	10 4/8	5 7/8	5 7/8	1 6/8	1 6/8	7 6/8	7 3/8	Sweet Grass Co., MT	Brad Zundel	Brad Zundel	1998	28
51	11 1/8	11 4/8	5 2/8	5 3/8	1 6/8	1 6/8	6 4/8	4 6/8	Horn Cliffs, AK	C. Don Wall	C. Don Wall	2002	28
50 6/8	10 2/8	10 1/8	6	6	1 6/8	1 6/8	6 5/8	5 6/8	Park Co., MT	Dustin J. Hartl	Dustin J. Hartl	2001	30
50 6/8	10 1/8	10 2/8	5 5/8	5 5/8	1 7/8	1 7/8	7 3/8	6 6/8	Beaver Co., UT	Patrick J. Gilligan	Patrick J. Gilligan	2002	30
50 6/8	10 3/8	10 3/8	5 5/8	5 5/8	1 6/8	1 6/8	7 5/8	7 2/8	Cub Lake, BC	Jeffrey A. Grant	Jeffrey A. Grant	2003	30
50 4/8	9 7/8	9 6/8	5 4/8	5 4/8	1 7/8	1 7/8	6 5/8	5 5/8	Revillagigedo Island, AK	Tarek C. Wetzel	Tarek C. Wetzel	2001	33

50 4/8	10 6/8	9 4/8	5 6/8	5 6/8	2	2	7 4/8	7 1/8	Middle River, BC	Eugene L. Webb	Eugene L. Webb	2001	33
50 4/8	9 2/8	9 1/8	6	5 7/8	2 1/8	2	7 4/8	7	Coles Lake, BC	Karl-Heinz Seitzinger	Karl-Heinz Seitzinger	2001	33
50 4/8	10 2/8	10 1/8	5 5/8	5 5/8	1 6/8	1 7/8	7 7/8	7 6/8	Tom Creek, BC	L. Dale Gaugler	L. Dale Gaugler	2001	33
50 4/8	10 2/8	9 7/8	5 7/8	5 7/8	1 7/8	1 7/8	8 1/8	8 1/8	Spatsizi Plateau, BC	Frank F. Flynn	Frank F. Flynn	2002	33
50 4/8	9 6/8	9 5/8	5 7/8	5 7/8	2	2	7 4/8	7 4/8	Stikine River, AK	Roy B.Hisler	Roy B.Hisler	2002	33
50 4/8	10 3/8	10 2/8	5 6/8	5 6/8	1 7/8	1 7/8	8 2/8	7 6/8	Dease Lake, BC	Kevin A. McLain	Kevin A. McLain	2003	33
50 4/8	10 2/8	10 1/8	5 4/8	5 4/8	1 7/8	1 7/8	6 5/8	6 1/8	Okanogan Co., WA	Blane E. Rogers	Blane E. Rogers	2003	33
50 4/8	10 1/8	10 1/8	5 4/8	5 4/8	2	2	7 2/8	6 7/8	Mt. Stinenia, AK	Bryan C. Bailey	Bryan C. Bailey	2003	33
50 4/8	10 5/8	10 4/8	5 5/8	5 5/8	1 6/8	1 6/8	7 2/8	6 3/8	Kechika River, BC	Stephen A. Nelson	Stephen A. Nelson	2001	33
50 2/8	10 7/8	11	5 4/8	5 4/8	1 5/8	1 5/8	8 3/8	8 1/8	Blue Lake, BC	Charles M. Bloom	Charles M. Bloom	2002	42
50 2/8	10 1/8	10 2/8	5 5/8	5 5/8	1 6/8	1 6/8	7 1/8	6 5/8	Deadwood River, BC	Mark A. Wayne	Mark A. Wayne	2000	42
50	9 5/8	9 7/8	5 5/8	5 5/8	1 7/8	1 7/8	5 4/8	3 7/8	Williston Lake, BC	Troy N. Ginn	Troy N. Ginn	2000	44
50	9 5/8	10	5 6/8	5 6/8	1 7/8	1 7/8	5 6/8	5 6/8	Cleveland Pen., AK	Rick M. Santos	Rick M. Santos	2000	44
50	10 1/8	10 3/8	5 5/8	5 5/8	1 6/8	1 6/8	7	6 1/8	Utah Co., UT	Kirk E. Winward	Kirk E. Winward	2001	44
50	10 2/8	10 2/8	5 5/8	5 5/8	1 6/8	1 6/8	8 3/8	8	Portlock Glacier, AK	Melvin S. Matthews	Melvin S. Matthews	2002	44
50	9 5/8	9 5/8	6	5 7/8	1 7/8	1 7/8	6 4/8	5 7/8	Elko Co., NV	Mike G. Harrigan	Mike G. Harrigan	2002	44
50	10 7/8	11	5 4/8	5 4/8	1 5/8	1 5/8	6 4/8	6	Park Co., MT	Mark D. Etchart	Mark D. Etchart	2002	44
49 6/8	9 4/8	9 5/8	5 6/8	5 6/8	1 6/8	1 6/8	7 2/8	6 3/8	Utah Co., UT	Michael C. Allen	Michael C. Allen	1997	51
49 4/8	9 2/8	9 4/8	5 6/8	5 6/8	1 7/8	1 7/8	6 4/8	6	Snohomish Co., WA	David C. Campbell, Jr.	John L. Campbell	1971	52
49 4/8	10 3/8	10 3/8	5 2/8	5 2/8	1 7/8	1 7/8	7 3/8	6 6/8	Elwyn Creek, BC	James R. Gabrick	James R. Gabrick	2000	52
49 4/8	9 6/8	9 6/8	5 6/8	5 6/8	1 7/8	1 7/8	7 2/8	7 1/8	Baker Co., OR	Slade H. Taylor	Slade H. Taylor	2001	52
49 4/8	9 2/8	8 6/8	6	6	2	2	6 2/8	5 4/8	Elko Co., NV	Charles H. Hone	Charles H. Hone	2002	52
49 4/8	10 1/8	10 1/8	5 5/8	5 4/8	1 6/8	1 6/8	8 2/8	7 7/8	Chugach Mts., AK	Randy Hicks	Randy Hicks	2002	52
49 4/8	9 7/8	9 6/8	5 7/8	5 7/8	1 5/8	1 5/8	8	7 5/8	Park Co., WY	Darell R. Brooks	Picked Up	2003	58
49 2/8	10 3/8	10 3/8	5 4/8	5 4/8	1 5/8	1 5/8	7 1/8	6 1/8	Chouteau Co., MT	Mark Sullivan	Mark Sullivan	2000	58
49 2/8	10	9 5/8	5 5/8	5 5/8	1 6/8	1 6/8	7	6 2/8	Dixon Glacier, AK	Colt A. Belmonte	Colt A. Belmonte	2002	60
49	10	10	5 3/8	5 3/8	1 6/8	1 6/8	9	8 7/8	Resurrection Bay, AK	Daniel D. Kreis	Daniel D. Kreis	2001	60
49	9 7/8	9 6/8	5 2/8	5 2/8	1 5/8	1 5/8	6 4/8	6 4/8	Columbia Glacier, AK	Roy K. Keefer	Roy K. Keefer	2001	62
48 6/8	9 6/8	9 6/8	5 4/8	5 4/8	1 5/8	1 4/8	5 7/8	5 3/8	Utah Co., UT	John L. Lundin	John L. Lundin	2002	63
48 4/8	9 4/8	9 3/8	5 6/8	5 6/8	1 4/8	1 5/8	6 4/8	5 5/8	Elko Co., NV	Marvin E. Davis	Marvin E. Davis	2001	63
48 4/8	9 3/8	9 6/8	5 4/8	5 4/8	1 5/8	1 5/8	6 2/8	6 1/8	Idaho Co., ID	Terry J. Saba	Terry J. Saba	2001	65
48 2/8	9 4/8	9 4/8	5 5/8	5 3/8	1 7/8	1 7/8	6	5	Lewis Co., WA	Mitchel J. Hausserman	Mitchel J. Hausserman	1975	65
48 2/8	10 1/8	9 7/8	5 4/8	5 4/8	1 5/8	1 6/8	6 7/8	5 6/8	Dease Lake, BC	Jason Seitz	Jason Seitz	1999	65
48 2/8	9 6/8	9 6/8	5 2/8	5 2/8	1 6/8	1 6/8	6 7/8	6 4/8	Wallowa Co., OR	Bill K. Girard	Bill K. Girard	2001	65
48 2/8	10	10	5 3/8	5 3/8	1 6/8	1 6/8	7	6 7/8	Park Co., MT	David K. Mize	David K. Mize	2001	65
48 2/8	10 1/8	9 6/8	5 4/8	5 4/8	1 6/8	1 5/8	8	7 5/8	Kaza Peak, BC	Gary Bartsch	Gary Bartsch	2002	65
48 2/8	10 4/8	10 5/8	5 5/8	5 5/8	1 5/8	1 6/8	7 4/8	7	Park Co., MT	John C. Gilbert	John C. Gilbert	2002	65
48	9 3/8	9	5 4/8	5 5/8	1 7/8	1 6/8	6 7/8	6 1/8	Adams Co., ID	E. Ray Simpson, Jr.	E. Ray Simpson, Jr.	2003	65
48	9 4/8	10 1/8	5 4/8	5 4/8	1 6/8	1 7/8	7 5/8	7 3/8	Gardner Creek, BC	Aaron C. Olson	Aaron C. Olson	2002	72
48	9 1/8	9	5 4/8	5 4/8	1 7/8	1 7/8	6	5 3/8	Duchesne Co., UT	John M. Wall	John M. Wall	2002	72
48	10	10 1/8	5 1/8	5	1 7/8	1 7/8	6 3/8	6 2/8	Stikine River, AK	Winston J. Davies	Winston J. Davies	2002	72

ROCKY MOUNTAIN GOAT

Oreamnos americanus americanus and related subspecies

Minimum Score 47

World's Record 56 6/8

Score	Length of Horn R.	L.	Circumference of Base R.	L.	Circumference at Third Quarter R.	L.	Greatest Spread	Tip to Tip Spread	Locality	Hunter	Owner	Date Killed	Rank
47 6/8	9 4/8	9 5/8	5 5/8	5 4/8	1 6/8	1 6/8	6 4/8	6	Findlay Creek, BC	Kevin Lethbridge	Kevin Lethbridge	2001	75
47 6/8	9 2/8	9 3/8	5 4/8	5 4/8	1 7/8	1 7/8	7	6 3/8	Pennington Co., SD	Todd H. Norby	Todd H. Norby	2001	75
47 6/8	9 4/8	9 4/8	5 3/8	5 3/8	1 6/8	1 6/8	7 4/8	6 6/8	Teton Co., WY	John J. Crump	John J. Crump	2002	75
47 4/8	9 2/8	8 5/8	5 5/8	5 5/8	1 7/8	1 7/8	6 4/8	6 6/8	Chelan Co., WA	L. Kevin Whitehall	L. Kevin Whitehall	1967	78
47 4/8	9 6/8	9 5/8	5 2/8	5 3/8	1 6/8	1 6/8	7 6/8	7 5/8	Park Co., MT	Paul A. Cockrell	Paul A. Cockrell	2000	78
47 4/8	8 7/8	9 1/8	5 4/8	5 5/8	1 6/8	1 6/8	6 2/8	5 7/8	Elko Co., NV	Sidney J. Cutting	Sidney J. Cutting	2001	78
47 4/8	9	9 2/8	5 5/8	5 5/8	1 6/8	1 6/8	6 6/8	6 3/8	Kodiak Island, AK	Larry L. Robinson	Larry L. Robinson	2002	78
47 2/8	9 2/8	9 5/8	5 3/8	5 3/8	1 5/8	1 5/8	6 6/8	5 5/8	Takshanuk Mts., AK	Larry V. Benda	Larry V. Benda	2000	82
47 2/8	10 1/8	10 1/8	5 1/8	5 1/8	1 5/8	1 5/8	7 1/8	6 4/8	Horn Cliffs, AK	Robin B. Cummings	Robin B. Cummings	2001	82
47 2/8	9 5/8	9 5/8	5 4/8	5 5/8	1 6/8	1 6/8	8 1/8	8 1/8	Mt. Meehaus, BC	Edward A. Petersen	Edward A. Petersen	2002	82
47	9 4/8	9 6/8	5 3/8	5 3/8	1 5/8	1 6/8	6 6/8	6 1/8	Lemhi Co., ID	Bryan K. Martin	Bryan K. Martin	2000	85
47	9	9 2/8	5 3/8	5 3/8	1 6/8	1 6/8	6 6/8	6 5/8	Lewis & Clark Co., MT	Steven M. Inabnit	Steven M. Inabnit	2001	85
53 4/8*	10 5/8	10 6/8	6 2/8	6 2/8	1 6/8	1 7/8	6 7/8	5 7/8	Lake Co., MT	Frank Boling	Frank Boling	1999	

* Final score subject to revision by additional verifying measurements.

MUSKOX

Ovibos moschatus moschatus and certain related subspecies

Minimum Score 105   New World's Record 129

Score	Length of Horn R.	L.	Width of Boss R.	L.	Circumference at Third Quarter R.	L.	Greatest Spread	Tip to Tip Spread	Locality	Hunter	Owner	Date Killed	Rank
129	29 5/8	28 3/8	11	11	6 2/8	5 4/8	29 1/8	27 1/8	Norman Wells, NT	Craig D. Scott	Craig D. Scott	2002	1
127 2/8	29 2/8	29 7/8	10 6/8	10 6/8	6	5 6/8	29 6/8	28 6/8	Kugluktuk, NU	Vicente S. Sanchez-Valdepenas	Vicente S. Sanchez-Valdepenas	1999	2
126 4/8	30 6/8	30 7/8	10 3/8	10 5/8	5 7/8	5 4/8	29 7/8	28 6/8	Coppermine River, NU	Robert M. Ortiz	Robert M. Ortiz	2003	3
125 6/8	29 7/8	29 3/8	10 3/8	10 5/8	6 1/8	6	28 7/8	27 3/8	Coppermine River, NU	William J. Smith	William J. Smith	2002	4
125	28 3/8	28 7/8	10 6/8	11 2/8	6	6 4/8	30 5/8	30 5/8	Kugluktuk, NU	Anton Gossein	Anton Gossein	2001	5
124 6/8	27 2/8	28 1/8	12	12	5 5/8	6 3/8	28 3/8	27	Kugluktuk, NU	Thomas L. Straka	Thomas L. Straka	2003	6
120 6/8	29 2/8	29 2/8	10 1/8	10 2/8	5 6/8	5 6/8	29 6/8	29	Kugluktuk, NU	Kent Deligans	Kent Deligans	2003	7
120 4/8	28	28 4/8	10	9 6/8	6	6 1/8	27 4/8	26 4/8	Kugluktuk, NU	Robert W. Ehle	Robert W. Ehle	2000	8
119 4/8	28 5/8	28 3/8	10 5/8	11 1/8	5 2/8	5 2/8	29	27 4/8	Kugluktuk, NU	William A. Keebler	William A. Keebler	2001	9
119 2/8	29	29 3/8	9 7/8	9 6/8	5 3/8	5 7/8	32 4/8	29 1/8	Rendez-vous Lake, NT	Ray E. Dukes	Ray E. Dukes	1999	10
119	29 3/8	29	10 1/8	10 3/8	5 2/8	5 3/8	28 1/8	25 6/8	Paulatuk, NT	Mark S. Rau	Mark S. Rau	2003	11
118 4/8	28 4/8	28 7/8	9 5/8	9 5/8	5 2/8	5 6/8	29 6/8	28 5/8	Kugluktuk, NU	Frank S. Noska IV	Frank S. Noska IV	2003	12
116 6/8	29 4/8	29 5/8	10 4/8	10 5/8	4 6/8	4 6/8	24 6/8	18 6/8	Horton River, NT	Marion H. Scott	Marion H. Scott	2003	13
116	27 3/8	28 5/8	9 5/8	9 5/8	5	5	24 7/8	24 1/8	Kugluktuk, NU	Michael Gajeske	Michael Gajeske	2001	14
114 6/8	23 2/8	26 4/8	10 6/8	10 5/8	6 6/8	5 7/8	24 6/8	24 4/8	Melbourne Island, NU	Brian Knusta	Brian Knusta	2002	15
114 4/8	26	26 1/8	9 7/8	9 6/8	5 2/8	5 2/8	25 2/8	22 5/8	Horton River, NT	Jerry K. Davis	Jerry K. Davis	1992	16
114	25 5/8	25 6/8	10 2/8	10 6/8	5 2/8	4 7/8	26 6/8	25 6/8	Ellice River, NU	Leo C. Potter	Leo C. Potter	1999	17
113 2/8	26 6/8	26 6/8	9 1/8	9 1/8	5	5 3/8	24 6/8	22 5/8	Rendez-vous Lake, NT	Dale A. Rivers	Dale A. Rivers	1992	18
112 6/8	27 4/8	26 4/8	9	8 7/8	6	5 2/8	27 1/8	25 6/8	Ellice River, NU	Paul W. Hansen	Paul W. Hansen	2001	19
112 6/8	28	27 4/8	8 5/8	8 4/8	5 3/8	5 4/8	27 6/8	27 4/8	Garfield Creek, AK	H. Appel & M.W. Smith	Howard Appel	2002	19
112 2/8	25 3/8	25 4/8	9 2/8	9 4/8	5 6/8	5 6/8	29	27	Melbourne Island, NU	Terry L. McVey	Terry L. McVey	1998	21
112	27 3/8	27 1/8	8 2/8	8 4/8	5 4/8	5 3/8	28 1/8	28	Nunivak Island, AK	Robert J. Condon	Robert J. Condon	2002	22
111 4/8	28 1/8	28	9 3/8	9 3/8	5	5 3/8	27 2/8	25 3/8	Kugluktuk, NU	George W. Windolph	George W. Windolph	2001	23
111 2/8	27 3/8	26 4/8	9 3/8	9 4/8	5 6/8		27 2/8	25 7/8	Rendez-vous Lake, NT	Jonathan M. Olson	Jonathan M. Olson	2000	24
110 4/8	25 2/8	25 2/8	8 6/8	8 5/8	5 3/8	5 3/8	28 4/8	28	Kougarok River, AK	Mark W. Smith	Mark W. Smith	2001	25
110	27 2/8	27 4/8	8 6/8	8 7/8	5 4/8	5	28 7/8	28 6/8	Nunivak Island, AK	Abed S. Radwan	Abed S. Radwan	2002	26
109 4/8	25 4/8	25 5/8	9 5/8	9 3/8	5	4 7/8	27 4/8	26 7/8	Victoria Island, NU	Richard E. Bennett	Richard E. Bennett	1991	27
109 4/8	26	25 3/8	9 7/8	9 6/8	5 2/8	5 1/8	29 1/8	26 6/8	Rendez-vous Lake, NT	Joe Novak	Joe Novak	2001	28
109 4/8	27	28 5/8	9 4/8	9 3/8	4 6/8	5 3/8	29 4/8	29 1/8	Nunivak Island, AK	Bill C. Hicks, Jr.	Bill C. Hicks, Jr.	2002	28
109	27	27	8 1/8	8 1/8	5 1/8	5 1/8	26 6/8	22 4/8	Rendez-vous Lake, NT	Jos Van Hage	Jos Van Hage	2000	30
108 6/8	27	25 6/8	9 1/8	8 7/8	5 4/8	5 1/8	26 3/8	24 1/8	Rendez-vous Lake, NT	Joe Hocevar	Joe Hocevar	2003	31
108 2/8	26 2/8	27	9	9	5	5 2/8	26 7/8	25 7/8	Gjoa Haven, NU	Chuck Adams	Chuck Adams	2002	32

MUSKOX

Ovibos moschatus moschatus and certain related subspecies

Score	Length of Horn R.	L.	Width of Boss R.	L.	Circumference at Third Quarter R.	L.	Greatest Spread	Tip to Tip Spread	Locality	Hunter	Owner	Date Killed	Rank
107 2/8	27 4/8	25	10 1/8	10 1/8	5 3/8	4 3/8	28 6/8	28	Kugluktuk, NU	George E. Mann	George E. Mann	2000	33
106 6/8	25 6/8	26 1/8	8 4/8	8 4/8	4 6/8	5	27 6/8	26 6/8	Nunivak Island, AK	Bud Junger	Bud Junger	2000	34
106 4/8	25 6/8	25 2/8	8 6/8	8 5/8	5 3/8	5 1/8	30 4/8	30 2/8	Nunivak Island, AK	Derek D. Nord	Derek D. Nord	2001	35
106 2/8	26 5/8	26 5/8	9 2/8	9 5/8	5 1/8	4 7/8	26 5/8	25 7/8	Ellice River, NU	David L. Gayer	David L. Gayer	2001	36
106	26 1/8	25 4/8	10 1/8	10 1/8	4 7/8	4 4/8	28 3/8	27 5/8	Ellice River, NU	Gary A. Rose	Gary A. Rose	2000	37
105 6/8	26 7/8	25 3/8	9 4/8	9 4/8	5 1/8	4 2/8	24 2/8	18 5/8	Rendez-vous Lake, NT	Metod Novak	Metod Novak	2001	38
105 4/8	27 1/8	26 6/8	9	8 6/8	4 2/8	4 2/8	26 5/8	25 6/8	Banks Island, NT	Clyde M. Sasser	Clyde M. Sasser	1999	39
105 2/8	26	27	7 7/8	7 6/8	5	5 2/8	29 7/8	29 5/8	Nunivak Island, AK	Dudley K. White	Dudley K. White	2003	40
105	26 4/8	26 1/8	8 3/8	8 2/8	4 5/8	4 5/8	28 6/8	28 4/8	Cape Mendenhall, AK	Todd D. Bergman	Todd D. Bergman	2002	41
105	27	27	8 3/8	8 2/8	4 5/8	4 3/8	27 3/8	26 4/8	Nunivak Island, AK	David A. Garganta	David A. Garganta	2002	41
105	25 4/8	26 5/8	8 2/8	7 7/8	4 5/8	5 2/8	26 2/8	25	Bekere Lake, NT	Michael D. Moore	Michael D. Moore	2002	41
105	26 5/8	27	8	8 2/8	4 4/8	5 1/8	28	27	Horton River, NT	Mary C. Scott	Mary C. Scott	2003	41
105	25 5/8	27 7/8	9 2/8	8 5/8	4 2/8	5 4/8	26 6/8	26 2/8	Baldy Mt., AK	Mark W. Smith	Mark W. Smith	2003	41

BIGHORN SHEEP

Ovis canadensis canadensis and certain related subspecies

Minimum Score 175   New World's Record 208 3/8

Score	Length of Horn R.	L.	Circumference of Base R.	L.	Circumference at Third Quarter R.	L.	Greatest Spread	Tip to Tip Spread	Locality	Hunter	Owner	Date Killed	Rank
208 3/8	47 4/8	46 5/8	15 7/8	15 7/8	12	11	23 1/8	23 1/8	Luscar Mt., AB	Guinn D. Crousen	Guinn D. Crousen	2000	1
202 1/8	45	44 7/8	15 6/8	15 6/8	11 6/8	11	24 6/8	24 1/8	Leyland Mt., AB	Guinn D. Crousen	Guinn D. Crousen	2001	2
200 7/8	44	44 7/8	17	16 7/8	8 6/8	9 6/8	26 1/8	25 7/8	Sanders Co., MT	Jack M. Greenwood	Jack M. Greenwood	2001	3
200 1/8	40 4/8	42 1/8	16 3/8	16 6/8	10 7/8	12	20 5/8	19 3/8	Jarvis Creek, AB	Picked Up	Robert E. Sonnenberg	2002	4
200 1/8	44 3/8	41 6/8	16 3/8	16 5/8	10 2/8	9 7/8	26 6/8	26 2/8	Fergus Co., MT	David J. Nygard	David J. Nygard	2003	4
197 1/8	41 7/8	42 2/8	16 1/8	16 2/8	10 1/8	9 6/8	23 4/8	18 2/8	Costilla Co., CO	Renee Snider	Renee Snider	2000	6
195 7/8	45	43 3/8	16 1/8	16 2/8	8 3/8	8 3/8	27 1/8	26 4/8	Lewis & Clark Co., MT	Steven J. King	Steven J. King	2001	7
195 4/8	42	43 4/8	15 6/8	15 6/8	10 1/8	9 1/8	26	25 3/8	Fergus Co., MT	Patricia A. Slivka	Patricia A. Slivka	2001	8
195 2/8	41 4/8	42 2/8	15 7/8	15 7/8	10 1/8	10	22 7/8	20 7/8	Taos Co., NM	Greg Koons	Greg Koons	2003	9
195	41 6/8	42 4/8	15 4/8	15 3/8	10 2/8	10	24 6/8	20 4/8	Taos Co., NM	Jennifer L. Chapel	Jennifer L. Chapel	2002	10
194 2/8	41 4/8	43 2/8	15 6/8	15 6/8	10	9 6/8	23 1/8	17 2/8	Broadwater Co., MT	Bud Breining	Bud Breining	2003	11
193 5/8	39 6/8	41 1/8	16 1/8	16 1/8	10 6/8	10	22 7/8	22 2/8	Granite Co., MT	Eric W. Burdette	Eric W. Burdette	2000	12
193 5/8	40 2/8	39 5/8	15 2/8	15 2/8	11 7/8	11	20 5/8	15 4/8	Wallowa Co., OR	Picked Up	OR Dept. of Fish & Wildlife	2002	12
193 1/8	38 6/8	41 1/8	16	16	10 2/8	10	23 5/8	23	Fergus Co., MT	Joan L. Gallentine	Joan L. Gallentine	1900	14
192 2/8	40 2/8	42 4/8	16 5/8	16 6/8	9 1/8	8 6/8	20 6/8	18 1/8	Nez Perce Co., ID	Paul Koslowski	Paul Koslowski	2001	15
191 6/8	40 4/8	41 6/8	16 3/8	16 3/8	8 5/8	8 4/8	21 7/8	21 5/8	Fergus Co., MT	Randy C. Orley	Randy C. Orley	2000	16
191 6/8	39 2/8	40 2/8	16 3/8	16 3/8	9 5/8	9 7/8	23 4/8	16 1/8	Pennington Co., SD	Scott E. Vander Meulen	Scott E. Vander Meulen	2000	16
190 7/8	43	42 3/8	14 3/8	14 4/8	10 2/8	10	25 7/8	25 6/8	Park Co., MT	Craig Kamps	Craig Kamps	2003	18
190 5/8	41 2/8	41 5/8	15 6/8	15 5/8	9 5/8	10	21 4/8	20 5/8	Taos Co., NM	Rick C. Hooley	Rick C. Hooley	2002	19
190 4/8	42 2/8	40 6/8	16 1/8	16 2/8	9 6/8	8 7/8	24 3/8	24 3/8	Silver Bow Co., MT	James A. Barnett	James A. Barnett	1990	20
190	38 7/8	39 7/8	16 2/8	16 1/8	9	9 4/8	23 7/8	22 1/8	Granite Co., MT	Richard N. King	Richard N. King	2001	21
190	44 4/8	43 4/8	14	14 1/8	10 2/8	10	23 3/8	23 3/8	Lewis & Clark Co., MT	Robert L. Freeman	Robert L. Freeman	2002	21
189 4/8	43	43	14 2/8	14 2/8	10 2/8	10	21 6/8	21 6/8	Mora Co., NM	Matthew D. Liljenquist	Matthew D. Liljenquist	2003	23
189 3/8	40 7/8	42 2/8	15 6/8	15 7/8	8 5/8	8 6/8	20 5/8	18 6/8	Sheep Creek, AB	Norman G. Miller	Norman G. Miller	2001	24
189	40 2/8	38 4/8	15 4/8	15 3/8	10 3/8	10	26 1/8	25 2/8	Fergus Co., MT	Mark B. Hathaway	Mark B. Hathaway	2003	25
188 7/8	38 7/8	41 6/8	15 4/8	15 4/8	9 3/8	9 7/8	23 2/8	19 6/8	Ewin Creek, BC	Marshall J. Collins, Jr.	Marshall J. Collins, Jr.	2001	26
188 3/8	38 7/8	40 2/8	15 5/8	15 7/8	10 1/8	10	22 4/8	20 4/8	Granite Co., MT	Michael R. Priddy	Michael R. Priddy	2002	27
188	39 6/8	38 6/8	16 4/8	16 4/8	8 5/8	9 1/8	21 3/8	20 7/8	Granite Co., MT	Anna F. Anderson	Anna F. Anderson	2002	28
187	38	36 4/8	16 2/8	16 4/8	9 7/8	10	25	19	Sanders Co., MT	Fred L. Cavill	Fred L. Cavill	2000	29
187	38 4/8	40	15 2/8	15 2/8	10 4/8	10	20 4/8	18 6/8	Granite Co., MT	Raymond M. Hanke	Raymond M. Hanke	2002	29
187	41 3/8	41 3/8	15 5/8	15 5/8	8 2/8	8 2/8	20 7/8	16 2/8	Grace Creek, BC	David A. Halko	David A. Halko	2002	29
186 6/8	40 6/8	39 6/8	15 4/8	15 5/8	9	8 5/8	22	22	Missoula Co., MT	Dustyn W. Strachan	Dustyn W. Strachan	2001	32

Ovis canadensis canadensis and certain related subspecies

Score	Length of Horn R.	L.	Circumference of Base R.	L.	Circumference at Third Quarter R.	L.	Greatest Spread	Tip to Tip Spread	Locality	Hunter	Owner	Date Killed	Rank
186 6/8	39 3/8	38 5/8	16 5/8	16 6/8	8 3/8	8 2/8	22	21 6/8	Sanders Co., MT	Richard J. Briskin	Richard J. Briskin	2002	32
186 5/8	38 6/8	39 1/8	15 7/8	15 7/8	9 3/8	9 2/8	22 5/8	19 5/8	Blaine Co., MT	Gerald A. Brown	Gerald A. Brown	2000	34
186 2/8	37	39	15 4/8	15 5/8	10 3/8	10	23 3/8	19	Granite Co., MT	Jeff J. Krier	Jeff J. Krier	2001	35
186 1/8	36 7/8	38 6/8	16 4/8	16 6/8	9 2/8	9 7/8	22	11 2/8	Emery Co., UT	Kenneth M. Labrum	Kenneth M. Labrum	2002	36
186	38 6/8	39 2/8	15 6/8	15 6/8	9 3/8	9 2/8	24 5/8	24	Pershing Co., NV	Sam S. Jaksick, Jr.	Sam S. Jaksick, Jr.	2001	37
185 7/8	37 7/8	43 4/8	16 1/8	16	8 3/8	8 3/8	26 4/8	26 4/8	Granite Co., MT	Dale A. Carpenter	Dale A. Carpenter	1999	38
185 7/8	39 7/8	36 4/8	16 1/8	16	9 7/8	9 4/8	23 6/8	21 2/8	Missoula Co., MT	Charles F. MacIntire	Charles F. MacIntire	2000	38
185	40 6/8	40 2/8	14 7/8	15	9 3/8	9 4/8	21 4/8	20 7/8	Granite Co., MT	Matt A. Noble	Matt A. Noble	2001	40
184 7/8	37 6/8	37 3/8	15 7/8	16	10 1/8	9 7/8	22 6/8	21 2/8	Silver Bow Co., MT	Leslie D. Barnett	Leslie D. Barnett	1994	41
184 4/8	41 4/8	36 4/8	15 6/8	15 6/8	9	8 4/8	31	30 3/8	Phillips Co., MT	Colby L. Loudon	Colby L. Loudon	2002	42
184 4/8	40 7/8	42 1/8	15 7/8	15 5/8	7 3/8	8	23 3/8	23	Fergus Co., MT	Mathew W. Birdwell	Mathew W. Birdwell	2002	42
184 3/8	39 3/8	38 6/8	15 4/8	15 4/8	9 1/8	9 6/8	22 4/8	21 4/8	Granite Co., MT	John A. Slevin	John A. Slevin	2001	44
184 3/8	39 2/8	39 3/8	14 4/8	14 6/8	10 5/8	10	20 6/8	16	Clearwater River, AB	Alan J. Douglas	Alan J. Douglas	2002	44
184 2/8	38	43 2/8	15	15	9 6/8	9 3/8	26 2/8	26 1/8	Ravalli Co., MT	Thomas J. O'Neill	Thomas J. O'Neill	2001	46
184 2/8	39 2/8	39 2/8	15 1/8	15 1/8	10	9 5/8	22 1/8	20 2/8	Condor Mt., AB	Keith C. Brown	Keith C. Brown	2001	46
184 1/8	39	39 3/8	14 7/8	15	10	9 7/8	24 6/8	24	Graham Co., AZ	James A. Jamison	James A. Jamison	2001	48
184	38 6/8	37	15 4/8	15 5/8	9 3/8	9 4/8	25 4/8	18 3/8	Blaine Co., MT	George Willeford	George Willeford	2000	49
184	38 3/8	38 3/8	15	14 7/8	10 6/8	10	21 2/8	14 3/8	Taos Co., NM	Dick A. Jacobs	Dick A. Jacobs	2001	49
184	39 4/8	41 2/8	16 2/8	16 3/8	7 4/8	7 4/8	24 6/8	24 4/8	Sanders Co., MT	Gary N. Hill	Gary N. Hill	2001	49
183 7/8	37 6/8	38 7/8	15 5/8	15 4/8	9 5/8	10	20 6/8	20 2/8	Granite Co., MT	Bruce Stell	Bruce Stell	2002	52
183 6/8	38 4/8	41 4/8	15 4/8	15 4/8	9 1/8	8 3/8	25 2/8	25 2/8	Diorite Creek, BC	Leon Cloarec	F.P. Bills Family	1936	53
183 4/8	39 6/8	39 4/8	15 4/8	15 4/8	9	8 6/8	22 4/8	20	Sanders Co., MT	S. Kim Elliott	S. Kim Elliott	2002	54
183 4/8	38 6/8	36 6/8	15 7/8	16	9 5/8	9 4/8	23 4/8	23 1/8	Elko Co., NV	Jim R. Marques	Jim R. Marques	2003	54
183 3/8	39 5/8	37 4/8	15	15	10	10	23 4/8	23 4/8	Blaine Co., MT	Leanna E. Olson	Leanna E. Olson	2000	56
183 3/8	39 5/8	39 4/8	15 3/8	15 3/8	8 5/8	9	18 6/8	18 1/8	Missoula Co., MT	Rich Lamb	Rich Lamb	2002	56
183 2/8	37 7/8	36 7/8	15 1/8	15 2/8	10 2/8	10	21 6/8	20 1/8	Deer Lodge Co., MT	Dan J. Burns	Dan J. Burns	2001	58
183 1/8	39 6/8	39 7/8	15 1/8	14 1/8	10 2/8	10	22 4/8	17 5/8	Taos Co., NM	James G. Petersen	James G. Petersen	1900	59
183 1/8	38 4/8	39 3/8	15 4/8	15 5/8	8 6/8	9 1/8	23 2/8	17 5/8	Taos Co., NM	Clinton L. Kuchan	Clinton L. Kuchan	2000	59
183 1/8	39 6/8	39 7/8	14 1/8	14 1/8	10 2/8	10	22 4/8	17 6/8	Taos Co., NM	James G. Petersen	James G. Petersen	2002	59
182 6/8	38 2/8	39	15	15 1/8	9 6/8	9 2/8	22	18 3/8	Teton Co., MT	Audie Anderson	Audie Anderson	2000	62
182 6/8	37 5/8	36 3/8	15 2/8	15 2/8	10 2/8	10	20 7/8	20 7/8	Chelan Co., WA	Kenneth R. Harris	Kenneth R. Harris	2002	62
182 5/8	37 6/8	37 3/8	16	16 1/8	9	9	20 5/8	14 5/8	Granite Co., MT	Gerald L. Fischer	Gerald L. Fischer	2000	64
182 4/8	41	44 2/8	15 1/8	15 1/8	7 4/8	7 6/8	24 3/8	23 4/8	Sanders Co., MT	Colin E. White	Colin E. White	2001	65

Score									Locality	Hunter	Owner	Date Killed	Rank
182 2/8	39	37 2/8	16	16 1/8	8 4/8	8 6/8	20 4/8	20 2/8	Missoula Co., MT	John B. Smith	John B. Smith	2002	66
182 2/8	37 5/8	39 1/8	15 3/8	15 3/8	9 2/8	8 7/8	23 3/8	23	Ravalli Co., MT	Virginia G. Karstetter	Virginia G. Karstetter	2003	66
182	37 3/8	38 3/8	15 3/8	15 3/8	9 2/8	8 6/8	21 4/8	18 5/8	Elk River, BC	W. Joe Putz	W. Joe Putz	2001	68
182	40	40 6/8	15	16	7 7/8	8 1/8	22 4/8	22 1/8	Mt. Allen, AB	Dale A. Fournier	Dale A. Fournier	2003	68
181 7/8	37 4/8	37 3/8	16 1/8	16	8 6/8	8 6/8		12 6/8	Pennington Co., SD	Tad B. Jacobs	Tad B. Jacobs	2001	70
181 6/8	38 1/8	37 3/8	15 6/8	16	9 1/8	8 5/8	22	19 4/8	Granite Co., MT	Guy D. Buyan	Guy D. Buyan	1999	71
181 6/8	38	37 6/8	16 1/8	16 2/8	8 1/8	8 1/8	21 1/8	19 2/8	Baker Co., OR	Steven W. Brooks	Steven W. Brooks	2001	71
181 4/8	39 2/8	37 4/8	15 4/8	15 4/8	9 3/8	8 5/8	23 7/8	19 7/8	Blaine Co., MT	Doug D. Stout	Doug D. Stout	2002	73
181 4/8	39 4/8	37	15	15	10 2/8	10	21	16 6/8	Fremont Co., CO	J. Chad Carter	J. Chad Carter	2003	73
181 3/8	38 7/8	37	15	15	9 5/8	10	18 6/8	17 7/8	Granite Co., MT	Randall L. Kanter	Randall L. Kanter	2001	75
181 1/8	35 3/8	41 2/8	15 7/8	16	8	8 6/8	22 6/8	22	Granite Co., MT	Shannon V. Taylor	Shannon V. Taylor	2003	76
181	37 5/8	39 1/8	14 4/8	14 4/8	9 5/8	9 3/8	21 3/8	18 3/8	Cadomin, AB	Carl Iacona	Picked Up	1968	77
180 7/8	39 7/8	38 2/8	15	15	10	10	20 6/8	20	Grant Co., NM	Naim S. Bashir	Naim S. Bashir	2002	78
180 6/8	37 3/8	36 5/8	15 2/8	15 3/8	10	10	23	18 7/8	Gilliam Co., OR	Jerry R. Tyrrell	Jerry R. Tyrrell	2001	79
180 6/8	38 5/8	38 1/8	14 7/8	14 7/8	9 4/8	9 4/8	23 4/8	23 1/8	Ravalli Co., MT	Richard J. Hayden	Carl Hayden	2001	79
180 4/8	34 6/8	37 6/8	15 5/8	15 4/8	9 7/8	10	21 2/8	19	Granite Co., MT	Cabela's, Inc.	Picked Up	1994	81
180 4/8	38 7/8	38 5/8	15 5/8	15 6/8	7 6/8	8 1/8	18 4/8	18 1/8	Lewis & Clark Co., MT	Bruce E. Keaster	Bruce E. Keaster	2000	81
180 4/8	35 4/8	37 4/8	15 7/8	16	9 6/8	9 1/8	26 5/8	25 4/8	Elko Co., NV	Michael J. Nannini	Michael J. Nannini	2002	81
180 3/8	35 6/8	36 5/8	15 5/8	16	10 2/8	10	21 2/8	18	Costilla Co., CO	David D. Dillon	David D. Dillon	2001	84
180 2/8	38 7/8	37 7/8	16 2/8	16	7 5/8	7 2/8	21 2/8	20 4/8	Granite Co., MT	Joseph F. Maloney	Joseph F. Maloney	2000	85
180 2/8	39	38 2/8	16 2/8	16 2/8	7 6/8	7 5/8	23 6/8	22 4/8	Sanders Co., MT	Jon W. Cole	Jon W. Cole	2000	85
180 2/8	37 6/8	36 4/8	16 4/8	16 4/8	7 6/8	7 6/8	26 1/8	18	Gunnison Co., CO	Oliver R. Biggers	Oliver R. Biggers	2001	85
180 2/8	37 6/8	38 6/8	14 3/8	14 5/8	9 5/8	9 2/8	22	19 4/8	Fremont Co., CO	Lonnie Lasha	Lonnie Lasha	2001	85
180 2/8	38 4/8	37 6/8	14 5/8	14 5/8	10 2/8	10	21 1/8	18 4/8	Gila Co., AZ	George F. Dennis, Jr.	George F. Dennis, Jr.	2002	85
180 2/8	40	40	15 6/8	14 7/8	7 4/8	7 4/8	17 4/8	17 4/8	Blaine Co., MT	Roy L. Thompson	Roy L. Thompson	2003	85
180 1/8	38 2/8	38 5/8	15 6/8	15 6/8	8 7/8	9 3/8	21 4/8	21 4/8	Lewis & Clark Co., MT	Brian L. Martinez	Brian L. Martinez	1999	91
180 1/8	38 7/8	39	14 7/8	14 7/8	11	11	21	14 2/8	Taos Co., NM	Branko Terkovich	Branko Terkovich	2001	91
180 1/8	38 5/8	40 6/8	14 1/8	14 1/8	8	8 1/8	26 3/8	25 4/8	Ravalli Co., MT	E. Earl Willard	E. Earl Willard	2001	91
180 1/8	39 7/8	36	14 2/8	14 1/8	10 1/8	10	23 2/8	17 6/8	Greenlee Co., AZ	Robert J. Stokes	Robert J. Stokes	2001	91
180 1/8	36 5/8	39 1/8	15 7/8	15 6/8	9 3/8	9 2/8	21 7/8	20 2/8	Broadwater Co., MT	Gerry R. Jones	Gerry R. Jones	2002	91
180 1/8	40 6/8	40 6/8	14 3/8	14 2/8	9 1/8	9 1/8	23 1/8	23 1/8	Lewis & Clark Co., MT	Anthony P. Swartz	Anthony P. Swartz	2002	91
180	42	41 2/8	15	15	7 3/8	7 3/8	21 7/8	21 3/8	Sanders Co., MT	Jeff A. Hockaday	Jeff A. Hockaday	2000	97
180	40 5/8	38 3/8	16 2/8	16 2/8	6 6/8	6 6/8	23 3/8	23 1/8	Ravalli Co., MT	Vicki Stiller	Vicki Stiller	2002	97
179 1/8	38 1/8	38	15 5/8	15 5/8	9	8 1/8	20 6/8	19	Lewis & Clark Co., MT	Thomas L. Davidson	Thomas L. Davidson	2000	99
179 1/8	38 4/8	45 3/8	14 1/8	14 2/8	7 6/8	8	25 3/8	25 2/8	Wallowa Co., OR	OR Dept. of Fish & Wildlife	Picked Up	2002	99
178 7/8	35 5/8	36	15 6/8	16	8 6/8	9	19	18 4/8	El Paso Co., CO	John V. Zenz	John V. Zenz	2001	101
178 6/8	37 2/8	37	14 6/8	14 6/8	10 2/8	9 5/8	23 4/8	21 4/8	Grant Co., OR	Chris G. Bozarth	Chris G. Bozarth	2001	102
178 3/8	38 7/8	38	15	15	8 5/8	8 2/8	21 3/8	15 6/8	Pennington Co., SD	Harry T. Lane	Harry T. Lane	2002	103
178 2/8	36 4/8	37 2/8	15 6/8	15 7/8	8 4/8	8 3/8	20 2/8	20	Elko Co., NV	Gregory S. Jackson	Gregory S. Jackson	2001	104
178 1/8	36	40 1/8	15 6/8	15 7/8	7 5/8	7 4/8	19 7/8	19 2/8	Deer Lodge Co., MT	Brent D. Perdue	Brent D. Perdue	2001	105

BIGHORN SHEEP

Ovis canadensis canadensis and certain related subspecies

Score	Length of Horn R.	L.	Circumference of Base R.	L.	Circumference at Third Quarter R.	L.	Greatest Spread	Tip to Tip Spread	Locality	Hunter	Owner	Date Killed	Rank
178	36 3/8	37 7/8	14 5/8	14 5/8	10	10	22 4/8	16 4/8	Granite Co., MT	Keith F. Koch	Keith F. Koch	2001	106
177 6/8	35 7/8	35 5/8	16 1/8	16	8 3/8	8 3/8	20 7/8	19 4/8	Ravalli Co., MT	Barbara Navarra	Barbara Navarra	2000	107
177 3/8	37 3/8	37 6/8	16	15 7/8	7 7/8	7 7/8	18 5/8	17 6/8	Granite Co., MT	Henry M. Kengerski	Henry M. Kengerski	2001	108
177 3/8	37 5/8	36	15 1/8	15 4/8	9 6/8	9	23 2/8	21	Chelan Co., WA	Garrett J. Grant	Garrett J. Grant	2003	108
177 1/8	37 1/8	36 6/8	15 4/8	15 3/8	8 2/8	8 4/8	24 7/8	24 7/8	Lemhi Co., ID	David J. Lechel	David J. Lechel	2002	110
176 6/8	37 2/8	37 6/8	14 6/8	14 5/8	8 7/8	9	25	24 4/8	Lake Co., OR	Jacob Lefebure	Jacob Lefebure	2003	111
176 4/8	38 4/8	37 6/8	14 6/8	14 6/8	8 2/8	8 5/8	22 4/8	22	Ravalli Co., MT	Dale E. Berry	Dorothy M. Berry	2000	112
176 3/8	36 2/8	38 1/8	14 7/8	14 6/8	8 3/8	8 2/8	22 7/8	22	Harney Co., OR	John D. McCollum, Jr.	John D. McCollum, Jr.	1998	113
176 2/8	36 7/8	36 1/8	15	15	9	9 3/8	21 4/8	15 5/8	Tombstone Mt., AB	Dean W. Hyslop	Dean W. Hyslop	2000	114
175 6/8	37 4/8	38	14 3/8	14 2/8	9	9 1/8	24 6/8	24 2/8	Lake Co., OR	Forris T.D. Sheridan	Forris T.D. Sheridan	2000	115
175 6/8	39 7/8	36 5/8	15 1/8	15 2/8	7 4/8	7 4/8	22 2/8	18 2/8	Lewis & Clark Co., MT	Chad M. Meidinger	Chad M. Meidinger	2003	115
175 4/8	36 2/8	36	15 1/8	15	9 5/8	9	23 2/8	19 4/8	Chelan Co., WA	Sean K. Duke	Sean K. Duke	2001	117
175	34 6/8	35 4/8	15	15	9 6/8	9 4/8	20 7/8	18	Blaine Co., MT	Kevin L. Salsbery	Kevin L. Salsbery	2002	118
197 4/8*	41 2/8	41 4/8	15 7/8	15 7/8	11	11	25	20 5/8	Drinnan Creek, AB	Dean B. Erickson	Dean B. Erickson	2002	

* Final score subject to revision by additional verifying measurements.

DESERT SHEEP

Ovis canadensis nelsoni and certain related subspecies

Minimum Score 165

World's Record 205 1/8

Score	Length of Horn R.	L.	Circumference of Base R.	L.	Circumference at Third Quarter R.	L.	Greatest Spread	Tip to Tip Spread	Locality	Hunter	Owner	Date Killed	Rank
180 5/8	37 7/8	40	15	14 6/8	9 2/8	9 2/8	28 7/8	21 5/8	Brewster Co., TX	Picked Up	TX Parks & Wildlife	2002	1
179 3/8	37 1/8	37 2/8	15 6/8	15 6/8	9 2/8	9 7/8	21 3/8	16 1/8	Hidalgo Co., NM	James A. Schneider	MaHUNT	2001	2
178 6/8	36 2/8	38 2/8	15 7/8	15 7/8	8 5/8	9	22 1/8	21 3/8	Mohave Co., AZ	Ernie Bombardieri	Ernie Bombardieri	2002	3
178 4/8	38	37 6/8	14	13 7/8	10 2/8	10	22 5/8	21 5/8	Coconino Co., AZ	Picked Up	Carl Iacona	1996	4
177 7/8	37 1/8	37 6/8	15 5/8	15 1/8	9 1/8	9 4/8	23 1/8	15 2/8	Sonora, MX	Donald W. Snyder	Donald W. Snyder	2001	5
177 2/8	36 4/8	36 4/8	15 5/8	14 5/8	10 1/8	10	22 2/8	17 2/8	La Paz Co., AZ	Bruce D. Kroeger	Bruce D. Kroeger	2002	6
175 6/8	37 4/8	39	15 3/8	15 3/8	8 4/8	8 6/8	21	21	Maricopa Co., AZ	Mark A.Thorsrud	Mark A.Thorsrud	2001	7
175	35 6/8	36 2/8	14 6/8	14 6/8	9	9	23 2/8	23 2/8	Maricopa Co., AZ	Matthew D. Liljenquist	Matthew D. Liljenquist	2002	8
174 7/8	34 5/8	35 6/8	15 1/8	15	9 3/8	9 7/8	21 5/8	19	Hidalgo Co., NM	James L. Daubendiek	James L. Daubendiek	2002	9
174 4/8	33 7/8	34 7/8	15 2/8	15	9 5/8	9 6/8	21	13 2/8	Hidalgo Co., NM	Glen A. Landrus	Glen A. Landrus	2002	10
174 2/8	34 6/8	35 4/8	15 1/8	15 1/8	9 7/8	9 7/8	23 6/8	23 6/8	Washington Co., UT	Margaret Barnett	Margaret Barnett	2001	11
174 1/8	38 1/8	37 4/8	14 2/8	14 3/8	9	8 6/8	22 2/8	21 6/8	Baja Calif, MX	Scott Jankowski	Scott Jankowski	2001	12
174	36	36	14 1/8	14 1/8	10 4/8	9 7/8	24 6/8	23	Hudspeth Co., TX	Robert H. Torstenson	Robert H. Torstenson	2001	13
173 7/8	36 4/8	35 3/8	15 3/8	15 1/8	9 2/8	9	22 1/8	21 1/8	Clark Co., NV	Bob Wells	Bob Wells	2002	14
173 1/8	36 1/8	36 4/8	14 4/8	14 4/8	9 3/8	9 1/8	22	16 1/8	Hidalgo Co., NM	James A. Schneider	MaHUNT	2000	15
173 1/8	35 2/8	36 5/8	14 5/8	14 6/8	9 1/8	9 6/8	21 1/8	16 4/8	Yuma Co., AZ	Heath Lewis	Heath Lewis	2002	15
172 3/8	41	41 3/8	13 3/8	13 4/8	8	8 3/8	28 2/8	28	Nye Co., NV	James G. Pedersen	James G. Pedersen	2000	17
172 2/8	36	36 4/8	14 3/8	14 5/8	9	8 6/8	22 7/8	22 4/8	Yuma Co., AZ	Dyanne L. Edwards	Dyanne L. Edwards	2000	18
172 2/8	36 4/8	35 6/8	15	15	8 5/8	8 5/8	23 6/8	23 6/8	San Bernardino Co., CA	Oliver R. Biggers	Oliver R. Biggers	2002	18
172 1/8	36 3/8	35 6/8	15 4/8	15 4/8	7 7/8	8	19	17 7/8	Sonora, MX	Kevin S. Small	Kevin S. Small	2002	20
171 6/8	37 5/8	37 1/8	14 4/8	14 4/8	8 2/8	8 4/8	24 6/8	24 6/8	Maricopa Co., AZ	Roxane R. Kelso	Roxane R. Kelso	2001	21
171 4/8	36 5/8	35 7/8	14 1/8	14 1/8	8 7/8	9	22 6/8	20 4/8	Gila Co., AZ	Earl R. LaForge	Earl R. LaForge	1991	22
171 4/8	35 1/8	34 3/8	14 6/8	14 6/8	10 2/8	9 5/8	23	19 4/8	Clark Co., NV	L. Alan Forman	L. Alan Forman	2001	22
171 3/8	35 5/8	34 4/8	15 5/8	15 3/8	8 5/8	9 1/8	23 6/8	21	Clark Co., NV	Mitch Buzzetti	Mitch Buzzetti	2001	24
171 3/8	36 5/8	36 6/8	15 2/8	15 1/8	8 1/8	8 2/8	18	16 5/8	Pima Co., AZ	Frank E. Zuern, Jr.	Frank E. Zuern, Jr.	2001	24
170 7/8	36	35 5/8	15 4/8	15 3/8	8	8	21 2/8	20 4/8	Mohave Co., AZ	Jeffrey J. Anderson	Jeffrey J. Anderson	2000	26
170 3/8	34 3/8	38 4/8	14	14 1/8	9 2/8	9 2/8	29	29	Mohave Co., AZ	Picked Up	Carl Iacona	PR1996	27
170 2/8	34	34	14 6/8	14 6/8	9	9	20 4/8	16 4/8	Yuma Co., AZ	James S. Lee	James S. Lee	2000	28
170 2/8	36 6/8	33 6/8	15	15	8 4/8	8 5/8	25	24 4/8	La Paz Co., AZ	Michael J. Bertoldi	Michael J. Bertoldi	2000	28
170 2/8	35 2/8	36 6/8	14 7/8	14 7/8	9	9 1/8	21 6/8	18	Clark Co., NV	Paul J. Harris	Paul J. Harris	2001	28
170 2/8	36	35 6/8	14 3/8	14 5/8	8 4/8	8 7/8	23 4/8	19	Clark Co., NV	William H. Taylor	William H. Taylor	2001	28
169 6/8	36 4/8	35 2/8	14 2/8	14 1/8	9	9	19 4/8	15 3/8	Yuma Co., AZ	Joseph M. Del Re	Joseph M. Del Re	2001	32

DESERT SHEEP

Ovis canadensis nelsoni and certain related subspecies

Score	Length of Horn R.	L.	Circumference of Base R.	L.	Circumference at Third Quarter R.	L.	Greatest Spread	Tip to Tip Spread	Locality	Hunter	Owner	Date Killed	Rank
169 6/8	35 2/8	32	14 6/8	14 7/8	10	9 4/8	23 3/8	22 2/8	Nye Co., NV	Mark R. Forsmark	Mark R. Forsmark	2002	32
169 4/8	35	35 2/8	14 6/8	14 7/8	9	8 7/8	20 6/8	20 4/8	Maricopa Co., AZ	Jay Senkerik	Jay Senkerik	2000	34
169 4/8	35 4/8	36 2/8	14 2/8	14 2/8	8 6/8	8 6/8	20 4/8	18 7/8	Sonora, MX	Normand Berube	Normand Berube	2001	34
169 2/8	33 2/8	33 4/8	14 4/8	14 6/8	9 4/8	10	20 1/8	14 4/8	Yuma Co., AZ	W. Jason Sherwood	W. Jason Sherwood	2001	36
169 2/8	35 7/8	35 5/8	14 6/8	14 6/8	8 4/8	8 4/8	18 2/8	17	Sonora, MX	Stephen A. Nelson	Stephen A. Nelson	2002	36
168 6/8	33 6/8	33 6/8	14 4/8	14 6/8	9	9	23 4/8	23 4/8	Mohave Co., AZ	Lawrence R. Lundin	Lawrence R. Lundin	2000	38
168 2/8	36 4/8	36	14 5/8	14 6/8	7 3/8	7 3/8	24 4/8	24 4/8	Lincoln Co., NV	Todd G. DeLong	Todd G. DeLong	2001	39
168 2/8	33 4/8	35 2/8	14 5/8	14 6/8	9 3/8	9	23 3/8	22 2/8	Brewster Co., TX	Doyle R. Powers	Doyle R. Powers	2002	39
168	36	34 6/8	13 5/8	13 5/8	8 7/8	9 3/8	21 4/8	20 2/8	Garfield Co., UT	Lee Howard	Lee Howard	2001	41
166 6/8	36	35 6/8	13 2/8	13 2/8	9 7/8	9 2/8	21 2/8	20 3/8	Clark Co., NV	Kelly Lewis	Kelly Lewis	2001	42
166 6/8	32 6/8	34	14 4/8	14 4/8	9 4/8	9 5/8	18	17 4/8	San Bernardino Co., CA	William H. Jones, Jr.	William H. Jones, Jr.	2001	42
165 7/8	35 2/8	34 7/8	14 6/8	14 6/8	8 1/8	7 6/8	21	15 2/8	Sonora, MX	A.J. Goertz	John McCall	2001	44
165 4/8	36 4/8	34 4/8	14 6/8	14 6/8	9 1/8	9	21	19 4/8	Maricopa Co., AZ	Sharon L. Duncan	Sharon L. Duncan	2000	45
165 1/8	33 5/8	31	15 4/8	15 4/8	8 3/8	8 1/8	22 5/8	22 2/8	Churchill Co., NV	Jason K. Arrien	Jason K. Arrien	2002	46
184 7/8*	38	38 5/8	17 1/8	17 2/8	8 3/8	8 4/8	20 2/8	15 5/8	Sonora, MX	Mirrel R. Kephart, Jr.	Mirrel R. Kephart, Jr.	2001	
184 4/8*	36 6/8	38	15 5/8	15 5/8	10 6/8	10	24	24	Clark Co., NV	Henry J. Moreda	Henry J. Moreda	2002	
182 6/8*	37 3/8	36 1/8	16	16 1/8	10 1/8	9 3/8	24 2/8	17 7/8	Sonora, MX	Dick A. Jacobs	Dick A. Jacobs	2000	
179 *	38 2/8	39 6/8	14 5/8	14 6/8	8 7/8	9	22 6/8	22 6/8	Gila Co., AZ	Donald W. Snyder	Donald W. Snyder	2002	

* Final score subject to revision by additional verifying measurements.

DALL'S SHEEP

Ovis dalli dalli and Ovis dalli kenaiensis

Minimum Score 160   World's Record 189 6/8

Score	Length of Horn R.	L.	Circumference of Base R.	L.	Circumference at Third Quarter R.	L.	Greatest Spread	Tip to Tip Spread	Locality	Hunter	Owner	Date Killed	Rank
177	40 1/8	39 7/8	15	15 1/8	7 1/8	7 1/8	23 1/8	21 4/8	Chugach Mts., AK	William J. Dunbar	William J. Dunbar	1994	1
173 6/8	45 1/8	42 5/8	13 1/8	13 2/8	6 5/8	6 4/8	26	26	Brooks Range, AK	Chris E. Kneeland	Chris E. Kneeland	2003	2
172 2/8	40 6/8	43	14 3/8	14 3/8	6 1/8	6 6/8	25 2/8	23 6/8	Chugach Mts., AK	William J. Dunbar	William J. Dunbar	1991	3
171 6/8	41 6/8	43 2/8	14 1/8	14 1/8	6 2/8	6 1/8	24 6/8	24 5/8	Talkeetna Mts., AK	Andrew G. Kelso	Andrew G. Kelso	2003	4
171 3/8	41	40 7/8	13 6/8	13 5/8	6 5/8	6 5/8	22 7/8	22 7/8	Chugach Mts., AK	Michael J. Pace	Michael J. Pace	2003	5
171 2/8	40 7/8	41 5/8	13 7/8	13 6/8	6 2/8	6 2/8	24 3/8	24	Chugach Mts., AK	Donald W. Snyder	Donald W. Snyder	2000	6
171 2/8	41 2/8	41 2/8	14 4/8	14 4/8	5 5/8	5 5/8	28 1/8	28	Mackenzie Mts., NT	Picked Up	Dan H. Whitelock	2002	6
170 5/8	43 6/8	44 1/8	13 2/8	13	6	5 7/8	27 7/8	27 6/8	Mt. Hesperus, AK	Scott T. Doxey	Scott T. Doxey	2000	8
170 5/8	41	41 5/8	14	14	5 7/8	5 7/8	27 5/8	27 3/8	Chugach Mts., AK	Glen A. Landrus	Glen A. Landrus	2001	8
170 3/8	46	42 1/8	13 1/8	12 7/8	6	5 3/8	28 7/8	28 5/8	Wrangell Mts., AK	James H. Duke, Jr.	James H. Duke, Jr.	1999	10
170	42	39	13 7/8	14 2/8	6 6/8	6 6/8	21	21	Mackenzie Mts., NT	William C. Mills	William C. Mills	1979	11
170	42 7/8	42 1/8	13 4/8	13 5/8	5 5/8	5 5/8	28	28	Alaska Range, AK	John F. Murray	John F. Murray	2000	11
168 6/8	41	41 6/8	14	13 7/8	5 7/8	5 6/8	29 2/8	29 2/8	Chugach Mts., AK	Craig Bade	Craig Bade	2003	13
168 3/8	38 7/8	38 2/8	14 6/8	14 6/8	6 5/8	6 5/8	23 4/8	23	Chugach Mts., AK	Craig R. Johnson	Craig R. Johnson	1979	14
166 4/8	40	40 4/8	13 7/8	13 7/8	5 7/8	5 7/8	24 6/8	24 4/8	Carcajou River, NT	Daniel L. Scharmer	Daniel L. Scharmer	2002	15
166 1/8	39 2/8	40 1/8	14 1/8	14 2/8	6	6 2/8	24 3/8	24 1/8	Arctic Red River, NT	Michael J. Buhler	Michael J. Buhler	2003	16
166	40 1/8	40 3/8	14 1/8	14 2/8	6 1/8	6 2/8	22 5/8	22 5/8	Ram River, NT	George A. Pickel	George A. Pickel	2002	17
165 4/8	40 4/8	41 2/8	13 1/8	13 1/8	6	6 2/8	24 5/8	24 5/8	Goat Creek, AK	Edward C. Joseph	Edward C. Joseph	2001	18
164 6/8	42 6/8	40	13 4/8	13 4/8	5 4/8	5 7/8	24 3/8	24 2/8	Godlin River, NT	Kent Deligans	Kent Deligans	2003	19
163 5/8	38 6/8	38 7/8	13 6/8	13 6/8	6 1/8	6 3/8	25 4/8	24 2/8	Chugach Mts., AK	Thomas P. Powers	Thomas P. Powers	2001	20
163 5/8	42 1/8	39 4/8	13 6/8	13 6/8	5 3/8	5	26	26	Mackenzie Mts., NT	Ken Trudell	Ken Trudell	2003	20
163 1/8	37 6/8	42 1/8	13	13	6 2/8	6 2/8	22	22	N. Fork Chandalar River, AK	Picked Up	Eugene M. Witt	PR2002	22
162 2/8	37 6/8	37 2/8	14	14 2/8	5 7/8	5 7/8	28 7/8	28 6/8	Billy Creek, AK	Richard C. Leach	Richard C. Leach	2002	23
162 1/8	38 6/8	39 1/8	13 7/8	13 7/8	5 1/8	5 4/8	24	24	Metal Creek Glacier, AK	W. David Ooten	W. David Ooten	2001	24
161 5/8	41 2/8	41 1/8	13 2/8	13 3/8	5 1/8	5 1/8	26 7/8	26 6/8	Necons River, AK	Thomas E. Farmer	Thomas E. Farmer	2000	25
161 4/8	38 6/8	38 4/8	13 4/8	13 4/8	5 7/8	5 6/8	22 5/8	22	Chugach Mts., AK	Ray Aderholt	Ray Aderholt	2001	26
161	37 2/8	37 6/8	13 6/8	13 7/8	6	6 1/8	25 6/8	25 6/8	Ram River, NT	Lawrence W. Dossman	Lawrence W. Dossman	2002	27
160 7/8	39	37 3/8	14	14	5 4/8	5 5/8	25 1/8	25 1/8	Mackenzie Mts., NT	Brent V. Trumbo	Brent V. Trumbo	2002	28
160 3/8	39 4/8	40 1/8	13 4/8	13 3/8	5 3/8	5 3/8	28 7/8	28 7/8	Kusawa Lake, YT	Jason F. Dennis	Jason F. Dennis	2002	29
173 7/8*	43 4/8	42 7/8	13 4/8	13 4/8	6 4/8	6 5/8	30	30	Sheenjek River, AK	Jerry D. Lees	Jerry D. Lees	2002	
171 6/8*	43 3/8	44 1/8	13 2/8	13	6	6 4/8	25 6/8	25 6/8	Chandalar River, AK	Reed J. Morisky	Reed J. Morisky	1999	

* Final score subject to revision by additional verifying measurements.

STONE'S SHEEP
Ovis dalli stonei

Score	Length of Horn R.	L.	Circumference of Base R.	L.	Circumference at Third Quarter R.	L.	Greatest Spread	Tip to Tip Spread	Locality	Hunter	Owner	Date Killed	Rank
174 6/8	39 3/8	42 3/8	14 4/8	14 3/8	6 6/8	6 3/8	23 6/8	24 6/8	Muncho Lake, BC	Donald L. Mann	Donald L. Mann	2000	1
174 1/8	43 7/8	41	13 7/8	14	6 3/8	6 2/8	23 6/8	23 6/8	Marker Lake, YT	Ronald G. Selby	Ronald G. Selby	2001	2
171 4/8	39 7/8	40 3/8	14 4/8	14 4/8	5 7/8	6 1/8	27 3/8	27 3/8	Gundahoo River, BC	A.J. Goertz	John McCall	2001	3
168 1/8	39 1/8	39 2/8	13 6/8	13 5/8	6 7/8	6 7/8	22	21 7/8	Muncho Lake, BC	Douglas J. Peterson	Douglas J. Peterson	2001	4
168 1/8	37 6/8	37 7/8	14 5/8	14 6/8	6 4/8	6 3/8	21 7/8	21 7/8	Prophet River, BC	Randy Pittman	Randy Pittman	2001	4
168	39 1/8	35 7/8	14	14 2/8	7 3/8	7 2/8	24	23 7/8	Prairie Creek, BC	Tom Foss	Tom Foss	2001	6
167	40 4/8	40 6/8	13 7/8	13 6/8	5 6/8	6 2/8	22 1/8	22 1/8	Gundahoo River, BC	Steven L. Bedell	Steven L. Bedell	2001	7
166 7/8	41 4/8	39 5/8	13 4/8	13 4/8	6 2/8	6 2/8	27	26 6/8	Walkout Creek, BC	Thomas E. Farmer	Thomas E. Farmer	2001	8
165 5/8	37 5/8	38 2/8	14 1/8	14 1/8	6 1/8	6 3/8	20 7/8	20 3/8	Muncho Lake, BC	Scott A. Limmer	Scott A. Limmer	2003	9
165	39 5/8	39 5/8	13 1/8	13 2/8	6 7/8	6 3/8	24 6/8	24 2/8	Edziza Peak, BC	Eric Guidobono	Eric Guidobono	2002	10
171 6/8*	45	38	14 3/8	14 4/8	6 4/8	6 3/8	25 3/8	25 3/8	Laurier Creek, YT	Shayne D. Parker	Shayne D. Parker	2000	
171 2/8*	39 3/8	40 5/8	14 4/8	14 4/8	7 5/8	6 6/8	26 2/8	25 7/8	Quash Creek, BC	Dick A. Jacobs	Dick A. Jacobs	2001	

* Final score subject to revision by additional verifying measurements.

OFFICIAL SCORE CHARTS FOR NORTH AMERICAN BIG GAME TROPHIES

250 Station Drive
Missoula, MT 59801
(406) 542-1888

BOONE AND CROCKETT CLUB®
OFFICIAL SCORING SYSTEM FOR NORTH AMERICAN BIG GAME TROPHIES

BEAR

	MINIMUM SCORES		KIND OF BEAR (check one)
	AWARDS	ALL-TIME	
black bear	20	21	■ black bear
grizzly bear	23	24	☐ grizzly
Alaska brown bear	26	28	☐ Alaska brown bear
polar bear	27	27	☐ polar

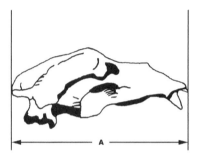

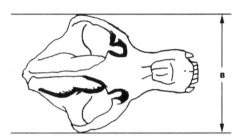

SEE OTHER SIDE FOR INSTRUCTIONS	MEASUREMENTS
A. Greatest Length Without Lower Jaw	14 5/16
B. Greatest Width	8 9/16
FINAL SCORE	22 4/16

Exact Locality Where Killed: **McCreary, Manitoba**

Date Killed: **Sept. 1998** Hunter: **John J. Bathke**

Owner: **John J. Bathke** Telephone #:

Owner's Address:

Guide's Name and Address:

Remarks: (Mention Any Abnormalities or Unique Qualities)

I, _____ **Caren Fish** _____ , certify that I have measured this trophy on _____ **03/16/2003** _____
　　　　　　PRINT NAME　　　　　　　　　　　　　　　　　　　　　　　　　　　　　　　　　MM/DD/YYYYY

at **Minnesota Deer Classic   St. Paul, Minnesota**
STREET ADDRESS　　　　　　　　　　　　　　　　　　　　　　CITY　　　　　　　　　　　　STATE/PROVINCE

and that these measurements and data are, to the best of my knowledge and belief, made in accordance with the instructions given.

Witness: _____ Signature: _____ I.D. Number
　　　　　　　　　　　　　　　　　　　B&C OFFICIAL MEASURER

INSTRUCTIONS FOR MEASURING BEAR

Measurements are taken with calipers or by using parallel perpendiculars, to the nearest **one-sixteenth** of an inch, without reduction of fractions. Official measurements cannot be taken until the skull has air dried for at least 60 days after the animal was killed. All adhering flesh, membrane and cartilage must be completely removed **before** official measurements are taken.

- **A. Greatest Length** is measured between perpendiculars parallel to the long axis of the skull, without the lower jaw and excluding malformations.
- **B. Greatest Width** is measured between perpendiculars at right angles to the long axis.

ENTRY AFFIDAVIT FOR ALL HUNTER-TAKEN TROPHIES

For the purpose of entry into the Boone and Crockett Club's® records, North American big game harvested by the use of the following methods or under the following conditions are ineligible:

- I. Spotting or herding game from the air, followed by landing in its vicinity for the purpose of pursuit and shooting;
- II. Herding or chasing with the aid of any motorized equipment;
- III. Use of electronic communication devices, artificial lighting, or electronic light intensifying devices;
- IV. Confined by artificial barriers, including escape-proof fenced enclosures;
- V. Transplanted for the purpose of commercial shooting;
- VI. By the use of traps or pharmaceuticals;
- VII. While swimming, helpless in deep snow, or helpless in any other natural or artificial medium;
- VIII. On another hunter's license;
- IX. Not in full compliance with the game laws or regulations of the federal government or of any state, province, territory, or tribal council on reservations or tribal lands;

Please answer the following questions:

Were dogs used in conjunction with the pursuit and harvest of this animal?
    Yes   No

If the answer to the above question is yes, answer the following statements:

1. I was present on the hunt at the times the dogs were released to pursue this animal.
    True   False

2. If electronic collars were attached to any of the dogs, receivers were not used to harvest this animal.
    True   False

To the best of my knowledge the answers to the above statements are true. If the answer to either #1 or #2 above is false, please explain on a separate sheet.

I certify that the trophy scored on this chart was not taken in violation of the conditions listed above. In signing this statement, I understand that if the information provided on this entry is found to be misrepresented or fraudulent in any respect, it will not be accepted into the Awards Program and 1) all of my prior entries are subject to deletion from future editions of **Records of North American Big Game** 2) future entries may not be accepted.

FAIR CHASE, as defined by the Boone and Crockett Club®, is the ethical, sportsman~~lik~~ ~~~~ ~~law~~ful pursuit and taking of any free-ranging wild, native North American big game animal in a manner that d~~~~ ~~~~ improper advantage over such game animals.

The Boone and Crockett Club® may exclude the entry of any an~~imal~~ ~~~~ ~~unethi~~cal manner or under conditions deemed inappropriate by the Club.

Date:_____ Signature of Hunter:_____
                  (SIG   IC.)

Date:_____ Signature of Notary or C

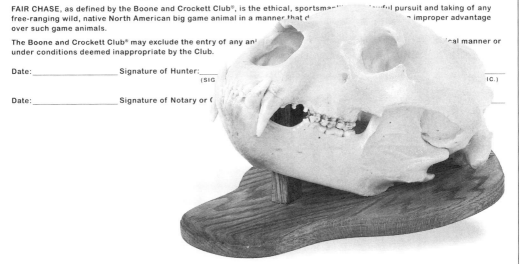

BOONE AND CROCKETT CLUB®
OFFICIAL SCORING SYSTEM FOR NORTH AMERICAN BIG GAME TROPHIES

COUGAR AND JAGUAR

MINIMUM SCORES		
	AWARDS	ALL-TIME
cougar	14 - 8/16	15
jaguar	14 - 8/16	14 - 8/16

KIND OF CAT (check one)

■ cougar
☐ jaguar

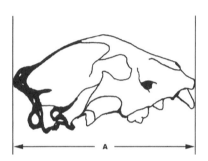

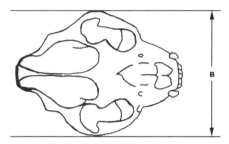

SEE OTHER SIDE FOR INSTRUCTIONS	MEASUREMENTS
A. Greatest Length Without Lower Jaw	9 4/16
B. Greatest Width	6 12/16
FINAL SCORE	16

Exact Locality Where Killed: **Archuleta County, Colorado**

Date Killed: **Dec. 2001**   Hunter: **Brian K. Williams**

Owner: **Brian K. Williams**   Telephone #:

Owner's Address:

Guide's Name and Address:

Remarks: (Mention Any Abnormalities or Unique Qualities)

I, _____ **Tom Watts** _____ , certify that I have measured this trophy on ___ **01/31/2002** ___
PRINT NAME   MM/DD/YYYY

at **Jicarilla Game and Fish Dept.   Dulce, New Mexico**
STREET ADDRESS   CITY   STATE/PROVINCE

and that these measurements and data are, to the best of my knowledge and belief, made in accordance with the instructions given.

Witness: _____   Signature: _____   I.D. Number | | | | |
                                              B&C OFFICIAL MEASURER

INSTRUCTIONS FOR MEASURING COUGAR AND JAGUAR

Measurements are taken with calipers or by using parallel perpendiculars, to the nearest **one-sixteenth** of an inch, without reduction of fractions. Official measurements cannot be taken until the skull has air dried for at least 60 days after the animal was killed. All adhering flesh, membrane and cartilage must be completely removed **before** official measurements are taken.

A. Greatest Length is measured between perpendiculars parallel to the long axis of the skull, without the lower jaw and excluding malformations.

B. Greatest Width is measured between perpendiculars at right angles to the long axis.

ENTRY AFFIDAVIT FOR ALL HUNTER-TAKEN TROPHIES

For the purpose of entry into the Boone and Crockett Club's® records, North American big game harvested by the use of the following methods or under the following conditions are ineligible:

I. Spotting or herding game from the air, followed by landing in its vicinity for the purpose of pursuit and shooting;
II. Herding or chasing with the aid of any motorized equipment;
III. Use of electronic communication devices, artificial lighting, or electronic light intensifying devices;
IV. Confined by artificial barriers, including escape-proof fenced enclosures;
V. Transplanted for the purpose of commercial shooting;
VI. By the use of traps or pharmaceuticals;
VII. While swimming, helpless in deep snow, or helpless in any other natural or artificial medium;
VIII. On another hunter's license;
IX. Not in full compliance with the game laws or regulations of the federal government or of any state, province, territory, or tribal council on reservations or tribal lands;

Please answer the following questions:

Were dogs used in conjunction with the pursuit and harvest of this animal?
    Yes   No

If the answer to the above question is yes, answer the following statements:

1. I was present on the hunt at the times the dogs were released to pursue this animal.
    True   False

2. If electronic collars were attached to any of the dogs, receivers were not used to harvest this animal.
    True   False

To the best of my knowledge the answers to the above statements are true. If the answer to either #1 or #2 above is false, please explain on a separate sheet.

I certify that the trophy scored on this chart was not taken in violation of the conditions listed above. In signing this statement, I understand that if the information provided on this entry is found to be misrepresented or fraudulent in any respect, it will not be accepted into the Awards Program and 1) all of my prior entries are subject to deletion from future editions of **Records of North American Big Game** 2) future entries may not be accepted.

FAIR CHASE, as defined by the Boone and Crockett Club®, is the ethical, sportsmanlike and lawful pursuit and taking of any free-ranging wild, native North American big game animal in a manner that does not give the hunter an improper advantage over such game animals.

The Boone and C⟨...⟩ ⟨...⟩imal that it deems to have been taken in an unethical manner or under conditi⟨...⟩

Date: _____

⟨...⟩SED BY AN OFFICIAL MEASURER OR A NOTARY PUBLIC.)

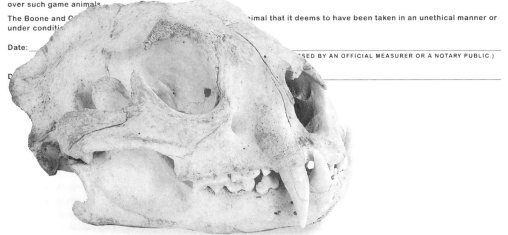

Records of
North American
Big Game

250 Station Drive
Missoula, MT 59801
(406) 542-1888

BOONE AND CROCKETT CLUB®
OFFICIAL SCORING SYSTEM FOR NORTH AMERICAN BIG GAME TROPHIES

MINIMUM SCORES		WALRUS	KIND OF WALRUS (check one)

	AWARDS	ALL-TIME
Atlantic	95	95
Pacific	100	100

KIND OF WALRUS (check one)
■ Atlantic
☐ Pacific

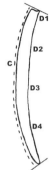

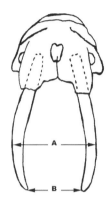

SEE OTHER SIDE FOR INSTRUCTIONS		COLUMN 1	COLUMN 2	COLUMN 3
A. Greatest Spread (If possible)	n/a	Right Tusk	Left Tusk	Difference
B. Tip to Tip Spread (If possible)	n/a			
C. Entire Length of Loose Tusk		24 4/8	25 1/8	5/8
D-1. Circumference of Base		6 6/8	6 4/8	2/8
D-2. Circumference at First Quarter		6 7/8	6 6/8	1/8
D-3. Circumference at Second Quarter		6 2/8	5 6/8	4/8
D-4. Circumference at Third Quarter		4 3/8	4 3/8	—
TOTALS		48 6/8	48 4/8	1 4/8

ADD	Column 1	48 6/8	Exact Locality Where Killed: **Foxe Basin, Nunavut**
	Column 2	48 4/8	Date Killed: **July 2001** Hunter: **Porter Hicks**
	Subtotal	97 2/8	Owner: **B&C National Collection** Telephone #:
SUBTRACT Column 3		1 4/8	Owner's Address:
FINAL SCORE		95 6/8	Guide's Name and Address:
			Remarks: (Mention Any Abnormalities or Unique Qualities)

I, _____ **Warren St. Germaine** _____ , certify that I have measured this trophy on ___ 11/07/2001 ___
PRINT NAME   MM/DD/YYYYY

at __ **54 Calder Crescent**   **Yellowknife, Northwest Territories** __
STREET ADDRESS   CITY   STATE/PROVINCE

and that these measurements and data are, to the best of my knowledge and belief, made in accordance with the instructions given.

Witness:_____ Signature:_____ I.D. Number
                                          B&C OFFICIAL MEASURER

COPYRIGHT © 2004 BY BOONE AND CROCKETT CLUB®

612

INSTRUCTIONS FOR MEASURING WALRUS

All measurements must be made with a 1/4-inch wide flexible steel tape to the nearest one-eighth of an inch. Enter fractional figures in eighths, without reduction. Tusks **should** be removed from mounted specimens for measuring. Official measurements cannot be taken until tusks have air dried for at least 60 days after the animal was killed.

A. Greatest spread is measured between perpendiculars at a right angle to the center line of the skull.

B. Tip to Tip Spread is measured between tips of tusks.

C. Entire Length of Loose Tusk is measured over outer curve from a point in line with the greatest projecting edge of the base to a point in line with tip.

D-1. Circumference of Base is measured at a right angle to axis of tusk. **Do not** follow irregular edge of tusk; the line of measurement must be entirely on tusk material.

D-2-3-4. Divide length of longer tusk by four. Starting at base, mark **both** tusks at these quarters (even though the other tusk is shorter) and measure circumferences at these marks.

ENTRY AFFIDAVIT FOR ALL HUNTER-TAKEN TROPHIES

For the purpose of entry into the Boone and Crockett Club's® records, North American big game harvested by the use of the following methods or under the following conditions are ineligible:

I. Spotting or herding game from the air, followed by landing in its vicinity for the purpose of pursuit and shooting;

II. Herding or chasing with the aid of any motorized equipment;

III. Use of electronic communication devices, artificial lighting, or electronic light intensifying devices;

IV. Confined by artificial barriers, including escape-proof fenced enclosures;

V. Transplanted for the purpose of commercial shooting;

VI. By the use of traps or pharmaceuticals;

VII. While swimming, helpless in deep snow, or helpless in any other natural or artificial medium;

VIII. On another hunter's license;

IX. Not in full compliance with the game laws or regulations of the federal government or of any state, province, territory, or tribal council on reservations or tribal lands;

I certify that the trophy scored on this chart was not taken in violation of the conditions listed above. In signing this statement, I understand that if the information provided on this entry is found to be misrepresented or fraudulent in any respect, it will not be accepted into the Awards Program and 1) all of my prior entries are subject to deletion from future editions of **Records of North American Big Game** 2) future entries may not be accepted.

FAIR CHASE, as defined by the Boone and Crockett Club®, is the ethical, sportsmanlike and lawful pursuit and taking of any free-ranging wild, native North American big game animal in a manner that does not give the hunter an improper advantage over such game animals.

The Boone and Crockett Club® may exclude the entry of any animal that it deems to have been taken in an unethical manner or under conditions deemed inappropriate by the Club.

Date:_____ Signature of Hunter:_____

(SIGNATURE MUST BE WITNESSED BY AN OFFICIAL MEASURER OR A NOTARY PUBLIC.)

Date:_____ Signature of Notary or Official Measurer:_____

Records of
North American
Big Game

250 Station Drive
Missoula, MT 5980●
(406) 542-1888

BOONE AND CROCKETT CLUB®
OFFICIAL SCORING SYSTEM FOR NORTH AMERICAN BIG GAME TROPHIES

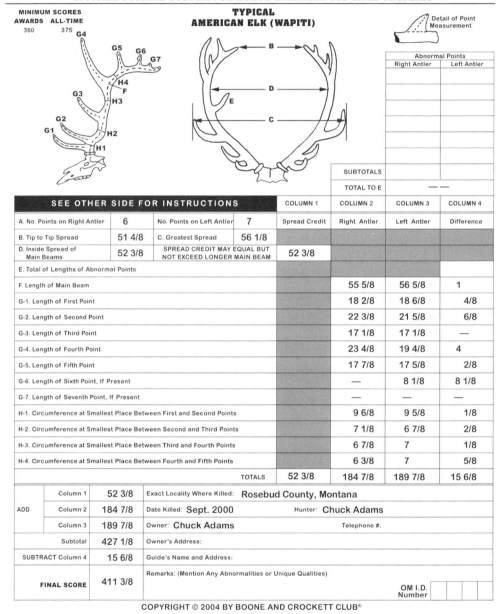

MINIMUM SCORES
AWARDS ALL-TIME
360   375

**TYPICAL
AMERICAN ELK (WAPITI)**

Detail of Point Measurement

Abnormal Points	
Right Antler	Left Antler

SUBTOTALS	
TOTAL TO E	— —

SEE OTHER SIDE FOR INSTRUCTIONS				COLUMN 1	COLUMN 2	COLUMN 3	COLUMN 4
A. No. Points on Right Antler	6	No. Points on Left Antler	7	Spread Credit	Right Antler	Left Antler	Difference
B. Tip to Tip Spread	51 4/8	C. Greatest Spread	56 1/8				
D. Inside Spread of Main Beams	52 3/8	SPREAD CREDIT MAY EQUAL BUT NOT EXCEED LONGER MAIN BEAM	52 3/8				
E. Total of Lengths of Abnormal Points							
F. Length of Main Beam					55 5/8	56 5/8	1
G-1. Length of First Point					18 2/8	18 6/8	4/8
G-2. Length of Second Point					22 3/8	21 5/8	6/8
G-3. Length of Third Point					17 1/8	17 1/8	—
G-4. Length of Fourth Point					23 4/8	19 4/8	4
G-5. Length of Fifth Point					17 7/8	17 5/8	2/8
G-6. Length of Sixth Point, If Present					—	8 1/8	8 1/8
G-7. Length of Seventh Point, If Present					—	—	—
H-1. Circumference at Smallest Place Between First and Second Points					9 6/8	9 5/8	1/8
H-2. Circumference at Smallest Place Between Second and Third Points					7 1/8	6 7/8	2/8
H-3. Circumference at Smallest Place Between Third and Fourth Points					6 7/8	7	1/8
H-4. Circumference at Smallest Place Between Fourth and Fifth Points					6 3/8	7	5/8
			TOTALS	52 3/8	184 7/8	189 7/8	15 6/8

ADD	Column 1	52 3/8	Exact Locality Where Killed: **Rosebud County, Montana**
	Column 2	184 7/8	Date Killed: **Sept. 2000** Hunter: **Chuck Adams**
	Column 3	189 7/8	Owner: **Chuck Adams** Telephone #:
	Subtotal	427 1/8	Owner's Address:
SUBTRACT Column 4		15 6/8	Guide's Name and Address:
FINAL SCORE		411 3/8	Remarks: (Mention Any Abnormalities or Unique Qualities)

OM I.D.
Number

COPYRIGHT © 2004 BY BOONE AND CROCKETT CLUB®

I, _____ Richard C. Berreth _____ , certify that I have measured this trophy on ___ 04/04/2004 ___

PRINT NAME   MM/DD/YYYY

at Cabela's   Kansas City, Kansas

STREET ADDRESS   CITY   STATE/PROVINCE

and that these measurements and data are, to the best of my knowledge and belief, made in accordance with the instructions given.

Witness: _____   Signature: _____   I.D. Number

B&C OFFICIAL MEASURER

INSTRUCTIONS FOR MEASURING TYPICAL AMERICAN ELK (WAPITI)

All measurements must be made with a 1/4-inch wide flexible steel tape to the nearest one-eighth of an inch. (Note: A flexible steel cable can be used to measure points and main beams only.) Enter fractional figures in eighths, without reduction. Official measurements cannot be taken until the antlers have air dried for at least 60 days after the animal was killed.

A. Number of Points on Each Antler: To be counted a point, the projection must be at least one inch long, with length exceeding width at one inch or more of length. All points are measured from tip of point to nearest edge of beam as illustrated. Beam tip is counted as a point but not measured as a point.

B. Tip to Tip Spread is measured between tips of main beams.

C. Greatest Spread is measured between perpendiculars at a right angle to the center line of the skull at widest part, whether across main beams or points.

D. Inside Spread of Main Beams is measured at a right angle to the center line of the skull at widest point between main beams. Enter this measurement again as the Spread Credit if it is less than or equal to the length of the longer main beam; if greater, enter longer main beam length for Spread Credit.

E. Total of Lengths of all Abnormal Points: Abnormal Points are those non-typical in location (such as points originating from a point or from bottom or sides of main beam) or pattern (extra points, not generally paired). Measure in usual manner and record in appropriate blanks.

F. Length of Main Beam is measured from the center of the lowest outside edge of burr over the outer side to the most distant point of the main beam. The point of beginning is that point on the burr where the center line along the outer side of the beam intersects the burr, then following generally the line of the illustration.

G-1-2-3-4-5-6-7. Length of Normal Points: Normal points project from the top or front of the main beam in the general pattern illustrated. They are measured from nearest edge of main beam over outer curve to tip. Lay the tape along the outer curve of the beam so that the top edge of the tape coincides with the top edge of the beam on both sides of point to determine the baseline for point measurement. Record point length in appropriate blanks.

H-1-2-3-4. Circumferences are taken as detailed in illustration for each measurement.

ENTRY AFFIDAVIT FOR ALL HUNTER-TAKEN TROPHIES

For the purpose of entry into the Boone and Crockett Club's® records, North American big game harvested by the use of the following methods or under the following conditions are ineligible:

I. Spotting or herding game from the air, followed by landing in its vicinity for the purpose of pursuit and shooting;

II. Herding or chasing with the aid of any motorized equipment;

III. Use of electronic communication devices, artificial lighting, or electronic light intensifying devices;

IV. Confined by artificial barriers, including escape-proof fenced enclosures;

V. Transplanted for the purpose of commercial shooting;

VI. The use of traps or pharmaceuticals;

VII. While swimming, helpless in deep snow, or helpless in any other natural or artificial medium;

VIII. On another hunter's license;

IX. Not in full compliance with the game laws or regulations of the federal government or of any state, province, territory, or tribal council on reservations or tribal lands;

I certify that the information on this chart was not taken in violation of the conditions listed above. In signing this statement, I understand that if the information provided on this entry is found to be misrepresented or fraudulent in any respect, it will not be accepted into the Awards Program and 1) all of my prior entries are subject to deletion from future editions of **Records of North American Big Game** and 2) future entries may not be accepted.

FAIR CHASE, as defined by the Boone and Crockett Club, is the ethical, sportsmanlike and lawful pursuit and taking of any free-ranging wild, native North American big game animal in a manner that does not give the hunter an improper advantage over such game animals.

The Boone and Crockett Club® may exclude the entry of any animal that it deems to have been taken in an unethical manner or under conditions deemed inappropriate by the Club.

Date: _____ Signature of Hunter: _____

(SIGNATURE MUST BE WITNESSED BY AN OFFICIAL MEASURER OR A NOTARY PUBLIC.)

Date: _____ Signature of Notary or Official Measurer: _____

250 Station Drive
Missoula, MT 59801
(406) 542-1888

BOONE AND CROCKETT CLUB®
OFFICIAL SCORING SYSTEM FOR NORTH AMERICAN BIG GAME TROPHIES

MINIMUM SCORES
AWARDS ALL-TIME
385   385

NON-TYPICAL
AMERICAN ELK (WAPITI)

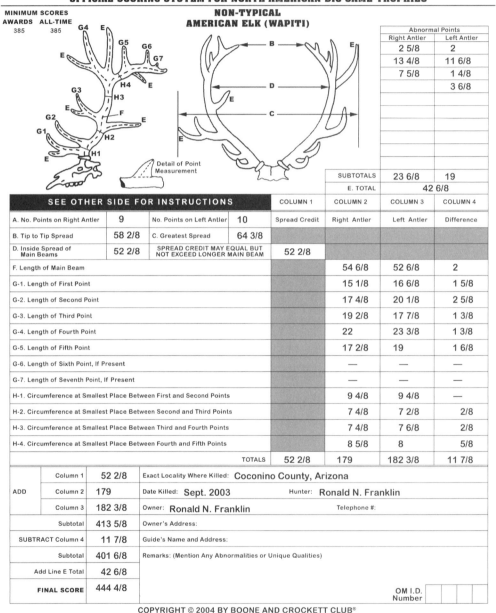

Abnormal Points	
Right Antler	Left Antler
2 5/8	2
13 4/8	11 6/8
7 5/8	1 4/8
	3 6/8
SUBTOTALS 23 6/8	19
E. TOTAL 42 6/8	

Detail of Point Measurement

SEE OTHER SIDE FOR INSTRUCTIONS			COLUMN 1	COLUMN 2	COLUMN 3	COLUMN 4
A. No. Points on Right Antler	9	No. Points on Left Antler 10	Spread Credit	Right Antler	Left Antler	Difference
B. Tip to Tip Spread	58 2/8	C. Greatest Spread 64 3/8				
D. Inside Spread of Main Beams	52 2/8	SPREAD CREDIT MAY EQUAL BUT NOT EXCEED LONGER MAIN BEAM	52 2/8			
F. Length of Main Beam				54 6/8	52 6/8	2
G-1. Length of First Point				15 1/8	16 6/8	1 5/8
G-2. Length of Second Point				17 4/8	20 1/8	2 5/8
G-3. Length of Third Point				19 2/8	17 7/8	1 3/8
G-4. Length of Fourth Point				22	23 3/8	1 3/8
G-5. Length of Fifth Point				17 2/8	19	1 6/8
G-6. Length of Sixth Point, If Present				—	—	—
G-7. Length of Seventh Point, If Present				—	—	—
H-1. Circumference at Smallest Place Between First and Second Points				9 4/8	9 4/8	—
H-2. Circumference at Smallest Place Between Second and Third Points				7 4/8	7 2/8	2/8
H-3. Circumference at Smallest Place Between Third and Fourth Points				7 4/8	7 6/8	2/8
H-4. Circumference at Smallest Place Between Fourth and Fifth Points				8 5/8	8	5/8
TOTALS			52 2/8	179	182 3/8	11 7/8

ADD	Column 1	52 2/8	Exact Locality Where Killed: **Coconino County, Arizona**
	Column 2	179	Date Killed: **Sept. 2003** Hunter: **Ronald N. Franklin**
	Column 3	182 3/8	Owner: **Ronald N. Franklin** Telephone #:
	Subtotal	413 5/8	Owner's Address:
SUBTRACT Column 4		11 7/8	Guide's Name and Address:
	Subtotal	401 6/8	Remarks: (Mention Any Abnormalities or Unique Qualities)
	Add Line E Total	42 6/8	
FINAL SCORE		444 4/8	OM I.D. Number

I, _____ Michael C. Cupell _____, certify that I have measured this trophy on __12/05/2003__
PRINT NAME   MM/DD/YYYYY

at __138 West Wood Drive__ __Phoenix, Arizona__
STREET ADDRESS   CITY   STATE/PROVINCE

and that these measurements and data are, to the best of my knowledge and belief, made in accordance with the instructions given.

Witness: _____ Signature: _____ I.D. Number [ ][ ][ ][ ]
                                              B&C OFFICIAL MEASURER

INSTRUCTIONS FOR MEASURING NON-TYPICAL AMERICAN ELK (WAPITI)

All measurements must be made with a 1/4-inch wide flexible steel tape to the nearest one-eighth of an inch. (Note: A flexible steel cable can be used to measure points and main beams only.) Enter fractional figures in eighths, without reduction. Official measurements cannot be taken until the antlers have air dried for at least 60 days after the animal was killed.

- A. **Number of Points on Each Antler:** To be counted a point, the projection must be at least one inch long, with length exceeding width at one inch or more of length. All points are measured from tip of point to nearest edge of beam as illustrated. Beam tip is counted as a point but not measured as a point.
- B. **Tip to Tip Spread** is measured between tips of main beams.
- C. **Greatest Spread** is measured between perpendiculars at a right angle to the center line of the skull at widest part, whether across main beams or points.
- D. **Inside Spread of Main Beams** is measured at a right angle to the center line of the skull at widest point between main beams. Enter this measurement again as the Spread Credit if it is less than or equal to the length of the longer main beam; if greater, enter longer main beam length for Spread Credit.
- E. **Total of Lengths of all Abnormal Points:** Abnormal Points are those non-typical in location (such as points originating from a point or from bottom or sides of main beam) or pattern (extra points, not generally paired). Measure in usual manner and record in appropriate blanks.
- F. **Length of Main Beam** is measured from the center of the lowest outside edge of burr over the outer side to the most distant point of the main beam. The point of beginning is that point on the burr where the center line along the outer side of the beam intersects the burr, then following generally the line of the illustration.
- G-1-2-3-4-5-6-7. **Length of Normal Points:** Normal points project from the top or front of the main beam in the general pattern illustrated. They are measured from nearest edge of main beam over outer curve to tip. Lay the tape along the outer curve of the beam so that the top edge of the tape coincides with the top edge of the beam on both sides of point to determine the baseline for point measurement. Record point length in appropriate blanks.
- H-1-2-3-4. **Circumferences** are taken as detailed in illustration for each measurement.

ENTRY AFFIDAVIT FOR ALL HUNTER-TAKEN TROPHIES

For the purpose of entry into the Boone and Crockett Club's® records, North American big game harvested by use of the following methods or under the following conditions are ineligible:

- I. Spotting or herding game from the air, followed by landing in its vicinity for the purpose of pursuing and shooting;
- II. Herding or chasing with the aid of any motorized equipment;
- III. Use of electronic communication devices, artificial lighting, or electronic light intensifying devices;
- IV. Confined by artificial barriers, including escape-proof fenced enclosures;
- V. Transplanted for the purpose of commercial shooting;
- VI. By the use of traps or pharmaceuticals;
- VII. While swimming, helpless in deep snow, or helpless in any other natural or artificial medium;
- VIII. On another hunter's license;
- IX. Not in full compliance with the game laws or regulations of the federal government or of any state, province, territory, or tribal council on reservations or tribal lands;

I certify that the trophy scored on this chart was not taken in violation of the conditions listed above. In signing this statement, I understand that if the information provided on this entry is found to be misrepresented or fraudulent in any respect, it will not be accepted into the Awards Program and 1) all of my prior entries are subject to deletion from future editions of **Records of North American Big Game** 2) future entries may not be accepted.

FAIR CHASE, as defined by the Boone and Crockett Club®, is the ethical, sportsmanlike and lawful pursuit and taking of any free-ranging wild, native North American big game animal in a manner that does not give the hunter an improper advantage over such game animals.

The Boone and Crockett Club® may exclude the entry of any animal that it deems to have been taken in an unethical manner or under conditions deemed inappropriate by the Club.

Date: _____ Signature of Hunter: _____
                                          (SIGNATURE MUST BE WITNESSED BY AN OFFICIAL MEASURER OR A NOTARY PUBLIC.)

Date: _____ Signature of Notary or Official Measurer _____

Records of
North American
Big Game

250 Station Drive
Missoula, MT 59801
(406) 542-1888

BOONE AND CROCKETT CLUB®
OFFICIAL SCORING SYSTEM FOR NORTH AMERICAN BIG GAME TROPHIES

ROOSEVELT'S AND TULE ELK

MINIMUM SCORES	AWARDS	ALL-TIME
Roosevelt's	275	290
Tule	270	285

KIND OF ELK (check one)
■ Roosevelt's
☐ Tule

Crown Points

	Right Antler	Left Antler
	2 4/8	3 2/8
	5 7/8	

I. Crown Points Total: 11 5/8

Abnormal Points

	Right Antler	Left Antler

Detail of Point Measurement

TOTAL TO E: — —

SEE OTHER SIDE FOR INSTRUCTIONS

		COLUMN 1	COLUMN 2	COLUMN 3	COLUMN 4
A. No. Points on Right Antler	9	No. Points on Left Antler 8	Spread Credit	Right Antler	Left Antler	Difference
B. Tip to Tip Spread	41	C. Greatest Spread 47 2/8				
D. Inside Spread of Main Beams	40 6/8	SPREAD CREDIT MAY EQUAL BUT NOT EXCEED LONGER MAIN BEAM	40 6/8			
E. Total of Lengths of Abnormal Points						
F. Length of Main Beam				54 1/8	57 5/8	3 4/8
G-1. Length of First Point				15 6/8	17 3/8	1 5/8
G-2. Length of Second Point				18 3/8	20 3/8	2
G-3. Length of Third Point				16 6/8	17 7/8	1 1/8
G-4. Length of Fourth Point				23 5/8	22 7/8	6/8
G-5. Length of Fifth Point				14 6/8	16 6/8	
G-6. Length of Sixth Point, If Present				5 2/8	2 3/8	
G-7. Length of Seventh Point, If Present				—	—	
H-1. Circumference at Smallest Place Between First and Second Points				8 2/8	9 4/8	1 2/8
H-2. Circumference at Smallest Place Between Second and Third Points				6 7/8	6 5/8	2/8
H-3. Circumference at Smallest Place Between Third and Fourth Points				7 1/8	7 1/8	—
H-4. Circumference at Smallest Place Between Fourth and Fifth Points				8 5/8	6 6/8	1 7/8
		TOTALS	40 6/8	179 4/8	185 2/8	12 3/8

ADD	Column 1	40 6/8	Exact Locality Where Killed: Benton County, Oregon
	Column 2	179 4/8	Date Killed: August 2002 Hunter: Jason S. Ballard
	Column 3	185 2/8	Owner: Jason S. Ballard Telephone #:
	Total of I	11 5/8	Owner's Address:
	Subtotal	417 1/8	Guide's Name and Address:
	SUBTRACT Column 4	12 3/8	Remarks: (Mention Any Abnormalities or Unique Qualities)
	FINAL SCORE	404 6/8	OM I.D. Number

COPYRIGHT © 2004 BY BOONE AND CROCKETT CLUB®

I, _____ Glenn W. Abbott _____, certify that I have measured this trophy on __10/19/2002__

PRINT NAME   MM/DD/YYYYY

at __24487 McCain Road   Monroe, Oregon__

STREET ADDRESS   CITY   STATE/PROVINCE

and that these measurements and data are, to the best of my knowledge and belief, made in accordance with the instructions given.

Witness: _____ Signature: _____ I.D. Number | | | |

B&C OFFICIAL MEASURER

INSTRUCTIONS FOR MEASURING ROOSEVELT'S AND TULE ELK

All measurements must be made with a 1/4-inch wide flexible steel tape to the nearest one-eighth of an inch. (Note: A flexible steel cable can be used to measure points and main beams only.) Enter fractional figures in eighths, without reduction. Official measurements cannot be taken until the antlers have air dried for at least 60 days after the animal was killed.

A. Number of Points on Each Antler: to be counted a point, the projection must be at least one inch long, with length exceeding width at one inch or more of length. All points are measured from tip of point to nearest edge of beam as illustrated. Beam tip is counted as a point but not measured as a point.

B. Tip to Tip Spread is measured between tips of main beams.

C. Greatest Spread is measured between perpendiculars at a right angle to the center line of the skull at widest part, whether across main beams or points.

D. Inside Spread of Main Beams is measured at a right angle to the center line of the skull at widest point between main beams. Enter this measurement again as the Spread Credit if it is less than or equal to the length of the longer main beam; if greater, enter longer main beam length for Spread Credit.

E. Total of Lengths of all Abnormal Points: Abnormal Points are those non-typical in location or pattern occurring below G-4. Measure in usual manner and record in appropriate blanks. **Note: do not confuse with Crown Points that may occur in the vicinity of G-4, G-5, G-6, etc.**

F. Length of Main Beam is measured from the center of the lowest outside edge of burr over the outer side to the most distant point of the main beam. The point of beginning is that point on the burr where the center line along the outer side of the beam intersects the burr, then following generally the line of the illustration.

G-1-2-3-4-5-6-7. Length of Normal Points: Normal points project from the top or front of the main beam in the general pattern illustrated. They are measured from nearest edge of main beam over outer curve to tip. Lay the tape along the outer curve of the beam so that the top edge of the tape coincides with the top edge of the beam on both sides of point to determine the base line for point measurement. Record point length in appropriate blanks.

H-1-2-3-4. Circumferences are taken as detailed in illustration for each measurement.

I. Crown Points: From the well-defined Royal on each end of beam, all points other than the normal points in their typical locations are Crown Points. This includes points occurring on the Royal, other normal points, on Crown Points, and on the bottom and sides of main beam after the Royal. Measure and record in appropriate blanks provided and add to score below.

ENTRY AFFIDAVIT FOR ALL HUNTER-TAKEN TROPHIES

For the purpose of entry into the Boone and Crockett Club's® records, North American big game harvested by the use of the following methods or under the following conditions are ineligible:

I. Spotting or herding game from the air, followed by landing in its vicinity for the purpose of pursuit and shooting;

II. Herding or pursuing with the aid of any motorized equipment;

III. Use of electronic communication devices, artificial lighting, electronic light intensifying devices;

IV. Confined by artificial barriers, including escape-proof fenced enclosures;

V. Transplanted for the purpose of commercial shooting;

VI. By the use of traps or pharmaceuticals;

VII. While swimming, helpless in deep snow, or helpless in any other natural or artificial medium;

VIII. On another hunter's license;

IX. Not in full compliance with the game laws or regulations of the federal government or of any state, province, territory, or tribal council on reservations or tribal lands;

I certify that the trophy scored on this chart was not taken in violation of the conditions listed above. In signing this statement, I understand that if the information provided is found to be misrepresented or fraudulent in any respect, it will not be accepted and any prior acceptance will be void, and the trophy is subject to deletion from future editions of **Records of North American Big Game** and future entries will not be accepted.

FAIR CHASE, as defined by the Boone and Crockett Club®, is the ethical, sportsmanlike and lawful pursuit and taking of any free-ranging wild, native North American big game animal in a manner that does not give the hunter an improper advantage over such game animals.

The Boone and Crockett Club® may exclude the entry of any animal that it deems to have been taken in an unethical manner or under conditions deemed inappropriate by the Club.

Date: _____

_____ (SIGNATURE MUST BE WITNESSED BY AN OFFICIAL MEASURER OR A NOTARY PUBLIC.)

Date: _____ _____ Notary or Official Measurer: _____

250 Station Drive
Missoula, MT 59801
(406) 542-1888

BOONE AND CROCKETT CLUB®

OFFICIAL SCORING SYSTEM FOR NORTH AMERICAN BIG GAME TROPHIES

TYPICAL
MULE DEER AND BLACKTAIL DEER

	MINIMUM SCORES	
	AWARDS	ALL-TIME
mule deer	180	190
Columbia blacktail	125	135
Sitka blacktail	100	108

KIND OF DEER (check one)
- ☑ mule deer
- ☐ Columbia blacktail
- ☐ Sitka blacktail

Detail of Point Measurement

Abnormal Points	
Right Antler	Left Antler
SUBTOTALS	
TOTAL TO E	

SEE OTHER SIDE FOR INSTRUCTIONS				COLUMN 1	COLUMN 2	COLUMN 3	COLUMN 4
A. No. Points on Right Antler	5	No. Points on Left Antler	5	Spread Credit	Right Antler	Left Antler	Difference
B. Tip to Tip Spread	25 4/8	C. Greatest Spread	31 6/8				
D. Inside Spread of Main Beams	25 2/8	SPREAD CREDIT MAY EQUAL BUT NOT EXCEED LONGER MAIN BEAM	24 5/8				
E. Total of Lengths of Abnormal Points							
F. Length of Main Beam					24 5/8	24 5/8	—
G-1. Length of First Point, If Present					4	3 7/8	1/8
G-2. Length of Second Point					20 1/8	18	2 1/8
G-3. Length of Third Point, If Present					12 6/8	12 6/8	—
G-4. Length of Fourth Point, If Present					13 3/8	13 6/8	3/8
H-1. Circumference at Smallest Place Between Burr and First Point					5	5 1/8	1/8
H-2. Circumference at Smallest Place Between First and Second Points					4 5/8	4 5/8	—
H-3. Circumference at Smallest Place Between Main Beam and Third Point					4 2/8	4	2/8
H-4. Circumference at Smallest Place Between Second and Fourth Points					4 4/8	4 4/8	—
			TOTALS	24 5/8	93 2/8	91 2/8	3

ADD	Column 1	24 5/8	Exact Locality Where Killed: **Summit County, Colorado**
	Column 2	93 2/8	Date Killed: **Nov. 2002** Hunter: **Robb R. Rishor**
	Column 3	91 2/8	Owner: **Robb R. Rishor** Telephone #:
	Subtotal	209 1/8	Owner's Address:
SUBTRACT Column 4		3	Guide's Name and Address:
FINAL SCORE		206 1/8	Remarks: (Mention Any Abnormalities or Unique Qualities)

OM I.D. Number

I, _____ C. R. Wenger _____ , certify that I have measured this trophy on __ 01/15/2003 __

PRINT NAME   MM/DD/YYYYY

at __189 Lemhi Backroad_____Salmon, Idaho_____

STREET ADDRESS   CITY   STATE/PROVINCE

and that these measurements and data are, to the best of my knowledge and belief, made in accordance with the instructions given.

Witness: _____   Signature: _____   I.D. Number | | | | |

B&C OFFICIAL MEASURER

INSTRUCTIONS FOR MEASURING TYPICAL MULE AND BLACKTAIL DEER

All measurements must be made with a 1/4-inch wide flexible steel tape to the nearest one-eighth of an inch. (Note: A flexible steel cable can be used to measure points and main beams only.) Enter fractional figures in eighths, without reduction. Official measurements cannot be taken until the antlers have air dried for at least 60 days after the animal was killed.

A. Number of Points on Each Antler: To be counted a point, the projection must be at least one inch long, with length exceeding width at one inch or more of length. All points are measured from tip of point to nearest edge of beam. Beam tip is counted as a point but not measured as a point.

B. Tip to Tip Spread is measured between tips of main beams.

C. Greatest Spread is measured between perpendiculars at a right angle to the center line of the skull at widest part, whether across main beams or points.

D. Inside Spread of Main Beams is measured at a right angle to the center line of the skull at widest point between main beams. Enter this measurement again as the Spread Credit **if** it is less than or equal to the length of the longer main beam; if greater, enter longer main beam length for Spread Credit.

E. Total of Lengths of all Abnormal Points: Abnormal Points are those non-typical in location such as points originating from a point (exception: G-3 originates from G-2 in perfectly normal fashion) or from bottom or sides of main beam, or any points beyond the normal pattern of five (including beam tip) per antler. Measure each abnormal point in usual manner and enter in appropriate blanks.

F. Length of Main Beam is measured from the center of the lowest outside edge of burr over the outer side to the most distant point of the Main Beam. The point of beginning is that point on the burr where the center line along the outer side of the beam intersects the burr, then following generally the line of the illustration.

G-1-2-3-4 Length of Normal Points: Normal points are the brow tines and the upper and lower forks as shown in the illustration. They are measured from nearest edge of main beam over outer curve to tip. Lay the tape along the outer curve of the beam so that the top edge of the tape coincides with the top edge of the beam on both sides of point to determine the baseline for point measurement. Record point lengths in appropriate blanks.

H-1-2-3-4 Circumferences are taken as detailed in illustration for each measurement. If brow point is missing, take H-1 and H-2 at smallest place between burr and G-2. If G-3 is missing, take H-3 halfway between the base and tip of G-2. If G-4 is missing, take H-4 halfway between G-2 and tip of main beam.

ENTRY AFFIDAVIT FOR ALL HUNTER-TAKEN TROPHIES

For the purpose of entry into the Boone and Crockett Club's ® _____ North American big game harvested by the use of the following methods or under the following conditions are ineligible:

I.   Spotting or herding game from the air, followed by landing in its vicinity for the purpose of pursuit and shooting;
II. Herding or chasing with the use of any motorized equipment;
III. Use of electronic communications for attracting, locating, or electronic light intensifying devices;
IV. Confined by artificial barriers, including escape-proof fenced enclosures;
V.   Transplanted for the purpose of commercial shooting;
VI. By the use of traps or pharmaceuticals;
VII. While swimming, helpless in deep snow, or helpless in any other natural or artificial medium;
VIII. On another hunter's license;
IX. Not in full compliance with the game laws or regulations of the federal government or of any state, province, territory, or tribal council.

I certify that the trophy scored on this chart was not taken in violation of the conditions listed above. In signing this statement, I understand that if the information provided on this entry is found to be misrepresented or fraudulent in any respect, it will not be accepted into the Awards Program and all of my prior entries are subject to deletion from future editions of **Records of North American Big Game** and future entries may not be accepted.

FAIR CHASE, as defined by the Boone and Crockett Club ®, is the ethical, sportsmanlike and lawful pursuit and taking of any free-ranging wild, native North American big game animal in a manner that does not give the hunter an improper advantage over such game animals.

The Boone and Crockett Club may exclude the entry of any animal that it deems to have been taken in an unethical manner or under conditions deemed inappropriate by the Club.

Date: _____   Signature of Hunter: _____

                              (SIGNATURE MUST BE WITNESSED BY AN OFFICIAL MEASURER OR A NOTARY PUBLIC.)

Date: _____   Signature of Notary or Official Measurer: _____

BOONE AND CROCKETT CLUB®

OFFICIAL SCORING SYSTEM FOR NORTH AMERICAN BIG GAME TROPHIES

NON-TYPICAL
MULE DEER AND BLACKTAIL DEER

	MINIMUM SCORES	
	AWARDS	ALL-TIME
mule deer	215	230
Columbia blacktail	155	155
Sitka blacktail	118	118

Abnormal Points	
Right Antler	Left Antler
6 4/8	6 6/8
2 4/8	3 1/8
3 2/8	8 4/8
5 1/8	6 6/8

Detail of Point Measurement

SUBTOTALS	17 3/8	25 1/8
E. TOTAL	42 4/8

SEE OTHER SIDE FOR INSTRUCTIONS	COLUMN 1	COLUMN 2	COLUMN 3	COLUMN 4
		Spread Credit	Right Antler	Left Antler	Difference
A. No. Points on Right Antler **9** — No. Points on Left Antler **9**				
B. Tip to Tip Spread **12 7/8** — C. Greatest Spread **25 6/8**				
D. Inside Spread of Main Beams **17 5/8** — SPREAD CREDIT MAY EQUAL BUT NOT EXCEED LONGER MAIN BEAM	**17 5/8**			
F. Length of Main Beam		21 7/8	20 4/8	1 3/8
G-1. Length of First Point, If Present		2 7/8	3 3/8	4/8
G-2. Length of Second Point		12 5/8	12 2/8	3/8
G-3. Length of Third Point, If Present		10 6/8	10 1/8	5/8
G-4. Length of Fourth Point, If Present		11 6/8	12 1/8	3/8
H-1. Circumference at Smallest Place Between Burr and First Point		4 2/8	4 3/8	1/8
H-2. Circumference at Smallest Place Between First and Second Points		4 1/8	4 1/8	—
H-3. Circumference at Smallest Place Between Main Beam and Third Point		3 3/8	3 3/8	—
H-4. Circumference at Smallest Place Between Second and Fourth Points		4 7/8	4 6/8	1/8
TOTALS	17 5/8	76 4/8	75	3 4/8

ADD	Column 1	17 5/8
	Column 2	76 4/8
	Column 3	75
	Subtotal	169 1/8
SUBTRACT Column 4		3 4/8
	Subtotal	165 5/8
ADD Line E Total		42 4/8
FINAL SCORE		**208 1/8**

Exact Locality Where Killed: **Polk County, Oregon**

Date Killed: **October 1962** — Hunter: **Frank S. Foldi**

Owner: **Steve D. Crossley** — Telephone #:

Owner's Address:

Guide's Name and Address:

Remarks: (Mention Any Abnormalities or Unique Qualities)

OM I.D. Number

I, _____ Roger L. Selner _____ , certify that I have measured this trophy on ___ 04/09/2003 ___
PRINT NAME   MM/DD/YYYYY

at _35230 S.E. Pine   Estacada, Oregon_____
STREET ADDRESS   CITY   STATE/PROVINCE

and that these measurements and data are, to the best of my knowledge and belief, made in accordance with the instructions given.

Witness: _____   Signature: _____   I.D. Number [ ][ ][ ]
                                                        B&C OFFICIAL MEASURER

INSTRUCTIONS FOR MEASURING NON-TYPICAL MULE DEER AND BLACKTAIL

All measurements must be made with a 1/4-inch wide flexible steel tape to the nearest one-eighth of an inch. (Note: A flexible steel cable can be used to measure points and main beams only.) Enter fractional figures in eighths, without reduction. Official measurements cannot be taken until the antlers have air dried for at least 60 days after the animal was killed.

A. Number of Points on Each Antler: To be counted a point, the projection must be at least one inch long, with length exceeding width at one inch or more of length. All points are measured from tip of point to nearest edge of beam as illustrated. Beam tip is counted as a point but not measured as a point.

B. Tip to Tip Spread is measured between tips of main beams.

C. Greatest Spread is measured between perpendiculars at a right angle to the center line of the skull at widest part, whether across main beams or points.

D. Inside Spread of Main Beams is measured at a right angle to the center line of the skull at widest point between main beams. Enter this measurement again as the Spread Credit if it is less than or equal to the length of the longer main beam; if greater, enter longer main beam length for Spread Credit.

E. Total of Lengths of all Abnormal Points: Abnormal Points are those non-typical in location such as points originating from a point (exception: G-3 originates from G-2 in perfectly normal fashion) or from bottom or sides of main beam, or any points beyond the normal pattern of five (including beam tip) per antler. Measure each abnormal point in usual manner and enter in appropriate blanks.

F. Length of Main Beam is measured from the center of the lowest outside edge of burr over the outer side to the most distant point of the main beam. The point of beginning is that point on the burr where the center line along the outer side of the beam intersects the burr, then following generally the line of the illustration.

G-1-2-3-4. Length of Normal Points: Normal points are the brow tines and the upper and lower forks as shown in the illustration. They are measured from nearest edge of main beam over outer curve to tip. Lay the tape along the outer curve of the beam so that the top edge of the tape coincides with the top edge of the beam on both sides of point to determine the baseline for point measurement. Record point lengths in appropriate blanks.

H-1-2-3-4. Circumferences are taken as detailed in illustration for each measurement. If brow point is missing, take H-1 and H-2 at smallest place between burr and G-2. If G-3 is missing, take H-3 halfway between the burr and tip of G-2. If G-4 is missing, take H-4 halfway between G-2 and tip of main beam.

ENTRY AFFIDAVIT FOR ALL HUNTER-TAKEN TROPHIES

For the purpose of entry into the Boone and Crockett Club's® records, North American big game harvested by the use of the following methods or under the following conditions are ineligible:

   I.   Spotting or herding game from the air, followed by landing in the purpose of shooting;

   II. Herding or chasing with the aid of any motorized

  III. Use of electronic communication devices, artificial lighting, or electron

  IV. Confined by artificial barriers, including escape-proof fenced enclosur

   V. Transplanted for the purpose of commercial shooting;

  VI. By the use of traps or pharmaceuticals;

 VII. While swimming, helpless in deep snow, or helpless in any other

VIII. On another hunter's license;

  IX. Not in full compliance with the game laws or regulations of the state, province, territory, or tribal council on reservations or tribal lands;

I certify that the trophy scored on this chart was not taken in violation of the conditions listed above. In signing this statement, I understand that if the information provided on this entry is found to be misrepresented or incorrect, it will not be accepted into the Awards Program and 1) all of my prior entries are subject to deletion from future editions of **Records of North American Big Game** 2) future entries may not be accepted.

FAIR CHASE, as defined by the Boone and Crockett Club®, is the ethical, sportsmanlike and lawful pursuit of any free-ranging wild, native North American big game animal in a manner that does not give the hunter an improper advantage over such game animals.

The Boone and Crockett Club® may exclude the entry of any animal that it deems to have been taken in an unethical manner or under conditions deemed inappropriate by the Club.

Date: _____   Signature of Hunter:_____
                                                (SIGNATURE MUST BE WITNESSED BY AN OFFICIAL MEASURER OR A NOTARY PUBLIC.)

Date: _____   Signature of Notary or Official Measurer: _____

250 Station Drive
Missoula, MT 59801
(406) 542-1888

BOONE AND CROCKETT CLUB®

OFFICIAL SCORING SYSTEM FOR NORTH AMERICAN BIG GAME TROPHIES

MINIMUM SCORES

	AWARDS	ALL-TIME
whitetail	160	170
Coues'	100	110

TYPICAL
WHITETAIL AND COUES' DEER

KIND OF DEER (check one)
■ whitetail
☐ Coues'

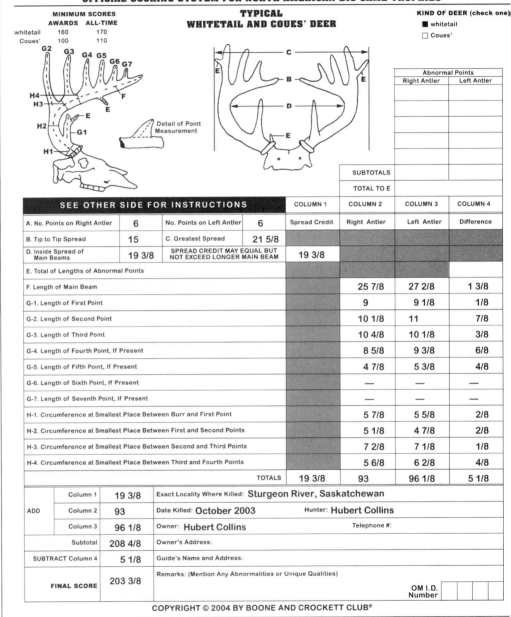

Detail of Point Measurement

Abnormal Points	
Right Antler	Left Antler

SUBTOTALS	
TOTAL TO E	

SEE OTHER SIDE FOR INSTRUCTIONS				COLUMN 1	COLUMN 2	COLUMN 3	COLUMN 4
A. No. Points on Right Antler	6	No. Points on Left Antler	6	Spread Credit	Right Antler	Left Antler	Difference
B. Tip to Tip Spread	15	C. Greatest Spread	21 5/8				
D. Inside Spread of Main Beams	19 3/8	SPREAD CREDIT MAY EQUAL BUT NOT EXCEED LONGER MAIN BEAM	19 3/8				
E. Total of Lengths of Abnormal Points							
F. Length of Main Beam					25 7/8	27 2/8	1 3/8
G-1. Length of First Point					9	9 1/8	1/8
G-2. Length of Second Point					10 1/8	11	7/8
G-3. Length of Third Point					10 4/8	10 1/8	3/8
G-4. Length of Fourth Point, If Present					8 5/8	9 3/8	6/8
G-5. Length of Fifth Point, If Present					4 7/8	5 3/8	4/8
G-6. Length of Sixth Point, If Present					—	—	—
G-7. Length of Seventh Point, If Present					—	—	—
H-1. Circumference at Smallest Place Between Burr and First Point					5 7/8	5 5/8	2/8
H-2. Circumference at Smallest Place Between First and Second Points					5 1/8	4 7/8	2/8
H-3. Circumference at Smallest Place Between Second and Third Points					7 2/8	7 1/8	1/8
H-4. Circumference at Smallest Place Between Third and Fourth Points					5 6/8	6 2/8	4/8
			TOTALS	19 3/8	93	96 1/8	5 1/8

ADD	Column 1	19 3/8	Exact Locality Where Killed: **Sturgeon River, Saskatchewan**
	Column 2	93	Date Killed: **October 2003** Hunter: **Hubert Collins**
	Column 3	96 1/8	Owner: **Hubert Collins** Telephone #:
	Subtotal	208 4/8	Owner's Address:
SUBTRACT Column 4		5 1/8	Guide's Name and Address:
FINAL SCORE		203 3/8	Remarks: (Mention Any Abnormalities or Unique Qualities)

OM I.D.
Number

COPYRIGHT © 2004 BY BOONE AND CROCKETT CLUB®

I, _____ **Allan Holtvogt** _____ , certify that I have measured this trophy on ___ **12/29/2003** ___

PRINT NAME   MM/DD/YYYYY

at   **Box 3**   **Big River, Saskatchewan**

STREET ADDRESS   CITY   STATE/PROVINCE

and that these measurements and data are, to the best of my knowledge and belief, made in accordance with the instructions given.

Witness: _____ Signature: _____ I.D. Number ☐ ☐ ☐ ☐

B&C OFFICIAL MEASURER

INSTRUCTIONS FOR MEASURING TYPICAL WHITETAIL AND COUES' DEER

All measurements must be made with a 1/4-inch wide flexible steel tape to the nearest one-eighth of an inch. (Note: A flexible steel cable can be used to measure points and main beams only.) Enter fractional figures in eighths, without reduction. Official measurements cannot be taken until the antlers have air dried for at least 60 days after the animal was killed.

A. Number of Points on Each Antler: To be counted a point, the projection must be at least one inch long, with the length exceeding width at one inch or more of length. All points are measured from tip of point to nearest edge of beam as illustrated. Beam tip is counted as a point but not measured as a point.

B. Tip to Tip Spread is measured between tips of main beams.

C. Greatest Spread is measured between perpendiculars at a right angle to the center line of the skull at widest part, whether across main beams or points.

D. Inside Spread of Main Beams is measured at a right angle to the center line of the skull at widest point between main beams. Enter this measurement again as the Spread Credit if it is less than or equal to the length of the longer main beam; if greater, enter longer main beam length for Spread Credit.

E. Total of Lengths of all Abnormal Points: Abnormal Points are those non-typical in location (such as points originating from a point or from bottom or sides of main beam) or extra points beyond the normal pattern of points. Measure in usual manner and enter in appropriate blanks.

F. Length of Main Beam is measured from the center of the lowest outside edge of burr over the outer side to the most distant point of the main beam. The point of beginning is that point on the burr where the center line along the outer side of the beam intersects the burr, then following generally the line of the illustration.

1-2-3-4-5-6-7. Length of Normal Points: Normal points project from the top of the main beam. They are measured from nearest edge of main beam over outer curve to tip. Lay the tape along the outer curve of the beam so that the top edge of the tape coincides with the top edge of the beam on both sides of the point to determine the baseline for point measurements. Record point lengths in appropriate blanks.

H-1-2-3-4. Circumferences are taken as detailed in illustration for each measurement. If brow point is missing, take H-1 and H-2 at smallest place between burr and G-2. If G-4 is missing, take H-4 halfway between G-3 and tip of main beam.

ENTRY AFFIDAVIT FOR ALL HUNTER-TAKEN TROPHIES

... the Boone and Crockett Club ... records ... North American big game harvested by the use of the ... er the following conditions are ...ible:

   ...potting or herding game from the air ...lowed ... purpose of pursuit and shooting;
   Herding or chasing with the aid of any motorized ...
   ...se of electronic communication devices, artificial ... ...tronic light intensifying devices;
   ...fined by artificial barriers, includ... ...scap... ...ed enclosures;
V.   ...nted for the purpose of comm... ...g;
VI.   ...of trade ... pharmaceutica...
VII.   Whil... ...less in deep snow ... ...pless in any other natural or artificial medium;
VIII. On anot... ...cense;
IX.   Not in full c... ...with the game ...r regulations of the federal government or of any state, province, territory, or tribal counc... ...vations or tr... ...nds;

I certify that the trophy sc... ... char... ...t taken in violation of the conditions listed above. In signing this statement, I understand that if t... ... on this entry is found to be misrepresented or fraudulent in any respect, it will not be accepted into the... ... 1) all of my prior entries are subject to deletion from future editions of **Records of North Americ...** ...re entries may not be accepted.

FAIR CHASE, as defined by t... ... ... Club®, is the ethical, sportsmanlike and lawful pursuit and taking of any free-ranging wild, native North ... ...ner ... ... animal in a manner that does not give the hunter an improper advantage over such game animals.

The Boone and Crockett Club® may ... ...y of any animal that it deems to have been taken in an unethical manner or under conditions deemed inappropr...

Date: _____ Signature ... _____

(...TURE MUST BE WITNESSED BY AN OFFICIAL MEASURER OR A NOTARY PUBLIC.)

Date: _____ Signature of Notary or Official Measurer: _____

250 Station Drive
Missoula, MT 59801
(406) 542-1888

BOONE AND CROCKETT CLUB®
OFFICIAL SCORING SYSTEM FOR NORTH AMERICAN BIG GAME TROPHIES

NON-TYPICAL
WHITETAIL AND COUES' DEER

MINIMUM SCORES		
	AWARDS	ALL-TIME
whitetail	185	195
Coues'	105	120

KIND OF DEER (check one)
- ☐ whitetail
- ■ Coues'

Abnormal Points	
Right Antler	Left Antler
4 3/8	1
1 6/8	2
1 1/8	1 1/8
1 3/8	1 1/8
6	5 3/8
2 5/8	5 4/8
	5 4/8
	3 1/8
	1 7/8
SUBTOTALS 17 2/8	26 5/8
E. TOTAL	43 7/8

Detail of Point Measurement

SEE OTHER SIDE FOR INSTRUCTIONS		COLUMN 1	COLUMN 2	COLUMN 3	COLUMN 4
		Spread Credit	Right Antler	Left Antler	Difference
A. No. Points on Right Antler **11**	No. Points on Left Antler **15**				
B. Tip to Tip Spread **4 7/8**	C. Greatest Spread **18 6/8**				
D. Inside Spread of Main Beams **12 3/8**	SPREAD CREDIT MAY EQUAL BUT NOT EXCEED LONGER MAIN BEAM **12 3/8**				
F. Length of Main Beam			20 4/8	19 3/8	1 1/8
G-1. Length of First Point			6 3/8	4 7/8	1 4/8
G-2. Length of Second Point			10 4/8	12 3/8	1 7/8
G-3. Length of Third Point			8	11	3
G-4. Length of Fourth Point, If Present			8 7/8	9 1/8	2/8
G-5. Length of Fifth Point, If Present			—	5 2/8	5 2/8
G-6. Length of Sixth Point, If Present			—	—	—
G-7. Length of Seventh Point, If Present			—	—	—
H-1. Circumference at Smallest Place Between Burr and First Point			4 6/8	4 6/8	—
H-2. Circumference at Smallest Place Between First and Second Points			4 3/8	4 6/8	3/8
H-3. Circumference at Smallest Place Between Second and Third Points			4 3/8	4 6/8	3/8
H-4. Circumference at Smallest Place Between Third and Fourth Points			4 7/8	5	1/8
	TOTALS	12 3/8	72 5/8	81 2/8	13 7/8

ADD	Column 1	12 3/8	Exact Locality Where Killed: **Graham County, Arizona**
	Column 2	72 5/8	Date Killed: **Prior to 1971** Hunter: **Native American**
	Column 3	81 2/8	Owner: **D.J. Hollinger & B. Howard** Telephone #:
	Subtotal	166 2/8	Owner's Address:
SUBTRACT	Column 4	13 7/8	Guide's Name and Address:
	Subtotal	152 3/8	Remarks: (Mention Any Abnormalities or Unique Qualities)
	ADD Line E Total	43 7/8	
	FINAL SCORE	196 2/8	OM I.D. Number

COPYRIGHT © 2004 BY BOONE AND CROCKETT CLUB®

I, _____ John T. Caid _____ , certify that I have measured this trophy on ___ 04/28/2004 ___
PRINT NAME   MM/DD/YYYY

at __ Cabela's   Kansas City, Kansas _____
STREET ADDRESS   CITY   STATE/PROVINCE

and that these measurements and data are, to the best of my knowledge and belief, made in accordance with the instructions given.

Witness: _____ Signature: _____ I.D. Number
                                                    B&C OFFICIAL MEASURER

INSTRUCTIONS FOR MEASURING NON-TYPICAL WHITETAIL AND COUES' DEER

All measurements must be made with a 1/4-inch wide flexible steel tape to the nearest one-eighth of an inch. (Note: A flexible steel cable can be used to measure points and main beams only.) Enter fractional figures in eighths, without reduction. Official measurements cannot be taken until the antlers have air dried for at least 60 days after the animal was killed.

A. Number of Points on Each Antler: To be counted a point, the projection must be at least one inch long, with the length exceeding width at one inch or more of length. All points are measured from tip of point to nearest edge of beam as illustrated. Beam tip is counted as a point but not measured as a point.

B. Tip to Tip Spread is measured between tips of main beams.

C. Greatest Spread is measured between perpendiculars at a right angle to the center line of the skull at widest part, whether across main beams or points.

D. Inside Spread of Main Beams is measured at a right angle to the center line of the skull at widest point between main beams. Enter this measurement again as the Spread Credit if it is less than or equal to the length of the longer main beam; if greater, enter longer main beam length for Spread Credit.

E. Total of Lengths of all Abnormal Points: Abnormal Points are those non-typical in location (such as points originating from a point or from bottom or sides of main beam) or extra points beyond the normal pattern of points. Measure in usual manner and enter in appropriate blanks.

F. Length of Main Beam is measured from the center of the lowest outside edge of burr over the outer side to the most distant point of the main beam. The point of beginning is that point on the burr where the center line along the outer side of the beam intersects the burr, then following generally the line of the illustration.

G-1-2-3-4-5-6-7. Length of Normal Points: Normal points project from the top of the main beam. They are measured from nearest edge of main beam over outer curve to tip. Lay the tape along the outer curve of the beam so that the top edge of the tape coincides with the top edge of the beam on both sides of the point to determine the baseline for point measurement. Record point lengths in appropriate blanks.

H-1-2-3-4. Circumferences are taken as detailed in illustration for each measurement. If brow point is missing, take H-1 and H-2 at smallest place between burr and G-2. If G-4 is missing, take H-4 halfway between G-3 and tip of main beam.

ENTRY AFFIDAVIT FOR ALL HUNTER-TAKEN TROPHIES

For the purpose of entry into the Boone and Crockett Club's records, North American big game harvested by the use of the following methods or under the following conditions are ineligible:

I.   Spotting or herding game from the air, followed by landing in its vicinity for the purpose of pursuit and shooting;
II. Herding or chasing with the use of motorized equipment;
III. Use of electronic devices for attracting, locating or observing game, or for guiding the hunter to such game, or using electronic light intensifying devices;
IV. Confined by artificial barriers, including escape-proof fenced enclosures;
V.   Transplanted for the purpose of commercial shooting;
VI. By the use of traps or pharmaceuticals;
VII. While swimming, helpless in deep snow, or helpless in any other natural or artificial medium;
VIII. On another's license;
IX. Not in full compliance with the game laws or regulations of the federal government or of any state, province, territory, or tribal council on reservations or tribal lands;

I certify that the trophy shown on this part was not taken in violation of the conditions listed above. In signing this statement, I understand that if the information provided on this entry is found to be misrepresented or fraudulent in any respect, it will not be accepted into the Awards Program and (1) all of my prior entries are subject to deletion from future editions of **Records of North American Big Game** and (2) future entries may not be accepted.

FAIR CHASE, as defined by the Boone and Crockett Club®, is the ethical, sportsmanlike and lawful pursuit and taking of any free-ranging wild, native North American big game animal in a manner that does not give the hunter an improper advantage over such game animals.

The Boone and Crockett Club® may exclude the entry of any animal that it deems to have been taken in an unethical manner or under conditions deemed inappropriate.

Date: _____ Signature of Hunter: _____
                                    (SIGNATURE MUST BE WITNESSED BY AN OFFICIAL MEASURER OR A NOTARY PUBLIC.)

Date: _____ Signature of Notary or Official Measurer: _____

Records of
North American
Big Game

250 Station Drive
Missoula, MT 59801
(406) 542-1888

BOONE AND CROCKETT CLUB®
OFFICIAL SCORING SYSTEM FOR NORTH AMERICAN BIG GAME TROPHIES

MOOSE

	MINIMUM SCORES	
	AWARDS	ALL-TIME
Canada	185	195
Alaska-Yukon	210	224
Wyoming	140	155

KIND OF MOOSE (check one)
- ☐ Canada
- ☐ Alaska-Yukon
- ■ Wyoming

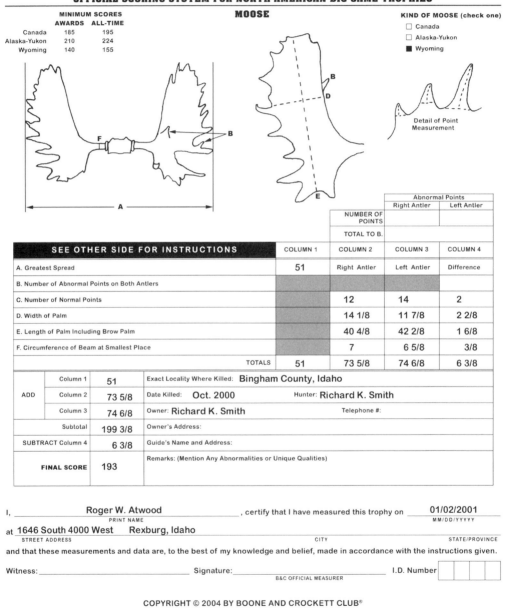

Detail of Point Measurement

		Abnormal Points	
		Right Antler	Left Antler
NUMBER OF POINTS			
TOTAL TO B.			

SEE OTHER SIDE FOR INSTRUCTIONS	COLUMN 1	COLUMN 2	COLUMN 3	COLUMN 4
A. Greatest Spread	51	Right Antler	Left Antler	Difference
B. Number of Abnormal Points on Both Antlers				
C. Number of Normal Points		12	14	2
D. Width of Palm		14 1/8	11 7/8	2 2/8
E. Length of Palm Including Brow Palm		40 4/8	42 2/8	1 6/8
F. Circumference of Beam at Smallest Place		7	6 5/8	3/8
TOTALS	51	73 5/8	74 6/8	6 3/8

ADD	Column 1	51
	Column 2	73 5/8
	Column 3	74 6/8
	Subtotal	199 3/8
SUBTRACT Column 4		6 3/8
FINAL SCORE		193

Exact Locality Where Killed: **Bingham County, Idaho**

Date Killed: **Oct. 2000**   Hunter: **Richard K. Smith**

Owner: **Richard K. Smith**   Telephone #:

Owner's Address:

Guide's Name and Address:

Remarks: (Mention Any Abnormalities or Unique Qualities)

I, _____ **Roger W. Atwood** _____ , certify that I have measured this trophy on __ **01/02/2001** __
PRINT NAME   MM/DD/YYYYY

at **1646 South 4000 West   Rexburg, Idaho**
STREET ADDRESS   CITY   STATE/PROVINCE

and that these measurements and data are, to the best of my knowledge and belief, made in accordance with the instructions given.

Witness: _____   Signature: _____   I.D. Number ☐☐☐☐
                                        B&C OFFICIAL MEASURER

INSTRUCTIONS FOR MEASURING MOOSE

Measurements must be made with a 1/4-inch wide flexible steel tape to the nearest one-eighth of an inch. Enter fractional figures in eighths, without reduction. Official measurements cannot be taken until antlers have air dried for at least 60 days after animal was killed.

A. Greatest Spread is measured between perpendiculars in a straight line at a right angle to the center line of the skull.

B. Number of Abnormal Points on Both Antlers: Abnormal points are those projections originating from normal points or from the upper or lower palm surface, or from the inner edge of palm (see illustration). Abnormal points must be at least one inch long, with length exceeding width at one inch or more of length.

C. Number of Normal Points: Normal points originate from the outer edge of palm. To be counted a point, a projection must be at least one inch long, with the length exceeding width at one inch or more of length. Be sure to verify whether or not each projection qualifies as a point.

D. Width of Palm is taken in contact with the under surface of palm, at a right angle to the inner edge of palm. The line of measurement should begin and end at the midpoint of the palm edge, which gives credit for the desirable character of palm thickness.

E. Length of Palm including Brow Palm is taken in contact with the surface along the underside of the palm, **parallel** to the inner edge, from dips between points at the top to dips between points (if present) at the bottom. If a bay is present, measure across the open bay if the proper line of measurement, parallel to **inner edge**, follows this path. The line of measurement should begin and end at the midpoint of the palm edge, which gives credit for the desirable character of palm thickness.

F. Circumference of Beam at Smallest Place is taken as illustrated.

ENTRY AFFIDAVIT FOR ALL HUNTER-TAKEN TROPHIES

For the purpose of entry into the Boone and Crockett Club's® records, North American big game harvested by the use of the following methods or under the following conditions are ineligible:

I. Spotting or herding game from the air, followed by landing in its vicinity for the purpose of pursuit and shooting;

II. Herding or chasing with the aid of any motorized equipment;

III. Use of electronic communication devices, artificial lighting, or electronic light intensifying devices;

IV. Confined by artificial barriers, including escape-proof fenced enclosures;

V. Transplanted for the purpose of commercial shooting;

VI. By use of traps or pharmaceuticals;

VII. While swimming, helpless in deep snow, or helpless in any other natural or artificial medium;

VIII. On another hunter's license;

IX. Not in full compliance with the game laws or regulations of the federal government or of any state, province, territory, or tribal council on reservations or tribal lands;

I certify that the trophy scored on this chart was not taken in violation of the conditions listed above. In signing this statement, I understand that if the information provided on this entry is found to be misrepresented or fraudulent in any respect, it will not be accepted into the Awards Program and 1) all of my prior entries are subject to deletion from future editions of **Records of North American Big Game** 2) future entries may not be accepted.

FAIR CHASE, as defined by the Boone and Crockett Club®, is the ethical, sportsmanlike and lawful pursuit and taking of any free-ranging wild, native North American big game animal in a manner that does not give the hunter an improper advantage over such animals.

The Boone and Crockett Club® may exclude the entry of any animal that it deems to have been taken in an unethical manner or under conditions deemed inappropriate by the Club.

Date: _____ Signature of Hunter: _____
(SIGNATURE MUST BE WITNESSED BY AN OFFICIAL MEASURER OR A NOTARY PUBLIC.)

Date: _____ Signature of Official Measurer: _____

Records of
North American
Big Game

250 Station Drive
Missoula, MT 59801
(406) 542-1888

BOONE AND CROCKETT CLUB®
OFFICIAL SCORING SYSTEM FOR NORTH AMERICAN BIG GAME TROPHIES

CARIBOU

MINIMUM SCORES		
	AWARDS	ALL-TIME
mountain	360	390
woodland	265	295
barren ground	375	400
Central Canada		
barren ground	345	360
Quebec-Labrador	365	375

KIND OF CARIBOU (check one)
- ☐ mountain
- ☐ woodland
- ■ barren ground
- ☐ Central Canada
- barren ground
- ☐ Quebec-Labrador

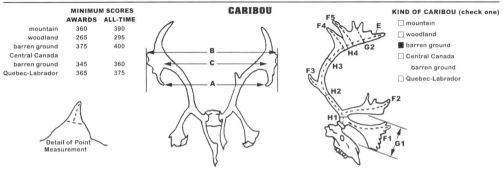

Detail of Point
Measurement

SEE OTHER SIDE FOR INSTRUCTIONS			COLUMN 1	COLUMN 2	COLUMN 3	COLUMN 4
A. Tip to Tip Spread		28 2/8	Spread Credit	Right Antler	Left Antler	Difference
B. Greatest Spread		36				
C. Inside Spread of Main Beams	34 1/8	SPREAD CREDIT MAY EQUAL BUT NOT EXCEED LONGER MAIN BEAM	34 1/8			
D. Number of Points on Each Antler Excluding Brows				15	12	3
Number of Points on Each Brow				4	4	
E. Length of Main Beam				55 3/8	54 2/8	1 1/8
F-1. Length of Brow Palm or First Point				18	19 3/8	
F-2. Length of Bez or Second Point				27 2/8	27 2/8	—
F-3. Length of Rear Point, If Present				4 3/8	5 4/8	1 1/8
F-4. Length of Second Longest Top Point				12 4/8	13 5/8	1 1/8
F-5. Length of Longest Top Point				17	14 7/8	2 1/8
G-1. Width of Brow Palm				6 4/8	9 2/8	
G-2. Width of Top Palm				8 3/8	10	1 5/8
H-1. Circumference at Smallest Place Between Brow and Bez Point				7	8 4/8	1 4/8
H-2. Circumference at Smallest Place Between Bez and Rear Point				5 5/8	5 4/8	1/8
H-3. Circumference at Smallest Place Between Rear Point and First Top Point				4 6/8	4 7/8	1/8
H-4. Circumference at Smallest Place Between Two Longest Top Palm Points				14 7/8	18 6/8	3 7/8
TOTALS			34 1/8	200 5/8	207 6/8	15 6/8

ADD	Column 1	34 1/8	Exact Locality Where Killed: **Shagak Bay, Alaska**
	Column 2	200 5/8	Date Killed: **Sept. 2002** Hunter: **James A. McIntosh**
	Column 3	207 6/8	Owner: **James A. McIntosh** Telephone #:
Subtotal		442 4/8	Owner's Address:
SUBTRACT Column 4		15 6/8	Guide's Name and Address:
FINAL SCORE		426 6/8	Remarks: (Mention Any Abnormalities or Unique Qualities)

OM I.D.
Number

COPYRIGHT © 2004 BY BOONE AND CROCKETT CLUB®

I, _____ Daniel R. Caughey _____ , certify that I have measured this trophy on _____ 05/01/2004 _____

PRINT NAME   MM/DD/YYYYY

at Cabela's   Kansas City, Kansas

STREET ADDRESS   CITY   STATE/PROVINCE

and that these measurements and data are, to the best of my knowledge and belief, made in accordance with the instructions given.

Witness: _____   Signature: _____   I.D. Number

                                                                B&C OFFICIAL MEASURER

INSTRUCTIONS FOR MEASURING CARIBOU

All measurements must be made with a 1/4-inch wide flexible steel tape to the nearest one-eighth of an inch. (Note: A flexible steel cable can be used to measure points and main beams only.) Enter fractional figures in eighths, without reduction. Official measurements cannot be taken until the antlers have air dried for at least 60 days after the animal was killed.

A. Tip to Tip Spread is measured between tips of main beams.

B. Greatest Spread is measured between perpendiculars at a right angle to the center line of the skull at widest part, whether across main beams or points.

C. Inside Spread of Main Beams is measured at a right angle to the center line of the skull at widest point between main beams. Enter this measurement again as the Spread Credit if it is less than or equal to the length of the longer main beam; if greater, enter longer main beam length for Spread Credit.

D. Number of Points on Each Antler: To be counted a point, a projection must be at least one-half inch long, with length exceeding width at one-half inch or more of length. Beam tip is counted as a point but not measured as a ___ re are no "abnormal" points in caribou.

E. Length of Main Beam is measured from the center of the lowest outside edge of burr over the outer sid ___ distant point of the main beam. The point of beginning is that point on the burr where the center line along ___ le of the beam intersects the burr, then following generally the line of the illustration.

F-1-2-3. Length of Points are measured from nearest edge o_ b_am o_er outer curve to tip. Lay the tape along ___ curve of the beam so that the top edge of the tape coincides ___ top _ge of the beam on both sides of p ___ mine the baseline for point measurement. Record point length ___ oriate blanks.

F-4-5. Length of Points are measured from the tip of the point to ___ beam ___ at a right angle to the b ___ dge of beam. The Second Longest Top Point **cannot** be a point bra ___ st Top Point.

G-1. Width of Brow is measured in a straight line from top edge t ___ ge, as illustrated, with measuremen ___ right angle to main axis of brow.

G-2. Width of Top Palm is measured from midpoint of lower edge of ___ n beam to midpoint of a dip between points, ___ dest part of palm. The line of measurement begins and ends at midpoi_ _f palm edges, which gives credit for palm thic ___ ss.

H-1-2-3-4. Circumferences are taken as illustrated for measuremen ___ If brow point is missing, take H-1 at smalles ___ int between burr and bez point. If ___ ear point is missing, ___ ake H-2 an_ H-_ ___ easurements at smallest place between be ___ nd first top point. Do not depress the ___ pe into any dips of th_ palm or m_ n be ___

ENTRY AFF___VIT FOR AL___UN___ER-T___KEN TROPHIES

For the purpose of entry into the Boone ___ ckett Clu_ ___ Amer___ n big game harvested by the u ___ of the following methods or under the following co___ ___ are i ___

   I.   Spotting or herding game from the air, foll___ by landing in it_ ___ for ___ purpose of pursuit an___ ___oting;

   II. Herding or chasing with the aid of any moto___ ___ ___uipment;

  III. Use of electronic communication dev___ a___ ia___ting, or electro___ ___ t intensifying d___ ___s;

  IV. Confined by artificial barriers, includi___ ___ l ___ of r___ encl___

   V. Transplanted for the purpose of commer___ ___o

  VI. By the use of traps or pharmaceuticals;

 VII. While swimming, helpless in deep snow, o___ ___s in any o___ ___al medium;

VIII. On another hunter's license;

  IX. Not in full compliance with the game laws or regulations of the ___ ince, territory, or tribal council on reservations or tribal lands;

I certify that the trophy scored on this chart was not taken in violati___ ___ state- ment, I understand that if the information provided on this entry i___ ___spect, it will not be accepted into the Awards Program and 1) all of my ___ ___ of **Records of North American Big Game** 2) future entries ___

FAIR CHASE, as defined by the Boone and Crockett Club® ___ any free-ranging wild, native North American big game anim___ ___age over such game animals.

The Boone and Crockett Club® may exclude the entry of any a___ that it deems t___ ___ner or under conditions deemed inappropriate by the Club.

Date: _____   Signature of Hunter: _____

                                          (SIGNATURE MUST BE WITNESSED BY AN O___ ___TARY PUBLIC.)

Date: _____   Signature of Notary or Official Measurer: _____

250 Station Drive
Missoula, MT 59801
(406) 542-1888

BOONE AND CROCKETT CLUB®
OFFICIAL SCORING SYSTEM FOR NORTH AMERICAN BIG GAME TROPHIES

MINIMUM SCORES
AWARDS   ALL-TIME
   80   82

PRONGHORN

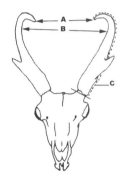
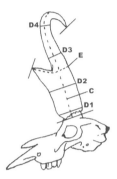

SEE OTHER SIDE FOR INSTRUCTIONS		COLUMN 1	COLUMN 2	COLUMN 3
A. Tip to Tip Spread	4 3/8	Right Horn	Left Horn	Difference
B. Inside Spread of Main Beams	10 1/8			
C. Length of Horn		17 2/8	17 2/8	—
D-1. Circumference of Base		7 2/8	7 2/8	—
D-2. Circumference at First Quarter		8 2/8	7 7/8	3/8
D-3. Circumference at Second Quarter		5 2/8	5 1/8	1/8
D-4. Circumference at Third Quarter		3 7/8	4	1/8
E. Length of Prong		7	6 1/8	7/8
TOTALS		48 7/8	47 5/8	1 4/8

ADD	Column 1	48 7/8	Exact Locality Where Killed: **Mohave County, Arizona**
	Column 2	47 5/8	Date Killed: **August 2002** Hunter: **David Meyer**
	Subtotal	96 4/8	Owner: **David Meyer** Telephone #:
	SUBTRACT Column 3	1 4/8	Owner's Address:
FINAL SCORE		95	Guide's Name and Address:
			Remarks: (Mention Any Abnormalities or Unique Qualities)

I, _____ Ralph C. Stayner _____ , certify that I have measured this trophy on ___ 10/16/2002 ___
PRINT NAME   MM/DD/YYYYY

at __ 4612 E. Fox Circle   Mesa, Arizona __
STREET ADDRESS   CITY   STATE/PROVINCE

and that these measurements and data are, to the best of my knowledge and belief, made in accordance with the instructions given.

Witness: _____   Signature: _____   I.D. Number ___
                                                        B&C OFFICIAL MEASURER

INSTRUCTIONS FOR MEASURING PRONGHORN

All measurements must be made with a 1/4-inch wide flexible steel tape to the nearest one-eighth of an inch. Enter fractional figures in eighths, without reduction. Official measurements cannot be taken until horns have air dried for at least 60 days after the animal was killed.

A. Tip to Tip Spread is measured between tips of horns.

B. Inside Spread of Main Beams is measured at a right angle to the center line of the skull, at widest point between main beams.

C. Length of Horn is measured on the outside curve on the general line illustrated. The line taken will vary with different heads, depending on the direction of their curvature. Measure along the center of the outer curve from tip of horn to a point in line with the lowest edge of the base, using a straight edge to establish the line end.

D-1. Circumference of Base is measured at a right angle to axis of horn. **Do not** follow irregular edge of horn; the line of measurement must be entirely on horn material.

D-2-3-4. Divide measurement C of longer horn by four. Starting at base, mark **both** horns at these quarters (even though the other horn is shorter) and measure circumferences at these marks. If the prong interferes with D-2, move the measurement down to just below the swelling of the prong. If D-3 falls in the swelling of the prong, move the measurement up to just above the prong.

E. Length of Prong: Measure from the tip of the prong **along the upper edge** of the outer side to the horn; then continue around the horn to a point at the rear of the horn where a straight edge across the back of both horns touches the horn, with the latter part being at a right angle to the long axis of horn.

ENTRY AFFIDAVIT FOR ALL HUNTER-TAKEN TROPHIES

For the purpose of entry into the Boone and Crockett Club's® records, North American big game harvested by the use of the following methods or under the following conditions are ineligible:

I. Spotting or herding game from the air, followed by landing in its vicinity for the purpose of pursuit and shooting;

II. Herding or ch_____ the aid of any motorized equipment;

III. Use of ele_____ communication devices, artificial lighting, or electronic light intensifying devices;

IV. Confine_____ tificial barriers, including_____ of fenced enclosures;

V. Transp_____ for the purpose of commercial sho_____

VI. By th_____ of traps or pharmaceuticals;

VII. Whil_____ ming, helpless in deep snow, or helple_____ any other natural or artificial medium;

VIII. On_____ r hunter's license;

IX. No_____ l compliance with the game laws or reg_____ s of the federal government or of any state, province, territory, or_____ council on reservations or tribal lands

I certify t_____ trophy scored on this chart was not t_____ violation of the conditions listed above. In signing this statement, I u_____ nd that if the information provided o_____ try is found to be misrepresented or fraudulent in any respect, it will not b_____ ted into the Awards Program and 1_____ ny prior entries are subject to deletion from future editions of **Records _____ th American Big Game** 2) futur_____ may not be accepted.

FAIR CHA_____ efined by the Boone and Crock_____ , is t_____ e ethical, sportsmanlike and lawful pursuit and taking of any free-rangi_____ native North American big g_____ manner that does not give the hunter an improper advantage over such_____ imals.

The Boone_____ ket_____ ub® may exclud_____ ny animal that it deems to have been taken in an unethical manner or under con_____ nappropriate_____

Date: _____   Signatur_____

(SIGNATURE MUST BE WITNESSED BY AN OFFICIAL MEASURER OR A NOTARY PUBLIC.)

Date: _____   Sign_____ ary or Official Measurer: _____

BOONE AND CROCKETT CLUB®
OFFICIAL SCORING SYSTEM FOR NORTH AMERICAN BIG GAME TROPHIES

BISON

MINIMUM SCORES	
AWARDS	ALL-TIME
115	115

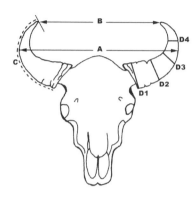

SEE OTHER SIDE FOR INSTRUCTIONS		COLUMN 1	COLUMN 2	COLUMN 3
A. Greatest Spread	19 5/8	Right Horn	Left Horn	Difference
B. Tip to Tip Spread	30			
C. Length of Horn		21 5/8	21 4/8	1/8
D-1. Circumference of Base		16	15 1/8	7/8
D-2. Circumference at First Quarter		13 3/8	13	3/8
D-3. Circumference at Second Quarter		10 6/8	10 6/8	—
D-4. Circumference at Third Quarter		5 4/8	5 4/8	—
TOTALS		67 2/8	65 7/8	1 3/8

ADD	Column 1	67 2/8	Exact Locality Where Killed: Coconino County, Arizona	
	Column 2	65 7/8	Date Killed: March 2002	Hunter: Duane R. Richardson
	Subtotal	133 1/8	Owner: Duane R. Richardson	Telephone #:
	SUBTRACT Column 3	1 3/8	Owner's Address:	
			Guide's Name and Address:	
FINAL SCORE		131 6/8	Remarks: (Mention Any Abnormalities or Unique Qualities)	

I, _____ Ralph C. Stayner _____ , certify that I have measured this trophy on ___ 06/06/2002 ___
PRINT NAME   MM/DD/YYYYY

at _ 4612 E. Fox Circle _ Mesa, Arizona
STREET ADDRESS   CITY   STATE/PROVINCE

and that these measurements and data are, to the best of my knowledge and belief, made in accordance with the instructions given.

Witness: _____ Signature: _____ I.D. Number ☐ ☐ ☐ ☐
B&C OFFICIAL MEASURER

INSTRUCTIONS FOR MEASURING BISON

All measurements must be made with a 1/4-inch wide flexible steel tape to the nearest one-eighth of an inch. Wherever it is necessary to change direction of measurement, mark a control point and swing tape at this point. Enter fractional figures in eighths, without reduction. Official measurements cannot be taken until horns have air dried for at least 60 days after the animal was killed.

- **A. Greatest Spread** is measured between perpendiculars at a right angle to the center line of the skull.
- **B. Tip to Tip Spread** is measured between tips of horns.
- **C. Length of Horn** is measured from the lowest point on underside over outer curve to a point in line with the tip. Use a straight edge, perpendicular to horn axis, to end the measurement, if necessary.
- **D-1. Circumference of Base** is measured at right angle to axis of horn. **Do not** follow the irregular edge of horn; the line of measurement must be entirely on horn material.
- **D-2-3-4. Divide measurement C** of longer horn by four. Starting at base, mark **both** horns at these quarters (even though the other horn is shorter) and measure the circumferences at these marks, with measurements taken at right angles to horn axis.

ENTRY AFFIDAVIT FOR ALL HUNTER-TAKEN TROPHIES

For the purpose of entry into the Boone and Crockett Club's® records, North American big game harvested by the use of the following methods or under the following conditions are ineligible:

- I. Spotting or herding game from the air, followed by landing in its vicinity for the purpose of pursuit and shooting;
- II. Herding or chasing with the aid of any motorized equipment;
- III. Use of electronic communication devices, artificial lighting, or electronic light intensifying devices;
- IV. Confined by artificial barriers, including escape-proof fenced enclosures;
- V. Transplanted for the purpose of commercial shooting;
- VI. By the use of traps or pharmaceuticals;
- VII. While swimming, helpless in deep snow, or helpless in any other natural or artificial medium;
- VIII. On another hunter's license;
- IX. Not in full compliance with the game laws or regulations of the federal government or of any state, province, territory, or tribal council on reservations or tribal lands;

I certify that the trophy scored on this c[...] was not taken in violation of the conditions listed above. In signing [...] statement, I understand that if the inform[...] provided on this entry is found to be misrepresented or fraudulent in any [...]ect, it will not be accepted into the Awar[...] gram and 1) all of my prior entries are subject to deletion from future edition[...] **Records of North American B[...] e 2)** future entries may not be accepted.

FAIR CHASE, as defined by the [...] nd Crockett Club®, is the ethical, sportsmanlike and lawful pursuit and taking of [...] free-ranging wild, native North [...] big game animal in a manner that does not give the hunter an improper adva[...] over such game animals.

The Boone and Crockett Club® ma[...] mal th[...] been taken in a[...] under conditions deemed inapprop[...]

Date:_____ Signature o[...]

PUBLIC.)

Date:_____ Signature of Notary or Offic[...]

250 Station Drive
Missoula, MT 59801
(406) 542-1888

BOONE AND CROCKETT CLUB®
OFFICIAL SCORING SYSTEM FOR NORTH AMERICAN BIG GAME TROPHIES

MINIMUM SCORES
AWARDS   ALL-TIME
47   50

ROCKY MOUNTAIN GOAT

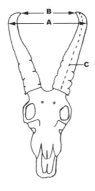

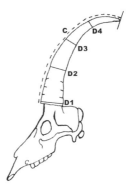

SEE OTHER SIDE FOR INSTRUCTIONS		COLUMN 1	COLUMN 2	COLUMN 3
A. Greatest Spread	6 1/8	Right Horn	Left Horn	Difference
B. Tip to Tip Spread	6 1/8			
C. Length of Horn		11 4/8	11 4/8	—
D-1. Circumference of Base		5 6/8	5 6/8	—
D-2. Circumference at First Quarter		4 7/8	4 6/8	1/8
D-3. Circumference at Second Quarter		3 4/8	3 3/8	1/8
D-4. Circumference at Third Quarter		2	2	—
TOTALS		27 5/8	27 3/8	2/8

ADD	Column 1	27 5/8	Exact Locality Where Killed: Vixen Inlet, Alaska
	Column 2	27 3/8	Date Killed: Oct. 2001 Hunter: Ross M. Groben
	Subtotal	55	Owner: Ross M. Groben Telephone #:
SUBTRACT Column 3		2/8	Owner's Address:
FINAL SCORE		54 6/8	Guide's Name and Address:
			Remarks: (Mention Any Abnormalities or Unique Qualities)

I, _____ **Tim Humes** _____ , certify that I have measured this trophy on ___ **12/17/2001** ___
                    PRINT NAME   MM/DD/YYYYY

at __ **1190 Terminal Way   Reno, Nevada** _____
        STREET ADDRESS   CITY   STATE/PROVINCE

and that these measurements and data are, to the best of my knowledge and belief, made in accordance with the instructions given.

Witness: _____   Signature: _____   I.D. Number [ ][ ][ ][ ]
                                                                        B&C OFFICIAL MEASURER

INSTRUCTIONS FOR MEASURING ROCKY MOUNTAIN GOAT

All measurements must be made with a 1/4-inch wide flexible steel tape to the nearest one-eighth of an inch. Wherever it is necessary to change direction of measurement, mark a control point and swing tape at this point. Enter fractional figures in eighths, without reduction. Official measurements cannot be taken until horns have air dried for at least 60 days after the animal was killed.

A. Greatest Spread is measured between perpendiculars at a right angle to the center line of the skull.

B. Tip to Tip spread is measured between tips of the horns.

C. Length of Horn is measured from the lowest point in front over outer curve to a point in line with tip.

D-1. Circumference of Base is measured at a right angle to axis of horn. **Do not** follow irregular edge of horn; the line of measurement must be entirely on horn material.

D-2-3-4. Divide measurement C of longer horn by four. Starting at base, mark **both** horns at these quarters (even though the other horn is shorter) and measure circumferences at these marks, with measurements taken at right angles to horn axis.

ENTRY AFFIDAVIT FOR ALL HUNTER-TAKEN TROPHIES

For the purpose of entry into the Boone and Crockett Club's® records, North American big game harvested by the use of the following methods or under the following conditions are ineligible:

I.   Spotting or herding game from the air, followed by landing in its vicinity for the purpose of pursuit and shooting;
II. Herding or chasing with the aid of any motorized equipment;
III. Use of electronic communication devices, artificial lighting, or electronic light intensifying devices;
IV. Confined by artificial barriers, including escape-proof fenced enclosures;
V.   Transplanted for the purpose of commercial shooting;
VI. By the use of traps or pharmaceuticals;
VII. While swimming, helpless in deep snow, or helpless in any other natural or artificial medium;
VIII. On another hunter's license;
IX. Not in full compliance with the game laws or regulations of the federal government or of any state, province, territory, or tribal council on reservations or tribal lands;

I certify that the trophy scored on this chart was not taken in violation of the conditions listed above. In signing this statement, I understand that if the information provided on this entry is found to be misrepresented or fraudulent in any respect, it will not be accepted into the Awards Program and 1) all of my prior entries are subject to deletion from future editions of **Records of North American Big Game** 2) future entries may not be accepted.

FAIR CHASE, as defined by the Boone and Crockett Club®, is the ethical, sportsmanlike and lawful pursuit and taking of any free-ranging wild, native North American big game animal in a manner that does not give the hunter an improper advantage over such game animals.

The Boone and Crockett Club® may exclude the entry of any animal that it deems to have been taken in an unethical manner or under conditions deemed inappropriate by the Club.

Date: _____ Signature of Hunter: _____ (SIGNATURE MUST BE WITNESSED BY AN OFFICIAL MEASURER OR A NOTARY PUBLIC.)

Date: _____ Signature of Notary or Official Measurer: _____

250 Station Drive
Missoula, MT 5980█
(406) 542-1888

BOONE AND CROCKETT CLUB®
OFFICIAL SCORING SYSTEM FOR NORTH AMERICAN BIG GAME TROPHIES

MINIMUM SCORES

AWARDS	ALL-TIME
105	105

MUSKOX

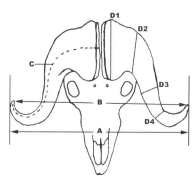

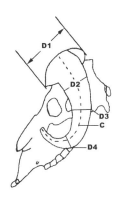

SEE OTHER SIDE FOR INSTRUCTIONS		COLUMN 1	COLUMN 2	COLUMN 3
A. Greatest Spread	29 1/8	Right Horn	Left Horn	Difference
B. Tip to Tip Spread	27 1/8			
C. Length of Horn		29 5/8	28 3/8	1 2/8
D-1. Width of Boss		11	11	—
D-2. Width at First Quarter		7 6/8	7 5/8	1/8
D-3. Circumference at Second Quarter		13	12	1
D-4. Circumference at Third Quarter		6 2/8	5 4/8	6/8
TOTALS		67 5/8	64 4/8	3 1/8

ADD	Column 1	67 5/8
	Column 2	64 4/8
Subtotal		132 1/8
SUBTRACT Column 3		3 1/8
FINAL SCORE		129

Exact Locality Where Killed: **Normal Wells, Northwest Territories**

Date Killed: **March 2002**   Hunter: **Craig D. Scott**

Owner: **Craig D. Scott**   Telephone #:

Owner's Address:

Guide's Name and Address:

Remarks: (Mention Any Abnormalities or Unique Qualities)

I, _____ **Albert C. England** _____ , certify that I have measured this trophy on ___ **04/30/2004**
PRINT NAME   MM/DD/YYYYY

at __ **Cabela's   Kansas City, Kansas** _____
STREET ADDRESS   CITY   STATE/PROVINCE

and that these measurements and data are, to the best of my knowledge and belief, made in accordance with the instructions given.

Witness: _____   Signature: _____   I.D. Number | | | |
                                                            B&C OFFICIAL MEASURER

INSTRUCTIONS FOR MEASURING MUSKOX

All measurements must be made with a 1/4-inch wide flexible steel tape and adjustable calipers to the nearest one-eighth of an inch. Enter fractional figures in eighths, without reduction. Official measurements cannot be taken until horns have air dried for at least 60 days after the animal was killed.

- **A. Greatest Spread** is measured between perpendiculars at a right angle to the center line of the skull.
- **B. Tip to Tip Spread** is measured between tips of horns.
- **C. Length of Horn** is measured along center of upper horn surface, staying within curve of horn as illustrated, to a point in line with tip. Attempt to free the connective tissue between the horns at the center of the boss to determine the lowest point of horn material on each side. Hook the tape under the lowest point of the horn and measure the length of horn, with the measurement line maintained in the center of the upper surface of horn following the converging lines to the horn tip.
- **D-1. Width of Boss** is measured with calipers at greatest width of the boss, with measurement line forming a right angle with horn axis. It is often helpful to measure D-1 before C, marking the midpoint of the boss as the correct path of C.
- **D-2-3-4. Divide measurement C** of longer horn by four. Starting at base, mark **both** horns at these quarters (even though the other horn is shorter). Then, using calipers, measure width of boss at D-2, making sure the measurement is at a right angle to horn axis and in line with the D-2 mark. Circumferences are then measured at D-3 and D-4, with measurements being taken at right angles to horn axis.

ENTRY AFFIDAVIT FOR ALL HUNTER-TAKEN TROPHIES

For the purpose of entry into the Boone and Crockett Club's® records, North American big game harvested by the use of the following methods or under the following conditions are ineligible:

- I. Spotting or herding game from the air, followed by landing in its vicinity for the purpose of pursuit and shooting;
- II. Herding or chasing with the aid of any motorized equipment;
- III. Use of electronic communication devices, artificial lighting, or electronic light intensifying devices;
- IV. Confined by artificial barriers, including escape-proof fenced enclosures;
- V. Transplanted for the purpose of commercial shooting;
- VI. By the use of traps or pharmaceuticals;
- VII. While swimming, helpless in deep snow, or helpless in any other natural or artificial medium;
- VIII. On another hunter's license;
- IX. Not in full compliance with the game laws or regulations of the federal government or of any state, province, territory, or tribal council on reservations or tribal lands;

I certify that the trophy scored on this chart was not taken in violation of the conditions listed above. In signing this statement, I understand that if the information provided on this entry is found to be misrepresented or fraudulent in any respect, it will not be accepted into the Awards Program and 1) all of my prior entries are subject to deletion from future editions of **Records of North American Big Game** 2) future entries may not be accepted.

FAIR CHASE, as defined by the Boone and Cr_____ sportsmanlike and lawful pursuit and taking of any free-ranging wild, native North American _____ does not give the hunter an improper advantage over such game animals.

The Boone and Crockett Club® may _____ to have been taken in an unethical manner or under conditions deemed inappr_____

Date:_____ Sig_____ _____ OFFICIAL MEASURER OR A NOTARY PUBLIC.)

Date:_____ S_____

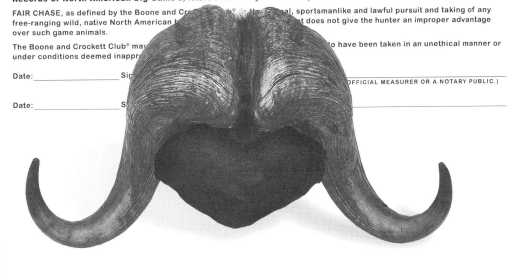

250 Station Drive
Missoula, MT 59801
(406) 542-1888

BOONE AND CROCKETT CLUB®
OFFICIAL SCORING SYSTEM FOR NORTH AMERICAN BIG GAME TROPHIES

SHEEP

MINIMUM SCORES	AWARDS	ALL-TIME
bighorn	175	180
desert	165	168
Dall's	160	170
Stone's	165	170

KIND OF SHEEP (check one)
- ■ bighorn
- ☐ desert
- ☐ Dall's
- ☐ Stone's

PLUG NUMBER

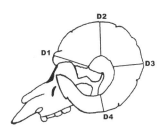

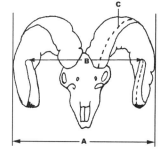

Measure to a
Point in Line
With Horn Tip

SEE OTHER SIDE FOR INSTRUCTIONS		COLUMN 1	COLUMN 2	COLUMN 3
A. Greatest Spread (Is Often Tip to Tip Spread)	23 1/8	Right Horn	Left Horn	Difference
B. Tip to Tip Spread	23 1/8			
C. Length of Horn		47 4/8	46 5/8	
D-1. Circumference of Base		15 7/8	15 7/8	—
D-2. Circumference at First Quarter		15 2/8	15 3/8	1/8
D-3. Circumference at Second Quarter		14 7/8	14 5/8	2/8
D-4. Circumference at Third Quarter		12	11 3/8	5/8
TOTALS		105 4/8	103 7/8	1

ADD	Column 1	105 4/8	Exact Locality Where Killed: Luscar Mt., Alberta
	Column 2	103 7/8	Date Killed: Nov. 2000 Hunter: Guinn D. Crousen
	Subtotal	209 3/8	Owner: Guinn D. Crousen Telephone #:
SUBTRACT Column 3		1	Owner's Address:
FINAL SCORE		208 3/8	Guide's Name and Address:
			Remarks: (Mention Any Abnormalities or Unique Qualities)

I, _____ Kenn Witt _____ , certify that I have measured this trophy on __ 01/28/2001 __
PRINT NAME   MM/DD/YYYYY

at __ 2200 Stemmons Freeway _____ Dallas, Texas _____
STREET ADDRESS   CITY   STATE/PROVINCE

and that these measurements and data are, to the best of my knowledge and belief, made in accordance with the instructions given.

Witness: _____ Signature: _____ I.D. Number □□□
B&C OFFICIAL MEASURER

COPYRIGHT © 2004 BY BOONE AND CROCKETT CLUB®

INSTRUCTIONS FOR MEASURING SHEEP

All measurements must be made with a 1/4-inch wide flexible steel tape to the nearest one-eighth of an inch. Enter fractional figures in eighths, without reduction. Official measurements cannot be taken until horns have air dried for at least 60 days after the animal was killed.

- **A. Greatest Spread** is measured between perpendiculars at a right angle to the center line of the skull.
- **B. Tip to Tip Spread** is measured between tips of horns.
- **C. Length of Horn** is measured from the lowest point in front on outer curve to a point in line with tip. **Do not** press tape into depressions. The low point of the outer curve of the horn is considered to be the low point of the frontal portion of the horn, situated above and slightly medial to the eye socket (not the outside edge). Use a straight edge, perpendicular to horn axis, to end measurement on "broomed" horns.
- **D-1. Circumference of Base** is measured at a right angle to axis of horn. **Do not** follow irregular edge of horn; the line of measurement must be entirely on horn material.
- **D-2-3-4. Divide measurement C** of longer horn by four. Starting at base, mark **both** horns at these quarters (even though the other horn is shorter) and measure circumferences at these marks, with measurements taken at right angles to horn axis.

ENTRY AFFIDAVIT FOR ALL HUNTER-TAKEN TROPHIES

For the purpose of entry into the Boone and Crockett Club's® records, North American big game harvested by the use of the following methods or under the following conditions are ineligible:

- I. Spotting or herding game from the air, followed by landing in its vicinity for the purpose of pursuit and shooting;
- II. Herding or chasing with the aid of any motorized equipment;
- III. Use of electronic communication devices, artificial lighting, or electronic light intensifying devices;
- IV. Confined by artificial barriers, including escape-proof fenced enclosures;
- V. Transplanted for the purpose of commercial shooting;
- VI. By the use of traps or pharmaceuticals;
- VII. While swimming, helpless in deep snow, or helpless in any other natural or artificial medium;
- VIII. On another hunter's license;
- IX. Not in full compliance with the game laws or regulations of the federal government or of any state, province, territory, or tribal council on reservations or tribal lands;

I certify that the trophy scored on this chart was not taken in violation of the conditions listed above. In signing this statement, I understand that if the information relating to this entry is found to be misrepresented or fraudulent in any respect, it will not be accepted into the Awards Program and all of my prior entries are subject to deletion from future editions of **Records of North American Big Game** and future entries may not be accepted.

FAIR CHASE, as defined by the Boone and Crockett Club®, is the ethical, sportsmanlike and lawful pursuit and taking of any free-ranging wild, native North American big game animal in a manner that does not give the hunter an improper advantage over such game animals.

The Boone and Crockett Club® may exclude the entry of any animal that it deems to have been taken in an unethical manner or under conditions deemed inappropriate by the Club.

Date:_____ Signature of Hunter: _____ (SIGNATURE MUST BE WITNESSED BY AN OFFICIAL MEASURER OR A NOTARY PUBLIC.)

Date:_____ Signature of Notary or Official Measurer: _____

TROPHY FIELD PHOTOS FROM THE 25TH AWARDS PROGRAM 2001-2003

Chad Farley and his father, Brian, spent three weeks together on the Alaskan tundra. The result — this monster grizzly bear, which scores 24 points – taken with a .300 Winchester Magnum and 180-grain Barnes X Bullet handloads.

Photograph courtesy of John C. Marsh

Photograph courtesy of Robert A. Elka

Photograph courtesy of Glen A. Landrus

TOP LEFT: Telegraph Creek, British Columbia, produced this Rocky Mountain goat scoring 51-6/8 points for John C. Marsh in August of 2001. A 165-grain Nosler Partition from his .300 Winchester Magnum dropped the billy from 328 yards. **BOTTOM LEFT:** Alaska's Chugach Mountains was the location of Glen A. Landrus' August 2001 Dall's sheep hunt. Glen used a 7mm Rem. Mag. to down this ram scoring 170-5/8 points. **RIGHT:** Robert A. Elka hunted with guide, Wes Berge, near Johiah Lake, British Columbia, to take this mountain caribou scoring 372-4/8 points in September 2000.

TOP: B&C Official Measurer, Frank S. Noska IV, stalked to within bow range to arrow this Moffat County, Colorado, pronghorn that scores 81-2/8 points. BOTTOM LEFT: Brian Hornberger traveled to Humbolt County, California, to take this 5x6 typical Columbia blacktail, which scores 136-1/8 points. BOTTOM RIGHT: In April 2003, John L. Lundin backpacked with his .300 Weatherby into the San Carlos Indian Reservation in Graham County, Arizona, to take this black bear that scores 20-6/16 points.

Photograph courtesy of Thomas R. Sherman

**Thomas R. Sherman took this Roosevelt's elk scoring 340-2/8 points. He harvested this
bull in Benton County, Oregon, in November 2002, only 500 yards from where
Jason S. Ballard downed the current World's Record Roosevelt's elk. Thomas was with
Jason when he took his bull two months earlier.**

Edward A. Petersen with his Rocky Mountain goat scoring 47-2/8 points taken from British Columbia's Mt. Meehaus in October 2002. Edward used a 7mm STW and 150-grain Barnes X Bullets to take this billy with 9-5/8-inch horns.

Photograph courtesy of Lori Ginn

Photograph courtesy of Bruce E. Young

Photograph courtesy of Rick C. Hooley

TOP: Lori J. Ginn, applied, drew the tag, and found this 156-2/8 point Wyoming moose in September 2002. She hunted in Beaverhead County with a .270 to fill her tag.
BOTTOM LEFT: Bruce E. Young hunted with Robert J. Seeds and Cougar Mountain Outfitters to take this tom that scores 15 points. The big tom was taken in Rio Arriba County, New Mexico, in November 2000. BOTTOM RIGHT: Rick C. Hooley took this bighorn sheep scoring 190-5/8 points from Taos County, New Mexico, in September 2002 while hunting with guide, Perry Harper. Rick was aided by the use of mules and a 140-grain bullet from his .270.

TOP: This 7x6 typical American elk was taken by Bennie J. Rossetto in October 2001 from Gila County, Arizona. The bull scores 379-5/8 points and was dropped by a 425-grain Hornady Great Plains load from a .54 caliber muzzleloader. BOTTOM LEFT: Charles A. Lantry poses with his Rich County, Utah, pronghorn scoring 83 points. The buck was taken in 2000 with his D'arcy Echols Winchester Legend rifle. BOTTOM RIGHT: Custer State Park in Custer County, South Dakota, was the site of Charles A. LeKites 2001 bison hunt. Charles used a .338 loaded with a 225-grain Swift A-Frame to down this bull, which scores 122 points.

Photograph courtesy of George A. Pickel

George A. Pickel is pictured here with his Dall's sheep taken near Ram River, Northwest Territories. The ram scores 166 points. George hunted with guide, Derrick Payne, in August 2002 using a 7mm Remington Magnum and 160-grain Trophy Bonded Bear Claws.

The McKay Lake region in the Northwest Territories is the site of numerous records book entries for Central Canada barren ground caribou. This was the case for Kevin R. Williams. His 368-4/8 point bull was taken there in September 2001.

Photograph courtesy of Jerry D. Lees

Photograph courtesy of Sidney G. Humphries

Photograph courtesy of Randy Pittman

TOP: Jerry D. Lees took this Alaska brown bear scoring 27-7/16 points near Wide Bay, Alaska, in May 2000. Jerry initially arrowed this boar from eight yards and tracked it into thick alders where one shot from a 7mm Magnum was used to end a very dangerous situation.

BOTTOM LEFT: Manitoba's Porcupine Provincial Forest produced this Canada moose scoring 197-4/8 points for Sidney G. Humphries in October 2001. BOTTOM RIGHT: Randy Pittman teamed up with guide, Dustin Peacock, to find this Stone's sheep scoring 168-1/8 points in the Prophet River area of northern British Columbia in October 2001.

Photograph courtesy of Zane D. Terry

Photograph courtesy of Garrett J. Grant

Photograph courtesy of Phillip W. DeShazo

TOP: Zane D. Terry worked with guide, Thomas Brunson, to locate and take this 381-5/8 point 6x6 American elk from White Pine County, Nevada, in November 2002.
BOTTOM LEFT: Seventeen-year-old Garrett J. Grant, took this bighorn sheep in September 2003 from Chelan County, Washington. The ram scores 177-3/8 points. Garrett used his .300 Remington Short Magnum for a 250-yard shot. BOTTOM RIGHT: Nevada's Unit 231 produced this typical mule deer scoring 180-7/8 points for Phillip W. DeShazo in October of 2001. Phillip was carrying a .300 Remington Ultra-Mag.

This split-beam, 10x5 non-typical whitetail deer was taken by Cochrane, Alberta, taxidermist, Jim Boland, in November of 2000. The buck scores 198-4/8 points. Jim commented, "This was four days of the most elusive buck I have ever hunted, then I got lucky."

Montana's Powder River County produced this pronghorn scoring 82-6/8 points for William P. Stuver in October 2002. William used a 100-grain bullet fired from his .25-06.

BOONE AND CROCKETT CLUB'S

Photograph courtesy of Cody L. Warren

Photograph courtesy of Jason House

Photograph courtesy of Steven R. Farr

TOP: Cody L. Warren and his wife, Megan, hold his typical mule deer scoring 191-7/8 points taken in October 2000 in Tooele County, Utah. BOTTOM LEFT: Jason House took this typical American elk, scoring 386-1/8 points, in Lincoln County, Nevada, in September 2001 using a 7mm Weatherby Magnum shooting 160-grain Nosler Partitions. BOTTOM RIGHT: Bison hunter, Steven R. Farr hunted the Henry Mountains of Garfield County, Utah, to take this bull scoring 128-6/8 points. He used a .338-.378 Weatherby and 250-grain Nosler Partitions.

Photograph courtesy of Michael M. Golightly

Photograph courtesy of Grant A. Medlin

Photograph courtesy of Hanspeter Giger

TOP: This typical Coues' whitetail deer was taken by Michael M. Golightly while hunting with Sonora Outfitters in Sonora, Mexico. The buck scores 112-3/8 points. BOTTOM LEFT: This 195-1/8 point typical mule deer was taken by Grant A. Medlin in Sonora, Mexico, in January 2002. The buck has a greatest spread of 34-6/8 inches. BOTTOM RIGHT: B&C Lifetime Associate Hanspeter Giger hunted Luna County, New Mexico, to take this pronghorn scoring 82-4/8 points in October 2001.

Jay Senkerik poses with his desert bighorn sheep, which scores 169-4/8 points. Jay went on a self-guided hunt in the Gila Bend Mountains of Maricopa County, Arizona, to find this once-in-a-lifetime ram.

Justin T. Dubay is pictured here with his Kodiak Island, Alaska, typical Sitka blacktail, which scores 102-2/8 points. Justin found this buck near Uganik Bay in October 2001.

Photograph courtesy of Bob J. Williams

Photograph courtesy of Daniel L. Scharmer

Photograph courtesy of Thomas J. O'Neill

TOP LEFT: Bob J. Williams traveled to McKay Lake, Northwest Territories, to find this Central Canada barren ground caribou scoring 371-2/8 points in September 2001. Bob used a .300 Weatherby and 165-grain Hornady loads to drop this bull. **BOTTOM LEFT:** Thomas J. O'Neill traveled to Tuck Creek, Alaska, to find this Alaska-Yukon moose scoring 232-4/8 points. Swollen rivers made for tough going, but Thomas took his bull with a .300 Winchester Magnum in September 2001. **RIGHT:** Daniel L. Scharmer holds his Dall's sheep scoring 166-4/8 points taken in July 2002 at the head of Ram River, Northwest Territories. Daniel hunted with guide, Gary Billings, and used his 7mm Magnum to down this 40-inch ram.

Photograph courtesy of Robert J. Beaulieu

Photograph courtesy of Douglas J. Hood

Photograph courtesy of John H. Noble

TOP: This Alaska brown bear was taken by Robert J. Beaulieu in April 2000 from Kodiak Island's Kizhuyak Bay. The big boar scores 26-4/16 points and fell to Robert's .375 H&H Magnum loaded with 300-grain Federal Trophy Bonded Bear Claws. BOTTOM LEFT: This 6x5 typical whitetail was taken by bowhunter Douglas J. Hood in Rock Island County, Illinois, in November 2002. The buck scores 180-4/8 points. BOTTOM RIGHT: John H. Noble III holds his Coconino County, Arizona, typical American elk taken in September 2003. The 6X6 bull scores 375-2/8 points.

Photograph courtesy of Jim Clary

This handsome 8x10 mule deer was taken with a bow by Jim Clary along the South Saskatchewan River, Saskatchewan, in October 2001. The non-typical buck scores 220-2/8 points.

Sharon R. Sterud dropped this 6x6 typical American elk in Sanpete County, Utah, using a .30-06 and a 180-grain boat tail. The bull scores 361-1/8 points and was taken in September 2002.

Photograph courtesy of Max G. Bauer, Jr.

Photograph courtesy of Margaret Barnett

Photograph courtesy of Delbert R. Oney

TOP: Max G. Bauer, Jr., and his son, Chad, pose with Max's bison from Custer County, South Dakota, taken in December 2001. The bull scores 118-4/8 points. BOTTOM LEFT: Washington County, Utah, produced this desert bighorn sheep for Margaret Barnett in October 2001. The ram scores 174-2/8 points. Margaret used a .270 loaded with 140-grain Federal Trophy Bonded Bear Claws. BOTTOM RIGHT: This impressive barren ground caribou was taken by Delbert R. Oney on Adak Island, Alaska, in September 2003. The bull scores 407-4/8 points.

Photograph courtesy of Bryan C. Bailey

Photograph courtesy of Colby L. Loudon

Photograph courtesy of Leo C. Potter

TOP: Bryan C. Bailey hunted Mount Stinenia, Alaska, to take this 10-1/8-inch Rocky Mountain goat in October 2003. The billy scored 50-4/8 points. BOTTOM LEFT: This Phillips County, Montana, bighorn sheep was taken by Colby L. Loudon in September 2002. The ram scores 184-4/8 points. BOTTOM RIGHT: Leo C. Potter poses with his 1999, Ellice River, Nunavut, muskox. The bull scores 114 points and was taken with a .300 Winchester Magnum shooting 180-grain Nosler Partitions.

Catherine D. Mower pictured here with her Summit County, Utah, Wyoming moose taken in September 2002. The bull scores 160-6/8 points.

This 81-point pronghorn was taken by Kurt D. Rued, in Garfield County, Montana, in October 2001. Kurt carried a .300 Remington Ultra-Mag. shooting 180-grain Nosler Partitions.

Photograph courtesy of Mike J. Ryan

Photograph courtesy of Harry E. Buzby III

Photograph courtesy of Vodne O. Chapoose

TOP: This black bear scoring 21-4/16 points was taken near Kelvington, Saskatchewan, in May 2002 by Mike J. Ryan. He used a .30-378 Weatherby and 180 gr. Barnes X Bullets. BOTTOM LEFT: Harry E. Buzby III poses with his 2001 barren ground caribou, taken from the Chulitna River region of Alaska. The bull scores 431-3/8 points. BOTTOM RIGHT: This non-typical mule deer, with a 33-2/8-inch outside spread, was taken by Vodne O. Chapoose in San Miguel County, Colorado, in November 2002. The 10x9 buck scores 239-1/8 points.

LEFT: This Dall's sheep, scoring 160-7/8 points, was taken in the Mackenzie Mountains of Northwest Territories by Brent V. Trumbo. He was guided by Tim Stephenson in August 2002. Brent used a Jack O'Connor classic – a .270 Winchester and 130-grain loads.
TOP RIGHT: Jack K. Mulder, traveled to Gull Lake, Alberta, in November 2001 to find this 10x9 non-typical whitetail that scores 206-2/8 points. **BOTTOM RIGHT:** Boone and Crockett Club Member, Mark B. Steffen, drew a non-resident moose tag and chose to hunt for his bull with a bow. Mark arrowed this Wyoming moose, scoring 167-2/8 points, in Sheridan County, Wyoming, in September 2003.

Photograph courtesy of Murl E. Seeley

Murl E. Seeley took this heavy-antlered, typical mule deer from Eagle County, Colorado, in November 2002. This classic 5x5 scores 184-3/8 points.

The Quebec-Labrador caribou was taken by Duane Armitage in September 2002. Duane hunted the Minto Lake region to arrow this great bull with a Mathews Feather Max and 100-grain Thunderheads. The bull scores 387 points.

Photograph courtesy of Mark Kayser

Photograph courtesy of Tyson N. Faucher

Photograph courtesy of Luke R. Viravec

TOP: Mark Kayser traveled west into Montana's Powder River County to take this 6x6 typical American elk scoring 363 points in October 2002. **BOTTOM LEFT:** Tyson N. Faucher used a .50-caliber muzzleloader to take this heavy-antlered, typical mule deer scoring 199-7/8 points near Pelletier Lake, Saskatchewan, in October 2003. **BOTTOM RIGHT:** Luke R. Viravec used a 7mm Remington Magnum and a 140-grain Nosler Ballistic Tip bullet to drop this grizzly bear scoring 24-5/16 points on Two Pete Mountain, Yukon Territory, in August 2001.

ACKNOWLEDGEMENTS
Boone and Crockett Club's
25th Big Game Awards, 2001-2003

Data compiled with the able assistance of:

Eldon L. "Buck" Buckner – Chairman, Boone and Crockett Club's Records Committee
Jack Reneau – Director of Big Game Records, Boone and Crockett Club
Ryan Hatfield – Assistant Director of Big Game Records, Boone and Crockett Club
George A. Bettas – Executive Director, Boone and Crockett Club
Sandra Poston – Office Manager, Boone and Crockett Club
Amy Hutchison – Customer Service Specialist, Boone and Crockett Club
Julie T. Houk – Director of Publications, Boone and Crockett Club
Keith Balfourd – Marketing Coordinator, Boone and Crockett Club
Emily McKeever – Controller, Boone and Crockett Club
Joanna Giffin – Assistant Controller, Boone and Crockett Club
Wendy Nickelson – File Clerk, Boone and Crockett Club

Copy Editing by:

Jack Reneau – Director of Big Game Records, Boone and Crockett Club
Ryan Hatfield – Assistant Director of Big Game Records, Boone and Crockett Club
George A. Bettas – Executive Director, Boone and Crockett Club
Sydney Rimpau – Bozeman, Montana

Pronghorn painting on dust jacket by:

Hayden Lambson – *Town Meeting* – Lambson Wildlife Originals, Pocatello, Idaho

Special Trophy Handling

Mark B. Steffen – B&C Member – Hutchinson, Kansas
Richard T. Hale – B&C Member – Ottawa, Kansas
H. Hudson DeCray – B&C Member – Bishop, California
David Morris – Northwest Big Game – Long Creek, Oregon
Larry Lack – Northwest Big Game – Thompson Falls, Montana
Glenn Abbott – B&C Official Measurer – Portland, Oregon
Dale Ream – B&C Official measurer – Unionville, Missouri
Missouri Show-Me Big Bucks Club – Unionville, Missouri
Dwaine Knouse – Cabela's – Kansas City, Kansas
Helen Stonhill – Cabela's – Sidney, Nebraska
Mark Dowse – Cabela's – Sidney, Nebraska
Travis Thomson – Cabela's – Sidney, Nebraska

Special Acknowledgement

Dick and Mary Cabela – Sidney, Nebraska
Jim Cabela – Sidney, Nebraska

Printed and bound by:

R.R. Donnelley & Sons Company
Crawfordsville, Indiana

Limited Editions binding by:

Roswell Book Binding
Phoenix, Arizona